Law, Governance and Technology Series

Volume 25

The *Law-Governance and Technology Series* is intended to attract manuscripts arising from an interdisciplinary approach in law, artificial intelligence and information technologies. The idea is to bridge the gap between research in IT law and ITapplications for lawyers developing a unifying techno-legal perspective. The series will welcome proposals that have a fairly specific focus on problems or projects that will lead to innovative research charting the course for new interdisciplinary developments in law, legal theory, and law and society research as well as in computer technologies, artificial intelligence and cognitive sciences. In broad strokes, manuscripts for this series may be mainly located in the fields of the Internet law (data protection, intellectual property, Internet rights, etc.), Computational models of the legal contents and legal reasoning, Legal Information Retrieval, Electronic Data Discovery, Collaborative Tools (e.g. Online Dispute Resolution platforms), Metadata and XML Technologies (for Semantic Web Services), Technologies in Courtrooms and Judicial Offices (E-Court), Technologies for Governments and Administrations (E-Government), Legal Multimedia, and Legal Electronic Institutions (Multi-Agent Systems and Artificial Societies).

More information about this series at http://www.springer.com/series/8808

David Wright • Paul De Hert
Editors

Enforcing Privacy

Regulatory, Legal and Technological Approaches

Springer

Editors
David Wright
Trilateral Research
London, UK

Paul De Hert
Faculty of Law and Criminology
Vrije Universiteit Brussel
Brussels, Belgium

ISSN 2352-1902 ISSN 2352-1910 (electronic)
Law, Governance and Technology Series
ISBN 978-3-319-25045-8 ISBN 978-3-319-25047-2 (eBook)
DOI 10.1007/978-3-319-25047-2

Library of Congress Control Number: 2016937934

Printed on acid-free paper

This Springer imprint is published by Springer Nature
The registered company is Springer International Publishing AG Switzerland

Contents

About the Authors

Jan Philipp Albrecht is from Germany, a member of the European Parliament (MEP) representing the group of the Greens/European Free Alliance. He is also vice-chair of the Committee on Civil Liberties, Justice and Home Affairs ("the LIBE Committee"), which has been shepherding the proposed data protection legislation through the parliament. His committee considered more than 4,000 proposed amendments.

Kirsten Bock is the legal counsel at the Data Protection Commissioner's office in Schleswig-Holstein, Germany, the Unabhängiges Landeszentrum für Datenschutz, ULD (Independent Centre for Privacy Protection). She was the initiator and head of the European Privacy Seal EuroPriSe and responsible for EuroPriSe certification criteria, policy and governance. She works with industry, government and NGOs on programmes, standards, best practice and regulation in privacy and data protection. Kirsten studied law and legal philosophy in Germany and the UK and has lectured in criminal and data protection law.

Gertjan Boulet is a Ph.D. candidate in law at the Vrije Universiteit Brussel (Free University Brussels, Belgium) and a consortium member of the EU-funded PHAEDRA project ("Improving Practical and Helpful cooperAtion betweEn Data PRotection Authorities"). His doctoral degree focuses on cross-border law enforcement investigations on the Internet.

Ana Brian Nougrères works as a lawyer and as a consultant at the Senate and Chamber of Representatives in Uruguay and teaches graduate and undergraduate students the principles of data protection and legal informatics at the School of Law of the public Uruguayan University (Facultad de Derecho, Universidad de la República). She is the director of the Privacy and Data Protection branch at Estudio Jurídico BrianN and Associates, based in Montevideo, Uruguay.

Chris Connolly is a director of Galexia, a privacy advocate and researcher and the author of significant reports on Safe Harbor compliance, privacy trustmarks and privacy regulatory structures.

Hannah Crowther is an associate solicitor at Bristows LLP. Her practice involves advising on a wide variety of data protection issues, ranging from large-scale compliance projects to individual subject access requests. She is also increasingly involved in contentious work, assisting clients in relation to data breaches, individual complaints and regulatory investigations.

Paul De Hert is a professor of law at Vrije Universiteit Brussel and an associate professor at the Institute of Law and Technology at Tilburg University. He has co-authored many articles and co-edited numerous books on data protection.

Alexander Dix is the Berlin commissioner for Data Protection and Freedom of Information and chairman of the International Working Group on Data Protection in Telecommunications (internationally known as the "Berlin Group").

Pam Dixon is a researcher, author and the founder and executive director of the World Privacy Forum, a public interest research group. Her work in privacy includes ground-breaking reports, books and testimony in the area of privacy regulation and public policy, medical identity theft and health privacy and privacy issues related to emerging technologies.

Robert Gellman is a privacy and information policy consultant, based in Washington, DC. He has also been chief counsel to a subcommittee in the US House of Representatives; a senior fellow, Center on Law and Information Policy, Fordham University School of Law; and a fellow at the Institute for Quantitative Social Science, Harvard University.

Hazel Grant is a partner and head of the Privacy and Information Law Group at Fieldfisher in London. She has had 20 years' experience of advising on data privacy matters and has advised on freedom of information law issues since the implementation of the law in England and Wales. Her work includes advising on general data privacy compliance issues for global businesses, carrying out privacy impact assessments in new public sector programmes and advising on data breaches, claims and enforcements. She is an editor of the *Encyclopedia of Data Protection and Privacy* and a contributing editor on data protection and freedom of information matters for the *Encyclopaedia of IT Law* (both Sweet and Maxwell).

Graham Greenleaf is professor of law and information systems at UNSW Australia. He has been involved in privacy issues for 40 years and is Asia-Pacific editor of *Privacy Laws & Business International Report*. His most recent book is *Asian Data Privacy Laws: Trade and Human Rights Perspectives* (OUP 2014). In

2010, he was made a member of the Order of Australia for his contributions to privacy protection and free access to legal information.

Billy Hawkes served as Ireland's data protection commissioner from 2005 to 2014. He also served as chair of INTERPOL's data protection oversight body, the Commission for the Control of Interpol Files (CCF). His previous career was in the Irish Civil Service.

David Jacobs was formerly consumer protection counsel at the Electronic Privacy Information Center. He is a graduate of the University of Wisconsin-Eau Claire and Harvard Law School. At Harvard, he was involved with the Cyberlaw Clinic at the Berkman Center for Internet and Society and worked as a research assistant to former professor John Palfrey.

Jacob Kohnstamm is the chairman of the Dutch Data Protection Authority (College bescherming persoonsgegevens), whose six-year term was renewed in August 2010. He was also chairman of the Article 29 Data Protection Working Party between 2010 and 2014.

Daniel Le Métayer is research director for INRIA, the French National Institute for Research in Computer Science and Control, and has been involved in various international projects on privacy, IT security, software design and analysis.

Artemio Rallo Lombarte is the chair of Constitutional Law of the Jaume I University of Castellón, Spain. While the director of the Spanish Data Protection Agency (2007–2011), he hosted the 31st International Conference of Data Protection and Privacy Commissioners in Madrid. He was also a director general of the Centre for Legal Studies of the Spanish Ministry of Justice from 2004 to 2007.

Hiroshi Miyashita is an associate professor, Faculty of Policy Studies, Chuo University, Tokyo. In 2012–2013, he was a visiting scholar at the Harvard Law School. He is also an advisor in the Office of Personal Information Protection, in the Cabinet Office.

Marc Rotenberg is the president and executive director of the Electronic Privacy Information Center (EPIC) in Washington, DC. He teaches information privacy law at Georgetown University Law Center and frequently testifies before Congress on emerging privacy and civil liberties issues.

James B. Rule has been doing research and writing on surveillance and privacy protection throughout his career. He is author, co-author or editor of four books and many articles on privacy and personal information. He has held teaching and research positions at MIT, Oxford University, the University of Bordeaux, Stony Brook University and the University of California, Berkeley, where he is now affiliated with the Center for the Study of Law and Society. He has also been a fellow at the Center for Advanced Study in the Behavioral Sciences at Stanford, the Institute for Advanced Study in Princeton and the Russell Sage Foundation in New York City. In addition to his academic writings, he also contributes to magazines and op-ed pages in publications such as *Dissent*, *The Washington Monthly*, *The New York Times* and *The Los Angeles Times*.

Blair Stewart is the assistant privacy commissioner of New Zealand. He was one of the pioneers of privacy impact assessment and wrote some of the first papers on PIA as well as New Zealand's influential *Privacy Impact Assessment Handbook*. He has been an ardent proponent of international privacy enforcement co-ordination in the International Conference of Data Protection and Privacy Commissioners, the Asia-Pacific Economic Cooperation (APEC), the Global Privacy Enforcement Network (GPEN) and other fora.

Dan Svantesson is a professor in the Faculty of Law in Australia's Bond University and editor of *International Data Privacy Law*.

Ivan Szekely social informatist, is an internationally known expert in the multidisciplinary fields of data protection and freedom of information. A long-time independent researcher, consultant and university lecturer, as well as former chief counsellor of the Hungarian Parliamentary Commissioner for Data Protection and Freedom of Information, Szekely is at present senior research fellow of the Open Society Archives at Central European University, associate professor at the Budapest University of Technology and Economics and advisory board member of the Eotvos Karoly Policy Institute. His research interests are focused on information autonomy, openness and secrecy, privacy, identity, memory and forgetting, and archivistics.

Peter van Dijk is the managing director of Galexia and an expert on global privacy compliance and cloud computing law and policy.

David Wright is Director of Trilateral Research, an enterprise based in London that he founded in 2004. He has been a partner in numerous European and UK privacy projects and is the author of many articles on privacy and surveillance in peer-reviewed journals. He was a principal co-editor of *Privacy Impact Assessment*, published by Springer in 2012, and co-editor of *Surveillance in Europe*, published by Routledge in 2014.

Chapter 1
Introduction to Enforcing Privacy

David Wright and Paul De Hert

1.1 Introduction

This book received its final edit at a crucial moment in the EU process of data protection reform with the finalisation of the trilogue negotiations between the European Parliament, Council and Commission, and the final stage of the arduous process of bringing the General Data Protection Regulation (GDPR) into law. The Regulation contains a new governance model that combines powerful data protection authorities (DPAs), along with increased co-operation, a lead DPA and a European Data Protection Board with real functional and financial independence and the power to issue binding decisions. Attention with regard to DPA co-operation and enforcement should be given particularly to GDPR Chapters VI (supervisory authorities) and VII (co-operation and consistency), the latter defining amongst others the powers of the Board in its consistency monitoring capacity.

The EU reform process was finalised in a rocky period when courts and DPAs started hitting the news with far-reaching actions and judgments.[1]

On 6 October 2015, the Court of Justice of the European Union (CJEU) issued the *Schrems* judgment, invalidating the European Commission's Decision of 2000 that recognised the adequacy of the EU-US Safe Harbor framework. In addition to this invalidation of the adequacy decision, the CJEU upheld the power of national DPAs to independently investigate international data transfers based on adequacy

[1] Linkomies, Laura, and Stewart Dresner, "Multinationals face increasing pressure from DPAs. A Belgian court supported the Belgian DPA's record breaking 250,000 Euros per day fine on Facebook", *Privacy Laws & Business*, Issue 138, 2015, pp. 1–4.

D. Wright (✉)
Trilateral Research, London, UK
e-mail: david.wright@trilateralresearch.com

P. De Hert
Faculty of Law and Criminology, Vrije Universiteit Brussel, Brussels, Belgium
e-mail: paul.de.hert@vub.ac.be; paul.de.hert@uvt.nl

D. Wright, P. De Hert (eds.), *Enforcing Privacy*, Law, Governance and Technology Series 25, DOI 10.1007/978-3-319-25047-2_1

decisions. The judgment is a must-read concerning enforcement. The Court sees it as a duty flowing from Article 12 of the EU Data Protection Directive and Article 8 of the EU Charter on Fundamental Rights that a DPA, even when there is an adequacy, must, with complete independence, investigate complaints. If the DPA finds a problem, it cannot disable the adequacy decision but must be able to challenge this decision in court.[2]

As DPA enforcement friendly as the *Schrems judgment* was, the *Weltimo judgment* delivered five days earlier was also important. On 1 October 2015, the Court decided in a case concerning a company based in Slovakia but offering services to Hungarians that when a DPA receives a complaint, it may exercise its investigative powers irrespective of the applicable law and before even knowing which national law is applicable.[3]

This book has been conceived in a wider landscape of reform both inside and outside Europe.[4] Bringing data protection and privacy to life, turning it from a paper existence into a reality is a common element in all these reforms.

This book tries to capture that development through the lens of enforcement, a term that denotes this process of turning paper into reality or, more eloquently, to translate a set of legal standards designed to influence human and institutional behaviour into social reality.[5] More is needed for effective and legitimate privacy arrangements than just and clear rules: enforcement can contribute to the legitimacy of these rules: regulators that are endowed with legitimate authority to define and impose norms can easily lose that authority if they have no effective way of enforcing these rules and, conversely, a regulator that achieves a high level of compliance will enhance its legitimacy.[6]

The book does not cover all possible aspects that could be dealt with under the banner of "enforcement" or that could be linked with broader themes. It is definitely

---

[2] See Cadiot, Sarah, and Laura De Boel, "Safe Harbor invalid: What to expect after the ruling?", *Privacy Laws & Business*, Issue 137, 2015, pp. 1, 3.

[3] See Soós, Andrea Klára, "ECJ clarifies meaning of territorial scope in DP Directive", *Privacy Laws & Business*, Issue 137, 2015, pp. 1, 5.

[4] For an overview of recent proposals for modernising information privacy law in the USA, the European Union, Australia and New Zealand, see Gunasekara, Gehan, "Paddling in unison or just paddling? International trends in reforming information privacy law", *International Journal of Law and Information Technology,* 2013, pp. 1–37. Also, on the matter of accountability in Australia, the United States (e.g., Title V, Gramm-Leach-Bliley Act of 1999) and Canada (e.g., Sch. 1, Principle 1, Personal Information Protection and Electronic Documents Act (PIPEDA), 2000), see Crompton, Malcolm, Christine Cowper and Christopher Jefferis, "The Australian Dodo Case: An Insight for Data Protection Regulation", *BNA World Data Protection Report*, Vol. 9, No. 1, 2009, pp. 5–8.

[5] Morgan, Bronwen, and Karen Yeung, *An introduction to Law and Regulation*, Cambridge University Press, 2007, p. 10.

[6] Reed, Chris, "Cloud Governance: The Way Forward" in Christopher Millard (ed.), *Cloud Computing Law*, Oxford University Press, 2013, p. 374.

not a book on "regulating" privacy, which is one of these possible broader themes. Within the stricter limits of the theme of enforcement, the book does not address all pending issues. The book does not look in detail at the role of the European Data Protection Supervisor (EDPS) or, for that manner, the future role of the European Data Protection Board[7] Equally, the organisational aspects of enforcement, such as the right for data protection authorities to prioritise their workflows is not covered and with upcoming court decisions on this aspect, we expect it to be an important legal topic in the future.

We view our book as predominantly pragmatic.

First, we need to say something about the terminology of "privacy" and "data protection". There is some discussion about the respective content of the terms, their similarities and differences.[8] Some authors use term "data privacy", embracing in particular the European understanding of "personal data protection" and the Anglo-Saxon one of "informational privacy", in order to "avoid terminology that might seem focused too much on a particular legal system".[9] In a similar vein of *what matters is the result*, we have not insisted on using a specific terminology and although the outcome is a book mainly on data protection, we have opted to use the term *privacy* on the cover, partly because we view "data protection" as one type of privacy. We prefer the wider term "privacy", because there are several types of privacy.[10] We think that regulators and privacy advocates should not circumscribe privacy to equate with only data protection. Other types of privacy deserve protection and enforcement too. While this book is primarily concerned with data protection, many of the measures discussed in these pages are applicable to the enforcement of all types of privacy.

---

[7] See De Hert, Paul and Vagelis Papakonstantinou, "The EDPS as a Unique Stakeholder in the European Data Protection Landscape, Fulfilling the Explicit and Non-explicit Expectations", in Hielke Hijmans and Herke Kranenborg (eds.), *Data Protection Anno 2014: How to Restore Trust? Contributions in honour of Peter Hustinx, European Data Protection Supervisor (2004–2014)*, Intersentia, 2014, pp. 237–252. See also "EDPS aims to be proactive and focus on external relations", *Privacy Laws & Business*, Issue 133, 2015, pp. 1–4.

[8] Gellert, Raphaël, and Serge Gutwirth, "The legal construction of privacy and data protection", *Computer Law & Security Review*, Vol. 29, 2013, pp. 522–530; González Fuster, Gloria, *The Emergence of Personal Data Protection as a Fundamental Right of the EU*, Springer, 2014; Lynskey, Orla, "Deconstructing Data Protection: The 'Added- Value' of a Right to Data Protection in the EU Legal Order", *International and Comparative Law Quarterly*, Vol. 63, 2014, pp. 569–597.

[9] Kuner, Chris, Fred H. Cate, Christopher Millard and Dan J. B. Svantesson, "Taking Stock after Four Years", *International Data Privacy Law*, Vol. 4, No. 2, 2014, pp. 87–88. See also Zalnieriute, Monika, "An international constitutional moment for data privacy in the times of mass-surveillance", *International Journal of Law and Information Technology*, Vol. 23, 2015, pp. 99–133.

[10] Clarke, Roger, "What's "Privacy"?." Version of 7 August 2006. http://www.rogerclarke.com/DV/Privacy.html. Finn, Rachel, David Wright and Michael Friedewald, "Seven Types of Privacy", in Serge Gutwirth, Yves Poullet et al. (eds.), *European data protection: coming of age?*, Springer, Dordrecht, 2013.

We also need to explicate the phrase "enforcing privacy". Enforcement typically means the activity of a regulator to ensure that third parties comply with a law or regulation or code. If regulators do not enforce laws or regulations or codes or do not have the resources, political support or wherewithal to enforce them, they effectively eviscerate and make meaningless such laws or regulations or codes, no matter how laudable or well-intentioned. This is the challenge that many regulators face: they do not have the resources or political support for enforcement to do their jobs effectively. In some cases, however, the mere existence of such laws or regulations combined with a credible threat to invoke them is sufficient for regulatory purposes. It may not be necessary to enforce privacy regulation against every company that fails to comply. Selective enforcement may be sufficient to send a message to all delinquent companies (as well as public sector or even third sector organisations) that they should get their houses in order. But the threat has to be credible. As some of the authors in this book make clear – it is a theme that runs throughout this book – "carrots" and "soft law" need to be backed up by "sticks" and "hard law".

In this book, we and our co-authors view privacy enforcement as an activity that goes beyond regulatory enforcement. In his chapter, Graham Greenleaf distinguishes between enforcement and compliance. He points out that there is often evidence of enforcement of national laws, but there is little information on the extent of compliance. In some sense, enforcing privacy is a task that befalls to all of us. This is a point that James Rule makes in his envoi to our book. Privacy advocates and members of the public play or can play an important role in enforcing privacy. For those of us old enough, we might recall the proclamation of Howard Beale, the veteran news presenter played by Peter Finch in the 1976 classic film *Network*: "Things have got to change. But first, you've gotta get mad! You've got to say, 'I'm as mad as hell, and I'm not going to take this anymore!'" This is where we are with the continuing intrusions upon privacy by governments, intelligence agencies and corporate warlords. It might serve their interests to say that privacy is dead, but it does not serve our interests, the interests of we the people, of a healthy, democratic society. In effect, we have to echo Howard Beale and say that we are as mad as hell and we are not going to take it anymore. Edward Snowden obviously felt this way. There are different ways to enforce privacy, in addition to those of the regulator. The essays in this book demonstrate some of the different ways by means of which we, collectively, can enforce privacy.

This brings us to a *second* point: the geographical scope of the book is global. Authors from all over the globe are participating and their valuable voices are heard in all four sections of the book: *countries, international, instruments, the future*. This explains why we have perspectives on international enforcement written by authors coming from several continents and why the country reports on Spain and Hungary are followed by reports on Japan, the US and Latin America. These reports are not structured in an identical way. A rigid format does not always guarantee vivid or interesting outcomes. To compensate for the relative freedom of direction accorded to authors, almost all authors participated in a closed workshop convened by the editors as a side event at the conference on *Computers, Privacy and Data Protection* held in Brussels in January 2014.

Third, respectful of the ambition of that important Brussels conference was the editors' decision not to limit the book to one group of authors, for instance, academics, but to consult a wider group of people willing to author a contribution – hence, the presence of activists, of officials working for data protection or privacy-related authorities and prominent policy-makers. Some of the more political voices are clustered in the *Future* section, with minimal editorial restriction so as to respect the energy, vision and willingness to impact on the policy agenda. To us, the chapters in that section will become useful testimony for subsequent researchers and with more than just tolerance, we accepted some of them being written in the first person singular.

1.2 Pragmatism and theory: two themes strike the attention

The choices discussed above are identical to the ones we made four years ago when we compiled *Privacy Impact Assessment*, a 523-page book allowing a multitude of authors with different geographical and professional backgrounds to speak out on a novel phenomenon that is developing globally but not at the same speed.[11] The reception of that book in terms of appreciation and sales was excellent and strengthened our belief that this kind of mixed book was indeed answering a need to go beyond strictly practical or academic books. We then and now opted to refrain from giving strict thematic direction or to ask contributors to test a certain hypothesis or theory.

We are well aware that out there is a burgeoning field of theory and evidence with regard to policy-making and especially regulatory policy. The choice to engage with that literature was left to the authors. Several authors, in particular those with an academic background such as Greenleaf and De Hert and Boulet have taken up the challenge. That does not mean that the book as a whole does not deliver cross-cutting themes that are theoretically relevant. Two themes strike the attention.

First, there is the theme of state regulation *v.* self-regulation. The latter is the central topic in the third chapter ("Failures of Privacy Self-Regulation in the United States"), but the theme echoes throughout other chapters as well. Law students are most familiar with state-controlled norm-setting and enforcement. The reality is far more complex and shows the existence in many domains of society of governance structures other than government structures, systems of rule-creation and enforcement that do not depend solely on state command-and-control, but instead involve participants from a wider community. An extreme form of governance is self-regulation, a model where those who are the primary subjects of the system's rules come together to agree a governance structure and undertake to abide by the rules it produces. The model is not absent, also in the context of the Internet. Think only of the rule-setting by major IT firms when developing the technological architecture. But the purely self-regulatory model is not a dominant one since governments and

[11] Wright, David, and Paul De Hert (eds.), *Privacy Impact Assessment*, Springer, Dordrecht, 2012.

states need to step in for a plurality of reasons (power, concern for privacy and other fundamental rights, etc.). Governance of this type is referred to as co-regulation, to be distinguished from governance purely by law, on the one hand, or self-regulation or contract on the other.[12] Reed rightly observes that co-regulation has become the predominant governance structure for those Internet activities extending beyond national boundaries,[13] but even for purely national arrangements, various factors can account for a turn to co-regulation.

The impact of these regulatory models on the theme of enforcement is evident; enforcement is a particular problem with self-regulatory governance systems because they tend to lack coercive mechanisms to sanction rule-breaking.[14] Self- and co-regulatory strategies need to be continuously monitored to see whether they keep their promises. The same, however, goes for state-controlled regulation. Too few are the studies critically examining the output of, for instance, the public authorities that are said to help safeguard our privacy and personal data. Enforcement, therefore, has become a key duty for all. The efforts of governments and big companies towards social sorting, categorisation, profiling and data matching erode individuality and propel us ever closer to Huxley's *Brave New World*. Invasions of privacy lead to a breakdown in trust. If we know that governments, big companies and other evil-doers are spying on us, without our consent, we are less likely to trust them. The loss of trust in social institutions leads to a loss of social capital; it creates a dysfunctional, distrusting society. Government and big companies know more and more about us, but we know less and less about them and about what they are doing with our personal data. Privacy is essential for trust in political and social institutions.

Second, but linked to the foregoing, there is the debate on the choice of enforcement instruments. Successful enforcement seems to demand coercive means of enforcing regulations, even if that coercion is used only as a last resort.[15] The importance of the recent actions by competent US authorities (the Federal Trade Commission in particular) to check on the firms that have accepted the Safe Harbor agreement is therefore more than significant. The whole EU policy agenda today seems to be turned towards creating more coercion and giving administrative enforcement powers to the national data protection authorities, but strangely enough, this book, at least several contributions to it, brings the message that "hard" powers need to be complemented by "soft" powers and that "sticks" are in need of "carrots". Billy Hawkes, former Irish data protection commissioner, says in his country the use of both "soft" and "hard" enforcement measures "is to bring about compliance rather than to punish. Even where punitive action is taken through the courts,

---

[12] Reed, Chris, "Cloud Governance: The Way Forward", in Christopher Millard (ed.), *Cloud Computing Law*, Oxford University Press, 2013, p. 362.

[13] "The most obvious reason why this should be so is that the Internet is global in reach, and thus cuts across the hierarchical structures of national law." Reed, ibid., p. 365.

[14] Ibid., p. 374.

[15] Ibid.

the objective is always to achieve compliance by the offending organisation and by other organisations in its sector." To achieve such outcomes, a DPA needs a range of "hard" and "soft" powers, as Hiroshi Miyazaki comments. Also important, as Billy Hawkes further notes, is the ability of the DPA to deploy the tools in its regulatory tool-box with flexibility and an ability and willingness to work closely with other regulators. These are, he says, key enablers for smaller DPAs. Other DPAs favour a tougher sanctions regime. Dutch DPA Jacob Kohnstamm says in his chapter that significant fines will help data protection authorities to carry out their task and that being able to impose sufficiently high fines can act as a deterrent to data controllers, leading to a higher degree of compliance. Billy Hawkes says that it is open to question whether the more punitive approach adopted in the Regulation will actually lead to a higher standard of compliance. In this regard, it is interesting to note that the Spanish regulator which had the highest fines and highest number of fines decided to "modulate" its fines, sticks in favour of a softer approach. The evidence shows that DPAs have some different approaches and regulatory philosophies. What does the empirical evidence suggest? Grant and Crowther in their capter suggest that fines need to be complemented by other instruments such as naming and shaming.

The "sticks and carrots" logic in regulation[16] is more than anecdotic: for the tortoise to move, both a stick and a carrot are needed; for a governing mechanism to work, both threats and incentives are needed. Under this perspective, the provisioning of sanctions – and not necessarily their imposition – and the increased load of obligations seem to hold the role of the stick in the earlier mentioned metaphor, which needs to be coupled, though, with a "carrot". The "carrot" implies providing for a "suitable" incentive, for an appropriate stimulation that would sufficiently tempt data controllers to move towards the inspired vision of "not mere compliance". The golden question in this regard is whether the respective legislative frameworks envisage carrots and whether choices between hard law and soft law, between carrots and sticks, are legitimate or, on the contrary, purely opportunistic. Taking this scheme seriously demands creativity. Taking that question into account, one could, for instance, defend the proposition that no notification of breaches – always bad for reputation – is needed when preventive security measures are taken. The awareness that Europe today is perhaps too focused on creating sticks, partly justifies chapters with experiences from abroad (negative, but also positive), chapters on the use of technology to regulate and enforce norms and chapters reflecting on the purposes of administrative fines as opposed to criminal fines. The wealth of detailed description in Chap. 2 teaches us that the work of data protection authorities cannot be presumed to impose sanctions alone.

[16] Morgan and Yeung, *op. cit.*, p. 101.

1.3 The structure of the book

For this volume, we have brought together experts in the field of enforcing privacy. Contributors to this book include privacy advocates, regulators, academics, lawyers, a technologist and a parliamentarian. In this volume, they consider different ways of enforcing privacy and different issues that arise in attempts to enforce privacy.

Following this Introduction, David Wright reviews the enforcement powers of data protection authorities, but makes the point that not all DPAs have all enforcement powers they need. Hence, DPAs often co-operate with each other and sometimes co-ordinate their enforcement actions as a way to leverage their shortage of resources. Nevertheless, they face various barriers to co-operation and co-ordination, which they are attempting to overcome. Wright's chapter sets the scene for the rest of the book, which considers various ways of enforcing privacy.

As mentioned above, the contributions to this book are clustered in four main sections. The first concerns countries, the second focuses on international mechanisms, the third on instruments and the fourth on challenges for the future.

The first section focuses on the US, Hungary, Japan, Spain and Latin America. Self-regulation puts the onus for enforcing privacy on individual organisations, but the title of Bob Gellman and Pam Dixon's chapter – "Failures of privacy self-regulation in the United States" – says it all: self-regulation is not an effective way of enforcing privacy. They back up their contention with various examples, including self-regulatory activities with the involvement of government, industry, academia and civil society.

Across the Atlantic, Ivan Szekely performs a case study of enforcing privacy and data protection in Hungary, where political factors undercut the regulator's powers, which has drawn criticism from the European Commission and others. The title of his chapter is "From a model pupil to a problematic grown-up", by which he means that Hungary initially led the way in eastern Europe's transition to democracy in the early 1990s, but then faltered. He concludes that Hungary's positive and negative experiments in enforcing privacy can serve as a model for both European and non-European countries.

In Japan, Hiroshi Miyashita explores the relative effectiveness of hard power and soft power as mechanisms for enforcing privacy. He also explores the differing enforcement approaches in Japan and Europe, as illustrated by the hacking of the Sony PlayStation Network.

Artemi Rallo, formerly Director of the Spanish Data Protection Authority (Agencia Española de Protección de Datos, AEPD), considers hard power and soft power too, but uses the terminology of sticks and carrots. Heretofore, Spain has had the toughest sanctions for breaches of its data protection law, but in recent years, the AEPD has modulated its "sticks" (relatively heavy fines) in favour of "carrots" (lower fines). The chapter explores whether this has made a difference in terms of enforcing privacy.

The first section of the book ends with a chapter on enforcing privacy in Latin America, with special attention paid to Uruguay, by Ana Brian Nougrères. Data protection legislation is a relatively new phenomenon in Latin America, but eight countries have adopted legislation since Argentina took the initiative in 2000. Argentina together with Uruguay has the distinction of meeting the adequacy standards set out in the EU's Data Protection Directive.

The second section of the book focuses on international mechanisms for enforcing privacy. There are various regional and thematic networks that help in this process, and one of these is the International Working Group on Data Protection in Telecommunications (IWGDPT), which is the subject of the chapter by Alexander Dix, the chairman of the IWGDPT. The first point that he makes is that privacy today can no longer be enforced on a national level only, an observation with which we fully agree. Dan Svantesson takes up the theme in his chapter on enforcing privacy across different jurisdictions. He considers jurisdictional issues that arise where there are differences in privacy laws, and then examines the implications of the International Covenant on Civil and Political Rights (ICCPR) on the enforcement of privacy across different jurisdictions.

Blair Stewart, New Zealand's Assistant Privacy Commissioner and a pioneer of privacy impact assessment, makes the case for mandatory breach notification as a means of enforcing privacy and, in particular, he discusses cross-border notification, an issue that has not had much air time until now. He argues that policy-makers and regulators must pay more attention to the parameters of cross-border notification if its potential is to be realised to the benefit of our globalised economy.

His Antipodean colleague, Graham Greenleaf, proposes "responsive regulation of data privacy" as a measure for assessing data privacy laws, which he does with regard to the 12 Asian countries that have such laws. Along the way, he makes some comparisons between Asia and Europe, especially in regard to their enforcement mechanisms. He points out that no Asian privacy regulator has yet levied fines measured in hundreds of thousands of US dollars, as is now a frequent occurrence in both Europe and the US.

Chris Connolly and Peter van Dijk bring us back to the Atlantic side of the planet with their chapter on enforcement and reform of the EU-US Safe Harbor agreement. That agreement has generated controversy ever since its introduction in 2000 as a way of sidestepping the adequacy requirements of Article 25 of the EU Data Protection Directive. As a means of enforcing privacy, the agreement has been less than effective, at least, not until very recently. They blame poor enforcement of the agreement. At the time this book goes to press, the European Commission and the US Department of Commerce are attempting to reach an agreement on a replacement for the original Safe Harbor agreement.

The third section of the book discusses instruments for enforcing privacy. Hazel Grant and Hannah Crowther consider how effective monetary penalties (or fines) have been at enforcing privacy, with a particular focus on the fines levied by the UK Information Commissioner's Office (ICO). They stress the importance of combining fines with other enforcement measures, such as "naming and shaming". Although the ICO has some of the highest fines in Europe at its disposition, they raise the question whether the UK's fines are too low to be effective. As they note, that question should go away when the European Data Protection Regulation comes into force. The Regulation contains a provision for fines of up to four per cent of a company's turnover.

Another important instrument for enforcing privacy is class action litigation. The US has had far more experience with class action suits than any other country. Marc Rotenberg, Director of the Electronic Privacy Information Center (EPIC), and his colleague David Jacobs delve into the intricacies of class action suits and, in particular, the efficacy of *cy pres* awards, the theory of which is to make the award to some entities on behalf of consumers where the awards to individual consumers would be nominal at best. *Cy pres* derives from the French phrase *si près*, which literally means "so near" or, in this context, "as near as possible".

Kirsten Bock's chapter poses the question of whether data protection certification and privacy seals are effective instruments for enforcing privacy or merely decorative. The answer is that it depends. She sets out various conditions that must be met in order for privacy seals or trustmarks to be effective.

Paul De Hert and Gertjan Boulet consider administrative and criminal law sanctions as remedies to infringements of data protection law. They reflect on the relative "silence" regarding enforcement under the European data protection legal framework. The Data Protection Regulation distinguishes between criminal and administrative sanctions. It makes administrative enforcement mandatory but leaves criminal enforcement optional. They contend that the lack of harmonisation of criminal law sanctions is unsatisfactory. They recommend that Member States define as clearly as possible what offences shall be considered criminal or administrative, and enforced by means of criminal and administrative law.

Regulators and individuals can enforce privacy through the use of technologies. Daniel Le Métayer takes us on a tour of privacy-enhancing technologies. However, as he points out, the adoption of these technologies is still rather limited, even if it is growing, especially in the aftermath of recent privacy breach scandals. He adds that we cannot evade the issue of trust in the technologies themselves, that recent history has shown that cryptographic tools that were considered as the cornerstone of many secure systems might very well have been either bugged or hacked by secret agencies and might thus have been a major source of leaked personal data for years. He concludes that technology can play a key role in enforcing privacy but should not be used in isolation or seen as a convenient way to forget about privacy.

The fourth and final section of the book addresses challenges for the future. Billy Hawkes, formerly data protection commissioner of Ireland, explores the challenges facing data protection authorities with limited (human) resources in enforcing privacy. He examines the enforcement approach of the Office of the Data Protection Commissioner (ODPC), focussing on its use of a combination of "soft" and "hard" enforcement tools. He examines in particular how the ODPC has used its audit tool in relation to Ireland-based multinational companies that process personal data in connection with the provision of services across the European Union. He also comments on how the ODPC has involved other DPAs in such investigations and how this situation might change under the Data Protection Regulation.

Billy Hawkes' counterpart in the Netherlands, Jacob Kohnstamm, follows with a chapter entitled "Getting our act together: European Data Protection Authorities face up to Silicon Valley". Kohnstamm speaks of the challenge facing DPAs in working more closely together across borders. His chapter reviews some joint investigations by European and other DPAs in the past decade or so, and then looks to the future to identify what is needed to facilitate better co-operation across borders. He comments that the biggest challenge for data protection authorities is getting organisations to acknowledge that privacy by design, transparency and respecting the personal nature of their customers' data is good for business. But another challenge is arriving at the point where data subjects can trust organisations to follow the rules.

The last chapter in this last section, written by Member of the European Parliament Jan Philipp Albrecht, is entitled "Regaining control and sovereignty in the digital age". He was the rapporteur for the European Parliament's position on the Data Protection Regulation. He contends that the Googles and Facebooks of this world "disempower us not only as customers who consume what they have to offer but also as citizens of democratic societies governed by the rule of law. They dictate their rules to us. This is particularly true of what drives and perpetuates the new economy: our 'personal data'". His challenge for the future is stark: "If things remain as they are, we shall be completely disenfranchised and easily fleeced in the digitised world. We shall find ourselves living in a totalitarian controlled society, which has come into existence and holds sway because these businesses gather vast amounts of information about us, and are becoming more entrenched in our daily lives." Albrecht's chapter may be a sombre assessment of the realpolitik in progressing data protection reform, but appropriate nevertheless. His chapter underscores the importance of enforcing privacy.

We asked privacy guru James Rule to write a kind of envoi for the book, his view on the future of privacy enforcement. He acknowledges as "impressive" the global community of professionals who enforce privacy codes, but says they face a complex and daunting array of forces against their efforts. He says that public indignation against privacy intrusions has resulted in the establishment or strengthening of privacy institutions. He concludes that the "defenders of privacy need to consider measures that will more greatly mobilise the attentions of individual data subjects". To that end, he recommends the development of "hard-hitting, galvanising appeals that will resonate with ordinary people's privacy concerns – and embed themselves in public attention, even in the absence of dramatic events like the Snowden revelations". He suggests three such galvanising appeals or "capsule" demands for "Strong Privacy" to help solidify an alliance between the public and professional privacy advocates.

Despite the cynicism of corporate warlords who declare that privacy is dead, the contributors to this book clearly do not agree. We, the editors, hope this book offers readers and policy-makers some insights into what works and doesn't work as measures to enforce privacy. If those insights translate into stronger measures and if this book creates greater resistance to those who proclaim the death of privacy, then we will have achieved our objective.

References

Clarke, Roger, "What's "Privacy"?." Version of 7 August 2006. http://www.rogerclarke.com/DV/Privacy.html.

Crompton, Malcolm, Christine Cowper and Christopher Jefferis, "The Australian Dodo Case: An Insight for Data Protection Regulation", *BNA World Data Protection Report*, Vol. 9, No. 1, 2009, pp. 5–8.

De Hert, Paul, and Vagelis Papakonstantinou, "The EDPS as a Unique Stakeholder in the European Data Protection Landscape, Fulfilling the Explicit and Non-explicit Expectations", in Hielke Hijmans and Herke Kranenborg (eds.), *Data Protection Anno 2014: How to Restore Trust? Contributions in honour of Peter Hustinx, European Data Protection Supervisor (2004–2014)*, Intersentia, 2014, pp. 237–252.

Finn, Rachel, David Wright and Michael Friedewald, "Seven Types of Privacy", in Serge Gutwirth, Yves Poullet et al. (eds.), *European data protection: coming of age?*, Springer, Dordrecht, 2013.

Gellert, Raphaël, and Serge Gutwirth, "The legal construction of privacy and data protection", *Computer Law & Security Review*, Vol. 29, 2013, pp. 522–530.

González Fuster, Gloria, *The Emergence of Personal Data Protection as a Fundamental Right of the EU*, Springer, 2014.

Gunasekara, Gehan, "Paddling in unison or just paddling? International trends in reforming information privacy law", *International Journal of Law and Information Technology*, 2013, pp. 1–37.

Hijmans, Hielke, and Herke Kranenborg (eds.), *Data Protection Anno 2014: How to Restore Trust? Contributions in honour of Peter Hustinx, European Data Protection Supervisor (2004–2014)*, Intersentia, 2014, pp. 237–252.

Kuner, Chris, Fred H. Cate, Christopher Millard, and Dan J. B. Svantesson, "Taking Stock after Four Years", *International Data Privacy Law*, Vol. 4, No. 2, 2014, pp. 87–88.

Lynskey, Orla, "Deconstructing Data Protection: The 'Added- Value' of a Right to Data Protection in the EU Legal Order", *International and Comparative Law Quarterly*, Vol. 63, 2014, pp. 569–597.

Privacy Laws & Business, "EDPS aims to be proactive and focus on external relations", Issue 133, 2015, pp. 1–4.

Reed, Chris, "Cloud Governance: The Way Forward", in Christopher Millard (ed.), *Cloud Computing Law*, Oxford University Press, 2013.

Wright, David, and Paul De Hert (eds.), *Privacy Impact Assessment*, Springer, Dordrecht, 2012.

Zalnieriute, Monika, "An international constitutional moment for data privacy in the times of mass-surveillance", *International Journal of Law and Information Technology*, Vol. 23, 2015, pp. 99–133.

Chapter 2
Enforcing Privacy

David Wright

2.1 Introduction

With the increasing intrusions by governments, big companies and others, privacy needs protection – and enforcers, especially regulators, to resist these depredations. Individuals simply do not have the powers necessary to counter those at the disposition of big companies and government agencies. Who are these enforcers? The preamble to the Additional Protocol to the Council of Europe's Convention 108 clearly states that "supervisory authorities, exercising their functions in complete independence, are an element of the effective protection of individuals with regard to the processing of personal data".[1] Former European Data Protection Supervisor Peter Hustinx has commented that the supervisory authorities [i.e., data protection authorities or DPAs] "have become an essential component of the data protection supervisory system in a democratic society".[2] This chapter describes the various powers that DPAs have to enforce privacy.[3]

---

[1] Council of Europe, Additional Protocol to the Convention for the Protection of Individuals with regard to Automatic Processing of Personal Data regarding supervisory authorities and transborder data flows, Strasbourg, 8 November 2001. http://conventions.coe.int/Treaty/EN/Treaties/HTML/181.htm. See also Council of Europe, Convention for the Protection of Individuals with regard to Automatic Processing of Personal Data, Strasbourg, 28 January 1981. http://conventions.coe.int/Treaty/en/Treaties/Html/108.htm

[2] Hustinx, Peter, Cahiers du Centre de Recherches Informatique et Droit (CRID), No. 31, "Défis du droit à la protection de la vie privée/Challenges of privacy and data protection law", Namur-Brussels, 2008, pp. 561–568.

[3] This chapter draws on research conducted by Trilateral Research as a partner in the EU-funded PHAEDRA project (www.phaedra-project.eu). A PHAEDRA II project was launched in January 2015. PHAEDRA II is somewhat different from its predecessor in the sense that is focused on

D. Wright (✉)
Trilateral Research, London, UK
e-mail: david.wright@trilateralresearch.com

D. Wright, P. De Hert (eds.), *Enforcing Privacy*, Law, Governance and Technology Series 25, DOI 10.1007/978-3-319-25047-2_2

However, DPAs are typically constrained by their varying powers and limited resources in enforcing privacy as effectively as they might like. That being the case, many DPAs are collaborating with each other to leverage their powers and those scarce resources. Nevertheless, there are barriers to co-operation and privacy enforcement co-ordination. But efforts are being made to overcome these barriers, as this chapter points out. Despite these efforts, some issues – and challenges – remain. The chapter concludes with some recommendations.

2.2 Enforcement powers

In the European Union, recital 100 of the Data Protection Regulation provides that supervisory authorities "should have in each Member State the same tasks and effective powers, including powers of investigation, corrective powers and sanctions, and authorisation and advisory powers, particularly in cases of complaints from individuals, and without prejudice to the powers of prosecutorial authorities under national law, to bring infringements of this Regulation to the attention of the judicial authorities and/or engage in legal proceedings. Such powers should also include the power to impose a temporary or definitive limitation, including a ban, on processing."[4] While supervisory authorities are expected to act with complete independence, their decisions may be appealed to the courts.

A variety of enforcement instruments are at the disposition of DPAs.[5] The principal ones are the following.

2.2.1 Receiving and investigating complaints

Complaints are a double-edged sword. On the one hand, a rising number of complaints shows that people are increasingly aware of their privacy. On the other hand, that rising number consumes more time from the data protection authorities. The UK Information Commissioner's Office received some 15,492 complaints in 2014 compared to 7421 complaints in 2011.[6]

Europe and, in particular, practical implementation of the proposed Regulation, but it too will focus on improving co-operation between DPAs in the enforcement of privacy.

[4] For a copy of the text agreed by the European Parliament, Council and Commission on 15 December 2015, see http://www.statewatch.org/news/2015/dec/eu-council-dp-reg-draft-final-compromise-15039-15.pdf

[5] The UK Information Commissioner's Office (ICO) lists the instruments at its disposition on its website. See ICO, "Taking action: data protection and privacy and electronic communications". http://ico.org.uk/what_we_cover/taking_action/dp_pecr

[6] Data provided by Adam Stevens in an e-mail dated 3 March 2015.

Article 51a of the Data Protection Regulation says that each supervisory authority shall be competent to deal with a complaint lodged with it.

Complaints can be an important source of data for DPAs, but a large number of complaints can overwhelm those with limited resources. Peter Hustinx has commented that

> Many authorities presently suffer because their activities are dominated by individual complaints. This may be for different reasons, but they tend to reinforce each other and limit the capacity of the authority to invest sufficient resources in important issues: firstly, a lack of alternatives for enforcement of rights by data subjects, and secondly, a lack of means for authorities to set their own priorities and to make selections.[7]

It would be regrettable if data protection authorities were obliged to deal with *all* complaints and requests for assistance without the possibility to exercise a reasonable discretion as to whether and how to deal with the matter. This may be a common approach for courts, and understandable from the point of view of general administrative law, but for data protection authorities with wide responsibilities and limited resources, it only means that individual cases will dominate the agenda at the expense of other matters.

The appropriate remedy for these problems should thus be twofold: first, encourage alternative courses of action for enforcement of data protection rights and, second, make sure that data protection authorities are able to set priorities and develop more flexible methods of dealing with individual complaints, including simple procedures and using them in support of ex officio inquiries against responsible parties.[8]

Not all DPAs respond to all complaints. An example is the Dutch DPA (College Bescherming Persoonsgegevens or CBP), who no longer follows up on all complaints it receives because of its scarce resources.

2.2.2 *Guidance and codes of practice*

DPAs offer guidance and codes of practice on, especially, sensitive or difficult issues. For example, the UK Information Commissioner's Office (ICO) has issued a data sharing code of practice providing practical advice to organisations that share personal data.[9] The code aims to help organisations to collect and share personal data in a way that complies with the law, is fair, transparent and in line with the rights and expectations of the people whose data is being shared. The ICO has also

[7] Hustinx, op. cit.

[8] Hustinx, op. cit.

[9] Version 2, released in December 2014, can be found here: https://ico.org.uk/for-organisations/guide-to-data-protection/data-sharing/

issued a code of practice for surveillance (or CCTV) cameras,[10] on subject access for organisations dealing with requests from individuals for personal information,[11] on privacy impact assessment,[12] on assessment notices,[13] employment practices,[14] big data[15] international data transfers,[16] and more.[17] It has also published a guide to data protection, which discusses the DP principles in great detail (80 pages)[18] and a guide to the Privacy and Electronic Communications Regulations (PECR).[19]

Other DPAs publish similar guides and codes of practice, sometimes in English in addition to the national language(s). For example, the CNIL has published a methodology for Managing Privacy Risks[20] and Measures for Managing Privacy Risks,[21] both in English, while the Hong Kong Privacy Commissioner has published a guidance on cross-border data transfers.[22] The Hungarian DPA has published a guidance on privacy impact assessment, also in English.

2.2.3 *Notices and warnings*

A regulator may require an organisation to provide it with whatever information it needs to carry out its functions. This is sometimes described as an "information notice". It differs from an "enforcement notice", whereby the regulator may require a data controller or data processor to take whatever steps it considers appropriate to comply with data protection legislation. Such steps could include correcting data, blocking data from use for certain purposes, or erasing data altogether. The ICO issues information notices that require companies in its jurisdiction to give it information should it require it.

---

[10] https://ico.org.uk/media/for-organisations/documents/1542/cctv-code-of-practice.pdf

[11] https://ico.org.uk/media/for-organisations/documents/1065/subject-access-code-of-practice.pdf

[12] https://ico.org.uk/media/for-organisations/documents/1595/pia-code-of-practice.pdf

[13] An assessment notice, or compulsory audit, enables the ICO to determine whether a data controller is complying with data protection principles. https://ico.org.uk/media/for-organisations/documents/1534/assessment_notices_code_of_practice.pdf

[14] https://ico.org.uk/media/for-organisations/documents/1064/the_employment_practices_code.pdf

[15] https://ico.org.uk/media/for-organisations/documents/1541/big-data-and-data-protection.pdf

[16] https://ico.org.uk/media/for-organisations/documents/1566/international_transfers_legal_guidance.pdf

[17] https://ico.org.uk/for-organisations/guidance-index/data-protection-and-privacy-and-electronic-communications/

[18] https://ico.org.uk/media/for-organisations/documents/1607/the_guide_to_data_protection.pdf

[19] https://ico.org.uk/for-organisations/guide-to-pecr/

[20] http://www.cnil.fr/fileadmin/documents/en/CNIL-ManagingPrivacyRisks-Methodology.pdf

[21] http://www.cnil.fr/fileadmin/documents/en/CNIL-ManagingPrivacyRisks-Measures.pdf

[22] http://www.pcpd.org.hk/english/resources_centre/publications/guidance/files/GN_crossborder_e.pdf

In Ireland, the Office of the Data Protection Commissioner (ODPC) may prohibit the transfer of personal data from the state to a place outside the European Economic Area. The ODPC can exercise this power by providing a written notice, called a "prohibition notice", to the data controller or data processor. In considering whether to exercise this power, the ODPC considers the need to facilitate international transfers of information. A prohibition notice may be absolute, or may prohibit the transfer of personal data until the person concerned takes certain steps to protect the interests of the individuals affected.[23]

An enforcement notice has the potential to have a far greater influence on a controller than even the heftiest fine: an order to cease processing personal data altogether. Whether the order only relates to certain types of data, or is confined to a limited period (for example, until the controller improves its compliance more generally), it has the potential to shut down a business for the duration of the notice. Consequently, this power is often regarded as the strongest weapon that a DPA has in its arsenal. Failure to comply with an enforcement notice is punishable by a fine, and constitutes a criminal offence. This means that any subsequent fine is potentially unlimited, but would have to be the subject of formal proceedings before a criminal court (entailing, amongst other things, that the offence be proved beyond reasonable doubt).[24]

2.2.4 *Naming and shaming*

When a DPA makes public the names of organisations that have seriously contravened data protection legislation, this is a practice known as "naming and shaming". Some DPAs are able to "name and shame"; others cannot or, at least, not until an organisation has been investigated and penalised. There are different views on how well naming and shaming actually works. Dutch DPA Jacob Kohnstamm is of the view that "Possible bad publicity is usually short-lived and does not tend to lead to the great losses in customers or money."[25]

The ICO and other DPAs recognise the power of publicity, as evidenced by their willingness to co-operate with the media. The ICO does not simply post monetary penalty notices (MPNs or fines) on its website for journalists to find, but frequently issues press releases, briefs journalists and uses social media. The ICO's public policy statement on communicating enforcement activities states that "the ICO aims to get media coverage for enforcement activities".[26] The policy contains a list of

---

[23] Hawkes, Billy, "Data Protection Enforcement: Challenges Facing Smaller Data Protection Authorities", this volume.

[24] Grant, Hazel, and Hannah Crowther, Chap. 13, this volume.

[25] Kohnstamm, Jacob, Chap. 19, this volume.

[26] ICO Corporate Affairs policy 'Communicating enforcement activities', 11 November 2010. https://ico.org.uk/media/about-the-ico/policies-and-procedures/1890/ico_enforcement_communications_policy.pdf

circumstances where the ICO is likely to seek publicity, including where it is a "new, extreme or first" instance, where publicity is likely to deter others, or where there is an opportunity for education and prevention. In France, this element of the penalty is formalised in the French Data Protection Act, under Article 46 of which the CNIL has a statutory power to seek publication of the penalty in newspapers and other media.[27]

2.2.5 *Mandatory PIAs*

While some DPAs encourage organisations in their jurisdictions to undertake privacy impact assessments (PIAs), few have made PIAs mandatory. They are mandatory for government departments and agencies in the UK, the US and Canada. PIAs (or data protection impact assessments) will be mandatory in the European Union when the new Data Protection Regulation comes into force where the processing of personal data poses "high risks" to data subjects. PIAs could be a formidable arrow in the regulatory quiver depending on how the European Commission implements the DPIA provision in practice. For example, if the EC subjects DPIAs to regulatory oversight or, at least, random inspection, then companies and public sector organisations will need to treat DPIAs seriously and produce credible DPIA reports. If they fail to produce adequate DPIAs, DPAs may refuse to authorise the initiation of a new database or other activity that risks intruding upon our privacy.

2.2.6 *Inspections, investigations and audits*

Most DPAs are able to conduct inspections, investigations and audits, in some cases only in response to a complaint, in other cases, on the DPA's own initiative. For example, the Australian DPA has the power to conduct investigations on its own initiative (not just in response to a complaint). The EC-funded PHAEDRA project[28] (in which the author was a partner) conducted a survey asking DPAs about their enforcement powers to which it received 21 responses. All but two of the respondents said they were able to conduct inspections. Only two respondents – the New Zealand Privacy Commissioner and the US Federal Trade Commission (FTC) – said they could not.

Not all DPAs can make unannounced inspections. In the same survey, most said they could make unannounced inspections, but four said they could not – from NZ, Ontario, the UK and the US. In an interview, one DPA said that unannounced inspections were better because if the inspection is announced in advance, the company can simply destroy evidence of wrong-doing.

[27] Grant and Crowther, Chap. 13, this volume.

[28] See www.phaedra-project.eu

2.2.7 Monetary penalties (fines)

Some DPAs are able to issue fines against those who have transgressed data protection rules, while others are not able to do so. The DPAs from Canada, Hong Kong, Lithuania, Mauritius, New Zealand, Ontario and Switzerland as well as the European Data Protection Supervisor (EDPS) are examples of those who don't have a power to impose fines directly. For those who can impose fines, the level of fines can vary significantly. The ICO can impose fines of up to £500,000, while CNIL can impose a fine of a maximum of €150,000 for a first time offender. The Spanish DPA (Agencia Española de la Protección de Datos, AEPD) can impose fines of more than €1 million (it imposed a fine of €900,000 against Google in December 2013 in connection with Google's unified privacy policy which would enable Google to mine personal data across all of its services for more highly targeted adverts). In December 2014, the Commissioner for Data Protection and Freedom of Information of the German state Rhineland-Palatinate imposed a fine of €1,300,000 on the insurance group Debeka. Even more recently, January 2015, the Dutch DPA has threatened Google with a fine of up to €15 million.[29]

In other cases, some DPAs need to go to court in order to get a fine imposed on a company that is not compliant with the law.

Hazel Grant and Hannah Crowther in their chapter in this volume note that legislators have adopted a variety of different "fining models" to enforce privacy obligations. Fines may take the form of an administrative penalty issued by a data protection authority, a civil penalty ordered by a court or, in some cases, a criminal penalty. The typical amounts of fines, the sorts of breaches that result in fines, and the typical profile of the recipients of fines also vary significantly between countries.[30]

Prior to issuing a fine – also known as a monetary penalty notice (MPN) – the ICO must issue a notice of intent to which the data controller may respond in its defence. In cases where the ICO thinks a data controller has breached the Data Protection Act 1998,[31] ICO gives the controller an opportunity to set out all of the steps it has taken to mitigate the breach, with a view to reducing the amount of any

---

[29] In January 2015, the College Bescherming Persoonsgegevens (CBP, the Dutch DPA) released a cease and desist order requiring Google to pay €60,000 per day, up to a maximum of €15 million, for violating Dutch data protection law. Google had until the end of February 2015 to change the way it handles personal data. The order requires Google to carry out three measures:

- Ask for "unambiguous consent" before it shares personal data of Internet users with its other services, such as Google Maps and YouTube, the video-sharing site
- Make it clear to users that Google is the owner of YouTube
- Amend its privacy policy to clarify what data is collected and how the data is used.

For more, see O'Donoghue, Cynthia, "Dutch data protection authority threatens Google with a €15 million fine", *Lexology*, 8 Jan 2015.

[30] Grant and Crowther, Chap. 13, this volume.

[31] http://www.legislation.gov.uk/ukpga/1998/29/contents

MPN that the ICO might impose.[32] The ICO takes various factors into account in determining the amount of a monetary penalty, including (1) the nature of the contravention, (2) the effect of the contravention, (3) behavioural issues, and (4) the impact on the data controller.

Under the Data Protection Regulation, once it is in force (expected in early 2018), DPAs would be empowered to fine companies up to 4 % of their annual global turnover.

2.2.8 Undertakings

The ICO has leveraged the threat of MPNs into an alternative enforcement mechanism: seeking contractual undertakings from data controllers to take certain remedial steps. Although the practice began before MPNs were initially introduced, the regulator can encourage data controllers to take steps to avoid an MPN and the resulting negative media coverage. Undertakings have significant advantages for the regulator. Since an undertaking is a more "co-operative" solution, it is less likely that a data controller will challenge it. An undertaking is simpler and easier to put in place. Furthermore, the ICO can put an undertaking in place quickly. The ICO entered into more than 20 undertakings in 2013 (compared to 18 MPNs and 7 enforcement notices), suggesting that the *threat* of an MPN may be an effective means to drive remedial action, at least after a breach has occurred.[33]

2.2.9 Refusal to register a new database

In EU countries, most DPAs require data controllers and processors to register their databases if they intend to process personal data. In some Member States (such as Ireland), the DPA has the power to refuse registration, which effectively means that the organisation concerned is prohibited from processing personal data.

2.2.10 Court orders

In many countries, the DPA has the power to seek a court order to force a potentially offending company or organisation to cease and stop its offending behaviour. If a company fails to comply with an order, the DPA could consider contempt of court and, accordingly, could issue an enforcement notice through the courts. Furthermore,

[32] Grant and Crowther, Chap. 13, this volume.

[33] Grant and Crowther, Chap. 13, this volume.

the regulator may also seek punitive damages and fines against the offending company for the perceived harm it has caused to privacy or data protection.

2.2.11 *Other powers*

In addition to the above principal enforcement powers, DPAs sometimes possess other powers. For example:

- The Bulgarian DPA is able to issue compulsory instructions on personal data protection.
- The Finnish Data Protection Ombudsman must be heard in the preparation of legislative or administrative reforms concerning the protection of personal rights and freedoms in the processing of personal data. In practice, this means that the Ombudsman provides statements and participates in working groups set up for the preparation and review of legislation. The public prosecutor must consult the Data Protection Ombudsman prior to bringing charges based on violations of the Personal Data Act. Courts of law are also obliged to hear the Ombudsman in cases concerning related issues.
- The Mauritius DPA said that the DPA 2004 makes provision for preservation orders, entry and search, requesting assistance from other authorities.
- The NZ Privacy Commissioner has these additional powers:

  (a) Enforceable codes of practice
  (b) Civil orders by tribunal
  (c) Compensation by tribunal
  (d) Subject access charging determinations (by Commissioner)

- The US SAFE WEB Act provides several other powers that assist the US Federal Trade Commission (FTC) in cross-border privacy enforcement. The FTC has the ability to maintain confidential information received from foreign sources, facilitating the receipt of non-public investigative information. The FTC can take action when US-based actions harm foreign consumers. The FTC can accept reimbursement for investigative assistance, and can participate in foreign staff exchanges. Finally, the FTC has power to enter into binding international agreements for mutual legal assistance in consumer protection matters.

Some DPAs are seeking even stronger enforcement powers. The ICO has said it would like to see custodial sentences for a breach of section 55 of the UK Data Protection Act, which involves a person knowingly or recklessly obtaining, procuring or otherwise processing personal data unlawfully.[34]

---

[34] Arthur, Charles, "European watchdogs order Google to rewrite privacy policy or face legal action", *The Guardian*, 5 July 2013. http://www.guardian.co.uk/technology/2013/jul/05/google-privacy-policy-legal-action

2.2.12 Privacy seals and trustmarks

Some DPAs, notably the CNIL and the ICO, have developed or are developing trustmarks. The first DPA-inspired privacy seal was the EuroPriSe seal, developed by the DPA from Schleswig-Holstein. Privacy seals are voluntary. To be able to use a privacy seal or trustmark, the applicant must meet and adhere to certain standards. As of mid-2015, the number of privacy seals awarded by DPAs is small, fewer than 100 in the case of each of CNIL and the EuroPriSe.

The use of privacy seals may stretch beyond the above three countries once the GDPR comes into force. Article 39 of the GDPR provides for a data protection seal. While the European Commission has commissioned a study of privacy seals, which considered several different options, and while the European Parliament has indicated its support for a privacy seal, the Commission has yet to propose a particular scheme.[35]

2.2.13 Obligatory data breach notifications

The European Commission has put in place specific rules to ensure that personal data breaches in the EU telecom sector are notified in the same way in each Member State. Under the revised ePrivacy Directive (2009/136/EC), when a personal data breach occurs, the provider has to report this to a specific national authority. Also, the provider has to inform the concerned subscriber directly when the breach is likely to adversely affect personal data or privacy. To ensure consistent implementation of the data breach rules across Member States, the Commission has adopted "technical implementing measures" – practical rules to complement the existing legislation – on the circumstances, formats and procedures for the notification requirements. These rules aim to ensure that all citizen-consumers receive equivalent treatment across the EU in case of a data breach, and that businesses can take a pan-EU approach to these problems if they operate in more than one country.[36]

Article 31 of the General Data Protection Regulation widens the scope of breach notifications to the supervisory authority. Once adopted, any organisation, not just from the telecom sector, would need to notify the host DPA of a data breach within 72 h of its occurrence.

---

[35] For more on privacy seals as a means of enforcing privacy, see the chapter by Kirsten Bock in this volume.

[36] http://ec.europa.eu/digital-agenda/en/eprivacy-directive-data-breach-notifications

2.2.14 *Public opinion*

Public opinion is, potentially, a powerful instrument at the disposition of DPAs. DPAs can harness it to enforce privacy on wayward companies and government departments.[37] Some of the larger DPAs are obviously more active and adept in their media relations than smaller ones. In interviews with DPAs in the context of the PHAEDRA project, several mentioned the utility of collaboration among DPAs in regard to communications with the media and public, particularly in the context of high profile issues. If DPAs collectively decide to delegate lead responsibility for an investigation to one DPA, then other DPAs may feel the need to explain to their public, including the media, what they have done and why they have delegated responsibility to some other DPA. In short, some DPAs have recognised the need to develop a common communications (or dissemination) strategy, especially in instances where they agree to some other DPA's taking the lead to investigate an issue on behalf of all DPAs. However, a DPA strategy for harnessing public opinion should go beyond explanation of investigations: it should build support for the exercise of enforcement powers and call for greater powers where existing powers are insufficient. Or more generally, DPAs need to harness public opinion on the importance of enforcing privacy and encouraging privacy-protective behaviour among individuals as well as corporate citizens.

2.3 Enforcement powers vary from one DPA to another

Not all DPAs have the complete catalogue of powers described above. Enforcement powers vary from one DPA to another, sometimes because of differences in law and sometimes because of differences in strategy. Some DPAs may prefer the "stick", while others prefer "carrots" and still others may prefer a combination.

Here are some examples of differences in powers:

- The Office of the Privacy Commissioner of Canada, the Dutch DPA and the Irish Office of the Data Protection Commissioner have not been able to levy fines directly, but the ICO, AEPD and CNIL can.
- ICO cannot investigate private sector entities without the consent of the target, whereas the Kosovo DPA can investigate public and private sector organisations.
- The US FTC cannot disclose an investigation underway, whereas in Norway DPA documents are public by default.
- ILITA, the Israeli DPA, cannot share criminal information but can share other information. CNIL cannot share any confidential information.

[37] DPAs can use a variety of tools to "harness" public opinion, such as press conferences, press releases, studies, etc.

At least in Europe, adoption of the new Data Protection Regulation will give DPAs greater and more uniform powers, including fines of up to four per cent of turnover, as mentioned above.

2.4 Co-operation and co-ordination as leverage

DPAs clearly recognise the benefits of co-operation and co-ordination with their peers. The proliferation of DPA networks reflects this reality. Among the benefits of the Global Privacy Enforcement Network (GPEN) and other regional and international networks is that it sends a message to industry that regulators are working together. Presumably, it will be increasingly difficult for companies to play one regulator off against another or to engage in "forum shopping".

Experience demonstrates the benefits of co-operation, which yields efficiencies for DPAs. It produces superior specific and broad-based outcomes. It leads to expedited resolutions and results. The Article 29 Working Party (WP) in Europe is the prime example of DPA co-operation and collaboration. Its Opinions hold far more weight than those of a single DPA. The Article 29 WP conducts investigations and develops Opinions that are beyond the resources of even the biggest of DPAs. Hence, participation by European DPAs in the Article 29 WP is a way of leveraging their scarce resources. Similarly, again in Europe, DPAs gain knowledge and contacts through their participation in the so-called Spring Conference and its associated case-handling workshop, which would not otherwise be so readily at their disposition.

Not all DPAs are able to contribute as fully as they might like to co-operative efforts with other DPAs. Their enabling legislation may constrain the extent to which they can contribute to international efforts at privacy enforcement. Such is the case with CNIL, among others. DPAs well recognise this issue. Accordingly, DPAs generally recognise that there needs to be various levels of co-operation and co-ordination, some of which will be applicable to some DPAs, but not others. The Global Cross Border Enforcement Co-operation Arrangement,[38] agreed at the 36th International Conference of Data Protection and Privacy Commissioners in Mauritius in October 2014, reflects this reality.

Building partnerships is an evolutionary process. Personally knowing other DPAs is an important element in making progress internationally. Such personal knowledge builds trust, which affects the extent to which DPAs can collaborate.

---

[38] http://www.privacyconference2014.org/media/16667/Enforcement-Cooperation-Agreement-adopted.pdf

2.5 Barriers to co-operation and co-ordination

Despite good will among DPAs, they still face various barriers to co-operation and co-ordination, some of which are described below.

2.5.1 *Results from the second PHAEDRA questionnaire*

In the PHAEDRA project, co-funded by the EU, the PHAEDRA consortium[39] asked DPAs: if a DPA requested some information from them in connection with an investigation, would they be able to gather or share it? Here are some of the responses we received to that question, which reveals the range of possibilities from no to yes to maybe:

- The Office of the Australian Information Commissioner (OAIC) said that, in relation to sharing investigation information with a DPA, section 43(2) of the Privacy Act 1988 would apply to any participation by the OAIC in joint enforcement action. That section currently provides that the investigation of complaints and own motion investigations "shall be conducted in private but otherwise in such manner as the Commissioner thinks fit". However, amendments to the Privacy Act on 12 March 2014 clarify that the Commissioner has the discretion to investigate in public or private. The amendment provides the OAIC with the flexibility to participate in joint enforcement action. Section 96 provides some additional parameters that limit the use or disclosure of the affairs of another person to that required in the performance of a duty under or in connection with the Privacy Act, or in the course of acting for or on behalf of the Commissioner. Gathering information (where sharing is permitted) for another DPA could present resource challenges depending on the size of the request. The OAIC's capacity to assist in a given matter needs to be assessed at the time of the request.
- The Bulgarian Commission for Personal Data Protection (CPDP) has the possibility to co-operate with other data protection authorities on different cases if the issues are within its competence.[40] However, it shares only the results from the performed inspection, not the information about the stages of the inspection.
- Article 64(2) of the Danish Act on Processing of Personal Data states that "The Data Protection Agency may further disclose data to supervisory authorities in other Member States to the extent that this is required in order to ensure compliance

---

[39] The consortium comprised Vrije Universiteit Brussel (Belgium), Trilateral Research (UK), Universidad Jaume I (Spain) and GIODO (the Polish data protection authority).

[40] For the Law for Protection of Personal Data, see https://www.cpdp.bg/en/index.php?p=element&aid=373-. For the Rules on the activity of the Commission for Personal Data Protection and its administration, see https://www.cpdp.bg/en/index.php?p=element&aid=36-. For Ordinance 1 on the minimum level of technical and organisational measures and the admissible type of personal data protection, see https://www.cpdp.bg/en/index.php?p=element&aid=632-

with the provisions of this Act or those of the data protection legislation of the Member State concerned."[41]

- The European Data Protection Supervisor (EDPS) said yes, in principle, to the extent necessary (see more detailed language in Article 46 sub (f) (i) of Regulation (EC) 45/2001: "shall cooperate…").[42] In the case of non-EU DPAs, the EDPS would take the same approach in principle. However, this may be subject to adequate levels of protection or adequate safeguards set out in a Memorandum of Understanding (MoU) or similar.
- The Estonian DPA said yes, it was entitled to do so by the Council of Europe's Convention 108, the EU Directive 95/46/EC (Art 28.6) and national law.[43]
- The Finnish Data Protection Ombudsman and Hungarian DPA said yes.[44]
- The Hong Kong Privacy Commissioner said it was possible to do so under sections 46.7–10 of the Personal Data (Privacy) Ordinance (Chapter 486, Laws of Hong Kong).[45]
- The Mexican Federal Institute for Access to Information and Data Protection (IFAI) said yes, as long as the DPA undertakes the responsibility of keeping the same provisions of privacy, confidentiality and discretion that the Federal Law on Protection of Personal Data Held by Private Parties (Article 60) requires of federal civil servants involved in investigations when they are in progress.[46]
- The Netherlands DPA said it was able to gather and share information in accordance with Article 61 (6) Dutch Data Protection Act (Wet bescherming persoonsgegevens).[47]
- The New Zealand Privacy Commissioner's Office said gathering information was possible, but depended on the type of information requested. In terms of sharing information, the Act provides the Commissioner with a reasonably broad discretion to disclose information where "in the Commissioner's opinion [the information] ought to be disclosed for the purposes of giving effect to [the Privacy] Act" (section 116). There are recommendations before the government for broadening the information-sharing regime with overseas authorities in accordance with the applicable OECD Recommendation.[48]

---

[41] http://www.datatilsynet.dk/english/the-act-on-processing-of-personal-data/read-the-act-on-processing-of-personal-data/compiled-version-of-the-act-on-processing-of-personal-data/

[42] https://secure.edps.europa.eu/EDPSWEB/webdav/site/mySite/shared/Documents/EDPS/DataProt/Legislation/Reg_45-2001_EN.pdf

[43] http://www.aki.ee/en/inspectorate (also link "Overview and Details")

[44] Its enabling legislation is here: http://www.tietosuoja.fi/27305.htm. An unofficial translation of the legislation can be found at http://www.finlex.fi

[45] http://www.pcpd.org.hk/english/ordinance/ordfull.html

[46] http://inicio.ifai.org.mx/_catalogs/masterpage/English.aspx

[47] http://wetten.overheid.nl/BWBR0011468/geldigheidsdatum_24-10-2013. There is no official translation into English.

[48] Organisation for Economic Co-operation and Development, OECD Recommendation on Cross-border Co-operation in the Enforcement of Laws Protecting Privacy, Paris, 2007. http://www.oecd.org/internet/ieconomy/38770483.pdf

- Singapore's Personal Data Protection Commission (PDPC) is required under its Personal Data Protection Act 2012 (PDPA)[49] to protect personal data and other confidential information gathered in the course of an investigation and is only permitted to share such information subject to strict conditions. Factors that may affect whether it can gather and share the information requested by another DPA include (amongst others) whether there is an ongoing investigation or breach of the PDPA in Singapore, the scope of the information requested and whether there is an appropriate co-operation agreement between the PDPC and the other DPA concerned.
- The Slovak Office of Personal Data Protection said any request from a partner DPA would be addressed within its scope of power. The Office is also open to joint investigation activities, trading of information, sharing of experiences, etc.[50]
- The Swiss Federal Data Protection and Information Commissioner (FDPIC)[51] said it can share information with some limitation (see Articles 13, 15 and 16 of Convention 108). The FDPIC will not exchange personal data without the expressed consent of the individual concerned.
- The UK ICO said it depends on the DPA requesting the information. Under Article 52 of the EU's Data Protection Regulation, there is an obligation to share such information with other EU DPAs. There are narrower legal obligations such as that under Convention 108, which places the obligation to share all non-personal data in relation to a case. Beyond these two European legal instruments, there is no obligation to share information. Therefore, it rests on a balance between the confidentiality obligations of an authority and the public interest of sharing that information with another regulator.[52]
- The US Federal Trade Commission (FTC) said it could gather and share information at the request of another DPA. The US SAFE WEB Act permits investigative assistance and information sharing, on certain conditions and subject to certain safeguards. The statute authorises the Commission to assist foreign law enforcement agencies in their investigations of, or enforcement proceedings against, "possible violations of laws prohibiting fraudulent or deceptive commercial practices, or other practices substantially similar to practices prohibited by any provision of the laws administered by the Commission", according to 15 U.S.C. § 46(j). Under section 6(j)(2)(A), the Commission may "conduct such investigation as the Commission deems necessary to collect information and evidence pertinent to the request for assistance, using all investigative powers authorized by [the FTC Act]" 15 U.S.C. § 46(j)(2)(A). The Act authorises the

---

[49] http://statutes.agc.gov.sg/aol/search/display/view.w3p;page=0;query=CompId%3A32762ba6-f438-412e-b86d-5c12bd1d4f8a;rec=0;whole=yes

[50] The English version of the Act No. 122/2013 Coll. on personal data protection and about amendment of other acts can be found here: http://www.dataprotection.gov.sk/buxus/docs/Act_12213-en_1.pdf?buxus=10c21c1ce0bd7e9f41a003a939f76f0b

[51] http://www.edoeb.admin.ch/org/00129/index.html?lang=en

[52] The UK Data Protection Act 1998 and all its amendments can be found via the link below: http://www.legislation.gov.uk/all?title=data%20protection%20Act

FTC to share confidential information in its files with foreign law enforcement agencies, subject to certain statutory safeguards [15 U.S.C. § 57b-2(b)(6)].[53]

As these responses to the PHAEDRA questionnaire clearly show, there is a range of provisions in the authorising legislation of DPAs and privacy enforcement authorities that restrict or allow or condition the sharing of information with other DPAs. We discuss such provisions in the following sections.

2.5.2 *Confidentiality and legal barriers*

The task of effective international enforcement outside of Europe is complicated by the absence of internationally accepted data protection standards and the potential conflict with the confidentiality obligations laid down in Article 49 of the new Data Protection Regulation and Article 15 of Convention 108.[54]

DPAs have discussed at length the issue of how far they can go in releasing confidential information (not personal data) to their counterparts in other countries, even if doing so would contribute to apprehending large companies who are not troubled by their compromising privacy. Existing legislation enabling either the DPA, privacy commissioner or PEA may prevent or hamper the sharing of information. Laws have differences in scope from one country to another.

---

[53] The FTC enforces privacy protections based on several general consumer protection laws and several sectoral laws:

- FTC Act: http://www.ftc.gov/ogc/ftcact.shtm;
- The Children's Online Privacy Protection Act: http://www.law.cornell.edu/uscode/text/15/chapter-91;
- Fair Credit Reporting Act: http://www.law.cornell.edu/uscode/15/1681.shtml;
- Gramm-Leach-Bliley Act: http://www.law.cornell.edu/uscode/uscode15/usc_sec_15_0000680 1DOUBLEHYPHENDOUBLEHYPHEN000-.html [Title V, subtitle A, of this Act requires the FTC, along with several other agencies, to issue regulations (see 16 CFR Part 313) ensuring that financial institutions protect the privacy of consumers' personal financial information];
- Do Not Call Registry Legislation. http://frwebgate.access.gpo.gov/cgi-bin/getdoc.cgi?dbname=108_cong_public_laws&docid=f:publ010.108.pdf;
- Fair and Accurate Credit Transactions Act of 2003. http://frwebgate.access.gpo.gov/cgi-bin/getdoc.cgi?dbname=108_cong_public_laws&docid=f:publ159.108.pdf;
- Controlling the Assault of Non-Solicited Pornography and Marketing Act of 2003 (CAN-SPAM Act). http://frwebgate.access.gpo.gov/cgibin/getdoc.cgi?dbname=108_cong_public_laws&docid=f:publ187.108.pdf;
- Health Information Technology ("HITECH") Provisions of American Recovery and Reinvestment Act of 2009, Title XIII, Subtitle D. http://www.ftc.gov/ogc/stat3/hitech-pub-l-111-5.pdf

[54] Hawkes, op. cit.

2.5.3 *Lack of resources*

A shortage of human resources is an equally serious barrier that constrains the extent to which DPAs can co-operate and co-ordinate investigations with each other. Many DPAs are faced with staff shortages. The following table lists the number of full-time equivalent staff in data protection authorities around the world in 2013.

Data protection authority	Number of employees
Albania	29
Australia	62
Bavaria	16
Belgium	50
Berlin	37
Bosnia & Herzegovina	24
Bulgaria	73
Canada	170
Colombia	20
Costa Rica	1 [28][a]
Cyprus	14
Czech Rep	100
Denmark	32
Estonia	18
Finland	20
France	171
Germany	80
Greece	39
Hong Kong	76
Hungary	59
Iceland	4
Ireland	26.5
Isle of Man	4
Israel	25
Italy	109
Japan[b]	2–13
Korea	40
Liechtenstein	2
Lithuania	30
Macau	31
Macedonia	26
Mexico	87
Moldova	18
Montenegro	15
Netherlands	80
New Zealand	30

(continued)

Data protection authority	Number of employees
Ontario	100
Poland	130
Portugal	26
Russia	298
Serbia	43
Singapore[c]	40
Spain	164
Slovak Republic	28
Slovenia	33
Sweden	40
Switzerland	22.7
Ukraine	43
UK	350
USA (FTC)	45
Uruguay	12
Vietnam	40

[a]The Costa Rican authority said it was soon to begin a major recruitment, which would result in staff numbers as indicated in the square brackets

[b]The Japanese Ministry of Economy, Trade and Industry (METI) responded to the questionnaire. In doing so, it noted that, in Japan, there was no authority dedicated to data protection. Each ministry enforces privacy in its own jurisdiction, and each ministry and external agency has a unit working on data protection. METI's response to the questionnaire joined answers from various ministries and agencies. Since then, Japan has established a data protection authority, as mentioned by Hiroshi Miyashita in Chapter 5. With regard to FTEs, METI said there are cases where some departments or units also co-operate on privacy issues.

[c]Singapore's Personal Data Protection Commission (PDPC) was formed in January 2013; hence, it is still ramping up its recruitment. It envisages 40–50 employees.

As can be seen from the above, most DPAs have fewer than 60 staff. Only a few have more than 60 staff members. A shortage of resources can affect even DPAs with larger staff numbers. One DPA may ask another DPA for support, information, or even action, and a response may go unanswered for some time. Many DPAs favour some form of time limits in an international privacy enforcement co-ordination arrangement governing the amount of time before a response to a request is due.

Berlin DPA Alexander Dix has described the problem (the challenge) of resource shortages with the following example:

> The Facebook case has highlighted a more generic problem of enforcing privacy rules against global players. The office of the Irish Data Protection Commissioner is undoubtedly understaffed[55] compared to other European jurisdictions such as France or Germany. This may have influenced the decision of Facebook and other US providers such as Google and LinkedIn to have their European headquarters in Ireland although other considerations

[55] The office had 30 members of staff at the time of the Facebook audit, with no legal expert among them.

(e.g., tax legislation) could well have played a more prominent role in this decision. It is obvious that auditing large companies such as Facebook strains the scarce resources of a small data protection authority to its limits. The Irish Commissioner's audit of Facebook led to some changes in the service of the company, e.g., in the field of face recognition. However, basically the Commissioner accepted the argument brought forward by Facebook that users had no choice but to pay for the service with their personal data. Without disputing that this was a correct interpretation of Irish law, the example shows two major deficiencies in transnational enforcement: as long as the material rules on data protection as well as the resources of data protection authorities differ even within Europe, there is considerable room for *forum shopping* for companies (European or non-European).[56]

Because many DPAs have limited staff, they do not have the range of competences needed to address many of the main challenges facing DPAs today. In some cases, as in Ireland, however, the DPA is able to recruit external expertise on a short-term basis.

2.5.4 *Lack of awareness*

In response to a PHAEDRA survey, some DPAs mentioned the difficulty of knowing "what's going on" or "what's happening". Their limited human resources are a factor in some DPAs having an imperfect understanding of the principal issues being discussed in the International Conference of Data Protection and Privacy Commissioners (ICDPPC) or GPEN or the Art. 29 Working Party or the International Working Group on Data Protection in Telecommunications (IWGDPT). Some DPAs said they might like to participate in a co-ordinated privacy enforcement initiative, but weren't always aware when such initiatives were being taken, or who was the lead DPA and how they might be able to contribute to the collective effort.

The UK ICO said there is lack of understanding about the legal provisions across the world about what can and cannot be shared before, during and after enforcement action. Whilst GPEN and, in Europe, the case-handling workshop are helping to address this issue of what some DPAs can and cannot share, lack of awareness is still an issue for various DPAs.

2.5.5 *Language capability*

There are 24 official languages in the European Union, but most international meetings are conducted in English, which is more or less the lingua franca. Even so, some DPAs have difficulties expressing themselves in English, which limits their ability to contribute effectively, to speak cogently at meetings and to prepare written contributions, no matter how earnest and desirous they are of doing so.

[56] Dix, Alexander, Chap. 8, in this volume.

2.5.6 Lobbying power of multinationals

Multinationals have been rather successful in watering down the new Data Protection Regulation,[57] although they did not get everything they wanted. The biggest multinationals such as Google and Facebook pour huge resources in lobbying against provisions with which they disagree and bring to bear the US government to support their efforts. To the extent that Silicon Valley is successful in watering down the provisions of the proposed Data Protection Regulation, it reduces the prospects for improved privacy enforcement and, with it, more effective co-ordination between DPAs. Their lobbying against such provisions drains away resources that DPAs could otherwise spend in co-operative arrangements with other DPAs instead of trying to blunt the power of multinationals. On the other hand, it could be argued that the lobbing power of multinationals creates a kind of "siege mentality" among DPAs and that, as a consequence, they do seek to resist corporate efforts to undermine privacy enforcement.

2.5.7 Recognition of PEAs

In the last few years, the term "PEA" (privacy enforcement authority) has come into currency. There are differences between data protection authorities, privacy commissioners and PEAs. The ICDPPC nominally accredits only those "autonomous" institutions that are not under the direction of a government ministry. Ideally, the DPA should be authorised and funded by Parliament. The GPEN is not so strict. DPAs, PCs and PEAs can all become members of the GPEN.

2.5.8 The Snowden revelations

Since June 2013, the Snowden revelations have become a standing, ongoing topic of discussion among DPAs. The revelations have raised many issues, many of which are still active (e.g., the Safe Harbor agreement). While the Snowden revelations are not a barrier as such for privacy enforcement by DPAs, they nevertheless have raised many issues[58] that challenge already limited resources even more. Also the indepen-

[57] See the chapters by Jacob Kohnstamm, Chap. 19, and Jan Philipp Albrecht, Chap. 20, in this volume.

[58] See especially the European Parliament resolution of 12 March 2014 on the US NSA surveillance programme, surveillance bodies in various Member States and their impact on EU citizens' fundamental rights and on transatlantic cooperation in Justice and Home Affairs (2013/2188(INI)). http://www.europarl.europa.eu/sides/getDoc.do?type=TA&language=EN&reference=P7-TA-2014-0230. See also the European Parliament Committee on Civil Liberties, Justice and

dence of some DPAs has come under constraint. To the extent that the revelations place greater demands on DPA resources, they indirectly impact DPA resources that might otherwise have been devoted to improving co-ordination. The Snowden revelations have also shown the limitations of DPAs in providing oversight of the intelligence agencies and their violation of citizens' fundamental rights.

2.6 Efforts being made to overcome these barriers

Within the European Union, co-operation is facilitated by the common requirements laid down in the Data Protection Directive (95/46/EC), including the obligation to co-operate as specified in Article 28.6 of the Directive. In the broader European framework, such co-operation is also facilitated by the Council of Europe Convention 108, with its obligation of mutual assistance between signatories spelled out in its Article 13.[59] Article 45 of the new Data Protection Regulation also provides for co-operation between DPAs. One novelty of the Regulation is that it encourages co-operation with DPAs beyond the EU, a provision not found in the old Data Protection Directive. Among other things, Article 45 states that

> In relation to third countries and international organisations, the Commission and supervisory authorities shall take appropriate steps to:
>
> (a) develop international co-operation mechanisms to facilitate the effective enforcement of legislation for the protection of personal data;
> (b) provide international mutual assistance in the enforcement of legislation for the protection of personal data, including through notification, complaint referral, investigative assistance and information exchange, subject to appropriate safeguards for the protection of personal data and other fundamental rights and freedoms….

Data protection authorities, privacy commissioners and PEAs have already been making efforts in various ways to improve co-operation, collaboration and co-ordination, especially since publication of the OECD Recommendation of 2007.[60] They are able to work together towards common goals. The European Commission and the OECD have supported efforts to gain greater leverage by increased collaboration. Among the various instruments and institutional arrangements for improving collaboration are the following:

Home Affairs (the "LIBE committee"), Report on the US NSA surveillance programme, surveillance bodies in various Member States and their impact on EU citizens' fundamental rights and on transatlantic cooperation in Justice and Home Affairs (2013/2188(INI)), 21 February 2014. http://www.europarl.europa.eu/sides/getDoc.do?pubRef=-//EP//TEXT+REPORT+A7-2014-0139+0+DOC+XML+V0//EN

[59] Hawkes, op. cit.

[60] OECD, op. cit., 2007. See fn 58.

2.6.1 *Instruments*

This section describes a few of the most important instruments that DPAs are using to improve co-operation and co-ordination efforts among themselves.

Memoranda of understanding

Several DPAs, PCs and PEAs have established MoUs, especially for sharing information and helping each other in investigations. Examples include the collaboration between the Office of the Privacy Commissioner of Canada (OPC) and the Dutch DPA in investigating What'sApp. Ireland has an MoU with the FTC, one with the OPC and another with the Office of the Australian Information Commissioner (OAIC). Some DPAs, such as that from Macedonia, have, relatively speaking, quite a few MoUs, while other DPAs have none. The purposes of MoUs vary, but often they are aimed at exchanging experience and information. MoUs are sometimes used as ways for overcoming legislative barriers to sharing information and/or co-operating in investigations. The FTC has signed MoUs on spam enforcement with the Australian Information Commissioner, Spanish Data Protection Authority and the ICO. Some European DPAs believe that MoUs are unnecessary and that Convention 108 and the EU Data Protection Directive are sufficient. Typically, MoUs are between two parties, but some regard the APEC Cross-border Privacy Enforcement Arrangement (CPEA) as essentially a multilateral MOU.

Revision of Convention 108

The Convention of the Council of Europe for the Protection of Individuals with regard to Automatic Processing of Personal Data, better known as Convention 108, opened for signature in 1981. It was the first legally binding international instrument in the data protection field. Convention 108 is open for accession by any country in the world and is not limited to member states of the Council of Europe. It has currently been ratified by 46 States, with the latest ratifications by Russia and Uruguay, while Morocco is in the process of ratification.

The Convention establishes a Consultative Committee (T-PD, which stands for *traité protection de données*), consisting of representatives of Parties to the Convention complemented by observers from other States (including Australia, Canada and the USA) and international organisations. It is responsible for interpreting the provisions, for improving implementation of the Convention, for preparing Recommendations and facilitating co-operation between the Parties in the form of bilateral assistance and exchanges of information.

The Council of Europe is in the process of updating the Convention, which is now more than 30 years old. The T-PD reached consensus on revisions at its meeting in November 2012. The Committee of Ministers set up an ad hoc Committee on data protection (CAHDATA), to finalise the revisions based on the proposals made by the T-PD.

Article 13 of the Convention deals with co-operation between Parties. The Parties agree to render mutual assistance to each other in order to implement the Convention. It also provides for one authority, at the request of another authority, to "furnish information on its law and administrative practice in the field of data protection" and to furnish "factual information relating to specific automatic processing carried out in its territory, with the exception however of the personal data being processed".

The current draft of the Convention also says that the supervisory authorities shall co-operate with one another by:

- providing mutual assistance by exchanging relevant and useful information;
- co-ordinating their investigations or interventions, or conducting joint actions;
- providing information and documentation on their law and administrative practice relating to data protection.[61]

The T-PD decided not to modify Article 13 in substance, but to add Article 12bis on requests for assistance between authorities. The Ad Hoc Committee on Data Protection (CAHDATA) meeting in April 2014 decided that the assistance request part should actually remain in Article 13 and, in December 2014, the committee approved the "modernised" text of the Convention,[62] but with reservations from the European Commission. The CAHDATA also instructed the CoE secretariat to prepare a draft amending Protocol and transmit it together with the draft Explanatory report to the Committee of Ministers for examination and adoption.[63] The Committee of Ministers is scheduled to discuss the CAHDATA item at its first meeting in 2016.

Proposed EU Data Protection Regulation

The new Data Protection Regulation promotes co-operation and co-ordination between and among DPAs. Article 55 says that "Supervisory authorities shall provide each other with relevant information and mutual assistance in order to implement and apply this Regulation in a consistent manner, and shall put in place measures for effective co-operation with one another."

As mentioned above, Article 45 goes even further, because it says the Commission and supervisory authorities shall develop effective co-operation mechanisms with third countries and international organisations, a provision not found in the Data Protection Directive.

---

61 http://www.coe.int/t/dghl/standardsetting/dataprotection/CAHDATA/CAHDATA%282014%2901_En_%20Working%20doc_Convention_108.pdf

62 http://www.coe.int/t/dghl/standardsetting/dataprotection/TPD_documents/CAHDATA-RAP03Abr_En.pdf

63 http://www.coe.int/en/web/human-rights-rule-of-law/-/data-protection-convention-the-cahdata-approved-the-modernisation-proposals

In addition, one of the tasks of the proposed European Data Protection Board (EDPB) listed in Article 66 is to

(e) promote the co-operation and the effective bilateral and multilateral exchange of information and practices between the supervisory authorities

In short, the proposed Data Protection Regulation determines that EU data protection authorities shall co-operate with each other in regard to some of the most important data protection enforcement powers – i.e., provision of information and mutual support regarding authorisations and consultations, inspections and investigations. Among its novelties, the proposed Regulation not only supports co-operation with supervisory authorities (also known as data protection authorities and/or privacy commissioners) in the EU Member States, but also in third countries with regard to enforcement of data protection legislation. This surely reflects an understanding of the importance of "raising the bar" with regard to data protection not just in Europe, but also around the world. Better enforcement around the world will discourage "forum shopping", whereby multinationals gravitate away from countries with tougher regulation towards countries with less demanding regulatory regimes.

A co-operation arrangement

As mentioned above, the 36th International Conference of Data Protection and Privacy Commissioners (ICDPPC) in Mauritius in 2014 adopted a Global Cross Border Enforcement Co-operation Arrangement, which culminated the work undertaken by the International Enforcement Co-ordination Working Group established at the 33rd Conference in Mexico City in 2011. The Working Group aimed to develop a common approach to cross-border case handling and enforcement co-ordination. The Arrangement addresses the sharing of enforcement-related information, including how such information is to be treated by recipients. Participants in the Arrangement commit to international cross-border privacy enforcement co-operation, particularly on reciprocity, confidentiality, data protection and co-ordination, but the Arrangement is not intended to create legally binding obligations or to affect existing obligations under other arrangements or international or domestic law. The proponents of the Arrangement regard it as a significant step forward in fostering privacy enforcement co-ordination. The Arrangement went through 16 iterations before it was finally agreed, which is perhaps a measure of how difficult and complex the subject of international privacy enforcement co-ordination is, which is the case not only within Europe, but also globally. It will be interesting to see how many countries subscribe to the Arrangement in the next few years.

2.6.2 *Institutional arrangements*

Data protection authorities, privacy commissioners and privacy enforcement authorities have created a range of institutional mechanisms, global, regional or thematic, to facilitate international co-operation. The most significant of these are the following:

International Conference of Data Protection and Privacy Commissioners (ICDPPC)

The ICDPPC is the biggest annual event bringing together more data protection authorities and privacy commissioners than any other. The conference is intended to facilitate co-operation and the exchange of information among accredited members, in particular regarding enforcement actions. The conference has both open and closed sessions. The closed session of the Conference is limited to just accredited DPAs and privacy commissioners, while the open session includes non-members, including representatives from industry, associations, lobbyists, consultancies, academics and others hoping to influence policy-making or to generate new business opportunities. The ICDPPC has adopted many resolutions over the years, some on specific issues, some on privacy and data protection rights and some on improving co-operation and co-ordination between DPAs.

In order to become members of the International Conference, supervisory authorities must be public entities created by appropriate legal instruments in their country, compatible with international legislation and instruments on data protection, with legal powers appropriate to their functions and with appropriate autonomy and independence. Public entities that do not meet these criteria but are involved with privacy and data protection can apply for observer status.[64]

The International Conference held in Warsaw in September 2013 issued a Resolution on international enforcement co-ordination.[65] The resolution built on previous resolutions encouraging co-operation in cross-border privacy enforcement.[66] It gave a fresh mandate to the International Enforcement Co-ordination Working Group (IECWG) (chaired by Office of the Privacy Commissioner of Canada and the UK's Information Commissioner's Office) tasked with developing a co-ordination arrangement by means of which DPAs could collaborate – to the extent that they can – on privacy enforcement co-ordination actions. Most DPAs supported a non-binding arrangement for privacy enforcement co-operation containing safeguards and guidelines. DPAs envisaged different levels or stages of

[64] PHAEDRA Deliverable D1, p. 105.

[65] http://www.priv.gc.ca/information/conf2013/res_04_coordination_e.asp

[66] PHAEDRA Deliverable D1, p. 106.

co-operation, taking into account different types of confidential information. These four stages are as follows:

Stage 1	Stage 2
Non confidential, unco-ordinated	Co-ordinated, GPEN Intranet, e.g., the Sweeps, Google Glass
Stage 3	Stage 4
Confidential	Co-ordinated
MoUs, GPEN alert tools	Enforcement, investigation actions

Another important point in the Warsaw resolution is that it expressed support for "the development of a secure information platform which offers a 'safe space' for privacy enforcement authorities to share confidential information and to facilitate the initiation and conduct of co-ordinated enforcement action and complement other international enforcement co-ordination mechanisms".

However, it remains unclear whether this clause was intended to support the development of a platform within the context of the ICDPPC or beyond it, e.g., the platform already established within GPEN.

Global Privacy Enforcement Network (GPEN)

The OECD initiated the GPEN in 2007 and hosts its website.[67] GPEN is focused on sharing information among PEAs and undertaking common actions (such as "the Sweep"[68]). One of the principal differences between the GPEN and the ICDPPC is that privacy enforcement agencies (PEAs) who are not accredited to the ICDPPC can be a member or participant in GPEN. The chairpersons of the ICDPPC enforcement co-ordination working group were also active members in GPEN. The number of GPEN members has continued to grow, from 11 when the OECD established it in 2007 to more than 50 members as of December 2015.[69]

While there might be the appearance of some competition between the ICDPPC and GPEN, the ICDPPC Warsaw resolution on International Enforcement Co-ordination explicitly recognised "that the Global Privacy Enforcement Network (GPEN) remains the only global network devoted solely to enforcement cooperation in which all privacy enforcement authorities can participate and encourages authorities to join GPEN and help make it more effective".

GPEN has been struggling to find the financial support for the development and maintenance of an alerting tool, based on the Sentinel alerting tool developed by the FTC.

At the initiation of the Canadian Privacy Commissioner, GPEN co-ordinated the first "Sweep" in 2013, which involved 19 PEAs (including DPAs and privacy

[67] https://www.privacyenforcement.net

[68] A "Sweep" is a co-ordinated investigation by Data Protection Authorities from around the world. For more information, see https://www.priv.gc.ca/media/nr-c/2013/nr-c_130506_qa_e.asp

[69] For a list of GPEN members, see https://www.privacyenforcement.net/about_the_network

commissioners) examining some 2000 websites to review if they had a privacy policy and the adequacy of those policies. PEAs say that the Sweep led to improvements by those that they targeted. The second Sweep, in May 2014, involving 26 PEAs, focused on the adequacy of privacy protection in mobile applications. The third Sweep took place in May 2015, involved about 30 DPAs, and focussed on websites and mobile apps specifically targeting minors. PEAs regard the Sweep as a significant, practical example of co-operation among PEAs that has led, and still is leading to improvements in privacy protections in the private sector.

Regional and sectorial organisations

In addition to the global mechanisms mentioned above, there is a range of regional mechanisms that foster international co-operation. Among them are the following:

- European Conference of Data Protection Authorities ("Spring Conference")[70]
- Article 29 Working Party[71]
- Council of Europe[72]
- Central and Eastern Europe Data Protection Authorities[73]
- Conference of Balkan Data Protection Authorities
- Asia-Pacific Economic Co-operation[74]
- Asia Pacific Privacy Authorities (APPA).[75]

Among the sectorial or thematic mechanisms are the following:

- Ibero-American Data Protection Network[76]
- Association of Francophone Data Protection Authorities[77]
- International Working Group on Data Protection in Telecommunications.[78]

Case-handling workshops

The "Case-Handling Workshops" for data protection authority employees take place twice a year and are intended to exchange information and experience on concrete cases. The Case-Handling Workshops are a series of events organised by a

---

70 http://www.coe.int/t/dghl/standardsetting/dataprotection/european-conference/

71 http://ec.europa.eu/justice/data-protection/article-29/index_en.htm

72 http://www.coe.int/t/dghl/standardsetting/DataProtection/default_en.asp

73 www.ceecprivacy.org

74 http://www.apec.org/Home/Groups/Committee-on-Trade-and-Investment/Electronic-Commerce-Steering-Group

75 http://www.appaforum.org

76 http://www.redipd.org/index-ides-idphp.php

77 http://www.afapdp.org

78 http://www.datenschutz-berlin.de/content/europa-international/international-working-group-on-data-protection-in-telecommunications-iwgdpt

different data protection authority each time[79] to help promote the exchange of information on case studies and practical issues at the operational level ("staff level"), as well as to increase general contacts between employees.

The Workshop is a sub-grouping of the Spring Conference, with overlapping participants drawn from the accredited membership of the Conference. It is not a policy-making workshop. Initially named the Complaints Handling Workshop, one of the aims of the Workshop was the use of a common procedure for handling international complaints. The initiative for the Workshop came from the Spring Conference held in Helsinki in 1999, in pursuit of Article 28(6) of EU Directive 95/46/EC requiring supervisory authorities to collaborate with each other. A revised Framework for Workshop activities was adopted in 2005[80] and a paper on the future of case-handling workshops in 2009.[81]

The Workshop generally lasts two full days. The Conference suggests the alternation between large and small authorities and supports the concept of joint hosting. It also suggests a "friends of the host" group comprising previous and future organisers to support the host. Topics for discussion are chosen in advance by the host DPA, although the Conference suggests a questionnaire for participants to advise this choice and to identify topics of the highest relevancy. The Conference also suggests at least one session dedicated to operational challenges of case-handling. Case studies (potentially drawn from the experience of the hosting DPA) are seen by the Conference as a method for achieving useful discussion and interaction.[82]

The Workshop also reports to the Article 29 Working Party. Decisions on the structure of the Workshop are made at the Conference. A report on the Workshop presented to the Conference in 2004 stated that:

> the Workshop has been a success in facilitating mutual day-to-day co-operation by the creation of a network of contacts between Data Protection Authorities at staff level. Also the website and related mailing list are regularly used for fast information requests to colleagues, information exchange and co-operation in the contexts of international complaints.[83]

While the Case-Handling Workshop appears to have been a success, its success could be further maximised by a platform or website for the Workshops, which would

[79] The 26th Case Handling Workshop was held in Skopje, Macedonia. http://www.privacy.mk/en/CHW

[80] European Privacy and Data Protection Commissioners' Conference, "Case Handling Workshop – Framework of activities", March 2005. www.giodo.gov.pl/data/filemanager_pl/665.pdf

[81] European Privacy and Data Protection Commissioner' Conference, "The future of the case handling workshops", Edinburgh, 23–24 April 2009. https://secure.edps.europa.eu/EDPSWEB/webdav/shared/Documents/Cooperation/Conference_EU/09-04-23_Edinburgh_case_handling_wk_EN.pdf

[82] An example of the cases considered by the Workshop can be found here: http://www.azlp.gov.ba/workshop/documents/?id=923

[83] The International Complaints Handling Workshop, "The International Complaints Handling Workshop: Evolution & Consolidation", Presented to the Spring Conference of European Data Protection Authorities, Rotterdam, 2004. http://www.giodo.gov.pl/data/filemanager_pl/667.pdf

offer continuity and a source of information, and by Spring Conference DPAs inviting non-European DPAs to the Workshops, which would help develop a common, harmonised approach to handling complaints, audits and enforcement.

2.6.3 *Some issues*

While DPAs have made considerable progress in improving co-operation and co-ordination by means of MoUs, institutional exhortations (Convention 108 Article 13, the 1995 Data Protection Directive Article 28, the new Data Protection Regulation Articles 45 and 55), conferences (ICDPPC, the Spring Conference, APPA), networks (the Spanish and French networks of DPAs), the exchange of information and informal contacts, nevertheless, they still must address fundamental issues, a few key examples of which follow.

Sharing information

While DPAs recognise the benefits of co-operation, sharing information has been and continues to be one of the particular challenges. Especially with regard to confidential information arising from an investigation, this has proven to be problematic. Some DPAs are legally constrained from sharing, especially, confidential information or, if it is possible, they must comply with some tightly defined exceptions.

Here are some examples:

In the UK, Article 59 (on Confidentiality of information) of the Data Protection Act 1998 states that

(1) No person who is or has been the Commissioner, a member of the Commissioner's staff or an agent of the Commissioner shall disclose any information which –

 (a) has been obtained by, or furnished to, the Commissioner under or for the purposes of [the information Acts],
 (b) relates to an identified or identifiable individual or business, and
 (c) is not at the time of the disclosure, and has not previously been, available to the public from other sources, unless the disclosure is made with lawful authority.

However, this prohibition is not quite total, as section 2 of Article 59 says that a disclosure of information is made with lawful authority if, inter alia, "the disclosure is necessary in the public interest". It would seem obvious that collaborating with other data protection authorities to investigate data protection offenders is in the public interest.

In France, Article 20 of the Loi Informatique et Libertés of 6 January 1978 (as amended)[84] states that

> Members and officers of the Commission are bound by a duty of confidentiality in respect of the facts, acts and information of which they have knowledge by virtue of their functions…

There is less "wiggle room" in the case of the French law compared to the UK Data Protection Act.

In Canada, Article 20 of the Personal Information Protection and Electronic Documents Act (PIPEDA, 2000, as amended) states that

> the Commissioner or any person acting on behalf or under the direction of the Commissioner shall not disclose any information that comes to their knowledge as a result of the performance or exercise of any of the Commissioner's duties or powers

However, subsection 2 has a public interest exception to the above. It says:

> The Commissioner may, if the Commissioner considers that it is in the public interest to do so, make public any information that comes to his or her knowledge in the performance or exercise of any of his or her duties or powers under this Part.

In the US, the Federal Trade Commission Act states that

> The custodian of any documentary material, written reports or answers to questions, and transcripts of oral testimony may deliver to any officers or employees of appropriate Federal law enforcement agencies, in response to a written request, copies of such material for use in connection with an investigation or proceeding under the jurisdiction of any such agency… The custodian may make such material available to any foreign law enforcement agency upon the prior certification of an appropriate official of any such foreign law enforcement agency, either by a prior agreement or memorandum of understanding with the Commission or by other written certification, that such material will be maintained in confidence and will be used only for official law enforcement purposes[85]

So the FTC can share information if it has a written request and is satisfied by who is requesting the information.

---

[84] Loi Informatique et Libertés Act N° 78–17 of 6 January 1978 on Information Technology, Data Files and Civil Liberties, amended by the following laws:

- Act of 6 August 2004 relative to the protection of individuals with regard to the processing of Personal Data
- Act of 13 May 2009 relative to the simplification and clarification of law and lighter procedures
- Law No. 2009-526 dated 13/05/2009
- Organic Law No. 2010-704 dated 28/06/2010
- Law No. 2011-334 dated 29 March 2011 relative to the défenseur des droits
- Ordinance No. 2011-1012 dated 24/08/2011

http://www.cnil.fr/fileadmin/documents/en/Act78-17VA.pdf

[85] Incorporating US SAFE WEB Act amendments of 2006, § 57b-2 Confidentiality (Sec. 21). http://www.ftc.gov/sites/default/files/documents/statutes/federal-trade-commission-act/ftc_act_incorporatingus_safe_web_act.pdf

While taking into account legal provisions on confidentiality, DPAs have been finding ways, as noted in previous sections of this chapter, of overcoming this barrier, if not in whole then at least in part.

Adoption of the Data Protection Regulation will make sharing confidential information easier, especially within the EU, but also with third countries, as Article 45 makes clear. The Global Cross Border Enforcement Co-operation Arrangement adopted at the 36th ICDPPC in Mauritius in September 2014 should also facilitate the sharing of information and improving privacy enforcement co-ordination. So, at least, we see the prospect for improvements in the ability to share information and to collaborate in privacy enforcement. The prospect is not a mirage.

Finding a lead authority to investigate

Within the EU and around the world, data protection authorities have debated the issue of a lead authority to investigate a particular case. Rather than having various DPAs investigating the same incident, one authority leading the investigation would save resources and increase efficiency. Further, DPAs have arrived at different conclusions and applied differing sanctions, if at all, against an offending company or institution. This is what happened when Google Street View cars were taking 360-degree photographic views of streets everywhere. The regulatory treatment of Google Street View varied significantly across the EU Member States and other countries around the globe. Such regulatory differences create a credibility gap ("Why do different DPAs reach different conclusions?") and the risk of forum shopping, whereby a multinational chooses to submit itself to a regulatory regime that it views as more accommodating than others.

DPAs have seen and recognised the risk of duplication of effort at a time when most of them are resource-constrained. Thus, Art. 29 WP members agreed that CNIL should take the lead in investigating Google's unified privacy policy, one applying across all Google services, which basically says that Google is free to mine personal data across all of its services. Several DPAs announced fines on Google on the same day or within days of each other. None of the fines made much difference in Google's revenue streams, but the co-ordinated action showed that DPAs believe there is strength in numbers. However, some DPAs have submitted to the author that one could interpret the result differently – i.e., that there were only half a dozen or so DPAs in Europe who banded together to send a message to Google – only half a dozen out of 28 countries.

The lead authority issue has created some disgruntlement on the part of DPAs elsewhere in Europe who believe the Silicon Valley giants have located their European headquarters in Ireland, partly because of the favourable tax arrangements, but also because the DPA there has limited resources, insufficient for a detailed investigation of the multinationals' data protection practices.

One-stop shop and consistency mechanism

The "one-stop shop" concept is the mirror image of the lead authority concept. The one-stop shop is an important element of the proposed Data Protection Regulation. Originally proposed by the European Commission, as Billy Hawkes explains in his chapter, the one-stop shop would mean that for any company with establishments in different EU Member States, only the DPA where it has its "main establishment" would be responsible for the data protection supervision of that company. The loss of direct oversight responsibility by other DPAs would be compensated for by a strong "consistency mechanism" under which the DPA of the "main establishment" would be obliged to work closely with other DPAs, with overall co-ordination being provided by the proposed European Data Protection Board (the successor to the Article 29 Working Party). The obligation to co-operate would include an obligation to include staff from other DPAs in investigations of companies operating across the EU.[86]

In order to increase the consistent application of the Regulation, provide legal certainty and reduce the administrative burden for data controllers and processors, the Commission proposed that one DPA monitors the activities of the controller or processor throughout the Union and takes the related decisions, where the processing of personal data takes place in more than one Member State. The DPA providing such a one-stop shop should be the supervisory authority of the Member State in which the controller or processor has its main establishment.

In January 2015, the European Council proposed that, in cross-border cases warranting the involvement of the DPAs of several (possibly all 28) Member States, the decision to be taken should be agreed jointly by all DPAs concerned (co-decision). This would ensure that all interests at stake are taken into account by allowing each DPA to defend its views. The lead DPA would then ensure its implementation via the main establishment of the controller or processor of the personal data at issue.[87]

According to the Council, the Commission's proposal could be interpreted as giving the lead authority exclusive jurisdiction for the supervision of the processing activities of the controller or the processor in all Member States (Article 51.2), which is a departure from the Data Protection Directive where the lead DPA has competence only within its own jurisdiction. The Council felt this would deprive the DPAs of other Member States of the possibility of exercising their powers regarding companies established in their Member States.

Recital 105 of the proposed Regulation states in part:

> (105) In order to ensure the consistent application of this Regulation throughout the Union, a consistency mechanism for co-operation between the supervisory authorities should be established. This mechanism should in particular apply where a supervisory authority intends to adopt a measure intended to produce legal effects as regards processing operations which substantially affect a significant number of data subjects in several Member States. It should also apply where any supervisory authority concerned or the Commission requests that such matter should be dealt with in the consistency mechanism.

---

[86] Hawkes, op. cit.

[87] http://www.statewatch.org/news/2014/nov/eu-dp-reg-one-stop-shop-14788-rev1-14.pdf

Jacob Kohnstamm (Chap. 19, in this volume) interprets the consistency mechanism as follows:

> In cross-border cases, however, there must be a lead supervisory authority that will be the contact point for the company and will be the sole authority to take a legally binding decision. It naturally takes this decision only after having consulted the other concerned authorities in an endeavour to reach consensus. And when a concerned supervisory authority, other than the lead, does not agree with the draft decision proposed by the lead authority, it should have the possibility to appeal to the European Data Protection Board (EDPB), who shall be able to adopt an opinion on the matter. The EDPB, in which all the data protection authorities of the Member States of the EU are assembled and is factually the successor of the Article 29 Working Party, shall decide whether or not to adopt an opinion on the specific case. If it decides to do so, this opinion shall be taken into account by the lead authority.[88]

Some Member States remain sceptical about the one-stop-shop approach in the Regulation, which would enable citizens to complain to their local data protection authority in respect of a breach anywhere in the EU.

Interoperability between Binding Corporate Rules (BCRs) and Cross-Border Privacy Rules (CBPRs)

A sign of the growing co-operation between data protection authorities around the world was presented by the first ever meeting of representatives of the Article 29 Working Party (WP29), in which all EU data protection authorities are assembled, and the Asia Pacific Economic Cooperation (APEC), held in Jakarta on 31 January 2013. The purpose of the meeting was to develop a set of tools to facilitate transfers of personal data for multi-national companies that operate both in Europe and the Asia-Pacific.

In the European Union, the Article 29 Working Party has Binding Corporate Rules (BCRs) to govern international data transfers by companies or groups of companies. These binding internal rules define a company's policies on data transfers in order to ensure adequate safeguards for personal data transferred from the European Union to third countries.

In 2012, APEC completed development of its Cross-Border Privacy Rules (CBPRs) for protection of personal data throughout the Asia-Pacific. Like the BCRs, CBPRs aim to ensure that a company's privacy policies meet established standards for the protection of personal information. Such policies must be validated by APEC-recognised Accountability Agents.

BCRs and CBPRs are based on a similar approach, which is the use of internal binding rules for cross-border transfers of personal data, subject to prior approval by EU Data Protection Authorities or by APEC-recognised Accountability Agents.

Experts from the Art. 29 WP and the APEC Data Privacy Sub-Group developed a practical tool (called a "referential") to map the respective requirements of the

---

[88] See Kohnstamm, Jacob, "Getting our act together: European Data Protection Authorities face up to Silicon Valley" in this volume.

BCRs and CBPRs. APEC endorsed the referential at its meeting of 27–28 February 2014. The Art. 29 WP adopted an opinion on it at its plenary meeting of 26–27 February 2014.[89]

This referential does not aim to achieve mutual recognition of both systems. However, it could serve as a basis for double certification. In any case, data protection policies of applicant international companies operating both in the EU and the APEC have to be approved respectively by the relevant bodies in the EU Member States and in the APEC economies, in accordance with the applicable approval procedures.[90]

The Article 29 Working Party and APEC are developing a shared roadmap in order to continue their co-operation in developing practical tools for use by companies doing business in Europe and the Asia-Pacific region. The prospect for interoperability – whereby the authorisation of a company by APEC is recognised and accepted by the Art. 29 WP, and vice versa – looms on the horizon.

Reciprocity is important

Some privacy enforcement authorities have made the point that reciprocity is important in building trust and co-operation with their peers. Reciprocity can be in the context of sharing information, but can also mean co-operation in a wider sense. DPAs requesting assistance of other DPAs in regard to investigations, inspections, audits, training or staff exchanges should think how they can reciprocate. It could be as simple as offering to reciprocate should the "donor" DPA need to request some information or inspection in the future. Or it could be in signing joint letters protesting the privacy intrusions of Google or Facebook or some other measure. In short, co-operation between DPAs should be seen as a two-way street.

The Irish DPA offers an interesting example of reciprocity that could alleviate some concerns with regard to the one-stop-shop model. As a DPA with limited resources, investigating or auditing corporate giants is a major challenge. However, the DPA is able to engage third party experts, including those from other DPAs, as "authorised officers". Engaging other DPAs in audits of companies providing services to EU users from an Irish base would be a way of assuaging concerns that the Irish DPA might not be able to conduct a thorough audit or might be more lenient than some other DPAs. This might also encourage reciprocal action by other DPAs in relation to the many European multinationals providing services to Irish residents. Such co-operative activity could also help to mitigate the resource constraints that apply to a small DPA.[91]

---

[89] Article 29 Data Protection Working Party, "Promoting Cooperation on Data Transfer Systems Between Europe and the Asia-Pacific", press release, 26 March 2013.

[90] Article 29 Data Protection Working Party, Opinion 02/2014 on a referential for requirements for Binding Corporate Rules, 27 February 2014. http://ec.europa.eu/justice/data-protection/article-29/documentation/opinion-recommendation/files/2014/wp212_en.pdf

[91] Hawkes, op. cit.

2.7 Conclusions and recommendations

Former European Data Protection Supervisor (EDPS) Peter Hustinx once said "it is crucial for independent supervisory authorities to regularly think about their own effectiveness, and to consider ways to measure and where necessary improve their performance".[92] DPAs need to think about the effectiveness of privacy enforcement measures as well as their own effectiveness in applying those measures. They are not the only guardians of privacy and data protection in Europe, but they are certainly the primary guardians. As such, they carry an enormous responsibility. They well and truly recognise that their effectiveness is enhanced by collaborating with each other, and that in numbers there is strength. The rest of us should applaud and support their efforts.

Nevertheless, there is a contradiction or ambiguity between the provisions in the Data Protection Directive (and its successor Regulation) and Convention 108 that oblige European DPAs or signatories to the Convention and national legislation empowering DPAs that frowns on the exchange of information, especially confidential information. One can only hope that the Regulation will do away with such ambiguity.

The Arrangement, agreed in Mauritius, rightly states that

> to effectively respond to data protection and privacy violations that affect multiple jurisdictions a multi-lateral approach is required and therefore appropriate mechanisms to facilitate the information sharing of confidential enforcement related material, and coordination of enforcement amongst privacy enforcement authorities to tackle said violations is much needed.

The Arrangement will appear to be on a successful trajectory as a global mechanism for improving enforcement co-ordination, as evidenced by the number of DPAs, PCs and PEAs who become signatories to it.

Among the mechanisms mentioned in the Arrangement are "secure electronic information sharing platforms to exchange enforcement related information, particularly confidential information about on-going or potential enforcement activities", and participants are encouraged to use and assist in the development of such platforms. Such a platform is under development in GPEN and could, as well, be developed in the context of the International Conference. It should be obvious that the International Conference needs a platform and a small permanent secretariat distinct from that of GPEN. As a minimum, the ICDPPC platform could include all resolutions and other documents adopted by the ICDPPC. As it stands now, one needs to hunt through various DPA websites to glean all such information. The small secretariat could maintain the website and could help DPAs hosting future ICDPPC meetings in organising the meeting.

---

[92] Hustinx, op. cit. Hustinx further observes that "no other fundamental right – except the right to a fair trial – is structurally associated with the role of an independent body to ensure its respect and further development. This right is special in the sense that it is considered to be in need of 'structural support' through the establishment of an independent authority with adequate powers and resources."

Similarly, while the Case-Handling Workshop appears to have been a success, its success could be further maximised by introducing a platform or website for the Workshops, which would offer continuity and a source of information, and by Spring Conference DPAs inviting non-European DPAs to the Workshops which would help develop a common, harmonised approach to handling complaints, audits and enforcement.

Enforcing privacy will be a never-ending struggle, but the willingness and efforts of most DPAs to co-operate and co-ordinate their privacy enforcement efforts show that progress is not only possible, but is actually happening.

References

Arthur, Charles, "European watchdogs order Google to rewrite privacy policy or face legal action", *The Guardian*, 5 July 2013. http://www.guardian.co.uk/technology/2013/jul/05/google-privacy-policy-legal-action

Article 29 Data Protection Working Party, Opinion 02/2014 on a referential for requirements for Binding Corporate Rules, 27 February 2014. http://ec.europa.eu/justice/data-protection/article-29/documentation/opinion-recommendation/files/2014/wp212_en.pdf

Article 29 Data Protection Working Party, "Promoting Cooperation on Data Transfer Systems Between Europe and the Asia-Pacific", press release, 26 March 2013.

Council of Europe, Additional Protocol to the Convention for the Protection of Individuals with regard to Automatic Processing of Personal Data regarding supervisory authorities and trans-border data flows, Strasbourg, 8 November 2001. http://conventions.coe.int/Treaty/EN/Treaties/HTML/181.htm

Council of Europe, Convention for the Protection of Individuals with regard to Automatic Processing of Personal Data, Strasbourg, 28 January 1981. http://conventions.coe.int/Treaty/en/Treaties/Html/108.htm

European Commission, Proposal for a Regulation of the European Parliament and of the Council on the protection of individuals with regard to the processing of personal data and on the free movement of such data (General Data Protection Regulation), COM(2012) 11 final, Brussels, 25 January 2012. http://ec.europa.eu/justice/data-protection/document/review2012/com_2012_11_en.pdf

European Parliament and the Council, Directive 95/46/EC of 24 October 1995 on the protection of individuals with regard to the processing of personal data and on the free movement of such data, Official Journal L 281, 23/11/1995, pp. 0031–0050

European Parliament Committee on Civil Liberties, Justice and Home Affairs (the "LIBE committee"), Report on the US NSA surveillance programme, surveillance bodies in various Member States and their impact on EU citizens' fundamental rights and on transatlantic cooperation in Justice and Home Affairs (2013/2188(INI)), 21 February 2014. http://www.europarl.europa.eu/sides/getDoc.do?pubRef=-//EP//TEXT+REPORT+A7-2014-0139+0+DOC+XML+V0//EN

European Privacy and Data Protection Commissioners' Conference, "Case Handling Workshop – Framework of activities", March 2005. www.giodo.gov.pl/data/filemanager_pl/665.pdf

European Privacy and Data Protection Commissioner' Conference, "The future of the case handling workshops", Edinburgh, 23–24 April 2009. https://secure.edps.europa.eu/EDPSWEB/webdav/shared/Documents/Cooperation/Conference_EU/09-04-23_Edinburgh_case_handling_wk_EN.pdf

Hustinx, Peter, Cahiers du Centre de Recherches Informatique et Droit (CRID), No. 31, "Défis du droit à la protection de la vie privée/Challenges of privacy and data protection law", Namur-Brussels, 2008, pp. 561–568.

International Complaints Handling Workshop, "The International Complaints Handling Workshop: Evolution & Consolidation", Presented to the Spring Conference of European Data Protection Authorities, Rotterdam, 2004. http://www.giodo.gov.pl/data/filemanager_pl/667.pdf
O'Donoghue, Cynthia, "Dutch data protection authority threatens Google with a €15 million fine", *Lexology*, 8 Jan 2015.
Organisation for Economic Co-operation and Development, OECD Recommendation on Cross-border Co-operation in the Enforcement of Laws Protecting Privacy, Paris, 2007. http://www.oecd.org/internet/ieconomy/38770483.pdf

Part I
Countries

Chapter 3
Failures of Privacy Self-Regulation in the United States

Robert Gellman and Pam Dixon

3.1 Introduction

3.1.1 Scope of this chapter

The principal purpose of this chapter is to review some of the history of privacy self-regulation in the United States, to consider the role of the Federal Trade Commission (FTC) in that history, and to evaluate whether privacy self-regulation has any long-term value. For reasons that will become clear, the history mostly covers the period from 1997 to 2007, with additional discussion of later events.

Privacy self-regulatory activities can be grouped under three broad categories, although the lines are not always sharp. *Industry*: of the activities under review here, five were mostly run by industry for industry. *Government*: two efforts included a degree of involvement by the federal government. *Joint*: in two other efforts, stakeholders including academics, consumer groups and privacy advocates played a role along with industry.

R. Gellman (✉)
Privacy and Information Policy Consultant, 419 Fifth Street SE,
Washington, DC 20003, USA
e-mail: bob@bobgellman.com

P. Dixon
Executive Director, World Privacy Forum, 3108 Fifth Avenue, Suite B,
San Diego, CA 92103, USA
e-mail: pdixon@worldprivacyforum.org

D. Wright, P. De Hert (eds.), *Enforcing Privacy*, Law, Governance
and Technology Series 25, DOI 10.1007/978-3-319-25047-2_3

3.1.2 Characteristics common to industry privacy self-regulation

For most industry-supported privacy self-regulatory efforts, a clear pattern developed in the years covered by this review. Reacting to pressure from FTC scrutiny and legislative interest, industry began privacy self-regulatory efforts, mostly motivated by the desire to avoid formal regulation. These self-regulatory activities typically were characterised by some or most of the following qualities:

- Self-regulatory organisations were most often based in Washington, DC, where potential regulators are.
- Self-regulatory organisations formulated their rules in secret, typically with no input from non-industry stakeholders, and the governing boards of privacy self-regulatory organisations typically did not have non-industry board members.
- Privacy self-regulatory rules covered only a fraction of an industry or covered an industry subgroup, leaving many business practices and many relevant players untouched. It was rarely apparent what percentage of an industry was covered by the rules.
- Privacy self-regulatory organisations were short-lived, typically surviving for a few years, and then diminishing or disappearing entirely when pressure faded.
- Privacy self-regulatory organisations were loudly promoted despite their limited scope and substance.
- Privacy self-regulatory organisations were structurally weak, lacking meaningful ability to enforce their own rules or maintain memberships. Those who subscribed to self-regulation were usually free to drop out at any time.
- Privacy self-regulatory organisations were typically underfunded, and industry financial support in some cases appeared to dry up quickly. There was no long-term plan for survival or transition.

3.2 Industry-supported self-regulatory programs for privacy

The history of privacy self-regulation presented here is not comprehensive. Some self-regulatory efforts disappeared without a trace. Activities within trade associations are difficult or impossible to assess from evidence available to those outside the associations. Nevertheless, this history captures the leading American industry-supported self-regulatory programs from 1997 to 2007.[1]

Another limitation is that a comprehensive analysis of the quality of each self-regulatory effort is not possible. The standards promulgated by the self-regulatory programs were often general and quickly became outdated because of technological

[1] Privacy seal programs arose during this period, but some disappeared entirely. The two most notable were BBBOnLine and TRUSTe, which, as a for-profit company, lacks sufficient credibility to warrant review here.

development and other changes. Audits or reviews of compliance with self-regulatory standards were often not attempted, not completed, not credible or not transparent. Original documents have disappeared. However, there is enough available information to describe the programs, their rise, their activities and, in most cases, their demise.

3.2.1 *Individual Reference Services Group*

The Individual Reference Services Group (IRSG) announced its establishment in June 1997 at an FTC workshop.[2] The group consisted of companies offering individual reference services that provided information that identifies or locates individuals.[3] The IRSG reported 14 "leading information industry companies" as members, including Acxiom, Equifax, Experian, Trans Union and Lexis-Nexis.[4]

The IRSG described its self-regulatory activities as a "self-imposed restriction on use and dissemination of non-public information about individuals in their personal (not business) capacity".[5] However, a principal purpose of the IRSG plan appeared to be to avoid any real regulation, and its announcement at an FTC event was not an accident. The IRSG eventually succeeded in achieving its primary goal of avoiding actual regulation. In a 1999 report to Congress, the FTC recommended that the industry be left to regulate itself despite some significant shortcomings.[6]

One of the IRSG principles called for an annual "assurance review" for compliance with IRSG standards.[7] The IRSG also required that a summary of the report and any subsequent actions taken be publicly available. While the IRSG website contained some evidence that at least some IRSG members conducted reviews, the IRSG did not make the reports public on its website so it is not possible to determine the quality of the reviews.[8]

After the threat of regulation diminished, the IRSG continued in existence for a few years. In September 2001, approximately four years after it was established (and less than one year after control of the federal government shifted from a

[2] Federal Trade Commission, *Individual Reference Services, A Report to Congress*, 1997. http://www.ftc.gov/bcp/privacy/wkshp97/irsdoc1.htm

[3] Individual Reference Services Group, Industry Principles – Commentary, 15 Dec 1997. http://www.ftc.gov/os/1997/12/irsappe.pdf

[4] http://web.archive.org/web/19990125100333/http://www.irsg.org

[5] Ibid. Two scholars who examined the IRSG principles said that they "set forth a weak framework of protections, allowing companies to sell nonpublic personal information 'without restriction' to 'qualified subscribers'". Solove, Daniel J., and Chris Jay Hoofnagle, "A Model Regime of Privacy Protection", *University of Illinois Law Review*, Vol. 2006, No. 2, 2006, pp. 357, 365.

[6] Federal Trade Commission, *Individual Reference Services, A Report to Congress*, Commission Recommendations, 1997. http://www.ftc.gov/bcp/privacy/wkshp97/irsdoc1.htm

[7] http://web.archive.org/web/20020210151622/www.irsg.org/html/3rd_party_assessments.htm

[8] See http://web.archive.org/web/20020215163015/www.irsg.org/html/irsg_assessment_letters-2000.htm

Democratic to a Republican Administration), the IRSG announced its termination.[9] The stated reason was that legislation – specifically the Gramm-Leach-Bliley Act (GLB) – made the self-regulatory principles no longer necessary.[10]

However, the legislation cited as the reason for termination did *not in fact regulate IRSG members*. The GLB Act provided that each *financial institution* has an "affirmative and continuing obligation to respect the privacy of its customers and to protect the security and confidentiality of those customers' nonpublic personal information".[11] A financial institution is a company that offers financial products or services to individuals, like loans, financial or investment advice, or insurance.[12] The IRSG companies – companies that provide information that *identifies* or *locates* individuals – were not financial institutions under GLB. It is also significant that GLB became law almost two years before the IRSG cited it as the reason for self-termination. GLB was a fig leaf that covered the lack of continuing industry support for the IRSG.

Why did the IRSG issue a deceptive statement about the reason for its termination? According to informal reports circulating at the time, IRSG members lost interest in supporting an expensive self-regulatory organisation because they no longer felt threatened by legislation or regulatory activities.

It is noteworthy that the FTC did not use its power to take action against unfair and deceptive trade practices to enforce the promises made by IRSG members.

3.2.2 The Privacy Leadership Initiative

A group of industry executives with members including IBM, Procter & Gamble, Ford, Compaq and AT&T established the Privacy Leadership Initiative (PLI) in June 2000.[13] PLI promptly began an ad campaign in national publications to promote industry self-regulation of online consumer privacy. According to a contemporary news account, the PLI initiative "follows a recent Federal Trade Commission recommendation that Congress establish legislation to protect online consumer privacy".[14]

A description of the PLI from its website in 2001 stated that the "purpose of the PLI is to create a climate of trust which will accelerate acceptance of the Internet and the emerging Information Economy, both online and off-line, as a safe and secure

[9] http://web.archive.org/web/20020202103820/www.irsg.org/html/termination.htm

[10] Ibid.

[11] 15 U.S.C. § 6801(a).

[12] 15 U.S.C. § 6809(3). See also Federal Trade Commission, *In Brief: The Financial Privacy Requirements of the Gramm-Leach-Bliley Act*, 2002. http://business.ftc.gov/documents/bus53-brief-financial-privacy-requirements-gramm-leach-bliley-act

[13] See Savage, Marcia, "New Industry Alliance Addresses Online Privacy", *Computer Reseller News*, 19 June 2000. http://technews.acm.org/articles/2000-2/0621w.html#item13

[14] Ibid.

marketplace".[15] Other accounts from the time support the notion that PLI's purpose was to promote self-regulation.[16]

By the middle of 2002, the threat of regulation had diminished enough so that PLI "transitioned" its activities to others. The BBBOnLine, a program of the Better Business Bureau system,[17] took over the PLI website (understandingprivacy.org). The BBBOnLine privacy program, which lasted longer than the PLI, is no longer operational, and its details are discussed below.

By the middle of September 2002, the transition of the website to BBBOnLine appeared to be complete.[18] However, by January 2008, the understandingprivacy.org website had changed entirely, offering visitors an answer to the question "Can microwave popcorn cause lung disease?"[19] By the beginning of 2011, the understandingprivacy.org website was controlled by Media Insights, a creator of "content-rich Internet publications".[20] Other Media Insights websites include BunnyRabbits.org, Feathers.org and PetBirdReport.com.[21]

In the end, PLI amounted to little more than an advertising campaign to promote, but not actually implement, self-regulation. PLI's termination drew no attention from the FTC.

3.2.3 *The Online Privacy Alliance*

Former Federal Trade Commissioner Christine Varney created the Online Privacy Alliance (OPA)[22] in 1998.[23] The OPA's earliest available webpage described the organisation as *a cross-industry coalition of more than 60 global corporations and*

---

[15] http://web.archive.org/web/20010411210453/www.understandingprivacy.org/content/about/index.cfm. See also http://web.archive.org/web/20010419185921/www.understandingprivacy.org/content/about/fact.cfm

[16] See, e.g., "Up for Sale: How Best to Protect Privacy on the Internet", Knowledge@Wharton, 19 March 2001. http://knowledge.wharton.upenn.edu/article.cfm?articleid=325

[17] Privacy Leadership Initiative, "Privacy Leadership Initiative Transfers Initiatives to Established Business Groups", press release, 1 July 2002, cited in Gellman, Robert, and Pam Dixon, "Many Failures: A Brief History of Privacy Self-Regulation in the United States", World Privacy Forum, 2011, at note 31. http://www.worldprivacyforum.org/pdf/WPFselfregulationhistory.pdf, http://goliath.ecnext.com/coms2/gi_0199-1872940/Privacy-Leadership-Initiative-Transfers-Initiatives.html

[18] http://web.archive.org/web/20020914095335/www.bbbonline.org/understandingprivacy

[19] http://web.archive.org/web/20080118171946/http://www.understandingprivacy.org

[20] http://www.mediainsights.com

[21] Ibid.

[22] The main webpages for the organisation are at www.privacyalliance.org. However, for a brief period starting in 2005, the Internet Archive shows that the organisation also maintained webpages at www.privacyalliance.com. The first pages reported by the Internet Archive for www.privacyalliance.org have a 2 Dec 1998 date.

[23] http://web.archive.org/web/19990209062744/www.privacyalliance.org/join/background.shtml

associations.[24] The first paragraph of the background page on its website stated clearly its interest in promoting self-regulation.[25]

In July 1998, the OPA released a paper describing "Effective Enforcement of Self-regulation".[26] In November 1999, a representative of the OPA appeared at an FTC workshop on online profiling and participated in a session on the role of self-regulation.[27] OPA self-regulatory principles were cited by industry representatives before the FTC and elsewhere.[28]

It is difficult to chart with precision the deterioration of the OPA. By all appearances, the OPA is defunct. A review of webpages available at the Internet Archive shows a decline of original OPA activities starting in the early 2000s. For example, the first webpage available for 2004 prominently lists OPA news, but the first item shown is dated March 2002 and the next most recent item is dated November 2001.[29] The OPA news on the first webpage available for 2005 shows four press stories from 2004, but the most recent OPA item was still November 2001.[30] By 2008, the OPA news on the first webpage available for that year showed two news stories from 2006, and no reported OPA activity more recent than 2001.[31] There is little or no evidence after 2001 of OPA activities or participation at the FTC.[32] The threat that fostered the creation of the OPA apparently had disappeared. Wikipedia categorises the OPA under *defunct privacy organizations*.[33]

The OPA website continues to exist and appears to have been reformatted and updated occasionally after 2008. The main OPA webpage also includes links to old OPA documents such as "Guidelines for Online Privacy Policies" (approximately 533 words) and "Guidelines for Effective Enforcement of Self-Regulation" (approximately 1,269 words). The website continues to offer old items, such as an OPA "Commentary to the Mission Statement and Guidelines" dated 19 November 1998.[34] In early 2013, the website reported that membership was "closed". Yet in January 2014, the website included links to some recent news stories, although the copyright date on its home page was 2011.

The list of members on its website as recently as May 2011 included at least one company (Cendant) that no longer existed at that time.[35] The membership page was

---

[24] Ibid.

[25] http://web.archive.org/web/19990209062744/www.privacyalliance.org/join/background.shtml

[26] http://web.archive.org/web/19981202200600/http://www.privacyalliance.org

[27] http://www.ftc.gov/bcp/workshops/profiling/991108agenda.htm

[28] See, e.g., Statement of Mark Uncapher, Vice President and Counsel, Information Technology Association of America, before the Federal Trade Commission Public Workshop on Online Profiling, 18 Oct 1999. http://www.ftc.gov/bcp/workshops/profiling/comments/uncapher.htm

[29] http://web.archive.org/web/20040122052508/http://www.privacyalliance.org

[30] http://web.archive.org/web/20050104085718/http://www.privacyalliance.org

[31] http://web.archive.org/web/20080201111641/http://www.privacyalliance.org

[32] www.ftc.gov

[33] http://en.wikipedia.org/wiki/Online_Privacy_Alliance

[34] http://www.privacyalliance.org/news/12031998-4.shtml

[35] http://web.archive.org/web/20110512024943/http://www.privacyalliance.org/members

not dated, and members number approximately 30, or less than half the number reported in 1998.

It is noteworthy that the FTC did not use its power to take action against unfair and deceptive trade practices to enforce the promises made by OPA members.

3.2.4 *The Network Advertising Initiative (1999–2007 version)*

The network advertising industry announced the formation of the Network Advertising Initiative at an FTC workshop in 1999. NAI issued its principles, a 21-page document, the next year.[36] The core concept – the opt-out cookie – has been criticised as a technical and policy failure, and it remains highly controversial.[37] The NAI is of particular note because the FTC voted on its creation, something that is quite rare.

When it began, NAI membership consisted of 12 companies, which was a fraction of the industry engaging in behavioural ad targeting. By 2002, membership hit a low of two companies.[38] This represented a significant lack of participation by the industry. When the NAI created a category of associate members who were not required to be in full compliance with the NAI standards, membership increased, with associate members outnumbering regular members by 2006. Eventually, the NAI eliminated the associate membership category.[39]

The NAI delegated enforcement of its standards to TRUSTe, an unusual action given that TRUSTe was a member of the NAI for one year.[40] Over several years, the scope of TRUSTe public reporting on NAI complaints decreased consistently until 2006, when separate reporting about NAI by TRUSTe stopped altogether.[41] There is no evidence that NAI members conducted the audits required by NAI principles. No information about audits of members was ever made public during this time.[42]

Much of the pressure that produced the NAI came from the FTC. Industry reacted in 1999 to an FTC behavioural advertising workshop, and the NAI self-regulatory principles were drafted with the support of the FTC.[43] Pressure from the FTC diminished or disappeared quickly, and by 2002, only two NAI members remained. When

---

[36] This section is adapted from a comprehensive review of the Network Advertising Initiative (NAI) published by the World Privacy Forum in 2007. *The Network Advertising Initiative: Failing at Consumer Protection and at Self-Regulation* at pp. 7–8. The WPF report contains citations and support for the conclusions presented here. http://www.worldprivacyforum.org/wp-content/uploads/2007/11/WPF_NAI_report_Nov2_2007fs.pdf

[37] Ibid., pp. 14–16.

[38] Ibid. at pp. 28–29.

[39] Ibid. at pp. 29–30.

[40] Ibid. at p. 25.

[41] Ibid. at pp. 33–36.

[42] Ibid. at p. 37.

[43] Ibid. at p. 9.

the FTC again showed interest in online behavioural advertising in 2008, the NAI began to take steps to fix the problems that had developed with its 2000 principles.[44] One of those steps was "promoting more robust self-regulation by today opening a 45-day public comment period concurrent with the release of a new draft 2008 NAI Principles".[45] NAI never sought public comment on the original principles.

Privacy remains an active issue in US politics, and that means that it is too soon to assess the quality or sincerity of the revival of NAI self-regulatory activities. The history presented in this chapter supports the notion that self-regulatory efforts only flourish when there is political and regulatory pressure for better privacy protections. The true test will come when that pressure fades because of a change in political leadership in the White House or a change in focus at the FTC.

There were substantive problems with the original NAI principles as well. The conclusion of a 2007 World Privacy Forum Report summarises the NAI failures:

> The NAI has failed. The agreement is foundationally flawed in its approach to what online means and in its choice of the opt-out cookie as a core feature. The NAI opt-out does not work consistently and fails to work at all far too often. Further, the opt-out is counter-intuitive, difficult to accomplish, easily deleted by consumers, and easily circumvented. The NAI opt-out was never a great idea, and time has shown both that consumers have not embraced it and that companies can easily evade its purpose. The original NAI agreement has increasingly limited applicability to today's tracking and identification techniques. Secret cache cookies, Flash cookies, cookie re-setting techniques, hidden UserData files, Silverlight cookies[46] and other technologies and techniques can be used to circumvent the narrow confines of the NAI agreement. Some of these techniques, Flash cookies in particular, are in widespread use already. These persistent identifiers are not transparent to consumers. The very point of the NAI self-regulation was to make the invisible visible to consumers so there would be a fair balance between consumer interests and industry interests. NAI has not maintained transparency as promised.
>
> The behavioral targeting industry did not embrace its own self-regulation. At no time does it appear that a majority of behavioral targeters belong to NAI. For two years, the NAI had only two members. In 2007 with the scheduling of the FTC's new Town Hall meeting on the subject, several companies joined NAI or announced an intention to join. Basically, the industry appears interested in supporting or giving the appearance of supporting self-regulation only when alternatives are under consideration. Enforcement of the NAI has been similarly troubled. The organization tasked with enforcing the NAI was allowed to become a member of the NAI for one year. This decision reveals poor judgment on the part of the NAI and on the part of TRUSTe, the NAI enforcement organization. Further, the reporting of enforcement has been increasingly opaque as TRUSTe takes systematic steps away from transparent reporting on the NAI. If the enforcement of the NAI is neither independent nor transparent, then how can anyone determine if the NAI is an effective self-regulatory scheme? The result of all of these and other deficiencies is that the protections promised to consumers have not been realized. The NAI self-regulatory agreement has

---

[44] See, e.g., Network Advertising Initiative, "Written Comments in Response to the Federal Trade Commission Staff's Proposed Behavioral Advertising Principles", April 2008. http://www.ftc.gov/os/comments/behavioraladprinciples/080410nai.pdf

[45] Ibid.

[46] Secret cache cookies, Flash cookies, cookie re-setting techniques, hidden UserData files, and Silverlight cookies cited in the quoted text are different methods used to track Internet users through techniques that either add text on a user's computer in places other than where "traditional" cookies reside or that make other modifications on a user's computer with the same intent.

failed to meet the goals it has stated, and it has failed to meet the expectations and goals the FTC laid out for it. The NAI has failed to deliver on its promises to consumers.[47]

The NAI self-regulatory effort that began in 1999 was a demonstrable failure within a few years. It is noteworthy that the FTC did not use its power to take action against unfair and deceptive trade practices to enforce the promises made by NAI members.

The 2014 version of the NAI is quite different from its predecessor. There are currently nearly 100 member companies, and the organisation now undertakes yearly, published audits. The organisation opened its newest guidelines up to privacy experts and advocates for review and comment. There have been clear changes and some improvements. Though its current leadership has been an improvement over the past, the long-term viability of the NAI remains uncertain.

3.2.5 BBBOnLine Privacy Program

The BBBOnLine Privacy Program began in 1998, in response to "the need identified by the Clinton Administration and businesses for a major self-regulation initiative to protect consumer privacy on the Net and to respond to the European privacy initiatives".[48] Founding sponsors included leading businesses, such as AT&T, GTE, Hewlett-Packard, IBM, Procter and Gamble, Sony Electronics, Visa and Xerox.[49] The program was operated by the Council of Better Business Bureaus through its subsidiary, BBBOnLine. There may have been some consumer group participation in the development of the BBBOnLine privacy program, but industry and BBB controlled the activities for the most part.

On paper, the BBBOnLine Privacy Program was much more extensive than many other efforts at the time. It included "verification, monitoring and review, consumer dispute resolution, a compliance seal, enforcement mechanisms and an educational component".[50] To qualify, a company had to post a privacy notice telling consumers what personal information is being collected, how it will be used and what choices consumers have in terms of use. Participants also had to verify security measures taken to protect their information, abide by their posted privacy policies, and agree to an independent verification by BBBOnLine. Companies had to

[47] World Privacy Forum, "The National Advertising Initiative – Failing at Consumer Protection and at Self-Regulation", p.39. http://www.worldprivacyforum.org/2007/11/report-nai-failing-at-consumer-protection-and-at-self-regulation/

[48] Better Business Bureau, "BBBOnLine Privacy Program Created to Enhance User Trust on the Internet", news release, 22 June 1998. http://web.archive.org/web/20110306180813/http://www.bbb.org/us/article/bbbonline-privacy-program-created-to-enhance-user-trust-on-the-internet-163

[49] Ibid.

[50] The earliest web presence for the BBB Online Privacy Program appeared at the end of 2000. http://web.archive.org/web/20010119180300/www.bbbonline.org/privacy

participate in the program's dispute resolution service,[51] a service that operated under a 17-page set of detailed procedures.[52] The dispute resolution service also publicly disclosed statistics about its operations.[53] As noted above, the BBBOnLine Privacy Program took over the Privacy Leadership Initiative website (understandingprivacy.org) when PLI ended operations in 2002. The BBBOnLine Privacy Program was considerably more robust than most, if not all, of the contemporary privacy self-regulatory activities.

It is difficult to determine how many companies participated in the BBBOnLine privacy program. A 2000 FTC report on online privacy said that "[o]ver 450 sites representing 244 companies have been licensed to post the BBBOnLine Privacy Seal since the program was launched" in March 1999.[54] Whether the numbers increased in subsequent years is unknown, but the number represents a tiny fraction of all websites and companies. It may be that the more rigorous requirements that BBBOnLine asked its members to meet was a factor in dissuading many companies from participating.

BBBOnLine stopped accepting applications for its privacy program sometime in 2007.[55] The specific reasons for termination are not clear, but it seems likely that it was a lack of support, participation and interest. Self-regulation for the purpose of avoiding real regulation is one thing, but the active and substantial self-regulation offered by BBBOnLine may have been too much for participants. BBBOnLine continues to operate other programs, including an EU Safe Harbor dispute resolution service,[56] but there is no evidence on its website of the original BBBOnLine privacy program.

As with the other self-regulatory programs discussed above, the FTC did not use its power to take action against unfair and deceptive trade practices to enforce the promises made by BBBOnLine members.

---

[51] http://web.archive.org/web/20010201170700/http://www.bbbonline.org/privacy/how.asp

[52] http://web.archive.org/web/20030407011013/www.bbbonline.org/privacy/dr.pdf

[53] See, e.g., http://web.archive.org/web/20070124235138/www.bbbonline.org/privacy/dr/2005q3.asp. While the BBBOnLine privacy program dispute procedures were better and more transparent than other comparable procedures, the BBBOnLine dispute resolution service was controversial in various ways. In 2000, for example, questions arose when the BBBOnLine Privacy Program, under pressure from a company that was the subject of a complaint, vacated an earlier decision and substituted a decision more favourable to the complaint subject.

[54] Federal Trade Commission, "Privacy Online: Fair Information Practices in the Electronic Marketplace, A Report To Congress", May 2000. http://www.ftc.gov/reports/privacy2000/privacy2000.pdf

[55] http://web.archive.org/web/20070830164536rn_1/www.bbbonline.org/privacy

[56] http://www.bbb.org/us/european-union-dispute-resolution. Annual reports for 2011 and 2012 show that BBBOnLine handled a few Safe Harbor complaints, but the reports contain limited information. See https://www.bbb.org/us/european-dispute-resolution/complaint-reports/

3.3 Self-regulatory activities with government involvement

Two privacy self-regulatory activities include formal roles for federal agencies. The Department of Commerce operates the Safe Harbor Framework, and the FTC oversees the Children's Online Privacy Protection Act safe harbor program. These self-regulatory activities share some characteristics with the industry self-regulatory programs discussed above, but these activities have differed as a result of government involvement.

3.3.1 *Department of Commerce Safe Harbor Framework*

The Safe Harbor Framework[57] operated by the Department of Commerce started in 2000 with an agreement between the Department and the European Commission.[58] The Safe Harbor Framework differs somewhat from the other self-regulatory activities discussed in this chapter because of the central role played by the Department. However, the Department's role in the Safe Harbor Framework did not prevent the deterioration of the Safe Harbor over time or stop the lack of compliance by companies that participated in the Safe Harbor. Safe Harbor has been the subject of significant scrutiny and negotiation by European DPAs and regulators. The most recent and significant negotiations of 2013–2015 were sparked in part by the revelations in the summer of 2013 regarding US National Security Agency access to European data, although the difficulties go back further than that.

The inception of Safe Harbor began with the adoption of the European Union's Data Protection Directive[59] in 1995 and its implementation in 1998. At that time, much of the concern about transborder data flows of personal information centered on the export restriction policies of the Directive. Article 25 of the Directive generally allows exports of personal data from EU Member States to a third country that *ensures an adequate level of protection*.[60] While the EU determined that some countries (e.g., Argentina, Canada and Switzerland[61]) provide an adequate level of

---

[57] This summary is adapted from an analysis of the Department of Commerce's international privacy activities published by the World Privacy Forum in 2010. The WPF report is "The US Department of Commerce and International Privacy Activities: Indifference and Neglect". The WPF report contains additional citations and support for the conclusions presented here. http://www.worldprivacyforum.org/pdf/USDepartmentofCommerceReportfs.pdf

[58] For Safe Harbor documents, see http://www.export.gov/safeharbor/eg_main_018237.asp

[59] European Parliament and the Council, Directive 95/46/EC of 24.10.1995 on the protection of individuals with regard to the processing of personal data and on the free movement of such data, OJ L 281, 23.11.1995. http://eur-lex.europa.eu/LexUriServ/LexUriServ.do?uri=CELEX:31995L0046:EN:HTML

[60] Other grounds for data exports are not relevant here.

[61] See http://ec.europa.eu/justice/data-protection/document/international-transfers/adequacy/index_en.htm

privacy protection according to EU standards, it has never made a similar determination with regard to the United States.

Restrictions on exports of personal data from Europe created some significant problems and uncertainties for both US and EU businesses, including online businesses. Pressured by the American business community, the Commerce Department intervened to resolve the threats to US business presented by the Data Protection Directive.

The 2000 Safe Harbor framework[62] was the result. Until the European Court of Justice invalidated the Safe Harbour Agreement in October 2015, it allowed US organisations to publicly declare that they will comply with the requirements. An organisation had to self-certify annually to the Department of Commerce in writing that it agreed to adhere to the Safe Harbor's requirements. The Safe Harbor Framework had its own standards, voluntary certification and some external method of enforcement so that it is similar to the other self-regulatory activities considered here.

Only organisations subject to the jurisdiction of the FTC or the Department of Transportation are eligible to participate. This limitation means that many companies, agencies and organisations that transfer personal information internationally cannot qualify for participation either in whole or in part.

Since its inception, three studies of the Safe Harbor Framework have been completed. The first was conducted in 2001 at the request of the European Commission Internal Market Directorate General.[63] The second, completed in 2004, was also requested by the European Commission Internal Market DG. An international group of academics conducted the study.[64] The third study from 2008 was prepared by Chris Connolly, director of an Australian consulting company with expertise in privacy, authentication, electronic commerce and new technology.[65]

Overall, the findings of the three studies were in agreement on the key problems with Safe Harbor at that time. Namely, companies that claimed to meet the Safe Harbor requirements were not actually in compliance with those requirements. Evidence from the three reports suggested that the number of companies not in compliance had increased over time.

While the Safe Harbor Framework was not a purely industry-run self-regulatory activity because of the role of the Department of Commerce, it shared some characteristics of industry self-regulatory activities, particularly a lack of compli-

---

[62] The Department of Commerce maintains a set of documents about the Safe Harbor Framework, including the original US-EU agreement, an overview, a list of companies in the Safe Harbor, and more. http://www.export.gov/safeharbor/eu/eg_main_018476.asp

[63] European Commission, "The Functioning of the US-EU Safe Harbor Privacy Principles", 21 September 2001. This study was reportedly published by the European Commission, but a copy has not been located on the EU's data protection webpage or elsewhere on the Internet. The study author is not identified in the document, but a Commission official publicly identified Professor Joel R. Reidenberg, Fordham University Law School, as the author, and the 2004 Study also identified Professor Reidenberg as the author. See 2004 Study at note 2.

[64] Centre de Recherche Informatique et Droit, "Safe Harbour Decision Implementation Study", 2004. http://ec.europa.eu/justice/policies/privacy/docs/studies/safe-harbour-2004_en.pdf. The report was prepared "at the request of the European Commission".

[65] Galexia, "The US Safe Harbor – Fact or Fiction"?, 2008. http://www.galexia.com/public/research/assets/safe_harbor_fact_or_fiction_2008/safe_harbor_fact_or_fiction.pdf

ance with the requirements. Until EU interest in Safe Harbor revived in 2014, enforcement had been rare. The Department had not apparently conducted or required audits of participants.

The initial shortcomings of the Safe Harbor Framework came to the attention of some data protection authorities in Europe. In April 2010, the Düsseldorfer Kreis, a working group comprising the data protection authorities of the 16 German länder with authority over the private sector, adopted a resolution applicable to those who export data from Germany to US organisations that self-certified compliance with the Safe Harbor Framework. The resolution instructs German data exporters to explicitly verify whether a self-certified data importer in the US actually complies with the Safe Harbor requirements.[66]

Until recently, the Commission appeared to ignore the known problems with Safe Harbor. However, in 2013, after the revelations of Edward Snowden regarding US security agency access to European data, Viviane Reding, EU Justice Commissioner who oversees data protection, announced that her office would review the Safe Harbor Framework. She stated that "it could be a loophole" that allowed companies to shift data to the US where "data protection standards are lower than our European ones".[67]

An important November 2013 European Commission report was highly critical of Safe Harbor and called for extensive reforms.[68] The report cited surveillance concerns nine times, and the report contained 13 recommendations for the continuation of Safe Harbor. These recommendations covered the areas of transparency, redress, enforcement, and access by US authorities.

By the Spring of 2015, negotiations for improving Safe Harbor were well underway, and 12 major points of agreement based on the 2013 recommendations had been reached between the US and the EU. The last remaining point to be negotiated, and certainly the most difficult point, has been the circumstances under which US national security bodies would have an exception to access data covered by the Safe Harbor agreement.[69]

In October 2015, the European Court of Justice ruled that the Safe Harbor program was invalid, making negotiations for a new Safe Harbor Agreement more complex. Another chapter in this book contains a more detailed review of the Safe Harbor program.

---

[66] Supreme Supervisory Authorities for Data Protection in the Nonpublic Sector (Germany), "Examination of the Data Importer's Self-Certification According to the Safe-Harbor-Agreement by the Company Exporting Data", revised version, 23 Aug 2010. http://www.datenschutz-berlin.de/attachments/710/Resolution_DuesseldorfCircle_28_04_2010EN.pdf?1285316129

[67] Chaffin, Joshua, "EU to review 'safe harbour' data privacy rule for US companies", *The Financial Times*, 19 July 2013. http://www.ft.com/intl/cms/s/0/285454b4-f091-11e2-929c-00144feabdc0.html

[68] European Commission, Communication from the Commission to the European Parliament and the Council on the Functioning of the Safe Harbour from the Perspective of EU Citizens and Companies Established in the EU, COM(2013) 847 final, Brussels, 11.27.2013. http://ec.europa.eu/justice/data-protection/files/com_2013_847_en.pdf

[69] Gardner, Stephen, "EU Cites U.S. Data Transfer Pact Progress Amid Privacy Regulation Reform Negotiations", Bloomberg BNA, 6 June 2015. http://www.bna.com/eu-cites-us-n17179891134/

3.3.2 Children's Online Privacy Protection Act

The safe harbor provision in the Children's Online Privacy Protection Act (COPPA)[70] is sometimes cited as a self-regulatory program. For that reason, COPPA is discussed here. However, it is crucial to note that COPPA self-regulation is significantly different from the others discussed in this chapter. The companies in a COPPA safe harbor must follow all the substantive standards established in the COPPA statute and FTC regulations, meaning that a participant in a COPPA safe harbor program must do everything that a non-participant must do *plus* bear the cost of the safe harbor. The standards cannot be changed by the participants in the self-regulatory program. The FTC formally oversees and approves COPPA safe harbor programs, a characteristic that other self-regulatory programs reviewed here lacked.[71]

Whether COPPA self-regulation is a success or failure is a subject for reasonable debate, but COPPA has fewer characteristics of failure than the industry self-regulation discussed earlier. For example, there is a formal input procedure for consumers, the COPPA safe harbor program has not disappeared and the FTC has enforced its COPPA regulations.

In effect, the COPPA safe harbor programs mostly engage in limited oversight of the statute and relieve the Commission of some of the burden. This may have some benefits to consumers and overall. It should not be surprising that industry participation in the safe harbor aspect of COPPA is minimal. The benefits to industry are narrow at best and non-existent at worst. The reason may be that self-regulation under a legislative scheme has little attraction when the principal purpose of industry self-regulation for privacy has been avoidance of regulation in the first place. The COPPA model does not appear to be in current use outside of this instance.

3.4 Joint self-regulatory efforts

The self-regulatory efforts in this category include projects with multiple participants, including government, industry, academia and civil society.

3.4.1 Platform for Privacy Preferences Project

The Platform for Privacy Preferences Project (P3P) is a technical standard for communicating the privacy policies of a website to those who use the website. A user can retrieve a standardised machine-readable privacy policy from a website and use

[70] 15 U.S.C. §§ 6501–6506. See http://business.ftc.gov/content/safe-harbor-program

[71] 15 U.S.C. § 6503.

the information to make a decision about how to interact with the website. Each user can match the privacy policy against the user's individual privacy preferences.

P3P allows a browser to understand a website privacy policy in a simplified and organised manner, without the need for a user to find and read a lengthy privacy policy. With the proper browser settings, P3P will automatically block any cookies from a website with a privacy policy that the user determined to be objectionable.

The Center for Democracy and Technology (CDT), a non-profit public policy group, supported the early work that eventually resulted in P3P.[72] CDT convened an Internet Privacy Working Group that drafted a mission statement, with companies, trade associations and consumer groups participating. Representatives of the Working Group made a presentation of a prototype at an FTC Workshop in 1997.[73]

Later in the same year, P3P became a project of the World Wide Web Consortium (W3C), the main international standards organisation for the World Wide Web. The working group included representatives of companies, academia and government.[74] The work of drafting the formal specification took some time, and version 1.0 was finally published at the end of 2000.[75] A later specification was published in 2006.[76]

Microsoft included support for P3P in its browser, Internet Explorer (version 6).[77] The Firefox browser from Mozilla also provided support.[78] The E-Government Act of 2002[79] included a requirement that federal agency websites translate privacy policies into a standardised machine-readable format,[80] and P3P is the only specification that meets the requirements.[81] It was a promising start.

However, the extent to which commercial websites and even government websites attempted to implement P3P or succeeded in doing so in the long term is highly uncertain. Professor Lorrie Faith Cranor published a review of P3P in 2008 that found P3P adoption increasing overall but that P3P adoption rates greatly vary across industries. Other findings are that P3P had been deployed on 10 % of the sites returned in the top 20 results of typical searches, and on 21 % of the sites in the top 20 results of e-commerce searches. A review of more than 5,000 websites in both 2003 and 2006 found that P3P deployment increased over that period, although

---

[72] For a fuller history of P3P and details on the actual technical standard, see Cranor, Lorrie Faith, *Web Privacy with P3P*, O'Reilly Media, Sebastopol, CA, 2002.

[73] Ibid., p. 45.

[74] Ibid. at 46.

[75] Ibid. at 53.

[76] http://www.w3.org/TR/P3P11

[77] See http://msdn.microsoft.com/en-us/library/ms537343%28VS.85%29.aspx

[78] See http://www-archive.mozilla.org/projects/p3p

[79] Public Law 107–347.

[80] See Office of Management and Budget, "Guidance for Implementing the Privacy Provisions of the E-Government Act of 2002", M-03-22, 2003. http://www.whitehouse.gov/omb/memoranda_m03-22

[81] See, e.g., Department of Health and Human Services, HHS-OCIO Policy for Machine-Readable Privacy Policies, Policy 2010–0001, 2010, section 4.2. http://www.hhs.gov/ocio/policy/hhs-ocio-2010_0001_policy_for_machine-readable_privacy_policies.html

there were decreases in some sectors. The review also found high rates of syntax errors among P3P policies, but much lower rates of critical errors that prevent a P3P user agent from interpreting them. Privacy policies of P3P-enabled popular websites were found to be similar to the privacy policies of popular websites that do not use P3P.[82]

The CyLab at Carnegie Mellon University published an analysis two years later that looked at more than 33,000 websites using P3P compact policies (CP) and "detected errors on 11,176 of them, including 134 TRUSTe-certified websites and 21 of the top 100 most-visited sites".[83] The study also found thousands of sites using identical invalid CPs that had been recommended as workarounds for Internet Explorer cookie blocking. Other sites had CPs with typos in their tokens or other errors. Fully 98 % of invalid CPs resulted in cookies remaining unblocked by Internet Explorer under its default cookie settings. The analysis concluded that it "appears that large numbers of websites that use [compact policies] are misrepresenting their privacy practices, thus misleading users and rendering privacy protection tools ineffective".[84] The study concluded that companies do not have sufficient incentives to provide accurate machine-readable privacy policies.[85]

In other words, the self-regulatory aspects of P3P do not appear to be working, with the CyLab study suggesting that lack of enforcement by regulators is a problem.[86] Neither P3P nor any industry trade association offers a P3P enforcement method.

P3P has some of the indicia of industry self-regulation in that it was inspired in part by FTC interest and motivated in part by an industry interest in avoiding legislation or regulation.[87] The involvement in P3P's development and promotion by consumer groups and the White House together with industry representatives differentiates P3P somewhat from the other industry efforts discussed earlier. Another differentiator is the legislative requirement that federal agencies use P3P or similar

---

[82] Cranor, Lorrie Faith, Serge Egelman, Steve Sheng, Aleecia M. McDonald and Abdur Chowdhury, "P3P Deployment on Websites", 7 Electronic Commerce Research and Applications 274–293, 2008. http://lorrie.cranor.org/pubs/%23p3p-deployment.html

[83] Leon, Pedro Giovanni, Lorrie Faith Cranor, Aleecia M. McDonald and Robert McGuire, "Token Attempt: The Misrepresentation of Website Privacy Policies through the Misuse of P3P Compact Policy Tokens", CMU-CyLab-10-014, 2010. http://www.cylab.cmu.edu/files/pdfs/tech_reports/CMUCyLab10014.pdf. The authors define compact policies in this way: "User agents, including Microsoft's Internet Explorer (IE) web browser, use CPs to evaluate websites' data collection practices and allow, reject, or modify cookies based on sites' privacy practices. CPs can provide a technical means to enforce users' privacy preferences if CPs accurately reflect websites' practices."

[84] Ibid.

[85] Ibid., p. 9.

[86] Ibid.

[87] See, e.g., Garfinkel, Simson, "Can a labeling system protect your privacy?", *Salon*, 11 July 2000. http://www.salon.com/technology/col/garf/2000/07/11/p3p. ("But P3P isn't technology, it's politics. The Clinton administration and companies such as Microsoft are all set to use P3P as the latest excuse to promote their campaign of 'industry self-regulation' and delay meaningful legislation on Internet privacy.")

technology. P3P shares sufficient characteristics with the self-regulatory programs discussed in this chapter to warrant its inclusion here.

Some privacy groups opposed P3P from the beginning, largely because of concerns that it would prevent privacy legislation from passing. Company views of the project also varied.[88] It is not clear how much attention P3P has received in recent years from companies or privacy groups.

Unlike some of the self-regulatory activities discussed earlier, P3P remains in use, at least technically. However, given the findings of the 2010 study of widespread misrepresentation of privacy policies by those using P3P, it is hard to call P3P any kind of success. Further, that study provides strong evidence of deliberate deception in implementation of P3P at some websites.

Internet users appear to have little knowledge of P3P, although public awareness may not be essential since the controls are built into browsers and users appear to be concerned about the privacy policies that P3P is designed to convey.[89] It is noteworthy that the FTC did not seek to enforce the promises made by commercial P3P participants using the Commission's power to take action against unfair and deceptive trade practices.

3.4.2 *NTIA's multi-stakeholder process*

The multi-stakeholder process of the National Telecommunications and Information Administration (NTIA) represents an attempt at a different model of self-regulation. The process began in July 2012, when the NTIA, an agency of the Department of Commerce, began to implement an Obama Administration plan for enforceable privacy codes of conduct developed though a multi-stakeholder process. The plan envisioned:

> open, transparent forums in which stakeholders who share an interest in specific markets or business contexts will work toward consensus on appropriate, legally enforceable codes of conduct. Private sector participation will be voluntary and companies ultimately will choose whether to adopt a given code of conduct. The participation of a broad group of stakeholders, including consumer groups and privacy advocates, will help to ensure that codes of conduct lead to privacy solutions that consumers can easily use and understand. A single code of conduct for a given market or business context will provide consumers with more consistent privacy protections than is common today….[90]

---

88 Cranor, Lorrie Faith, *Web Privacy with P3P*, O'Reilly Media, Sebastopol, CA, 2002, p. 56.

89 See Egelman, Serge, Janice Tsai, Lorrie Faith Cranor and Alessandro Acquisti, "Timing Is Everything? The Effects of Timing and Placement of Online Privacy Indicators", CHI '09: Proceedings of the SIGCHI Conference on Human Factors in Computing Systems, 2009. http://www.guanotronic.com/~serge/papers/chi09a.pdf

90 The White House, "Consumer Data Privacy in a Networked World: A Framework for Protecting Privacy and Promoting Innovation in the Global Digital Economy", Feb 2012. http://www.whitehouse.gov/sites/default/files/privacy-final.pdf

The plan expected that any privacy code of conduct would be enforced by the FTC using its power to take action against unfair and deceptive trade practices.[91] The lack of any evidence that the Commission actually used its enforcement powers against privacy self-regulatory codes did not appear to be a factor in the strategy.

The first multi-stakeholder process started with an announcement on 5 March 2012,[92] and the first meeting of participants occurred on 12 July 2012.[93] The topic of the first effort was mobile application transparency. That is, one element of fair information practices (transparency) for one set of functions (applications) for one class of technology (mobile devices). Meetings were open to the public, and consumer and privacy groups worked together with industry and trade associations to develop a consensus code of conduct. The apparent last meeting took place on 25 July 2013, more than a year after the first meeting. The product of the process was the "Short Form Notice Code of Conduct to Promote Transparency in Mobile App Practices".[94] The notice established several privacy benchmarks, including the first standard for notice to users about biometric use and about sharing of data with information resellers, or data brokers.

Some but not all participating stakeholders reached consensus on the code. They included, in particular, the Application Developers Alliance and several large industry trade groups such as CTIA – The Wireless Association and the Online Publishers Association. TRUSTe was also a signatory, as was the American Civil Liberties Union. However, not all participants in the process supported the final draft. Some industry trade groups such as the Digital Advertising Alliance and some consumer and privacy groups did not, in the end, agree.

In announcing its dissent, the Consumer Federation of America, a leading consumer group, said:

> It is not surprising that the product is so flawed given the problems with the process itself. There was never any clear procedure for how it would work and what would constitute success. There was no legal framework on which the code could be built, so that even terms such as "user data" are not clear and universally understood. The last meeting of the stakeholder group yesterday was as confusing as the process has been all along, with a "vote" being taken that allowed multiple attendees from the same companies or organizations to vote and resulted in no clear consensus. The groups that drafted the code, a small subset of the stakeholders, simply declared victory and the process ended.[95]

Not everyone involved agreed with this analysis. The drafting group included members of civil society, privacy groups, consumer groups and trade associations. Some in the drafting group issued statements that the code took an incremental, but

[91] Ibid. at 27.

[92] Federal Register, Vol. 77, No. 43, 5 Mar 2012, p. 13098. http://www.ntia.doc.gov/files/ntia/publications/fr_privacy_rfc_notice_03052012_0.pdf

[93] See generally http://www.ntia.doc.gov/other-publication/2013/privacy-multistakeholder-process-mobile-application-transparency

[94] http://www.ntia.doc.gov/files/ntia/publications/july_25_code_draft.pdf

[95] Grant, Susan, Consumer Federation of America, "CFA on the NTIA Short Form Notice Code of Conduct to Promote Transparency in Mobile Applications", 26 July 2013. http://www.consumerfed.org/news/693

important step forward. For example, the ACLU said that the code was a "modest but important step forward for consumer privacy".[96]

Many things remain uncertain about the first multi-stakeholder process. Some application developers based in the US are now using the code, following advice of their trade associations. The trade association for application developers created an automated tool to facilitate application of the code. The number of app developers who plan to implement the code is unknown; however, the 30,000 members of the Application Developers Alliance are reportedly implementing the code. It is also not clear how the code will be interpreted or if it can or will be updated as technology changes. Further, it is not known if the FTC will take any enforcement action to require those who promise to implement the code to actually live up to their promises. In the first multi-stakeholder process, the FTC was very clear that they would not be offering a "safe harbor" for companies that chose to voluntarily comply with the code. This position from the FTC denied the NTIA an important negotiating tool. It is unclear what long-term impact this might have. The initial impact, however, appears to have been deleterious to the process, making it less attractive to app developers and publishers.

The positive aspect of the multi-stakeholder process was the facilitation of a discussion involving consumers and industry on substantive issues. Most privacy self-regulatory efforts did not provide for any participation by consumer representatives. The disjointed response to the multi-stakeholder process makes it difficult to predict whether the resulting code will grow into a lasting success or will simply fade from use over time. Although there is no formal oversight or reporting, the NTIA made a statement that more than 200 million people are using the mobile app short form notice through the companies that have implemented it.[97] There is no independent verification of actual or continuing use, and there is no process for updating the standards.

Whether future multi-stakeholder efforts will produce results is unknown. The second multi-stakeholder process has not gone well, and may well produce a document without meaningful – or perhaps any – input from advocates. In 2014, the Department of Commerce commenced a second multi-stakeholder process on the topic of commercial facial recognition products.[98] The NTIA is again playing a "facilitating role" as a convener of the discussions.

The discussions began in February 2014, and over time the advocacy communities and industry representatives failed to find common ground, despite engagement in the process. This was especially true regarding the issue of consent – industry

---

[96] American Civil Liberties Union, "Mobile App Code of Conduct an Important Step Forward", 25 July 2013. https://www.aclu.org/technology-and-liberty/mobile-app-code-conduct-important-step-forward. Statements of support also came from ADA, Consumer Action and others.

[97] NTIA, "Remarks of Assistant Secretary Strickling at the Internet Governance Forum USA", 16 July 2015. http://www.ntia.doc.gov/speechtestimony/2015/remarks-assistant-secretary-strickling-internet-governance-forum-usa-07162015

[98] See generally http://www.ntia.doc.gov/other-publication/2013/privacy-multistakeholder-process-facial-recognition-technology

would not concede any ground on this particular issue. As a result, in June 2015, after more than a year of meetings, the privacy, civil liberties, and advocacy groups staged a very public walkout, abandoning the NTIA facial recognition stakeholder process.[99] Industry and the administration continued on with the process without the consumer groups' input or involvement.

The public interest groups wrote, in part:

> At this point, we do not believe that the NTIA process is likely to yield a set of privacy rules that offers adequate protections for the use of facial recognition technology. We are convinced that in many contexts, facial recognition of consumers should only occur when an individual has affirmatively decided to allow it to occur. In recent NTIA meetings, however, industry stakeholders were unable to agree on any concrete scenario where companies should employ facial recognition only with a consumer's permission.[100]

For its part, the administration commented that "Multistakeholder processes work best when a broad range of stakeholders with differing viewpoints fully participate. Most importantly, stay in the room."[101] The final outcome of the proceeding is not clear whatsoever at this point.

Several more NTIA multi-stakeholder processes are set to move forward, a process on drones, and one on cybersecurity. Based on the first two proceedings, the next two will likely prove to be a challenging process. An uncertainty going forward is the ongoing role of the Department of Commerce. The next President or the next Secretary of Commerce may choose not to continue the multi-stakeholder process, which could leave previous work without a sponsor. It is much too early to evaluate the longevity or value of the multi-stakeholder process, however, it can be said with confidence that the process has been difficult at best.

3.5 Federal Trade Commission and privacy self-regulation

A constant background issue in privacy self-regulation is the role of the FTC in enforcement of any self-regulatory code. A full analysis of the FTC's powers is beyond the scope of this chapter. Some of the Commission's limits and history nevertheless offer a gloss on the topic, as noted in the following points.

First, the Commission does not have authority over the entire US economy. In general, it has limited or no authority over privacy activities of federal, state and local agencies, most non-profit organisations, and many commercial entities engaged in transportation, insurance, banking and telecommunications.

---

99 Center for Democracy and Technology, "CDT Withdraws from the NTIA Facial Recognition Process", 16 June 2015. https://cdt.org/blog/cdt-withdraws-from-the-ntia-facial-recognition-process/. A joint statement came from the nine groups remaining in the process at that time.

100 "Privacy Advocates' Statement on NTIA Facial Recognition Process", 16 June 2015. https://www.dropbox.com/s/g7cdhl66p5um7dn/Privacy%20advocates%20statement%20on%20NTIA%20facial%20recognition%20process%20-%20FINAL.pdf?dl=0

101 Ibid at 96.

Second, the Commission has "vigorously promoted self-regulatory efforts",[102] beginning with its support for the IRSG effort in 1997 and continuing through its 2012 report. In that report, the Commission acknowledged the shortcomings of privacy self-regulation: "self-regulation has not gone far enough" and "there has been little self-regulation".[103] Nevertheless, the Commission urged "industry to accelerate the pace of its self-regulatory measures to implement the Commission's final privacy framework".[104] The Commission still somehow sees a role for privacy self-regulation notwithstanding the lesson of past failures. Intriguingly, Commission staff appeared lukewarm on the NTIA proceedings, leading some to wonder about a possible rivalry between the two agencies over privacy roles.

One reason for the Commission's continuing interest in self-regulation despite the known failures of self-regulation may be the limits of the FTC's jurisdiction. As a practical matter, the Commission cannot engage in broad rulemaking for privacy, although it has some rulemaking authority under specific statutes such as COPPA. The Commission has been able to use its power to prevent unfair or deceptive trade practices for some general privacy enforcement activities. Many of those activities rely on companies making promises and not fulfilling those promises. That constitutes deception. Self-regulation provides the promises that the Commission can seek to enforce, but the Commission has not done so.

Third, along with its push for more privacy self-regulation, the Commission at the same time called on Congress "to consider enacting baseline privacy legislation".[105] Note, however, that this recommendation did not call for legislation. It only asked Congress to *consider* enacting legislation, an attenuated recommendation that lacks force or conviction, especially since privacy legislation was and remains before the Congress, with little prospect of passage.[106] However, it is also likely true that a more positive statement from the FTC would not have had any greater influence on the legislative process.

Fourth, while the role of the Commission as a privacy enforcer has been much touted, the actual results are less impressive. A comparison of FTC efforts with those of another privacy enforcement agency based on reported activities though the middle of 2013 is instructive.

---

[102] Federal Trade Commission, "Protecting Consumer Privacy in an Era of Rapid Change: Recommendations For Businesses and Policymakers", 2012, p. ii. http://ftc.gov/os/2012/03/120326privacyreport.pdf

[103] Ibid., p. 11.

[104] Ibid. at 13.

[105] Ibid. at 13.

[106] The FTC has a longer history of favouring and disfavouring federal privacy legislation. In 2000, during a Democratic administration, the Commission affirmatively *recommended* passage of online privacy legislation. Federal Trade Commission, "Privacy Online: Fair Information Practices in the Electronic Marketplace: A Report to Congress", 2000, p. 36. http://www.ftc.gov/ reports/privacy2000/ privacy2000.pdf. In 2001, during a Republican Administration, the Commission backed off and called only for better enforcement. See Testimony of FTC Chairman Timothy J. Muris Before the Subcommittee on Commerce, Trade and Consumer Protection of the House Energy and Commerce Committee, 7 Nov 2001. http://www.ftc.gov/os/2001/11/muris011107.htm

The Office of Civil Rights at the federal Department of Health and Human Services is the enforcement agency for health privacy and security rules issued under the authority of the Health Insurance Portability and Accountability Act (HIPAA).[107] The HIPAA privacy rule took effect in 2003 and the security rule in 2009. A recent study found that during the 10-year period ending in April 2013, the OCR received 80,836 complaints through its patient complaint system. Of these, 28,981 fell within the OCR's jurisdiction. Most of these complaints (19,726) revealed a HIPAA violation, and the OCR required covered entities to change the way they implemented HIPAA requirements. For the decade, the OCR found about 2,000 violations per year.[108]

Contrast that with the FTC, which reports that during the 15-year period ending in February 2013, the Commission brought 153 cases, or about 10 a year.[109] Even allowing for somewhat increased Commission activity in recent years, the OCR brought more than 100 cases for each one that the FTC brought. While comparisons between agencies may be unfair because of differing authorities and budgets, the relative paucity of activity at the Commission speaks for itself.

3.6 Conclusion

Privacy self-regulation has generally failed when industry acts by itself behind closed doors. It is unclear whether joint consumer-industry efforts will succeed. Whether the new multi-stakeholder process can succeed is uncertain. A joint industry-consumer self-regulatory effort might succeed if (a) it were narrow in focus; (b) the efforts were deemed important enough by industry to overcome the fear of increased liability; (c) the process for negotiation were well-defined and more efficient; (d) the result included a process for benchmarking success and for addressing technological change; and (e) long-term enforcement was meaningful. Self-regulatory enforcement actions by the FTC have been scarce in the privacy arena. The failure of the Commission to take action against any of the failed privacy self-regulatory efforts cited in this chapter has repeatedly been noted here.

The only route left seems to be legislation, but the prospects for broadly applicable privacy legislation at present appear poor. Most see the 114th Congress (2015–2016) as broadly dysfunctional. While many privacy bills and legislative proposals continue to circulate, there is scant political consensus about what to do. Even a more effective Congress rarely produces results in the absence of consensus.

---

[107] See generally 45 C.F.R Parts 160–164. http://www.hhs.gov/ocr/privacy/hipaa/administrative/combined/hipaa-simplification-201303.pdf

[108] Melamed, Dennis, "HIPAA/HITECH Act Enforcement: 2003–2013 The Role of Patient Complaints In Medical Privacy and Data Security", 2013. http://www.melamedia.com/White_Papers.html

[109] http://business.ftc.gov/legal-resources/8/35

The Obama Administration supported privacy legislation in its 2012 White Paper,[110] but an actual draft bill was not released by the White House until February 2015.

Overcoming the institutional and legislative barriers to privacy legislation or to other forms of privacy regulation may take more public pressure combined with industry recognition that the American status quo for privacy is worse than other alternatives. Whether there is a genuine prospect that the US will seriously address privacy regulation any time soon remains to be seen.

References

American Civil Liberties Union, "Mobile App Code of Conduct an Important Step Forward", 25 July 2013. https://www.aclu.org/technology-and-liberty/mobile-app-code-conduct-important-step-forward

Better Business Bureau, "BBBOnLine Privacy Program Created to Enhance User Trust on the Internet", news release, 22 June 1998. http://web.archive.org/web/20110306180813/http://www.bbb.org/us/article/bbbonline-privacy-program-created-to-enhance-user-trust-on-the-internet-163

Centre de Recherche Informatique et Droit, "Safe Harbour Decision Implementation Study", 2004. http://ec.europa.eu/justice/policies/privacy/docs/studies/safe-harbour-2004_en.pdf. The report was prepared "at the request of the European Commission".

Center for Democracy and Technology, "CDT Withdraws from the NTIA Facial Recognition Process", 16 June 2015. https://cdt.org/blog/cdt-withdraws-from-the-ntia-facial-recognition-process/

Chaffin, Joshua, "EU to review 'safe harbour' data privacy rule for US companies", *The Financial Times*, 19 July 2013. http://www.ft.com/intl/cms/s/0/285454b4-f091-11e2-929c-00144feabdc0.html

Cranor, Lorrie Faith, *Web Privacy with P3P*, O'Reilly Media, Sebastopol, CA, 2002.

Cranor, Lorrie Faith, Serge Egelman, Steve Sheng, Aleecia M. McDonald and Abdur Chowdhury, "P3P Deployment on Websites", Electronic Commerce Research and Applications, Vol. 7, 2008, pp. 274–293. http://lorrie.cranor.org/pubs/%23p3p-deployment.html

Department of Health and Human Services, HHS-OCIO Policy for Machine-Readable Privacy Policies, Policy 2010–0001, 2010. http://www.hhs.gov/ocio/policy/hhs-ocio-2010_0001_policy_for_machine-readable_privacy_policies.html

Egelman, Serge, Janice Tsai, Lorrie Faith Cranor and Alessandro Acquisti, "Timing Is Everything? The Effects of Timing and Placement of Online Privacy Indicators", CHI '09: Proceedings of the SIGCHI Conference on Human Factors in Computing Systems, 2009. http://www.guanotronic.com/~serge/papers/chi09a.pdf

European Commission, "The Functioning of the US-EU Safe Harbor Privacy Principles", Study prepared by Professor Joel R. Reidenberg, Fordham University Law School, 21 September 2001.

European Commission, Communication from the Commission to the European Parliament and the Council on the Functioning of the Safe Harbour from the Perspective of EU Citizens and Companies Established in the EU, COM(2013) 847 final, Brussels, 27 November 2013. http://ec.europa.eu/justice/data-protection/files/com_2013_847_en.pdf

[110] The White House, "Consumer Data Privacy in a Networked World: A Framework for Protecting Privacy and Promoting Innovation in the Global Digital Economy", 2012. http://www.whitehouse.gov/sites/default/files/privacy-final.pdf

European Parliament and the Council, Directive 95/46/EC of 24.10.1995 on the protection of individuals with regard to the processing of personal data and on the free movement of such data, OJ L 281, 23 November 1995. http://eur-lex.europa.eu/LexUriServ/LexUriServ.do?uri=CELEX:31995L0046:EN:HTML

Federal Register, Vol. 77, No. 43, 5 Mar 2012. http://www.ntia.doc.gov/files/ntia/publications/fr_privacy_rfc_notice_03052012_0.pdf

Federal Trade Commission, *Individual Reference Services, A Report to Congress*, Commission Recommendations, 1997. http://www.ftc.gov/bcp/privacy/wkshp97/irsdoc1.htm

Federal Trade Commission, "Privacy Online: Fair Information Practices in the Electronic Marketplace, A Report To Congress", May 2000. http://www.ftc.gov/reports/privacy2000/privacy2000.pdf

Federal Trade Commission, *In Brief: The Financial Privacy Requirements of the Gramm-Leach-BlileyAct*,2002.http://business.ftc.gov/documents/bus53-brief-financial-privacy-requirements-gramm-leach-bliley-act

Federal Trade Commission, "Protecting Consumer Privacy in an Era of Rapid Change: Recommendations For Businesses and Policymakers", 2012. http://ftc.gov/os/2012/03/120326privacyreport.pdf

Galexia, "The US Safe Harbor – Fact or Fiction"?, 2008. http://www.galexia.com/public/research/assets/safe_harbor_fact_or_fiction_2008/safe_harbor_fact_or_fiction.pdf

Gardner, Stephen, "EU Cites U.S. Data Transfer Pact Progress Amid Privacy Regulation Reform Negotiations", Bloomberg BNA, 6 June 2015. http://www.bna.com/eu-cites-us-n17179891134/

Garfinkel, Simson, "Can a labeling system protect your privacy?", *Salon*, 11 July 2000. http://www.salon.com/technology/col/garf/2000/07/11/p3p

Grant, Susan, Consumer Federation of America, "CFA on the NTIA Short Form Notice Code of Conduct to Promote Transparency in Mobile Applications", 26 July 2013. http://www.consumerfed.org/news/693

Individual Reference Services Group, Industry Principles – Commentary, 15 Dec 1997. http://www.ftc.gov/os/1997/12/irsappe.pdf

Leon, Pedro Giovanni, Lorrie Faith Cranor, Aleecia M. McDonald and Robert McGuire, "Token Attempt: The Misrepresentation of Website Privacy Policies through the Misuse of P3P Compact Policy Tokens", CMU-CyLab-10-014, 2010. http://www.cylab.cmu.edu/files/pdfs/tech_reports/CMUCyLab10014.pdf

Melamed, Dennis, "HIPAA/HITECH Act Enforcement: 2003–2013 The Role of Patient Complaints In Medical Privacy and Data Security", 2013. http://www.melamedia.com/White_Papers.html

Muris, Timothy J., Testimony of FTC Chairman Timothy J. Muris Before the Subcommittee on Commerce, Trade and Consumer Protection of the House Energy and Commerce Committee, 7 Nov 2001. http://www.ftc.gov/os/2001/11/muris011107.htm

Network Advertising Initiative, "Written Comments in Response to the Federal Trade Commission Staff's Proposed Behavioral Advertising Principles", April 2008. http://www.ftc.gov/os/comments/behavioraladprinciples/080410nai.pdf

National Telecommunications and Information Agency (NTIA), "Remarks of Assistant Secretary Strickling at the Internet Governance Forum USA", 16 July 2015. http://www.ntia.doc.gov/speech-testimony/2015/remarks-assistant-secretary-strickling-internet-governance-forum-usa-07162015

Office of Management and Budget, "Guidance for Implementing the Privacy Provisions of the E-Government Act of 2002", M-03-22, 2003. http://www.whitehouse.gov/omb/memoranda_m03-22

"Privacy Advocates' Statement on NTIA Facial Recognition Process", 16 June 2015. https://www.dropbox.com/s/g7cdhl66p5um7dn/Privacy%20advocates%20statement%20on%20NTIA%20facial%20recognition%20process%20-%20FINAL.pdf?dl=0

Privacy Leadership Initiative, "Privacy Leadership Initiative Transfers Initiatives to Established Business Groups", press release, 1 July 2002, cited in Robert Gellman, and Pam Dixon, "Many Failures: A Brief History of Privacy Self-Regulation in the United States", World Privacy Forum, 2011. http://www.worldprivacyforum.org/pdf/WPFselfregulationhistory.pdf

Savage, Marcia, "New Industry Alliance Addresses Online Privacy", *Computer Reseller News*, 19 June 2000. http://technews.acm.org/articles/2000-2/0621w.html#item13

Solove, Daniel J., and Chris Jay Hoofnagle, "A Model Regime of Privacy Protection", *University of Illinois Law Review*, Vol. 2006, No. 2, 2006, pp. 357, 365.

Supreme Supervisory Authorities for Data Protection in the Nonpublic Sector (Germany), "Examination of the Data Importer's Self-Certification According to the Safe-Harbor-Agreement by the Company Exporting Data", revised version, 23 Aug 2010. http://www.datenschutz-berlin.de/attachments/710/Resolution_DuesseldorfCircle_28_04_2010EN.pdf?1285316129

Uncapher, Mark, Statement of Mark Uncapher, Vice President and Counsel, Information Technology Association of America, before the Federal Trade Commission Public Workshop on Online Profiling, 18 Oct 1999. http://www.ftc.gov/bcp/workshops/profiling/comments/uncapher.htm 15 U.S.C. § 6809(3)

Wharton School of the University of Pennsylvania, "Up for Sale: How Best to Protect Privacy on the Internet", Knowledge@Wharton, 19 March 2001. http://knowledge.wharton.upenn.edu/article.cfm?articleid=325

The White House, "Consumer Data Privacy in a Networked World: A Framework for Protecting Privacy and Promoting Innovation in the Global Digital Economy", Feb 2012. http://www.whitehouse.gov/sites/default/files/privacy-final.pdf

World Privacy Forum, *The Network Advertising Initiative: Failing at Consumer Protection and at Self-Regulation*, 2007. http://www.worldprivacyforum.org/wp-content/uploads/2007/11/WPF_NAI_report_Nov2_2007fs.pdf

World Privacy Forum, "The US Department of Commerce and International Privacy Activities: Indifference and Neglect", 2010. http://www.worldprivacyforum.org/pdf/USDepartmentofCommerceReportfs.pdf

Chapter 4
From a Model Pupil to a Problematic Grown-Up: Enforcing Privacy and Data Protection in Hungary

Ivan Szekely

4.1 Introduction

When the new democracies of Central and Eastern Europe had to implement the rights of the western world, they had to choose the particular mechanisms of enforcement. Among these new rights and freedoms, the information rights, which included the right to privacy and data protection, featured prominently in the priority list of the democratic transition. In the 1990s, Hungary proved to be a model pupil in the creation of the system of information rights and, through the establishment of an ombudsman-type institution to safeguard data protection, it also led the way in developing the enforcement mechanisms. For more than 15 years, the data protection ombudsman headed one of the most successful new democratic institutions in Hungary, while the country itself served as an example to the other new democracies of the region. However, the government that took power in 2010 decided to abolish the institution in 2012, dismissing the data protection ombudsman before the end of his mandate and setting up a new government authority for enforcing of the data protection laws. This amounted to a paradigm change in the enforcement mechanisms, and the method chosen to carry this out provoked strong criticism from several international organisations. While it is still too early to assess the impact of the paradigm change and the performance of the new authority, the story of enforcing privacy and data protection in Hungary can definitely offer important lessons for other new democracies. This chapter describes and analyses how privacy has been enforced (or not) in Hungary since its transition to a democracy in the early 1990s.

History tells us that in the case of those countries that experienced an abrupt change in their political and social system as they moved from a closed, authoritarian

I. Szekely (✉)
Vera and Donald Blinken Open Society Archives (OSA), Central European University,
Arany Janos u. 32, 1051 Budapest, Hungary
e-mail: szekelyi@ceu.edu

D. Wright, P. De Hert (eds.), *Enforcing Privacy*, Law, Governance and Technology Series 25, DOI 10.1007/978-3-319-25047-2_4

regime or an outright dictatorship to a more open, democratic system based on western liberal values and the rule of the law, the codification of the new rights and freedoms, together with the formation and functioning of their enforcement methods and institutional system, and the public's respect for them, tend to show a characteristic pattern in their evolution.

In the period immediately after the democratic transition, these rights and freedoms are usually regarded as being of the highest importance; some of them, for example, the right of assembly or the freedom of information, often become the symbols of, and the practical tools for, staging a break with the old political system. The sufficiently active and professionally well prepared countries, which are usually the most successful in codifying the new rights at this early stage – and not merely in an ad hoc manner but proceeding systematically in transforming the entire legal system on the basis of the western standards of constitutionality – have reason to feel historically lucky, in the sense that in subsequent periods of far less favourable circumstances, they are able to preserve the basic institutions of democracy and the rule of the law. The first period of euphoria is almost invariably followed by a period when people discover that the new rights and the new legal institutions will not be able to solve the country's social and, more importantly, economic problems, while the more liberal environment will allow the influential players of the old regime to retain their former influence and control. The formation of the new economic and political power structures begins, in which the realisation of the individual freedoms might seem to act as a limiting factor; and within a few years, a new generation emerges, whose members are no longer interested in the past and only care for the present, and whose main ambitions concern material goods, individual advancement and the development of new power structures in the interests of which they are sometimes willing to transgress legal and ethical norms.[1] All these together lead to the erosion of the respect for, and importance of, the constitutional values and the new rights and freedoms, and the process is usually accompanied by a decline in the acceptance of both the enforcement methods and associated institutions.

This chapter does not discuss the democratisation processes of the countries of the cultural East, where the substantive acceptance of both the influence of the western values and the rights and freedoms understood in the western sense pose fundamental theoretical and practical problems anyway. Instead, it focuses on the "new democracy" of Hungary, a representative of the region that for a prolonged period had belonged to the Soviet bloc and followed a Soviet-type political and social model. The above-referenced evolution pattern reveals distinct, country-specific features within the region; the time and the scale of the changes vary from country to country. Nevertheless, there are historical experiences of general validity, which might even serve as instructive lessons for some new democracies to emerge in the future.

---

[1] For an analysis of freedom of information in Central and Eastern Europe, see Szekely, Ivan, "Central and Eastern Europe: Starting from Scratch", in Ann Florini (ed.), *The Right to Know: Transparency for an Open World*, Columbia University Press, 2007, pp. 116–142.

The right to privacy is one of the fundamental rights, which made their appearance in the legal framework of the new democracies either during the turbulent years of democratic transition or in the period immediately following. The countries concerned (the former communist countries of Central and Eastern Europe, the so-called Soviet Bloc) did not have the necessary time to fully develop these rights and to incorporate them in their legal and institutional practices in the course of a long, organic development, so as to consolidate their social embeddedness or interiorisation, i.e., to become an accepted part of the social fabric. As a result, the rights to privacy and data protection had to be imported from the practices of the more fully developed democracies, along with many other legal principles and norms. In addition, suitable points had to be found for linking them to the existing legal and institutional traditions, and even to the current legislative framework, especially in those countries where the democratic transition had been completed without bloodshed, through the peaceful transfer of power. In the context of Hungary, the implementation of these new laws is of great interest, since, on the one hand, it provides an excellent example of the establishment of the new legal order and the consolidation of the institutional and enforcement system and related practices, while on the other hand, it faithfully illustrates the vulnerability of a system considered to be firmly established and well functioning, along with its sensitivity to changes in the political environment, and thus – not at all independently of the international trends in the enforcement of privacy law – it reveals radical changes in the model.

The following pages briefly outline the emergence of privacy and data protection legislation in Hungary after the democratic transition in the 1990s, mainly concentrating on the formation of the enforcement mechanisms and the associated institutions. The chapter then describes the political and social context and the functioning of the new institutions, and discusses the fundamental changes that have taken place in the political and legal system since the early 2010s. This chapter has a special focus on the enforcement model of privacy and data protection laws. Next, it analyses those aspects of the legal and enforcement guarantees in the privacy and data protection laws that are specific to Hungary, revealing the origins of these developments and pointing out the causes and consequences of recent changes in them, while also mentioning the main differences between the two models. After that, the chapter demonstrates the differences between the two models through a few typical examples of the mandates and the roles of the former data protection ombudsman and the present data protection authority, respectively.

Since the history of enforcing privacy and data protection legislation is far from its end in Hungary, we conclude our analysis by posing a few open questions, followed by a few general recommendations for the new democracies in area of privacy and data protection taking into account historical experiences.

4.2 A brief history and context

Before the Second World War, Hungary was still not in the position to generate demand for western-type information rights and to organically build it into the country's legal system; during the decades after the war, it was no longer in the position to do so. That could only take place in the hectic period around the 1989 democratic transition, almost as if to make up for the lost decades. The scant legal precedent mostly came via those comrades who had encountered the ideas and expectations of information rights, including privacy and data protection, at conferences abroad, manifested in the introduction of some new provisions in the Communist legal system, partly as a result of a cautious adoption of western expectations, and partly simply due to some misunderstandings.[2] The most important and most substantive precedent was the creation of a multidisciplinary experts' team,[3] which worked under the auspices of the Central Statistical Bureau (KSH): it collected the international examples of data protection and freedom of information; it developed the legal regime for the new information law still before the democratic transition, including a draft proposal for the combined data protection and freedom of information law.

There was a negotiated transfer of political power, a "velvet revolution" of some sort. The platform of the negotiations was called the Opposition Roundtable (EKA), which brought together the leaders, spokespersons and experts of the old and the new regime. Even the participants of EKA could sense that they were in fact making decisions about the transformation of the political and legal system without consulting the people, so they tried to establish legal institutions, which would belatedly allow the citizens to have a direct say in the running of public affairs. As Laszlo Solyom, participant of EKA (who later became President of the newly established Constitutional Court, and then President of the Republic), stated at a conference held recently[4], the EKA made three "gestures" to the people: the establishment of the institution of ombudsman ("the people's advocate"),[5] the introduction of the *actio popularis* (the option to turn to the Constitutional Court directly) and the creation of the conditions for holding referendums.[6]

A milestone on the road to the creation of the data protection law was the 1991 decision of the Constitutional Court, in which it declared the use of the universal personal ID number to be unconstitutional, expounded the principles of information self-determination patterned on the German model, and ordered the Parliament to

[2] For example, data protection was often confused with data security.

[3] Laszlo Solyom was among the members of this group, as were Laszlo Majtenyi, the first data protection ombudsman, and the author of this chapter.

[4] Conference on the institution of constitutional complaint, organised by the Eotvos Karoly Policy Institute on 21 February 2014, in the OSA (Vera and Donald Blinken Open Society Archives at Central European University), Budapest.

[5] The data protection ombudsman became one of them.

[6] Solyom followed here an earlier analysis by Laszlo Majtenyi, presented at the conference "Two constitutions (1989–2011)" held at OSA on 21 March 2011.

create a data protection law. Parliament passed the law in 1992, without a single opposing vote. This combined data protection and freedom of information bill prescribed the establishment of an independent supervisory body, the office of a parliamentary commissioner with ombudsman-like powers. However, this only took place in the summer of 1995, together with the election of the other two parliamentary ombudsmen.

The data protection ombudsman (Parliamentary Commissioner for Data Protection and Freedom of Information), who was responsible for supervising the enforcement of both information rights, functioned between 1995 and 2011 and his office was one of the most successful institutions of the new democracy, the practices of which were taken as a model by several similar institutions in the West. As for Hungary, it became something of a model country among the new democracies in the area of the introduction of information rights. Nevertheless, the political leadership that took power in 2010 abolished the institution and dismissed the data protection ombudsman before the end of his mandate, creating instead a government authority – which was not a legal successor – effective from January 2012.

4.3 Characteristic features: the causes and the consequences

Constitutional values become part of the legal framework only when their codification is followed by the establishment of enforcement mechanisms. The laws come to life and become socially embedded only after these values have been accepted both by the institutions and administrators of the public sphere and the civilian population, when these laws are widely understood and when the legal institutions are broadly used.

The question about the extent to which these constitutional values – including privacy – became interiorised both by the public and the political elite during the turbulent years of democratic transition and the extent to which they had been latently present in the period before the transition is worth asking. During the decades before the democratic transition, such questions were primarily addressed by a Hungarian institute unique in the entire Soviet bloc, the Mass Communication Research Center (TK). Throughout its existence between 1969 and 1991, the TK – in its final years, renamed as Hungarian Institute for Public Opinion Research (MKI) – carried out investigations in the areas of public opinion and mass communication, operating on a generous budget, maintaining a very high professional standard, and using the most up-to-date methodologies developed in the western world. However, the first democratically elected government after the transition abolished the institute on the grounds of its former co-operation with the old regime; the research continued in the 1990s within a different organisational framework, based on a less coherent methodological foundation.[7] Happily, young researchers can

[7] The research centres and private polling firms, which now mostly work as the Hungarian subsidiaries of international polling companies, originally were formed from the institute's professional

benefit from empirical studies that had already been conducted prior to the democratic transition[8] and that continued into the 1990s.[9]

From the viewpoint of our topic, a survey conducted in 1988–1989[10] is perhaps the most important: this was the first effort in the region to conduct a comprehensive survey about public opinion concerning privacy, data sensitivity and trust in data-handling organisations. An analysis of the findings showed that people had substantive views about these apparently rather abstract issues, and although these opinions were somewhat unformed, with the help of multivariable methods, the main patterns of views can be demonstrated. According to these, crucial factors were sensitivity to privacy issues, receptiveness to trust and order, and pro and anti-computer attitudes.[11] Although the respondents in general revealed a considerable degree of mistrust towards the proprietors and representatives of information power, the overwhelming majority of them were compliant data subjects: resistance to data requests was rarely recorded.[12]

The interiorisation of values is important, since the task of raising awareness for the rights and values of privacy and data protection, or more generally the job of working out the system of information rights and developing the enforcement mechanisms and the associated institutions, mostly fell on an elite team, which embarked on these tasks well before the period of the democratic transition. In some sense, therefore, the establishment of the new system of information rights can be regarded as an "elitist" initiative, which in numerous situations has become a useful reference point for the political system in connection with the western democracies or the international organisations, yet for the entirety of the public administration or

---

and human resources. Thanks to the TK researchers' passion of collecting, copies of the research materials, and in some cases even the data files, have survived and have, since 2013, been available for research at the OSA. (Fonds HU OSA 420, see http://osaarchivum.org/db/fa/420.htm.)

[8] The important question one needs to ask is how far can one trust the data of public opinion polls recorded under a dictatorial regime, and whether what the respondents say can be accepted as their own opinions. Participants of the conference "TK 3.0: Did People Lie in Kadar's Hungary?", which was held in April 2013 at the OSA concurred in the view – in harmony with earlier professional opinions – that the surveys conducted by TK had yielded authentic information about public opinion; it came with the price that certain parts of these research results could never be published before the democratic transition.

[9] Much can be learned from the comparison of two surveys, which used similar methodology to find out about what was better in Hungary than in the West in public opinion. In 1981, a considerable majority of the respondents thought better of the Hungarian situation in all of the areas (including the general moral condition of society, the well-balanced lives of families, and the freedom of opinion), while by 1987, the scenario had radically turned around. A retrospective analysis of these surveys can show not only the changes in values, but also the radical weakening of the regime's legitimacy in these years. See Vasarhelyi, Maria, "Lattuk-e, hogy jon?" [Did we see it coming?] *Jel-Kep,* No. 3–4, 2010, pp. 91–97.

[10] The research documentation and the data files are now held in the OSA.

[11] Szekely, Ivan, Janos Tolgyesi and Gabor Varnai, *Information privacy in Hungary. Survey report and analysis*, Hungarian Institute for Public Opinion Research, Budapest 1991.

[12] The complete English-language study is available at http://www.sscqueens.org/sites/default/files/Information_Privacy_in_Hungary.pdf

the broad segments of the population, it is becoming a familiar and accepted idea only slowly and gradually.

In view of the fact that in the period before the democratic transition, people had only a limited ability to realise the right to privacy, or even to learn about its content, readers may be surprised by the first data protection ombudsman's assessment of the situation, who wrote the following in his first report:

> The sensitivity of Hungarian society to data protection and the right to informational self-determination is more advanced than was previously anticipated. Data protection does not represent a luxury demand of people of higher social standing or educational level, and the sensitivity to data protection cannot be closely attributed to social standing: It spreads across Hungarian society from the unemployed homeless to the highest ranking citizens.[13]

Indeed, such a positive assessment was supported by the surveys conducted in the 1990s to test knowledge and legitimacy[14]; subsequently, the knowledge index of the office of the data protection ombudsman increased,[15] while the trust index declined[16] (this can be seen as another example of the evolution patterns mentioned in the Introduction). Parallel with this, new voices arose in the changing political landscape, which questioned the extent of data protection laws and the need for the enforcement mechanism, while a radical right-wing politician went as far as saying that the office of the data protection ombudsman should be abolished, because the concept of data protection is alien to the Hungarian national spirit.[17]

From a legal perspective, the consolidation of privacy and data protection legislation proceeded in instalments, in a typical top-down fashion: first, the basic provisions were inserted in the Constitution; next, the newly established Constitutional Court issued rulings to expound its content, after which the Data Protection Act was formulated and work on sector-specific laws began, and finally the independent supervisory body was established.[18] The model had three distinct features: (1) the rights

---

[13] Majtenyi, Laszlo (ed.), *The first three years of the Parliamentary Commissioner for Data Protection and Freedom of Informatio*n, ABI, Budapest, 1998, p. 11.

[14] According to a 1998 survey by Szonda Ipsos, 43 % of the population knew about the data protection ombudsman, and the ombudsman's office in general ranked fourth in the list of most trusted institutions (after the President of the Republic, the Constitutional Court and the respondent's favourite political party).

[15] According to the results of the survey repeated 10 years later, in 2008, 46 % of the respondents had heard about the institution of data protection ombudsman, which earned Hungary second place among the countries of the European Union (Flash Eurobarometer 225, http://ec.europa.eu/public_opinion/flash/fl_225_en.pdf).

[16] According to a 2008 survey by Szonda Ipsos, the trust index of the institution of ombudsman dropped from 63 to 52 % in 10 years (it must be pointed out, however, that the trust for institutions in general was also declining at the time).

[17] Istvan Csurka, chairman of the Hungarian Justice and Life Party, Spring 2001. See http://www.origo.hu/itthon/20010426antidemokratikus.html [in Hungarian]. The political attacks led to the obstruction of the first data protection ombudsman's re-election; the post was eventually filled after a 6-month delay.

[18] Although the possibility of enforcement through court action already existed before the introduction of the independent supervisory body, this hardly ever happened in practice. (This partly proved that there was a real need for the creation of a specialised supervisory and enforcement institution.)

to privacy and data protection which were elevated to the status of fundamental rights enshrined in the Constitution; (2) informational self-determination conceived along the lines of the German model (thus raising the standard above the minimum level required by the Council of Europe and the European Union); and (3) an ombudsman-type supervisory body. A further characteristic of the legislative model was the structural division of general law versus sectoral laws: the data protection law – covering both the public sector and the private sector – laid down the fundamental rules for handling personal data in a codex-like manner, while the sectoral laws and regulations mainly contained the detailed provisions and, most notably, the exceptions; in matters not covered by the sectoral rules, the provisions of the data protection law automatically applied.[19]

With the exception of the type and mandate of the independent supervisory body, all the rest of these characteristic features have survived down to the present day (even though the codex-like character of the data protection law has partially eroded due to the numerous exceptions and subsequently introduced legislative changes).

So how can the characteristic features of the Hungarian model be explained? On top of the historical, legal and administrative traditions (traditions that reached Hungary with a delay and manifested themselves only in a twisted way in the decades prior to the democratic transition), one of the causes was provided by the specific experiences of the dictatorial regime and by the effort of the new system's constitutional fathers to raise the level of the legal guarantees of the new democratic establishment as high as possible, as a precaution against a possible reversal of the democratic process, should a future power try to take back the newly gained and codified rights.[20] This, too, contributed to the fact that the level of data protection in Hungary – similarly to other, post-dictatorial countries – was set at a level that in many respects was distinctly higher than the minimum standard for European democracies. Other factors that contributed to the development of the model were the legal systems of western, most notably European, democracies, the legal and institutional models they had developed, and the practical knowledge they had gained in the realisation of privacy and data protection.[21]

However, the role, erudition and approach of certain prominent persons cannot be overlooked – this was especially important in regions where the reforms and the changes had an "elitist" character, advanced by a vanguard of professionals, rather than some plebeian mass movements. The prime mover in the adoption of the German model – including the concept of informational self-determination – was the law professor Laszlo Solyom, who in the second half of the 1980s studied on a

---

[19] For more on this, see Szekely, Ivan, and Mate Daniel Szabo, "Privacy and data protection at the workplace in Hungary", in Sjaak Nouwt, Berend R. de Vries and Corien Prins (eds.), *Reasonable Expectations of Privacy? Eleven Country Reports on Camera Surveillance and Workplace Privacy*, IT & Law Series, T.M.C. Asser Press, The Hague, 2005, pp. 249–284 [pp. 252–255].

[20] The political elite of the democratic transition proved to be less circumspect in making the *whole* of the constitutional system impervious to these kinds of changes, as vividly demonstrated by the recent political changes related to constitutionality.

[21] In the collection and analysis of these, the earlier mentioned interdisciplinary team working under the aegis of the KSH played a prominent role.

research grant at the Johann Wolfgang Goethe University in Frankfurt[22] under the supervision of Spiros Simitis, a prominent scholar of German and EU data protection legislation, whose name was associated with the drafting of the first data protection law[23] and who filled the office of data protection ombudsman in the province of Hessen for 15 years. In a broader sense, Solyom also prodded the Hungarian Constitutional Court into adopting certain practices, and occasionally even the concrete reasoning, of the Constitutional Court of Germany. Solyom was later elected as the first, and probably the most influential, president of the Hungarian Constitutional Court; he eventually became President of Hungary in the period between 2005 and 2010.

The other person who had a major influence on developments in the area of data protection in Hungary was Laszlo Majtenyi. He learned about the Scandinavian model of the ombudsman system while studying on a scholarship in Norway. Through the articles he published in professional and public journals, he presented this model to the Hungarian experts in charge of developing the new legal and administrative system, personally making tremendous efforts to integrate it into the Hungarian legal and administrative system. As Hungary's first data protection ombudsman, Majtenyi was responsible for creating the legal environment for the ombudsman system, developing the rules of operation and defining the main priorities of its activities.[24] Of course, the influence of one person would not have been enough to bring about the establishment of the ombudsman system in Hungary: the process was greatly aided by the view – widely held in the countries of Central and Eastern Europe – that the introduction of a previously unknown institution, the office of the ombudsman, could work as some kind of a panacea in solving the country's problems concerning public administration, civil rights protection and the self-correction mechanism of the new democratic system in general.

4.4 Enforcement models and alternatives

In the period following the establishment of the data protection ombudsman, three types – or models – for enforcing privacy and data protection laws appeared in the Hungarian legal system. The most robust among them was the functioning of the data protection ombudsman, which was based on a powerful mandate to investigate

---

[22] Later on, when he was already President of the Republic, the university awarded Laszlo Solyom an honorary doctorate ("Sterne unserer Jugend – Ehrendoktorwürde des Fachbereichs Rechtswissenschaft für den Ungarischen Staatspräsidenten Prof. László Sólyom", *UniReport* 7, 15 November 2006, p. 2. http://www2.uni-frankfurt.de/44481170/unireport_07-2006.pdf).

[23] The federal state of Hessen, 1970.

[24] Although the official title of the – by now abolished – position was Parliamentary Commissioner, the public usually referred to him as data protection ombudsman, just as they did to the other two varieties of parliamentary commissioners.

and a weak mandate to enforce: in other words, it had the characteristic features associated with the activities of the ombudsman, exerting an influence through recommendations and voluntary compliance, as well as through the power of publicity. Its investigative powers were among the strongest within the structure of the State, surpassing even the powers of the other parliamentary ombudsmen: it could request information from any of the data controlling organisations within both the state and the private sector in all matters related to personal data (or data of public interest); it could inspect or copy all documents and enter all offices where data were processed, and in these activities, it could not be hindered by state secrets, trade secrets or other confidential information.[25] As the annual reports of the data protection ombudsman have shown, its weak powers to enforce were accompanied by the high rate of voluntary compliance, which proves the success of the ombudsman model.

However, even the data protection ombudsman's powers mixed investigative authority with enforcement authority, although the few enforcement-type authorities assigned to it from the beginning were associated with its other main task, the supervision of access to public information – and classified state secrets, as a limiting factor. If the ombudsman thought that the classification of some information, or its time limit, was unjustified, he could instruct the data controller to modify or abolish it.[26] The data controller concerned then had the right to appeal to the court against such an instruction, as an example of the checks and balances between organisations of the State.

After the amendment of the law in 2003 – initiated in order to counter the slight decline in the number of voluntary compliances – the data protection ombudsman was empowered to issue binding decisions as part of his competences related to the protection of personal data: once the data controller refused to accept the ombudsman's recommendation, the latter gained the authority to issue a binding decision to prohibit or to suspend the further processing of data, to delete or destroy the personal data processed illegally, or to suspend the forwarding of the data to a foreign country. But in practice, the ombudsman resorted to this power only in cases when all his other options had been exhausted, as he continued to perceive his role as an ombudsman. On the other hand, the duties of data controllers became more robust and better defined: data controllers had 30 days to respond to communications (recommendations or decisions) from the ombudsman, the same time period they had to appeal against decisions in court. However, the proceedings hardly ever reached that stage, and if they did, they mostly took the form of a trial case, in which the data controllers usually withdrew their appeals before the court's issuing its decision. In general, it is fair to say that even in this period, the investigations of the data protection ombudsman – when they confirmed the unlawful processing of personal data – mostly ended with the data controller's compliance, and in those few instances when he felt the need to issue a binding decision, these were mostly carried into effect. These characteristic features of the data protection ombudsman's mode of operation survived right until the abolition of the institution.

---

[25] Act LXIII of 1992, Section 26 (1).

[26] Section 26 (4) [renumbered as (5) after a subsequent modification].

Although the data controllers' willingness to accept the ombudsman's recommendations and decisions could be observed as a rule throughout the period, some of the data controllers resorted from the start to the tactic of deftly evading compliance with the measures required by the ombudsman. One method of such evasions was formal compliance, when the data controller accepted the ombudsman's recommendations at the level of declarations, but continued with the substandard or unlawful data processing in practice.[27] A similar practice could be observed in connection with the various government offices, which tried to ward off the ombudsman's critical or inconvenient remarks in his legally required evaluation of any draft legislation by failing to send the ombudsman's office a copy, or by sending it only at the last minute. This, of course, could also have resulted from simple carelessness (although that, too, would say a lot about the prestige of the data protection ombudsman's office in the government's eyes), but the assumption of intentionality would not be too far-fetched. This practice took several forms (the data protection ombudsmen all made a note of these in their annual reports), one of which was sending drafts running to hundreds of pages without marking the places where the ombudsman's comments were required, in the hope that his assistants may have missed the relevant passages; or sending large volumes of texts on a Friday afternoon, with a return date by Monday morning. The element most likely to draw criticism in connection with the involvement of the ombudsman in the legal review process was the decision to put it in the general review round, where his opinion counted as only one among the views of many other organisations, occasionally as many as 50, and so in the end, it hardly received the necessary attention. A more appropriate solution – one that was more in line with the legal status of the ombudsman – would have been if the government, in the course of the preparatory phase of the legal drafting – had first held a preliminary consultation among the governmental bodies, before sending the agreed draft proposal to the data protection ombudsman, who then could have added his own remarks and recommendations to it, which – in the case of parliamentary legislation – could have been presented to Parliament alongside the government's proposal.

The other method of formal compliance was based on a ruse analogous to the practice of journalists under the communist regime of earlier times, who added a "red tail"[28] to their articles. The "red tail" treatment in the form of a "data protection tail" was applied every time when a blatantly unlawful method of data processing (to which the ombudsman was likely to object) was announced and the data controllers wanted to promote it. In introducing a new plan, which concerned the processing of personal data, or sometimes even in launching an entire system developed

27 This mostly happened in the case of service providers with a large number of domestic clients, according to the experience of the author who had, earlier on, worked as an expert and advisor – naturally, bound by very strict secrecy obligations.

28 In the period of the thawing of the communist ideology during the Kadar regime, journalists were able to praise the achievements of the capitalist system almost in any areas, providing they ended the article with a turn of phrase something like "the future belongs to communism" or "the world's leading power is the Soviet Union" – this was to what the term "red tail" referred.

without the involvement of the data protection ombudsman, they invariably ended their presentation with the turn of phrase "in full compliance with the relevant sections of the data protection laws" – even when the system in question had obviously been created and operated in violation of the provisions of the data protection law. Finally, in addition to the tactics of evasion and deceit, open resistance to the data protection laws and the data protection ombudsman had also raised its head by around 2005; it was led by the experts of the efficiency-conscious bureaucracy (former supporters of data protection legislation), allying themselves with the representatives of the information industry, who had earlier looked upon the centralisation of registries and personal identification systems, and their legitimate use for any purpose, as the "modern" ideal. These efforts were taken on by the Institute for Computer Science and Control, Hungarian Academy of Sciences (SZTAKI),[29] which took care to also invite a former data protection ombudsman as well as some independent experts in data protection[30] – making sure, of course, that any dissenting opinions by the latter remain in the minority, and occasionally seeing to it that those views were watered down in the minutes taken at the discussions.[31]

All in all, it is fair to say that the office of the data protection ombudsman has successfully foiled the attempts to soften the information rights regime. However, in some areas, the data protection ombudsman was only able to accomplish moderate results, and these were all related to issues of enforcement. One of these issues concerned the running of the central data protection register, which contained the most important information related to data processing and data controllers, and which is accessible to anyone. The system providing online access to the register itself took long years to complete and the design of the user-friendly interface left much to be desired, but it was mainly in the area of improving the slack discipline in reporting in the various sectors of data controllers that the ombudsman and his office proved less successful or at least inactive. The data protection law required data controllers to file an annual report about the number of personal data requests they turned down each year, and the specific grounds they cited (the ombudsman annually issued a call in the official bulletin to that effect). And while they were not obliged to provide information about the successful requests, the ombudsman – on a voluntary basis – encouraged the data controllers to do so. Neither the range, nor the information

[29] The broader framework of the initiative was the establishment of an ad hoc committee by the President of the Academy of Sciences in 2005, which dealt with "the conceptual issues of information society and the most burning problems of society management (sic) at the moment". The chairman of the committee was the academy member Tibor Vamos, the president of SZTAKI.

[30] When the committee completed its report in May 2006, Laszlo Solyom, whose "persuasion" the committee regarded as crucial, fulfilled the office of the President of the Republic. The incumbent data protection ombudsman was not invited to participate in the committee's work.

[31] This lobby eventually was successful, in the space for manoeuvring created after Laszlo Solyom's term as President of the Republic had ended, the institution of the data protection ombudsman had been abolished, the constitution had been rescinded and the new law replacing the data protection law had been passed, clearing the way to revoking the ban on the standardised and universal personal identification number, which had been one of the symbols of opposition to the dictatorial regime in the area of information law.

content of these reports can be described as satisfactory; for this reason, it is impossible to draw conclusions from this data.[32]

Several data protection ombudsmen questioned the usefulness and functionality of the data protection register and the filed information on turned-down requests, but that was not what mattered most: it was the use of the single search and retrieval system for data of public interest that explained the ombudsmen's moderately successful supervisory authority. Rather than his mandate to protect personal data, the ombudsman's authorisation to act in matters regarding the accessibility of public information was affected by the system: the law of 2005 on the freedom of electronic information[33] made it mandatory for government organisations, local government agencies and other organisations performing public functions to display certain information relating to their operation and financial record on Internet websites, and to register the metadata of this information in a standardised search and retrieval system for data of public interest. Interested citizens can then access current and relevant public information through this standardised system. But a precondition is for the organisations obligated to provide information to register in the standardised system and to regularly update the data and documents for the website. Compliance with the requirement to register and to update – regardless of the technical adequacy of the system – was very poor; moreover, the ombudsmen did not make the necessary effort to encourage co-operation on the one hand, and to sanction failure to comply with a legal obligation on the other.

Finally, we must point out that during the 17 years that passed between the establishment and the abolition of the data protection ombudsman's office, the different personalities of the three data protection ombudsmen greatly determined the character of the institution's activities. Experience has shown that all ombudsman-type institutions are, by their nature, highly susceptible to the leaders' personality, and since they have considerable freedom in shaping the operative rules of their institutions themselves, the institutions end up reflecting the approaches and priorities of their leader. To sum it up briefly, the first data protection ombudsman, Laszlo Majtenyi, emphasised the ombudsman-like character of the institution; the second ombudsman, Attila Peterfalvi, focused more on the efficient functioning of the office, while András Jori, the third and last ombudsman (who was dismissed from the job before his term expired), paid special attention to the data protection aspects of new technologies.[34]

The second type of enforcement, enforcement through public proceedings, appeared in specific sectors of data processing, such as telecommunication or banking, where the supervisory body overseeing the legal provisions of the activities

---

32 The ombudsman regularly gave a detailed account of this activity in his annual reports.

33 Act XC of 2005 – its provisions were later incorporated into Act CXII of 2011, which replaced the data protection law.

34 The similarities and differences between the respective approaches of the three data protection ombudsmen were revealed to the public at a roundtable discussion held during the last international professional conference before the abolition of the institution ("Data Protection Commissioner: 1995–2011", 28 September 2011).

in the given area was also responsible for monitoring compliance with, and sanctioning violations of, the relevant sector-specific laws of data protection. From time to time, this additional possibility and the accompanying public authority character turned out to be useful for the data protection ombudsman, too: when the data controllers in these sectors failed to comply with the data protection ombudsman's recommendation or decision – and a court proceeding was not possible[35] – the ombudsman could turn to the body supervising the given area and ask the supervisors either to penalise the data controller or to enforce the acceptance of the recommendation or decision through other available disciplinary measures. Such actions could be taken in the financial and telecommunication sector, among others, where the supervisory bodies have already imposed high penalties for the illegal and unnecessary practice of photocopying personal identification documents. Such co-operation in some areas increased the efficiency of enforcement and, as a result, the data controllers started to take the data protection ombudsman's recommendations and decisions more seriously.

The third, traditional type of enforcement was legal action in a court of law. This course has always been open to both data subjects and data controllers, yet it was relatively rarely taken, in comparison to the number of proceedings taken by the data protection ombudsman. In contrast to the thousands of applications sent annually to the ombudsman, the number of court actions in data protection cases was limited. Our study of these court cases was greatly facilitated by the Compendium of Court Decisions, an institution created by the Electronic Freedom of Information Act of 2005, with online access open to anyone. This database reveals that, on the one hand, in the majority of cases with some bearing on this subject, the processing of personal data does not form an essential point of the case and, on the other hand, both the data controllers and the data subjects regard the personal data related to customer relationship and customer service as data forming part of the business procedure, rather than as personal data in the sense of data protection law.[36]

Whether it was about data subjects worrying about the possible violation of their data protection rights or about data controllers considering the data subjects' legal actions as unjustified, what the people in question needed to consider was the relative advantages and disadvantages of the different procedures. Adjudication by the data protection ombudsman was cost-free – regardless of the outcome – while a court procedure involved certain costs (court fees, lawyers' fees and stamp duties). Even if you would not exactly describe it as fast, the ombudsman's procedure was quicker than court action (despite the fact that the data protection law required the courts to hear such cases in priority proceedings). On top of that, the ombudsman's

[35] In this way, the data controllers in fact had withdrawn behind the walls of passive resistance; as the ombudsman had no means to enforce the decision an impasse followed in the execution of the data protection law.

[36] This latter phenomenon was confirmed by the empirical research conducted in an ongoing EU FP7 research project, IRISS (http://www.irissproject.eu), in the course of which the researchers attempted to access their own personal data on the basis of their rights guaranteed under the data protection laws in various countries, including Hungary.

procedure was more predictable, since it was quite easy to take the evolution of a single person's quasi case law and extrapolate from that the position the ombudsman would likely take on certain questions. However, in a court case – both at a court of first instance and an appeal court – the decisions frequently diverged, even in similar cases. This resulted partly from the independence of the judiciary, partly from the acceptance or rejection of the evidence, but partly also from a slight degree of inexperience in data protection cases on the judges' part.[37] These factors, therefore, unequivocally speak in favour of the data protection ombudsman's procedure. On the other hand, a court decision is binding, while the data protection ombudsman's decisions – at least in the initial period – were not mandatory, and even when that changed, his decisions could only be enforced to a limited degree in practice.

The legislators tried to keep the ombudsman's procedure separate from the court procedure by offering these two paths to the data subjects as alternative courses of action. The data protection ombudsman was not entitled to act in those cases that either were being investigated in court or had already been adjudicated in a court of law.[38] At the same time, an ongoing investigation by the data protection ombudsman did not limit the court's authority, so those who wanted to exhaust both channels had to go about it in the right order: they first had to file a complaint with the data protection ombudsman, and only when that investigation was over could they turn to the court. Although the two investigations were independent from one another, the judge could be influenced by the professional opinion of the data protection ombudsman.

We must also briefly mention the role of the "fourth enforcement model" (self-regulation) in the execution of the data protection provisions. After the mid-1990s – following the enactment of the data protection act – a number of sector-specific acts were passed, which made it obligatory for each of the various organisations in the data protection sectors to draft their own internal data protection regulation,[39] as well as to appoint an internal data protection officer.[40] Naturally, the internal data protection regulations could not be in contradiction with the current laws, although they could define the actual content of their interpretation and enforcement in the practices of the various organisations dealing with processing of personal data. The 2003 amendment of the data protection act made it obligatory to prepare such regulations – and to appoint internal data protection officers – in a broad circle,

[37] Given their training and practical work, the judges understandably display more competence in the traditional branches of law (civil law, criminal law, etc.) and have difficulty identifying with the approach more closely related to the fundamental rights laid down in the Constitution. In their arguments, they tend to rely on the civil code, rather than on the data protection law or the sector-specific provisions of data protection regulations. Only a small number of judges are conversant with information rights (even though the first data protection ombudsman had still made the effort to regularly organise joint professional consultations with representatives of the judiciary, with whom he discussed actual problems in the interpretation of the law).

[38] Act LXIII of 1992, Section 24. a), Section 27 (1).

[39] For example, the 1995 law on direct marketing or the 1997 law on data protection in health care.

[40] See the data protection law in health care.

which prompted massive efforts in both drafting such regulations and launching training courses for the data protection officers.

In both areas, one can encounter numerous misunderstandings in the practices of data protection experts and advisors. In some parts, the regulations simply copied certain chapters of the data protection act, without containing the crux of the matter: the internal division of tasks, the responsibilities and the details of the data processing procedures. Some of the internal data protection officers were not quite clear about their own role: whether they were "moles" or "agents" sent out to report to the ombudsman on the internal irregularities or, quite the opposite, their job was to cover up the unlawful practices in their company's data management so as to protect it from both the complaining data subjects and the data protection ombudsman. Naturally, it was neither: their actual task was to represent the interests of the organisation, while staying within the boundaries of the law. In other words, their job was to invent and apply data management processes, so as to enable their organisation to carry out its main task in an efficient (or in the business sector, profitable) manner, while obeying both the letter and the spirit of the data protection law. Privacy policies had already been available for the data subjects, and especially for the users of Internet services, as early as the 1990s, but a real proliferation in this regard took place in the first years of the new millennium. The quality and the content of these information materials varied vastly: some provided the data subjects with specific information, others only contained generalities, and some claimed things about the processing of personal data that were simply not true. Finally, there were those who only wished to win the confidence of the customers with some advertisement-type message. According to a survey conducted in 2005,[41] in the case of a considerable number of Hungarian webpages, online privacy policies were either completely lacking or were incomplete; the most informative were the webpages of the Hungarian branches of international companies, although even these mostly contained texts translated from the parent company's information leaflets, rather than locally relevant information.

4.5 Political changes and a new model in enforcing data protection

In 2010, 20 years after the democratic transition, Hungary witnessed some major changes, both in politics and in legislation. The political party that won an absolute majority at the parliamentary elections abolished the constitution,[42] changed the official name of the country,[43] dismissed a good part of the judiciary, limited the

[41] Laszlo, Gabor, "Magyarorszagi weboldalak adatvedelmi nyilatkozatainak elemzese" [Analyisis of privacy policies on Hungarian webpages], in Ivan Szekely and Mate D. Szabo (eds.), *Szabad adatok, vedett adatok* [*Open data, protected data*a, BME GTK ITM, Budapest 2005, pp. 95–114.

[42] This was replaced by a new Basic Law, designed for a similar purpose.

[43] The designation "Republic" disappeared from the official name of the country.

authority of the constitutional court, placed the media under strong government influence, and introduced a centralised system of political leadership and institutional framework. The new leadership seriously weakened the constitutional framework that had previously been patterned on a western model, its institutional guarantees and system of checks and balances, and used its parliamentary majority to abolish or transform the organisations of the State, including the institution of parliamentary ombudsmen. In the course of this, it repealed the data protection act in force and summarily dismissed the incumbent data protection ombudsman as of 1 January 2012. The new political leadership basically denounced the democratic regime of the previous 20 years as illegitimate and, as a symbolic expression of this, it precluded the constitutional court's decisions issued from legal precedence from being used as legal precedents.[44] These incidents, along with many others, prompted the European Commission to launch accelerated infringement proceedings against Hungary[45] in January 2012, which resulted in the Commission's rebuking the ruling political elite for curbing the independence of the National Bank and the data protection authority as well as over the measures affecting the judiciary.[46] The Venice Commission of the Council of Europe[47] put forward similar criticisms on several occasions.[48] In response to these admonishments, the political leadership was forced to introduce minor changes in the wording of the laws, but the previous status quo was not restored.

The 1992 data protection act was replaced with Act CXII of 2011, which, while preserving the cornerstones of the earlier law, strengthened the positions of the data controllers at the expense of the protection of data subjects, and replaced the institution of data protection ombudsman with a government body, the data protection authority, NAIH (Hungarian National Authority for Data Protection and Freedom of Information). To the superficial observer, the change may seem formal (especially in view of the fact that a former – more precisely, the second – data protection ombudsman, Attila Peterfalvi, was appointed as head of the new authority), even though the difference between the two supervisory bodies, the parliamentary ombudsman's office and the data protection authority, is substantial. This is clearly shown in the text of the laws defining the mandates of the institutions: the data

[44] For a critical review of the changes, see http://ekint.org/ekint_files/File/hungarian_ngos_assessing_the_draft_constitution_of_hungary_20110412_k.pdf and http://ekint.org/ekint/ekint_angol.news.page?nodeid=551

[45] http://europa.eu/rapid/press-release_IP-12-24_en.htm?locale=fr

[46] In its April 2012 bulletin, the Committee announced that it had accepted the Hungarian responses in the area of the national bank as adequate, while in the case of the judiciary and the data protection authority, it upheld its criticism.

[47] The European Commission for Democracy through Law – better known as the Venice Commission, as it meets in Venice – is the Council of Europe's advisory body on constitutional matters. It provides legal advice to its Member States and, in particular, to help states wishing to bring their legal and institutional structures into line with European standards. http://www.venice.coe.int/WebForms/pages/?p=01_Presentation

[48] http:// www. academia. edu/1760582/ The_Venice_Commissions_opinions_on_Hungary_and_the_Hungarian_Governments_responses_-_Summarising_table

protection ombudsman's task is "to protect the rights and freedoms afforded by the Constitution for the protection of personal data and access to information of public interest", while the new authority is responsible "to oversee and promote the enforcement of the rights to the protection of personal data and access to public information and information of public interest". Phrasing it differently, the data protection ombudsman seems to be above codified law in the sense that he is responsible primarily for protecting fundamental rights and thus he can occasionally go against the legislation in force in the interest of protecting constitutional values, he is empowered to turn to the constitutional court, while the new authority is merely responsible for overseeing compliance with the provisions of the data protection laws.

These two institutions have different positions within the structure of the State: the data protection ombudsman was elected by Parliament, and was obliged to report to Parliament only, while the new authority is one among the many government offices, and its head is appointed by the Hungarian president at the recommendation of the prime minister. Although the independence of the new authority is nominally guaranteed under the new data protection law, his actual independence is questionable, especially in comparison with the independence of the data protection ombudsman's office.[49] The European Commission criticised the legislation related to the appointment and dismissal of the head of the new authority (these were later modified by the Hungarian political leadership), but even beside that, one can question the practical independence of the new authority in dealing with any improper data handling by other branches of government. – In this regard, we discuss below some ongoing independent research.

Naturally, the two institutions envisioned their own roles differently: the data protection ombudsman primarily relied on the powers of persuasion and public openness in enforcing his recommendations and decisions, while the NAIH prefers to operate through administrative fines and other forms of sanctions.

The question can be posed – leaving aside the changes in the political environment – whether it was really necessary to reform the institution of the data protection ombudsman, and what other options, beside establishing a government authority, would have been conceivable and feasible. While still in office, Andras Jori, the last data protection ombudsman, developed a concept,[50] which would have renamed the ombudsman's title as Information Commissioner and instead of the earlier method of financing – a joint budget with the other parliamentary ombudsmen – it would have had a separate budget, thus guaranteeing the institution's full independence. Jori submitted the concept to the committee responsible for drafting

[49] While we know of a number of supervisory authorities in long-established democracies that have managed to remain independent regardless of their integration into the government structure, in the case of the new democracies, there are several factors that can endanger the genuine independence of such agencies.

[50] Jori, Andras, "The end of independent data protection supervision in Hungary – a case study", in Serge Gutwirth, Ronald Leenes, Paul de Hert, Yves Poullet (eds.), *European Data Protection: Coming of Age*, Springer, Dordrecht, 2013, pp. 395–406.

the Basic Law that came to replace the Constitution, but the committee made no use of it in its work.[51]

Thus, while the new arrangement combines all three models of data protection enforcement, their relative strength, as well as the relationship between them, has shifted considerably. The main emphasis is on legal enforcement, even though the NAIH took over some of the tasks of its predecessor: it continues to have the power to make recommendations, both general and specific, to specific data controllers.[52] The way to a court procedure in data protection cases is still open, although the separation between the new authority's activities and the courts' enforcement role is less clear now than it was earlier: in certain cases, the authority itself can turn to the court; it also has the power to intervene in court procedures initiated by others.[53]

4.6 Edifying cases

It is too early to draw general conclusions from the authority's track record after just 3 years, nevertheless, it appears that it is the mass-scale enforcement authority function that poses the most serious problems for the NAIH: it still has not been able to bring the data protection register up to date (this is the reason it has not collected the registration fee), and it cancelled the option of accessing the registry via the Internet – hopefully, only temporarily. Furthermore, the supervision of the standardised search and retrieval system for data of public interest has produced no visible result: although the interface of the web service has been updated, there has been no improvement in the compliance rate.

While the NAIH is not a legal successor of the data protection ombudsman's institution, the new law on data protection obligates the new authority to take over from the data protection ombudsman's office all of the cases still open at the time of switchover. We can best demonstrate the difference between the two institutions' visions of their own roles by presenting cases that either spread across the switchover period or occurred in the practice of both institutions and had a similar character.

One of the cases the NAIH inherited from the data protection ombudsman concerned the data protection aspects of a populist campaign by the government taking power in 2010. As part of that campaign, the government circulated nationwide a questionnaire as a means of "national consultation", which was designed to formally legitimise the government's actions, to increase its popularity and to run a registry on the political preferences of the respondents. In the course of the 2011 campaign, these questionnaires were mailed to the country's entire population as political

[51] In the opinion of the author – who was among the founders of the institution of data protection ombudsman – the strengthening of the official powers would have been reconcilable with the role and parliamentary legitimation of the ombudsman.

[52] Act CXII of 2011, Section 38 (4) c).

[53] Section 38 (3) d), e).

direct marketing, using the database of the central population registration office.[54] Still in office at the time, the data protection ombudsman initiated a meeting with the authorities concerned[55] before sending out the questionnaires, because in his opinion numerous infringements of the law had been committed in the handling of the data in connection with the campaign. The authorities ignored the ombudsman's concerns and the campaign went ahead. Subsequently, the data protection ombudsman published a statement in June 2011 – thus executing its "soft" powers – in which he called on the authorities to cease the illegal processing of data, pointing out that the responses to the questionnaires could only be recorded in an anonymised manner, and they had to be destroyed after the act of recording. Since the authorities failed to comply fully with this request, the risk of linking the personal identification data to the recorded opinions continued to exist. At that point, the ombudsman, making full use of the powers vested in him, issued a decision ordering the destruction of the personal data related to the questionnaires and banning the creation of the database formed by personal data gathered for the purpose of direct mailing.[56]

The authorities concerned decided to challenge the data protection ombudsman's decision in court, but the court proceeding did not start until 2012, by which time the institution of the data protection ombudsman had been abolished – presumably in line with the intentions of the authorities. At the first session of the trial, it was the new data protection authority, NAIH, which represented the data protection ombudsman's position, and the two authorities mutually agreed to terminate the proceedings with immediate effect. The NAIH passed a decision, in which it reversed the earlier decision of the data protection ombudsman, stating that the data of those respondents, who had indicated their consent to future communication in a signed agreement, did not have to be deleted (in ordering the destruction of all the data, the data protection ombudsman had objected to a different aspect of processing personal data). In addition to the diverging professional approaches, it was evident that the new authority did not wish to go against the government: it founded its entire professional argument on a single provision of law,[57] thus forsaking the protection of the data subjects and offering instead a compromise solution to the government, as data controller, for the execution of its planned action.[58]

---

[54] For example, one of the sections enquired whether the pharmaceutical lobby should be brought down, because "they take billions out of people's pockets", while another asked whether education should be adjusted to the real demands of the economy, etc. A similar "national consultation" was conducted in May 2015 "on immigration and terrorism".

[55] Central Office for Public Administrative and Electronic Public Services (KEK KH).

[56] http://www.jogiforum.hu/hirek/25999 [in Hungarian].

[57] Attila Peterfalvi, President of the NAIH, already demonstrated that he tends to offer a narrow interpretation of the law in a high-profile case back in the days when he was still data protection ombudsman, and that incident paradoxically earned him the Big Brother Award – the ironic title awarded by civil society actors to institutions or persons doing their best to erode people's private lives. The case concerned the right of department stores to fit their changing rooms with cameras, which Peterfalvi defended as legal on the grounds that the customers had been informed about it.

[58] When the government carried out a similar campaign in 2012, entitled as National Consultation, it had previously changed the law in order to make its actions legally unassailable. Nevertheless, in

It is worth comparing two very similar cases, one investigated by the data protection commissioner, the other by the new authority. In 1997, two journalists independently from one another approached the data protection ombudsman about gaining access to the scientific work of politicians as public figures. The journalists wanted to read the doctoral theses of leading politicians, including the incumbent prime minister, Gyula Horn, but the institutions holding the dissertations rejected their request. The data protection ombudsman stated that limiting the freedom of information can only be constitutionally justified if it is deemed necessary to ensure the realisation of another fundamental right. He determined that the right to read books in a library's holding primarily belonged to the authorised users of the library (especially in the case of limited-access libraries of universities or university departments), but in view of the author's being a well-known politician and public figure, this right can also be extended to persons outside the circle of membership.[59]

In 2012, an applicant turned to the NAIH for an opinion concerning the possibility of getting access to the academic theses of various public figures, including the current and the previous prime ministers, according to press reports. In its response, the authority stated that "there are no legal regulations prescribing that the content of an academic thesis must be made accessible to anyone on the grounds that it qualifies as public data on account of its being in the public interest." Therefore, in the authority's opinion, a higher education institute had complete autonomy in deciding who can access the institution's academic theses. In addition, the document pointed out that the politicians had written their dissertations before becoming public figures.[60]

Although the reasoning of the NAIH contains legally valid elements (not to mention the fact that the 1997 petition was not simply about dissertations, but academic work in general, for which a legal requirement of public access was much easier to justify), it is clear that the data protection ombudsman had given priority to the information rights of the citizens, while the NAIH recognized the primacy of university autonomy.

As part of a recent research project, the NAIH's financial penalty policy was investigated on the basis of the information published on the authority's homepage. An analysis of the data has revealed that the NAIH's official procedures ending with a decision very rarely concern data controllers associated with government or local government agencies, and this rate is even lower with regard to decisions establishing culpability. Incidentally, the non-private data controllers (among the few data controlling agencies rebuked) are mostly local governments, with only a few other

---

the view of the Eotvos Karoly Policy Institute (EKINT), a non-governmental organisation formed by internationally recognised experts on data protection law, led by the first data protection ombudsman, the government's data collection through questionnaires still remained unlawful, which prompted EKINT to ask for an investigation of NAIH in a petition submitted in June 2012. However, NAIH declined to launch an investigation. See http://ekint.org/ekint/ekint.news.page?nodeid=537 [in Hungarian].

[59] Case no. 198/A/1997. See Majtenyi, Laszlo (ed.), The first three years of the Parliamentary Commissioner for Data Protection and Freedom of Information, ABI, Budapest, 1998.

[60] http://www.naih.hu/files/1033_V_2012-2.pdf [in Hungarian].

public authorities here and there. With regard to the fines levied, the data show that the NAIH imposed heavier penalties on private data controllers than on data controllers associated with public authorities, in terms of individual fines, the sum total of the fines and the average figure.[61] On the basis of this information, the researcher has concluded that the constitutionally stated independence of the data protection authority is no guarantee of its relative independence from the organisations it supposedly supervises.[62]

4.7 Open questions

The European Commission initiated an infringement action in January 2012 in reaction to Hungary's abolishment of the institution of data protection ombudsman, but it has failed to produce any result (the Hungarian authorities did not reverse their decision). The Commission then filed a case at the European Court in Luxemburg against Hungary for violating EU law. In December 2013, the Advocate General of the European Court published his opinion on this issue, in which he advised the Court to reprimand Hungary.[63] In its judgment of 8 April 2014, the Court ruled that *by prematurely bringing to an end the term served by the supervisory authority for the protection of personal data, Hungary has failed to fulfil its obligations under EU law*.[64] The only consequence of the judgment was that the Hungarian government offered an apology and financial compensation to the dismissed Commissioner for his loss of salary, however, the abolished institution has not been restored.

Whether the new authority will be able to demonstrate a growing independence in its future handling of governmental data controllers will be seen in the forthcoming period. This will be judged from various high-profile cases, the authority's statements and role perception, as well as from the relevant statistical analyses. Even if we only consider its narrowly interpreted tasks associated with its capacity as a public authority, most notably the tasks of maintaining the data protection registry and running the standardised search and retrieval system for public data, it is doubtful how it will be able to fulfil these in the future. How seriously data controllers will take their obligations and how closely they will follow the instructions of the authority, whether they comply with the tasks the law designates to them only in

---

[61] During the first 31 months of the NAIH's operation, only 5 % of the fines were levied on state data controllers and 95 % on private organisations.

[62] See Szabo, Mate D., and Fanny Hidvegi, "Ket itelet es vegrehajtasuk" [Two judgments and their enforcement], *Fundamentum*, Issue 4, 2014, pp. 69–82.

[63] "Hungary violates EU law on ending data protection ombudsman's contract, says European Court official", *Daily News Hungary*, 10 December 2013. http://dailynewshungary.com/hungary-violates-eu-law-on-ending-data-protection-ombudsmans-contract-says-european-court-official/

[64] Court of Justice of the European Union, Press Release No 53/14, Luxembourg, 8 April 2014. Judgment in Case C-288/12, Commission v Hungary. http://curia.europa.eu/jcms/upload/docs/application/pdf/2014-04/cp140053en.pdf

form or also in essence will depend on the authority's successes in discharging these tasks, and nowhere more so than in the area of Internet services.

However, besides the data controlling organisations, the general public, too, has a legitimate interest in learning about the new authority. In early 2013, one year after its establishment, the new authority commissioned a public opinion poll entitled "The Public Conception of the Situation of Data Protection in Hungary".[65] According to the results of the survey based on personal interviews of 2,000 people, 31 % of the Hungarian population had heard about the Hungarian National Authority for Data Protection and Freedom of Information, which was considerably less than the corresponding figure for the former data protection ombudsman (see Flash Eurobarometer 225). Six per cent of the respondents knew the head of the authority by name; this is similar to the last data protection ombudsman's name recognition, but both fell far below the name recognition of the first ombudsman (23 %).[66] Only 5 % of the respondents knew of the authority's activities, according to their own assessment. It is worth noting that only three out of ten people were satisfied with the Hungarian regulation of data protection (29 %) and freedom of information (31 %).

These data show that the authority needs to expend more effort in informing the public about its activities, as most people have heard about the establishment of the new authority only in connection with the abolition of the data protection ombudsman's office and the highly critical EU report that followed it. However, name recognition by itself is not enough: the organisation responsible for effective data protection also needs to win the respect of the general public. Due to its character, an authority is less sympathetic to the public and the data controllers than an ombudsman, so only time will tell how successful the new enforcement model of data protection, along with the institution representing it, will be in gaining the public's trust.

4.8 Conclusions

Overall, the codification and enforcement of the data protection laws can be described as a success story in Hungary's post-communist history. The incorporation of the right to privacy and data protection in the legal system and the self-regulatory documents was achieved in a proper measure in the first period of the democratic transition, along with the institution-building related to the enforcement of data protection laws. The recent political changes have transformed the system of institutions, changed the enforcement model of the data protection regime and modified its legal guarantees. In other words, with regard to enforcing privacy in

[65] Nezopont Institute, "Az adatvedelem magyarországi helyzetenek tarsadalmi megitelese" [The public conception of the situation of data protection in Hungary], February-March 2013. http://www.naih.hu/files/adatved-kozvelkut-2013-03.pdf [in Hungarian].

[66] Laszlo Majtenyi's subsequent public activities, in which constitutional issues and data protection cases have played a central role, probably also contributed to his greater recognition.

Hungary, the former model pupil among the new members of the community of democratic countries has become a problematic grown-up. However, even the combined effects of these changes have failed to destroy the framework and enforcement mechanisms of data protection law, and this can be viewed as one of the lasting results of the democratic transition of 1989.

Although the political, ideological and legal changes in Hungary form an unusual mix, which pushes the limits of the European system of values, the changes introduced in the type of data protection supervisory authority, and in its enforcement model, do not go against the general trend in Europe. While in the years during the democratic transition, the ideal – not only in the former satellite states of the Soviet Union – was a data protection supervisory institution of high legitimacy that contained elements of the ombudsman system, in recent years, the value of administrative powers has increased. This is understandable in the sense that the volume of personal data processing has increased by many orders of magnitude in the past decade, the associated technology and its monitoring possibilities have become more complex, while the data controllers – including the Internet superpowers – comply with the data protection law only formally, at best. This changed scenario calls for a more austere supervisory body with stronger administrative powers. In an indirect manner, this trend is reinforced by the institutional consequences of the legal separation of data protection from privacy in the Charter of Fundamental Rights of the European Union, as well as the EU's planned reforms of the data protection system (including, among others, the mandatory co-operation between data protection agencies and the planned establishment of the European Data Protection Board). The change in the data protection model is not the central element in the judgment of the Court of Justice of the European Union cited above, not even the dubious relative independence of the new authority: it is the mode of dismissal of an incumbent data protection ombudsman that lies at the heart of the case. Having said that, the independence and the role perception of the ombudsman will be greatly missed in all future cases, when in the interest of the realization of fundamental rights the constitutional values would have to be defended even against legal regulations in force, or when in a high-profile case the ombudsman would have to turn to the population to give publicity to a case, or when he would have to mediate between partners in data management cases of strategic importance.

The Hungarian history of enforcing privacy and data protection provides numerous lessons for countries recently freed from dictatorial political and social systems and for the new democracies of the future. We have seen that the euphoria of democratic transition, along with the rising stature of new rights and freedoms, tends to be short-lived, therefore, permanent guarantees of the new information rights must be created, both at the legal and the institutional level, in this brief, initial period. And as for the legal guarantees of the rights, it is better to set them at a level that is higher than the minimum requirement of international standards, partly in order to set the norms high in a society freed from a dictatorial system, partly to anticipate their probable future erosion and to ensure that they remain at a reasonable level even after the attempts to limit them. To wait until large parts of the population demand the codification and realisation of these rights would be a serious mistake.

Nor is it useful to suggest that information rights are the luxury of developed countries and that a transition country has no resources for such luxury, because a new democracy will probably never reach the stage of socially interiorising the information rights. Furthermore, the country may not even reach the status of a developed country, because there is a strong interconnection between the implementation of information rights and welfare.[67] The Hungarian example has clearly shown that the establishment of the legal system and the creation of the institutional system have been successful, but the social awareness and acceptance of the law has not been completed, which has made the task of the opposing forces easier.

Privacy and data protection are just two of the fundamental rights of crucial importance in the democratic establishments of the twenty-first century. Similar advice can be given in establishing and enforcing other rights and freedoms, although information rights require special attention. Compared to other fundamental rights, they are less visible and less tangible, while they provide the basic foundations for the realisation of other rights. Without free access to public information, no informed, participatory democracy can exist; without the protection of privacy, there can be no freedom of speech.

Hungary is a small country, which never belonged to the club of Europe's great economic or political powers. This is not the reason why her political and legal experiments are important: rather, they are important, because they can serve as examples, both positive and negative, for European and non-European countries alike, and – with regard to the spread and threshold level of the shared European framework – for the European Union itself.[68] If nothing else, this alone makes it worthwhile to watch closely the unfolding developments in the enforcement of privacy and data protection in Hungary.

References

Daily News Hungary, "Hungary violates EU law on ending data protection ombudsman's contract, says European Court official", 10 December 2013. http://dailynewshungary.com/hungary-violates-eu-law-on-ending-data-protection-ombudsmans-contract-says-european-court-official/

Darch, Colin, and Peter G. Underwood, *Freedom of Information and the Developing World. The Citizen, the State and Models of Openness*, Chandos Publishing, 2009.

European Commission, Data Protection in the European Union: Citizens' perceptions. Analytical Report, Flash Eurobarometer 225, February 2008. http://ec.europa.eu/public_opinion/flash/fl_225_en.pdf

[67] See, for example, Darch, Colin, and Peter G. Underwood, *Freedom of Information and the Developing World. The Citizen, the State and Models of Openness*, Chandos Publishing, 2009.

[68] See, for example, Scheppele, Kim Lane, Testimony, U.S. Commission on Security and Cooperation in Europe, Hearing on "The Trajectory of Democracy – Why Hungary Matters", 19 March 2013. http://lapa.princeton.edu/hosteddocs/hungary/Scheppele%20Testimony%20Helsinki%20Commission%2019March13.pdf

Jori, Andras, "The end of independent data protection supervision in Hungary – a case study", in Serge Gutwirth, Ronald Leenes, Paul de Hert and Yves Poullet (eds.), *European Data Protection: Coming of Age*, Springer, Dordrecht, 2013, pp. 395–406.

Laszlo, Gabor, "Magyarorszagi weboldalak adatvedelmi nyilatkozatainak elemzese" [Analyisis of privacy policies on Hungarian webpages], in Ivan Szekely and Mate D. Szabo (eds.), *Szabad adatok, vedett adatok [Open data, protected data]*, BME GTK ITM, Budapest 2005, pp. 95–114.

Majtenyi, Laszlo (ed.), *The first three years of the Parliamentary Commissioner for Data Protection and Freedom of Information*, ABI, Budapest, 1998.

Nezopont Institute, "Az adatvedelem magyarországi helyzetenek tarsadalmi megitelese" [The public conception of the situation of data protection in Hungary], February-March 2013. http://www.naih.hu/files/adatved-kozvelkut-2013-03.pdf [in Hungarian]

Parliamentary Commissioner for Data Protection and Freedom of Information (ed.), *Annual Reports of the Parliamentary Commissioner for Data Protection and Freedom of Information*, Budapest, 1995–2010. https://81.183.229.204:51111/dpc/index.php?menu=reports

Scheppele, Kim Lane, Testimony, U.S. Commission on Security and Cooperation in Europe, Hearing on "The Trajectory of Democracy – Why Hungary Matters", 19 March 2013. http://lapa.princeton.edu/hosteddocs/hungary/Scheppele%20Testimony%20Helsinki%20Commission%2019March13.pdf

Szabo, Mate D., and Fanny Hidvegi, "Ket itelet es vegrehajtasuk" [Two judgments and their enforcement], *Fundamentum*, Issue 4, 2014, pp. 69–82.

Szekely, Ivan, Janos Tolgyesi and Gabor Varnai, *Information privacy in Hungary. Survey report and analysis*, Hungarian Institute for Public Opinion Research, Budapest 1991. http://www.sscqueens.org/sites/default/files/Information_Privacy_in_Hungary.pdf

Szekely, Ivan, and Mate Daniel Szabo, "Privacy and data protection at the workplace in Hungary", in Sjaak Nouwt, Berend R. de Vries and Corien Prins (eds.), *Reasonable Expectations of Privacy? Eleven Country Reports on Camera Surveillance and Workplace Privacy*, IT & Law Series, T. M. C. Asser Press, The Hague, 2005, pp. 249–284.

Szekely, Ivan, "Central and Eastern Europe: Starting from Scratch", in Ann Florini (ed.), *The Right to Know. Transparency for an Open World*, Columbia University Press, 2007, pp. 116–142.

Szonda Ipsos, "Az Orszaggyulesi Biztosok ismertsege es megitelese a lakossag koreben" [Knowledge of and opinion about Parliamentary Commissioners in the population], Budapest, December 1998.

Szonda Ipsos, "Az orszaggyulesi biztosok ismertsege es megitelese a magyar lakossagban" [Knowledge of and opinion about Parliamentary Commissioners in Hungarian population], Research Report, Budapest, March 2008.

UniReport 7, "Sterne unserer Jugend – Ehrendoktorwürde des Fachbereichs Rechtswissenschaft für den Ungarischen Staatspräsidenten Prof. László Sólyom", 15 November 2006. http://www2.uni-frankfurt.de/44481170/unireport_07-2006.pdf

Vasarhelyi, Maria, "Lattuk-e, hogy jon?" [Did we see it coming?], *Jel-Kep*, No. 3–4, 2010, pp. 91–97.

Chapter 5
A Tale of Two Privacies: Enforcing Privacy with Hard Power and Soft Power in Japan

Hiroshi Miyashita

5.1 Introduction: Two powers of enforcement

In the world of politics, there are two powers: hard power and soft power. According to Professor Joseph Nye, hard power is military and economic might which often forces others to change their position, whereas soft power – "getting others to want the outcomes that you want – co-opts people rather than coerces them".[1] If enforcement means to bring something into effect, both hard power and soft power are necessary for enforcement.

In the world of privacy protection, these two powers apply when one wants a legal sanction or when the other seeks to persuade. Both are compatible, but society often chooses one of the two approaches based on its culture and social norms of privacy.

This Chapter explores these two forms of enforcement mechanisms from a comparative perspective and demonstrates how they function in a particular society. Hard power may be widely recognised as an effective means of protecting the right to privacy, but many still doubt the effectiveness of soft power without examining its experience. My intention is not to oversimplify these two powers of privacy; rather, I will focus on the relative effectiveness of using either power depending on the situation. I believe both are useful instruments for privacy regulators and shields for effective privacy protection.

---

[1] Nye, Joseph, *Soft Power: The Means to Success in World Politics*, Public Affairs, 2004, p. 5.

H. Miyashita (✉)
Faculty of Policy Studies, Chuo University,
742-1, Higashinakano, 192-0393 Hachioji, Tokyo, Japan

Harvard Law School, Visiting Scholar, Cambridge, Massachusetts, USA

Office of Personal Information Protection, Cabinet Office, Tokyo, Japan
e-mail: hmiya.64r@g.chuo-u.ac.jp

D. Wright, P. De Hert (eds.), *Enforcing Privacy*, Law, Governance and Technology Series 25, DOI 10.1007/978-3-319-25047-2_5

Japan has adopted an exceptional system of privacy enforcement. Although there has been, until recently, no independent supervisory authority to enforce the law powerfully, its enforcement has worked to some extent. Why? The answer may lie in Professor Nye's soft power in the world of privacy. This Chapter demonstrates from the experiences of Japan what I call "privacy as soft power" as distinct from the "privacy as hard power" known as law enforcement or coercion. Hard power, which is often used in Europe, is desirable in some instances, but this Chapter points out, in light of Japanese experience, that soft power based on privacy as a cultural value and social norms may also be effective in some cases, but the evidence suggests that enforcing privacy may be more effective if both hard and soft powers are used.

5.2 Two approaches to privacy

5.2.1 London and Tokyo

We have seen the two different types of enforcement used in relation to the same data breach case in London and Tokyo.[2] In April 2011, it was revealed that the Sony PlayStation Network had been hacked. Approximately 77 million users' personal information, including names, addresses, dates of birth and account passwords, had been leaked throughout the world, and more sensitive data such as credit card details were also at risk. The attack could have been prevented if appropriate technical measures had been taken.

In the United Kingdom, the Information Commissioner's Office (ICO) responded by fining Sony a sum of £250,000.[3] In its decision, the ICO held that the data controller had failed to ensure that the network platform service provider kept up with technical developments. The ICO also pointed out both aggravating and mitigating features in determining the amount of the monetary penalty, carefully scrutinising (1) the nature of the contravention, (2) the effect of the contravention, (3) behavioural issues, and (4) the impact on the data controller. The ICO concluded that such a contravention would cause substantial damage or distress to the data subjects.

In Japan, this incident resulted not in a sanction, but rather, a piece of advice as an administrative measure by the Ministry of Economy, Trade and Industry. After conducting an investigation, the Ministry simply pointed out that the submission of the report on the security breach to the Ministry had been late and requested that security measures be improved, in the form of an administrative direction based on

[2] Although the UK Information Commissioner's Office is based in Wilmslow, London is used here as a metonymy, i.e., to represent the UK or, more particularly, the UK approach to privacy enforcement.

[3] Information Commissioner's Office, "Sony fined £250,000 after millions of UK gamers' details compromised", news release, 24 January 2013. http://ico.org.uk/news/latest_news/2013/ico-news-release-2013

the Act on the Protection of Personal Information.[4] In the absence of any sanction, Sony first made public apologies at a press conference and on its homepage. Second, Sony voluntarily gave users free downloads and free services of PlayStation Plus for 30 days without being ordered to do so by the Ministry or courts. Even without any penalty being imposed on Sony by the Ministry, its share price fell four per cent over night as a result of the security breach.[5]

The ICO's courageous decision may be regarded as hard power entailing a legal sanction in order to change the corporation's behaviour. In contrast, the Japanese approach indicates soft power by social and cultural enforcement in order to rebuild trust with customers. In London, the monetary penalty sought to address the damage and distress of data subjects. Under the British approach, a fine may be more effective in altering the corporate mentality and deterring future security breaches, whereas in Tokyo, the public apologies and voluntary compensation went some way to regaining public trust and rebuilding a close relationship with customers. In the Japanese business climate, the risk of reputational damage and loss of customer trust may be more serious for corporations than paying fines in data breach cases.

Both were compatible in restoring the rights of data subjects, but the means of enforcing privacy diverged between the United Kingdom and Japan. It is convincing to resort to sanctions as a hard power in the United Kingdom. It is reasonable to rely on social trust as a soft power in Japan. The UK and Japan share the fundamental value of privacy, but the means to realise this shared value may vary. It is not correct to simplify or overstate the differences in enforcing privacy between UK and Japan. Yet, the different means of enforcing privacy in the Sony PlayStation Network case between London and Tokyo show us the distinctive features of privacy enforcement mechanisms. As long as privacy is not the product of logic, cultures of privacy matter and differ, as do the practices of enforcing privacy. A means of enforcing privacy is embedded in each social and cultural value. Thus, there is no good or bad in enforcing privacy in terms of culture and social norms. The two different means of enforcement in the same case have confirmed the diversity and complexities of enforcing privacy.

5.2.2 *Hard and soft power*

Now we can recognise the two important means of enforcing privacy. Although I admit that I will simplify the two powers in spite of their diversities and complexities, we may be able to distinguish the hard and soft power of enforcing privacy by considering the following issues.

---

[4] For the UK enforcement approach, see Carey, Peter, *Data Protection: A Practical Guide to UK and EU Law Fourth Edition*, Oxford University Press, 2015.

Ministry of Economy, Trade and Industry, Instruction based on the Act of the Protection of Personal Information against Sony Computer Entertainment, 27 May 2013.

[5] *Nikkei Shimbun*, Sony lost four per cent shares in the stock market: disgust of the personal information leakage, 29 April 2011, p. 13.

First of all, who enforces privacy? Hard power premises a strong enforcement power on the part of the regulator. The ICO and other European countries have independent supervisory authorities. These authorities are given real investigative powers to enforce privacy under the new EU Data Protection Regulation (Art. 28). Some already have such powers. For instance, in March 2011, the French data protection authority, CNIL, used its strong power of investigation by onsite inspection to impose a fine of €100,000 on Google for engaging in unlawful collection of personal data.[6] On the other hand, under a soft power regime, it may be the society as a whole that plays a crucial function in enforcing privacy without coercion. A data protection authority may assist in the promotion of a privacy culture through soft enforcement.

Second, why is privacy enforced? There may be no single reason to enforce privacy; rather, it may be for a multitude of reasons. Regulators may be motivated to enforce privacy by punishing or deterring the wrongful act of a corporation. In some cases, sanctions may be necessary for the compensation of proprietary damages and the distress suffered by consumers. The ultimate reason to enforce privacy through the use of legal sanctions is to protect the fundamental rights of the data subject. This may be true in the soft-power world, but the main motivation for enforcement by soft power originates from regaining the trust of customers and avoiding the reputational damage of corporations.

Third, what is the outcome of enforcement? The enforcement action in a single case should have a social message. The EU Data Protection Regulation provides for a fine of up to four per cent of the corporation's annual worldwide turnover for non-compliance. A fine is an excellent instrument for those regulators who prefer hard power to deter negligence and non-compliance. A fine may also have the incidental effect of promoting compliance by other organisations, so the impact of a fine may be substantial. However, once again, regulators using soft power wish to co-opt people rather than coerce them in order to achieve some degree of social enforcement.

5.3 Privacy and soft power in Japan

5.3.1 Soft power and decency

Soft power is "the ability to get what you want through attraction rather than coercion or payment. It arises from the attractiveness of a country's culture, political ideals, and policies."[7] Privacy may originally have been understood to be both enforced by soft and hard power when it was articulated. At the ages of 34 and 71,

---

[6] CNIL, "Google Street View: CNIL pronounces a fine of 100,000 Euros" (Pour approfondir Délibération n°2011-035 de la formation restreinte prononçant une sanction pécuniaire à l'encontre de la société GOOGLE Inc.), 21 March 2011.
http://www.cnil.fr/fileadmin/documents/La_CNIL/actualite/D2011-035.pdf

[7] Nye, op. cit., p. x.

Louis Brandeis defended "decency" as the source of his right to privacy. In 1890, Brandeis, as a Boston lawyer, criticised "breaches of decency and propriety"[8] by the press. In 1928, as a Supreme Court Justice, he censured that "[d]ecency, security and liberty alike demand that government officials shall be subjected to the same rules of conduct that are commands to the citizen."[9] For Brandeis, "decency" was the penetrating word of his right to privacy, "the right most valued by civilized men", to attack the "unclean hands"[10] disrupting personal relationships and interfering with private life.

The seed of the soft power of privacy has grown in the Restatement of Torts as "decent standards": namely, in relation to the publication of private facts, "[t]he limitations, in other words, are those of common decency".[11] Later on, Professor Robert Post pronounced "rules of civility".[12] According to Post, privacy rules of civility are judged by the reasonable person, who is meant to embody the general level of moral judgement of the community. Thus, the civility rules enforced by courts are a kind of expression of generally accepted norms in a society under conditions of cultural heterogeneity.

Needless to say, the story of privacy enforcement developed as hard power with legislative support over the course of a century. Nevertheless, one should not ignore the development of privacy as soft power in the United States, and its impact can also be seen in Japan.

The Japanese concept of privacy was originally based on the notion that the people should respect community values by giving up their own private lives.[13] *Murahachibu* is the idea that one will be excluded from the village and have one's links with it severed due to breach of trust and social norms.[14] From the viewpoint of respecting trust and social norms, this may be similar to the Jewish Bible saying, "If a man has a wall running alongside his neighbour's wall… if there are windows, he must leave a clear space of four cubits whether above or below or opposite"[15] to

[8] Warren, Samuel D., and Louis D. Brandeis, "The Right to Privacy", *Harvard Law Review*, Vol. 4, No. 5, 15 Dec 1890, p. 216. Brandeis considered breach of "contract" or "property" to be too narrow, so he used breach of "decency" instead. See Pember, Don R., *Privacy and the Press: The Law, the Mass Media, and the First Amendment*, University of Washington Press, 1972, p. 53.

[9] *Olmstead v. United States*, 277 U.S. 438, 485 (1928) (Brandeis, J., dissenting). Justice Brandeis regarded the snooping government as "evil-minded rulers" and "lawbreakers". Ibid., p. 479.

[10] Ibid., p. 483 (Brandeis, J., dissenting).

[11] *Restatement (Second) of Torts*, §652D, Comment h. (1977) at 391.

[12] Post, Robert C., *Constitutional Domains: Democracy, Community, Management*, Harvard University Press, 1995, pp. 64–67.

[13] See generally Miyashita, Hiroshi, "The Evolving Concept of Data Privacy in Japanese Law", *International Data Privacy Law*, Vol. 1, No. 4, 2011, p. 229.

[14] The observation of the Japanese concept of breach of trust is the basis of privacy. See Rosen, Dan, "Private Lives and Public Eyes: Privacy in the United States and Japan", *Florida Journal of International Law*, Vol. 6, No. 1, 1990, p. 141.

[15] *Mishnah Baba Bathra* 22a. In addition, the Jewish concept of *tikkun olam*, the duty that each of us has to heal a broken world, seems to have influenced Brandeis's privacy. See Chemerinsky, Erwin, "Rediscovering Brandeis's Right to Privacy", *Brandeis Law Journal*, Vol. 45, No. 3, 2007, p. 643.

respect privacy. In Japan, a cultural value of privacy was originally created through respect for the "rules of civility".

Based on this social norm, Professor Masami Ito, who would later be the first Justice of the Supreme Court of Japan to defend the right to privacy, wrote in 1963 that "crystallization of the legal protection of the right to privacy, despite its diverse contents, is proof of the enjoyment of a certain level of culture in its society".[16] Professor Ito indicated that it is the social and cultural conditions, not just the legal text, that protect the right to privacy in Japan. Japan has invented its original enforcement mechanism in privacy legislation along with its social norms and cultural value of privacy.

5.3.2 *Institutional uniqueness in Japan*

Without coercion, we have seen the force of soft power in enforcing privacy laws in Japan. Before I explain the substantive aspects of the Japanese enforcement mechanism, I will briefly summarise the institutional uniqueness under the Act on the Protection of Personal Information of 2003.

In its unique mechanism, Japan did not have any independent supervisory authority until the new Specific Personal Information Protection Commission was established in January 2014.[17] In the private sector, each ministry enforces its guidelines in the areas under its control, co-ordinated by the Consumer Affairs Agency. For example, the Financial Services Agency enforces the law in the case of bank data breaches. Each ministry has the power to collect reports (Art. 32 of the Act on the Protection of Personal Information), to give advice (Art. 33), and to recommend and make orders (Art. 34).[18] There has, however, been no case of criminal penalty or order issued by a ministry since the Act entered fully into force in 2005. This is because the businesses that were found to have data breaches followed the instructions given by the relevant ministry, meaning there was no need for a further order or penalty.[19]

---

[16] Ito, Masami, *Puraibashiii no Kenri* [*The Right to Privacy*], Iwanami Shoten, 1963, p. 7. A year after Professor Ito's publication, the Tokyo District Court, for the first time in history of Japan, affirmed that "the right to privacy is recognized as the legal protection or the right so as not to be disclosed of private life" ('After the Banquet' case). Judgment of Tokyo District Court, 28 Sep. 1964, *Hanreijiho* vol. 385, p. 12.

[17] See Miyashita, Hiroshi, The New ID Number System and Personal Information Protection in Japan, *Sungkyunkwan Journal of Science & Technology Law*, Vol. 8, No.1, 2014, p. 39.

[18] In fiscal year (FY) 2013, there were two cases of collection of reports on incidents, by the Financial Services Agency: Consumer Affairs Agency, *Study on the Implementation Status of Businesses on the Protection of Personal Information*, October 2014, p. 2 [in Japanese].

[19] In the public sector, there was one criminal prosecution of a case by the National Tax Administration Agency in FY 2012: Ministry of Internal Affairs and Communications, *Implementation Status of the Protection of Personal Information of Administrative Organs and the Incorporated Administrative Agencies in FY 2012*, August 2013, p. 29 [in Japanese].

Why did Japan adopt such an original enforcement system? There may be both historical and political reasons. First, historically, some of the ministries had their own guidelines on personal information before the Bill on the Protection of Personal Information was first submitted to the Diet in 2001.[20] Accumulation of best practices on the protection of personal information in certain business sectors encouraged their divisional structure in the administration even after the new Act entered into force. As for political reasons, the current Acts on the Protection of Personal Information were discussed in the Diet at a time of small government and decentralisation under the administration of Junichiro Koizumi.[21] Thus, it was clearly against the political trend at that time to establish a new independent public authority at national level.

From these backgrounds, Japan adopted the competent ministry system, together with other complementary mechanisms, to promote the autonomous effort of privacy protection. One advantage of this system is that the competent minister can enforce the Act on the Protection of Personal Information by making use of the administrative experience in that business sector.[22] In order to complement the competent minister system due to the limited resources, the authorised organisations for the protection of personal information have investigative powers delegated to them by the ministries, including the collection of reports and materials, instruction, recommendations and orders.[23]

Second, this decentralised privacy regime in Japan may also have merit in terms of assisting consumers. Consumers can submit their complaints to each ministry, local government or authorised organisations in light of the scale of the data breach. The multiple channels of dispute resolution provide consumers with a choice.

I believe the decentralised system with a bottom-up approach may be suitable for using soft power to enforce privacy in the Japanese culture. The next section discusses two issues as a reflection of soft power under the Japanese legal regime, namely, the trustmark system and data breach notifications.

---

[20] See, e.g., Ministry of Internal Affairs and Communications (then Ministry of Posts and Telecommunications), *Guidelines on the Protection of Personal Information in Telecommunications*, 1991; Ministry of Economy, Trade and Industry (then Ministry of International Trade and Industry), *Guidelines on the Protection of Personal Information with regard to Computer Processing in Private Sector*, 1997.

[21] Koizumi was Prime Minister from 2001 to 2006. See also Miyashita, Hiroshi, *Policies on the Protection of Personal Information* [*Kojin Joho no Shisaku*], Choyokai, 2010, p. 110.

[22] Sonobe, Itsuo, *Commentary on the Protection of Personal Information* [*Kojin Joho Hogoho no Kaisetsu*], Gyosei, 2005, p. 213.

[23] As of October 2014, there were 39 authorised organisations, which handled 505 complaints from consumers with 140 instructions in FY 2013.

5.3.3 *Trustmark system*

Interest in certification is growing in the world of privacy. In the United States, trustmarks have been widely used for website privacy, and new certification schemes, such as CNIL's data protection label, have started recently.[24] In Japan, trustmarks represent the largest feature of the soft power mechanism. The Japan Information Processing Development Cooperation (JIPDEC), an organisation authorised by the Ministry of Economy, Trade and Industry and Ministry of Internal Affairs and Communications, has been operating the trustmark known as "PrivacyMark" since April 1998.[25] As of December 2014, there were more than 13,000 PrivacyMark-certified companies.

The goal of the PrivacyMark system is to enhance consumer awareness and promote the proper handling of personal information. The PrivacyMark system operates on the basis of JIS Q 15001:2006 (Japan Industrial Standards) with supplementary guidelines.[26] The review process is conducted by an assessment body, which determines whether the privacy policy and internal privacy management system meet the objective criteria. Its fee depends on the size of business, ranging from 300,000 yen (€2,100) to 1,200,000 yen (€8,400), plus a renewal fee every two years. One good motivation for companies is that a de facto condition for tendering for government contracts is that they have secured an adequate level of protection of personal information. Accredited companies must notify data breach cases to JIPDEC.[27] Consumers can submit complaints to JIPDEC with respect to personal information handling by both certified and non-certified corporations.[28] According to one survey, 28.3 % of consumers responded that they either know or have seen the PrivacyMark.[29] In trusting data processing, 54.5 % of the companies regard the PrivacyMark as the selection criterion.[30] Certification may work in business-to-business (B2B) activities, particularly in trusting data processing, but in the context of businesses-to-consumers (B2C), roughly one-third of consumers

---

[24] For an excellent comparative study on privacy seal schemes, see Rodrigues, Rowena, David Wright and Kush Wadhwa, "Developing a Privacy Seal Scheme (That Works)", *International Data Privacy Law*, Vol. 3, No. 2, 2013, p. 100.

[25] English information is available at http://privacymark.org/index.html

[26] *Guidelines for Personal Information Protection Management System Implementation based on JIS Q 15001*: 2006. http://privacymark.org/reference/pdf/PMS%20guideline.pdf

[27] There were 1,627 data breach cases reported to JIPDEC in FY 2013. JIPDEC, *The Trend and Cautions in the Reported Incidents on Handling Personal Information in FY 2013*, 25 Aug 2014 [in Japanese].

[28] In FY 2013, 368 cases were submitted to JIPDEC and 354 cases were resolved. JIPDEC, *The Overview of Coping with Consumer Consultations in FY 2013*, 30 Sep 2014 [in Japanese].

[29] For a recent empirical study on the importance of trustworthiness and reputation, see Orito, Yoko, Kiyoshi Murata and Yasunori Fukuta, "Do Online Privacy Policies and Seals Affect Corporate Trustworthiness and Reputation?", *International Review of Information Ethics*, Vol. 19, 2013, p. 52.

[30] Consumer Affairs Agency, *Study on the Implementation Status of Businesses on the Protection of Personal Information*, March 2012, p. 62 [in Japanese].

recognise it. Thus, its impact on consumer protection may be limited in the context of B2C business.

The revocation process was discussed when a printing company, which had leaked 8,640,000 items of personal information, was finally instructed by JIPDEC in March 2007 to improve its operations, with no revocation of its accreditation.[31] In November 2014, JIPDEC decided on revocation in the case of the educational company, Benesse Corp, because inadequate security measures led to the leakage of information relating to more than 20 million customers.[32] In addition, there were false application cases in the process of review where JIPDEC rejected the applications with suspension of the reapplication for one year.[33]

Law enforcement should follow up in serious data breach cases, but certification in Japan is operated by private organisations. Oversight by a public authority should be considered to promote a more effective certification system. In 2007, a law reform body, the Quality-of-Life Policy Council, expressed the opinion that "the certification system on information security is a useful means to enhance the level of security management for the protection of personal information".[34] The trustmark was formed as a kind of co-regulation operated by private organisations expressly authorised by the government since the Japanese Government had not considered a formal legal regime at that stage. Again, the trustmark is a form of self-regulation, but it spread among a great number of companies, including small to medium-sized enterprises. Certification works in Japan because of the risk of reputational damage and social distrust in the event of misuse. It can also be said that the effectiveness of certification is grounded on the trustworthiness and reputation management of privacy protection in Japan. Certification may have played an important role in raising awareness among businesses and consumers by a bottom-up approach.

The trustmark scheme has also attracted attention outside Japan in the area of data transfers. JIPDEC launched a system of mutual recognition between the Korean Association for ICT Promotion and the Dalian Software Industry Association (54 agreements of mutual recognition as of June 2010). In fact, 29.7 % of Japanese companies engage in data exchanges with foreign entities, and nearly half of the companies (49.4 %) indicated the need for regulations on data transfer and outsourcing.[35] The Asia-Pacific Economic Cooperation (APEC) has also been seeking Cross-Border Privacy Rules (CBPRs), and Japan formally joined CBPRs in April 2014

---

[31] JIPDEC, *Decision of "Request" to Dai Nippon Printing Co. in the Data Breach Case*, 23 March 2007. This decision indicated the possibility of revocation if the company did not follow the requested measures.

[32] JIPDEC, *Decision of Benesse Corp.*, 26 Nov 2014. This case involved a security breach by an employee who stole over 20 million personal information items for selling to several data brokers.

[33] JIPDEC, *Decision of the false application in the process of review*, 14 Nov 2014.

[34] Quality-of-Life Policy Council, *Summary of Opinions on the Protection of Personal Information*, 29 June 2007.

[35] Consumer Affairs Agency, *Study on the Implementation Status of Businesses on the Protection of Personal Information*, March 2012, pp. 110, 112 [in Japanese].

by making use of its trustmark experience.[36] TRUSTe, a US-based certification company, has since been recognised as the first Accountability Agent in these cross-border rules, meaning that the trustmark scheme is likely to be a promising bridge in the APEC region.[37] Furthermore, the EU is interested in trustmarks and the proposed EU Data Protection Regulation clearly includes privacy seals and certification.[38]

In February 2014, both the Article 29 Working Party on Data Protection and APEC published a cross-reference, as a practical checklist for organisations, between the approval of Binding Corporate Rules (BCRs) in the EU and certification of Cross-Border Privacy Rules in APEC. "Significant differences may exist between the requirements generally imposed by national DPAs in the EU for BCR authorisation, in particular those deriving from EU data protection laws, and the CBPR program requirements."[39] At this time, it is true that "some BCR and CBPR requirements are not fully compatible",[40] but this cross-reference is the first step to extending the trustmark practices and influence of soft power in Japan and the APEC region to the rest of the world, with transparency allowing for sufficient input from stakeholders.[41]

5.3.4 Data breach notification and voluntary compensation

A data breach notification system is recognised at state level in the United States and some European countries. Data breach cases are almost always reported by the media, and reputational damage is the most significant impact for businesses and public institutions. The Basic Policy on the Protection of Personal Information, endorsed by Cabinet, provides that "it is important for the business to publicize all the facts of the incident to the extent possible from the viewpoint of avoidance of similar incidents and the prevention of secondary damage."[42] Here, the Basic Policy

---

[36] APEC Electronic Commerce Steering Group, Joint Oversight Panel, Findings Report regarding Japan's intent to participate in the CBPR system, 25 Apr 2014.

[37] APEC Electronic Commerce Steering Group, Joint Oversight Panel, Recommendation Report on APEC Recognition of TRUSTe, 19 February 2013 as amended 18 June 2013.

[38] European Commission, Proposal for a Regulation of the European Parliament and of the Council on the Protection of Individuals with regard to the Processing of Personal Data and the Free Movement of Such Data, Brussels, 25 January 2012, Art. 39.

[39] Article 29 Working Party, Opinion 02/2014 on a referential for requirements for Binding Corporate Rules submitted to National Data Protection Authorities in the EU and Cross Border Privacy Rules submitted to APEC CBPR Accountability Agents, adopted on 27 February 2014, p. 8.

[40] Ibid.

[41] See Kuner, Christopher, *Transborder Data Flows and Data Privacy Law*, Oxford University Press, 2013, p. 180.

[42] Cabinet Decision, *Basic Policy on the Protection of Personal Information*, 2 April 2004. The Basic Policy is the formal legal document based on Art. 7 of the Act to provide the basic direction regarding promotion of policies on the protection of personal information.

simply mentions the importance to publicise the facts of incidents, which is understood as non-mandatory, but in reality, businesses report data breach incidents to data subjects and the relevant ministries.

In practice, the guidelines set by each ministry, which are supplementary documents to the Act on the Protection of Personal Information, lay down the necessity of notification of such incidents to the ministry and data subjects. For instance, the Financial Services Agency has created a designated report form for data breaches, including minor incidents such as sending faxes or mail to the wrong numbers or addresses, which are to be submitted monthly. The report form should include (1) the name of the data protection officer, (2) date of the breach, (3) date of becoming aware of such breach, (4) types, contents, volume and degree of sensitivity of information, (5) encryption measures, (6) place of the breach, (7) cause of the breach, (8) background, (9) notification to the data subject(s), (10) publication, (11) contents and means of publication, (12) analysis of the cause, and (13) preventive measures. A "data breach" means any personal data leaked outside the organisation, which must report even very minor cases with encrypted personal data to the Consumer Affairs Agency. There is no time limit to report, but the guidelines require an "immediate report to the Agency".[43] In the Sony case, the Ministry noted the lateness of the report on the incident, published about a week after the company first became aware of the incident.

In the private sector, 366 data breach cases were reported to the Agency by each ministry in FY 2013.[44] Most of the cases were relatively small data breach incidents (66 % of the cases involved disclosure of the information of no more than 500 persons) and occurred due to human carelessness by an employee or third party (68 %). Nevertheless, all of these minor and carelessness cases were reported to the ministries and 89 % of them were reported to the data subjects.

In the public sector, there were 818 data breach cases at administrative organs and 1,816 cases at incorporated administrative agencies during the same period.[45] The mere mishandling of letters and transmission of faxes to wrong numbers accounted for more than half (54.6 %) at administrative organs, whereas the loss or mishandling of letters was the largest cause of incidents (67.1 %) at incorporated administrative agencies. This is because mailing incidents and human error do inevitably occur when dealing with personal information. Most of these incidents at administrative organs (61.1 %) and incorporated administrative agencies (96.6 %) were notified to data subjects in FY 2012.

---

[43] Financial Services Agency, *Guidelines on the Protection of Personal Information in the Financial Sector*, 20 November 2009; *Q &A on the Protection of Personal Information in Financial Corporations* [in Japanese].

[44] Consumer Affairs Agency, *Implementation Status of the Protection of Personal Information in FY 2013*, October 2014 [in Japanese].

[45] Ministry of Internal Affairs and Communications, *Implementation Status of the Protection of Personal Information of Administrative Organs and the Incorporated Administrative Agencies in FY 2012*, August 2013 [in Japanese].

Under the Japanese practice of data breach notification, it is fair to say that the corporations report to the competent ministry and notify the data subjects because they wish to regain the public's trust. Hiding data breaches may be regarded as a betrayal of both customers and citizens at large. Clearly, the invisible enforcement with compliance and accountability is firmly rooted in Japanese privacy governance.

Some may be surprised not just to see the precise data breach notifications, but also the voluntary compensation paid to customers in Japan. To give a few examples, there was a case of a security breach by a local bank in which the president of the bank resigned in circumstances where the Financial Services Agency had imposed no penalty, but merely made a recommendation.[46] Voluntary compensation has been demonstrated in cases where a securities firm sent 10,000-yen (about €70) gift cards to 50,000 customers with apologies after a former employee sold their personal information[47] and an insurance company paid a total of 500 million yen (about €3.5 million) in compensation for leaking an estimated 32,000 items of personal information.[48] These business practices were well established before the Act on the Protection of Personal Information was implemented. For instance, Yahoo BB sent gift cards after the personal information of more than 4.5 million of its users was leaked in 2004.[49] One local government paid the costs of relocating a data subject after her restricted residential records were disclosed to her former husband in a domestic violence case.[50] All of these examples demonstrate the voluntarily paid compensation to data subjects and clear responsibility of the data controller to provide effective remedies. The competent ministry or courts may impose additional legal sanctions, but data subjects generally appear to have been satisfied with the voluntary compensation already provided.

The practice of data breach cases in Japan has shown that the soft power mechanism for enforcing protection of personal information has been functioning well in the context of Japanese social norms and cultural values. The lack of sanctions handed down is not always a negative.

---

[46] Financial Services Agency, Administrative Decision on Michinoku Bank, 20 May 2005. See also *Nikkei Shimbun*, Michinoku Bank lost 1.31 million consumers' information, 23 Apr 2005, p. 39.

[47] Financial Services Agency, Administrative Decision on Mitsubishi UFJ Securities, 25 June 2009. See also *Nikkei Shimbun*, Financial Services Agency issued recommendation to Michinoku Bank: the first time under the Act on the Protection of Personal Information, 20 May 2009, p. 4.

[48] Financial Services Agency, Administrative Decision on Alico Japan, 24 February 2010. See also *Nikkei Shimbun*, Alico's apology money: 500 million yen in total, 7 Oct 2009, p. 4.

[49] The Court also took into account the payment of voluntary compensation and deducted that amount from the total compensation. Judgment of Osaka District Court on 19 May 2006, *Hanrei Jiho*, Vol. 1948, p. 122.

[50] *Nikkei Shimbun*, Disclosing the domestic violence victim's new address: mishandling a mail in Kashiwa city, 20 Nov 2013 (evening edition), p. 15.

5.4 Overcoming the weakness of soft power

5.4.1 *The design of privacy enforcement in Japan*

The design of privacy enforcement in Japan originated in the 1970s when mere ex post facto judicial remedies were essential, but not adequate as preventive measures in a computerised society.[51] With the historical complexities of privacy laws between the national and local levels and different policies between the various ministries, the Japanese approach towards enforcing privacy, under the current privacy laws, gives consumers multiple choices to submit complaints, which are dealt with by the competent ministers, authorised personal information protection organisations (for example, JIPDEC), National Consumer Affairs and local governments. This decentralised system has the beauty of flexibility and diversity for individuals to enforce situational privacy ranging from consumer information to employment contexts.

The fundamental philosophy of designing privacy enforcement is based on the Japanese concept of data privacy, the core value of which is freedom from unlawful interference by the government, namely, "the freedom not to disclose one's personal information to a third party without good reason and not to have it made public under Article 13 of the Constitution".[52] Here, the classic attitude of data privacy in Japan is the exclusion of interference with private life by the state.[53] In other words, a privacy infringement between private parties cannot be regarded as an issue of constitutional rights, but the parties can resolve and prevent such infringements through the designated channel offered by privacy legislations and social norms.

So far, I have described the strengths of privacy as soft power, but one should acknowledge its weaknesses as well. Soft power alone is not enough for privacy protection. These weaknesses of soft power may accelerate the use of hard power in some cases.

Here, I will mention some defects of Japanese privacy law. These are already recognised by the Japanese Government, which is preparing to reform the current law in 2015. The Bill was approved by the cabinet decision in March 2015 and approved by the Diet in September 2015.[54] The law reform plan includes, among other things, issues relating to the enforcement authorities, criminal sanctions against the illegal use of personal data and improvements in the exercise of the right.

---

[51] See Horibe, Masao, *Contemporary Privacy* [Gendai no Puraibashiii], Iwanami, 1980, p. 206.

[52] Judgment of Supreme Court, 6 March 2008, *Minshu* Vol. 62, No. 3, p. 665. Article 13 of the Constitution provides: "All of the people shall be respected as individuals. Their right to life, liberty, and the pursuit of happiness shall, to the extent that it does not interfere with the public welfare, be the supreme consideration in legislation and in other governmental affairs."

[53] The Supreme Court held that the Constitution does not directly apply to private parties, but the general regulations in the Civil Code may provide a solution in certain contexts. See Judgment of Supreme Court on 12 December 1973, *Minshu* Vol. 27, No. 11, p. 1536 (Mitsubishi Jushi Case).

[54] Cabinet Decision on the Amendment on the Act of the Protection of Personal Information, 10 March 2015; IT Strategic Headquarters, the Cabinet, Policy Outline of the Institutional Revision for Utilization of Personal Data, 24 June 2014; Policy on the System Review on the Use of Personal Data, 20 December 2013.

5.4.2 *Inconsistent enforcement*

The most essential component of using soft power to enforce privacy is social support and community norms. Without social support, soft power may just cause disorder in privacy protection. Social enforcement is mainly created by citizens and businesses, but the social and community norms vary to such an extent that there is no streamlined privacy governance.

Japan may have had some advantage in promoting social enforcement thanks to the lack of a single supervisory authority. In addition to the PrivacyMark scheme of private organisations, local governments have their own ordinances encouraging the original trustmark in their regions (for example, the PD mark in Kanagawa Prefecture). Exemptions for small to medium-sized enterprises are eliminated by some ordinances. Ministries' guidelines give detailed explanations on privacy protection in their own business sectors. All of these multiple channels have aided the development of privacy governance in Japan, but none of this levelling-up of privacy governance has led to a single unified social norm of privacy protection for several reasons.

First, there is an inconsistency in enforcement depending on the business sector. The evidence clearly shows that some business sectors are very progressive, such as the financial, telecommunications and general business sectors, but we have not seen any enforcement cases in education, healthcare or transportation. The system of competent ministers may, after all, have brought more sectionalism into administration.

Second, data breach cases often overlap between multiple business sectors so that corporations need to identify which ministry has authority to enforce the law. Consumers are not concerned which ministry will supervise the issue so long as the remedies are timely, but it takes time to provide a remedy when the data breach involves multiple ministries.

Finally, sometimes when corporations consider the privacy aspects of their projects, they have no legal reference at all. They first have to look at the text of the Act on the Protection of Personal Information and then the guidelines and commentaries set by each ministry. The competent ministry system has increased the burden for businesses, and a "one-stop shop" is particularly desirable in an age of big data.

In this sense, the supervisory authority with the power of coercion and sanction may overcome these weaknesses of soft power.

5.4.3 *Weak rights, strong governance*

Soft power requires all data controllers to respect the right to privacy as a community norm. While it is true that people can exercise their right to privacy, in reality, soft power may sometimes detach the privacy management system from the demand for the right to privacy.

As for trustmarks, it is desirable that data controllers prove their responsible privacy management by using such marks, but it is by no means certain that consumers will have adequate knowledge of their meaning. What is worse, multiple certifications will only confuse consumers – food labels, Internet security seals and now privacy seals. The same is true of privacy policy statements. Companies write detailed explanations of their use of personal data with security measures, but the longer and more detailed the privacy policies are, the more inconvenient or unrealistic it is for consumers to read them.[55]

After all, the soft power approach encourages a levelling-up of standards of privacy protection by social norms, which does not necessarily represent the consumer's choice. So the legal aspect of the right to privacy may be relatively weak and mild, depending on the social context.

My analysis of the weak privacy right can be explained by the Supreme Court's decision regarding the *Juki-Net* resident registration network system. *Juki-Net* commenced full operation in 2003 for the purpose of "promotion of convenience of the residents and rationalization of the administration of local governments". Key identification information as to the name, address, date of birth, gender and residential code of every citizen is managed on the network. There was much resistance and opposition to *Juki-Net* from both citizens and local governments.

The Supreme Court's decision of 6 March 2008 upheld the constitutionality of *Juki-Net*. The Court's reasoning seems to depart from the traditional rights-oriented review. Although the Court admitted that protection did exist for "the freedom not to disclose one's personal information to a third party without good reason and not to have it made public under Article 13 of the Constitution",[56] it held that

> *Juki-Net* has no defects either in a technical and legal sense so there is no concrete risk that identification information would be disclosed or made public without the legal ground and regulations or beyond the legitimate administrative purpose. ... Therefore, the storage and use of identification information of the appellees as residents operated by the administrative organs do not disclose personal information to a third party nor make it public, which does not constitute a violation of freedom guaranteed by Article 13 of the Constitution, even in the absence of the consent of the individuals.

Here, according to the Court, the crucial reasoning of the constitutionality of *Juki-Net* is its privacy governance and security management.[57] It is not the privacy right, but rather the privacy governance that determines the constitutionality of the

---

[55] See Solove, Daniel J., "Privacy Self-Management and the Consent Dilemma", *Harvard Law Review*, Vol. 126, No.7, 2013, pp. 1880–1903 [p. 1888].

[56] Judgment of Supreme Court, 6 March 2008, *Minshu*, Vol. 62, No. 3, p. 665.

[57] This decision is not understood as recognition of the right to control one's personal information, according to the law clerk (chosakan) explanations. See Masumori, Tamami, *Explanations on the Supreme Court Cases in 2008* [Saiko Saibansho Hanrei Kaisetsu Minjihen], p. 141. On the contrary, since the 1970s, most constitutional scholars defended the right to control one's personal information. See, e.g., Sato, Koji, "The Constitutional Position on Privacy: A Comparative Study of Japan and the United States [Puraibashii no Kenri (Sono Kohotekisokumen) no Kenporontekikosatsu]", *Hogaku Ronso* Vol. 86, No. 5, 1970, p. 12.

operation of *Juki-Net*.[58] In other words, the logic of the Court indicates the possibility of unconstitutional operation in *Juki-Net* once its security management departs from the appropriate standard, which is not the right criterion for sustaining privacy.

It is ironic that the soft power enforcement of the right to privacy may have resulted from a lack of a fundamental philosophy of the right to privacy coupled with inconsistent enforcement.[59] Needless to say, the right to privacy is fully respected and firmly rooted under Japanese judicial precedents, but the Court may be willing to push social enforcement rather than legal and rights-oriented enforcement in the face of rapid changes in technology. Reshaping the right to privacy by way of hard power enforcement will be the future task for Japanese privacy protection.

5.5 Conclusion: Use both powers

Enforcing privacy is not an easy task since privacy is an evolving concept with universal value. Nevertheless, regulators have invented some useful tools of communication to share their best practices in enforcing privacy. We have already seen global dialogue in the annual International Conference of Data Protection and Privacy Commissioners, the Global Privacy Enforcement Network (GPEN), based on the OECD Recommendation on Cross-border Co-operation in the Enforcement of Laws Protecting Privacy in 2007, APEC Cross-border Privacy Rules, and various regional meetings. These international fora will enhance the enforcement mechanisms within individual countries through the sharing of best practices.

The decision by the ICO in the Sony case had a clear impact in streamlining the enforcement of privacy law by the use of hard power. The overall soft power approach in that case illustrates the significance of social norms and cultural values of privacy in Japan. We have seen the convergence of two powers. It is noteworthy that the leading law enforcement data protection authority, CNIL, encourages digital education as soft power in France. In Japan, the core of the privacy law reform is about law enforcement and investigation. Again, it is wrong to simply label the European approach as hard power enforcement and Japanese approach as soft power enforcement. Both soft and hard powers have their benefits, which regulators, consumers and businesses desire. The enforcement of privacy is dependent on the choice of the societal and cultural values.

When we talk about privacy enforcement at the international level, it is important to consider the diversities and complexities of privacy protection, but such cultural differences are no excuse for failing to comply with international standards. Rather, they are a source of experimentation toward best privacy protection, and each region may be a laboratory of privacy ideals. Louis Brandeis, the founding father of the

[58] Yamamoto, Tatsuhiko, "The Right to Privacy [Puraibashii no Kenri]", *Jurist*, No. 1412, 2010, p. 87.

[59] For a critique of Japanese privacy laws, see Greenleaf, Graham, *Asian Data Privacy Laws*, Oxford University Press, 2014 p. 228–265.

right to privacy, insisted that the "state may, if its citizens choose, serve as a laboratory; and try novel social and economic experiments without risk to the rest of the country".[60] The laboratory of privacy protection may also be enhanced as long as the regional or national experiments function properly. Sharing best practices from multiple laboratories is surely a good way to promote international standards of privacy protection. After all, "[t]o stay experimentation in things social and economic is a grave responsibility".[61]

References

Article 29 Working Party, Opinion 02/2014 on a referential for requirements for Binding Corporate Rules submitted to National Data Protection Authorities in the EU and Cross Border Privacy Rules submitted to APEC CBPR Accountability Agents, adopted on 27 February 2014.

Carey, Peter, *Data Protection: A Practical Guide to UK and EU Law*, Fourth Edition, Oxford University Press, 2015.

Chemerinsky, Erwin, "Rediscovering Brandeis's Right to Privacy", *Brandeis Law Journal*, Vol. 45, No. 3, 2007.

Greenleaf, Graham, *Asian Data Privacy Laws*, Oxford University Press, 2014.

Horibe, Masao, Contemporary Privacy [Gendai no Puraibashiii], Iwanami, 1980.

Ito, Masami, Puraibashiii no Kenri [The Right to Privacy], Iwanami Shoten, 1963.

Kuner, Christopher, *Transborder Data Flows and Data Privacy Law*, Oxford University Press, 2013.

Masumori, Tamami, Explanations on the Supreme Court Cases in 2008 [Saiko Saibansho Hanrei Kaisetsu Minjihen].

Miyashita, Hiroshi, "The Evolving Concept of Data Privacy in Japanese Law", *International Data Privacy Law*, Vol. 1, No. 4, 2011.

Miyashita, Hiroshi, The New ID Number System and Personal Information Protection in Japan, *Sungkyunkwan Journal of Science & Technology Law*, Vol. 8, No.1, 2014.

Miyashita, Hiroshi, Policies on the Protection of Personal Information [Kojin Joho no Shisaku], Choyokai, 2010.

Nye, Joseph, *Soft Power: The Means to Success in World Politics*, Public Affairs, 2004.

Orito, Yoko, Kiyoshi Murata and Yasunori Fukuta, "Do Online Privacy Policies and Seals Affect Corporate Trustworthiness and Reputation?", *International Review of Information Ethics*, Vol. 19, 2013.

Pember, Don R., *Privacy and the Press: The Law, the Mass Media, and the First Amendment*, University of Washington Press, 1972.

Post, Robert C., Constitutional Domains: Democracy, Community, Management, Harvard University Press, 1995.

Rodrigues, Rowena, David Wright and Kush Wadhwa, "Developing a Privacy Seal Scheme (That Works)", *International Data Privacy Law*, Vol. 3, No. 2, 2013.

Rosen, Dan, "Private Lives and Public Eyes: Privacy in the United States and Japan",

Restatement (Second) of Torts, §652D, Comment h. (1977).

Sato, Koji, "The Constitutional Position on Privacy: A Comparative Study of Japan and the United States [Puraibashii no Kenri (Sono Kohotekisokumen) no Kenporontekikosatsu]", Hogaku Ronso Vol. 86, No. 5, 1970.

---

[60] *New State Ice Co. v. Liebmann*, 285 U.S. 262, 311 (1932) (Brandeis, J., dissenting).

[61] Ibid.

Solove, Daniel J., "Privacy Self-Management and the Consent Dilemma", *Harvard Law Review*, Vol. 126, No.7, 2013.

Sonobe, Itsuo, Commentary on the Protection of Personal Information [Kojin Joho Hogoho no Kaisetsu], Gyosei, 2005.

Yamamoto, Tatsuhiko, "The Right to Privacy [Puraibashii no Kenri]", Jurist, No. 1412, 2010.

Warren, Samuel D., and Louis D. Brandeis, "The Right to Privacy", *Harvard Law Review*, Vol. 4, No. 5, 15 December 1890.

Chapter 6
The Spanish Experience of Enforcing Privacy Norms: Two Decades of Evolution from Sticks to Carrots

Artemio Rallo Lombarte

6.1 Introduction[1]

For the last 20 years, Spain has had the most severe sanctions for breaches of its data protection law.[2] The enforcement of data protection under Spanish law is built on four pillars: (1) resolving complaints on the rights of access, rectification, erasure and objection; (2) investigating complaints lodged with the Spanish data protection agency (Agencia Española de Protección de Datos, AEPD) for any legal breach; (3) providing effective powers of investigation to the AEPD; (4) and, particularly, imposing an extremely hard level of sanctions (fines) on the private sector.[3]

[1] This chapter draws on research funded by the Spanish Ministry of Economy and Competitiveness (DER 2012-34764) and the Jaume I University (P1-1B2012-12) on the reform of the European data protection system.

[2] The AEPD has received numerous invitations to explain its enforcement experience. See, for example, the papers presented by the author: "The role of the Spanish DPA in safeguarding privacy and its influence in the wider world", 21st Annual International Conference, St. John's College, Cambridge, 9 July 2008; "Sanction mechanisms against any breach of data protection rules", VIII Data Protection Latin American Meeting, Mexico City, 29–30 September 2010; "Auditing and enforcement at the Spanish DPA", Conference on Cross-Border Data Flow & Privacy, Washington, DC, 15 October 2007; "The AEPD, independent authority for the protection of personal data", Journée d' études sur le droit à protection des données au Maroc et en Espagne", University of Rabat, 2010; "What is in the National and International Data Protection Agenda?", presentation at the Computers, Privacy & Data Protection conference, Brussels, 25–27 January 2011, published in Serge Gutwirth, Ronald Leenes, Paul De Hert and Yves Poullet (eds.), *European Data Protection: in good health*?, Springer, Dordrecht, 2012; "What's on the regulatory agenda: hear from the regulators", 32nd International Conference of Data Protection and Privacy Commissioners, Jerusalem, 2010.

[3] The best example is the resolution of the AEPD 2892/2013, which imposed a fine on Google of €900,000 in a case involving the unification of its privacy policies in 2012. Identical facts drove the

A.R. Lombarte (✉)
Public Law, Jaume I University, Ferrandis Salvador Avenue 50 8-1-A, Castellón 12100, Spain
e-mail: rallo@uji.es

D. Wright, P. De Hert (eds.), *Enforcing Privacy*, Law, Governance and Technology Series 25, DOI 10.1007/978-3-319-25047-2_6

Spain's approach to sanctions has its origins in the first Data Protection Act (1992), specifically Act 5/1992, regulating the automated processing of personal data (LORTAD).[4] For nearly two decades, most of the basic features of the sanctions regime laid down by LORTAD have remained intact.

6.1.1 *A catalogue of high fines*

The LORTAD established a "modulation" of fines that the AEPD could impose on companies and other organisations. These fines are the highest in Europe and have remained almost intact to date: (1) minor fines ranged from €600 (today, €900) to €60,000; (2) serious: from €60,001 (today, €40,001) to €300,000; (3) very serious: from €300,001 to €600,000. In the last decade, the AEPD has imposed fines totaling more than €206 million (Table 6.1).

The severity of the fines the regulator can impose for various infringements has led to claims that the data protection law is "unconstitutional" because it breaches the principle of proportionality. However, the LORTAD contemplates a gradation in fines according to several mitigating or aggravating circumstances: the nature of the rights breached or the volume of data processed, the benefits obtained, and the intentionality and the repetition of infringements.

In practice, although the AEPD could impose higher fines, it has generally imposed sanctions closer to the baseline (or minimum) of each category of fine. Today, following the reform of the data protection Act in 2011, the baselines are €900, €40.001 and €300,001. In fact, the Spanish National Court (SNC) has stated that "in the vast majority of cases, sanctions … imposed by the Data Protection Agency, and … confirmed by this Court, [are] in the minimum amount." (SNC Judgment 16 February 2005). The LORTAD gave the AEPD the power to adopt an additional measure with an extraordinary executive impact, known as the "immobilisation" of data, which means that the AEPD has the power to order the cessation of use of illicit transfer of data. This power is more than a sanction; it is a measure aimed at safeguarding the processing of personal data. This power can be exercised any time, even as a preventive measure; however, the AEPD has rarely exercised this power. In reality, the power of the AEPD to declare an "immobilisation" has not produced the expected effect because data flows have continued – despite proceedings against serious infringements to the law arising from unlawful automated processing.

French data protection authority (Commission nationale de l'informatique et des libertés, CNIL) to impose a €150,000 fine on Google on 8 January 2014. Then European Justice Commissioner Viviane Reding described both fines as "pocket money" for Google. See Reding, Viviane, "The EU Data protection reform: helping businesses thrive in the digital economy", 19 January 2014. http://europa.eu/rapid/press-release_SPEECH-14-37_en.htm

[4] LORTAD = Ley Orgánica 5/1992, de 29 de octubre, de Regulación del Tratamiento Automatizado de los Datos de Carácter Personal.

Table 6.1 The value of fines almost trebled in the decade 2002–2012

	2002	2003	2004	2005	2006	2007	2008	2009	2010	2011	2012	Total
Fines (€000)[a]	7,989	8,372	16,439	21,105	24,422	23,263	22,013	24,872	17,497	19,500	21,054	€206 million+

[a]Rallo, Artemi, "Data Protection in Europe: the Spanish Data Protection Agency", Georgetown University Law Center, Washington, April, 2010, pp. 10–12. A sectoral approach to these data can be found in the Annual Reports of the AEPD

6.1.2 A typology of infringements

LORTAD identified many kinds of infringements, but some critics have said the description of these infringements is riddled with "imprecision, ambiguity, coincidences and overlaps".[5]

The LORTAD's typology of infringements is a response to the principles that safeguard the fundamental right to personal data protection: quality principle, the right to inform, consent, special protection of sensitive data, security of data, duty of secrecy and protection against data transfer without prior consent.

"Minor" infringements include formal or documentary mistakes and breaches of information, rectification and erasure rights, but these infringements could be regarded as serious in other situations and punished accordingly.

"Serious" infringements are those where there is unambiguous evidence of infringing behaviour such as the controller's not having notified a database, not having obtained consent, having breached the duty of secrecy or lacking adequate security measures. Serious infringement could also include the amplitude of certain infringement types – for example, breaching principles and guarantees of laws and regulations under Art. 44.3.d of the LOPD.[6]

"Very serious" infringements deserve a correspondingly strong regulation, which, however, is rarely exercised, except in certain cases, such as those involving the fraudulent collection of data, unlawful international transfers of data or unlawful processing that breaches fundamental rights. Other breaches involving the unlawful transfer of data or violations of the confidentiality of sensitive data have figured in various proceedings.

6.1.3 Investigating "all" claims and complaints lodged with the AEPD

Since its establishment, the AEPD has processed and resolved all of the individual complaints it has received against data controllers and processors, in line with the provisions of the data protection Act and/or Spanish administrative law. On the one hand, the LORTAD gave to the AEPD a generic function to "ensure compliance with the data protection legislation" – in particular, regarding the rights of access, rectification and erasure of data – and to "take care of all claims and complaints lodged by individuals". On the other hand, the Spanish legislation regulating administrative proceedings has required the AEPD to initiate administrative proceedings

[5] Calvo Rojas, Eduardo, "El régimen sancionador de la Ley Orgánica 15/1999, de 13 de diciembre, de protección de datos de carácter personal. El principio de proporcionalidad", *La potestad sancionadora de la Agencia Española de Protección de Datos*, Cizur Menor (Navarra), AEPD-Aranzadi, 2008, pp. 20–21.

[6] The Ley Orgánica 15/1999 de Protección de Datos de Carácter Personal (LOPD, the Data Protection Law 15/1999) superseded the LORTAD.

(protecting rights, investigating and sanctioning) in compliance with regulations and constitutional or legal provisions.

Data protection law grants to all citizens a right of access to their personal data, rights to rectify, erase and/or object to it. If an organisation does not comply with these requirements, citizens can lodge complaints with the AEPD, which must resolve them within a maximum of six months, which may be subject to judicial review.

The following table shows the explosive growth of claims for protecting rights of access, rectification, erasure and objection (AREO) in the AEPD. Two-thirds are related to the right of erasure and a quarter to the right of access (Table 6.2).

The growth of the AEPD enforcement activity is due to the extraordinary increase in complaints and claims of breaches of data protection law (Table 6.3).

These figures show that the number of complaints multiplied by almost 12 times in the space of a decade. And there is no reason to doubt that this trend will continue into the future. During the AEPD's first 10 years, all claims and complaints received were subject to an inspection aimed at verifying the facts of each complaint and evaluating a potential infringement. Investigations ended with the AEPD either closing the file on a complaint or opening administrative proceedings leading to a sanction against the infringing organisation.[7]

However, the explosive growth of complaints forced the AEPD to scrutinise its approach to prevent the collapse of its inspection and sanction powers.[8]

Heretofore, the AEPD has not adopted the "selective to be effective" principle[9] whereby a data protection authority chooses to investigate only certain complaints, rather than all complaints, in keeping with its limited resources. Instead, the AEPD

Table 6.2 The number of claims increased almost five times in the decade 2002–2012

	2002	2003	2004	2005	2006	2007	2008	2009	2010	2011	2012
Protection of AREO	393	541	463	592	632	849	1,229	1,947	1,830	1,939	2,193

Table 6.3 The number of complaints increased more than 10-fold in the decade 2002–2012

	2002	2003	2004	2005	2006	2007	2008	2009	2010	2011	2012
Complaints	723	574	978	1,158	1,282	1,624	2,362	4,136	4,302	7,648	8,594

[7] For a detailed description of this procedure, see López Calvo, J., "Actividad inspectora y procedimiento administrativo sancionador en materia de protección de datos personales", *La potestad sancionadora de la Agencia Española de Protección de Datos*, AEPD-Aranzadi, Cizur Menor (Navarra), 2008, pp. 253–267.

[8] On the difficulty of managing the growing flood of claims and complaints to the AEPD, see Rallo, Artemi, "Strengths and weaknesses of enforcement: the Spanish case", London Initiative Workshop: "selective to be effective", London, 13 Dec 2007.

[9] However, in favour of the AEPD adopting a "selective" approach are E. Espín Templado (referencing the Public Prosecutor's Office), J. Tornos Mas (pointing to the limited resources of the AEPD) and A. Huergo Lora in *La potestad sancionadora de la Agencia Española de Protección de Datos*, AEPD-Aranzadi, Cizur Menor (Navarra), 2008, pp. 132, 135 and 158.

Table 6.4 How the AEPD dealt with complaints

Annual increase[a]	2009	2010	2011	2012	Increase 2011/2012
Abandonment	222	229	337	448	32.94 %
Refusal	1,967	2,240	2,993	4,756	58.90 %
File	920	1,044	901	1,153	27.97 %
Total	3,109	3,513	4,240	6,357	
Complaints	4,136	4,302	7,648	8,594	

[a]AEPD, *Memoria Anual*, 2012, p. 70. www.agpd.es

performs a rigorous review of all of the claims and complaints it receives, even though it does not open an investigation in many cases because the individuals concerned abandon the complaint or because the AEPD does not find sufficient merit in the complaint. The AEPD may turn down a complaint for various reasons: (1) the data protection law may not be applicable because the complaint is outside the scope of the law or because the complainant is a legal person or pretends to be seeking data protection for deceased persons or the complaint actually involves consumer rights; (2) the complaint lacks the minimum evidence needed to justify an investigation; (3) the complaint concerns other fundamental rights (freedom of expression, right of association, right to due process) more than the right to data protection; (4) there are more effective ways to safeguard the right to data protection than imposing a sanction (for example, erasure of data on the Internet). The following table shows the increase in the number of complaints received and how they were handled (Table 6.4).

The comparison between total figures for complaints lodged with the AEPD during the past years and the volume of complaints abandoned by the complainants and dismissed by the AEPD shows the rigor applied by the Agency in its initial analysis by limiting investigations of little relevance or remote viability. The volume of complaints rejected *ab initio* doubled in four years (2009–2012). In the same period, three-quarters of the complaints did not result in any inspection. Especially striking is the increase in 2012 compared to 2011 of proceedings abandoned (33 %), refused (59 %) and filed[10] (28 %).

6.1.4 *Effective investigation powers*

The LORTAD introduced a control system primarily supported by making "face-to-face investigations" by AEPD inspectors. The LORTAD gives AEPD inspectors the power to inspect files subject to "gathering how much information [is needed] to be accurate for the fulfillment of its tasks". For this purpose, inspectors have the status of a "public authority" (which means they have the corresponding legal protection

[10]"filed" means the AEPD closed the case because it lacked evidence or did not merit an investigation.

in the administrative and criminal fields). To obstruct the exercise of their powers is a serious infringement. Inspectors are empowered to: (1) require the data controller to display or submit documents and data and examine them in situ; (2) inspect physical and logical equipment used for the data processing; (3) access the data controller's premises. If a company fails to produce the documents and information sought by the AEPD within a specified period of time, then it is committing a serious infringement.

6.1.5 *Differences in liability between the public and private sectors*

While companies may suffer stiff fines, the AEPD treats infringements committed by public administrations differently. In the latter case, the AEPD Director generally only issues a resolution declaring a breach of data protection law and ordering the public administration to adopt appropriate measures to stop and correct the effects of the infringement. The AEPD reports this resolution to the Ombudsman (who is a Commissioner appointed by the Parliament for protecting human rights), and proposes, where appropriate, the initiation of disciplinary proceedings against officials. Finally, the offending public body must inform the AEPD about the measures and actions it is adopting to correct the situation. Although it is clear that so many sanctioning resolutions against public bodies have resulted in improvements to data protection, this supervisory model, more than a sanctioning procedure strictu sensu, looks like a bureaucratic procedure with the appearance of impunity for obvious reasons: (1) not imposing fines marks a difference with other types of administrative infringements (for example, those of an environmental nature); (2) by not opening disciplinary proceedings against public officials; (3) by the bureaucratic passivity of the Ombudsman upon receipt of resolutions issued by the AEPD; (4) and by the traditional lack of monitoring by the AEPD of the corrective measures that the infringing public body must adopt. But in the last five years, at the request of the Ombudsman, the AEPD has proceeded to monitor the implementation of these corrective measures (Table 6.5).

Table 6.5 Sanctions to the private sector and public bodies

	2002	2003	2004	2005	2006	2007	2008	2009	2010	2011	2012
Private sector	128	148	189	279	301	342	535	621	591	505	863[a]
Public bodies	13	28	28	52	106	49	59	71	61	81	33

[a]For example, the AEPD Annual Report 2012 shows that most of the sanctions were imposed on the telecommunications sector (73 % of the total, €15,368,938), which is in line with a nearly constant trend throughout the previous decade. Three of the main telecommunications operators accounted for 71 % of the total amount of fines. In addition, the AEPD imposed fines of more than one million euro in the financial sector (€2,853,000, or 13.5 % of total fines) and utilities such as energy or water (€1,270,000 or 6.03 %). However, the numerous sanctions imposed on video surveillance (32 %) represented only 1.60 % of the total fines

The differences in sanctions imposed on private companies and public bodies have been considered traditionally as a "privilege", a breach of European competition law, without constitutional protection. The difference in sanctioning approach seems caused by the legislator's wishing to avoid economic sanctions against public bodies that face difficulties in complying with data protection legislation. On the other hand, there have been voices that have argued in favour of this difference in approaches as "sufficient, reasonable and rational"[11] because the unnecessary imposition of fines against public bodies would ultimately negatively affect citizens.

"Humanising" the sanctions regime

LORTAD was repealed and replaced by the Act 15/1999 for Data Protection (LOPD), which transposed the EU Data Protection Directive 95/46/EC in Spain, but without substantially changing the existing sanctioning regime. All key elements of the LORTAD regime were almost literally reinstalled by the LOPD. In addition, a number of seemingly minor novelties in the LOPD have proven to have a strong impact in practice:

6.1.6 The continuity of the sanctioning regime

The categories of infringements remained almost the same under the new law (for example, breaches of confidentiality were considered a minor infringement; only if sensitive data was affected was it considered a serious infringement). However, the typology of infringements in both Acts (LORTAD and LOPD) resulted in a flood of serious infringements, which entailed the risk of fines ranging from €60.001 to €300,000.

An analysis of the period 2006–2009 shows that serious infringements constituted two-thirds of the total (followed in importance by minor infringements). In addition,

Table 6.6 Types of infringements: prevalence of serious infringements

	2006	2007	2008	2009
Minor	111	108	105	152
Serious	308	323	520	527
Very serious	43	43	35	33
Total	462	474	660	712

For an analysis of the evolution of the sanction regime, see Rallo, Artemi, "Development of the Agency's audit and sanctions policy in Spain: Trends regarding investigations, fines and other sanctions", *23rd Annual International Conference*, St. John's College, Cambridge, 5 July 2010 and "The regulator's Priorities. View of the Spanish DPA", IAPP Europe Data Protection Congress, Paris, 2010

[11] Rebollo Puig, Manuel, *La potestad sancionadora de la Agencia Española de Protección de Datos* (AAVV), Cizur Menor (Navarra), AEPD-Aranzadi, 2008, p. 105.

Table 6.7 Modulating criteria in section 45.4 LOPD

	Total 2006	Total 2007	Total 2008	2008 modulated sanctions	Total 2009	2009 modulated sanctions	Total 2010	Total 2011	Total 2012
Minor	111	108	105	**50**	152	**61**			
Serious	308	323	520	**190**	527	**219**			
Very serious	43	43	35	**4**	33	**3**			
Total	462	474	660	**244**	712	**283**	591	505	863
Without modulation			416		429			136	166

Comparative figures are in Rallo, Artemi, "Development of the Agency's audit and sanctions policy in Spain. Trends regarding investigations, fines and other sanctions", *23rd Annual International Conference*, St. John's College, Cambridge, 5 July 2010. Completed with AEPD, *Memoria Annual*, 2012, p. 71

while very serious infringements showed a decline, serious infringements showed an extraordinary increase, almost doubling during that period and increasing by 38 % between 2007 and 2008 (Table 6.6).

The LOPD established a range of fines in three main groups (€600–60,000, €60.001–300,000 and €300.001–600,000). But, according to mitigating or aggravating circumstances (nature of the rights breached, volume of data processed, benefits obtained, intentionality and repetition of infringements[12]), the LOPD has allowed an extensive application of the minimum fines, as reflected in the following table (Table 6.7).

An analysis of sanctions imposed in the 2008–2009 biennium shows the wide application of the criteria for a range of fines, as provided for in section 45.4 LOPD. In 2008, 47 % of infringements were minor, 37 % were serious and 11 % were very serious. In 2009, 40 % of infringements were minor, 41 % were serious and 9 % were very serious. In addition, in 2008, modulated infringements were 37 % of the total; in 2011, 73 %; and 80 %, in 2012.

However, there was no widespread application of the modulating criteria until the 2011 legal reform; the expansive application of section 45.5 LOPD criteria enabled the AEPD to modulate fines downwards to the minimum levels.

6.1.7 *The new downgrading clause of fines: the qualified reduction of guilt*

The LOPD includes criteria for downgrading fines based on the following ratio: the AEPD could accept a "qualified reduction of the guilt of the infringer or of the unlawful facts". The agency can establish the amount of the fine taking into account the severity of immediately preceding infringements in relation to the current

[12] The AEPD uses these criteria to "modulate" fines; in other words, the level of fines depends on the circumstances of each case.

(punishable) case (section 45.5). That means that before imposing a potentially "very serious" sanction for an infringement, the AEPD can impose fines corresponding to "serious" infringements or, where appropriate, it can impose fines for "serious infringements" if it recognised a qualified reduction of the infringer's guilt or of the unlawful facts.

Initially, the High Court interpreted restrictively this downgrading clause, requiring its application only exceptionally, when duly justified and qualified by circumstances that merited a "reduction of guilt or illegality".[13] In fact, the High Court, which has overturned National Court judgments, has taken account of section 45.5 LOPD by estimating the infringer's motivation instead of making mere "dialectical speculations" (Judgment of 18 March 2005). The National Court translated this restrictive criterion in the following terms: "This is a rule to be applied with precise weighting, and only in cases in which the guilt and illegality are substantially mitigated and address the circumstances of the particular case, so that it recognises legal sensitivities, is guided by justice, and imposes a penalty appropriate to the infringement. Such discretion is justified on an exceptional basis and in extreme cases" (Judgment of 14 December 2006).

In addition, before the risk of confusing "mitigating circumstances" (modulating fines in each grade) with the "qualifying circumstances of guilt reduction" (to downgrade the infringement), the latter possibility saw little application until 2007 when the AEPD began to explain the circumstances for applying this "downgrading clause of fines" provided for in section 45.5 LOPD.[14] Examples of such circumstances are the following:

- *Companies merge*: the infringement was performed by a company that later merged, was absorbed or acquired by another and the latter had implemented measures that would have avoided the infringement.
- *Exceptional failure*: the infringer had a proper protocol for data collection that, exceptionally, failed.
- *Technical difficulties*: the infringement was difficult to detect but was not the result of negligent action or an erroneous application of law.
- *Immediate corrective reaction*: the infringer reacted immediately, to minimise the effects of the infringement, or worked diligently to rectify the situation in a reasonable time.
- *Training measures*: the infringer adopted and implemented training measures for employees about data protection compliance.
- *Data subject "provocation"*[15]: the data subject did not act diligently, was partly responsible for the breach or induced an error by the infringer.

---

[13] High Court Judgments of 7 March 2006 and 17 April 2007. The High Court Judge E. Espín Templado wrote in favour of this restrictive application in *La potestad sancionadora de la Agencia Española de Protección de Datos*, AEPD-Aranzadi, Cizur Menor (Navarra), 2008, p. 131.

[14] Related cases highlighting various examples of the application of section 45.5 LOPD can be found in the AEPD Annual Reports from 2007 to 2010 (www.agpd.es).

[15] In fact, as J.M. Fernández López and J. Tornos Mas explain, a phenomenon resulting from the severity of the sanctions regime has been the *blackmail pathology* to the LOPD infringer demanding economic compensation to avoid complaints in the AEPD, *La potestad sancionadora de la*

- *Real security measures*: the company had a system of security measures even if it did not comply with all formal obligations.
- *Unqualified infringer*: the infringer was an individual or a small or medium-sized enterprise without technical qualification.
- *Immediate self-incrimination*[16]: the infringer spontaneously recognised his guilt at the beginning of the proceedings.

The situations described above responded to the urgent need for adapting the sanctioning strategy, according to the experience of a decade and a half of repressive actions with, on the one hand, the "humanisation" of the sanctioning model and, on the other hand, the promotion and encouragement of data protection and good compliance practices (Table 6.8).

A detailed comparison of the 2008–2009 figures is illustrative. In 2008, 71 % of very serious infringements were lowered to serious and 39 % of the serious infringements were transformed into minor. In 2009, 79 % of the very serious infringements were downgraded to serious and 36 % of the serious were reduced to minor. In the following years, 69 % (2010), 71 % (2011) and 35 % (2012) of the serious and very serious infringements were downgraded.

The new AEPD goals, which were drafted with widespread consensus, are:

(a) to recognise and mitigate the severity of the sanctioning regime which did not differentiate between big companies and small organisations, or even individuals without specific qualifications in data protection;
(b) to note that numerous breaches did not have their origins in a clear willingness to breach data protection law but on a misunderstanding;
(c) to recognise certain difficulties and exceptions in the applicability of data protection law regarding breaches offset by the most diligent and immediate damage containment;
(d) to encourage the implementation of proactive measures (such as employee training plans and security measures) as a means of alleviating potential infringements (Table 6.9).

The comparative analysis of the total of fines by year and its correlative number of sanctions imposed on the private sector offers conclusive considerations of interest to our purposes here:

- 2006 marks a turning point in AEPD sanctioning rigour – according to the average value of fines/sanctions – with fines totalling more than €24 million.
- Until 2006, the progressive increase in annual sanctions and fines was striking and showed a continuing ascent, with a significant sprouting of fines over sanctions. On the one hand, sanctions increased by 15 % (2003), 28 % (2004),

Agencia Española de Protección de Datos, AEPD-Aranzadi, Cizur Menor (Navarra), 2008, pp. 90, 91 and 137.

[16] A recurrent question about the applicability of this downgrading clause was if this "guilt qualified reduction" could be applied to subsequent infringement behaviour. In favour, M. Rebollo Puig recalls the existence of the criminal mitigation circumstance of spontaneous remorse. See *La potestad sancionadora de la Agencia Española de Protección de Datos*, AEPD-Aranzadi, Cizur Menor (Navarra), 2008, p. 117.

Table 6.8 Modulating criteria in section 45.5 LOPD

	2008 Sanctions	2008 Gradated sanctions	2009 Sanctions	2009 Gradated sanctions	2010 Sanctions	2010 Gradated sanctions	2011 Sanctions	2011 Gradated sanctions	2012 Sanctions	2012 Gradated sanctions
Minor	105	–	152	–						
Serious	520	**204**	527	**193**						
Very serious	35	**25**	33	**26**						
Total	660	**229**	712	**219**	591	**182**	505	**145**	863	**308**

AEPD, *Memoria Annual*, 2012, p. 71. www.agpd.es. For a review of these comparative figures, see Rallo, Artemi, "Development of the Agency's audit and sanctions policy in Spain: Trends regarding investigations, fines and other sanctions", 23rd Annual International Privacy Laws and Business Conference, St. John's College, Cambridge, 5–7 July 2010.

Table 6.9 Comparison of the evolution between fines and sanctions

	2002	2003	2004	2005	2006	2007	2008	2009	2010	2011	2012	Total
Fines (€ 000)[a]	7,989	8,372	16,439	21,105	24,422	23,263	22,013	24,872	17,497	19,500	21,054	>206 million
Private sector sanctions	128	148	189	279	301	342	535	661	591	505	863	
Warnings in writing										312	352	
Hypothetical average fine/ sanction (€000)	62	57	87	76	81	68	41	38	30	24	17	

Rallo, Artemi, "Data Protection in Europe: the Spanish Data Protection Agency", Georgetown University Law Center, Washington, DC, April, 2010, pp. 10–12

47 % (2005) and 7 % (2006). In total, over the 5-year period 2002–2006, imposed sanctions more than doubled (with an increase of 238 %). On the other hand, fines went up 5 % (2003), 49 % (2004), 22 % (2005) and 14 % (2006). In total, the fines more than tripled, increasing over the same period of 2002 and 2006 by 327 %.

- The four-year 2007–2010 period highlights the new strategy of modulating and downgrading sanctions. As a result of greater social awareness and increasing complaints, imposed sanctions continued growing at a breakneck pace: in the four years from 2007 to 2010, sanctions nearly doubled (196 %) while fines were reduced by 28 %.

The best statistical resource to demonstrate the progressive reduction in the severity of sanctions resulting from the downgrading of fines promoted by AEPD since 2007 lies in the evolution of the ratio between fines and sanctions. The five-year period 2002–2006 showed the highest average values: €87,000 (2004), €76,000 (2005) and €81,000 (2006). But the period from 2007 to 2010 demonstrates a reduction: €68,000 (2007), €41,000 (2008), €38,000 (2009) and €30,000 (2010).

- Finally, the 2011–2012 biennium reflects the impact of the 2011 data protection Act reform regulating the prior AEPD enforcement practice by introducing criteria for modulating and downgrading fines. Hypothetically, if the warnings in writing were considered as sanctions, we can observe that the rebound in the total volume of fines does not detract from the reduced average value of sanctions: €24,000 (2011) and €17,000 (2012).

In short, this model of modulating and downgrading fines opened the door to a new strategy that would combine a mandatory sanctioning regime with proactive responsibility measures (accountability) for companies and private organisations. The AEPD has, in effect, ushered in a reform of the data protection law adopted in 2011.

6.1.8 *Publicity of sanctions on the AEPD website*

Although the AEPD failed in its attempts to introduce a "naming and shaming" provision in the LOPD,[17] Act 62/2003 later included this provision. Henceforth, the AEPD could make public on its website the sanctions it levied after it had notified recipients. Although publicity of the AEPD sanctions does not have the formal nature of a sanction, there is no doubt that this provision constitutes a *material* sanction for companies and organisations because it affects their reputation and could, consequently, affect their business.

[17] As J.M. Fernández Lopez, former AEPD Director, remembers in *La potestad sancionadora de la Agencia Española de Protección de Datos*, AEPD-Aranzadi, Cizur Menor (Navarra), 2008, p. 90.

6.2 Reform of the LOPD sanctioning regime (2011)

For almost a decade, business organisations had called for reform of the data protection sanctioning regime (first, in the LORTAD and, later, in the LOPD). The advertising and marketing sector[18] was particularly vocal as they were the main recipients of severe fines and claimed high compliance costs and competitive disadvantages over similar business sectors in other European countries.

Echoing this claim,[19] during the parliamentary proceedings in the *Congreso de los Diputados* of the Sustainable Economy bill, the Catalan Parliamentary Group (Convergencia i Unió) submitted an amendment that sought to reform the complete sanctioning regime by proposing: (1) a significant revision of the infringements catalogue aimed at downgrading existing sanctions; (2) a reduction of the type and amount of fines (minor, up to €6,000; serious, €6,000 to €60,000; and very serious, from €60,000 to €300,000)[20]; (3) a new warning in writing to first-time infringers as an alternative to the first sanction.

However, the parliamentary proposal invited the AEPD to propose an alternative amendment. The AEPD accepted the challenge and developed an alternative proposal that would substantially revise the sanctioning regime. The AEPD proposal for an amendment gained wide support in the Senate and became Final Section 56 of the Act 2/2011 of Sustainable Economy that reformed sections 43–46 and 49 of the LOPD.

The new sanctions regime proposed by the AEPD was based on the following pillars:

---

[18] As shown in the *Landwell Report on proposed amendment to the LOPD* drawn up at the behest of the Spanish Federation of E-commerce and Direct Marketing (FECEM) in March 2007. See also the speech of L. Llairó Canal, representative of FECEM, in *La potestad sancionadora de la Agencia Española de Protección de Datos*, AEPD-Aranzadi, Cizur Menor (Navarra), 2008, pp. 123–126.

[19] J. Jané Guash, Convergència i Unió parliamentary spokesman in the *Congreso de los Diputados*, set out his party's position, which is outlined in *La potestad sancionadora de la Agencia Española de Protección de Datos*, AEPD-Aranzadi, Cizur Menor (Navarra), 2008, pp. 120, 230–232.

[20] The Catalan Parliamentary Group justified this reduction by comparing it to figures from other European countries: in Spain, an unlawful transfer of data for advertising could reach from €300,001 to €600,000 (although mitigating circumstances could reduce this range to €60.001–€300.000). In Germany, a similar offence could be penalised at a maximum of €50,000; in France, it would only be sanctioned if it failed to fulfil the warning in writing from the CNIL with a fine exceeding €60,000 – because a first breach is only fined up to €150,000; in the Netherlands, to €4,537; in Belgium, a fine not exceeding €100,000; in Portugal, €9,975; in Italy, between €10,000 and €60,000. See *Boletín Oficial de las Cortes Generales*, Congreso de los Diputados, A, No. 60–14, 11/10/2010, pp. 364–367.

6.2.1 *Maintenance of the maximum level of fines*

Spanish sanctions have traditionally been characterised by the severity of fines and lowering these would have sent a message to the whole of society that data protection was being relaxed instead of being regarded as a social necessity.[21] When that high level was established two decades ago, some might have considered it excessive, but current socio-economic circumstances and sanctioning systems implemented in nearby countries (France and the United Kingdom) or in the process of being adopted (notably the sanctions contained in the new EU Data Protection Regulation are much higher – up to four per cent of a company's turnover) demonstrate that lowering the fines would have an adverse effect.

6.2.2 *Revision of the infringements typology*

After two decades in force, the infringement typology in the Data Protection Act had shown that some types of infringements were unnecessary and that its wide scope required delimitation. This reform also allowed identification of some "aggravated" infringements (such as failure to comply with the duty of confidentiality and the unlawful transfer of non-sensitive data).

6.2.3 *Expansion of criteria for modulating and downgrading fines*

The heavy fines provided for in Spanish legislation have pushed the AEPD to consolidate the practice of imposing the amount corresponding to the base of each grade – €600 (today, €900), €60,001 (today, €40,001) and €300,001 – making largely ineffective and almost unnecessary the modulation criteria provided for in section 45.4 LOPD regarding the nature of rights breached, volume of data processed, benefits, intentionality and repetition of infringement.

Interestingly, while it may seem contradictory, the 2011 reform not only maintained the above criteria but expanded them significantly to include the following:

- Continued infringements
- The infringer's data processing activity

[21] The qualified opinion of the High Court judge, E. Calvo Rojas, claimed that "the risk of sanction is not as dissuasive as it should be… the amount of fines, while not negligible, does not guarantee that it will be entirely neutralized by the illegal profit… particularly relevant in the data protection field is the black figure of unpunished infringements". See "El régimen sancionador de la Ley Orgánica 15/1999, de 13 de diciembre, de protección de datos de carácter personal: El principio de proporcionalidad", op. cit., p. 30.

- The infringer's volume of business
- Nature of damages
- Accreditation that, prior to the breach, the infringer had implemented appropriate procedures for data collection and processing, so that the infringement could be seen as an anomaly and not due to a lack of diligence on the part of the infringer
- Any other circumstance that could be relevant to determine the degree of illegality and guilt of the infringement.

The extension of mitigating or aggravating circumstances aimed to avoid regulatory arbitrariness and to give more legal certainty to stakeholders. At the same time, section 45.5 LOPD allows the AEPD to impose for very serious infringements fines appropriate for serious infringements, and smaller fines for minor infringements.

The 2011 reform standardised circumstances that allow "a qualified reduction of guilt or illegality" and extended circumstances for the application of fines. It improved legal certainty by establishing that the imposition of fines arises "from the *significant* concurrence of *several* criteria". It also added several circumstances whereby guilt could be reduced.[22] The new circumstances included the following:

- the infringer would have resolved the problem in a diligent way;
- the complainant conduct would have contributed to the infringement;
- the infringer spontaneously recognized his guilt;
- the breach was committed by a different entity which subsequently merged with another company.

The review of this wide range of mitigating and aggravating circumstances and the typology of infringements aimed to modulate fines and to downgrade sanctions. The AEPD's interpretation of the LOPD has had these effects:

- A reduction in a potential fine of €600,000–€40,001 – or from €300,000 to €900 – in so many cases in which an infringer (a natural person or small business entity) is not aware (like many people) of data protection rules and had spontaneously recognised his guilt and worked diligently to correct an irregularity of little impact or economic benefit. An example of such an infringement is a data controller's publication of data about owners in a housing estate on a public notice board. Ultimately, the modulation and downgrading of fines were intended to humanise a sanctioning regime which was targeted at large companies in banking, utilities, telecommunications, advertising, etc., which could be fatal for small companies but not dissuasive for large companies.[23]

---

[22] J. Tornos Más had already advanced a range of cases for the application of this downgrading clause – partially coincident with AEPD – for their inclusion in the Spanish Data Protection Regulation. See "Potestad sancionadora de la Agencia Española de Protección de Datos y principio de proporcionalidad", *La potestad sancionadora de la Agencia Española de Protección de Datos*, AEPD-Aranzadi, Cizur Menor (Navarra), 2008, pp. 49–50.

[23] Casino Rubio, M., *La potestad sancionadora de la Agencia Española de Protección de Datos*, AEPD-Aranzadi, Cizur Menor (Navarra), 2008, p. 87.

- Flexibility, so the AEPD would not need to unduly punish organisations and companies that were typically compliant with data protection legislation, but exceptionally, perhaps for reasons beyond their control, had committed an infringement, but had responded diligently to mitigate its effects. The AEPD regarded this new sanction regime as having a salutary effect on accountability.

6.2.4 *A warning in writing for the first infringement*

The LOPD reform introduced a new reactive mechanism against data protection breaches as a central tool in its sanctioning system: the warning in writing. It is, without a doubt, a legal instrument alien to the Spanish tradition of enforcement – but it exists in other nearby countries (e.g., France[24]) and is expected to be widely used across Europe[25] – because it is an alternative to direct sanctions. This mechanism responds to the widespread perception that many legal breaches are not the result of an intentional violation of data protection law but a lack of knowledge of this fundamental right and thus the first-time infringer merits a second chance.

The Spanish regulation of the warning in writing is far from a blind and automatic application, and is subject to rules and limits contained in section 45.6 of the LOPD:

- Instead of obliging the AEPD to impose mandatory fines, section 45.6 empowers the AEPD to exercise its discretion in certain circumstances.
- Although the warning in writing is not a sanction per se, it will not be adopted as a reflex action in response to any complaint, but it will be issued only following comments from both the complainant and infringer.
- The warning in writing will only be adopted after assessing the facts and the "significant" fulfillment of criteria for modulation and downgrading provided for in the LOPD.
- The AEPD can only issue a warning in writing to the first-time infringer: it is specifically excluded from issuing a warning in writing to the infringer who has been punished or warned before (even where the facts of the case are different).
- A warning in writing will not apply to very serious infringements.

---

[24] Section 45 of the French Act 1978-17 on Computing and Freedoms, last amended by Act 2011-334, includes the following sanctioning mechanism: "1. La formation restreinte de la Commission nationale de l'informatique et des libertés peut prononcer, après une procédure contradictoire, un avertissement à l'égard du responsable d'un traitement qui ne respecte pas les obligations découlant de la présente loi. Cet avertissement a le caractère d'une sanction."

[25] The new EU Data Protection Regulation points out in its sanction regime that "in case of a first breach, a written warning may be sent and it shall not impose any sanction, if: (a) a physical person carries out the processing of personal data without commercial interest, (b) or a company or organization employing less than 250 workers processes personal data only as ancillary activity of its main activity."

Table 6.10 Warning in writing and sanctions

	2007	2008	2009	2010	2011	2012
Economic sanctions	342	535	661	591	505	863
Warning in writing					312 (38 %)	352 (29 %)

- An AEPD warning in writing gives the infringer the opportunity to adopt corrective measures. If it fails to do so, sanctioning proceedings will start.

As might have been predicted, despite the restrictive conditions for adopting a warning in writing, this new enforcement tool has had a remarkable impact (Table 6.10).

The 2011–2012 biennium shows an overview of the impact of the sanctioning regime and, in particular, the role that the warning in writing is playing and may play in the future.

If the warning in writing is considered useful for a first infringement and added to the sanctions imposed in 2011 and 2012, figures show, again, the explosive increase in these years of AEPD sanctioning activity: 123 % more sanctions issued in 2011 than in 2010 and in 2012, an increase of 149 % (compared to 2011) or 183 % (over 2010).

However, after the 2011 reform, this evolution did not have an identical increase in economic sanctions and fines due to the number of warnings in writing: in 2011, warnings in writing accounted for 38 % (312) of the total number of adopted sanctions and, in 2012, for 29 % (352).

In 2011 and 2012, more than 70 % of warnings in writing were concentrated in the video surveillance sector followed by Internet services, professional activities, housing estates and land agent activities. However, the AEPD did not adopt warnings in writing – and therefore proceeded to inspect and, where appropriate, to sanction – in cases (1) where there was a lack of reduction of guilt or illegality involving impersonation on social networks on the Internet or fraudulent data collection on the Internet; (2) involving disclosure of sensitive data because of security breaches via the Internet or in judicial documents; (3) where the infringer was engaged in a high volume of data processing activity.[26]

The AEPD wanted to "humanise" the LOPD sanctioning system – first, by the practice of applying modulating and downgrading criteria in 2007–2010 and, second, with the 2011 legal reform. These reforms have largely fulfilled its ambitions, as evidenced by the AEPD 2011 Annual Report: "Just 14 % of fines were imposed without mitigation because in 86 % of cases sanctions have been modulated by warnings in writing or applying the mitigation criteria provided for paragraphs 4 and 5 of section 45 LOPD."[27]

---

[26] AEPD, *Memoria Anual*, 2011 and 2012. www.agpd.es

[27] AEPD, *Memoria Anual*, 2011, p. 23.

6.2.5 *A false legend: AEPD financing by fines as cause of its loss of objectivity*

A significant part of the prestige, authority and legitimacy earned by the AEPD inspection and sanctioning activity in the last 20 years has been lost because of the widespread belief – inside and beyond Spanish borders – that the extraordinary number and amount of fines imposed by the AEPD has been motivated by an AEPD effort to ensure it is self-financing and, therefore, able to maintain its own existence.

It is true that the AEPD finances almost all of its expenses with revenue from fines. This financial regime has remained unchanged since the AEPD was established in 1993; none of the legislative reforms since then has modified this status quo.[28]

Section 35.4 of the LOPD specifies that the AEPD should, for the fulfillment of its purposes, set out

- the economic resources at its disposition established annually in the national budget – which are marginal and purely testimonial – and
- its assets, including properties, products and incomes, and any other resources to which it may be legally entitled.

The AEPD Organizational Regulation from 1993 came with these provisions and states that the AEPD financial resources would be integrated by "incomes, ordinary and extraordinary arising from the exercise of its activities". This is the legal provision that enables the AEPD to finance itself by means of the fines that have been integrated into the AEPD budgets during the last two decades.

A different matter is to evaluate the effect of this funding model on AEPD sanctioning activity: the loss of the AEPD objectivity in the exercise of its sanctioning functions is an allegation that deserves an explanation and response.[29] The following are germane:

1. AEPD inspection and sanctioning activity is ineluctably mandated to comply with the law. Sanctioning without a pre-existing legal basis would be an unambiguous form of corruption.
2. The number of fines imposed by the AEPD does not have any correlation with the evolution of its annual budget. The AEPD budget increases or reductions show a strong difference with the ongoing increase in the number of fines. The latter do not generate an increase in AEPD human and material resources because this money remains in the AEPD bank accounts and is unavailable without other legal basis.
3. The draft AEPD budget is determined by the general guidelines laid down by the Government and Parliament. Budget changes are authorised by the AEPD

[28] *Diario de Sesiones del Congreso de los Diputados*, Committees, 2004, No. 154, p. 28.

[29] For an introductory analysis, see Gómez-Juarez Sidera, "Estudio del régimen sancionador de la LOPD", *Revista Española de Protección de Datos*, No. 4, January-June, 2008, pp. 159–173.

Director only when they do not increase its amount; the Minister of Economy or the Government must authorise any supplementary or extraordinary surpluses. The list of AEPD jobs is approved by the Government; AEPD jobs must comply with civil service legislation and staff salaries must be in accordance with the annual budgetary Act. In other words, AEPD human and material resources are indifferent to the amount of imposed fines (as evidenced by the gap between the explosive increase of complaints and the progressive increase of fines and limitations in the AEPD human and material resources).

4. During the last decade, the AEPD has implemented a strategy of reducing economic sanctions, first, by modulating and reducing fines and, subsequently, by proposing a legal reform in 2011 directly aimed at mitigating the repressive strategy. It would be illogical and contradictory if AEPD needed to fine companies to ensure it is self-financing.

6.3 Conclusion

As this paper shows, Spanish data protection law provides the toughest sanctioning regime in Europe. Since 1992, the effective protection of personal data has been sustained in inspections, investigations and, where appropriate, sanctions of all complaints lodged with the Data Protection Spanish Agency. However, with the 1999 and 2011 legislative reforms, this strict sanctioning system has been balanced by a preventive strategy that stimulates effective enforcement of such legislation.

The sanction regime laid down in the LORTARD (1992) changed with the LOPD (1999) and opened the door to "humanisation" of the sanctioning regime and a proactive strategy. The LOPD reform (2011) has integrated repression and proactivity in the same enforcement strategy. The analysis presented in this chapter shows that the evolution from sticks to carrots has been just as effective, if not more so, as enforcing privacy using the big stick approach.

References

Agencia Española de la Protección de Datos (AEPD), *Memoria Anual*, 2012. www.agpd.es

Calvo Rojas, Eduardo, "El régimen sancionador de la Ley Orgánica 15/1999, de 13 de diciembre, de protección de datos de carácter personal. El principio de proporcionalidad", in AEPD (ed.), *La potestad sancionadora de la Agencia Española de Protección de Datos*, Aranzadi, Cizur Menor (Navarra), 2008, pp. 20–21.

Casino Rubio, M., in AEPD (ed.), *La potestad sancionadora de la Agencia Española de Protección de Datos*, Aranzadi, Cizur Menor (Navarra), 2008.

Congreso de los Diputados, *Boletín Oficial de las Cortes Generales*, A, No. 60–14, 11/10/2010, pp. 364–367.

Espín Templado, E., in AEPD (ed.), *La potestad sancionadora de la Agencia Española de Protección de Datos*, Aranzadi, Cizur Menor (Navarra), 2008.

Fernández López, J.M., and J. Tornos Mas, in AEPD (ed.), *La potestad sancionadora de la Agencia Española de Protección de Datos*, Aranzadi, Cizur Menor (Navarra), 2008.

Gómez-Juarez Sidera, "Estudio del régimen sancionador de la LOPD", *Revista Española de Protección de Datos*, No. 4, January-June 2008, pp. 159–173.

Gutwirth, Serge, Ronald Leenes, Paul De Hert and Yves Poullet (eds.), *European Data Protection: in good health?*, Springer, Dordrecht, 2012.

López Calvo, J., "Actividad inspectora y procedimiento administrativo sancionador en materia de protección de datos personales", in AEPD (ed.), *La potestad sancionadora de la Agencia Española de Protección de Datos*, Aranzadi, Cizur Menor (Navarra), 2008, pp. 253–267.

Rallo, Artemi A., "Strengths and weaknesses of enforcement: the Spanish case", London Initiative Workshop: "Selective to be effective", London, 13 Dec 2007.

Rallo, Artemi A., "Data Protection in Europe: the Spanish Data Protection Agency", Georgetown University Law Center, Washington, DC, April 2010, pp. 10–12.

Rallo, Artemi A., "Development of the Agency's audit and sanctions policy in Spain: Trends regarding investigations, fines and other sanctions", 23rd Annual International Privacy Laws and Business Conference, St. John's College, Cambridge, 5–7 July 2010.

Rebollo Puig, Manuel, in AEPD (ed.), *La potestad sancionadora de la Agencia Española de Protección de Datos* (AAVV), Aranzadi, Cizur Menor (Navarra), 2008.

Reding, Viviane, "The EU Data protection reform: helping businesses thrive in the digital economy", 19 January 2014. http://europa.eu/rapid/press-release_SPEECH-14-37_en.htm

Tornos Más, J., "Potestad sancionadora de la Agencia Española de Protección de Datos y principio de proporcionalidad", in AEPD (ed.), *La potestad sancionadora de la Agencia Española de Protección de Datos*, Aranzadi, Cizur Menor (Navarra), 2008.

Chapter 7
Data Protection and Enforcement in Latin America and in Uruguay

Ana Brian Nougrères

7.1 Introduction

This chapter focuses on the evolution of the Latin American system for enforcing privacy and data protection in the last few years. Only 10 years ago, in the Latin American region, one would think of privacy as a fundamental right, and look for its foundations in sectoral regulation and in national constitutions. The Red IberoAmericana de Protección de Datos (the Ibero-American Data Protection Network) has had an important influence in the transformation of Latin American interest in data protection and its enforcement. Nowadays, in a process that is still ongoing, comprehensive laws on data protection have been adopted in many Latin America countries (Argentina 2000, Uruguay 2008, Mexico 2010, Peru 2011, Costa Rica 2011, Nicaragua 2012, Colombia 2012, Dominican Republic 2013). An analysis of the data protection systems of these countries tends to show how they follow the European approach to data protection.

A. Brian Nougrères (✉)
School of Engeneering, Universidad de Montevideo, Montevideo, Uruguay

Senate and Chamber of Representatives, Uruguayan Parliament, Montevideo, Uruguay

School of Law, Universidad de la República, Montevideo, Uruguay
e-mail: ana.brian@estudiojuridicobriann.com.uy

D. Wright, P. De Hert (eds.), *Enforcing Privacy*, Law, Governance and Technology Series 25, DOI 10.1007/978-3-319-25047-2_7

Argentina and Uruguay have met the adequacy standards set out in the EU Data Protection Directive (95/46/EC) as confirmed in Decision 2003/490/EC[1] and Decision 2012/484/EC[2] respectively.

This chapter reviews data protection in eight Latin American countries, particularly Uruguay. The country ratified the Convention for the Protection of Individuals with Regard to Automatic Processing of Personal Data (Convention 108 of the Council of Europe), which entered into force on 1 August 2013, making it the 45th country to be party to the Convention and the first non-European country to do so. Consequently, this chapter provides a more concise breakdown of the Uruguayan data protection system, analysing the scope of the law, the most important definitions, the recognition of data protection principles, its regime for international data transfers and the enforcement system.

The chapter analyses enforcement from several points of view. To focus on education and awareness, it examines some key articles from Uruguayan media as well as the Uruguayan data protection authority. The results of a preliminary study made on an unrepresentative sample of the Uruguayan population are shown. From the data collected, Brazil appears as a country that has a certain interest in the topic. The results of a Colombian survey are described too. Concerning sanctions, this chapter provides a comparative analysis of eight Latin American countries and their legal regimes. Finally, it examines some old and new examples of international co-operation.

7.2 Evolution of Data Protection Systems in Latin America

7.2.1 From habeas data to the European model

Data protection concerns appear in Latin America as a consequence of the growing importance of information technology and the assumption of the potential of information technologies to manipulate the rights of freedom, life and human dignity.

Technology has advanced to such an extent that a new design of the world has formed; people have adopted new ways to communicate, and human socialisation and interaction have changed as well. Changes can be observed at work, in education, culture, social development as well as the approach to health problems. Information has become a vital asset.

In this context, on one hand, data protection appears as one of the most important guarantees for individuals, as it makes possible the planning of the fundamentals of

---

[1] http://eur-lex.europa.eu/legal-content/EN/TXT/?uri=CELEX:32003D0490

[2] European Parliament and the Council, Commission Implementing Decision of 21 August 2012 pursuant to Directive 95/46/EC of the European Parliament and of the Council on the adequate protection of personal data by the Eastern Republic of Uruguay with regard to automated processing of personal data. http://eur-lex.europa.eu/legal-content/EN/TXT/PDF/?uri=CELEX:32012D0484&rid=1

human development in democracy, giving each citizen the possibility to express his or her opinion on public affairs, but also, on the other hand, generating serious risks, facilitating the use, match, organisation and comparison of data, which can be used to limit and control areas of individual freedom.

The law must stand to prevent discrimination and violation of human rights whenever there is a risk that collection and handling of information may be a factor in political, social or economic domination. Thus, the right to data protection is crucial for the development of free people in democratic societies.

At this point, the protection of personal data appears as a human right that requires our attention beyond the special consideration of the topic by the law. That is to say, even taking into account that Latin American legal systems do not follow the regime of the common law, even in the countries where there is no law regulating data protection, there is usually a bill of rights that can be applied to protect citizens and their personal data.

Personal data of Latin American individuals has always been protected as a right inherent to the human condition or a right that derives from the republican form of government. The Uruguayan Constitution (1967) is not an exception, and it provides that the application of the sections of the Constitution that acknowledge individual rights as well as those awarding rights and imposing duties on public authorities should not be impeded by the lack of pertinent regulations. Rights are protected using analogous law, general principles and generally accepted doctrines. Similar rules that appeal to doctrines to be applied when there is no specific regulation exist in other South American countries.

In addition, some Latin American constitutions regulate the habeas data action in an explicit way.[3] The habeas data action constitutes a quick and effective procedure that can be used for the protection of personal data. Originally aimed to obtain data, this action has come to guarantee the right of individuals for an adequate protection of their data. This is the case in Brazil,[4] Paraguay,[5] Peru,[6] Ecuador[7] and Venezuela,[8] with some differences in their regimes. The Constitution of Argentina, with similar conditions and purpose, regulates an "amparo action".[9] The habeas data action might be used to obtain information, to know the purpose of the collection of information, to correct data, to dissociate data, to reserve data, to encrypt data, to update data, etc.[10] However, from a practical perspective, this habeas data regime generally

---

[3] Wikipedia defines habeas data as a remedy designed to protect, by means of an individual complaint presented to a constitutional court, the image, privacy, honour, information self-determination and freedom of information of a person. http://en.wikipedia.org/wiki/Habeas_data

[4] 1988, Section 5 LXXII, LXXVII.

[5] 1992, Section 135.

[6] 1993, modified in 1995, Section 200 n° 3.

[7] 1998, modified in 2008, Section 92 (previously Section 94).

[8] 1999, Section 281.

[9] 1994, Section 43.

[10] Puccinelli, Oscar, "Evolución histórica y análisis de las diversas especies, subespecies, tipos y subtipos de habeas data en América Latina: un intento clasificador con fines didácticos", *Universitas*, No. 107, 2004, pp. 471–501. http://www.redalyc.org/articulo.oa?id=82510714

provides an "after the fact" solution that is rather expensive for individuals and does not offer adequate levels of certainty, given the difficulties in proving damages.

Other constitutions have rules about data protection: Among them are those of Portugal,[11] Colombia,[12] Argentina,[13] Bolivia,[14] Brazil,[15] Ecuador,[16] Honduras,[17] Mexico,[18] Nicaragua,[19] Panama,[20] Paraguay,[21] Peru,[22] Dominican Republic,[23] Venezuela[24] and Guatemala.[25] Other Latin American countries have a jus naturalistic point of view of data protection, and – when no explicit data protection law exists – the data protection principles are protected as part of the rights inherent to the human condition or personality that derive from the republican form of government.

A comparative law perspective shows there are several models for the protection of personal data, which we call systems. The fundamentals of all these systems are the data protection principles; they always imply an evaluation of data flows and the creation of rules for data processing, which include rights and responsibilities for the data owner and the data holder. Depending on time and space, the systems vary, the characteristics of consent are different, the need for an independent and autonomous data protection authority varies, the application of penalties has differences. Notwithstanding, there are certain patterns that enable us to classify data protection systems with a basis in general laws, systems organised by sectors of activities (health, financial, statistics, etc.) and systems based on binding corporate rules.

Nowadays, Latin America is changing its position on data protection. Its regime, as mentioned above, was characterised by a jus naturalistic approach and by the right of habeas data enabling individuals to complain in order to protect their privacy, honour, self-determination, and providing the way to correct registries, to update data, to take care of their personal information in order to keep it confidential. In addition to this, regulations following the European model are being implemented.

Nevertheless, this approach does not guarantee that Latin American countries have a proper way to enforce data protection, as it is not possible to transpose an enforcement regime as a natural human right if there is no regulation on the topic.

---

[11] 1976, Section 35.

[12] 2003, Section 15.

[13] 1994, Section 43.

[14] 2004, Section 130.

[15] 1988, Section 5, LXXII.

[16] 1998, modified in 2008, Section 66 n° 19 and 92.

[17] 2005, Section 182.

[18] 2007, Section 6; 2009 Section 16 and 73 XXIX-O, 2011 Section 20 C.V.

[19] 1987, Section 26.

[20] 2004, Section 42, 44.

[21] 1992, Section 135.

[22] 1993, Section 2 n° 6.

[23] 2010, Section 44 n°2 and 70.

[24] 1999, Section 28 and 281.

[25] 1985, Section 31.

Thus, in this period, the lack of enforcement measures characterises the Latin American regime on data protection.

Adopting the European system implies that international data transfers are prohibited unless the third country provides a certain degree of protection of the data. The European system has an integrated data protection framework that Latin America does not have, a framework that makes it easier for companies to transfer data from one country to another, and that makes it easier for data protection authorities to enforce effective control. The lack of integration of Latin American countries makes it difficult to transfer data complying with all regulations. Harmonisation and integration appear as important challenges that should be taken up by Latin American countries.

We can observe, too, a lack of independence in data protection authorities, who need to work autonomously to have the due authority to enforce the regime. For that purpose, data protection authorities need economic and human resources, as they confront the limited budgets allocated in public sectors. Thus, another challenge is to provide Latin American authorities with the necessary dose of independence and autonomy to proceed with their duties and to enforce the regime in places where it is regulated. Last but not least, more important efforts should be made in order to face the challenge of educating individuals and generating awareness of data protection principles.

Even though regulation is taking shape in Latin America following the model of the European system, there is much to be done to achieve the levels of protection that we can find in Europe and North America.

As the approach to data protection differs in the European Union and in the United States, and both try to influence Latin America's system, the role of companies becomes more important. It is especially important for companies to attend to the needs of international data flows. This is the reason why companies need to assume a proactive role, being transparent even if the law does not oblige them to be, complying with the rules even if no other company complies with them, building reputation, generating trust. This is the challenge for foreign companies that do business in Latin America. The same applies to Latin American companies that aim to do business outside Latin America. The challenge for Latin American countries is to offer a clear legal framework within which enterprises can develop their business.

7.2.2 *The Role of the Ibero-American Data Protection Network*

In the Latin American scene, the European model based on Directives 1995/46/EC and 2002/58/EC appears as an instrument that gives special importance to harmonisation between European countries and in the international framework, and subordinates the free movement of personal data to the existence of a minimum level of protection, which provides equal protection among states. It establishes a special regime for international data transfers, has special dispositions for the personnel in charge of the treatment of the information, develops the principle of quality of data, brings the concept of legitimate interest as a way to legitimate the processing of information, develops certain systems of self-regulation, reinforces the authority of the data protection authorities and creates the Article 29 Working Party.

At this point, several milestones should be mentioned when we consider regulation of personal data in Latin America. The first milestone coincided with the Ibero-American Summit of Heads of State and Government, held in Santa Cruz de la Sierra, Bolivia, in November 2003. Its Declaration states: "We are conscious that personal data protection is a fundamental right and we highlight the importance of Latin American regulatory initiatives to protect privacy such as the Declaration of La Antigua, Guatemala, June 2003, in which the Ibero-American Data Protection Network (Red IberoAmericana de Protección de Datos) was created, open to all countries of IberoAmerica."[26] Thus, data protection began to appear as a topic to be considered on the agenda of some legislators in Latin America.

The second milestone was the creation in 2003 of the Data Protection Ibero-American Network,[27] which the above-mentioned Declaration specially recognises. It was established as a result of the initiative put forward by the Spanish data protection authority on the occasion of the II Encuentro IberoAmericano de Protección de Datos, held in La Antigua, Guatemala, in 2003. This permanent forum, organised by the Spanish data protection agency and co-ordinated by its Secretary, has worked since its inception in the promotion of laws that guarantee data protection in the Latin American community, has worked hard to establish open channels of dialogue between Latin American countries, academic exchange, co-operation and seeking the goal of harmonised regulation.

The various documents[28] approved in the meetings of this forum constituted inspirational texts at a time when data protection regimes were beginning to be developed in Latin America. Seminars were held several times a year, which contributed to the training of government employees and public officials in data protection.

The approval of the document entitled "Guidelines for Ibero-American regulation in Data Protection" is the third milestone.[29] The document consists of recommendations for those Latin American countries that are leading a regulatory process in data protection modelled after the European system. If we study the recently adopted Latin American laws, we can recognise the concepts of the Guidelines in them.

[26] Secretaría General Iberoamericana, "Declaración de Santa Cruz de la Sierra: la inclusión social, motor del desarrollo de la Comunidad Iberoamericana", XIII Cumbre IberoAmericana de Jefes de Estado y de Gobierno, November 2003, section 45. http://segib.org/documentos/esp/DeclaraciondeSantaCruz.pdf

[27] More information about the Ibero-American Data Protection Network can be found here: http://www.redipd.org/index-ides-idphp.php

[28] Red Iberoamericana de Protección de Datos, "Declaración de Lisboa", V Encuentro Iberoamericano de Protección de Datos, 2007. http://www.redipd.org/documentacion/common/declaracion_2007_V_encuentro_es.pdf

[29] Brian Nougrères, Ana, "V Encuentro Iberoamericano de protección de datos personales. Declaración de Lisboa. Directrices para la armonización de la protección de datos en la comunidad Iberoamericana", *Anuario de Derecho Informático*, Tomo VIII, Fundación de Cultura Universitaria, Montevideo, Uruguay, 2009, pp. 497–516.

After considering its scope, terminology and basic principles (loyalty, lawfulness, purpose, proportionality, quality, transparency, responsibility, consent), these Guidelines analyse the peculiarities of international data flows and the rights of the data subject (access, rectification, deletion, opposition), encouraging the States to create mechanisms for the data subject to make proper use of his or her rights. These mechanisms consist of procedures for the prevention of infractions, the existence of proper supervisory staff, education, awareness, inspections, the performance of privacy impact assessment, the validation of self-regulation agreements, claims before the authorities and lawsuits.

A fourth milestone was that of the general Assembly of the Organisation of American States (OAS) in its 41st Ordinary Period of Sessions by Resolution AG/RES.2514 (XXXIX-O/09), which took account of the growing importance of privacy and data protection and the need to facilitate international data transfers. Consequently, the Department of International Law of the Secretariat for Legal Affairs of the OAS elaborated a document entitled "Preliminary Principles and Recommendations on Data Protection (The Protection of Personal Data)".[30] The document brings data protection to the consideration of OAS authorities, referring to laws on the topic of some countries and to the principles of access to public information and data protection.

7.3 Data protection systems in Latin America

As mentioned above, in the last 10 years or so, several Latin American countries have adopted laws on data protection that follow the European approach. The following section provides a short overview of these laws. Its aim is to show how the European data protection system has been adopted by several Latin American countries.

7.3.1 Argentina (2000)

Formal aspects

Laws regulating data protection in accordance with the European system made their first appearance in Latin America in Argentina with Law N° 25.326, which was passed in 2000. Three years later, the European Union recognised Argentina as having an appropriate standard of data protection.[31]

[30] Department of International Law of the Secretariat for Legal Affairs of the Organization of American States, "Preliminary Principles and Recommendations on Data Protection (The Protection of Personal Data)". http://www.oas.org/dil/CP-CAJP-2921-10_rev1_corr1_eng.pdf

[31] Commission Decision 2003/490/EC of 30 June 2003 pursuant to Directive 95/46/EC of the European Parliament and of the Council on the adequate protection of personal data in Argentina.

Scope

The law applies to personal data registered in any media, within public or private domains. The same regime is used for legal persons if they have domicile in Argentina (sections 1 and 2 of the law).

Definitions

For the purpose of the law, personal data is any kind of information that refers to an identified or identifiable person (section 2).

Principles

The principles stated in the law are: lawfulness (section 3), quality (section 4), access (section 4), informed consent (sections 5 and 6), security (section 9) and confidentiality (section 10).

International data transfers

The principle of limitation of subsequent data transfers appears in section 12 with some exceptions.

Data Protection Authority[32]

The Data Protection Authority rests on a National Direction (Direccción Nacional de Protección de Datos Personales), which has autonomous functions and depends on the Ministry of Justice and Human Rights, Secretary of Justice, Legislative Affairs and Human Rights of the central government of Argentina. The DPA Director is appointed by the Presidency with the agreement of the Senate, for a four-year term and he or she must be selected from persons with data protection experience. The DPA is assisted by a Consultant Council, composed of representatives from the Ministry of Justice, a judge, the chambers of companies who provide credit information, the central bank of Argentina, a consumers' association, the Argentinean institute of standardisation and insurance companies. These associations, mentioned in section 29 of Regulation N° 1558/2001, are invited to form the Consultant Council, but have no obligation to do so.

---

http://eur-lex.europa.eu/LexUriServ/LexUriServ.do?uri=CELEX:32003D0490:EN:HTML. See also section 25(6) of Directive 95/46/EC of the European Parliament and the Council of 24 October 1995 on the protection of individuals with regard to the processing of personal data and on the free movement of such data.

[32] Dirección Nacional de Protección de Datos Personales, Ministerio de Justicia y Derechos Humanos, Presidencia de la Nación. http://www.jus.gob.ar/datos-personales.aspx/

Rights, procedures and sanctions

Individuals have the right to information (sections 13 and 15), access (section 14), rectification, updating or suppression (section 16), confidentiality (section 16 of Regulation N°1558/2001). Non-compliance with the regulations may result in administrative sanctions, fines, suspension, closure or cancellation of the file, the register or the database (section 31). The judiciary may order criminal sanctions in cases involving false information or the disclosure of information that violates confidentiality or security protocols (section 32). A quick action to the judiciary (called "amparo") offers the possibility to the data subject of enforcing his or her rights in compliance with the principles on data protection and its regulation (section 33). Judicial resolutions must be registered with the data protection authority.

7.3.2 *Mexico (2010)*

Formal aspects

In 2007, the Mexican Congress reformed the Constitution (Constitución Política de los Estados Mexicanos), section 6 of which considers that personal data should be protected and that the disclosure of personal information contained in public files should be given special consideration. In 2009, sections 16 and 73 of the Constitution were modified and the rule becomes applicable to data held by private persons too as a consequence of the approval of several dispositions (Ley Federal de Transparencia y Acceso a la Información Pública Gubernamental and its corresponding regulation, Ley Federal de Protección de Datos Personales en Posesión de Particulares and its regulation). From then on, individual Mexican States began to regulate private databases containing personal data, with some peculiarities depending on the state involved.[33]

Scope

The Ley Federal de Protección de Datos Personales en Posesión de Particulares applies to personal data in possession of natural or legal persons in the private sector (with exceptions). The Ley Federal de Transparencia y Acceso a la Información Pública Gubernamental applies to personal data in the public domain.

[33] Instituto Federal de Acceso a la información pública, "Estados que cuentan con Legislación en Materia de Protección de Datos Personales en entes Públicos/Privados y Órgano encargado de su protección". http://www.redipd.org/legislacion/common/legislacion/mexico/Matriz_Datos_Personales_Estados_DVPEM_17_junio.pdf

Definitions

According to section 3.V. of the Ley Federal de Protección de Datos Personales en Posesión de Particulares, personal data is any information concerning an identified or identifiable natural person.

Principles

The principles stated in the law are lawfulness, consent, information, quality of the data, purpose, loyalty, proportionality, liability, security and confidentiality.

International data transfers

The general principle states that international data transfers are permitted when they are communicated in a privacy notice and the purpose is determined by the data subject. The privacy notice must contain a specific reference to consent for international data transfers (section 36 of the Ley Federal de Protección de Datos Personales en Posesión de Particulares). The law provides for certain cases in which consent is not required for international data transfers (section 37).

Data Protection Authority

The Mexican Data Protection Authority is the Instituto Federal de Acceso a la Información y Protección de Datos (IFAI). In 2013, IFAI informed the Congress about progress concerning data protection[34] as follows. Of the investigations carried out, 35 % concerned the private sector, 51 % the public sector, and the rest concerned both private and public sectors. Regarding sanctions, five procedures obliged five companies to pay fines totalling 21 million Mexican pesos (approximately US $1.5 million). The companies that were fined were from different sectors: pharmaceuticals, banking, sports, savings and health care. IFAI guarantees due process according to its data protection regulations. The IFAI report addresses other measures. Between them, we can see that consumer interest in data protection is growing: the number of telephone calls to IFAI and visits to its website have experienced considerable growth. Consumers seem mainly interested in privacy policies and have concerns about the regulations and the exercise of their rights of access, rectification, opposition and correction. Awareness, education and co-operation are key IFAI goals. Sections 210, 211 and 211 bis of the Criminal Code (Código Penal Federal) of 2009 contain provisions regarding criminal actions related to data protection and access.

---

[34] IFAI, "Informe al Congreso de la Unión respecto a la Protección de Datos Personales", 2013. http://inicio.ifai.org.mx

7.3.3 *Peru (2011)*

Formal aspects

On 3 July 2011, Peru published the Personal Data Protection Act No. 29.733,[35] which established a data protection authority. A regulation concerning its practical application was approved in March 2013 (Decreto Supremo N° 003-2013-JUS[36]).

Scope

The Peruvian data protection law is applicable to data subjects registered in any kind of media if the processing is done in Peru. Its administration covers both the public and private sectors. Section 3 admits two exceptions to that general principle. The first refers to databases created by natural persons for purposes related to their private or family life. The second exception concerns databases of the public administration concerning defence, public security, investigation and crime control.

Definitions

The law defines personal data in section 2.4 as any information about a natural person identified or identifiable by reasonably used means.

Principles

The law states some principles (lawfulness, consent, purpose, proportionality, quality, security, standardisation, due process, confidentiality), and states the importance of other principles not specially enunciated (section 12).

International data transfers

Section 15 of the law prohibits data transfers to countries that do not provide adequate levels of protection of personal data. The exceptions in section 15 include consent, international agreements, cases of international judicial co-operation, international co-operation in cases related to terrorism or dealing with illegal drugs or corrupt bank transfers, cases concerning the health of individuals, or when there is another disposition that refers to an exception to the application of section 15.

---

[35] Congreso de la República, Ley 29733 de Protección de Datos Personales, Diario Oficial El Peruano, Lima, Perú, 3 July 2011, pp. 445746–445753.

[36] Ministerio de Justicia y Derechos Humanos, Decreto Supremo N° 003-2013-JUS, Diario Oficial El Peruano, Lima, Peru, 22 March 2013, pp. 491320–491334.

Data Protection Authority[37]

Reporting to the Secretary of Justice and Human Rights, the Autoridad Nacional de Protección de Datos Personales has plans to open offices across Peru. It acts under the counsel of ONGEI (Oficina Nacional de Gobierno Electrónico e Informática), which is in charge of e-government in Peru and which reports to the President of the Council of Secretaries of State (Presidencia del Consejo de Ministros). ONGEI acts as a counseling institute, approves regulations and resolutions and has powers of inspection and enforcement.

Rights, procedures and sanctions

The Peruvian data protection authority can apply sanctions and its decisions are final. The procedures may begin at the initiative of the DPA or at the initiative of the data subject. The fact that the decisions are final opens the possibility of a contentious administrative action. The sanctions can be of different degrees of importance and the graduation is legally explained in sections 38–40 of the law. The law also offers the possibility of imposing fines. The action of habeas data is a possible procedure for the data subject, which can be used independently from the administrative procedure. A registry implemented according to the regulation shall contain the name of anyone sanctioned, the sanction imposed and the injunction issued. The DPA can also initiate criminal proceedings.[38]

7.3.4 Costa Rica (2011)

Formal aspects

On 7 July 2011, Costa Rica passed a comprehensive data protection law, N° 8968,[39] on the protection of persons in the processing of personal data, based on the European approach. In March 2013, the Tribunal Supremo de Elecciones published its regulation.[40] In April 2013, the President, together with the Secretary of Public

[37] Dirección General de Protección de Datos Personales. http://www.minjus.gob.pe/proteccion-de-datos-personales/

[38] According to laws N° 27309 (17 July 2000), N° 30096 (22 October 2013), N° 301171 (10 March 2014) and the Criminal Code (sections 154, 156, 157, 161–164 and 207).

[39] Asamblea Legislativa de la República de Costa Rica, "Protección de la persona frente al tratamiento de sus datos personales", La Gaceta N°170, 5 September 2011. http://www.archivonacional.go.cr/pdf/ley_8968_proteccion_datos_personales.pdf

[40] Presidencia de la República de Costa Rica and Ministro de Justicia y Paz, "Decreto Ejecutivo n° 37554-JP – Reglamento a la Ley de Protección de la Persona Frente al Tratamiento de sus Datos Personales", Alcance Digital N°42, LA Gaceta N° 45, 5 March 2013. http://www.tse.go.cr/pdf/normativa/reglamentoleyproteccionpersona.pdf

Finance and the Secretary of Science, Technology and Telecommunications, approved Directriz 046-H-MICITT on Cloud Computing for the Public Sector.

Scope

The law applies to personal data registered in databases, public or private, manual or automated, with the exception of those maintained for internal, personal or domestic purposes, if they are not to be sold or commercialised.

Definitions

The definition of personal data is comprehensive of all data that identifies a person or makes him or her identifiable. The data can be processed manually or by computer, and it can be processed by public or private persons. There are two exceptions in section 3 of the Regulation. The first is given to databases with internal, personal or domestic purposes, that can't be commercialised. The second is credit-related databases.

Principles

Section I of the law analyses the basic principles and rights: the right of self-determination (section 4 with the limitations imposed in section 8), informed consent (section 5), quality of information (section 6), the right of access and rectification (section 7). Security and confidentiality are also addressed in sections 10 and 11.

Data transfers

The data contained in databases can only be transferred when the data subject gives his or her express consent for the transfer (section 14 of the law and section 40 of the Regulation), under the conditions stated in the legal dispositions.

Data Protection Authority

The data protection authority is called PRODHAB (Agencia de Protección de Datos de los Habitantes). It reports to the Secretary of Justice and Peace, but has a certain degree of autonomy. It is in charge of its own resources and budget, and makes its own decisions with independence. The Director of PRODHAB takes nationwide decisions. He must have an academic degree relevant to data protection and must be well known professionally and morally. The Director is forbidden to have any relation with companies that collect or store personal data, as a legal representative or employee. The prohibition persists for two years after the person completes his or her functions at the company. The same impediment works for husband or wife, and for relatives until third degree of consanguinity or affinity. The same prohibitions apply to technical and administrative staff, who are elected by competition and on merit and are due the right of confidentiality and to ensure professional secrecy.

Rights, procedures and sanctions

All procedures can begin by a claim of the data subject or by the PRODHAB by itself. All claims must be presented at the PRODHAB. These procedures have very short deadlines. PRODHAB can undertake inspections. The decisions of the PRODHAB are subject to appeal. In case the PRODHAB orders those responsible for a database to proceed as required by the data subject, if those responsible for the database do not act as ordered, a fine might be imposed according to the importance of the offence (minor, serious or very serious). In addition to issuing fines, PRODHAB may initiate criminal proceedings, according to sections 196 bis, 217 bis and 229 bis of the Criminal Code.

7.3.5 Colombia (2012)

Formal aspects

The Colombian Congress passed a comprehensive law on data protection, N° 1581,[41] in 2012, completing the regulations of Law N° 1266[42] of 2008. In 2013, Regulation N° 1377[43] came into effect also regulating Law N° 1581. The text contains provisions on self-regulation and establishes the obligation of setting out policies for the processing of information, when an organisation registers a database. It permits the use of binding corporate rules to facilitate international transfers of data within the same group of companies.

---

[41] Congreso de Colombia, Ley Estatutaria N° 1581 "Por el cual se dictan disposiciones generales para la protección de datos personales", Colombia, 17 October 2012. http://www.alcaldiabogota.gov.co/sisjur/normas/Norma1.jsp?i=49981

[42] Congreso de la República de Colombia, Ley Estatutaria N° 1266 de 2008, "Por la cual se dictan las disposiciones generales del Hábeas Data y se regula el manejo de la información contenida en bases de datos personales, en especial la financiera, crediticia, comercial, de servicios y la proveniente de terceros países y se dictan otras disposiciones", Colombia, 31 December 2008. https://www.icetex.gov.co/dnnpro5/Portals/0/Documentos/Pagos/Ley1266.pdf

[43] Presidencia de la Republica y Ministerio de Comercia, Industria y Turismo de la Republica de Colombia, Decreto N° 1377 de 2013, "Por el cual se reglamenta parcialmente la ley 1581 de 2012", Colombia, 27 June 2013. http://www.alcaldiabogota.gov.co/sisjur/normas/Norma1.jsp?i=53646#0

Scope

The law applies to all personal data processed in Colombian territory or wherever Colombian law is applicable. Some exceptions apply according to section 2 of the law and section 2 of the Regulation. These include databases and files maintained in a personal or domestic environment, with the limitations established by the Constitutional Court in Judgment C-748 of 2011. Databases and files dealing with security and national defence, prevention, detection, monitoring and control of money laundering and financing terrorism; databases and files that contain information related to intelligence and counterintelligence (statutory Law N° 1621 of 2013 applies); databases and files of journalistic information and other editorial contents; databases and files related to financial, credit and commercial information are partially excluded according to Law N° 1266 of 2008. Databases and files that refer to population census are partially excluded according to Law N° 79 of 1993.[44]

Definitions

Personal data is any information related or that can be related to one or various natural persons who are identified or may be identified.

Principles

The principles stated in the law include lawfulness, purpose, freedom, proportionality, quality, transparency, access, security and confidentiality. The list of principles is open, and new principles might be added of equal value.

International data transfers

Section 26 of the law forbids international data transfers to countries with non-adequate levels of data protection.

Data Protection Authority

The data protection authority in Colombia depends on the Superintendencia de Industria y Comercio, by means of a delegated authority for data protection. The head of the authority is called Superintendente Delegado. Its budget depends on the general budget of Colombia.

[44] Remolina Angarita, Nelson, *Tratamiento de datos personales. Aproximación internacional y comentarios a la Ley 1581 de 2012*, Legis Editores SA, Bogotá, 2013, pp. 127–131.

Rights, procedures and sanctions

The data subject has the right to access, update and rectify his or her personal data, to ask for proof of consent, to be informed about the use of his or her personal data by the database controller, as well as to present claims according to the law and to ask for explanations. Depending on the case, the authority may impose fines according to the criteria in section 24 of the law, depending on how serious the infraction is.

Criminal offences

Several criminal offences may arise, according to Law N° 1273 of 2009. The penalty for such offences may consist of increasing the sanction imposed, for example, if the sanction imposed was a fine, the regulator could add another sanction consisting of a prohibition to act as a professional because the illegal act was done on a public server, or over official networks, or with a terrorist intention. Other criminal offences include interception of data (section 269 C of the Criminal Code), informatics harm (269), blocking of a network or an informatics system (269 B), and abusive access to an informatics system (269 A).

7.3.6 Nicaragua (2012)

Formal aspects

Law N° 787[45] of 29 March 2012 governs data protection in Nicaragua.

Scope

The law applies to data from natural and legal persons, which can be stored in public or private files.

Definitions

Personal data is all information that identifies a person or may make him or her identifiable.

---

[45] Asamblea Nacional de la República de Nicaragua, "Ley de Protección de Datos Personales N° 787", Diario Oficial La Gaceta, N°61, Nicaragua, 29 March 2012. http://legislacion.asamblea.gob.ni/normaweb.nsf/9e314815a08d4a6206257265005d21f9/e5d37e9b4827fc06062579ed0076ce1d?OpenDocument

Principles

The principles considered by the law are: proportionality, consent, purpose, confidentiality and security.

International data transfers

Section 14 of the law generally forbids international data transfers. The exceptions are: international collaboration with the judiciary, exchange of personal health data, epidemic research, banking transactions according to the law, transfers made to comply with international treaties ratified by Nicaragua or transfers that support international co-operation between intelligence agencies in regard to the crimes specified in section 14. There is a special procedure for the data transfers established in section 15, which attends the adequate compliance with data protection principles. It also establishes the obligation of communicating the transfer to the national data protection authority, which must be done once the transfer is done.

Data Protection Authority

The authority is the Dirección de Protección de Datos Personales, which reports to the Secretary of Finance. There is a Director in charge of the office.

Rights, procedure and sanctions

The rights of the data subject include: right to access his or her personal information, to rectify, modify, suppress, add, include, update or delete personal information. In addition to this, the data controller must guarantee access to the personal information collected within 10 days, and provide information on the methods of its compilation and the reasons why the data was collected, as well as information about any transfers of the data.

The rights to rectify, modify, suppress, include, update or delete shall be free of charge. The authority may conduct inspections and impose administrative sanctions such as subpoenas, suspension of the processing of personal data, closure or deletion of the files or databases, temporarily or definitively. The data subject may also use the data protection action to enforce his or her rights. The data protection authority may initiate a criminal action in the courts.

7.3.7 *Dominican Republic (2013)*

Formal aspects

The national Congress of the Dominican Republic approved Law N° 172-13,[46] titled Organic Law on Data Protection, on 13 December 2013.

Scope

The law applies to the protection of personal data stored in files, registers, databases or any other media, public or private, and aims to facilitate access to information. Section 4 sets out four exceptions to the application of the law: (1) data stored by natural persons on personal or domestic activities; (2) files the purpose which is investigation and intelligence-gathering for the prevention and punishment of crime; (3) files referring to deceased persons; (4) processing of data of legal persons and persons who work with legal persons if it only consists of name, surname, job, postal or virtual address, telephone and fax.

Definitions

When the law refers to personal data, it is referring to any information in numbers, letters, graphics, sound or any other medium that identifies a natural person or that makes him or her identifiable.

Principles

These concern lawfulness, quality, accuracy, access, information, purpose, consent, security, secrecy and loyalty.

International data transfers

These are only permitted in the cases set out in section 80, i.e., with the consent of the data subject; health data in cases determined by the law; bank transfers; transfers according to free trade agreements; international co-operation; execution of contracts; execution of pre-contractual measures; public interest; judicial international aid; transfer required by an international institution.

[46] Congreso Nacional de la República Dominicana, "Ley 172-13. Ley Orgánica sobre Protección de Datos de Carácter Personal", Dominican Republic, 13 December 2013. http://www.redipd.org/legislacion/common/legislacion/rep_dominicana/Ley_172_13_Proteccion_Datos_Caracter_Personal.pdf

Data Protection Authority

There are several data protection authorities. The authority named by section 30 of the law for the processing and exchange of information on credit history is the Superintendencia de Bancos. In regard to the public sector,[47] the Dirección General de Ética e Integridad Gubernamental (DIGEIG) and the Ministerio de Administración Pública act as data protection authorities according to Laws N° 200-04 and N° 41-08.

Rights, procedures and sanctions

Individuals have the right to consult their data in files or databases, as well as the right of access, rectification, deletion or opposition. The procedures are strict and protective of the data subject. Notwithstanding the reparation of the harm, the local data protection authority may impose fines according to section 84. Section 85 explains civil sanctions. Section 86 considers criminal sanctions, fines and remedies for the harm caused. Criminal actions can be filed according to Law N° 53-07.

7.4 Uruguay

Uruguay is playing a leading role in data protection in Latin America: it was the second Latin American country (after Argentina) to be recognised by the European Commission as a country that ensures an adequate level of data protection,[48] and it is the first non-European country to ratify Convention 108 of the Council of Europe.[49]

---

[47] Barinas, Berenice, Directora de Transparencia Gubernamental en la Dirección General de Ética e Integridad Gubernamental (DIGEIG), unreleased.

[48] European Parliament and the Council, Commission Implementing Decision of 21 August 2012 pursuant to Directive 95/46/EC of the European Parliament and of the Council on the adequate protection of personal data by the Eastern Republic of Uruguay with regard to automated processing of personal data. http://eur-lex.europa.eu/legal-content/EN/TXT/PDF/?uri=CELEX:32012D0484&rid=1

[49] Asamblea General del Poder Legislativo de la República Oriental del Uruguay, Ley 19.030, Convenio N°108 del Consejo de Europa para la protección de las personas con respecto al tratamiento automatizado de datos de carácter personal y Protocolo Adicional al convenio para la protección de las personas con respecto al tratamiento automatizado de datos de carácter personal, a las autoridades de control y a los flujos transfronterizos de datos. http://www.parlamento.gub.uy/leyes/AccesoTextoLey.asp?Ley=19030&Anchor=

7.4.1 *Formal aspects*

Law N° 18.331 of 11 August 2008[50] ("the Law") and its Regulation N° 414/009[51] of 31 August 2009 ("the Regulation") are the core of the Uruguayan data protection system, which follows the European data protection legal framework. Consequently, on 21 August 2012, the European Commission decided that Uruguay ensures an adequate level of protection within the meaning of section 25(6) of the Data Protection Directive (95/46/EC). Moreover, in 2013, Uruguay acceded to Convention 108 and its Additional Protocol.

7.4.2 *Scope of the Law and the Regulation*

The Uruguayan data protection regime applies to personal data likely to be collected, processed or subsequently used in any way, registered within public or private domains (section 3 of the law). If applicable, the same regime covers data of legal persons (section 2 of the law). However, both section 3 of the law and section 2 of the Regulation provide that the regime introduced by the law shall not be applicable in three situations. First, the Law shall not apply to domestic databases, which are defined by the Regulation as those developed in a strictly private sphere, such as files of letters or personal agendas. Second, the law shall not apply to databases that were created under or are regulated by specific provisions. Specific regulations, such as sectoral laws, regulate certain data, such as health data, statistics, children's data, financial data, and exchange of personal data within public offices. Third, the law does not apply in cases of public security, defence, state security, investigation and repression of crime.

These regulations apply when the processing of personal data is performed through databases or controllers located in Uruguay and executing their activities in Uruguay (section 4 a of the Regulation). If the database or controller is not located in Uruguay but the data is processed using means located in Uruguay, the Uruguayan law will be applicable (section 3 b of the Regulation). In the event that these means, located in Uruguay, are used only for transfers, the law requires the controller to appoint a representative with domicile and permanent residence in Uruguayan territory (section 3 of the Regulation).

[50] Asamblea General del Poder Legislativo de la República Oriental del Uruguay, Ley N° 18.331. Protección de datos personales y acción de habeas data. http://www.parlamento.gub.uy/leyes/AccesoTextoLey.asp?Ley=18331&aNCHOR=

[51] Presidencia de la República en Consejo de Ministros, Decreto 414/009. http://archivo.presidencia.gub.uy/_web/decretos/2009/08/813.pdf

7.4.3 *Definitions*

Section 4 D of the law defines personal data as any information referring to an identified or identifiable person. This definition includes information related to a legal person. Sensitive data are defined in section 4 E as data that reveal the racial or ethnic origins of a person, his or her political preferences, moral or religious beliefs, labour union affiliations and information related to health or sexual life. Section 4 D of the Regulation clarifies that the term health data includes data concerning degrees of disability of disabled persons as well as genetic information. The law defines a data processor as the person who performs the processing of personal data by itself or with other persons or institutions, on behalf of the data controller. The processing can be performed by a public authority or a private institution, a physical person or a legal entity, according to section 4 H of the law. The person responsible for the database or for the processing of personal data is the person who owns the database or the person who decides on its purpose, contents and use. This might be a physical or a legal person, a public entity or a private institution.

7.4.4 *Principles*

The Uruguayan law sets out various data protection principles. Informed consent, the basic principle of the Uruguayan data protection system, is regulated by section 9 of the law and Chapter III of the Regulation. Data should be processed for specific purposes, and can be used and transferred under the purpose limitation principle, stated in sections 5c and 6. Data should be accurate, appropriate, relevant and not excessive in relation to the purpose for which it is transferred and processed, according to sections 7 and 8. The transparency rule determines the obligation to inform the data subject about the processing of his or her data (section 13). Data controllers and processers must adopt technical and organisational measures to ensure security, the requirements for which appear in sections 5, 7, 8, 10 and 11 of the law and Chapter IV of the Regulation. In particular, the principle of limitation of subsequent transfers follows the European system of data protection, prohibiting transfers of personal data if a third country does not ensure an adequate level of data protection.

7.4.5 *International data transfers*

As stated above, the law prohibits transfers of personal data, unless the third country ensures an adequate level of data protection. Similarly, successive transfers of personal data from a third destination country to another country may only be permitted if an adequate level of protection is ensured. Following the European system, the

Uruguayan regime provides some exceptions to the general principle regarding prohibition of transfers. The first exception refers to situations in which the Uruguayan data protection authority authorises one transfer, or several transfers, of personal data to a third party country that, even though it does not ensure adequate level of protection, has a controller who offers adequate safeguards for the protection of privacy, of the rights of the individuals, and of the exercise of their rights. Such safeguards may result from contractual clauses.

Additionally, there are other exceptions excluded from authorisation, such as: (1) the unambiguous consent of the individual to the proposed transfer; (2) when the transfer is required for the execution of a contract between the individual and the controller, or for the implementation of pre-contractual measures taken at the request of the individual; (3) when the transfer is required for the formation or execution of a contract, or for a contract that will be executed in the interest of the individual between the controller and a third party; (4) when the transfer is needed or is legally required to safeguard an important public interest, or in order to recognise, exercise or defend a right in court proceedings; (5) when the transfer is needed in order to safeguard an individual's vital interest; (6) when the transfer is delivered from a registry which, according to the law, is intended to provide information to the public, and is open for public consultation, or by a person who can demonstrate a legitimate interest, provided that they fulfil the legally established requirements for doing so.

Finally, another set of exceptions to the general principle is regulated in the following terms: (1) international judicial co-operation, according to the relevant international instrument, be it a treaty or a convention, in accordance with the circumstances of the case; (2) exchange of medical data, when it is required in order to treat the person in question for reasons of public health or hygiene; (3) bank transfers or exchanges, with regard to the respective transactions, and in accordance with applicable law; (4) agreement under international treaties to which Uruguay is a party; (5) international co-operation between agencies to combat organised crime, terrorism or drug trafficking.

7.4.6 Data protection authority

The name of the Uruguayan data protection authority, created by section 31 of the law, is Unidad Reguladora y de Control de Datos Personales (URCDP). The management of the URCDP is in charge of an Executive Council, composed of three members. The first one is the Executive Director of AGESIC (the Uruguayan public authority in charge of all issues related to e-government and the information society). The other two members of the Executive Council are appointed by the Executive Power of the Republic.[52]

---

[52] The acts of the "Poder Ejecutivo" are those of the President of the Republic acting by himself or with one or several Secretaries of State (e.g., Secretary of Agriculture, of Foreign Affairs, of Defence, etc.).

The Executive Council works with the assistance of an Advisory Council of five members. Three are appointed by the Parliament, the Supreme Court and the Public Ministry; one represents academia and another the private sector.

The URCDP acts as the supervisory authority; it provides assistance and advice to individual data subjects regarding data protection; it establishes rules and regulations. It is also in charge of the register of databases. It monitors compliance with regulations, security and confidentiality. It issues opinions and has the power to request information and investigate topics related to privacy and protection of personal data, as well as applying enforcement mechanisms.

7.4.7 Rights and procedures

According to the regulations (sections 13–17 and 37–45 of the law and 9–14 and 29–33 of the Regulation), individuals have the right of access to all information which concerns them as well as the right to rectify all inaccurate data, the right to update data that concerns them, the right of inclusion and the right of deletion or opposition. This means that the data subject can demand any correction, updating, inclusion or deletion of personal data held in a database in the terms that follow.

Regarding the right of access, the data subject must request access to the equivalent of a controller of the database.[53] The database controller has to respond within five days. If the database controller thinks that the claim is not applicable, he must justify his refusal. The information must be provided clearly, with an explanation that can be easily understood. It should include all of the information referring to the data subject, and should not include the personal data of other people. It can be provided in written form, by electronic records, by telephone, images or any other means the data subject may prefer. If the database controller does not respond to the data subject's request, the data subject can make use of additional safeguards.

The data protection authority can study the case at the request of the data subject or upon its own initiative. In both cases, the authority can use its power of inspection before coming to terms in a resolution. The inspection can take place in the buildings housing the database or in any other building used by the database controller. In case the URCDP needs to enter a private home, it will need an authorisation or warrant from a competent judge. The DPA can inspect documents, books and files stored in a computer or in paper records. If needed, the URCDP can copy them or hold them for six days to study them. If necessary, the judiciary can extend this term.

The URCDP can also require the presence of the accused at its offices or even the presence of third persons in order to gain information. Any person who does not

[53] In Uruguay, we have two figures (proprietary and responsible); the law does not consider the existence of a controller: both proprietary and responsible of the database do what the controller does.

comply with an order to provide information to the URCDP can be fined (up to US $60,000). The URCDP can also order the suspension of the database for five days or its closure. If the data protection authority orders its closure, the judiciary can intervene within three days. If the judge appointed to study the case does not issue a resolution, the data protection authority proceeds with the closure. If the judge understands that it is not correct to proceed with the closure of the database, the data protection authority must obey its determination immediately, rescinding the adopted measure, even if the judge does not decide within three days.

Decisions of the URCDP are subject to appeal. There is also the legal possibility to file a habeas data action with the judiciary. In this case, the data subject presents the case to a judge, the accused is given the opportunity to articulate a defence, then evidence will be taken to trial, and the judge decides. The procedure is quick, the terms are short and cannot be extended.

Deletion of data will not proceed when there is a valid contract between the database controller and the data subject. Otherwise, the database controller must prove the data was deleted, and has the obligation of indicating if there has been a cession or a transfer of any of the suppressed data and identify the person to whom it was transferred.

7.4.8 Sanctions

According to the URCDP,[54] in 2012, it received 38 consultations and 89 complaints. The sanctions imposed by the Uruguayan data protection authority were divided as follows: two observations, one warning and one fine. In 2013, the URCDP received 31 queries and 43 complaints. The sanctions imposed were two observations, three warnings and four fines.[55] During 2014, the URCDP processed 19 consultations and 35 complaints. The sanctions imposed were eight observations, four warnings and 15 fines; one closure of the database was requested following its due procedure.[56]

If the sanctions applied by the Uruguayan data protection authority do not have the expected effect, the legislation provides procedural mechanisms for stronger enforcement, where the complainant is entitled to use judicial remedies, such as the

[54] Unidad Reguladora y de Control de Datos Personales, "*Memoria Anual 2012*". http://www.datospersonales.gub.uy/wps/wcm/connect/7e75d68040bc925f9debdfff29651486/Memoria+URCDP+2012.pdf?MOD=AJPERES&CONVERT_TO=url&CACHEID=7e75d68040bc925f9debdfff29651486

[55] Unidad Reguladora y de Control de Datos Personales, "*Memoria Anual 2013*". http://www.datospersonales.gub.uy/wps/wcm/connect/b875f280442d54e1a8d2e96d575befd1/Memoria+URCDP+2013.pdf?MOD=AJPERES&CONVERT_TO=url&CACHEID=b875f280442d54e1a8d2e96d575befd1

[56] Unidad Reguladora y de Control de Datos Personales, "Memoria Anual 2014". E-book. Limited edition.

habeas data action, which is a quick procedure enabling the data subject to take the data controller to court.

7.4.9 *Crimes*

Even though the Uruguayan Data Protection Act does not consider criminal acts specifically, other legislation may apply in cases related to data protection. For example: Law N° 18.600 refers to data contained in electronic documents; fraud is punished according to the Criminal Code (section 347); data protection of children is considered in Law N° 17559 and N° 17815; electronic surveillance is regulated by Law N° 18494. An Informatics Crimes Bill[57] is considering identity theft, non-authorised access to informatics systems, informatics harm, informatics fraud and abuse of personal data. The bill establishes fines and penalties of three to eight years in jail according to the crime committed.

7.5 Enforcement

There are three main courses of action to enforce privacy. The first is education and generating awareness. The second is the imposition of administrative sanctions (warnings, fines, suspension or closure of databases), civil penalties or criminal proceedings. The third relates to international co-operation.

7.5.1 *Education and awareness*

All data protection authorities are concerned about education and awareness, and they work at it at different levels and with different budgets.

In the case of Uruguay, the URCDP web page[58] shows an online course and several actions undertaken in 2013. The first action consisted of meetings with directors and employees of the ministry of agriculture. The second consisted of participation at a seminar aimed at policemen and discussed data protection, information security, data breaches, cyber bullying, intelligence and education. Officials from different levels at the Ministry of Interior Affairs participated. URCDP also

[57] Presidencia de La República, Consejo de Ministros, "Delitos Informáticos", 16 May 2014. http://archivo.presidencia.gub.uy/sci/proyectos/2014/05/mec_1229.pdf

[58] Unidad Reguladora y de Control de Datos Personales, *Memoria Anual 2013*, pp. 38–40. http://www.datospersonales.gub.uy/wps/wcm/connect/b875f280442d54e1a8d2e96d575befd1/Memoria+URCDP+2013.pdf?MOD=AJPERES&CONVERT_TO=url&CACHEID=b875f280442d54e1a8d2e96d575befd1

met with telecommunications operators. It conducted two activities concerning children, giving school teachers illustrative documents and organising a competition between schools related to the value of data. It also provided training to informatics companies and to the College of Accountants and of Real Estate Administrators.

During 2014, the online course continued on the URCDP web page and the competition for school students got a new 2014 edition. At the same time, some educational actions took place. The first one consisted of visits to different parts of the country with lectures to employees and lawyers of public offices in Canelones, Colonia, Flores, Maldonado, Paysandú, Rivera and San José. The lectures were on e-government and data protection and given to a total of 235 participants. Several meetings focused on awareness were organised with educational authorities (ANEP, UTU, CODICEN, Ceibal, INJU, centros MEC) as well as IICA and the mayoralties of Canelones and Rocha. As exposed by the URCDP, its intention is to generate a group of educated and conscious people on data protection who will be responsible for promulgating the concepts across the country.[59] One might assume that the Snowden revelations would have had a good effect in raising awareness about privacy – and they did influence the press – but it is not so apparent that they have influenced the general population of our countries. An analysis of the Uruguayan press revealed different reactions. In October 2013 when *El País*[60] carried a story about the reactions of Brazil, Mexico, France and Germany to electronic spying by the NSA,[61] some reader comments suggested they did not make the connection with data protection.

When Facebook made public the number of requests from law enforcement agencies for access during the first semester of 2013, a Uruguayan newspaper[62] carried an analysis that showed 12,000 requests came from the US and 14,000 from the rest of the world. Some numbers are interesting: India made 3,000 requests, Brazil made 715, Chile made 215. The 715 requests from Brazil involved 857 Facebook accounts and the information released by the company was on 33 % of the cases. Chile requested information on 215 cases related to 340 accounts, and it succeeded with 68 % of its petitions. Readers made no comments on this story. Nor did they make any comments on similar information released by Yahoo.[63]

---

[59] Unidad Reguladora de Control de Datos Personales, "Memoria Anual URCDP 2014".

[60] One of the two most read newspapers by Uruguayans.

[61] AFP, ANSA, AP, "Espionaje irrita a los aliados de EE.UU, que piensan en represalias", published in *El País*, 26 Oct 2013. http://www.elpais.com.uy/mundo/espionaje-irrita-aliados-ee-uu.html#article-comments

[62] Emol, GDA, "Facebook detalla la cantidad de solicitudes de información en 2013", published in *El País*, 27 August 2013. http://www.elpais.com.uy/vida-actual/facebook-detalla-cantidad-solicitudes-informacion.html

[63] AFP, "Yahoo! también recibió miles de solicitudes de información", published in *El País*, 18 June 2013. http://www.elpais.com.uy/vida-actual/yahoo-recibio-miles-solicitudes-informacion.html

When Apple made public the fact that, during the first semester of 2013, US authorities asked for information between 4,000 and 5,000 times, generally in regard to criminal investigations, disappeared children, suicides or lost people, the news[64] did not receive any comments from readers.

The arrest of Google's most senior executive in Brazil, in September 2012, after the company failed to take down YouTube videos attacking a local mayoral candidate,[65] and the statistics of Google's transparency index,[66] show that requests for subject access as a consequence of a suspicion of defamation is especially noteworthy in this country (with 34 % of judicial petitions and 10 % of administrative petitions). They indicate a certain consideration of data protection. When we examine the subject of access requests to Google, privacy and security appear in fourth place (after electoral law and identity theft), with 6 % of judicial orders and 2 % of orders coming from State authorities. Identity theft, which appears in third place in Google's transparency statistics, accounts for 7 % of judicial petitions for access and 2 % of disclosure orders received from police or other administrative authorities.

Preliminary studies of a non-demonstrative sample of the population in Uruguay aged 22 and older show that 33 % of the population regard what is being offered as an exchange for their data before releasing them. With regard to privacy, people's major concern is that they might suffer from identity theft of their credit cards (37 %). Nineteen per cent of the sample share data in social networks exclusively with family and friends. Thirty-eight per cent declare that they personally did not have any security breach during the last five years and 50 % assured that they would not approve the use of cookies at the websites they visit. Forty-three per cent never read an entire privacy policy. Forty-eight per cent feel that they are in control of their personal data. The most popular way of protecting privacy is to use a long password for e-mails (28 %). Thirty-eight per cent of those surveyed declared that neither companies nor government organisations respect their personal data, but only 3 % said that they filed a claim under the data protection law. Forty-nine per cent consider that their data are used for different purposes to those authorised by the data subject, and 59 % consider the importance of consent to legitimate the use of personal data by third parties. Thirty-five per cent understand that privacy policies are abusive, 55 % disagree with the fact that search engines collect their data. Eighty-four per cent believe that the data protection authority of their country cannot defend them adequately if a security breach occurs or if their personal data are collected by means of the Internet from other countries.

---

[64] AFP, "Apple recibió 4.000 pedidos de la NSA", published in *El País*, 17 June 2013. http://www.elpais.com.uy/vida-actual/apple-recibio-pedidos-nsa.html

[65] Brocchetto, Marilia, "Autoridades de Brasil liberan al director de Google en ese país", CNN Mexico, 26 Sept 2012. http://mexico.cnn.com/mundo/2012/09/26/autoridades-de-brasil-liberan-al-director-de-google-en-ese-pais

[66] Google, "Informe de Transparencia", 2010–2013. http://www.google.com/transparencyreport/removals/government/BR/

Similar research on 573 responses in Colombia[67] drew the following conclusions. Fifty-four per cent of those surveyed have a pragmatic vision of data protection and would share their personal data depending on what is offered in exchange. Their major concern about privacy is fear that they might become the object of an identity theft of their credit cards (25 %). They share personal data on social networks only with family and friends (49 %). Fifty-nine per cent did not suffer a violation of their privacy in the last five years. Eighty-one per cent would not like Internet sites using cookies to track their surfing interests. Sixty-six per cent have never read a complete privacy policy. Eighty per cent feel that they are not in control of their personal data. When asked about options recently adopted to protect privacy, 20 % admitted they had opted for a long password on their e-mail. Fifty-three per cent believe that personal data are not respected in either the public or private sectors. Seventy-eight per cent have never filed a complaint about violation of their personal data. Ninety-seven per cent believe in the importance of personal consent or authorisation for the collection and use of personal data, but 79 % believe that companies and the State use their personal data for purposes different from those to which they consented or are lawful. Seventy-six per cent understand that privacy policies and security policies in social networks are abusive. Eighty-seven per cent disagree that search engines collect their data and 84 % believe that the data protection authority of their country cannot defend them adequately if a security breach occurs or their personal data are collected via the Internet from other countries.

7.5.2 Administrative sanctions, civil penalties and crimes

The following table shows the sanctions applied by Latin American countries that approved comprehensive laws on data protection. The sanctions were imposed according to what is stated in Law N° 25326 of Argentina, Law N° 18331 of Uruguay, Mexican Ley Federal de Protección de Datos Personales en Posesión de Particulares, Law N° 29733 of Peru, Law N° 8968 of Costa Rica, Law N° 787 of Nicaragua, Law N° 1581 of Colombia and Law N° 172-13 of Dominican Republic.

[67] Remolina, Nelson, "Resultado de la encuesta privacidad y datos personales (Colombia)", in Observatorio Ciro Angarita Barón sobre la protección de datos personales en Colombia, Universidad de los Andes, 17 Feb 2014. http://habeasdatacolombia.uniandes.edu.co/wp-content/uploads/Resultados-encuesta-sobre-privacidad-20141.pdf

	Argentina	Uruguay	México	Peru	Costa Rica	Nicaragua	Colombia	Dominican Republic
Law	25326	18331	Ley Federal de Protección de Datos Personales en Posesión de Particulares	29733	8968	787	1581	172-13
Date	04/10/2000	18/08/2008	05/07/2010	03/07/2011	07/07/2011	29/03/2012	17/10/2012	13/12/2013
Penalties								
Warning	√	√	√		√	√		
Fine	√	√	√	√	√		√	√
Suspension of the database	√	√					√	
Suspension of activities regarding treatment of personal data						√	√	√
Closure or cancellation of the file or database	√	√				√	√ (for sensitive data)	
Closure of the business							√	
Reparation of damages	√	√	√	√	√	√	√	√
Criminal penalties	√	√	√	√	√	√	√	√

The above table leads us to several conclusions. Indeed, economic penalties are the most popular among these countries and fines can be imposed in all of the countries surveyed, with the exception of Nicaragua. The civil reparation of damages and the imposition of criminal penalties appear to be the most popular instruments of enforcement, with no exceptions.

Unlawful practices by database controllers have different consequences. Argentina, Uruguay and Colombia regulate the suspension of the database. The laws of Nicaragua, Colombia and Dominican Republic enable the suspension of activities regarding the treatment of personal data. The laws of Argentina, Uruguay, Mexico and Nicaragua also provide mechanisms for the closure or deletion of the file or database, which is possible in Colombia only in cases involving sensitive data. Additionally, only in Colombia can a closure of the business be ordered.

Analysing the case of Uruguay, we can observe that the sanctioning procedures do not appear as highly applied, especially if we consider the data shown by the URCDP in June 2015.[68] As a matter of fact, during 2014, the sanctions imposed by the URCDP were eight observations, four warnings and 15 fines, as mentioned previously. One closure of a database was requested following its due procedure. During 2014, there were a total of 28 sanctions.

During the first semester of 2014, Colombia imposed 19 fines totalling US $252,000.[69]

7.5.3 *International co-operation*

In Latin America, we are far from achieving ideal data protection systems that work well with international transfers through the Internet, we must assume, thus, that from the international point of view the tools available for data protection are not enough;[70] anyway, co-operation must undoubtedly be the foundation of data protection, a principal instrument for the international enforcement of privacy principles.

The Ibero-American Network on Data Protection is a good example of co-operation as well as the exchange of knowledge and mutual assistance, as mentioned above. When it was created, nobody would have guessed the extent to which it would influence data protection systems towards the European standard.

---

[68] "URCDP presentó memoria 2014". http://www.datospersonales.gub.uy/inicio/institucional/noticias/urcdp+presento+memoria+2014+y+lanzo+concurso+tus+datos%2C+tu+decision

[69] "Informe sanciones primer semestre 2014", "Sanciones en materia de protección de datos personales", p. 15. http://www.sic.gov.co/drupal/sites/default/files/files/informe_consolidado_sanciones_1_2014_VERSION_SIC.pdf

[70] Remolina, Nelson, "Recolección internacional de datos personales: un reto del mundo post-internet", XXIII Edición del Premio de Protección Datos Personales, AEPD, 2014. "El sistema jurídico nacional, internacional o global no da respuestas útiles a los retos del ciberespacio. Es necesario crear un derecho para la nueva realidad socio tecnológica del siglo XXI. Para esto, es urgente que los reguladores se den cuenta que el mundo cambió después de internet y que las herramientas jurídicas del siglo XX son obsoletas e insuficientes."

Nevertheless, it has not generated any instrument to combat the problems from a lack of international co-operation.

Another good example of engaging in co-operation is the Warsaw Declaration on the "appification" of society issued in September 2013. In that Declaration, the 35th International Conference of Data Protection and Privacy Commissioners stated: "If encouraging a better privacy practice does not resort to sufficient effect, the commissioners will be ready to enforce the legislation in a global effort to reclaim user control. The privacy and data protection commissioners around the world intend to use the coming year to make serious steps in improving privacy and data protection in this area and will revisit the subject."[71]

The Resolution on Enforcement Co-operation[72] adopted by the 36th International Conference of Data Protection and Privacy Commissioners resolved to continue encouraging efforts to bring more effective co-operation in cross-border investigation and enforcement in appropriate cases, to accept the Global Cross Border Enforcement Co-operation Arrangement as a possible basis to facilitate enforcement co-operation, to continue working in co-ordination and enforcement and to support the development of a secure international information platform as stated in the Declaration.

These two declarations of intention show that enforcement is on the agenda of the most important fora and that the effort to provide adequate solutions on the topic is present in data protection authorities worldwide.

The EU Data Protection Directive also provides mechanisms for co-operation between the parties, such as that developed by the Article 29 Working Party when it decides on the adequacy of data protection systems of third countries. As well, Convention 108 of the Council of Europe and its Additional Protocol promote investigation and interventions to generate spaces of co-operation.

These legal instruments, nonetheless, have a scope of action that is limited only to those countries that met the adequacy standards set out in the EU Data Protection Directive 95/46/EC or to those that ratified Convention 108, respectively.

In addition, new mechanisms of international co-operation such as the Global Privacy Enforcement Network (GPEN) have appeared. This network was created in response to a Recommendation of the OECD governments adopted in 2007, and adopted an Action Plan in 2012. Its participants are privacy enforcement authorities responsible for enforcing laws or regulations protecting personal data and that have powers to conduct investigations or pursue enforcement proceedings. It seeks the exchange of information, encourages training opportunities and sharing of enforcement know-how, expertise and good practice, promotes dialogue, creates, maintains and supports processes or mechanisms of co-operation and undertakes or supports specific activities accordingly.

---

[71] International Conference of Data Protection and Privacy Commissioners, "Declaration of Warsaw", September 2013. https://privacyconference2013.org/web/pageFiles/kcfinder/files/ATT29312.pdf

[72] http://www.privacyconference2014.org/media/16605/Resolution-International-cooperation.pdf

The PHAEDRA Project ("Improving Practical and Helpful Co-operation between Data Protection Authorities") appears as an interesting effort to improve practical co-operation and co-ordination between data protection agencies, privacy commissioners and privacy enforcement authorities. Conscious that international enforcement is one of the weakest points in privacy and data protection governance, this consortium,[73] co-funded by the European Union under its Fundamental Rights and Citizenship programme, focuses on instruments for enforcing privacy, measures and factors to improve co-operation and co-ordination between data protection authorities and development of a repository for privacy enforcement authorities.

Both the Global Privacy Enforcement Network (GPEN) and the PHAEDRA Project constitute interesting efforts towards achieving a better level of international co-operation with regard to enforcement.

Notwithstanding these co-operation mechanisms, many more efforts are needed in order to fulfil Latin America's need for integration and harmonisation of data protection practices. This need is even more important if we consider that the United States has always had an important commercial influence over Latin America and that the European adequacy standard on data protection has acquired great importance in Latin America during the last decade.

7.6 Conclusions

During the last 10 years, Latin America has developed a different data protection regime. With Uruguay leading with the adequacy declaration according to the Data Protection Directive and the ratification of Convention 108, other Latin American countries are following. Data protection laws following the European model have been passed and number eight at present (Argentina, Uruguay, Mexico, Peru, Costa Rica, Nicaragua, Colombia and the Dominican Republic) and are increasing.

However, European data protection authorities exhibit an important degree of integration not yet matched by Latin America. This remains a challenge, one to which some difficulties will arise. Data protection authorities need to be more autonomous and independent, they need bigger budgets and more human resources. Only after achieving better degrees of autonomy will the authority to enforce effectively appear and, consequently, new forms of co-operation will materialise. It is evident that data protection systems are different in the United States and in the European Union, and both regimes have an important influence in Latin American countries.

How should Latin America respond to the challenges it faces?

First, the companies should assume a proactive role, clarifying how the company handles personal data, following all regulations, going beyond strict compliance.

---

[73] The PHAEDRA consortium has four partners: Vrije Universiteit Brussel (Belgium), Trilateral Research (UK), Inspector General for Personal Data Protection (GIODO) and Universidad Jaume I (Spain).

The companies need to build a positive reputation in Latin America, to generate trust in their products, services and brands, and by these means, they will get an edge over competitors.

Latin America needs to work on generating new processes of integration, while being aware of the legal dimensions of information security and what this implies in terms of privacy and data protection. Latin American countries must offer clear legal frameworks, give data protection authorities the means to work autonomously and with independence, to have true authority to enforce their privacy regimes, and continue educating and generating awareness among their populations.

References

Agencia de Protección de Datos de la Comunidad de Madrid, *Repertorio de Legislación y Jurisprudencia sobre Protección de Datos*, Civitas Ediciones SL, Madrid (España), 2004.

Arenas Ramiro, Mónica, *El derecho fundamental a la protección de datos personales en Europa*, Tirant lo Blanch, Valencia, Spain, 2006.

Brian Nougrères, Ana, "Seminario sobre marcos normativos en materia de protección de datos personales. Declaración de la Antigua y exposición sobre la situación en Uruguay", *Anuario de Derecho Informático*, Tomo IV, Fundación de Cultura Universitaria, Montevideo, Uruguay, 2005.

Brian Nougrères, Ana, "Reporte sobre el III Encuentro Iberoamericano de protección de datos y Declaración de Cartagena de Indias", *Anuario de Derecho Informático*, Tomo V, Fundación de Cultura Universitaria, Montevideo, Uruguay, 2006.

Brian Nougrères, Ana, "De la protección de datos personales y la cooperación internacional", *Anuario de Derecho Informático*, Tomo VI, Fundación de Cultura Universitaria, Montevideo, Uruguay, 2007

Brian Nougrères, Ana, "Reporte sobre el IV Encuentro Iberoamericano de protección de datos personales", *Anuario de Derecho Informático*, Tomo VI, Fundación de Cultura Universitaria, Montevideo, Uruguay, 2007.

Brian Nougrères, Ana, "El sistema legal uruguayo de protección de datos personales", in *Revista de Derecho, Comunicaciones y Nuevas Tecnologías 3*, Facultad de Derecho de la Universidad de los Andes, Colombia, 2007, pp. 3–30.

Brian Nougrères, Ana, "V Encuentro Iberoamericano de protección de datos personales. Declaración de Lisboa. Directrices para la armonización de la protección de datos en la comunidad Iberoamericana", *Anuario de Derecho Informático*, Tomo VIII, Fundación de Cultura Universitaria, Montevideo (Uruguay), 2009, pp. 497–516.

Brian Nougrères, Ana, *Protección de datos personales en Uruguay*, Ed. Tejeiro, Montevideo, Uruguay, 2009.

Brian Nougrères, Ana, "New Data Protection Laws in South America: Argentina, Uruguay", *The IAPP Privacy Academy 2011*, Dallas, 2011.

Brian Nougrères, Ana, "Data protection in the IberoAmerican Region*", Data Guidance*, 2012.

Brian Nougrères, Ana, "Iberoamérica: la evolución en la protección de datos personales", *The Public Voice 2012 Conference "Privacy rights are a global challenge*, Punta del Este, Uruguay, 2012.

Brian Nougrères, Ana, "Uruguay – Data Protection Overview", *Data Guidance*, in Comissão Nacional de Protecção de dados (ed.), *Colóquio Proteger os dados pessoais. Um desafio constante*, Fundação Calouste Gulbenkian, Lisboa, Portugal, 2004.

Chandler, Anupam, Lauren Gelman and Margaret Jane Radin, *Securing Privacy in the Internet Age*, Stanford University Press, Stanford, CA, 2008.

Chirino Sanchez, Alfredo, "Autodeterminación informativa y Estado de Derecho en la sociedad tecnológica. Una contribución al estudio de los retos y problemas existentes para alcanzar la protección del ciudadano ante el tratamiento electrónico de sus datos", unreleased.

Council of Europe, *Data protection. Compilation of Council of Europe texts*, Strasbourg, France, 2010. http://www.coe.int/t/dghl/standardsetting/dataprotection/dataprotcompil_en.pdf

Davara Rodríguez, Miguel Ángel, "Protección de datos", in *Anuario de derecho de las tecnologías de la información y de las comunicaciones (TIC) 2002*, Fundación AIRTEL Vodafone, Davara & Davara Asesores Jurídicos, Madrid, 2002.

Davara Fernández de Marcos, Isabel, "Protección de datos de carácter personal en Mexico: problemática jurídica y estatus normativo actual", *Protección de datos personales. Compendio de lecturas y legislación*, H Camara de Diputados, IFAI, ITAM, Alonso Editores, Mexico City, 2010, pp. 73–111.

Del Peso Navarro, Emilio, Ramos Gonzáles and Miguel Ángel, *Confidencialidad y seguridad de la información*, Ediciones Díaz de Santos SA, Madrid, 1994.

Delpiazzo, Carlos E., "Protección de los datos personales en tiempos de internet. El nuevo rostro del derecho a la intimidad", *Revista de Derecho de la Universidad Católica del Uruguay*, Amalio M. Fernández, Montevideo, Uruguay, 2002.

Delpiazzo, Carlos E., *Protección de Datos Personales y Acceso a la Información Pública*, Fundación de Cultura Universitaria, Montevideo, Uruguay, 2009.

Doneda, Danilo, *Da privacidade à proteção de dados pessoais*, Renovar, Rio de Janeiro, 2006.

Dozo, Dolores, and Pablo Martínez Quijano, *Glosario Iberoamericano de Protección de Datos*, Agencia Española de Protección de Datos, Habeasdat, 2013. http://www.redipd.org/noticias_todas/2014/tribuna/common/GLOSARIO_PDP.pdf

Durán Martínez, Augusto, *Estudios sobre derechos humanos*, Universidad Católica del Uruguay, Ingranussi, Montevideo (Uruguay), 1999.

Durán Martínez, Augusto, *Derecho a la protección de datos personales y al acceso a la información pública. Leyes Nª 18.331, de 11 de agosto de 2008 y Nª 18.381, de 17 de octubre de 2008*, Amalio M. Fernández, Montevideo (Uruguay), 2009.

European Union Agency for Fundamental Rights (FRA), *Access to data protection remedies in EU Member States*, Publications Office of the European Union, Luxembourg, 2013. http://fra.europa.eu/sites/default/files/fra-2014-access-data-protection-remedies_en_0.pdf

European Union Agency for Fundamental Rights (FRA), *Handbook on European data protection law*, Publications Office of the European Union, Luxembourg, 2014. http://fra.europa.eu/sites/default/files/fra-2014-handbook-data-protection-law-2nd-ed_en.pdf

Greenleaf, Graham, "The Influence of European Data Privacy Standards Outside Europe: Implications for Globalisation of Convention 108", *International Data Privacy Law*, Vol. 2, Issue 2, 2012.

Greenleaf, Graham, "Uruguay starts Convention 108's global journey with accession", International Report. *Privacy Laws & Business*, Issue 122, April 2013, pp. 20–23.

Hernández Crespo, Lourdes, "La Red Iberoamericana de Protección de Datos", *Agencia Española de Protección de Datos*, No. 12, July 2007, pp. 136–137.

H. Cámara de Diputados, Instituto Federal de Acceso a la Información Pública and Instituto Tecnológico Autónomo de México, *Protección de Datos Personales. Compedio de lecturas y legislación*, Alonso Editores, Mexico City, 2010.

Instituto de Acceso a la Información Pública del Distrito Federal, *Manual de autoformación sobre la Ley de Protección de Datos Personales para el Distrito Federal*, Corporación Mexicana de Impresión S.A. de C.V., Mexico City, 2009.

Kohnstamm, Jacob, "Effectiveness of personal data protection principles in the changing world", *International Data Protection Conference 2011*, Hungarian Official Journal Publisher, Budapest, 2011.

Marabotto Lugaro, Jorge, "Protección de Datos Personales y Garantías Constitucionales", *Ponencias del VI Congreso Iberoamericano de Derecho e informática*, Montevideo, Uruguay, 1998.

McEwen, Julie, and Stuart S. Shapiro, *U.S. Government Privacy. Essential Policies and Practices for Privacy Professionals*, The MITRE Corporation, IAPP, 2009.

Möller Méndez, Enrique Javier, and Ana Brian Nougrères, "Legal Responsibility for Information Technology Issues in Uruguay", *Cybercrime & Security*, March 2005, pp. 1–14.

Murillo de la Cueva, Pablo Lucas and José Luis Piñar Mañas, *El derecho a la autodeterminación informativa*, Fundación Coloquio Jurídico Europeo, Madrid, 2009.

Nauwelaerts, Wim, "The Belgian Privacy Commission's New Guidance on Information Security", *Bloomberg BNA World Data Protection Report*, Vol. 13, No. 5, May 2013. http://www.informationpolicycentre.com/files/Uploads/Documents/Centre/Belgian_Privacy_Commission_New_Guidance.pdf

Organisation for Economic Co-operation and Development (OECD), *Policies for Information Security & Privacy*, Paris, 2009.

Organisation for Economic Co-operation and Development (OECD), *The OECD privacy framework*, 2013. http://www.oecd.org/sti/ieconomy/oecd_privacy_framework.pdf

Perez Luño, Antonio Enrique, *Derechos Humanos, Estado de Derecho y Constitución*, 3rd ed., Editorial Tecnos, Madrid, 2010.

Privacy this week, "Latin America: Uruguay receives adequacy recognition from EU Commission", 4 Sept 2012. http://www.dataguidance.com/dataguidance_privacy_this_week.asp?id=1857

Privacy this week, "Uruguay accedes to Convention 108; Morocco to follow", 18 Apr 2013. http://www.dataguidance.com/dataguidance_privacy_this_week.asp?id=2012

Piñar Mañas, José Luis, Álvaro Canales Gil and Ma. José Blanco Antón, *Protección de datos personales de carácter personal en Iberoamérica. II Encuentro Iberoamericano de Protección de Datos, La Antigua – Guatemala, 2-6 de junio de 2003, Red Iberoamericana de Protección de Datos*, Agencia Española de Protección de Datos, Tirant lo Blanch, Valencia, Spain, 2005.

Piñar Mañas, José Luis, "El derecho fundamental a la protección de datos personales", *Protección de Datos de Carácter Personal en Iberoamerica*, Tirant lo Blanch, Valencia, Spain, 2005.

Piñar Mañas, José, *La Red Iberoamericana de Protección de Datos. Declaraciones y Documentos. Declarations and documents*, Agencia Española de Protección de Datos, Tirant lo Blanch, Valencia, Spain, 2006.

Piñar Mañas, José Luis, *¿Existe la privacidad?*, Universidad CEU San Pablo, Madrid, 2008.

Risso Ferrand, Martín J., *Derecho Constitucional*, Tomo I, Fundación de Cultura Universitaria, Montevideo, Uruguay, 2005.

Risso Ferrand, Martín J., "Control de la regularidad constitucional de las leyes que limitan o restringen derechos humanos en el derecho uruguayo", *Revista de Derecho III Universidad Católica Konrad Adenauer*, Amalio Fernández, Montevideo, Uruguay, 2000.

Real, Alberto Ramón, *Los principios generales del derecho como fuentes de derecho administrativo en el derecho positivo uruguayo*, Fundación de Cultura Universitaria, Montevideo, Uruguay, 2001.

Remolina Angarita, Nelson, *Tratamiento de datos personales. Aproximación internacional y comentarios a la Ley 1581 de 2012*, Legis Editores SA, Bogotá, Colombia, 2013.

Rodotà, Stefano, *A vida na sociedade da vigilância. A privacidade hoje*, Translated by Danilo Doneda and Luciana Cabral Doneda, Renovar, Rio de Janeiro, 2008.

Rodotà, Stefano, "Tecnología y derechos fundamentales", *Revista Datos Personales*, No. 8, Madrid, 2004.

Rundle, Mary, and Chris Konley, *Ethical Implications of Emerging Technologies: A Survey*, UNESCO, Paris, 2007. http://unesdoc.unesco.org/images/0014/001499/149992e.pdf

Saxby, Steve, "The International Journal of Technology Law and Practice", *Computer Law & Security Review*, Vol. 29, Issue 5, October 2013.

Simitis, Spiros, "Los fundamentos politicos y sociales de la protección de datos", *Revista Datos Personales*, No.17, Madrid, 2005.

Solove, Daniel J., "A taxonomy of privacy", in *University of Pennsylvania Law Review*, Vol. 154, No. 3, January 2006. https://www.law.upenn.edu/journals/lawreview/articles/volume154/issue3/Solove154U.Pa.L.Rev.477%282006%29.pdf

Solove, Daniel J., and Paul M. Schwartz, *Privacy law fundamentals*, IAPP, 2011.

Suñe, Emilio, *Tratado de Derecho Informático*, Vol. I, Ed. 2, Madrid, 2002.

Swiss Association of Privacy Commissioners, *Data Protection in Federal States: Supervision and Cooperation in the Field of Police and Justice*, Federal States Data Protection Authorities, Privatim, Schulthess, Vol. 4, Zurich, 2009.

Walter, Jean-Philippe, "The modernization of the convention of the Council of Europe for the protection of individuals with regard to automatic processing of personal data (ETS No. 108): moving from a European Standard towards a universal standard for data protection?", *International Data Protection Conference 2011*, Hungarian Official Journal Publisher, Budapest, 2011.

Part II
International Mechanisms

Chapter 8
The International Working Group on Data Protection in Telecommunications: Contributions to Transnational Privacy Enforcement

Alexander Dix

8.1 Introduction

Privacy today can no longer be enforced on a national level only. This recognition led to the formation in 1980 of the International Working Group on Data Protection in Telecommunications (also known as the "Berlin Group", because the Berlin Commissioner initiated it and has convened it ever since). For more than 30 years, the Group has worked in a specific, but ever more important, sector to formulate principles, recommendations and guidance for regulators, controllers and data subjects. Such principles are the first prerequisite for co-ordinated enforcement. At the same time, the Group has provided a unique global platform for an extensive exchange of information, which has led to common and co-ordinated enforcement actions against controllers such as Google. This chapter describes how the Berlin Group has contributed to privacy enforcement.

Data protection authorities have recently shifted their focus nationally and internationally from consultation and persuasion to enforcement. Indeed, some authorities even argue that they cannot do both – use a carrot and carry a big stick – at the same time. However, the majority of privacy regulators – depending of course on the legal framework within which they are operating – take the view that they can and should combine the two methods. Indeed, consultation and persuasion can be seen as one – and sometimes the most effective – way of enforcing privacy. In some jurisdictions, supervisory authorities have no (or at least no meaningful or efficient) sanctioning powers at their disposal. This unsatisfactory state of affairs in Europe will change when the General Data Protection Regulation comes into force in

A. Dix (✉)
Berlin Commissioner for Data Protection and Freedom of Information,
Friedrichstr. 219, D-10969 Berlin, Germany
e-mail: dix@eaid-berlin.de

D. Wright, P. De Hert (eds.), *Enforcing Privacy*, Law, Governance and Technology Series 25, DOI 10.1007/978-3-319-25047-2_8

early 2018. At any rate, enforcement in the stricter legal sense of imposing sanctions on controllers (if the legal framework provides for it) will always be the last step in a process. At the beginning of this process, especially in the transnational context, there is a need to analyse the commonalities and differences in national legal systems and to find ways to narrow differences in interpretation or to formulate a possible consensus on policies where there are no legal rules yet.

In this field, the International Working Group on Data Protection in Telecommunications has made considerable impact on consensus-building in the increasingly important telecoms and Internet sector within the community of data protection authorities. This Working Group has also turned into an important platform to share information that could be essential for national enforcement actions. Finally, the Group has provided for useful practical exchanges and comparisons between different enforcement cultures.

8.2 History and remit of the Working Group

In 1980, when the Berlin Data Protection Commissioner for the first time invited colleagues and experts to discuss the consequences of the so-called "new media" for the protection of privacy, he did so to allow for an informal exchange of views and to provide a platform to share experiences in different legal systems. At that time, telecommunications and media seemed to be a rather specialised area of data processing and data protection. With the advent of the Internet and its development into a "global mass medium", large parts of the processing of personal data take place via telecommunications and often are Internet-based. The 1980 meeting turned out to be the nucleus of the International Working Group on Data Protection in Telecommunications. This Group continues to meet twice a year (in Berlin in autumn and abroad in spring) and due to its regular venue, it is internationally also known as the "Berlin Group".

In 1989 – only weeks before the Berlin Wall collapsed – the 11th International Conference of Data Protection and Privacy Commissioners met in Berlin and adopted three resolutions. In the "Berlin Resolution",[1] the Conference referred to the rapid development of worldwide telecommunications and to rules regulating transborder data flows following the Convention 108 of the Council of Europe. In a second resolution,[2] the Conference specifically addressed the International Working Group on Data Protection and Telecommunications and chose the following words:

[1] Cf. Berliner Beauftragter für Datenschutz und Informationsfreiheit, International Documents on Data Protection in Telecommunications and Media 1983–2013, p. 30. The book contains all resolutions, working papers and memoranda adopted by the International Conference and the Berlin Group until 2013. These and all later documents are available at http://datenschutz-berlin.de/content/europa-international/international-working-group-on-data-protection-in-telecommunications-iwgdpt

[2] Ibid., p. 32.

> When we express opinions or make decisions on our countries, we have to take into account the international dimension of telecommunications networks and services. Information on events taking place beyond our national borders cannot be provided to us by our national operators only. Networks and services do not always develop at the same time or at the same pace in our countries. Experience has shown that the efficiency of data protection in this field depends – beyond mere principles – on practical measures... This is why the Conference agrees that this Working Group should continue its work in Berlin. Each delegation should have the opportunity to present its experiences in detail (analysis of the problems, possible solutions, adopted solutions).

These sentences describe well the remit of the Berlin Group and the resolution as a whole is considered to be the founding document of this Group, although it was only adopted nine years after the first meeting. In a third resolution, the Berlin Conference adopted recommendations drafted by the Working Group on data protection issues related to Integrated Services Digital Networks (ISDN).[3] Along these lines, the European members of the Working Group in 1990 adopted a Memorandum on the Proposal of the European Commission for a Council Directive on ISDN.[4] This was the first and last time that the Berlin Group specifically addressed a European regulatory issue. From then on, it focussed on subjects of an international nature. Today, the Group includes participants from outside Europe as well as Europeans. It has so far met in all continents except Africa.

8.3 Strength through informality

Since its first meeting, the Berlin Group has maintained its informal character. There are no written rules of procedure and therefore no formal process of invitation or admission. However, certain practices have been developed over the years. The Secretariat of the Group prepares the meetings and sends out the agenda, which is agreed at the start of each meeting. The Group includes representatives of data protection authorities, members of Internet governance bodies such as the Internet Engineering Task Force (IETF), independent experts and scientists. Representatives of Internet service providers such as Google, Facebook and Twitter have been invited to the meetings to present their policies and services.

Traditionally, the first item on the agenda concerns country reports from each jurisdiction, which in most cases are circulated before the meeting. Highlights of these reports are discussed in the Group. These country reports contain valuable practical information on issues, cases and enforcement procedures. Not only are they an inventory of different enforcement cultures but also they contribute to harmonised responses to global controllers, particularly Internet service providers. One notable example of how important this information-sharing tool has been in the history of the Group took place at the Granada meeting of the Working Group in

[3] Ibid., p. 35.

[4] Ibid., p. 102. The ISDN Directive was later replaced by the E-Privacy Directive 2002/58/EC.

2010. It was here that CNIL, the French data protection regulator, informed members of the Group for the first time about their findings that Google, while shooting pictures for their Street View service, was also covertly collecting data (including payload data such as passwords) from wireless access points. This led to administrative enforcement as well as criminal proceedings in various countries around the globe, including the United States. In several countries, regulators imposed fines, which were duly paid by Google.[5] Google said it stopped its Street View vehicles from harvesting Wi-Fi data.

The Group has adopted a large number of Reports, Opinions, Working Papers and Memoranda on a wide range of telecommunications- and Internet-related issues. One or more delegations draft these documents, which are then discussed during the meetings. After informal agreement on the contents, each document goes into a written procedure where the Secretariat circulates it not only to the participants in the meeting where it was discussed but also to all data protection authorities and experts who have participated in previous meetings. The Secretariat integrates proposed changes into the final text if they do not change the substance and publishes the final version online. In all other cases, the draft document is tabled again at the following meeting of the Group.

Initially, the Berlin Group adopted common positions. Since autumn 2001, the documents adopted by the Group are described as working papers or reports or guidance. This does not signal a change in substance and is in line with the practice of the Art. 29 Working Party of European data protection authorities. The documents accepted by the Berlin Group have no legally binding character. This may facilitate the consensus-building process in the Group, but it does not mean that the documents are without practical effect. Notably, the Budapest-Berlin Memorandum (Report and Guidance on Data Protection and Privacy on the Internet, 1996[6]), the Rome Memorandum (Report and Guidance on Privacy in Social Network Services, 2008[7]), the Sofia Memorandum (Report and Guidance on Road Pricing, 2009), the Granada Charter of Privacy in a Digital World (2010) and the Sopot Memorandum on Cloud Computing – Privacy and data protection issues (2012) had considerable impact on the international legal discourse as well as on policy-making and enforcing existing standards in certain countries. The Budapest-Berlin Memorandum was first discussed in Budapest in 1995 and finally adopted in Berlin 1996. It is one of the earliest documents addressing general and specific privacy issues linked with Internet use. In response to those who claim that the Internet cannot be regulated, the Memorandum referred to Prof. Joel Reidenberg's statement that "with power over physical situs points (users and infrastructure), states have… a potent tool in the ability to impose and enforce a certain degree of liability on networks and their

[5] The highest fine amounted to €1 million and was imposed by the Italian Data Protection Authority in April 2014 and paid by Google.

[6] Cf. footnote 1, p. 84.

[7] This and the three following documents mentioned in the text are available online, cf. footnote 1.

participants."[8] In many instances, the decision to enter the Internet and how to use it is subject to legal conditions under national data protection law.[9]

On several occasions, working papers adopted by the Berlin Group preceded and triggered similar and more extensive or specific papers in the Art. 29 Working Party or resolutions adopted by the International Conference of Data Protection and Privacy Commissioners to which the Berlin Group regularly reports. The example of ISDN (1998) was mentioned above. Later examples included search engines, the ISO privacy standard and social network services. Numerous other working papers have dealt with topics such as:

- telecommunications and privacy in labour relations (1997)
- cryptography (1997[10])
- reverse directories (1998)
- interception of private communications (1998)
- privacy-enhancing technologies on the World Wide Web (1998)
- intelligent software agents (1999)
- speaker recognition and voice analysis technology in telecommunications (1999)
- detection of fraud in telecommunications (2000)
- infomediaries (2000)
- copyright management (2000)
- online profiles (2000)
- registration of domain names (2000)
- publication of personal data contained in publicly available documents on the Internet (2000)
- data protection aspects of the Convention on Cyber-Crime of the Council of Europe (2000 and 2008)
- privacy and location information in mobile communication services (2001)
- data protection and online voting in parliamentary and other governmental elections (2001 and 2005)
- data protection aspects of digital certificates and public-key infrastructures (2001)
- childrens' privacy online – the role of parental consent (2002)
- use of unique identifiers in telecommunication terminal equipment: the example of IPv6 (2002)
- web-based telemedicine (2002)
- intrusion detection systems (2003)
- privacy and processing of images and sounds by multimedia messaging services (2004)

---

[8] Reidenberg, Joel, "Governing Networks and Rule-Making in Cyberspace", *Emory Law Journal*, Vol. 45, 1996, p. 911 [p. 929].

[9] Cf. footnote 1, p. 125.

[10] This Common Statement was in fact the only statement that was not adopted unanimously by the Working Group; the French CNIL did not take part in the adoption and the UK Data Protection Registrar had reservations.

- potential privacy risks associated with wireless networks (2004)
- freedom of expression and right to privacy regarding online publications (2004)
- means and procedures to combat cyber-fraud in a privacy-friendly way (2004)
- cyber security curricula integrating national, cultural and jurisdictional (including privacy) imperatives (2004)
- web browser caching of personal information in cybercafés (2005)
- online availability of electronic health records (2005)
- Internet telephony (VoIP) (2006)
- trusted computing, associated digital rights management technologies and privacy (2006)
- cross-border telemarketing (2007)
- e-ticketing in public transport (2007)
- privacy issues in the distribution of digital media content and digital television (2007)
- data protection and e-waste (2009)
- privacy risks in the re-use of e-mail accounts and similar information society services (2009)
- use of deep packet inspection for marketing purposes (2010)
- mobile processing of personal data and security (2010)
- Event Data Recorders (EDR) on vehicles (2011)
- electronic micropayment on the Internet (2011)
- privacy by design and smart metering: minimise personal information to maintain privacy (2011)
- web tracking and privacy (2012)
- publication of personal data on the web, website contents indexing and the protection of privacy (2013)
- privacy and aerial surveillance (2013).

The Berlin Group has discussed alternatives to face-to-face meetings such as video conferencing. Due to the disproportionate costs (compared to travel costs) such technology would cause, particularly for small data protection authorities, the Group has decided to continue meetings in person. As long as the technology costs do not decrease decisively, compromise solutions such as virtual workspaces and telephone conferences will be envisaged.

8.4 Harmonising national enforcement strategies: three examples

An early example of the kind of influence the Berlin Group has had on national enforcement strategies concerns databases of images depicting buildings. As early as in 1999, the Group adopted a Common Position[11] on this issue in which it dis-

[11] Cf. footnote 1, p. 168.

cussed the emerging business model of companies shooting pictures with cameras mounted on cars and selling them in digitised form on CD-ROMs. The Group stressed that there was a difference between an individual taking pictures of buildings and a company systematically collecting images of all buildings in a city or in all greater cities of a country for commercial purposes. The Group expressly recommended that national legislation – where this was not already the case – should provide the data subject (house owners, tenants) with a right to object against the systematic collection of such image data referring to his dwelling for commercial purposes.

This recommendation was taken up by German data protection authorities when Google started collecting data for its Street View service in 2008. They managed to get assurances from Google that a right to object would be implemented, which actually happened. However, despite the fact that the German members of the Berlin Group shared this information at the Granada meeting in 2010, Google did not implement such a right to object in other jurisdictions. A Swiss Federal Court imposed specific requirements on Google regarding the Street View service which did not include the right to object. Later, Google stopped the service in Germany and Switzerland altogether without giving any specific reasons. German data protection authorities still require the right to object whenever other companies offer comparable services.

The field of cloud computing offers a demonstration of how national enforcement may lead to international co-ordination in the framework of the Berlin Group. The Danish data protection authority (Datatilsynet) took the lead when they stopped a project by the City of Odense which had planned to outsource the whole processing of citizens' and staff data to a large US cloud service provider. However, since this company refused to disclose the name of the city in which jurisdiction the data were to be processed, the Datatilsynet stopped the project because it was impossible to evaluate the legality of this cloud computing exercise. Triggered by this case, the Berlin Group in 2012 adopted the Sopot Memorandum on Cloud Computing – Privacy and data protection issues[12] in which it stressed that the jurisdiction and place where a cloud provider is processing personal data may not be kept secret. Moreover, the level of data protection should not be lower in the cloud than with the original controller. After the revelations by Edward Snowden in 2013, this has become even more important.

In the field of social network services, the Berlin Group with the Rome Memorandum[13] adopted another early set of recommendations on privacy in social network services which influenced the discussions in the International Conference[14]

[12] Cf. footnote 1.

[13] Cf. footnote 1.

[14] 30th International Conference of Data Protection and Privacy Commissioners, Resolution on Privacy Protection in Social Network Services, 17 Oct 2008. http://www.bfdi.bund.de/EN/PublicRelations/Publications/functions/IntDSK_table.html?nn=410160&gtp=410186%3D2

as well as in the Art. 29 Working Party.[15] The Rome Memorandum called on regulators inter alia to introduce the right to pseudonymous use – i.e., to act in a social network service under a pseudonym – where not already part of the regulatory framework. In Germany, this has been the *lex lata* since 1997. The big social networks, Facebook, Google+ and Twitter, differ in their treatment of pseudonyms. Whereas Twitter has allowed for pseudonyms from the start, Facebook has always excluded the use of pseudonyms. Google in its social network service initially excluded pseudonyms as well, but changed its policy in 2011. Since then, Google allows for pseudonyms that are visible on the platform after registration under a real name. So two large social network service providers have followed the recommendation by the Berlin Group in this respect. Facebook, however, upholds its policy of excluding pseudonyms altogether and has been backed in this respect by the Irish Data Protection Commissioner in his extensive audit because the Irish legislature has not provided for a right to pseudonymous use. This shows that the recommendations adopted by the Berlin Group cannot by themselves bring about an international harmonisation of legal standards. But they can at least influence the discussion and describe best practices that should be adopted by corporations acting in this field.

Pseudonymous use is only one of numerous privacy issues linked with social network services. The Facebook case has highlighted a more generic problem of enforcing privacy rules against global players. The Office of the Irish Data Protection Commissioner is undoubtedly understaffed[16] compared to other European jurisdictions such as France or Germany. This may have influenced the decision of Facebook and other US providers such as Google and LinkedIn to have their European headquarters in Ireland although other considerations (e.g., tax legislation) could well have played a more prominent role in this decision. It is obvious that auditing large companies such as Facebook strains the scarce resources of a small data protection authority to its limits. The Irish Commissioner's audit of Facebook led to some changes in the service of the company, e.g., in the field of face recognition. However, basically the Commissioner accepted the argument brought forward by Facebook that users had no choice but to pay for the service with their personal data. Without disputing that this was a correct interpretation of Irish law, the example shows two major deficiencies in transnational enforcement: as long as the material rules on data protection as well as the resources of data protection authorities differ even within Europe, there is considerable room for *forum shopping* for companies (European or non-European). Furthermore, data protection laws and the agencies enforcing them need support from anti-trust law and anti-trust regulators.

---

[15] Article 29 Data Protection Working Party, Opinion 5/2009 on online social networking, WP 163, Brussels, Adopted on 12 June 2009. http://ec.europa.eu/justice/policies/privacy/docs/wpdocs/2009/wp163_en.pdf

[16] The Office had 30 members of staff at the time of the Facebook audit, with no legal expert among them.

Facebook has a near monopoly in Europe (with differences in the EU Member States).[17] Therefore, users have no real choice: if they want to stay in contact with most of their friends who are on Facebook, they cannot simply leave the platform and look for a more privacy-friendly network.

The new EU General Data Protection Regulation – once finally in force – should solve some of these issues. In particular, it will harmonise the regulatory standards and provide for a consistency mechanism between national data protection authorities in Europe. If there is a lead authority dealing with non-European companies as a "one-stop shop", it will have to co-operate more closely with other data protection authorities in other European countries to which these companies are directing their services.

8.5 International standards as a basis for global enforcement

Apart from the more specific examples mentioned above, the International Working Group has from the outset stressed the importance of common international legal standards in particular on telecommunications secrecy. This is particularly relevant after Edward Snowden's revelations have shown that even intelligence agencies in democratic states are massively collecting metadata as well as content data routinely without any specific suspicion on the basis of the "haystack" principle: In order to find a needle, you first have to pile up a haystack. Keywords such as "Full take" or "Mastering the Internet" indicate that these agencies accept hardly any legal limitations in their pursuit to guarantee "national security". They have apparently gone out of control. The European Data Protection Supervisor has aptly labeled this as "wild-west methods". There has been a massive loss of trust in the Internet and telecommunications services as a consequence.

The papers adopted by the Berlin Group consistently show how important the guarantee of telecommunications secrecy is in the information age. The Budapest-Berlin Memorandum of 1996[18] called for national and international law to state unequivocally that the process of communicating (e.g., via electronic mail) is also protected by the secrecy of telecommunications and correspondence. The Berlin Group then even suggested that "an international oversight mechanism should be established which could build on the existing structures such as the Internet Society and other bodies."[19] In their "Ten Commandments to protect Privacy in the Internet World" of 2000,[20] the Group referred to the remarks made by Justice Michael Kirby

[17] This is discussed in greater detail in Harbour, Pamela Jones, "The Transatlantic Perspective: Data Protection and Competition Law", in Hielke Hijmans and Herke Kranenbourg (eds.), *Data Protection anno 2014: How To Restore Trust?*, Contributions in honour of Peter Hustinx, European Data Protection Supervisor (2004–2014), Intersentia, Cambridge, UK, 2014, pp. 225–236.

[18] Cf. footnote 1, p. 126.

[19] Ibid.

[20] Cf. footnote 1, p. 214.

in his keynote speech at the International Conference of Data Protection and Privacy Commissioners in Hong Kong in 1999 where he called for new privacy principles adapted to contemporary technology. To this end, the Berlin Group proposed ten principles to be incorporated in multilateral privacy agreements or to be adopted as a separate document. These principles are

- Informational separation of powers (the equivalent of network neutrality)
- Telecommunications secrecy
- Data austerity (the equivalent of privacy by design)
- Right to anonymity
- Virtual right to be alone (e.g., the right not to be found by a search engine)
- Right to security (specifically the right to encrypt one's messages)
- Restriction on secondary use
- Transparency
- Subject access to personal data
- International complaints resolution.

These principles are still valid and necessary today but they have so far not been taken up by drafters of international agreements. In 2002, the Berlin Group in Auckland adopted a Working Paper on Telecommunications Surveillance[21] supporting the proposals made by the European Parliament in its resolution on the existence of a global system of interception of private and commercial communications (ECHELON) and called for their worldwide implementation. The Group stressed that these proposals had not lost their validity after the terrorist attacks of 11 September 2001. However, it was not until the whistleblower Edward Snowden made the world aware in summer 2013 that the US National Security Agency and the other intelligence agencies of the "Five Eyes" that had initiated ECHELON were systematically collecting metadata as well as content data on an industrial basis without any effective control. The Article 29 Working Party has stated that "metadata often yield information more easily than the actual contents of our communications do.… [I]n Europe metadata are personal data and should be protected".[22]

The Berlin Group reacted to these revelations by adopting the Working Paper on the Human Right to Telecommunications Secrecy in September 2013. Only weeks later, the 35th International Conference of Data Protection and Privacy Commissioners in Warsaw called for anchoring data protection and the protection of privacy in international law,[23] thereby reiterating calls which the Conference had made on earlier occasions in Montreux (2005), Madrid (2009) and Jerusalem (2010). Eventually, the Snowden revelations led to an initiative by the governments of Brazil, Germany, Switzerland and other countries to introduce a resolution into

---

[21] Cf. footnote 1, p. 234.

[22] Article 29 Data Protection Working Party, Opinion 04/2014 on surveillance of electronic communications for intelligence and national security purposes, WP 215, Brussels, Adopted on 10 April 2014. http://ec.europa.eu/justice/data-protection/article-29/documentation/opinion-recommendation/files/2014/wp215_en.pdf

[23] http://www.bfdi.bund.de/EN/PublicRelations/Publications/functions/IntDSK_table.html?nn=410160

the UN General Assembly on the protection of Privacy in the Digital Age, which was unanimously adopted on 18 December 2013.[24] Although this document, like all General Assembly Resolutions, lacks legally binding effect and – as "soft law" – is a political compromise, it starts the process of discussing possible international agreements to extend and enforce the protection of privacy in the twenty-first century. This process will take time, but its beginning has been long overdue.

8.6 Conclusions

The International Working Group on Data Protection in Telecommunications has made significant contributions to the international enforcement of privacy rules. Its remit is confined to telecommunications but this limitation is becoming more and more irrelevant due to the spread of online communications, particularly on the Internet, "at break-neck speed", as the European Commission once put it. In an era of ubiquitous surveillance on an industrial scale, the development and visible enforcement of global rules on telecommunications secrecy is crucial to regain the necessary trust in any form of remote communication provided by third parties.

References

Article 29 Data Protection Working Party, Opinion 5/2009 on online social networking, WP 163, Brussels, Adopted on 12 June 2009. http://ec.europa.eu/justice/policies/privacy/docs/wpdocs/2009/wp163_en.pdf

Article 29 Data Protection Working Party, Opinion 04/2014 on surveillance of electronic communications for intelligence and national security purposes, WP 215, Brussels, Adopted on 10 April 2014. http://ec.europa.eu/justice/data-protection/article-29/documentation/opinion-recommendation/files/2014/wp215_en.pdf

Berliner Beauftragter für Datenschutz und Informationsfreiheit, International Documents on Data Protection in Telecommunications and Media 1983–2013. http://datenschutz-berlin.de/content/europa-international/international-working-group-on-data-protection-in-telecommunications-iwgdpt

Harbour, Pamela Jones, "The Transatlantic Perspective: Data Protection and Competition Law", in Hielke Hijmans and Herke Kranenbourg (eds.), *Data Protection anno 2014: How To Restore Trust?*, Contributions in honour of Peter Hustinx, European Data Protection Supervisor (2004–2014), Intersentia, Cambridge, UK, 2014.

International Conference of Data Protection and Privacy Commissioners, Resolution on Privacy Protection in Social Network Services, 30th International Conference, 17 Oct 2008. http://www.bfdi.bund.de/EN/PublicRelations/Publications/functions/IntDSK_table.html?nn=410160&gtp=410186%3D2

Reidenberg, Joel, "Governing Networks and Rule-Making in Cyberspace", *Emory Law Journal*, Vol. 45, 1996.

[24] http://www.in.com/news/scitech/united-nations-adopts-resolution-to-protect-privacy-in-digital-age-51995799-in-1.html

Chapter 9
Enforcing Privacy Across Different Jurisdictions

Dan Svantesson

9.1 Introduction

In any context where there are differences in substantive law, jurisdictional issues arise. In light of the considerable differences in various data privacy laws, questions of jurisdiction and applicable law are of crucial importance. This chapter explores how such issues may impede the effective operation of data privacy laws – a topic that so far has gained surprisingly little attention. Concepts such as jurisdiction, recognition and enforcement – are of central importance to the topic addressed, and they are complex and developing. This chapter argues that *investigative jurisdiction* should be recognised as distinct to the jurisdiction to make rules, adjudicate disputes and enforce the law.

The chapter also argues that extraterritorial claims of jurisdiction may fill a function even where they are difficult to enforce. However, such claims must be expressed in more sophisticated terms than the binary test found in the current and forthcoming EU law, as well as in other data privacy laws around the globe.

In addition to a discussion of the legal considerations where data privacy agencies (DPAs) are seeking to enforce privacy across different jurisdictions, this chapter pays attention to the legal issues that arise where individuals are doing so. In this context, it notes that such private actions may have greater potential for being recognised and enforced in other countries compared to actions by DPAs. However, not all legal systems recognise privacy infringements as actionable under private law.

Next, the chapter discusses and analyses both successful and unsuccessful attempts by major Internet companies to rely on a particular corporate structure to meet legal challenges. It concludes that, while perhaps tactically useful in the short-term,

D. Svantesson (✉)
Faculty of Law, Bond University, University Drive, 4229 Gold Coast, QLD, Australia
e-mail: Dan_Svantesson@bond.edu.au; dasvante@bond.edu.au

D. Wright, P. De Hert (eds.), *Enforcing Privacy*, Law, Governance and Technology Series 25, DOI 10.1007/978-3-319-25047-2_9

such arguments are strategically unwise in that they create the image of major Internet corporations seeking to avoid the real issue of whether they reasonably should be forced to block the content in question.

Finally, the chapter examines the implications the International Covenant on Civil and Political Rights (ICCPR) may have on the enforcement of privacy across different jurisdictions. Here, Article 17(2) of the ICCPR, when read together with Article 2(1), appears to be a source of international law that urges signatory states to make fairly wide jurisdictional claims in relation to the protection of the privacy of people within their jurisdiction or territory.

9.1.1 Context

In light of the considerable differences in various countries' data privacy laws, questions of jurisdiction and applicable law are of crucial importance. Under a frank (some would say discourteous) analysis, the reasons for the lack of attention to these questions[1] may be attributable to the following factors: (1) experts in public international law have typically hidden behind the thinking on jurisdictional issues presented some 80 years ago in the Harvard Draft Convention on Jurisdiction with Respect to Crime 1935[2]; (2) in general, data privacy lawyers have lazily either presumed they understand the complex issues involved and therefore can ignore them, or simply put these issues into the "too hard" basket; and (3) scholars in the field of private international law (or "conflict of laws") have generally not yet even understood that jurisdictional issues in data privacy law are a major challenge within their field.

In any case, the importance of further work on the topic cannot be doubted.

9.1.2 Objectives

The challenges that arise in the context of enforcing privacy across different jurisdictions may be approached from different perspectives. We can distinguish enforcement by data privacy agencies from attempts by individuals to enforce privacy across different jurisdictions. Both these situations are discussed below.

---

[1] The rare examples of literature engaging with the topics addressed here include the writings of Professor Lee Bygrave (see, e.g., Bygrave, Lee A., *Data Privacy Law: An International Perspective*, Oxford University Press, Oxford, 2014; Dr Chris Kuner (see, e.g., Kuner, Christopher, *Transborder Data Flows and Data Privacy Law*, Oxford University Press, Oxford, 2013; Lokke Moerel (see, e.g., Moerel, Lokke, "The Long Arm of EU Data Protection Law: Does the Data Protection Directive Apply to Processing of Personal Data of EU Citizens by Websites Worldwide?", *International Data Privacy Law*, Vol. 1, No. 1, 2011 [pp. 23, 24]; and Professor Dan Svantesson (see, e.g., Svantesson, Dan, *Extraterritoriality in Data Privacy Law*, Ex Tuto Publishing, Copenhagen, 2013).

[2] See further: "Introductory Comment to the Harvard Draft Convention on Jurisdiction with Respect to Crime 1935", *American Journal of International Law*, 29 Supp 443, 1935.

The aim of this chapter is to introduce key considerations regarding jurisdiction, recognition and enforcement. I discuss, and give examples of, cross-border enforcement attempts by data privacy agencies, and such attempts by individuals. I also analyse in some detail the way the adoption of particular corporate structures are being used in the context of enforcing data privacy. I then turn to the impact of the International Covenant on Civil and Political Rights and pay particular attention to the online environment. Such a focus is easily justifiable in light of the fact that:

> When one examines academic writings, case law, and legislation relating to international jurisdiction, it becomes clear that, prior to the Internet, there never existed a situation in which a state purported to extend the application of its law to many millions of entities in different countries around the world based on the fact that they were accessible by, or processed data of, citizens of the home jurisdiction.[3]

9.1.3 *Methodology*

The objectives outlined above will be pursued through the method of legal dogmatic analysis. Thus, while this chapter examines the law of a selection of different jurisdictions, the main aim is not a comparative analysis as such. As stated above, the objective rather is to examine jurisdictional issues that affect the enforcement of privacy. Further, while examples mainly will be drawn from the European context, no claim is made of providing a comprehensive study of any particular jurisdiction. Rather, examples are drawn, in a somewhat eclectic manner, from a range of jurisdictions.

9.2 Key considerations

9.2.1 *Jurisdiction*

Any attempt at enforcing privacy laws takes its point of departure in the question of jurisdiction. In domestic cases, jurisdictional issues do not typically present any real concern. But as soon as a dispute has some form of international element, jurisdictional issues arise. In an increasingly global world, with data effortlessly flowing across national borders, more and more disputes have some form of international element, thus giving rise to issues of jurisdiction.

Wherever more than one country is willing to accept jurisdiction over a particular matter, the party initiating proceedings has a choice as to where to bring those proceedings. Critics of such a choice have termed it "forum shopping", and the

[3] Kuner, Christopher, *European Data Protection Law: Corporate Compliance and Regulation, 2nd ed.*, Oxford University Press, Oxford, 2007, pp. 123–124.

choice made will obviously affect the applicable law and, indeed, the outcome of the proceedings.

So far, experts have mainly discussed forum shopping in the context of cross-border defamation – in many ways a "cousin" to data privacy law. However, with an increase in data privacy actions, we may well also witness a rise in forum shopping in relation to data privacy law. After all, many such disputes will involve data processed in more than one jurisdiction, and affected individuals may have a choice of forum.

Such a development may not necessarily be a bad thing. Indeed, as Juenger points out: "But what is worse, from the perspective of their clients, than counsel who lack the imagination to ponder the advantages of wisely selecting among available fora?"[4] Juenger also notes the observation by Siehr[5] that "forum shopping may be beneficial because it allows an escape from substandard law"[6] and stresses that:

> [I]n practice choice-of-law considerations play but a minor role in counsel's selection of a forum. Attorneys usually serve their own convenience by litigating in their home territory. Some counsel, and their more sophisticated clients, may ponder the strategical advantages of different legal systems. But their choice of forum is generally influenced by such procedural considerations as cost, the quality of the trial bench and bar, the availability of evidence and of discovery devices, as well as the general legal climate of the particular country.[7]

At the same time, it is important that lawmakers create rules that prevent, or are resistant to, *abusive forum shopping*. As noted by Vischer: "As concurrent jurisdictions will always exist, international law can only propose remedies against excessive forum shopping".[8]

In any event, it is customary to distinguish between three different forms of jurisdiction:

1. Prescriptive (or legislative) jurisdiction;
2. Judicial (or adjudicative) jurisdiction; and
3. Enforcement jurisdiction.

Prescriptive (or legislative) jurisdiction relates to the power to make law in relation to a specific subject matter. Judicial (or adjudicative) jurisdiction, as the name suggests, deals with the power to adjudicate a particular matter. Enforcement jurisdiction relates to the power to enforce the law put in place, in the sense of, for example, arresting, prosecuting and/or punishing an individual under that law.

---

[4] Juenger, Friedrich K., "American and European Conflicts Law", *American Journal of Comparative Law*, Vol. 30, 1982, p. 128.

[5] Siehr, Ernst, "Domestic Relations in European Private International Law: European Equivalents to American Evolutions in Conflict of Laws", *American Journal of Comparative Law*, Vol. 30, 1982, p. 37.

[6] Ibid., p. 47.

[7] Ibid., p. 129.

[8] Vischer, F., "General Course on Private International Law", *Recueil des cours*, Vol. 232, 1992-I, p. 224 [p. 227].

However, elsewhere,[9] I have proposed that we distinguish a fourth category – a category of particular relevance for fields such as data privacy. This additional type of jurisdiction – that I call '*investigative jurisdiction*' – relates to the power to investigate a matter and must be kept separate from the jurisdiction to make rules, adjudicate disputes and enforce the law.

The instances where investigative jurisdiction plays a central role are numerous in the context of data privacy law and in areas such as consumer protection – areas where complaints often are best pursued by bodies such as privacy commissioners, ombudsmen and consumer protection agencies. Indeed, the crucial importance of distinguishing investigative jurisdiction from other forms of jurisdiction was at the core of a 2007 decision by the Federal Court of Canada. In *Lawson v Accusearch Inc dba Abika.com*,[10] the Privacy Commissioner of Canada was forced to defend, in court, her decision to decline to investigate a complaint made by Lawson of the Canadian Internet Policy and Public Interest Clinic against a US-based corporation. Harrington J of the Federal Court stated that:

> I agree with her [the Privacy Commissioner of Canada] that PIPEDA [*Personal Information Protection and Electronic Documents Act*] gives no indication that Parliament intended to legislate extraterritorially…. [However, the] Commissioner does not lose her power to investigate because she can neither subpoena the organization nor enter its premises in Wyoming.... It would be most regrettable indeed if Parliament gave the Commissioner jurisdiction to investigate foreigners who have Canadian sources of information only if those organizations voluntarily name names. Furthermore, even if an order against a non-resident might be ineffective, the Commissioner could target the Canadian sources of information.
>
> I conclude as a matter of statutory interpretation that the Commissioner had jurisdiction to investigate, and that such an investigation was not contingent upon Parliament having legislated extraterritorially[.][11]

To conclude this section, it is useful to reflect on the central role the question of jurisdiction plays in law, not least where law is applied to modern communications technology:

> What remains clear, however, is that questions of jurisdiction arise at the epicentre of the intersection of technology-mediated commerce and social governance; jurisdictional determinations tacitly address the social balance between providing incentives for entrepreneurship and providing recourse for harms. Through jurisdictional determinations, our courts make assessments regarding the social value of competing economic and personal interests.[12]

---

[9] Svantesson, Dan, *Extraterritoriality in Data Privacy Law*, Ex Tuto Publishing, Copenhagen, 2013 and Svantesson, Dan, "The Extraterritoriality of EU Data Privacy Law – Its Theoretical Justification and Its Practical Effect on U.S. Businesses", *Stanford Journal of International Law*, Vol. 50, No. 1, Winter 2014, pp. 53–117.

[10] *Lawson v Accusearch Inc dba Abika.com* [2007] 4 FCR 314.

[11] Ibid., pp. 28, 42, 43.

[12] Matwyshyn, Andrea M., "Of Nodes and Power Laws: A Network Theory Approach to Internet Jurisdiction Through Data Privacy", *Northwestern University Law Review*, Vol. 98, 2003–2004, p. 493 [p. 494].

9.2.2 *Recognition and enforcement*

Recognition means basically that the foreign judgment has the effect it has in its state of origin, while the enforcement of a foreign judgment means to "compel compliance ...through means such as attachment, committal, fine, sequestration, or execution".[13] Thus, as noted in *Dicey, Morris and Collins on the Conflict of Laws*, "while a court must recognize every foreign judgment which it enforces, it need not enforce every foreign judgment which it recognizes".[14]

Typically, the starting point is that the effective reach of a legal decision in one jurisdiction does not go beyond the borders of that jurisdiction. Thus, a decision by a Norwegian court is effective in Norway only. However, the ineffectiveness of this system is widely recognised and, as a result, arrangements are made amongst states for the mutual recognition and enforcement of judgments.

Nevertheless, getting a judgment recognised and enforced in a foreign jurisdiction is seldom easy and, in fact, the general complexity of getting foreign judgments recognised and enforced in a forum in which the defendant has assets works as a protection for defendants in international litigation. Indeed, in a sense, this area of law is self-balancing in that, for example, the severity of an action typically determines the size and significance of the resulting claim, which in turn determine whether such a claim is likely to be pursued across borders. Further, while a claimant is more likely to pursue a large, financially strong defendant across borders, such a defendant is better placed to ensure compliance with the applicable law in the first place and, indeed, better placed to defend an action than is a small, financially weak party.

One important consideration in the context of data privacy law is that, while judgments in private civil law disputes commonly are subject to mutual recognition arrangements, judgments in public, administrative and criminal disputes typically are not subject to such arrangements. Thus, from the perspective of this issue, the classification of data privacy law as private or public may be of great significance. Further, the private/public distinction is, of course, of relevance when we compare cross-border enforcement attempts by data privacy agencies and such attempts by individuals.

9.3 Enforcing privacy across different jurisdictions

Data protection authorities are often equipped, or at least expected, to actively enforce the data privacy laws of their respective countries. However, the actual level of enforcement activity appears limited in many countries with data privacy laws. Studies show that the low levels of compliance are due not so much to lack of formal

[13] Nygh, P., and P. Butt, *Butterworths Concise Australian Legal Dictionary*, 2nd ed., Butterworths, Sydney, 1998.

[14] L. Collins et al. (eds.), *Dicey, Morris and Collins on the Conflict of Laws*, 14th ed., Sweet and Maxwell, London, 2006, p. 567.

enforcement powers but rather to the fact that DPAs have not been given sufficient funding and other resources to expand their enforcement efforts.[15]

If the enforcement efforts are limited on the domestic level, they are, with a few notable exceptions, largely absent in the cross-border setting. This is, of course, only natural given that cross-border actions typically are more costly and complicated and require a greater commitment of resources. Considering also that the actual effectiveness of cross-border actions may depend on the co-operation of overseas agencies, it is no surprise that focus is placed on domestic matters where the lack of resources makes impossible the investigation of all matters arising.

The effect, however, is that there is little a data subject can hope for when an offender based overseas has infringed their data privacy rights. Thus, to a degree, the often overly wide claims of extraterritorial jurisdiction made in data privacy laws around the globe are symbolic in nature. At least in some instances, this is directly acknowledged. For example, in discussing the then proposed extraterritorial dimension of the *Personal Data Protection Act 2012* enacted in Singapore, the Ministry of Information, Communications and the Arts (MICA) observed:

> MICA is cognisant of the implementation challenges. In particular, where the organisation in question has no presence in Singapore, it would be difficult to carry out investigations into any complaint made in relation to an activity of the organisation, or to proceed with any enforcement action against the organisation. However, such coverage would act as deterrence for overseas companies to engage in activities that might result in a breach of the PDPA, and provide consistent treatment for local vis-à-vis overseas organisations with data-related operations in Singapore.[16]

This important quote highlights two reasons why extraterritorial claims are made despite the potential enforcement difficulties. First, there is a symbolic value in showing an attempt at treating domestic and foreign organisations equally. And second, the claim of an extraterritorial effect may have a deterrent effect. Elsewhere,[17] I have discussed this in terms of "bark jurisdiction" as opposed to a real attempt at "bite jurisdiction" – through the claim of extraterritoriality, states assert the international legitimacy of their attempts to protect the privacy of their residents.

---

[15] Bygrave, Lee A., *Data Privacy Law: An International Perspective*, Oxford University Press, Oxford, 2014, p. 189.

[16] Public Consultation Issued by Ministry of Information, Communications and the Arts – Proposed Personal Data Protection Bill, 19 March 2012.

[17] Svantesson, Dan, *Extraterritoriality in Data Privacy Law*, Ex Tuto Publishing, Copenhagen, 2013 and Svantesson, Dan, "The Extraterritoriality of EU Data Privacy Law – Its Theoretical Justification and Its Practical Effect on U.S. Businesses", *Stanford Journal of International Law*, Vol. 50, No. 1, Winter 2014, pp. 53–117.

Bygrave sees this "regulatory overreaching" as a problem[18] – a view apparently embraced by several other leading commentators such as Maier,[19] Kuner,[20] Reed[21] and Moerel.[22] Kuner has argued that laws that lack the means of being enforced undermine the legal system.[23] However, such a risk is small where the parts of the law that are difficult to enforce are not dominant or even close to being the dominant feature of the legal system in question.[24] One need only consider those situations where people in abusive dictatorships cling onto the notion of human rights even though those rights are unlikely to be upheld. Morally justifiable law – including morally justifiable law that cannot be enforced – has a quality that cannot, and should not, be ignored. And maybe this is exactly where we reach the core of this issue – moral justification.

In her excellent book on jurisdiction and the Internet, Kohl states: "It is enforceability that really matters, not actual enforcement."[25] She then proceeds to note that at least in the transnational context the reason for the importance of enforceability "lies often not simply, or even mainly, in inducing a fear of a sanction in the case of non-compliance, but rather in affirming the foreign law's legitimacy".[26]

Thus, perhaps it can be said that the relevance and value of bark jurisdiction depends on whether the jurisdictional claim, and the substantive law to which it relates, is morally justifiable. Where it is morally justifiable, it is perilous for the

[18] Bygrave, Lee, "Determining Applicable Law Pursuant to European Data Protection Legislation", *Computer Law & Security Report*, Vol. 16, Issue 4, August 2000, pp. 252–257 [p. 252].

[19] Maier, Bernhard, "How Has the Law Attempted to Tackle the Borderless Nature of the Internet?", *International Journal of Law and Information Technology*, Vol. 18, No. 2, 2010, p. 161.

[20] Kuner, Christopher, "Data Protection Law and International Jurisdiction on the Internet (Part 2)", *International Journal of Law and Information Technology*, Vol. 18, No. 3, Autumn 2010, pp. 227–247 [p. 235].

[21] Reed, Chris, "Making Laws for Cyberspace", Oxford University Press, Oxford, UK, 2012, pp. 189–204 [p. 49].

[22] Moerel, Lokke, "The Long Arm of EU Data Protection Law: Does the Data Protection Directive Apply to Processing of Personal Data of EU Citizens by Websites Worldwide?", *International Data Privacy Law*, Vol. 1, No. 1, February 2011, pp. 28–46.

[23] Kuner, op. cit., 2010, pp. 235–6, making reference to works such as: Hart, H. L. A., *The Concept of Law, 2nd ed.*, Oxford University Press, Oxford, 1997 and Kelsen, Hans, *General Theory of Law and State*, Transaction Publishers, New Brunswick, NJ, 2005.

[24] A view also supported by legal theorists focused on "obedience" as a crucial component of the concept of law. See Kelsen's observation that "[w]ithin a legal order which as a whole is efficacious there may occur isolated norms which are valid and which yet are not efficacious, that is, are not obeyed and not applied even when the conditions which they themselves lay down for their application are fulfilled." (Kelsen, Hans, *General Theory of Law and State* (translated by Anders Wedberg), The Lawbook Exchange Ltd, Clark, NJ, 2011, p. 119).

[25] Kohl, Uta, *Jurisdiction and the Internet – Regulatory Competence over Online Activity – Regulatory Competence in the Online World*, Cambridge University Press, Cambridge, UK, 2007, p. 205.

[26] Ibid.

target of the claim to ignore it,[27] and where it is not morally justifiable, it is perilous for the country making the claim to make the jurisdictional claim. In light of all this, I do not think it accurate to view bark jurisdiction or regulatory overreaching as problems per se.

9.3.1 *The EU approach as an example*

Given its status amongst the data privacy laws of the world, the relevant EU law is a natural example to focus the discussion. And while the approach to the territorial scope of the EU data privacy law will change through the transition from the current Directive[28] to the Regulation,[29] I will start by discussing the Directive's approach.

The European Data Protection Directive 1995

As pointed out by Bygrave, jurisdictional rules are not normally included in data protection law.[30] In fact, "[t]he provisions of Art. 4 [of the Data Protection Directive] constitute the first and only set of rules in an international data protection instrument to deal specifically with the determination of applicable law".[31] The cause of this may be traced to a statement in the Explanatory Memorandum to the 1980 OECD *Privacy Guidelines*:

> The Expert Group has devoted considerable attention to issues of conflicts of laws, and in the first place to the questions as to which courts should have jurisdiction over specific issues (choice of jurisdiction) and which system of law should govern specific issues (choice of law). The discussion of different strategies and proposed principles has confirmed the view that at the present stage, with the advent of such rapid changes in technology, and given the non-binding nature of the Guidelines, no attempt should be made to put forward specific, detailed solutions. Difficulties are bound to arise with respect to both the

---

[27] As Kohl notes: "The fact is that being perceived as a law-breaker is not good for business." (Ibid., p. 208). To this, I would add the reservation that the damage done by being perceived as a law-breaker, at least in part, depends on whether the law being broken is seen as morally justifiable or not.

[28] European Parliament and the Council, Directive 95/46/EC on the protection of individuals with regard to the processing of personal data and on the free movement of such data, 24 October 1995.

[29] European Commission, Proposal for a Regulation of the European Parliament and of the Council on the Protection of Individuals with Regard to the Processing of Personal Data and on the Free Movement of Such Data (General Data Protection Regulation), COM(2012) 11 final, Brussels, 25 January 2012.

[30] Bygrave, op. cit., 2000, p. 253.

[31] Ibid.

> choice of a theoretically sound regulatory model and the need for additional experience about the implications of solutions which in themselves are possible.[32]

Given the uniqueness of the EU's jurisdictional rules for data privacy, Kuner correctly concludes that:

> EU law is thus particularly important in this regard, since the EU rules on applicable law and jurisdiction represent a trail-blazing attempt to deal with the subject which may have considerable influence on similar rules that might be adopted in other regions.[33]

For our purposes here, the most important provision is Article 4, which makes clear that:

> 1. Each Member State shall apply the national provisions it adopts pursuant to this Directive to the processing of personal data where:...

(a) the processing is carried out in the context of *the activities of an establishment of the controller on the territory of the Member State*; when the same controller is established on the territory of several Member States, he must take the necessary measures to ensure that each of these establishments complies with the obligations laid down by the national law applicable;
(b) the controller is not established on the Member State's territory, but in a place where its *national law applies by virtue of international public law*;
(c) the controller is not established on Community territory and, for purposes of processing personal data *makes use of equipment, automated or otherwise, situated on the territory* of the said Member State, unless such equipment is used only for purposes of transit through the territory of the Community. [Emphasis added.]

[32] Organisation for Economic Co-Operation and Development (OECD), *Guidelines on the Protection of Privacy and Transborder Flows of Personal Data* (adopted by the OECD Council on 23 September 1980, Doc C(80)58/FINAL), para 74. In the same *Guidelines*, it was also noted at paragraph 75:

> As regards the question of choice of law, one way of approaching these problems is to identify one or more connecting factors which, at best, indicate one applicable law. This is particularly difficult in the case of international computer networks where, because of dispersed location and rapid movement of data, and geographically dispersed data processing activities, several connecting factors could occur in a complex manner involving elements of legal novelty. Moreover, it is not evident what value should presently be attributed to rules which by mechanistic application establish the specific national law to be applied. For one thing, the appropriateness of such a solution seems to depend upon the existence of both similar legal concepts and rule structures, and binding commitments of nations to observe certain standards of personal data protection. In the absence of these conditions, an attempt could be made to formulate more flexible principles which involve a search for a 'proper law' and are linked to the purpose of ensuring effective protection of privacy and individual liberties. Thus, in a situation where several laws may be applicable, it has been suggested that one solution could be to give preference to the domestic law offering the best protection of personal data. On the other hand, it may be argued that solutions of this kind leave too much uncertainty, not least from the point of view of the data controllers who may wish to know, where necessary in advance, by which national systems of rules an international data processing system will be governed.

[33] Kuner, Christopher, *European Data Protection Law: Corporate Compliance and Regulation*, 2nd ed., Oxford University Press, Oxford, 2007, p. 110.

As to the purpose of this Article, it is worth observing:

> [T]he intent of the drafters was not to provide a comprehensive jurisdictional and choice of law framework for data processing anywhere in the world, but first to ensure that data flows function properly within the EU, and second to prevent the possibility of evading EU rules through the relocation of data processing to third countries.[34]

In more detail, as pointed out by the European Commission in relation to the 1992 Amended Proposal for the Directive, the intention of Article 4 is to avoid two possibilities: (1) "that the data subject might find himself outside any system of protection, and particularly that the law might be circumvented in order to achieve this"[35] and (2) "that the same processing operation might be governed by the laws of more than one country".[36]

Considering that it can escape no one that non-EU parties caught by Article 4 remain bound by the laws of the place in which they are established or from which they operate, the reference to "the laws of more than one country" must be presumed to refer to the laws of more than one EU country. Thus, the EU Directive is an instrument primarily aimed at regulating the internal data flow within the EU and to prevent so-called *fraude à la loi* (fraudulent evasion). Nevertheless, Article 4 of the Directive also has an external dimension: in a sense, it deals both with the external scope of EU law and the issue of which national law applies.[37]

The first ground – the default rule – for jurisdiction canvassed in Article 4(1) is focused on an "establishment" of the territory of the Member State (Article 4(1)(a)). The de facto scope of Article 4(1)(a) is completely dependent on the definition of "establishment", and the Directive does not provide any definition of this key term.[38]

However, clarity is emerging through a dispute between Google Spain SL and Google Inc on the one hand and the Spanish DPA – Agencia Española de Protección

---

[34] Ibid., p. 111.

[35] COM (92) 422 final – SYN 287, 15 October 1992, 13. Recital 20 in the preamble to the Directive gives some additional guidance as to this goal:

> Whereas the fact that the processing of data is carried out by a person established in a third country must not stand in the way of the protection of individuals provided for in this Directive; whereas in these cases, the processing should be governed by the law of the Member State in which the means used are located, and there should be guarantees to ensure that the rights and obligations provided for in this Directive are respected in practice.

[36] Ibid. For an interesting example of the intra-European conflicts that may arise, refer to the ongoing dispute between Facebook Ireland Ltd and Facebook Inc on the one hand and the Independent Data Protection Authority of Schleswig-Holstein (Germany) on the other hand (Piltz, Carlo, "*Facebook Ireland Ltd. / Facebook Inc. v Independent Data Protection Authority of Schleswig-Holstein, Germany*—Facebook is not subject to German data protection law", *International Data Privacy Law*, Vol. 3, No. 3, 2013, pp. 210–212.

[37] See Opinion 9/2010 of the Article 29 Working Party, notably on p. 5 and 10.

[38] Recital 19 in the preamble of the Directive, however, includes the following: "establishment on the territory of a Member State implies the effective and real exercise of activity through stable arrangements; whereas the legal form of such an establishment, whether simply branch or a subsidiary with a legal personality, is not the determining factor in this respect".

de Datos (AEPD) – on the other hand (Case C-131/12). The Opinion of Advocate General Jääskinen, delivered 25 June 2013, is enlightening. Importantly, the Advocate General emphasises that it is no wonder that data protection experts have had difficulties in interpreting Article 4 in relation to the Internet,[39] and that due to developments in communications technology "the potential scope of application of the Directive in the modern world has become be surprisingly wide."[40] In fact, Advocate General Jääskinen stressed that:

> In the current setting, the broad definitions of personal data, processing of personal data and controller are likely to cover an unprecedently wide range of new factual situations due to technological development. This is so because many, if not most, websites and files that are accessible through them include personal data, such as names of living natural persons. This obliges the Court to apply a rule of reason, in other words, the principle of proportionality, in interpreting the scope of the Directive in order to avoid unreasonable and excessive legal consequences. This moderate approach was applied by the Court already in *Lindqvist*, where it rejected an interpretation which could have lead to an unreasonably wide scope of application of Article 25 of the Directive on transfer of personal data to third countries in the context of the internet.[41]

This approach, to which I have elsewhere referred as taking a "consequence focus",[42] is to be commended. In dealing with fast-moving technology, it is crucial for the law to look to the option having the most favourable consequences for the future.

In any case, on the core topic of whether Google Inc could be viewed as an establishment in Spain for the purpose of Article 4(1)(a), Advocate General Jääskinen noted that:

> Google Inc. is a Californian firm with subsidiaries in various EU Member States. Its European operations are to a certain extent coordinated by its Irish subsidiary. It currently has data centres at least in Belgium and Finland. Information on the exact geographical location of the functions relating to its search engine is not made public. Google claims that no processing of personal data relating to its search engine takes place in Spain. Google Spain acts as commercial representative of Google for its advertising functions. In this capacity it has taken responsibility for the processing of personal data relating to its Spanish advertising customers. Google denies that its search engine performs any operations on the host servers of the source web pages, or that it collects information by means of cookies of non registered users of its search engine.
>
> […]
>
> In my opinion the Court should approach the question of territorial applicability from the perspective of the business model of internet search engine service providers. This, as I have mentioned, normally relies on *keyword advertising* which is the source of income and, as such, the economic *raison d'être* for the provision of a free information location tool in the form of a search engine.
>
> […]
>
> I would adhere to the Article 29 Working Party's conclusion to the effect that the business model of an internet search engine service provider must be taken into account in the

[39] Opinion of Advocate General Jääskinen in *Google Spain SL, Google Inc. v Agencia Española de Protección de Datos (AEPD)*, Case C-131/12, para 61.

[40] Ibid., para 29.

[41] Ibid., para 30.

[42] Svantesson, Dan, "What is 'Law', if 'the Law' is Not Something That 'Is'? A Modest Contribution to a Major Question", *Ratio Juris*, Vol. 26, No. 3, September 2013, pp. 456–485 [p. 474].

> sense that its establishment plays a relevant role in the processing of personal data if it is linked to a service involved in selling targeted advertisement to inhabitants of that Member State.
>
> Moreover, even if Article 4 of the Directive is based on a single concept of controller as regards its substantive provisions, I think that for the purposes of deciding on the preliminary issue of territorial applicability, an economic operator must be considered as a single unit, and thus, at this stage of analysis, not be dissected on the basis of its individual activities relating to processing of personal data or different groups of data subjects to which its activities relate.
>
> In conclusion, processing of personal data takes place within the context of a controller's establishment if that establishment acts as the bridge for the referencing service to the advertising market of that Member State, even if the technical data processing operations are situated in other Member States or third countries.[43]

I return to this type of corporate structure issue below.

The CJEU took a similar but slightly different approach on this issue:

> In the light of that objective of Directive 95/46 and of the wording of Article 4(1)(a), it must be held that the processing of personal data for the purposes of the service of a search engine such as Google Search, which is operated by an undertaking that has its seat in a third State but has an establishment in a Member State, is carried out 'in the context of the activities' of that establishment if the latter is intended to promote and sell, in that Member State, advertising space offered by the search engine which serves to make the service offered by that engine profitable.
>
> In such circumstances, the activities of the operator of the search engine and those of its establishment situated in the Member State concerned are inextricably linked since the activities relating to the advertising space constitute the means of rendering the search engine at issue economically profitable and that engine is, at the same time, the means enabling those activities to be performed.[44]

Looking at the case more broadly, however, it is clear that while Advocate General Jääskinen took a consequence-focused approach throughout, the Court opted, in large parts, for a more narrow literal approach. The Court discussed in detail whether the functions carried out by Google Search amounted to data "processing", and whether Google was a data "controller" under the relevant EU law, and answered both these questions in the affirmative. This meant that Google was responsible for its search results completely independently of the possible liabilities of the publishers, such as the newspaper in this case.

In turn, this means that even if certain content, such as the newspaper reporting relating to Mr Mario Costeja González, can lawfully be uploaded to the Internet, it may be unlawful for Google to list such content in its search results. In light of this, I have suggested that it is incorrect to speak of this matter as a "right to be forgotten". Rather, what we are dealing with is a selective "duty to be forgetful".[45]

---

43 Opinion of Advocate General Jääskinen in *Google Spain SL, Google Inc. v Agencia Española de Protección de Datos (AEPD)* (Case C-131/12), paras 63–67.

44 *Google Spain and Inc. v. Agencia Española de Protección de Datos (AEPD) and Mario Costeja González*, C-131/12, paras 55–56.

45 Svantesson, Dan, "'Right to be Forgotten' v. 'Duty to be Forgetful', and the Importance of Correct Labelling", 23 August 2014. http://blawblaw.se/2014/08/%e2%80%98right-to-be-forgotten%e2%80%99-v-%e2%80%98duty-to-be-forgetful%e2%80%99-and-the-importance-of-correct-labelling/

At any rate, for the EU, there are practical advantages in the approach taken by the CJEU. It means that, by controlling the search engines, it can affect at least the likelihood of personal information being found online even where the information is provided by a party located outside the EU:

> Given the ease with which information published on a website can be replicated on other sites and the fact that the persons responsible for its publication are not always subject to European Union legislation, effective and complete protection of data users could not be achieved if the latter had to obtain first or in parallel the erasure of the information relating to them from the publishers of websites.[46]

The reference in Article 4(1)(c) to making use of "equipment, automated or otherwise, situated on the territory" possesses a somewhat mystical character and has proven difficult to apply, not least in the Internet setting. The term "equipment" may be misleading and, indeed, the term is probably best understood more in the sense of "means" – referring to the German and French versions of the Directive – though it is not so vague as to connote simply an abstract business method or technique.[47] Perhaps the greatest controversy about Article 4(1)(c) has arisen in the context of cookies. However, that topic falls outside the scope of this chapter.

9.4 The European Data Protection Regulation

One fundamentally important difference between the Directive discussed above and the Regulation[48] discussed here is that, since the Directive: (1) predates extensive cross-border Internet communication; (2) was mainly concerned with intra-EU data flows; and (3) was not designed to provide a comprehensive jurisdictional and choice of law framework for data processing anywhere in the world, it is unsurprising that it fails to adequately address our modern technology-driven world characterised by extensive and intense cross-border interaction.[49] In contrast, any flaws associated with the Regulation cannot be so easily excused.

---

[46] Case C-131/12 *Google Spain SL, Google Inc. v Agencia Española de Protección de Datos, Mario Costeja González* [2014] ECLI:EU:C:2014:317, at para 84.

[47] For more on the interpretation of Article 4(1)(c), consider, e.g., Dammann, Ulrich, and Spiros Simitis, *EG-Datenschutzrichtlinie*, Nomos Verlagsgesellschaft, Baden Baden, 1997, p. 129 and Schartum, Dag Wiese, and Lee A. Bygrave, "Utredning av behov for endringer i personopplysningsloven" [Report on the need for changes to the Personal Data Act], report commissioned by the Norwegian Ministry of Justice and Ministry of Modernisation (now Ministry of Government Administration and Reform), March 2006, p. 60.

[48] European Commission, Proposal for a Regulation of the European Parliament and of the Council on the Protection of Individuals with Regard to the Processing of Personal Data and on the Free Movement of Such Data (General Data Protection Regulation), COM(2012) 11 final, Brussels, 25 January 2012.

[49] Another important difference between a directive and a regulation is that a regulation is directly applicable in all Member States, whereas Member States need to transpose a directive and, in so doing, there may be some differences in how Member States do so – which has been the case in instance of the transposition of the 95/46/EC Directive.

Yet, the approach to extraterritoriality put forward in the Regulation is only a minor improvement on that of the Directive. While we may have hoped for a seismic change, we were presented with an approach clearly "cut from the same cloth" as the current one. Article 3 reads as follows:

1. This Regulation applies to the processing of personal data in the context of the activities of an establishment of a controller or a processor in the Union, regardless of whether the processing takes place in the Union or not.
2. This Regulation applies to the processing of personal data of data subjects who are in the Union by a controller or processor not established in the Union, where the processing activities are related to:
   (a) the offering of goods or services, irrespective of whether a payment of the data subject is required, to such data subjects in the Union; or
   (b) the monitoring of their behaviour as far as their behaviour takes place within the European Union.
3. This Regulation applies to the processing of personal data by a controller not established in the Union, but in a place where the national law of a Member State applies by virtue of public international law.

This provision seems likely to bring all providers of Internet services such as websites, social networking services and app providers under the scope of the Regulation as soon as they interact with data subjects who are in the Union. While this can be said to be the case already under the current EU approach to extraterritoriality, the new approach, as found in the proposed Regulation, goes even further or, at a minimum, more clearly emphasises the significant extraterritorial dimension of the data privacy law.

9.4.1 *The broader implications*

The above has focused on the approach to extraterritoriality taken in the EU. However, to complete the picture of the regulatory landscape globally, or near globally, with which active companies are faced, one also needs to take account of the fact that several other jurisdictions also have data privacy laws with extraterritorial reach. For example, such a reach is found in the data privacy laws of Australia, Singapore, the Philippines, Cape Verde, South Africa, Malaysia, India and the US. Taken together, this creates a complex regulatory matrix of often overlapping, and occasionally contradictory, data privacy laws. The need for reform ought to be self-evident.

Elsewhere,[50] I have proposed a departure from the binary approach adopted in data privacy laws around the world; that is, the rules of extraterritoriality are

---

[50] Svantesson, Dan, "A 'Layered Approach' to the Extraterritoriality of Data Privacy Laws", *International Data Privacy Law*, Vol. 3, No. 4, 2013, pp. 278–286.

structured so that organisations are either caught by the entire data privacy law in question, or they escape it altogether. This unsophisticated approach manages to be both overzealous and inadequate at the same time.

As an example, the EU Data Protection Regulation contains rules of diverse nature. Some rules, such as the rule requiring companies to have a designated Data Protection Officer,[51] are administrative in nature imposing a financial and regulatory burden. Other rules are much less intrusive and merely aim at abuse prevention such as the rule found in most data privacy laws seeking to discourage unauthorised and unreasonable disclosure or other use of personal data. Given this diversity, it is inappropriate to apply the same threshold test for the applicability of these rules to foreign parties such as globally active Internet intermediaries. In other words, we need different tests regulating when such a party has to comply with these rules. We need to examine laws, such as the Regulation, in detail and assign each rule to a layer, with each layer associated with a different threshold of application. So, for example, I have proposed that we divide the relevant rules into three layers.[52]

The applicability of rules falling within the first layer – the "abuse-prevention layer" – may reasonably be broad and may affect foreign parties as soon as they have contact with the state in question. The applicability of rules falling within the second layer – the "rights layer" – may be guided by a test along the lines of the US law's familiar "minimum contact" test first formulated in the *International Shoe Co. v. Washington*[53]:

> [D]ue process requires only that in order to subject a defendant to a judgment in personam, if he be not present within the territory of the forum, he have certain *minimum contacts* with it such that the maintenance of the suit does not offend '*traditional notions of fair play and substantial justice*'.[54] [Emphasis added.]

Finally, I have proposed that, at least in the context of data privacy, the rules belonging to the third layer – the "administrative layer" – ought to be applied restrictively so as to only affect foreign parties where they have an ongoing, systematic and substantive presence in the state in question.

[51] See, e.g., Article 35(1) of the Proposal for a Regulation of the European Parliament and of the Council on the Protection of Individuals with Regard to the Processing of Personal Data and on the Free Movement of Such Data (General Data Protection Regulation), COM(2012) 11, Brussels, 25 Jan. 2012.

[52] Svantesson, Dan, "A 'Layered Approach' to the Extraterritoriality of Data Privacy Laws", *International Data Privacy Law*, Vol. 3, No. 4, 2013, pp. 278–286.

[53] *International Shoe Co. v. Washington*, 326 US 310 (1945).

[54] Ibid., p. 316.

9.5 Individuals enforcing privacy across different jurisdictions

Discussions of data privacy matters are largely confined to a focus on data privacy laws such as the EU Directive and Regulation referred to above and, e.g., the *Privacy Act 1988* (Cth) in Australia. However, such a narrow focus is inadequate in the discussion of the enforcement by data privacy across different jurisdictions. Increasingly, actions are taken directly by individuals against the offending party.

Before discussing the jurisdictional aspects of such actions, a few observations must be made about the foundations upon which such actions rely; after all, not all legal systems have reached the maturity of recognising privacy infringements as actionable under private law. For example, despite numerous calls for a tort of, or statutory cause of action for, privacy infringement, Australia has so far failed to implement such a private law action. One argument overlooked in the Australian discussion of the pros and cons of a statutory cause of action for privacy infringement is directly relevant for this chapter.

As noted above, states are typically unwilling to recognise and enforce foreign judgments rendered within the ambit of administrative, public and criminal law. However, states are much more accommodating of private law judgments, such as judgments rendered based on a tort of, or statutory cause of action for, privacy infringement. Thus, from the perspective of international recognition, such actions have a clear advantage over actions taken based on traditional data privacy laws such as the Australian *Privacy Act 1988* (Cth).

9.5.1 Vidal-Hall & Ors v Google Inc [2014] EWHC 13 (QB) as an example

Vidal-Hall & Ors v Google Inc [2014] EWHC 13 (QB) is an important data privacy case for several reasons.[55] Most importantly, while an action for "misuse of personal information" was established through a string of other judgments, *Vidal-Hall & Ors v Google Inc* dispelled any lingering doubt that may have existed as to the nature of such a tort in English law. However, a different aspect of the case makes it relevant here. The Court was tasked with assessing whether the claimants could serve outside the jurisdiction at Google Inc's Mountain View headquarters.

[55] For discussions of this case, see e.g.: Richardson, Megan, "The Battle for Rights – Getting Data Protection Cases to Court", *Oslo Law Review*, Issue 1, 2015, pp. 23–35; Solove, Daniel J., and Neil Richards, "Privacy Law: From a National Dish to a Global Stew", 14 April 2015. http://www.techpolicy.com/Blog/April-2015/Privacy-Law-From-a-National-Dish-to-a-Global-Stew.aspx and Tene, Omer, "The European Privacy Judicial Decision of a Decade: Google v. Vidal-Hall", 2 April 2015. https://privacyassociation.org/news/a/the-european-privacy-judicial-decision-of-a-decade-google-v-vidal-hall/

The procedural history of the matter was that the claimants had been granted permission by the Master [judicial official] on 12 June 2013 to serve the relevant claim on Google Inc in California. Two months later, Google sought an order "declaring that the English court has no jurisdiction to try these claims, and setting aside service of the claim form, and the order of the Master".[56] Importantly, Google stressed that it accepted that, in some circumstances, it may be subject to the jurisdiction of the English courts but that in this particular case, the conditions required for permission to be granted for service out of the jurisdiction had not been fulfilled.

The relevant conditions are outlined in the *Civil Procedure Rules*. More specifically, the claimants sought to base their case on the following four grounds allowing for service outside the jurisdiction:

(2) A claim is made for an injunction ordering the defendant to do or refrain from doing an act within the jurisdiction.

(9) A claim is made in tort where (a) damage was sustained within the jurisdiction; or (b) the damage sustained resulted from an act committed within the jurisdiction.

(11) The whole subject matter of a claim relates to property located within the jurisdiction.

(16) A claim is made for restitution where the defendant's alleged liability arises out of acts committed within the jurisdiction.

The latter two grounds were added late in the proceedings and were dismissed by the Court.[57] Those grounds will consequently not be discussed further. However, it is worth noting that the Court stated that:

> The question whether "property" includes information of the kind here in question may not arise for consideration at any trial. It is a question of law of some difficulty. If it is to be argued on an application to set aside (or to oppose) permission to serve out, then in my judgment it should be argued in circumstances where the parties have had a proper opportunity to put the relevant evidence and submissions of law before the court.
>
> I take a similar view in relation to the claim in restitution and ground (16). That claim is the subject of very little elaboration by the Claimants, whether in the Particulars of Claim, or in the evidence.[58]

I will address the Court's reasoning on each of the two first grounds separately. However, before doing so, I note a general observation of far-reaching significance. At one point, the Court said: "This is a controversial question of law in a developing area, and it is desirable that the facts should be found. It would therefore be the better course in the present case that I should not decide this question on this application."[59]

While the Court made the statement in a specific context (the meaning of damages), it was also sending a signal that, when dealing with developing areas such as Internet law, courts may be willing to give a relatively liberal interpretation of the

---

[56] Vidal-Hall & Ors v Google Inc [2014] EWHC 13 (QB), at para 6.

[57] Ibid., para 142.

[58] Ibid., paras 140–141.

[59] Ibid., para 102.

Civil Procedure Rules so as to allow a claim to reach trial rather than apply those Rules strictly and thereby prevent the matter going to trial.

9.5.2 The injunction argument

The claimants sought to rely on alleged past and current privacy-infringing behaviour by Google to support their claim for an injunction. However, having noted that an injunction "will be granted only if the court finds there is an appreciable risk that (absent an injunction) the defendant will in the future interfere with the claimant's rights",[60] the Court had no difficulty in disposing of the injunction argument. It noted: "The uncontradicted evidence of Google Inc is that it ceased the conduct complained of, and has destroyed the information of the Claimants which gave rise to the conduct that affected the Claimants."[61] Importantly, the Court also noted:

> [T]he fact, if it be such, that Google Inc has on other occasions interfered with the privacy rights of other persons is not a basis on which the court could contemplate issuing an injunction in the present case. This view is supported by the fact that the Claimants have not in fact included in their Particulars of Claim any pleading of the other conduct which is referred to only in the witness statement of Mr Tench.... I think it very unlikely that a court would permit the Claimants in this case to adduce evidence of what Mr Tench refers to as alleged wrongdoing by Google Inc against other individuals, in particular given that it occurred in other parts of the world, governed by laws other than the law of England.[62]

9.5.3 The tort argument

The most complex matter before the Court was whether the claimants could rely upon a claim in tort where either: (a) damage was sustained within the jurisdiction or (b) the damage sustained resulted from an act committed within the jurisdiction. To understand the Court's reasoning on this point, a few words about the dispute's background are in order.

The claim was made by three users of Apple's Safari Internet browser, and related to Google having used cookies to collect personal information about the claimants without their consent and in a manner contrary to the browser's privacy settings. Each of the claimants stated that they had suffered distress and anxiety as a result of Google's conduct. In more detail, this discomfort had been caused by the fact that targeted advertisement revealing information about the claimants had appeared on their screens as a result of the personal information collected by Google. As such advertisement may reveal numerous types of sensitive personal

---

[60] Ibid., para 43.

[61] Ibid., para 44.

[62] Ibid., para 47.

information, the risk of third persons seeing the advertisement caused the said distress and anxiety.

The first obstacle for the claimants is found in the fact that actions for "misuse of personal information" originate in the equitable cause of action for breach of confidence, not in a tort. The Court, however, applying the reasoning that "[t]he fact that dogs evolved from wolves does not mean that dogs are wolves",[63] concluded that the tort of "misuse of personal information" is a tort within the meaning of the relevant section of the *Civil Procedure Rules*.

While a side issue in a chapter dealing with the enforcement of data privacy law, the Common Law tradition's preoccupation with looking in the rear-view mirror, and law's general tendency to categorise concepts may cause unnecessary difficulties in the application of the law. It must be seen as a systems failure when such a degree of resources must be dedicated to a question such as whether an action for "misuse of personal information" is to be classed as an action in tort or an action in equity.

The second main obstacle for the claimants was whether damages in the context of ground (9)(a) encompasses the type of damages they claimed to have suffered. The Court made the point "that damage is not confined to physical or economic harm is demonstrated by the fact that permission may be given to serve out of the jurisdiction in claims for libel".[64] This reasoning may be questionable given that defamation very well may give rise to economic harm. In any case, pointing to *Mosley v News Group Newspapers Ltd* [2008] EMLR 679, the Court concluded that "[d]amages for distress are recoverable in a claim for misuse of private information".[65] The Court did not expressly address the question of *where* the damages were suffered. This is presumably due to the fact that the claimants had been present within the jurisdiction. Thus, the Court concluded that the claim for "misuse of private information" fell within ground (9)(a). It would have been valuable had the Court explored this dimension in some detail. After all, one can imagine situations where a focus on the place of damages may become controversial; e.g., where the advertisement deemed to cause the distress and anxiety is displayed on the claimant's screen while outside the country of domicile (and perhaps geographically restricted so as to not appear in the country of domicile). However, the brunt of the distress and anxiety was suffered in the country of domicile. Would it be acceptable for a claimant to take action in the country of domicile in such a case even though an attempt has been made to avoid the controversial advertisement appearing in that country?

While made in *obiter*, the Court's reasoning in relation to ground (9)(b) has potential implications for future disputes and deserves detailed scrutiny. In the context of identifying the location of the act committed resulting in the damage sustained, the Court foremost relied on traditions stemming from defamation law:

> Damage is alleged to have arisen from what the Claimants, and potentially third parties, have, or might have, seen on the screens of each Claimant. That is what in libel is referred to as publication, and was referred to as publication by the Court of Appeal in *Douglas*,

[63] Ibid., para 57.

[64] Ibid., para 74.

[65] Ibid.

> cited at para 61 above ("The cause of action is based on the publication in this jurisdiction and the complaint is that private information was conveyed to readers in this jurisdiction."). So publication to the Claimants plainly was effected in this jurisdiction.[66]

However, this part of the case deserves greater scrutiny than was provided in the judgment. Indeed, too much is taken for granted. Where gratuitous statements are provided, courts are, in my view, obligated to take great care in providing clear reasoning that will make future tasks of courts easier to address. Justice Tugendhat failed to do so in this matter. My chief concern is that the Court, without any explanation or reasoning, adopted defamation law principles to a non-defamation law situation that, in fact, is distinguished from defamation law in important regards.

Why should we attach significance to the same locus for the tort of "misuse of personal information" as we do for defamation? The answer might be that in the tort of "misuse of personal information", we focus on where the content is published to the data subject, in a manner similar to how defamation law focuses on the publication of the defamatory content to a third person. Thus, if the data subject brings up the content of concern on the computer screen while in England, the content is published in England.

The problem with this reasoning is that, as in defamation matters, the involvement of a third party is a necessary component of the complaint in the case at hand – the damages were said to stem from the risk of a third person seeing the content. What if the advertisement only appeared while the claimants were overseas, where they are known by no one? Further, the exact requirement of involvement of a third person must be analysed in detail. In defamation law, publication to a third person is a necessary component. However, in relation to the tort of "misuse of personal information", the damages may, as in this case, stem from the mere *risk* of such publication. Further, while publication to persons who do not previously know the victim may suffice in defamation matters, it seems hard to argue that the advertisement being seen by a by-passing stranger would be a sufficient ground for the tort of misuse of personal information.

Taken together, these important differences necessitate a detailed justification as to why defamation principles should be applied in determining the relevant locus for the tort of misuse of personal information. Perhaps such a justification can be advanced. However, it cannot simply be taken for granted.

Finally, on the text on ground (9)(b), without any comment on its validity, the Court noted how Mr Tomlinson (acting for the claimants) referred to *Ashton Investments Ltd v Rusal*[67]:

> [S]ignificant damage occurred in England where the [claimant's] server was improperly accessed [from Russia] and the confidential and privileged information was viewed and downloaded… I also consider that substantial and efficacious acts occurred in London as well as in Russia. That is where the hacking occurred and where access to the server was achieved.[68]

---

[66] Ibid., para 77.

[67] *Ashton Investments Ltd v Rusal* [2006] EWHC 2545 (Comm) [2007] 1 Lloyd's Rep 311.

[68] Paras 62–63 of *Ashton Investments Ltd v Rusal* [2006] EWHC 2545 (Comm) [2007] 1 Lloyd's Rep 311 as presented in *Vidal-Hall & Ors v Google Inc* [2014] EWHC 13 (QB), at para 78.

If transferrable to the tort of misuse of personal information, this may support the notion that the collection of information occurs at the location of the source as well as at the location of the collecting party. However, in this case, the damage was not the collection but the risk of publication to relevant third persons. Thus, the relevant act for the sake of ground (9)(b) was not the collection but the presentation of the advertisement on the claimant's screen.

9.6 Other issues in enforcing privacy across different jurisdictions

In addition to what has been discussed above, two matters deserve particular attention when examining challenges that arise in the context of enforcing privacy across different jurisdictions.

9.6.1 Corporate structure issues

Major Internet businesses, such as Google and Facebook, have found themselves in courtrooms around the globe. Particulars have been provided above about two such matters. Both in data privacy disputes and in disputes in other fields, such as defamation, there are numerous examples of globally active Internet companies seeking to avoid the jurisdiction of courts by referring to the particular corporate structure they have adopted.

In this regard, a recent dispute involving Facebook in Brazil is illustrative. In the briefest terms possible, the case involved allegedly defamatory postings on Facebook resulting in a Brazilian celebrity seeking the removal of those postings in Brazil. Facebook unsuccessfully fought the matter with the result that the Court ordered Facebook to remove the content within 48 h. Failure to do so would result in Facebook's being blocked in Brazil.

The Court's reaction is telling when Facebook sought to complicate the proceedings by arguing that Facebook Inc and Facebook Ireland Ltd, located in the United States and Ireland respectively, rather than Facebook Brazil, were the appropriate defendants. The Court expressed the view that (1) this argument was an "outrageous disregard" of Brazilian sovereignty; (2) Facebook is not a sovereign country superior to Brazil; and (3) if Facebook wants to operate in Brazil, it is subject to the Brazilian laws, regardless of where the parent companies are incorporated.[69]

---

[69] Frosio, Giancarlo, "A Brazilian Judge Orders Facebook off Air if It Fails to Remove a Defamatory Discussion", 7 October 2013. http://cyberlaw.stanford.edu/blog/2013/10/brazilian-judge-orders-facebook-air-if-it-fails-remove-defamatory-discussion. Note also Opinion of Advocate General Jääskinen delivered on 25 June 2013 in Case C-131/12 (*Google Spain SL Google Inc. v Agencia Española de Protección de Datos* (AEPD) *Mario Costeja González*).

A similar, but less animated, reaction can be seen, for example, in the Advocate General's Opinion in *Google Spain SL, Google Inc v Agencia Española de Protección de Datos (AEPD)* discussed above.[70] And it should be recalled that the CJEU did in the end claim jurisdiction over Google Inc despite this type of argument being raised.

Elsewhere, however, courts have reached the directly opposite conclusion. For example, in *A v Google New Zealand Ltd*, the plaintiff took action against Google New Zealand Ltd as a result of Google's not removing search results (and associated links) of a potentially defamatory character to the degree desired by the plaintiff. While the case raises interesting questions of the extent to which Google may be held liable for the search results it presents, the issue of main interest here is that the action was met by Google New Zealand Ltd's arguing that "the plaintiff has the wrong defendant, in that its ultimate parent company, Google Inc (incorporated and resident in the United States of America), owns and operates the search engine."[71] The plaintiff was unsuccessful in its attempt to convince the Court that Google New Zealand Ltd's alleged ability to influence Google Inc to block search results meant that it was sufficiently connected to the publication of the defamatory content. The Court concluded that the fact that Google New Zealand Ltd may be able to influence Google Inc to act in a particular manner cannot be seen to make Google New Zealand Ltd sufficiently connected to the publication as such. Otherwise, as pointed out by Google New Zealand Ltd, it may be subject to a court order (to remove the relevant search results) with which it simply does not have the power to comply.[72]

Similarly, in the Australian case *Duffy v Google INC & Anor*,[73] a qualified researcher in the fields of clinical medicine and public health sought an interlocutory injunction against Google Inc and Google Australia Pty Ltd as a result of their refusal to remove certain search results allegedly defaming the plaintiff. One of the more interesting points in the case is that the plaintiff suggested the following as justifying the conclusion that Google Australia Pty Ltd had the ability to remove the search results in question: "After the plaintiff's proceedings were served on Google Australia,…but before they served on Google Inc, six of the URL links that were the subject of her claim were removed from the domain www.google.com.au."[74] While this undeniably hints at a degree of influence, the Court correctly noted that there is a difference between being able to influence another party so as to achieve a particular outcome and having control over a matter.[75]

In light of this and other factors taken into account by the Court, the order sought was refused against Google Australia Pty Ltd. Importantly, the Court in the *Duffy*

---

[70] Opinion of Advocate General Jääskinen delivered on 25 June 2013 in Case C-131/12 (*Google Spain SL Google Inc. v Agencia Española de Protección de Datos (AEPD) Mario Costeja González*), at para 55.

[71] *A v Google New Zealand Ltd* [2012] NZHC 2352, at para 4.

[72] Ibid., para 33.

[73] *Duffy v Google INC & Anor* [2011] S; ADC 178.

[74] Ibid., para 24.

[75] Ibid., para 25.

case saw "considerable force" in Google Inc's argument that "it would be inequitable to require Google Inc to remove material from its index database in circumstances where its competitors are free to publish the same material."[76]

In my view, while perhaps tactically useful in the short-term, this type of corporate structure argument – a form of reverse forum shopping – is strategically unwise in that it creates the impression that major Internet corporations are seeking to avoid the real issue of whether they reasonably should be forced to block the content in question.

9.6.2 *The effect of the International Covenant on Civil and Political Rights*

The International Covenant on Civil and Political Rights (ICCPR)[77] is, at least in theory, the most important articulation of the right to privacy. Article 17 reads as follows:

1. No one shall be subjected to arbitrary or unlawful interference with his privacy, family, home or correspondence, nor to unlawful attacks on his honour and reputation.
2. Everyone has the right to the protection of the law against such interference or attacks.

In the context of enforcing data privacy across borders, the question then arises (as) to what extent this right to privacy may be (so) enforced. Article 2(1) of the ICCPR offers some guidance to answer that question:

> Each State Party to the present Covenant undertakes to respect and to ensure to all individuals within its territory and subject to its jurisdiction the rights recognized in the present Covenant, without distinction of any kind, such as race, colour, sex, language, religion, political or other opinion, national or social origin, property, birth or other status.

It seems possible to argue that the phrase "to respect and to ensure to all individuals *within its territory and subject to its jurisdiction* the rights recognized in the present Covenant" (emphasis added) expresses two separate requirements rather than a double requirement. From that vantage point, Article 17 means that each signatory state has an obligation to provide legal protection against unlawful attacks on the privacy of people subject to its jurisdiction and those present within its territory, regardless of the origins of the attacks.

While this interpretation is potentially controversial under the rules of jurisdiction under international law, ICCPR General Comment 16 supports it: "Provision must also be made for everyone effectively to be able to protect himself against *any*

[76] Ibid., para 36.

[77] International Covenant on Civil and Political Rights, Art. 17, 16 Dec 1966, S. Treaty Doc. No. 95–20, 999 U.N.T.S. 171 {Hereinafter ICCPR}.

unlawful attacks that do occur and to have *an effective remedy against those responsible*"[78] [emphasis added].

If material originating in state A negatively affects the privacy of a person in state B, state B is arguably failing to provide "an effective remedy against those responsible" unless its laws provide for jurisdictional and legislative claims over the offender in state A. It can, of course, be said that even such a jurisdictional claim does not in itself provide "an effective remedy against those responsible" unless it can also be enforced. However, state B in our example cannot be required to do more than what is in its power to do.

In other words, Article 17(2) of the ICCPR, when read together with Article 2(1), appears to be a source of international law that urges signatory states to make fairly wide jurisdictional claims in relation to the protection of the privacy of people within their jurisdiction or territory.[79] This expansive interpretation of the ICCPR, suggesting an extraterritorial state responsibility for the protection of privacy, may be controversial. However, it seems to be a natural and logical consequence of the wording and structure of the ICCPR. Moreover, it has parallels in other areas of human rights law.[80]

Finally, in this context, we need to take note of how the object and purpose of the International Covenant on Civil and Political Rights impacts the question:

> [W]hile the jurisdiction of States is primarily territorial, it may sometimes be exercised outside the national territory. Considering the object and purpose of the International Covenant on Civil and Political Rights, it would seem natural that, even when such is the case, States parties to the Covenant should be bound to comply with its provisions.
>
> The constant practice of the Human Rights Committee is consistent with this. Thus, the Committee has found the Covenant applicable where the State exercises its jurisdiction on foreign territory.[81]

9.7 Conclusions

In the above, I have sought to highlight some of the numerous issues that arise in the context of enforcing privacy across different jurisdictions. The Chapter has examined the complexities of the concepts of jurisdiction, recognition and enforcement. It then examined the legal issues involved in data privacy agencies seeking to enforce privacy across different jurisdictions. In doing so, it referred to the current

---

78 Human Rights Committee, *General Comment No. 16: The Right to Respect of Privacy, Family, Home and Correspondence, and Protection of Honour and Reputation* (1988). http://www2.ohchr.org/english/bodies/hrc/comments.htm

79 Svantesson, Dan, "Fundamental Policy Considerations for the Regulation of Internet Cross-border Privacy Issues", *Policy and Internet*, Vol. 3, No. 3, 2011, Article 7.

80 Gibney, Mark, and Sigrun Skogly (eds.), *Universal Human Rights and Extraterritorial Obligations*, University of Pennsylvania Press, Philadelphia, 2010.

81 De Schutter, Olivier, et al., "Commentary to the Maastricht Principles on Extraterritorial Obligations of States in the Area of Economic, Social and Cultural Rights", *Human Rights Quarterly*, Vol. 34, 2012, pp. 1084–1169 [p. 1105].

and forthcoming EU law. Then, using a recent decision by the Queen's Bench Division of the High Court of Justice, it analysed the increasingly important alternative of individuals seeking to enforce privacy across different jurisdictions. Finally, it examined issues relating to corporate structures and the implications of the ICCPR.

While the above lends itself to several conclusions, one such conclusion – perhaps the most important conclusion – must be that this area of study will only grow in importance over the years to come. And we may again recall the relative immaturity of, and lacking attention given to, the discussions of enforcing data privacy across different jurisdictions.

I have no doubt that it will take years before we can see some level of stability in this field where there is a predictable consistency amongst the different courts as to how these issues are approached. And until such stability emerges, both data processors and data controllers, as well as data subjects, will be operating in a difficult landscape indeed.

References

A v Google New Zealand Ltd [2012] NZHC 2352.

Ashton Investments Ltd v Rusal [2006] EWHC 2545 (Comm) [2007] 1 Lloyd's Rep 311.

Bygrave, Lee A., *Data Privacy Law: An International Perspective*, Oxford University Press, Oxford, 2014.

Bygrave, Lee, "Determining Applicable Law Pursuant to European Data Protection Legislation", *Computer Law & Security Report*, Vol. 16, Issue 4, August 2000, pp. 252–257.

Collins, L. et al. (eds.), *Dicey, Morris and Collins on the Conflict of Laws*, 14th ed., Sweet and Maxwell, London, 2006.

Dammann, Ulrich, and Spiros Simitis, *EG-Datenschutzrichtlinie*, Nomos Verlagsgesellschaft, Baden Baden, 1997.

De Schutter, Olivier, et al., "Commentary to the Maastricht Principles on Extraterritorial Obligations of States in the Area of Economic, Social and Cultural Rights", *Human Rights Quarterly*, Vol. 34, 2012, pp. 1084–1169.

Duffy v Google INC & Anor [2011] SADC 178.

European Commission, Proposal for a Regulation of the European Parliament and of the Council on the Protection of Individuals with Regard to the Processing of Personal Data and on the Free Movement of Such Data (General Data Protection Regulation), COM(2012) 11 final, Brussels, 25 January 2012.

European Parliament and the Council, Directive 95/46/EC on the protection of individuals with regard to the processing of personal data and on the free movement of such data, 24 October 1995.

Frosio, Giancarlo, "A Brazilian Judge Orders Facebook off Air if It Fails to Remove a Defamatory Discussion", Center for Internet and Society at Stanford Law School, 7 October 2013. http://cyberlaw.stanford.edu/blog/2013/10/brazilian-judge-orders-facebook-air-if-it-fails-remove-defamatory-discussion

Gibney, Mark, and Sigrun Skogly (eds.), *Universal Human Rights and Extraterritorial Obligations*, University of Pennsylvania Press, Philadelphia, 2010.

Google Spain and Inc. v. Agencia Española de Protección de Datos (AEPD) and Mario Costeja González", C-131/12.

Hart, H. L. A., *The Concept of Law*, 2nd ed., Oxford University Press, Oxford, 1997.

Human Rights Committee, *General Comment No. 16: The Right to Respect of Privacy, Family, Home and Correspondence, and Protection of Honour and Reputation*, 1988.
International Covenant on Civil and Political Rights, Art. 17, 16 Dec 1966, S. Treaty Doc. No. 95–20, 999 U.N.T.S. 17.
International Shoe Co. v. Washington, 326 US 310, 1945.
Introductory Comment to the Harvard Draft Convention on Jurisdiction with Respect to Crime 1935, *American Journal of International Law*, 29 Supp 443, 1935.
Juenger, Friedrich K., "American and European Conflicts Law", *American Journal of Comparative Law*, Vol. 30, 1982.
Kelsen, Hans, *General Theory of Law and State* (translated by Anders Wedberg), The Lawbook Exchange Ltd, Clark, NJ, 2011.
Kohl, Uta, *Jurisdiction and the Internet – Regulatory Competence over Online Activity – Regulatory Competence in the Online World*, Cambridge University Press, Cambridge, UK, 2007.
Kuner, Christopher, "Data Protection Law and International Jurisdiction on the Internet (Part 2)", *International Journal of Law and Information Technology*, Vol. 18, No. 3, Autumn 2010, pp. 227–247.
Kuner, Christopher, *European Data Protection Law: Corporate Compliance and Regulation*, 2nd ed., Oxford University Press, Oxford, 2007
Kuner, Christopher, *Transborder Data Flows and Data Privacy Law*, Oxford University Press, Oxford, 2013.
Lawson v Accusearch Inc dba Abika.com, 4 FCR 314, 2007.
Maier, Bernhard, "How Has the Law Attempted to Tackle the Borderless Nature of the Internet?", *International Journal of Law and Information Technology*, Vol. 18, No. 2, 2010.
Matwyshyn, Andrea M., "Of Nodes and Power Laws: A Network Theory Approach to Internet Jurisdiction Through Data Privacy", *Northwestern University Law Review*, Vol. 98, 2003–2004.
Richardson, Megan, "The Battle for Rights- Getting Data Protection Cases to Court", *Oslo Law Review*, Issue 1, 2015, pp. 23–35.
Moerel, Lokke, "Back to Basics: When Does EU Data Protection Law Apply?", *International Data Privacy Law*, Vol. 1, No. 2, May 2011, pp. 92–110.
Moerel, Lokke, "The Long Arm of EU Data Protection Law: Does the Data Protection Directive Apply to Processing of Personal Data of EU Citizens by Websites Worldwide?", *International Data Privacy Law*, Vol. 1, No. 1, February 2011, pp. 28–46.
Nygh, P., and P. Butt, *Butterworths Concise Australian Legal Dictionary*, 2nd ed., Butterworths, Sydney, 1998.
Opinion of Advocate General Jääskinen in *Google Spain SL, Google Inc. v Agencia Española de Protección de Datos (AEPD)*, Case C-131/12.
Organisation for Economic Co-operation and Development (OECD), *Guidelines on the Protection of Privacy and Transborder Flows of Personal Data*, Doc C(80)58/FINAL, adopted by the OECD Council on 23 September 1980.
Piltz, Carlo, "*Facebook Ireland Ltd. / Facebook Inc. v Independent Data Protection Authority of Schleswig-Holstein, Germany*—Facebook is not subject to German data protection law", *International Data Privacy Law*, Vol. 3, No. 3, 2013, pp. 210–212.
Public Consultation Issued by Ministry of Information, Communications and the Arts – Proposed Personal Data Protection Bill, 19 March 2012.
Reed, Chris, "Making Laws for Cyberspace", Oxford University Press, Oxford, UK, 2012.
Schartum, Dag Wiese, and Lee A. Bygrave, "Utredning av behov for endringer i personopplysningsloven" [Report on the need for changes to the Personal Data Act], report commissioned by the Norwegian Ministry of Justice and Ministry of Modernisation (now Ministry of Government Administration and Reform), March 2006.
Siehr, Ernst, "Domestic Relations in European Private International Law: European Equivalents to American Evolutions in Conflict of Laws", *American Journal of Comparative Law*, Vol. 30, 1982.

Solove, Daniel J., and Neil Richards, "Privacy Law: From a National Dish to a Global Stew", 14 April 2015. http://www.techpolicy.com/Blog/April-2015/Privacy-Law-From-a-National-Dish-to-a-Global-Stew.aspx

Svantesson, Dan, "'Right to be Forgotten' v. 'Duty to be Forgetful', and the Importance of Correct Labelling", 23 August 2014. http://blawblaw.se/2014/08/%e2%80%98right-to-be-forgotten%e2%80%99-v-%e2%80%98duty-to-be-forgetful%e2%80%99-and-the-importance-of-correct-labelling/

Svantesson, Dan, "A 'Layered Approach' to the Extraterritoriality of Data Privacy Laws", *International Data Privacy Law*, Vol. 3, No. 4, 2013, pp. 278–286.

Svantesson, Dan, "Fundamental Policy Considerations for the Regulation of Internet Cross-border Privacy Issues", *Policy and Internet*, Vol. 3, No. 3, 2011, Article 7.

Svantesson, Dan, "The Extraterritoriality of EU Data Privacy Law – Its Theoretical Justification and Its Practical Effect on U.S. Businesses", *Stanford Journal of International Law*, Vol. 50, No. 1, Winter 2014, pp. 53–117.

Svantesson, Dan, "What is 'Law', if 'the Law' is Not Something That 'Is'? A Modest Contribution to a Major Question", *Ratio Juris*, Vol. 26, No. 3, September 2013, pp. 456–485.

Svantesson, Dan, *Extraterritoriality in Data Privacy Law*, Ex Tuto Publishing, Copenhagen, 2013.

Tene, Omer, "The European Privacy Judicial Decision of a Decade: Google v. Vidal-Hall", IAPP, 2 April 2015. https://privacyassociation.org/news/a/the-european-privacy-judicial-decision-of-a-decade-google-v-vidal-hall/

Vidal-Hall & Ors v Google Inc [2014] EWHC 13 (QB)

Vischer, F., "General Course on Private International Law", *Recueil des cours*, Vol. 232, 1992-I. Opinion 9/2010 of the Article 29 Working Party.

Chapter 10
Cross-Border Breach Notification

Blair Stewart

10.1 Introduction

Mandatory breach notification as a means of enforcing privacy is one of the most promising new ideas to enter the regulatory and enforcement debate in recent years. There has been widespread take-up of the idea at state level in the USA since 2002 when California became the first state to enact a law making it mandatory for companies to notify individuals whose personal information is put at risk by a security breach. Breach notification has been the subject of intense study around the world and has been adopted or recommended for adoption in Asia, Europe, North America and Australasia.

The approach is poised to become a recommended or required practice under several international instruments. For instance, the European Commission included it in the General Data Protection Regulation (GDPR), which will replace the EU Data Protection Directive adopted in 1995. The Organisation for Economic Co-operation and Development (OECD) has recommended breach notification as a means of ensuring data controller accountability. APEC is likely to head in the same direction as the OECD.[1] It is quite conceivable that within five years, breach

[1] In February 2015, APEC's Electronic Commerce Steering Group (ECSG) endorsed a plan to update the APEC Privacy Framework in six priority areas based upon changes to the OECD Privacy Guidelines, including adding breach notification as part of the recommended remedies where privacy protections are violated. See Asia-Pacific Economic Co-operation, "APEC Privacy Framework Stocktake: Comparative Review against 2013 Updates to OECD Privacy Guidelines", Paper prepared by Australia, Canada, New Zealand for the APEC ECSG Privacy Subgroup Meeting, 1 February 2015. http://mddb.apec.org/Documents/2015/ECSG/DPS1/15_ecsg_dps1_006.pdf

B. Stewart (✉)
Office of the Privacy Commissioner, 51 Shortland Street, Auckland 1010, New Zealand
e-mail: Blair.Stewart@privacy.org.nz

D. Wright, P. De Hert (eds.), *Enforcing Privacy*, Law, Governance and Technology Series 25, DOI 10.1007/978-3-319-25047-2_10

notification will be mandatory in the majority of economies that have data protection and privacy laws or regulatory schemes.

Breach notification (and indeed most regulation) is imposed at domestic level. However, it is becoming more common for breaches of the type that warrant notification by multinational companies that hold the personal information of individuals from many jurisdictions. In such cases, companies may face legal obligations to notify consumers in some jurisdictions but not in others. As notification laws become more widespread, companies face a patchwork of obligations to notify consumers in various jurisdictions in accordance with differing regimes.

Anyone with a role in developing effective privacy law and consumer protection in e-commerce should consider the advantages and implications of cross-border breach notification now, while the roll-out of notification laws and standards are at a sufficiently early stage in most economies. In doing so, there is a good chance to promote coherent international approaches. Promising approaches may emerge to promote better outcomes for all stakeholders both in the current phase, where there are mandatory obligations covering only a small number of affected data subjects, and in the longer term, where there may be multiple laws bearing upon the same breach.

Academics and other experts have already undertaken a lot of analysis of the strengths and shortcomings of notification laws enacted at state level in the USA. Some commentators have suggested that the early laws overreached themselves, mandating unwarranted notifications, and that cost effectiveness would be improved by setting higher thresholds and, in some cases, involving enforcement authorities. Acting upon such lessons may help ensure that the next generation of breach notification laws are better targeted and more effective. There also remains some scepticism about the effectiveness of some models of notification laws. However, this chapter does not seek to cover this well-trodden ground. Rather, it seeks to extend the discussion to the problems, opportunities and best approaches to notification to affected individuals across national and regional boundaries.

In exploring the issues, we need to keep in mind the perspectives of various stakeholders who may be called upon to shape, make, police or act upon such notices. The key stakeholders include:

- data subjects – both those in the locale of the breach and in other jurisdictions;
- data controllers – operating various business models and possibly subject to multiple laws;
- privacy enforcement authorities – and other regulators and public authorities;
- domestic law-makers and international policy-makers.

The perspectives of various stakeholders are discussed further below.

10.2 Opportunities and challenges

Breach notification across borders offers real opportunities for achieving data protection objectives. However, there are challenges as well. By exploring the issues, we can gain insights to fully leverage the opportunities and minimise the problems.

What are some of the opportunities offered by cross-border breach notification?

- **Effective remedial action**: Notification to individuals across borders may empower those individuals to act locally, neatly side-stepping some of the perennial difficulties in global harmonisation of privacy standards and remedies.
- **Fit with modern business models**: Business models that result in companies operating across borders, or holding data offshore, should also have the technical capability easily to give notice to individuals affected by a breach wherever they reside.
- **Building trust**: A mechanism that places remote consumers in an equal position to local consumers in the event of problems should help build trust in e-commerce by directly addressing consumer unease about having their information held in another jurisdiction.
- **Equity**: An effective scheme for notifying consumers both within the jurisdiction and beyond may ensure that individuals who are equally at risk as a result of a breach are treated equally in terms of remedial assistance.

However, cross-border notification also carries special problems, such as the following:

- **Communication**: There may be practical difficulties in designing notices that will be meaningful to a diverse range of recipients. There may be language issues.
- **Usefulness**: Notices should include information that will be of practical assistance to individuals affected by a breach but exactly what that information should be may differ by locality (e.g., availability of call centre assistance, existence of relevant or tailored local remedies).
- **Legal**: There remain notable differences in various laws between both the notification obligations (such as thresholds and timing obligations) and the privacy rights and remedies of the affected individuals. For instance, some laws require notification in all cases within various fixed timeframes, while others expressly allow for notice to be delayed or dispensed with in certain circumstances. Some laws provide that notified consumers have certain explicit entitlements, while others are silent or entitlements to general consumer or data protection laws that vary considerably and may not be applicable to individuals outside the jurisdiction.

By highlighting the substantial advantages of cross-border breach notification, while acknowledging some of the practical and legal difficulties, we hope that new insights will emerge on cross-border issues in order to:

- influence international principles in relation to breach notification;
- contribute to better design of domestic laws;
- enable data controllers better to prepare themselves for cross-border notification;
- enable privacy enforcement authorities to offer guidance, and undertake compliance activities, in ways that will maximise the best interests of individuals regardless of where they live.

10.3 A few issues from perspectives of stakeholders

10.3.1 Data subjects

How would individuals expect to be treated in the event of a significant breach of their personal data? Surely if *some* individuals affected by a company's breach receive notices, *all* equally affected individuals would expect to be notified? To do otherwise – for instance, to notify individuals in the company's home jurisdiction only – would raise justifiable concerns by consumers who felt their interests were not being adequately protected. The consumers concerned will not necessarily understand or care that the company may feel that it is constrained to act in a discriminatory way by a local law. The result may be an ongoing loss of trust in the company beyond what the original breach may have warranted. The mistrust may extend to other companies from that jurisdiction or reinforce general unease about cross-border consumer commerce.

In the event that a company does equally notify consumers in various jurisdictions, what might be the expectations of consumers? Options might seem to include a notice framed to meet the home jurisdiction's precise requirements, a standardised global notice or notices tailored to national or regional markets. Consumers would be unlikely to welcome a notice full of details relevant to another jurisdiction's laws but inapplicable to themselves. Expectations might perhaps differ between consumers in jurisdictions with a privacy law compared to those without – but their respective risks may be equal. Circumstances may also be relevant. If there is a need to act rapidly to protect their security interests, organisations might prefer a simple global notice with a promise of follow-up to delay while the organisation that suffered the breach tailors information to particular markets.

We need to make a distinction between treatment of data subjects and their legal rights. Well-informed consumers know that applicable laws differ between jurisdictions. They may understand that the processes and legal rights in their jurisdiction may differ somewhat from those applying to equally situated consumers in another jurisdiction. However, they will nonetheless expect to be treated fairly like the company's other customers and to be promptly and sufficiently advised about protecting their interests following the breach.

Data subjects may have preferences about how they would like to be notified, for example, by letter, telephone call or electronic message. Although such preferences may not always be able to be accommodated in the cross-border context or in the fraught circumstances of a major breach, data controllers and regulators should nonetheless consider this aspect. Data controllers should consider their relationship with consumers. For instance, consumers might not expect contact from an offshore processor used by a bank, for example. Consumers might mistrust an e-mailed message from the bank because they suspect phishing.

10.3.2 Data controllers

Data controllers will normally be the entities that must manage breaches and be subject to notification obligations. Accordingly, they will have the greatest interest in the practicalities of notification including across borders.

Data controller attitudes to cross-border breach notification may be influenced by their own circumstances. For example, a company principally operating in one jurisdiction may never have considered the implications for its foreign customers in the event of a breach and be baffled when confronted by one. A multinational corporation, by contrast, is likely to have sophisticated compliance systems, be familiar with data privacy requirements in other jurisdictions and quite likely be operating a single global policy aligned with the most onerous regulatory regime in the economies in which it operates. A company operating in one jurisdiction may need outside assistance and direction to manage a breach while a multinational may be quite capable on its own but desire that regulatory requirements for notification be clear and ideally harmonious or, at least, compatible between jurisdictions.

Breach notification is a remedial approach of equal relevance to public bodies and to companies. However, the laws of some countries make a distinction between organisations in the public and private sectors and that may have implications for cross-border notification. In principle, if individuals outside the jurisdiction are affected by a public sector breach, they should be notified along with local residents.

Data controllers may also need to be aware of varying legal requirements in privacy and breach notification laws but also other types of laws as well. For instance, there might be laws that address particular types of information (e.g., financial or employment), cyber-security and national security. There might also be general laws touching on matters such as giving notice (for instance, as to whether electronic notification suffices to meet statutory requirements), liability and insurance.

A few of the practical issues arising from cross-border breach notification include the following:

- Is it appropriate to prioritise notification to certain groups in advance of others? While the detail of applicable law may differ, in principle, it might seem reasonable to treat groups of affected individuals differently based upon, say, levels of risk. The circumstances of individuals affected by the same breach might also suggest a need to notify one group first (e.g., between customers that need to reset a password and those who don't). However, is it appropriate to differentiate by location? Is it acceptable for a global company to favour residents in its home economy over individuals based in another jurisdiction? To this mix might be added that social media give individuals the opportunity to spread the word beyond a company's selected targets which may diminish a company's ability to delay groups of notifications for very long.
- How is the practice of cross-border notification affected by multiple notification laws? Are these laws conflicting or reinforcing? It will be unfortunate if one applicable law says that notification should be delayed to enable law enforcement forensic enquiries to be completed while another says that notice must be given within, say, 24 h.

10.3.3 *Privacy enforcement authorities*

There is diversity in the make-up of privacy enforcement authorities and some variation in roles they are expected to perform under notification laws. Some authorities may simply prosecute companies that fail to notify individuals when required by a notification law. Some notification laws may mandate notification to the authority, which may then order notification to affected individuals if warranted. Some authorities may actively oversee compliance while others may act only on consumer complaints. Typically, consumers will expect privacy enforcement authorities to promote the objectives of the notification law by giving guidance to industry about how to comply.

Whatever the law says in one jurisdiction, the authority should consider the position of affected individuals that reside in other jurisdictions. If the authority gives guidance to industry or the public, this aspect should be addressed as a matter of legal compliance or recommended good practice.

Authorities should also review their own practices to see whether their actions adequately take account of the needs of consumers residing outside the jurisdiction who may be adversely affected by a breach within the jurisdiction.

As a matter of law reform, authorities should also consider whether their existing or proposed laws inhibit cross-border notification or create unnecessary barriers to making desirable notifications. Do laws explicitly discriminate on the basis of location? In the absence of explicit discrimination, does the law inhibit cross-border notification by requirements that cannot easily be satisfied for a cross-border notice?

Does the law allow for fewer or additional steps in the case of cross-border notifications? If a law is highly prescriptive, would it be useful to allow greater flexibility for cross-border notices or to substitute other more appropriate requirements?

One practice that might be useful where a breach has cross-border implications is to inform the privacy enforcement authority in the jurisdiction where affected consumers reside. This need not substitute for notification directly to affected individuals but act as a supplement. Keeping other authorities "in the loop" may benefit the company and affected individuals. If laws do not prescribe such an approach, it will simply be a matter of good practice. Experience will build up over time on how best to facilitate such notifications and to guide data controllers about how best, practically speaking, to involve other authorities. Improved co-ordination amongst authorities will assist in supporting efforts at cross-border notification to, and in support of, consumers following major breaches.

10.3.4 Non-privacy regulators and authorities

While the focus of this chapter is privacy law and privacy enforcement authorities, major breaches warranting notification to consumers can also raise issues under other laws and for other regulatory and enforcement bodies. One example is a breach resulting from criminal action where the police may launch a criminal investigation. Another is where the breach leaves network infrastructure vulnerable which may lead to action by those responsible for cyber security.

Privacy enforcement authorities should give careful consideration to the implications of notification in such circumstances. This usually involves a question of timing – will notification prejudice an ongoing investigation? If so, further issues arise in relation to statutory interpretation and public policy: Should notification go ahead notwithstanding some prejudice to an investigation or should notification be postponed, potentially to the detriment of the individuals concerned? The complication of cross-border notification may arise in relation to how much deference notification laws give to these competing investigative interests.

10.3.5 Law-makers

To date, it is likely that most notification laws or regulations do not explicitly address the position of affected consumers in other jurisdictions. Whether the lack of explicit provision is a problem will depend on the competence of the legislature or regulator, the wording and interpretation of each law and the terms of other applicable laws (e.g., those dealing with interpretation or the giving of legal notices). For example, a notification law might simply speak of notification to "affected individuals" which may be open to various interpretations, some of which may be sufficiently broad to accommodate cross-border notification while other interpretations may be more restrictive, implicitly limited to affected individuals within a jurisdiction.

Existing and proposed notification laws should be examined to make sure that they are effective in ensuring data controllers are equally accountable for all of the personal information they hold and not just that relating to domestic residents. However, this need not mean that the law must mandate exactly the same notification requirements for all consumers – there may be advantage to third-country consumers to allow the data controller some latitude in giving notice, for example, by using languages other than one mandated in the home jurisdiction.

Another matter to consider is the role and powers of the privacy enforcement authority. Some updating of the powers to co-operate with authorities in other jurisdictions may be desirable to get the best results.

10.3.6 International policy-makers

Most of the major international instruments on privacy will, before long, recommend or require that domestic privacy law include breach notification. The OECD has already done so in its 2013 update of its 1980 Privacy Guidelines and APEC, the Council of Europe and the EU are expected to follow in update of their frameworks, regulations and treaties. International policy-makers should develop such instruments or guide their implementation, and be alive to the advantages and practical challenges in cross-border notification.

The working groups associated with the major international organisations active in privacy policy are well placed to study the cross-border effects of notification laws and to offer recommendations or guidance on general and specific issues. Some problems may become apparent only after a significant number of domestic laws have been in operation for a while. Other problems may perhaps be avoided by proactive research and policy advice on emerging issues.

Perhaps it might be possible to develop some general principles to guide data controllers, regulators or domestic legislators that focus on the need to protect individuals at risk, and give effect to their privacy rights, regardless of their physical location? Such an approach may go beyond the modest scope of this chapter but would seem in keeping with other international policy work on ensuring that companies remain accountable for the information they process no matter where in the world they hold it.

10.4 Conclusion

As a means of enforcing privacy, breach notification is emerging as a significant new tool in the toolbox of the world's privacy enforcement authorities. It is a regulatory response that seems well attuned to the changes and challenges in the data processing landscape. However, most attention to breach notification to date has focused on domestic compliance. As notification laws become more widespread, companies may be faced with a patchwork of obligations to notify consumers in various jurisdictions in accordance with differing regimes. Obligations may be conflicting, unclear, incomplete or contradictory. This author recommends that notification laws and standards be designed to ensure that coherent and complementary approaches to cross-border notification are taken that will promote better outcomes for all stakeholders, particularly consumers, but also the businesses that must comply with the new laws. More attention must now be paid to the cross-border aspects of notification if the full potential of the approach is to be realised to the benefit of our globalised economy.

Reference

Asia-Pacific Economic Co-operation, "APEC Privacy Framework Stocktake: Comparative Review against 2013 Updates to OECD Privacy Guidelines", Paper prepared by Australia, Canada, New Zealand for the APEC ECSG Privacy Subgroup Meeting, 1 February 2015. http://mddb.apec.org/Documents/2015/ECSG/DPS1/15_ecsg_dps1_006.pdf

Chapter 11
Responsive Regulation of Data Privacy: Theory and Asian Examples

Graham Greenleaf

11.1 Introduction

What standards can we apply when attempting to assess, or to compare, data privacy laws (DPLs)? This chapter first considers the alternatives, then proposes one answer to that question. This approach is then applied to a brief survey of the 12 Asian countries that currently have DPLs covering all or a very substantial part of their private sectors (and sometimes the public sector as well), and the results are reported in summary fashion. Some comparisons between Asia and Europe are made along the way.[1]

11.2 International standards for data privacy enforcement

It is more difficult to determine standards for appropriate or sufficient enforcement of a data privacy regime than to describe standards for the privacy principles that such regimes should implement.[2] Nevertheless, some objective standards are needed if data protection regimes are to be analysed critically, and compared.

---

[1] Parts of this chapter are based on parts of Chaps. 3 and 18 of Greenleaf, Graham, *Asian Data Privacy Laws: Trade and Human Rights Perspectives*, Oxford University Press, 2014, to which reference should be made for details. Significant developments up to August 2015 have been taken into account.

[2] For an attempt to determine such standards for data privacy principles, see Greenleaf, ibid., Chap. 3 Sect. 3.3.

G. Greenleaf (✉)
Law and Information Systems, University of New South Wales (UNSW), Sydney, NSW, Australia
e-mail: graham@austlii.edu.au

D. Wright, P. De Hert (eds.), *Enforcing Privacy*, Law, Governance and Technology Series 25, DOI 10.1007/978-3-319-25047-2_11

It is necessary to distinguish compliance from enforcement. There is often available evidence of enforcement of national laws,[3] including statistics and case studies (both formal decisions and complaint summaries). The extent of compliance with each law (as distinct from enforcement of it) by companies or agencies is a different matter. Usually, little or no information on compliance levels is available because few sociological studies of compliance are done. This chapter only considers the extent of enforcement, not the extent of compliance.

Two broad approaches to enforcement standards can be taken. The first is to look for internationally accepted standards specific to privacy enforcement, from such sources as international agreements, peer-determined standards set by organisations of data protection authorities (DPAs), or suggestions made by expert commentators. The second is to consider the more general standards by which regulatory regimes are assessed, of which the most relevant to data privacy enforcement is "responsive regulation" theory.

This section therefore starts by considering what international instruments provide, what data protection Commissioners recommend and what leading authors propose. These are only dealt with briefly here, as none provides a sufficient answer in itself.

11.2.1 Standards required by international data protection instruments

International data privacy agreements embodying only the minimum '1980s' privacy standards have little of value to say about standards for enforcement. The 1980 OECD Privacy Guidelines[4] are non-prescriptive in relation to enforcement, encouraging both legislation and self-regulation, "reasonable means" for individuals to exercise their rights, "adequate sanctions and remedies", and no unfair discrimination against data subjects.[5] The 2013 revision of the OECD Guidelines[6] is, however,

[3] For example, see available evidence of enforcement of all national data privacy laws in Asian jurisdictions in Greenleaf, ibid., Chaps. 4, 5, 6, 7, 8, 9, 10, 11, 12, 13, 14, 15, and 16.

[4] *OECD Guidelines on the Protection of Privacy and Transborder Flows of Personal Data* (OECD, Paris, 1981); adopted as a Recommendation of the Council of the OECD, 23 September 1980.

[5] OECD Privacy Guidelines, Art. 19: "In implementing domestically the principles set forth in Parts Two [Basic Principles of National Application] and Three [Basic Principles of International Application], Member countries should establish legal, administrative or other procedures or institutions for the protection of privacy and individual liberties in respect of personal data. Member countries should in particular endeavour to: (a) adopt appropriate domestic legislation; (b) encourage and support self-regulation, whether in the form of codes of conduct or otherwise; (c) provide for reasonable means for individuals to exercise their rights; (d) provide for adequate sanctions and remedies in case of failures to comply with measures which implement the principles set forth in Parts Two and Three; and (e) ensure there is no unfair discrimination against data subjects."

[6] Organisation for Economic Co-operation and Development 2013 *OECD Privacy Guidelines and Supplementary Explanatory Memorandum*, 2013. http://www.oecd.org/sti/ieconomy/2013-oecd-privacy-guidelines.pdf. The 2013 Guidelines and the "OECD Cross-border privacy law enforce-

stronger in relation to enforcement,[7] including recommendations for a privacy management programme, mandatory data security breach, establishment of privacy enforcement authorities (PEAs) and increased transparency.

The APEC Privacy Framework is as non-prescriptive as the original 1980 OECD Guidelines, and does not require any particular means of implementation of the Privacy Principles.[8] Anything from complete self-regulation unsupported by legislation, through to legislation-based national privacy agencies, is acceptable.[9] Revision may occur,[10] but is unlikely to go beyond the 2013 OECD revisions.

The Council of Europe (CoE) Convention 108[11] in 1981 only required that state parties provide "appropriate sanctions and remedies". However, its Additional Protocol in 2001[12] requires considerably more to align it with the EU Data Protection Directive (95/46/EC). In particular, it rkequires that supervisory authorities (DPAs) function in "complete independence", and their decisions must be able to be appealed to the courts. They must have powers to hear complaints, investigate and intervene, to engage in legal proceedings or bring matters to the attention of the courts and to co-operate with other supervisory authorities.

The European Union's Data Protection Directive[13] (1995) called for all of the enforcement measures required by Convention 108 and its Protocol, plus additions. Data subjects must have a judicial remedy, and be able to obtain compensation for damage. The supervisory authority must be able to carry out prior checking of processing posing particular risks, and to keep a register of notified processing. These requirements in the two European instruments are the most concrete enforcement requirements in international agreements, not shared with the OECD and APEC agreements. Both are likely to be strengthened in the near future.[14]

---

ment co-operation" have also been re-badged as the "OECD Privacy Framework". http://www.oecd.org/sti/ieconomy/oecd_privacy_framework.pdf

[7] For a more detailed discussion, see Greenleaf, *Asian Data Privacy Laws*, op. cit., Chap. 19, Sect. 19.3.1.

[8] APEC Privacy Framework Part IV Section A ('Guidance for domestic implementation'), provisions I–VI, particularly II. The APEC Cross-Border Privacy Framework may differ: see Greenleaf, op. cit., Chap. 19, Sect. 19.2.

[9] Greenleaf, Graham, "Five years of the APEC Privacy Framework: Failure or promise?", *Computer Law & Security Review*, Vol. 25, Issue 1, 2009, pp. 28–43.

[10] A decision to revise the APEC Framework was made in 2014, but is not yet implemented.

[11] Council of Europe, *Convention for the Protection of Individuals with Regard to Automatic Processing of Personal Data* (CETS no. 108, opened for signature 28 January 1981, entered into force 1 October 1985).

[12] Council of Europe, *Additional Protocol to the Convention for the Protection of Individuals with Regard to Automatic Processing of Personal Data, regarding Supervisory Authorities and Transborder Data Flows* (ETS no. 181, opened for signature 8 November 2001, entered into force 1 July 2004).

[13] Directive 95/46/EC of the European Parliament and of the Council of 24 October 1995 on the protection of individuals with regard to the processing of personal data and on the free movement of such data (O.J.L. 281, 23 November1995, pgs. 31ff).

[14] The proposed EU Regulation and "modernised" CoE Convention may include improved means to exercise rights, but that is a matter for the future.

Another influential statement of enforcement standards is the EU Article 29 Working Party's interpretation of what types of enforcement mechanisms and levels of effectiveness constitute adequate enforcement in relation to the Directive.[15] The requirements can be summarised as follows[16]:(i) *Delivery of a good level of compliance* with the content rules (data protection principles), characterised by a high degree of awareness among data controllers of their obligations, and among data subjects of their rights and the means of exercising them, effective and dissuasive sanctions, and systems of direct verification of compliance; (ii) Provision of *support and help to individual data subjects* in the exercise of their rights, including institutional mechanism allowing independent investigation of complaints; and (iii) Provision of *appropriate redress* to the injured party where rules are not complied with, involving independent adjudication which allows compensation to be paid and sanctions imposed. This approach focuses on the results to be achieved, not on particular enforcement mechanisms, because of the wide varieties of legal systems, national legal cultures, and levels of economic and technical development in the countries to which it is addressed. The approach of the Article 29 Working Party is in many ways consistent with the "responsive regulation" approach discussed later in this chapter.

Standards that can be derived from international data privacy instruments are far less precise in relation to data privacy enforcement than they are in relation to data privacy principles, but (as with Principles) there is a higher European (EU and CoE) standard with more precision. The 2013 OECD Guideline revisions still do not approximate this. The revisions to these two European standards currently in progress are likely to widen the gap.

11.2.2 Standards proposed by DPAs collectively

The International Conference of Data Protection and Privacy Commissioners (ICDPPC) in 2009 adopted the so-called Madrid Resolution,[17] Part VI of which, on "Compliance and Monitoring", proposed that data privacy laws should include numerous enforcement-related measures falling into four main categories: (i) Encouragement through domestic law of proactive measures by data controllers; (ii) Monitoring by independent supervisory authorities; (iii) Co-operation and co-ordination between supervisory authorities nationally and internationally; and

[15] Article 29 Working Party, "Transfers of personal data to third countries", 24 July 1998; Article 29 Working Party, "First orientation on Transfers of Personal Data to Third Countries", 26 June 1997.

[16] This statement is derived from joint work with Lee Bygrave for the European Commission.

[17] International Conference of Data Protection and Privacy Commissioners, *International Standards on the Protection of Data Protection and Privacy* ("Madrid Resolution"), 5 November 2009. http://www.privacyconference2009.org/dpas_space/space_reserved/documentos_adoptados/common/2009_Madrid/estandares_resolucion_madrid_en.pdf

(iv) Liability of data controllers for pecuniary and non-pecuniary damage caused by breaches, including a right to compensation, with direct recourse to the courts and appeals against DPA decisions.

Although it seems to have had little direct impact after five years, this collective proposal by DPAs deserves attention as peer review of the compliance and enforcement provisions that a data privacy law should contain. However, it does not specify what mix of compensation, compliance orders, civil/administrative penalties, or criminal/penal provisions should be provided, or say anything about the role of publicity (transparency) in relation to breaches and remedies.

There is considerable work in recent years by DPAs and PEAs (Privacy Enforcement Authorities) to develop co-operation in relation to cross-border privacy issues, in forums such as GPEN (Global Privacy Enforcement Network), APEC's Cross-border Privacy Enforcement Arrangement (CPEA), and most recently the *Global Cross Border Enforcement Cooperation Arrangement* announced by the International Conference of Data Protection and Privacy Commissioners (ICDPPC).[18]

11.2.3 Standards suggested by commentators: Bennett and Raab's analysis

Most leading authors in the field of data privacy have given only limited consideration to the question of the desirable standard for enforcement mechanisms in a data privacy law.[19] Bennett and Raab give the most detailed analysis,[20] arguing that "there exists no satisfactory way of evaluating or measuring the approximation of regulatory laws and mechanisms to the goal of protecting privacy".[21] They discuss many different approaches to measuring the achievements of privacy laws and privacy regulators, concluding that it is necessary to focus on "the data protection system as a whole" "as a system of interacting parts", and not isolated components of it. Without suggesting any recipe, they say a highly efficacious data protection system would comprise (in summary): a strong law, an assertive regulatory authority, data controllers committed to compliance, market incentives to comply, a vigilant and

[18] See Greenleaf, Graham, "Global data privacy laws 2015: Data privacy authorities and their organisations", *Privacy Laws & Business International Report*, No. 134, April 2015.

[19] For example, see discussion in Greenleaf, Graham, *Asian Data Privacy Laws*, in Christopher Kuner (ed.), *European Data Protection Law: Corporate Compliance and Regulation*, second edition, Oxford University Press, 2007, part 1 G 'Enforcement of the Law', pp. 50–56 and Appendix 13, and Bygrave, Lee, *Data Protection Law: Approaching its Rationale, Logic and Limits*, Kluwer, 2002, pp. 70–84.

[20] Bennett, Colin, and Charles Raab, *The Governance of Privacy: Policy Instruments in Global Perspective*, MIT Press, 2006, pp. 235–268.

[21] Ibid., p. 239.

activist citizenry and use of privacy-enhancing technologies.[22] The result is "a process that involves organizational change and learning, and that involves an elaborate implementation network of persons and organizations engaged in the collaborative, albeit often conflictual, production of data protection".[23] Clearly, they are not evaluating only a law on paper, but including all matters associated with enforcing it and encouraging compliance with it.

Bennett and Raab conclude that the complexity of this process is such as to make overall performance measurement so difficult that "the only reliable subjects for evaluation seem to be procedural, involving rules, codes, sanctions and decisions that may lead to protection of privacy but do not themselves represent privacy as such"[24]: proxies for privacy, so to speak. They are right that this is a matter of measuring outputs, not outcomes (privacy), but (in my view) some proxies are closer to the real thing than others, although usually only *ex post facto*: amounts of compensation paid, employment or credit restored, apologies published and invasive systems or processes terminated. They do not enumerate what DPA powers are desirable for optimal enforcement, arguing that the existence of a DPA is "the sine qua non of good privacy protection" and necessary to establish a "privacy culture".[25]

11.2.4 The limits of international standards

Consensus on how to measure effective enforcement of data privacy principles, and therefore provide a standard against which privacy laws and authorities can be measured (or, more optimistically, aim to achieve) is clearly more elusive than to state the competing standards for data privacy principles. However, considered broadly, the systemic approach proposed by Bennett and Raab's analysis, the approach of the Article 29 Working Party, and the range of functions advocated by the ICDPPC peer assessment, are all largely consistent. There is also a high level of consensus, though not universal agreement, that such a data protection system at least requires a dedicated DPA, and the rights of individuals to obtain compensation for breaches and to bring matters before a court if they need to.

These approaches are valuable, but they do not tell us what inter-relationships are necessary between the components of a data protection system for the internal dynamics to be effective. We now turn to the approach that, in my view, is best able to explain key elements of how the necessary dynamic can be achieved.

---

[22] Ibid., pp. 263–4.

[23] Ibid., p. 265.

[24] Ibid., p. 266.

[25] Ibid., p. 134.

11.3 Responsive regulation and data privacy

The theory of responsive regulation provides one of the best ways to describe the complexity of the relationships between the achievement of objectives and the provision and use of appropriate enforcement mechanisms. In doing so, it also (in effect) recommends how regulators can best use the powers they have, in order to achieve their regulatory objectives.

11.3.1 Responsive regulation theory

Ayres and Braithwaite first encapsulated in 1992[26] the centrality of a hierarchy of sanctions, the best-known element of what has come to be known as responsive regulation theory[27]:

> the achievement of regulatory objectives is more likely when agencies display both a hierarchy of sanctions and a hierarchy of regulatory strategies of varying degrees of interventionism. The regulatory design requirement we describe is for agencies to display two enforcement pyramids with a range of interventions of ever-increasing intrusiveness (matched by ever-decreasing frequency of use). Regulators will do best by indicating a willingness to escalate intervention up those pyramids or to deregulate down the pyramids in response to the industry's performance in securing regulatory objectives.
>
> Finally, it is argued that the greater the heights of tough enforcement to which the agency can escalate (at the apex of its enforcement pyramid), the more effective the agency will be at securing compliance and the less likely that it will have to resort to tough enforcement. Regulatory agencies will be able to speak more softly when they are perceived as carrying big sticks.

Responsive regulation has, however, always involved much more than a pyramid of sanctions. In more recent work,[28] Braithwaite has stressed that there is both a pyramid of sanctions and a pyramid of supports. The supports pyramid includes (at its base) education, praise for progress in achieving regulatory aim, and (toward its peak) prizes and legislated benefits for compliance.[29] The theory posits that regulators should prioritise the pyramid of supports as the least costly way of achieving large-scale regulatory compliance, and only "when that fails to solve specific problems sufficiently, the regulator moves to the right … and starts to move up a pyramid of sanctions".[30]

---

[26] Ayres, Ian, and John Braithwaite, *Responsive Regulation: Transcending the Deregulation Debate*, Oxford University Press, 1992, pp. 35–52.

[27] Ibid., pp. 5–6.

[28] Braithwaite, John, "The essence of responsive regulation", Fasken Lecture, *University of British Colombia Law Review*, Vol. 44, No. 3, 2011, pp. 475–520.

[29] See the support pyramid diagram in Braithwaite, ibid., p. 482.

[30] Braithwaite, ibid., p. 481.

Braithwaite also stresses that responsive regulation contains a "storytelling orientation" where stories about the implementation of each level of the enforcement pyramid – both successes and failures – are made known to the various classes of stakeholders in the regulatory system (including those regulated, the intended beneficiaries, and those responsible for assessing its effectiveness). Braithwaite has applied this to privacy regulation.[31] Use of each level of sanction must be visible to all parties. In my interpretation, this is part of the transparency element of enforcement.

There are many elements in responsive regulation theory,[32] only some of which are of direct relevance to privacy regulation. Five propositions summarise basic elements of the sanctions pyramid (but worth stating for those not familiar with the theory):

1. Effective regulation requires *multiple types of sanctions* of escalating seriousness.
2. It is an enforcement *pyramid*: sanctions at the top get used far less than the cheaper bottom layers.
3. All forms of sanctions must be *actually used* when necessary, for credibility to be retained.
4. Use of each level of sanction must be *visible* to those regulated, consumers and the representatives of both.
5. The higher levels are *incentives* for those who are regulated to make the lower levels work.

Responsive regulation theory, therefore, posits (in part) a pyramid or hierarchy of enforcement options, credible use of the whole pyramid of options, and various types of transparency and feedback mechanisms. It is readily adapted to the context of data privacy regulation in many respects. However, in the area of data privacy, where all laws have been significantly complaint driven, my view is that it is necessary to distinguish two pyramids of sanctions, one comprising the reactive sanctions appropriate to responding to complaints (plus "own motion" investigations of individual instances of suspected breaches), and a second pyramid of systemic enforcement sanctions that are not complaint-driven. It would cause conceptual and descriptive confusion to combine the two.

Responsive regulation theory, as developed by Ayres and Braithwaite, has received a range of criticisms,[33] including that it has been "less successful in regulatory environments with large populations of regulatees and insufficient resources for visits, inspections, or other regular checks, and where detection of non-compliance

[31] John Braithwaite, comments in an address to an APEC Privacy seminar, Canberra, January 2007.

[32] Braithwaite in 2010 reformulated it in nine propositions, only one of which refers directly to the pyramid of sanctions: Braithwaite, "The essence of responsive regulation", p. 476.

[33] For a summary, see Kingsford-Smith, Dimity, "A harder nut to crack: Responsive regulation in the financial sector", *University of British Colombia Law Review*, Vol. 44, No. 3, 2011, pp. 695–742 [pp. 705–709].

is difficult".[34] This description fits most privacy regulators, but is only an argument that the classic approaches of responsive regulation do not work *as well* in these circumstances, not that they do not work at all or that the theory is defective. To say that privacy regulation is difficult and often marked by its absence and ineffectiveness would surprise no one familiar with the privacy field, nor that success in privacy regulation will need to emphasise different aspects of the responsive regulation toolbox than would be the case with, say, the regulation of nursing homes, coal mines or telecommunications providers. In particular, in my view, the visibility of the use of sanctions has to be achieved much more actively where there is no tightly-knit industry with which to communicate.

11.3.2 Applying responsive regulation to data privacy laws

Responsive regulation theory, when applied to privacy regulation (building on Bennett and Raab's approach), provides ways of analysing and comparing the enforcement aspect of DPLs. First, we can ask in relation to each country whether the range of sanctions (both reactive and systemic) and the supports provided by the law provide a sufficient range of each to make responsive regulation possible, including not only different types but sufficient high upper ends ("big sticks"). Different mixes may achieve this, allowing for the wide differences of legal and administrative traditions between these countries.

Second, we can at least compare the track record of each country's regulator in providing transparency of enforcement, which is particularly necessary for data privacy regulation. Third, if there is sufficient transparency in relation to remedial outputs, this may make possible assessment of whether all types (and degrees) of sanctions are being used. While these are only Bennett and Raab's proxies for privacy protection, they may be the best measure of evaluation – and comparison – available. They are discussed in more detail later.

It might be possible to construct an enforcement pyramid of ideal and global (universal) enforcement mechanisms, against which a country's data privacy laws could be compared. But its value would be limited, because successful responsive regulation is context dependent,[35] and is likely to differ across the legal, bureaucratic and business cultures in Asia. A somewhat more realistic approach, but one where context must still be borne in mind, may be to start with the enforcement mechanisms and sanctions already included in the data privacy laws of Asian

---

[34] Ibid., p. 695.

[35] The approach needed to achieve successful responsive regulation, Braithwaite says, is always context dependent upon such factors as the types of industries being regulated, the nature of the principles being enforced and the resources available to regulators and others given the state of development of the country concerned: Braithwaite, John, "Responsive regulation and developing economies", *World Development*, Vol. 34, No. 5, 2006, pp. 884–98.

countries, which would give a regional rather than universal standard of comparison.[36] That approach is, in my view, preferable to surrendering all attempts at comparison to contextual relativism.

11.3.3 Types of enforcement mechanisms: balancing sanctions, supports and transparency

The mechanisms through which the objectives of enforcement can be achieved in the field of data privacy fall into four main categories: (i) reactive sanctions (responses to individual instances of potential breaches of data privacy principles or legal requirements); (ii) systemic sanctions (proactive steps aimed at preventing breaches or detecting situations likely to result in breaches); (iii) compliance supporting measures (education and training, information services, awards, etc.) which support those who are trying to comply with the regulatory goals; and (iv) transparency measures. Each is discussed further in parts 4–8 of this chapter, and the extent to which it is utilised in Asian jurisdictions.

The approach proposed here to assess and compare the enforcement aspects of data privacy laws therefore emphasises the need for (i) a wide range of types of enforcement measures, including those enabling data subjects to take independent enforcement action (including court actions); (ii) both reactive and systemic enforcement measures; (iii) a range of possible severity of penalties (from "slap on the wrist" to "big stick"); (iv) measures supporting compliance in addition to those dealing with breaches; (v) regulators who demonstrably use all sanctions, and all levels of severity; and (vi) transparency, including transparency in how sanctions are applied in practice. An effective regulatory system in relation to privacy requires all these dimensions.

11.4 Comparing enforcement measures in Asian jurisdictions

Having identified desirable components of a privacy enforcement system, we now move to compare the enforcement measures of the Asian jurisdictions with data privacy laws. The laws of 12 jurisdictions are compared.[37] The comparison here is general, with section references omitted (but readily available elsewhere[38]), in order

---

[36] This is in effect what is done in Greenleaf, *Asian Data Privacy Laws*, Chap. 18, and its comparative table of enforcement mechanisms in the 10 most comprehensive current data privacy laws in Asia.

[37] This comparison is derived in part from Chap. 17 of Greenleaf, op. cit., 2014. For the details of the laws of each jurisdiction, see the relevant country chapters in Part II of that book.

[38] Greenleaf, ibid., Part II (Ch. 4, 5, 6, 7, 8, 9, 10, 11, 12, 13, 14, 15, and 16).

to make comparisons readable. For the same reason, all fines, etc., are also given in US dollars, to make comparisons easier. Six of these laws are comprehensive, covering both the public and private sectors: Hong Kong SAR,[39] Japan,[40] South Korea,[41] Macau SAR,[42] the Philippines[43] (not yet in force) and Taiwan.[44] Three others cover most of the private sector (India,[45] Malaysia[46] and Singapore[47]), and a further three (China,[48] Vietnam[49] and Indonesia[50]) have data privacy laws that only cover their e-commerce and consumer sectors.

A 2013 study of data protection remedies in the 28 European Union (EU) Member States by the EU Agency for Fundamental Rights (FRA)[51] found that, even with the harmonising effect of the EU Data Protection Directive on these countries' laws, sanctions that DPAs are empowered to impose differ between Member States, and that complainants had strong preferences for some remedial measures over others. This study is a useful touchstone throughout this chapter for comparisons with the equivalent position across Asia. Kuner noted in 2007 that although there was considerable enforcement of EU data protection law, "the imposition of penalties is often not particularly visible", with fines and other penalties often not being a matter of public record in various EU Member States.[52] Since then, penalties appear to have become more frequent, larger and more visible in the EU, but systematic evidence of this (like the FRA report) is still limited.

---

39 Personal Data (Privacy) Ordinance 1995 (Hong Kong SAR); see Greenleaf, *Asian Data Privacy Laws*, Chap. 4.

40 Act on the Protection of Personal Information 2003 (Japan) and related legislation; see Greenleaf, *Asian Data Privacy Laws*, Chap. 8.

41 Personal Information Protection Act 2011 (South Korea); see Greenleaf, *Asian Data Privacy Laws*, Chap. 5.

42 Personal Data Protection Act 2005 (Macau SAR); see Greenleaf, *Asian Data Privacy Laws*, Chap. 9.

43 Data Privacy Act 2012 (Philippines); see Greenleaf, *Asian Data Privacy Laws*, Chap. 12.

44 Personal Data Protection Act 2010 (Taiwan); see Greenleaf, *Asian Data Privacy Laws*, Chap. 6.

45 Information Technology (Reasonable Security Practices and Procedures and Sensitive Personal Data or Information) Rules 2011 (India); see Greenleaf, *Asian Data Privacy Laws*, Chap. 15.

46 Personal Data Protection Act 2010 (Malaysia); see Greenleaf, *Asian Data Privacy Laws*, Chap. 11.

47 Personal Data Protection Act 2012 (Singapore); see Greenleaf, *Asian Data Privacy Laws*, Chap. 10.

48 SC-NPC Decision on Internet Information Protection 2012 (China), SC_NPC Amendments to the Consumer Law 2013 (China), and subsidiary legislation; see Greenleaf, *Asian Data Privacy Laws*, Chap. 7.

49 Law on Information Technology 2006 (Vietnam); see Greenleaf, *Asian Data Privacy Laws*, Chap. 13.

50 Regulation on the Operation of Electronic Systems and Transactions 2012 (Indonesia); see Greenleaf, *Asian Data Privacy Laws*, Chap. 13.

51 European Union Agency for Fundamental Rights, *Access to data protection remedies in EU Member States* (FRA, 2013).

52 Kuner, Christopher, *European Data Protection Law*, second edition, Oxford University Press, 2007, pt. 1.G "Enforcement of the Law", pp. 50–57; see also Appendix 13, "Selected enforcement measures".

11.5 Choice, and independence, of privacy enforcement agency

The question of what type or types of enforcement agencies are used, and their independence, is the starting point for a comparison of enforcement measures.

11.5.1 *Data protection authorities or ministry-based enforcement?*

The de facto global standard in data privacy laws covering the whole private sector is a separate data protection authority, found in 99 out of 109 jurisdictions that currently have data privacy laws.[53] The majority of Asian jurisdictions have such specialised DPAs: Hong Kong SAR, Macau SAR, Singapore, Malaysia and the Philippines (not yet appointed). South Korea's new law in 2011 added a DPA (two if you count its specialised mediation body as well) while retaining a significant degree of ministry-based enforcement and one central co-ordinating ministry, so it can be said to have a mixed DPA/ministry enforcement model.

Asia also has the only notable global exceptions, with ministry-based enforcement still in place in Taiwan and Japan (but being replaced there), to some extent in India, and in the sector-based (e-commerce and/or consumer sector) laws in China, Vietnam and Indonesia

However, Japan has now enacted a law with a DPA (the Specific Personal Information Protection Commission) the scope of which is limited to its new ID system, but is also enacting to establish a DPA with responsibilities for all private sector uses of personal data.[54]

In the Association of Southeast Asian Nations (ASEAN) countries, there is acceptance of the DPA model where sector-wide laws have been enacted (Singapore, Malaysia, the Philippines), and in the Thai Bill. It seems likely that the DPA model will become the norm in ASEAN. In India, all versions of the proposals for reform of India's laws include a national DPA,[55] and that is likely to be the eventual result, particularly given the difficulties that India's current laws have in obtaining acceptance from the European Union as adequate. It remains to be seen whether China, Vietnam, Indonesia, Thailand and other Asian countries will follow the dominant

[53] Greenleaf, Graham, "Global data privacy laws 2015: 109 countries, with European laws now in a minority", *Privacy Laws & Business International Report*, No. 133, 2015, pp. 14–17.

[54] Greenleaf, Graham, "Japan: Toward international standards – except for 'big data'", *Privacy Laws & Business International Report*, No. 135, 2015, pp. 12–14.

[55] Greenleaf, Graham, "India's Draft the Right to Privacy Bill 2014 – Will Modi's BJP Enact it?", *Privacy Laws & Business International Report*, No. 129, 2014, pp. 21–24. http://ssrn.com/abstract=2481796

model of a DPA, but perhaps the lack of independence of the DPAs of Singapore and Malaysia (discussed in the following) will provide a model. Asia differs from Europe.

11.5.2 *Independence of Data Privacy Authorities (DPAs)*

There are international standards for the independence of DPA. Five of seven relevant international instruments require some form of independence.[56] Twelve attributes contributing to independence (based on these instruments and expert commentary) can be identified.[57] Analysis of their distribution across the six Asian jurisdictions that have DPAs shows[58] that six of the attributes of independence are frequently found (i.e., 4/7 instances or more).[59] Malaysia's requirement that the DPA must follow the instructions of a Minister (not found elsewhere) would weigh heavily against any assessment of independence.

Based on this approach, the DPAs of Hong Kong and South Korea (and the DPA in the Indian draft Bill) appear to have the most independence,[60] and the DPAs of Macau, Singapore and Malaysia the least. However, despite its lack of formal independence, the Macau DPA has demonstrated considerable independence from government, and this may also occur with the Singaporean and Malaysian DPAs (their laws only came into full operation during 2014). Part of the explanation for the lack of independence of Singapore's and Malaysia's DPAs may be that they are unusual among the 97 DPAs that have so far been created worldwide[61] because they are the only two that have jurisdiction over the private sector but not the public sector.[62] These two are not watchdogs on government, unlike other DPAs, so the strong and obvious need for other DPAs to be independent of the government over which there must be a watchdog do not apply to them with the same strength.[63]

A different model of a DPA may be emerging in Asia than in the Europe: that of a specialised data privacy agency, but one with limited independence from government.

---

[56] Greenleaf, Graham, "Independence of data privacy authorities: International standards and Asia-Pacific experience", *Computer Law & Security Review*, Nos. 28(1) & (2), 2012. http://ssrn.com/abstract=1971627

[57] Greenleaf, ibid., Part 1; summarised in Greenleaf, *Asian Data Privacy Laws*, op. cit., 2014, Ch. 3, Sect. 3.4.4.

[58] Greenleaf, *Asian Data Privacy Laws*, op. cit., Ch. 18, Sect. 18.2.2.

[59] These results may be under-estimates for some jurisdictions, if other laws provide the attribute.

[60] See table in Greenleaf, *Asian Data Privacy Laws*, op. cit., Ch. 18, Sect. 18.2.2.

[61] Greenleaf, Graham, "Scheherazade and the 101 Data Privacy Laws: Origins, Significance and Global Trajectories", *Journal of Law, Information and Science*, Vol. 23, No. 1, 2014, section "The Prevalence of DPAs". http://www.jlisjournal.org/abstracts/greenleaf.23.1.html. There are 10 more DPLs since that article, all with DPAs.

[62] Which is in part a reflection of the democratic deficits in these semi-democratic regimes.

[63] Greenleaf, *Asian Data Privacy Laws*, op. cit., Ch. 3, Sect 3.3.5.

11.6 Reactive sanctions: complaints, investigation, and remedies

Reactive sanctions, measures taken in response to particular situations where it appears that privacy principles are being, or have been, breached, are the principal means of enforcement of data privacy laws in Asian countries. The situations come to light either as a result of complaints received by DPAs (or Ministries), or from media reports resulting in own-motion investigations by DPAs (or Ministries). In contrast, systemic enforcement mechanisms, discussed in the next section, have relatively little use as yet. Six categories of reactive measures are then discussed, with overall conclusions concerning the availability of each measure across Asia, but not the details, which are available elsewhere.[64]

More than 20 different types of reactive sanctions are possible under at least one current Asian data privacy law.[65] The ranking of such sanctions by degree of seriousness can be a matter of reasonable disagreement, and will vary between countries depending on cultural perceptions. The range of severity of each sanction may also vary greatly in its application (an escalation model), such as a fine which might range from $100 to hundreds of thousands of dollars. Nevertheless, the range of reactive sanctions available under the data privacy laws of an individual country can usefully be compared against what is in use elsewhere (as is done in the following parts of this chapter).

11.6.1 DPA and ministry investigation types and powers

In the EU, the Fundamental Rights Agency (FRA) found that complaints to DPAs were preferred to judicial remedies, for reasons including that "DPAs do not necessitate high costs; their complaint procedure is shorter and less complex; and the procedure does not demand legal representation."[66]

Acts in those Asian jurisdictions with a DPA have clearly-described complaint systems, and the DPAs have sufficient powers to investigate complaints, often with strong powers to compel answers, obtain documents and inspect premises. In the three jurisdictions that do not yet have DPAs (Japan, Taiwan and India), there are no transparent or effective systems for individuals to make complaints to the ministries that are supposed to supervise the data privacy laws.

The DPAs in Hong Kong, Singapore and the Philippines are explicitly empowered to initiate investigations of their own volition (own-motion or suo moto investigations). In practice, the Macau and South Korean DPAs do so, and there is some

---

[64] Greenleaf, *Asian Data Privacy Laws*, op. cit., Ch. 18.

[65] See Greenleaf, *Asian Data Privacy Laws*, Ch. 3, fn. 74 (pp. 70–71) for one attempt at a 22-step categorisation by seriousness of measures in use in Asian data privacy laws.

[66] EU FRA, *Access to data protection remedies*, p. 8.

evidence of ministries in Japan, Taiwan, China and Vietnam doing so. Most DPAs (or ministries) have the ability to use their enforcement powers following such own-motion investigations. The Adjudicating Officer (AO) system in India is only reactive.

Provisions for complaints by classes or groups of complainants, with consequent remedies to benefit all members of the class, are included in the laws of half of the Asian jurisdictions (Hong Kong, Taiwan, South Korea, and – for court actions only – China and Vietnam). They are obviously important, not only in relation to mass data spills. Japan has no specific procedures for class complaints (or court actions) in its Act. Complaints to the Malaysian DPA can only be by individuals, with no provision for representative complaints.

Overall, Asian jurisdictions with specialist DPAs have more effective systems to trigger investigations, and to pursue actions by groups of complainants.

11.6.2 DPA and ministry powers to decide and enforce decisions

DPAs and ministries may have a broad range of enforcement powers: compliance orders; administrative penalties (fines); compensation orders; mediation roles (or referral powers); "name and shame" publication.[67] Rights of appeal from their decisions are important.

Compliance orders

Most DPAs can issue orders requiring data controllers to comply with privacy principles (or other Act requirements) whenever a breach is found, with failure to comply constituting a criminal offence (and possibly with other consequences). Compliance orders include powers to order access to or correction of personal records where this was improperly denied. The Malaysian law has the same deficiency as the pre-2012 Hong Kong law: the DPA cannot issue enforcement notices unless breaches are continuing or likely to be repeated. In Japan, the relevant ministry can issue compliance orders, but they only issue recommendations to companies, and even then only rarely. In Taiwan, the power to order remedial actions is also provided, but used rarely. In India, AOs may issue compliance orders but none has done so. Administrative sanctions apply to any violations of Vietnam's e-commerce regulations, but the provisions are not specific. Ministries in China are empowered to issue a wide range of compliance and other orders.

DPAs do not normally have powers to issue or seek injunctions against threatened or likely breaches that have not yet occurred.

---

[67] See Wright, Ch. 2, this volume.

Administrative penalties (fines)

In the EU, the most common course of action taken by DPAs is issuing a fine or pecuniary sanction, based on data from 19 EU states.[68] Over a three-year period, such administrative fines were frequent in some countries such as Spain (1715 instances), the Czech Republic (279), and Estonia (101), but much less so in others. The maximum possible fines varied widely between national laws, with the high end of the scale occupied by Spain (€600,000), the UK (£500,000), France (€300,000) and Greece (€150,000). Judicial fines often have comparable maximum amounts, as discussed later.

Singapore's DPA carries the biggest stick, and the only one comparable with many European countries, allowing it to require payment of a financial penalty up to S$1 million (US$790,000) if an organisation is not complying with any of the privacy principles. Some other Asian DPAs or Ministries are able to issue such fines or administrative penalties for breaches, but some still have no such powers, including in Hong Kong, Malaysia and the Philippines. Contraventions of any of the substantive principles of the Macau law are offences carrying maximum fines of either US$5,000 or US$10,000. In Taiwan, companies can be subjected (as an alternative to criminal prosecutions) to an administrative fine by a ministry, up to US$15,000 for or breaches of more important provisions, and company officers can be fined similarly unless they can prove they fulfilled their duty to prevent such a breach. In South Korea, a list of minor offences may be enforced by administrative penalties. Chinese ministries can issue fines up to US$82,250 where there are no illegal earnings, and confiscate illegal earnings, or impose a fine 10 times the illegal earnings. In Vietnam, there can be administrative sanctions for any breaches of principles, but the amounts of fines are not specified.

Compensation orders by DPAs or ministries

In Europe, although the Data Protection Directive requires that compensatory damages be available, and in most EU countries, judicial authorities can award damages,[69] but DPAs cannot do so.

In Asia, until recently, South Korea's specialised mediation bodies were the only Asian example of a DPA empowered to order payment of compensation. This is a routine part of data protection enforcement in South Korea (occurring in 76 % of mediations in favour of the complainant in the 2011–2014), though payments are small, and the proposed settlement may be rejected by either party (who may then go to court). Vietnam has specific provisions allowing compensation, but examples are not known. The Philippines DPA (when established) will be able to order such payments, with no maximum limit specified. The other jurisdictions have no such provisions, though some allow compensation to be sought via the courts (discussed

[68] EU FRA, *Access to data protection remedies*, p. 21.

[69] EU FRA, *Access to data protection remedies*, p. 21.

below). A unique South Korean element is that company privacy officers have a function of providing "remedial compensation" before matters ever get to a DPA: compensation is built into the South Korean system at all levels.

Mediation by DPA or third party referrals

All DPAs in Asia attempt to mediate to find a mutually acceptable solution to complaints. For example, Hong Kong's DPA states that in recent years about 10 % of complaints are resolved by mediation, although this function is not mentioned in its law. Mediation is explicitly encouraged in the laws of South Korea, Vietnam, the Philippines and (in considerable detail) Singapore.

Name-and-shame publication of decisions

Versions of "name and shame" are surprisingly common. Where parties in breach may be named in public reports and thus press releases, this is a significant sanction in itself (as distinct from the transparency function of reporting). The Hong Kong DPA has led the way in naming respondents, as a sanction, whenever section 48 (2) reports of breaches are published (averaging, 7 per year since 2011). Macao and South Korea also have explicit provisions that treat publication of details of breaches as an additional punishment, but have used "name and shame" less often than Hong Kong. In other jurisdictions, the legislation is ambiguous. China requires that violations be logged by the telecommunications management organs in the social credit register of a regulated entity, and published. Vietnam uses a similar technique. It seems that Japan's ministries never use "name and shame", unless a respondent has already been outed by the media. Other laws do not make any provision for such a sanction (Malaysia, Singapore, India).

Appeals from DPA decisions

All Asian jurisdictions with current DPAs (thus excluding the Philippines) allow appeals from their decisions, although there is considerable variation in the grounds and avenues of appeal.[70] Japan and Taiwan do not have specific provisions for appeals from ministry decisions, but those decisions are not based on individual complaints in any event. In Taiwan, administrative review of such decisions is common. In China and Vietnam, there is also a general right of appeal against administrative decisions. In India, the appeals body (Cyber Appellate Tribunal) has not been functioning since India's data privacy rules commenced.

---

[70] For details of these variations, see Greenleaf, *Asian Data Privacy Laws*, p. 516.

11.6.3 Criminal offences

The FRA found that in almost all EU countries, a variety of criminal sanctions and penalties can be imposed by judicial bodies. It says "the courts can issue warnings; publicise any judgment made; prohibit an individual from managing the processing of data in the future; and compel those responsible for the violation to undertake community service. In addition, in all EU Member States the courts can impose fines, issue prison sentences or combine both."[71] The maximum fines that can be imposed in EU countries vary greatly, from US$12,000, up to US$415,000 (€300,000) in France, and no maximum imposed on UK courts.[72] The new EU Data Protection Regulation, expected to be in force in 2018, provides for fines of up to four per cent of an organisation's turnover.

Across Asia, criminal prosecutions are one of the most commonly used means of data privacy enforcement. In comparison with Europe, Asian courts are only able to impose low financial penalties. Every jurisdiction has some criminal offences in its legislation, although not necessarily for breaches of provisions of the data privacy law. Offences in the criminal code are often used in Taiwan and Macau and China, instead of using offences located in the data privacy laws themselves. In Hong Kong, criminal prosecutions have been used in the past because of a lack of other enforcement mechanisms.

Malaysia is unusual in that breaches of any one of its Act's seven data privacy principles constitutes an offence carrying a maximum fine of US$100,000. However, in many Asian jurisdictions (Hong Kong, Japan and Singapore), a breach of the principles in the Act is not an offence in itself: there must first be an enforcement order issued by a DPA or ministry, and non-compliance with that order. The maximum fines for contravention of an enforcement notice are low (under US$100,000), and in Japan a derisory US$3,000 (with no occurrences).. In other jurisdictions, breaches of some specified principles constitute offences, or damage to individuals triggers an offence (Taiwan), without need for breach of an enforcement order. This applies to a broad range of provisions in the Philippines, or in Macau, with maximum penalties under US$50,000. In South Korea, the maximum fine for "normal" breaches is US$100,000, but extraordinarily high penalties ("surcharges") are being added by new amendments where resident registration (RR) numbers or commercial sales of data are involved.[73]

Data protection laws increasingly include offences by third parties (not only data controllers or processors) involving wrongful acquisition, sale or purchase of personal data. Such provision on trafficking in personal data have been added to most new or revised data privacy laws in Asia (including Hong Kong, the Philippines,

---

[71] EU FRA, *Access to data protection remedies*, p. 22. Fine ranges are given for many other countries as well.

[72] EU FRA, *Access to data protection remedies*, p. 22.

[73] For details of offences in these countries, see Greenleaf, *Asian Data Privacy Laws*, op. cit., pp. 517–18.

Malaysia, China and Vietnam).[74] A high profile Chinese case of illegally obtaining personal data has resulted in jail sentences for a UK and a US citizen.[75] Some such offences committed by third parties are clearly needed in any comprehensive data privacy law.

11.6.4 Access to judicial remedies by data subjects

In the EU, courts are able to issue compliance orders and injunctions in relation to breaches of data privacy laws, but the scope of such orders varies a great deal between countries.[76] In most EU Member States, according to the FRA, "judicial authorities can award damages for violations, although guidelines on award amounts vary,"[77] and non-pecuniary orders can be made in some cases. The range of awards that courts can make varies widely between jurisdictions, but is less than US$30,000 in all jurisdictions they considered. However, the FRA found that compensation was not a major motivating factor for complainants.[78]

In Asia, there is a right to seek compensation through court actions in most data privacy laws, the exceptions being Malaysia and Japan. Equivalent rights may also arise under the Civil Code in some civil law jurisdictions, but not in common law jurisdictions. The conditions for compensation actions are various. In the Philippines, the Act requires an offence to have occurred before compensation can be sought. Vietnam's e-commerce and consumer laws allow any breaches of the privacy principles to result in a claim for compensation through the courts. China's laws are specific that there is a right to compensation, and it is likely that this could occur under the tort law. In South Korea, complainants must pursue compensation before the civil courts, but has pro-complainant procedural rules.

Singaporean complainants must proceed before a court to obtain injunctions or damages, and it is unclear they must prove a contravention ab initio (despite a prior finding by the DPA). In Hong Kong, a similar provision allowing a civil action for compensation before the courts has not resulted in any compensation being ordered in nearly 20 years, but procedural amendments in 2012 reduced the likelihood of costs being awarded against plaintiffs, and made it make it easier for a plaintiff to prove in court matters that have already been investigated by the DPA.

So, while compensation actions through courts are possible in most jurisdictions, they have not occurred in some (Hong Kong, India), while in others it is as yet too

---

[74] For details of offences in these countries, see ibid., p. 519.

[75] Livingston, Scott, and Greenleaf, Graham, "China Whys and wherefores: Illegal provision of personal data under Chinese law", *Privacy Laws & Business International Report*, No. 131, 2014, pp. 1–5. http://ssrn.com/abstract=2541570

[76] EU FRA, *Access to data protection remedies*, p. 22.

[77] Ibid., p. 21.

[78] Ibid., p. 7.

early (Singapore and the Philippines), and otherwise it is difficult to obtain examples of cases and amounts typically paid (Macau, Taiwan, South Korea).

Litigation assistance to complainants

The FRA found that in the EU, merely providing a legal right to compensation before a court was rarely sufficient, and that data subjects worried about the lack of legal assistance available and the "difficulty in obtaining information about procedures and insufficient knowledge of remedies".[79] Hong Kong's 2012 amendments mean the Privacy Commissioner can assist complainants to obtain evidence from respondents, and in some cases may provide legal aid. There are no equivalent legal aid provisions applying to DPAs in other Asian jurisdictions, and none allows them to intervene in civil court cases on behalf of plaintiffs.

11.7 Systemic sanctions (compliance measures)

The preventive and deterrent objectives of enforcement can often be best achieved through systemic mechanisms, which are not used in reaction to any single complaint (also often called "proactive" measures). These can include: registration systems (general, or more often selective); audits and inspections, appointment of data protection officers, design or default requirements in information systems and privacy impact assessments. Systemic measures may also be ranked in a pyramid structure, in order of highest cost of application (and resulting infrequency of application) at the top, down to those placed at the bottom being measures of generic application where it is possible to spread the cost burden across a wide range of respondents (businesses and agencies). As with reactive sanctions, the greater variety of systemic sanctions a data privacy regulator has at its disposal, the stronger is the potential effectiveness of its enforcement system.

Six types of systemic enforcement measures are already in use in Asian jurisdictions,[80] as discussed below. They have only been used infrequently in Asian data privacy laws, both old and new. They have had some impact through the more established laws, particularly in South Korea, in Macau, in various ways in Hong Kong, and through quasi-mandatory guidelines in Japan and Taiwan. Singapore and the Philippines do not have any explicit systemic compliance measures in their legislation. Nor do Japan and Taiwan, but their ministry-based enforcement model

[79] EU FRA, *Access to data protection remedies*, p. 8.

[80] These include, from most costly to least costly: privacy impact assessments required; DPA inspection and/or audit of personal data systems; data user registration and publication (sensitive systems only); data protection officer (DPO) required; accountability requirements of a data processor; and openness of data processing procedures.

would lend itself to ministries having such powers as part of their general supervisory functions in an industry. Similar considerations apply in China and Vietnam.

11.7.1 Six systemic enforcement measures in use

(i) The only Asian jurisdiction to yet require a data protection officer with extensive and onerous obligations, defined qualifications for appointees and defined independence of action, is South Korea. India has a vague requirement for a data protection officer to be appointed.

(ii) DPA inspections or compliance audits of personal data systems can be required in Hong Kong, South Korea, Macao and Malaysia. In Hong Kong, the DPA has exercised its powers to carry out formal inspections of personal data systems on four occasions. Instead, it carries out informal compliance checks (220 in 2012–2013, mostly in the private sector). In China and Vietnam, periodic inspections, and publication of their results, are the main means of systemic enforcement.

(iii) There are no comprehensive registration schemes in Asia. Registration of data controllers in particular categories considered to be of higher risk can be required in Macau (applied in the public sector) and Hong Kong (postponed until EU intentions become clear). Malaysia's registration scheme is primarily for revenue-raising. Cancellation of registration is used as a punitive enforcement measure equivalent to cancellation of a licence to process data in Asia. While China does not have a data privacy registration system, suspension or termination of business operations, websites or licences are among the available range of administrative sanctions.

(iv) Privacy impact assessments (PIAs) can be required in South Korea, but only for public sector entities. No other Asian jurisdiction has specific provisions for privacy impact assessments of potentially dangerous systems. Macau's prior checking system could be used in a similar fashion. PIAs have not become a common practice in Hong Kong (but have occurred), or elsewhere in Asia.

(v) Where a DPA issues codes of conduct that are not merely advisory but have some legal effect, this is a form of systemic regulation because it makes the application of general privacy principles more precise for a particular industry sector, and therefore makes more clear what standards data controllers in that industry sector must observe. Provisions for codes do occur in Asian laws, but are little used, and have differing effects. Under Macau's unused provisions, DPA approval of a code has no effect on its legal validity. Similarly, non-compliance with Hong Kong's codes (of which there are two) does not itself amount to a contravention of the law, but may raise a rebuttable legal presumption against the data controller concerned. The Philippines DPA will be able to approve codes, but their relationship to the Act is unstated, and potentially reduces statutory rights. The Malaysian DPA will also be able to approve codes carrying penalties for non-compliance. In Japan and Taiwan, ministry guidelines for particular sectors are to some extent like statutory codes of conduct in other jurisdictions, because of the regulatory powers that ministries exercise in each sector. Extensive use of them is made in both countries.

(vi) Openness of processing procedures is required where jurisdictions implement the OECD openness principle, in theory as a deterrent against non-compliance. This requires data controllers to provide information about data processing practices to any person who enquires (including NGOs or the media), and not only to data subjects. Hong Kong is the only Asian jurisdiction implementing such a provision in relation to its private sector, though it can in effect be provided by freedom of information or right to information (FOI or RTI) laws in relation to the public sectors of other countries that have such laws (South Korea, Japan and India).

11.8 Systemic supports for compliance

Braithwaite and other responsive regulation theorists stress the importance of systemic measures that support compliance by regulatees. There are many types of support that DPAs or other regulators can give to those data controllers or processors (or their advisers) who wish to do the right thing. DPAs or ministries provide numerous compliance supports in Asian jurisdictions.[81] Responsive regulation also places a high value on citizen-consumers knowing their privacy protection rights and responsibilities. In various Asian jurisdictions similar support facilities are sometimes provided for both adults and schoolchildren, including educational materials, prizes and awards, and even television dramatisations about privacy. These measures can also be described as incentives or more colloquially as carrots (as opposed to sticks).[82] The long-established supervisory bodies in Hong Kong and South Korea invest a significant proportion of their resources in creative ways to assist both data controllers and data subjects to understand their obligations and rights. Singapore is starting to do likewise. Ministries in Japan and Taiwan invest considerable resources in developing guidelines for compliance in their industry sectors.

---

[81] These include: training courses; freely accessible training and educational materials; non-compulsory guidelines; compliance advisory services; assistance in conducting voluntary audits and PIAs; compliance seals and marks; and compliance prizes and awards.

[82] The notion of "nudges" to support compliance is related to this approach: For an overview, see "Nudge theory" (Wikipedia). http://en.wikipedia.org/wiki/Nudge_theory

11.9 Transparency: the evidence of enforcement

11.9.1 Types of transparency required in data protection

Responsive regulation requires transparency in the use of sanctions: use of each level of sanction must be visible to those regulated, consumers and the representatives of both. Without the right forms of publicity and transparency, in the context of privacy regulation, data controllers and processors, and their advisers, will not obtain market signals about the costs of non-compliance, and thus will have no incentive to institute steps to improve compliance, or settle complaints of non-compliance in a non-adversarial manner. Also, data subjects and their advisers will not get the message that they can use data privacy laws to vindicate their rights, or know "the going rate" for types of breaches. Without transparency, there is unlikely to be effective regulation.

Data privacy conflicts are only rarely elevated to the level of a decision by a court or a quasi-judicial tribunal, or even to the formal enforceable decisions of a regulator (DPA). Publication of all such decisions at these three levels is essential to transparency, but they usually do not exist in sufficient numbers to clarify how details of the law are in practice being interpreted, or what remedies (if any) are being received by individual complainants. These matters are hidden in the anonymous resolution of complaints, usually by mediation, carried out by DPAs.[83] These are too numerous (and typically too trivial) for publication of detailed complaint summaries of all of them, and the cost and administrative burden on the DPA would be unjustifiable. Preparation and publication of a selection of such case summaries is sufficient to illustrate important legislative interpretations by the DPA, and the typical remedies that may result from a range of complaint types. No DPAs take the next step in transparency, by establishing objective criteria for selecting which complaints to summarise.[84]

Complaint statistics, usually included in annual reports, often only indicate the subject area of complaints, numbers of complaints received compared with numbers resolved, and outcomes in the sense of the numbers of complaints found justified, dismissed without investigation, etc. However, the most valuable statistics are rarely provided, such as how many complainants received how much compensation, the numbers of complaints resulting in apologies, or changes to practices, or other remedies. Such statistics cover the bulk of complaints that do not result in summaries, and can give as good an objective measure of an enforcement system as it is realistic to expect.

Three types of transparency are therefore useful in data privacy regulation: (i) publication of formal complaint decisions and authorisations by DPAs, and of court decisions; (ii) publication of an illustrative selection of informal complaint resolutions by DPAs; and (iii) publication of statistics concerning penalties and remedies.

---

[83] Bygrave notes that this both hinders transparency and can obscure the positive achievements of DPAs: Lee Bygrave, *Data Privacy Law: An International Perspective*, OUP, 2014, p. 189.

[84] Greenleaf, Graham, "Reforming Reporting of Privacy Cases: A Proposal for Improving Accountability of Asia-Pacific Privacy Commissioners". http://ssrn.com/abstract=512782

11.9.2 Transparency of data privacy regulation in Asia

Publication of formal decisions may be implied to be required by law, but is not expressly required. Publication of complaint summaries is always only a practice adopted by a DPA or Ministry. The desired transparency is more likely to be provided by information published centrally and with consistency, and so is much more likely to be provided by a DPA rather than scattered across ministries (as a comparison of Japan or Taiwan with, say, Hong Kong or Macau illustrates).

Some DPAs in Asia (Hong Kong, Macau and various Korean bodies) report around 20–30 complaint summaries per year, usually in enough detail to explain the main legal issues and the DPA's response, and sometimes with a recommended standard form of citation for their summaries. All allow third-party republication.[85] Macau has the highest publication rate, publishing summaries of 28 % of complaints investigated during its first six years. The DPAs in Singapore, Malaysia and the Philippines have not yet handled any complaints, and the requirements of their laws are unclear. Ministries in Japan and Taiwan do not publish complaint summaries, a significant failure of their ministry-based systems. However, there are quite a few reported cases in Taiwan's courts. In India, there is nothing to report. Meaningful comparisons between the extent of transparent reporting in Europe and Asia, is not yet possible because of inadequate data at both ends.

Statistical reporting of remedial outcomes is the weakest aspect of the reporting practices in Asian jurisdictions, and probably elsewhere. Korea's mediation committees do publish such data. The Hong Kong DPA has stated it intends to do this in future. Macau's DPA publishes statistics of the number of complaints resulting in sanctions but few details. Japan's Cabinet and its Consumer Agency have at various times made efforts to publish some enforcement statistics, but there are few remedies to report.

Macau's DPA publishes considerable details of various types of systemic enforcement, particularly authorisation decisions concerning data matching, data exports and similar matters. Hong Kong's DPA publishes detailed reports as a result of any formal inspection, and publishes briefer details in its annual report of more informal compliance checks. There is no systemic enforcement to report in Taiwan, Japan or India.

[85] The complaint summaries and appeal decisions of 17 DPAs to be searched together, including those available from Hong Kong, Macau and South Korea: see *International Privacy Law Library* (World Legal Information Institute). http://www.worldlii.org/int/special/privacy/

11.10 Conclusions: effective and responsive regulation in Asia?

Based on the detailed analysis of the enforcement aspects of all Asian data privacy laws which this chapter summarises, it is possible to reach some conclusions about whether responsive regulation of data privacy is possible, or being achieved, in Asia. The recent increase in the number of new and reformed privacy laws in Asia gives ample examples of regulatory options to compare, but only a few Asian jurisdictions have had operational data privacy laws long enough for their effectiveness in practice to become apparent.

As discussed earlier, responsive regulation in the privacy context requires:

1. A diverse range of regulatory measures (a toolkit), sufficient to allow graduated responses to breaches of different forms of seriousness, and to complement reactive measures with systemic measures and with incentives;
2. A track record of actually using all the enforcement measures available to them;
3. A reasonable degree of transparency in regularly publishing details of the complaints they investigate and resolve, and the remedies that result.

The best regulatory toolkits (in theory) are found in South Korea and Macau, which have the widest range of enforcement mechanisms. Each jurisdiction's laws have been in force for long enough to assess their use. Hong Kong's DPA has since 2012 a much broader range of enforcement measures, adding some bite to the current Commissioner's insistent bark. Singapore has a variety of potentially strong enforcement mechanisms, notably the "million dollar fine". The Philippines also has a wide range of measures, again, in theory. It will take some years before an assessment of either law can be made concerning whether the sanctions are used and used effectively. The Malaysian law is lacking almost any enforcement measures, and those it has suffer from the same deficiencies as the pre-reform Hong Kong law. Japan's law has negligible enforcement measures, and even those are not being used, but its law is now being reformed. Taiwan's 2011 reformed Act has reasonable enforcement measures, but the ministries have made little use of them as yet. India has some ambiguous measures, but they are not used.

Concerning a track record of enforcement, Japan, Taiwan and India (the three ministry-based models of enforcement) are roughly equivalent in inactivity and do not provide responsive regulation. Despite its previously defective toolkit, Hong Kong's DPA has vigorously and publicly attempted to make the maximum use of all enforcement measures in its possession in recent years, particularly the name-and-shame approach. In a very small jurisdiction, Macau's DPA has used a range of quite different powers consistently and vigorously. South Korea's various DPAs and ministry agencies have in combination been effective in a much larger jurisdiction than either Hong Kong or Macau.

As discussed in the preceding section, Hong Kong, Macau and Korea also have the greatest transparency in the operation of their laws. Further comparison is unnecessary, because all three of these DPAs satisfy the three basic criteria for responsive regulation (though only recently in Hong Kong's case), even though all have room for improvement.

Responsive regulation is therefore alive in Asian privacy regulation, even if it is not yet state of the art. One major caveat, however, is that no Asian privacy regulator has yet levied fines measured in hundreds of thousands of US dollars, as is now a frequent occurrence in both Europe and the US (via its FTC). With the exceptions of Korea and Singapore, they do not have the formal powers to do so, let alone use them. So there is an open question whether the "big stick" is yet big enough in Asian jurisdictions to act as any deterrent to breaches by multinational information giants, or perhaps even the largest domestic companies. While there may be a good deal of responsiveness in some jurisdictions, effectiveness is probably still lacking in relation to the largest-scale privacy invaders.

A final conclusion is that Ministry-based privacy regulation appears to have failed, but is not yet dead. Japan, Taiwan and India, the three jurisdictions that only include ministry-based enforcement, produce little that can be recognised as enforcement of their laws, irrespective of how strong or weak the principles in their laws may be. The three success stories are the three longest-established DPAs (although South Korea is a mixed model). Singapore, Malaysia and the Philippines cannot yet contribute to our understanding of responsive privacy regulation in practice in Asia.

References

Article 29 Working Party, "First orientations on Transfers of Personal Data to Third Countries – Possible Ways Forward in Assessing Adequacy", 26 June 1997. http://ec.europa.eu/justice/policies/privacy/docs/wpdocs/1997/wp4_en.pdf

Article 29 Working Party, "Transfers of personal data to third countries: Applying Articles 25 and 26 of the EU data protection directive", 24 July 1998. http://ec.europa.eu/justice/policies/privacy/docs/wpdocs/1998/wp12_en.pdf

Ayres, Ian, and John Braithwaite, *Responsive Regulation: Transcending the Deregulation Debate*, Oxford University Press, 1992.

Bennett, Colin, and Charles Raab, *The Governance of Privacy: Policy Instruments in Global Perspective*, MIT Press, 2006.

Braithwaite, John, "The essence of responsive regulation", Fasken Lecture, *University of British Colombia Law Review*, Vol. 44, No. 3, 2011, pp. 475–520.

Braithwaite, John, "Responsive regulation and developing economies", *World Development*, Vol. 34, No. 5, 2006, pp. 884–898.

Bygrave, Lee, *Data Protection Law: Approaching its Rationale, Logic and Limits*, Kluwer, 2002.

Bygrave, Lee, *Data Privacy Law: An International Perspective*, Oxford University Press, 2014.

Council of Europe, Convention for the Protection of Individuals with Regard to Automatic Processing of Personal Data (CETS no. 108, opened for signature 28 January1981, entered into force 1 October 1985).

Council of Europe, Additional Protocol to the Convention for the Protection of Individuals with Regard to Automatic Processing of Personal Data, regarding Supervisory Authorities and Transborder Data Flows (ETS no. 181, opened for signature 8 November 2001, entered into force 1 July 2004).

European Parliament and the Council, Directive 95/46/EC of the European Parliament and of the Council of 24 October 1995 on the protection of individuals with regard to the processing of personal data and on the free movement of such data, O.J.L. 281, 23 November1995.

European Union Agency for Fundamental Rights, *Access to data protection remedies in EU Member States*, FRA, 2013.

Greenleaf, Graham, "Reforming Reporting of Privacy Cases: A Proposal for Improving Accountability of Asia-Pacific Privacy Commissioners", 2004. http://ssrn.com/abstract=512782

Greenleaf, Graham, "Five years of the APEC Privacy Framework: Failure or promise?", *Computer Law & Security Review*, Vol. 25, Issue 1, 2009, pp. 28–43.

Greenleaf, Graham, "Independence of data privacy authorities: International standards and Asia-Pacific experience", *Computer Law & Security Review*, Vol. 28, Nos. 1–2, 2012. http://ssrn.com/abstract=1971627

Greenleaf, Graham, *Asian Data Privacy Laws: Trade and Human Rights Perspectives*, Oxford University Press, 2014.

Greenleaf, Graham, "India's Draft the Right to Privacy Bill 2014 – Will Modi's BJP Enact it?", *Privacy Laws & Business International Report*, No. 129, 2014, pp. 21–24. http://ssrn.com/abstract=2481796

Greenleaf, Graham, "Scheherazade and the 101 Data Privacy Laws: Origins, Significance and Global Trajectories", *Journal of Law, Information and Science*, Vol. 23, No. 1, 2014. http://www.jlisjournal.org/abstracts/greenleaf.23.1.html

Greenleaf, Graham, "Global data privacy laws 2015: Data privacy authorities and their organisations", *Privacy Laws & Business International Report*, No. 134, April 2015.

International Conference of Data Protection and Privacy Commissioners, *International Standards on the Protection of Data Protection and Privacy* ("Madrid Resolution"), 5 November 2009. http://www.privacyconference2009.org/dpas_space/space_reserved/documentos_adoptados/common/2009_Madrid/estandares_resolucion_madrid_en.pdf

Kingsford-Smith, Dimity, "A harder nut to crack: Responsive regulation in the financial sector", *University of British Colombia Law Review*, Vol. 44, No. 3, 2011, pp. 695–742 [pp. 705–709].

Kuner, Christopher, *European Data Protection Law: Corporate Compliance and Regulation*, second edition, Oxford University Press, 2007.

Livingston, Scott, and Graham Greenleaf, "China Whys and wherefors: Illegal provision of personal data under Chinese law", *Privacy Laws & Business International Report*, No. 131, 2014, pp. 1–5. http://ssrn.com/abstract=2541570

Organisation for Economic Co-operation and Development, *OECD Guidelines on the Protection of Privacy and Transborder Flows of Personal Data*, Paris, 1981; adopted as a Recommendation of the Council of the OECD, 23 September 1980.

Organisation for Economic Co-operation and Development, *2013 OECD Privacy Guidelines and Supplementary Explanatory Memorandum*, 2013. http://www.oecd.org/sti/ieconomy/2013-oecd-privacy-guidelines.pdf

Chapter 12
Enforcement and Reform of the EU-US Safe Harbor Agreement

Chris Connolly and Peter van Dijk

12.1 Context

The EU/US Safe Harbor Framework[1] is a compromise agreement between two very different approaches to data protection, and as a result it has many limitations.

This chapter examines the history and current practice of enforcement of the Safe Harbor, including individual complaints, and the oversight and enforcement of the regulatory requirements that are imposed on Safe Harbor members. The chapter also discusses attempts at reform of the Safe Harbor.

12.2 Establishment of the Safe Harbor in 2000

Data protection is a fundamental right for European Union citizens. However, the extent of this protection once any personal data leaves Europe has been a longstanding concern. The 1995 Directive on the protection of individuals with regard to the processing of personal data and on the free movement of such data (95/46/EC)[2] attempts to address this issue by establishing a series of restrictions (and exceptions) relating to the transfer of personal data outside Europe.

[1] Safe Harbor background information and official documentation is available at: http://www.export.gov/safeharbor/

[2] European Parliament and the Council, Directive 95/46/EC of the European Parliament and of the Council of 24 October 1995 on the protection of individuals with regard to the processing of personal data and on the free movement of such data, O.J.L. 281, 23 November 1995. http://eur-lex.europa.eu/legal-content/EN/TXT/PDF/?uri=CELEX:01995L0046-20031120&from=EN

C. Connolly (✉) • P. van Dijk
Galexia, Sydney, NSW, Australia
e-mail: chrisc@galexia.com

D. Wright, P. De Hert (eds.), *Enforcing Privacy*, Law, Governance and Technology Series 25, DOI 10.1007/978-3-319-25047-2_12

The key provision is Article 25(1) which prohibits EU Member States from allowing the transfer of personal information to countries that do not have adequate protections in place. Importantly, Article 25(6) allows the European Commission to determine that a country has "adequate" privacy protections, and the EC has exercised this power on numerous occasions.

While the EC has never determined that the US *in its entirety* provides adequate protection, it did negotiate a compromise over the period 1999–2000, known as the EU-US Safe Harbor Framework that applies to a small sub-set of US businesses. The compromise was developed and promoted by the US Department of Commerce and the negotiations were lengthy and controversial.[3] The final agreement was reached despite the opposition of the European Parliament, and published in July 2000.[4]

Under this agreement, certain US companies (not all industry sectors are covered) can voluntarily self-certify that they comply with the Safe Harbor Principles, and thereby be "deemed" in compliance with Directive 95/46/EC.

The agreement is subject to numerous additional rules and tests. For example, the Safe Harbor Principles must be read and interpreted in conjunction with the Safe Harbor Frequently Asked Questions (or FAQs), which contain more detailed implementation rules. The Principles must also be read and interpreted in conjunction with a range of enforcement assurances provided by the Department of Commerce, the Federal Trade Commission and the Department of Transportation.

Finally, the agreement between the European Commission and the US can be suspended or terminated at any time by the European Commission if they believe it is not being implemented correctly or effectively enforced.

In practice, the key enforcement agency is the Federal Trade Commission (there are very few Safe Harbor members who fall under the jurisdiction of the Department of Transportation). The FTC's enforcement powers rely heavily on Sect. 5 of the Federal Trade Commission Act, which prohibits "unfair or deceptive acts or practices" in or affecting commerce. Section 5 can typically be applied where a company (usually through its website privacy policy) falsely claims to comply with specific privacy principles or standards – including the Safe Harbor Privacy Principles. Section 5 has been used as the "hook" for every Safe Harbor enforcement action to date in the US.

---

[3] See, for example, the Working Party on the Protection of Individuals with regard to the Processing of Personal Data, Opinion 7/99 On the Level of Data Protection provided by the "Safe Harbor" Principles as published together with the Frequently Asked Questions (FAQs) and other related documents on 15 and 16 November 1999 by the US Department of Commerce, Adopted on 3 December 1999. http://ec.europa.eu/justice/policies/privacy/docs/wpdocs/1999/wp27en.pdf

[4] European Commission, Commission Decision of 26 July 2000 pursuant to Directive 95/46/EC of the European Parliament and of the Council on the adequacy of the protection provided by the safe harbour privacy principles and related frequently asked questions issued by the US Department of Commerce (2000/520/EC). http://eur-lex.europa.eu/legal-content/EN/TXT/PDF/?uri=CELEX:02000D0520-20000825&from=EN

12.3 Early history: 2000–2008

During the first eight years of operation of the Safe Harbor, no enforcement actions were reported.

However, during this period, the Safe Harbor was the subject of two external reviews commissioned by the European Commission (2002 and 2004) and one independent review by Galexia (2008a), an Australian consultancy and advocacy organisation.

The two European Commission reviews were:

> European Commission, The application of Commission Decision on the adequate protection of personal data provided by the Safe Harbor Privacy Principles, 13 February 2002. http://ec.europa.eu/justice_home/fsj/privacy/docs/adequacy/sec-2002-196/sec-2002-196_en.pdf
>
> European Commission, The implementation of Commission Decision on the adequate protection of personal data provided by the Safe Harbor Privacy Principles, 20 October 2004. http://ec.europa.eu/justice/policies/privacy/docs/studies/safe-harbour-2004_en.pdf

These European Commission reviews noted gradual growth in the membership of the Safe Harbor, but they also raised serious questions about non-compliance and the complete absence of any Safe Harbor related enforcement activity. Indeed, the 2004 European Commission review openly questioned the "lack of interest by the FTC in Safe Harbor implementation and enforcement" at that time.[5]

The US Department of Commerce and the FTC completely ignored the findings and recommendations of these reviews, and no changes were made to the Safe Harbor during this period. Over time, the decision to ignore these reviews has had a significant negative impact on the operation of the Safe Harbor.

In 2008, Galexia completed a detailed study of the Safe Harbor.[6] The study was not commissioned or funded by any third party and had no official status. It was simply part of a series of research articles on self-regulatory privacy frameworks.[7]

The study identified widespread problems with the level of privacy protection being provided by Safe Harbor members. Most of the issues had been identified in the earlier European Commission studies, but those studies had only examined a small sample of Safe Harbor members. The 2008 Galexia study examined all 1,597 companies on the Department of Commerce Safe Harbor list. This approach helped

---

[5] Dhont, Jan, María Verónica Pérez Asinari and Prof. Dr. Yves Poullet, *Safe Harbour Decision Implementation Study*, with the assistance of Prof. Dr. Joel R. Reidenberg and Dr. Lee A. Bygrave, for the European Commission, Internal Market DG, 19 April 2004, p. 91. http://ec.europa.eu/justice/policies/privacy/docs/studies/safe-harbour-2004_en.pdf

[6] Connolly, Chris, *Safe Harbor: Fact or Fiction?*, Galexia, 2008a. http://www.galexia.com/public/research/assets/safe_harbor_fact_or_fiction_2008/print-index.html

[7] The other two reports in the series were: Connolly Chris, *Trustmarks Struggle to Protect Privacy*, Galexia, 2008b. http://www.galexia.com/public/research/assets/trustmarks_struggle_20080926/trustmarks_struggle_public-Coverage.html and Connolly, Chris, "Privacy White Lists: Don't Be Fooled", *Privacy Laws and Business International*, Issue 98, 2009, pp. 9–12. http://www.galexia.com/public/research/articles/research_articles-pa09.html

to capture the attention of the public, and the study received widespread attention amongst both US and EU stakeholders.

The key findings from the Galexia study were:

- 206 organisations claimed on their public websites to be members of the Safe Harbor when they were not current members. Many of these false claims had continued for several years.
- 36 of these 206 false claimants were also accredited by a third party as being current members of their Safe Harbor trustmark scheme (e.g., TRUSTe and BBB).
- 73 organisations claimed to be members of a Privacy Trustmark Scheme when they were not current members of those schemes, or they claimed to be members of schemes that no longer existed.
- 209 organisations selected a dispute resolution provider that was not affordable. These included the American Arbitration Association (AAA) and the Judicial Arbitration Mediation Service (JAMS), which at that time cost thousands of dollars to access. Organisations either failed to disclose these costs or required the consumer to share these costs.

Following the review, Galexia observed some minor improvements in relation to the provision of privacy policies,[8] but the US Department of Commerce did not address the other issues raised in the report.

The US Department of Commerce publicly rejected and dismissed the key findings and recommendations of the Galexia report, and as a consequence the report had no significant impact on levels of compliance within the Safe Harbor. This was the third review that failed to achieve any significant reform.

12.4 The 2009 false claim cases

The three Safe Harbor reviews had all raised concerns about false claims of Safe Harbor membership and the lack of enforcement by the Federal Trade Commission. This issue did receive some attention, and in 2009 the Federal Trade Commission (FTC) took action against six companies who had made false claims.[9]

However, the impact of the cases was very limited:

- The FTC took action against only six companies (Galexia had provided a list of more than 200 false claims to the US authorities).
- All of the companies were small.

[8] "The US Department of Commerce announced that it will review the privacy policies of participants in the Safe Harbor program to ensure that they clearly indicate adherence to the Safe Harbor Privacy Principles." Department of Commerce, Presentation at *Conference on Cross Border Data Flows, Data Protection and Privacy*, Washington, November 2009, summarised at: http://www.jeitosa.com/wp-content/uploads/2010/12/HARRIS_-_DATA_PRIVACY_12-2009.pdf

[9] See the Appendix for full case details.

- None of the companies belonged to a trustmark scheme, despite a high proportion of false claims having a link with trustmark schemes.
- The companies faced no sanctions – they were simply required not to make a false claim in the future.
- One case (Directors Desk) did more harm than good, as the FTC refused to prevent the company from forcing consumers to use an expensive mediation service for complaints.
- All six companies subsequently left the Safe Harbor.

Following the six cases, the number of false claims continued to rise steadily.

12.5 2011–2012: enforcement action by the FTC for substantive breaches

After another long lull in Safe Harbor enforcement activity, the FTC took action against three companies in 2011/2012 for substantive breaches of the Safe Harbor.

In 2011, Facebook and Google were found to have misled consumers about their privacy practices, and agreed to consent orders not to mislead consumers about their compliance with the Safe Harbor principles (amongst other orders). In 2012, Google was found to be in breach of the consent order and paid a substantial fine.

In 2012, MySpace was found to have misled consumers in a similar case. The consent order included Safe Harbor compliance, but MySpace left the Safe Harbor immediately.

The three cases had a more positive impact on Safe Harbor compliance than the earlier 2009 cases. They dealt with substantial issues, they involved large companies, they included an actual sanction (in one case), and two of the companies stayed in the Safe Harbor.

Some commentators have misunderstood the nature of the three *initial* cases and they are often cited as evidence of "robust enforcement" of the Safe Harbor. However, they are more accurately described as a reflection of the light-touch approach to enforcement that has been adopted by the FTC in Safe Harbor cases. There are no actual sanctions for a *first* breach, but heavy penalties for any *subsequent* breach.

The misunderstanding occurs because some commentators believe the orders in the initial cases (for example, the orders requiring audits and external compliance reports for 20 years) are themselves a significant sanction. However, as can be seen in the following table, the FTC orders for a first breach merely re-state the existing Safe Harbor requirements.

Existing Safe Harbor requirement[10]	FTC consent orders[11]
Must provide accurate information regarding the purpose and extent of collection and disclosure of personal information	Must not misrepresent the purpose and extent of collection and disclosure of personal information
Must inform consumers regarding their participation in Safe Harbor	Must not misrepresent compliance with privacy self-regulatory schemes including Safe Harbor
Must establish a comprehensive privacy compliance verification plan	Must establish a comprehensive privacy compliance plan
Must conduct "regular" independent testing and produce an **annual** privacy compliance report, signed off by the corporate officer	Must conduct an independent privacy compliance assessment **every two years**
Verification reports to be made available to the regulator or consumer on request	Compliance reports to be sent to the FTC every two years. Consumers can only access them using FOI
Orders last for the duration of Safe Harbor membership	Orders last for 20 years

It is important to remember that the Safe Harbor is a self-regulatory scheme, backed up by light touch regulation from the FTC for organisations breaching the Safe Harbor for the first time. The only potential for serious sanctions is for subsequent or systemic breaches. Any other characterisation of the scheme has the potential to mislead consumers about its true nature.

12.6 2013: The European Commission review

In May 2013, the Snowden revelations came to light regarding mass surveillance of individuals by the NSA and other agencies. These revelations gave added impetus and a higher profile to concerns about Safe Harbor compliance. However, they were not the only source of concern regarding the Safe Harbor and complaints by European regulators and consumer and privacy advocates had continued throughout the period 2009–2013.

In June 2013, the European Commission began work on a review of the Safe Harbor and, in November 2013, it issued a report recommending 13 specific reforms that would be necessary to restore trust in the Safe Harbor.[12]

[10] These requirements are taken from the Safe Harbor Privacy Principles and FAQs. http://www.export.gov/safeharbor/

[11] These sanctions are from Federal Trade Commission, A closer look at the Myspace Order: Part 2, 10 May 2012. https://www.ftc.gov/news-events/blogs/business-blog/2012/05/closer-look-myspace-order-part-2. Similar sanctions appear in all the key cases.

[12] European Commission, Communication from the Commission to the European Parliament and the Council on the Functioning of the Safe Harbour from the Perspective of EU Citizens and Companies Established in the EU, COM (2013) 847 final, Brussels, 27 November 2013. http://ec.europa.eu/justice/data-protection/files/com_2013_847_en.pdf

The recommendations were (in summary):

1. Self-certified companies should publicly disclose their privacy policies.
2. Privacy policies of self-certified companies' websites should always include a link to the Department of Commerce Safe Harbour website.
3. Self-certified companies should publish privacy conditions of any contracts they conclude with subcontractors.
4. The Department of Commerce should clearly flag on the Safe Harbor website all companies that are not current members of the scheme.
5. The privacy policies on companies' websites should include a link to the relevant alternative dispute resolution (ADR) provider and/or EU panel.
6. ADR should be readily available and affordable.
7. The Department of Commerce should monitor more systematically ADR providers.
8. Following the certification or recertification of companies under the Safe Harbour, a certain percentage of these companies should be subject to *ex officio* investigations of effective compliance of their privacy policies.
9. Whenever there has been a finding of non-compliance, following a complaint or an investigation, the company should be subject to follow-up specific investigation after one year.
10. In case of doubts about a company's compliance or pending complaints, the Department of Commerce should inform the competent EU data protection authority.
11. False claims of Safe Harbour adherence should continue to be investigated.
12. Privacy policies of self-certified companies should include information on the extent to which US law allows public authorities to collect and process data transferred under the Safe Harbour. In particular, companies should be encouraged to indicate in their privacy policies when they apply exceptions to the Safe Harbor principles to meet national security, public interest or law enforcement requirements.
13. It is important that the national security exception foreseen by the Safe Harbour Decision is used only to an extent that is strictly necessary or proportionate.

Some of these recommendations had been made in previous reviews of the Safe Harbor but US authorities had ignored them. One of the recommendations (number 6) merely restated an existing requirement of the Safe Harbor that had been in place since 2000, but US authorities had never enforced it. However, some of the recommendations represented a new approach to Safe Harbor compliance and enforcement, particularly recommendations 3, 8, 12 and 13.

By June 2014, the European Commission reported that it expected to reach agreement on all of the recommendations.[13] The implementation of these recom-

[13] European Commission, "EU-U.S. Justice Ministerial in Athens: Vice-President Reding welcomes U.S. announcement on data protection umbrella agreement", Statement 14/208, 25/06/2014. http://ec.europa.eu/commission_2010-2014/reding/multimedia/news/2014/06/20140625_en.htm

mendations would result in the biggest improvement in Safe Harbor compliance in the history of the Framework.

At the time of writing, some of the recommendations have been implemented or work has commenced on their implementation.

For example, hundreds of organisations have updated their privacy policies, usually to comply with Principle 7. Principle 7 is known as the enforcement principle, but in practice it deals largely with the provision of affordable, independent dispute resolution. Actual enforcement is left to the FTC. The US Department of Commerce states that since March 2013, the Department has refused to register (or renew) a Safe Harbor member who does not comply with Principle 7 in its privacy policy. The new requirement is that organisations must disclose the name and contact details of their dispute resolution provider in their public privacy policies.[14] This might seem like a very simple and straight-forward requirement and it has been part of the Department of Commerce's Safe Harbor guidance since 2000, but it has never been enforced.

Even today, this requirement seems to have passed by many major companies, including Google and Twitter, but there are plenty of examples of improvements in the months following the release of the European Commission review in November 2013. For example, major companies like Amazon have correctly identified their Safe Harbor dispute resolution provider for the first time. Overall, this change should be relatively easy to implement.

In addition, steps have been taken by the US Department of Commerce in mid-2014 to address the issue of the affordability of two of the dispute resolution schemes. Safe Harbor Principle 7 requires members to provide consumers with access to an affordable and independent dispute resolution scheme. All of the previous Safe Harbor reviews have found that hundreds of members were failing to comply with this requirement. Many members had chosen expensive mediation schemes such as the American Arbitration Association (AAA) or the Judicial Arbitration Mediation Service (JAMS) as their provider. At the time of previous reviews, these schemes cost thousands of dollars to access for EU consumers. As a result of these costs, neither scheme has received a single complaint in the 15 years of operation of the Safe Harbor (this contrasts with the thousands of complaints received by the free dispute resolution providers).

The Department of Commerce had previously strenuously denied that this was an issue or that this was a breach of the Safe Harbor. As recently as December 2013, the Department was still denying that this was an issue on its public website.[15] The FTC had also refused to treat this as a breach of the Safe Harbor in a key case in 2009.[16]

[14] Department of Commerce, "Key Points Concerning the Benefits, Oversight, and Enforcement of Safe Harbor", December 2013. http://www.export.gov/static/Safe%20Harbor%20Key%20Points%2012-2013_Latest_eg_main_068867.pdf

[15] Ibid.

[16] Federal Trade Commission, Directors Desk LL, 19 January 2010. https://www.ftc.gov/enforcement/cases-proceedings/0923140/directors-desk-ll

However, in late 2013/early 2014, this picture began to change. For the first time in the long history of the Safe Harbor, the FTC made a statement suggesting that dispute resolution services should be affordable for consumers. Their exact words were: "Consumers should not have to pay substantial fees simply to have their complaints heard."[17]

Then, in late 2013, one of the major dispute resolution providers – JAMS – published a new statement on its website stating that all Safe Harbor mediation would now be free for consumers. Previously, the JAMS International Mediation Rules had required consumers to pay 50 % of the costs. This change affects about 150 companies. (Although many Safe Harbor members still insist that JAMS costs are payable by consumers in their Privacy Policies.)

The Department of Commerce is also reported to have written to Safe Harbor members (in early 2014) who use the AAA as their dispute resolution provider, insisting that they change to an affordable provider or leave the Safe Harbor.[18] This report has not been confirmed but, if correct, this change would impact about 400 companies. (This applies to firms who use the generic AAA service, which is expensive, rather than the AAA/ICDR Safe Harbor service, which is subsidised for EU consumers.)

These changes are intriguing, as they are taking place many years after the requirement for "affordable" dispute resolution was first introduced, and many years after these important issues were raised in complaints and in the various reviews of the Safe Harbor. Although neither the FTC nor the Department of Commerce has made any public acknowledgment, these changes have also been influenced by the submission of several hundred complaints to the FTC (copied to the Department of Commerce and the European Commission) involving companies who failed to provide affordable dispute resolution.

The issue is not yet completely resolved, as dozens of Safe Harbor members, including large household names, still threaten consumers with arbitration fees in their privacy policies. Here are just a few examples of the words currently used by Safe Harbor members:

> Both parties will bear equally the cost of arbitration.
>
> Arbitrators will have the power to award recovery of all costs and fees.
>
> The prevailing party shall be entitled to recover its costs and reasonable attorneys' fees.
>
> [Company X] will assume the costs of the administrative fees if the mediator makes a written recommendation that finds [Company X] in breach of its duties pursuant to the Safe Harbour.

Once these threats are removed, it seems that the Safe Harbor requirement for affordable dispute resolution, first enshrined in 2000, will finally be implemented. It has been a long and sometimes bitter campaign.

---

[17] Brill, Julie, "At the Crossroads", Keynote Speech at the IAPP Europe Data Protection Congress, 11 Dec 2013, Brussels, Belgium. http://www.ftc.gov/sites/default/files/documents/public_statements/crossroads-keynote-address-iapp-europe-data-protection-congress/131211iappkeynote.pdf

[18] Grande, Allison, "EU-US Safe Harbor Members Warned Over Arbitrator's New Fee", Law360, New York, 5 June 2014 (subscription required). http://www.law360.com/articles/545209/eu-us-safe-harbor-members-warned-over-arbitrator-s-new-fee

12.7 2014–2015: more FTC consent orders for false claims

Following the Snowden revelations and the launch of the European Commission's investigation into the Safe Harbor in 2013, there has been a new wave of FTC enforcement activity in relation to false claims of Safe Harbor membership.

In June 2014, the FTC issued final consent orders in 14 cases where companies had made false claims of Safe Harbor membership.[19] In all 14 cases, the companies were previous Safe Harbor members who had allowed their membership to lapse, but still claimed to be members on their websites (for periods ranging from six months to eight years). None of the 14 cases involved companies who were *never* Safe Harbor members.

Although some of the 14 cases involve multiple breaches of the Safe Harbor, the FTC only issued draft consent orders in relation to the false claims. However, they did address some other breaches as side issues in the period between the draft consent orders and final orders (for example, important corrections were made to privacy policies during this period, following comments raised by advocates).

Interestingly, three of the cases related to companies that were also reported to US authorities in 2009. It is unclear why no public action was taken at that time. Perhaps it was because the 2009 report was "informal", rather than a formal complaint.

These 14 cases are similar to the 2009 consent orders. However, the companies involved are larger, and four of the companies had links to trustmark schemes (specifically TRUSTe). About half the companies have now re-joined the Safe Harbor.

A further two cases were settled by the FTC in May 2015 (TES Franchising and American International Mailing).[20] In both cases, the company had made a false claim of Safe Harbor membership. While the cases were similar to the previous false claim cases, the TES Franchising case also raised two new issues.

First, the company was found to have made an additional false claim in relation to its membership of TRUSTe. Their privacy policy claimed that its privacy practices were certified by TRUSTe, but this claim was untrue. This type of false claim is very common, not just in relation to TRUSTe, but also in relation to other privacy certification providers.

Second, the company was found to have misled consumers regarding the potential costs of independent dispute resolution. Their privacy policy stated that dispute resolution would be provided by an expensive US private mediation firm, when in fact they had self-certified to the Department of Commerce that dispute resolution would be provided for free by a European service. The FTC noted that this false claim was "likely to deter EU citizens from attempting to take advantage of the dispute resolution services offered by the company". This is the first (and only) time

---

[19] See the Appendix for full case details.

[20] See the Appendix for full case details.

that the US authorities have acknowledged the deterrent effect of the expensive private mediation firms that have operated in the Safe Harbor throughout its history. The case is a significant departure from the decision in the Directors Desk case in 2009, in which use of the same private mediation firm was ruled not to be a breach of the Safe Harbor framework.

Finally, in August 2015, the FTC settled a group of 13 additional cases.[21] In seven of the cases, the companies were previous Safe Harbor members who had allowed their membership to lapse, but were still claiming to be members in their privacy policies and advertising. This subset of seven cases simply follows the previous pattern of cases against prior members.

However, in a major diversion from previous enforcement activity, the other six cases were all companies who had never even applied to be members of the Safe Harbor. These were cases of straightforward deception.

In all of these 29 false claim cases between 2014 and 2015, the US authorities issued no specific sanctions. There were no apologies, notices to consumers, fines, compensation or any other specific requirements beyond a requirement to comply with the existing Safe Harbor rules. This is in keeping with the FTC's light-touch regulatory approach for the first breach by an organisation. The deterrent effect of these cases is questionable. Since the FTC began this series of cases in 2013, the overall number of false claims of Safe Harbor membership has continued to grow. In the absence of a fine or a specific sanction, it is difficult to see how the growth in Safe Harbor false claims can be addressed.

12.8 Outstanding issues

It is clear that a combination of the Snowden revelations, the European Commission recommendations and a massive wave of individual complaints in the period 2013–2015 has led to a series of significant improvements in Safe Harbor compliance and governance. However, a number of important compliance issues still need to be addressed.

12.8.1 Safe Harbor fraud

The European Commission report and the recent FTC cases have attempted to address the issue of false claims of Safe Harbor membership. However, the majority of cases only cover situations where a *former* member has allowed its membership to lapse.

[21] See the Appendix to this chapter for full case details.

A different type of false claim occurs where a company claims to be a Safe Harbor member, but it has *never* been a member. This is straight-forward fraud. These cases are surprisingly common. The FTC did prosecute one company in this category in early 2009.[22] There were then no cases in this category between 2009 and 2015. The issue was also not discussed in any of the recent reviews or documents on Safe Harbor compliance. Finally, in August 2015, the FTC raised complaints against six companies for making this type of fraudulent claim – a tiny fraction of the number of companies behaving in this way.

Safe Harbor compliance will only improve when this type of fraud is eliminated, so that consumers can be confident that companies claiming to provide Safe Harbor protection are legitimate members. Much more work needs to be done in order to eliminate Safe Harbor fraud.

12.8.2 Safe Harbor exclusions

The Safe Harbor can sometimes provide an ad hoc form of privacy protection. Levels of protection will vary as companies join the Safe Harbor and leave (and sometimes re-join). Within the Safe Harbor, members can also choose to exclude certain categories of data (online, offline, human resources and customer data) and these exclusions are typically only noted on the DOC website – not in individual privacy policies.

These basic exclusions can cause some difficulty and confusion for consumers, but a new type of exclusion appearing in many Safe Harbor privacy policies is even more alarming.

When organisations use some trustmark schemes, notably TRUSTe, as their dispute resolution provider for the Safe Harbor, the privacy policy often excludes key categories of personal information from coverage, leaving a significant gap in Safe Harbor protection.

These organisations still claim that they are complying with the Safe Harbor, even when their main business activity appears to be specifically excluded from Safe Harbor dispute resolution.

There are hundreds of members that use these exclusions. Some examples of the typical wording used in these exclusions are:

> The program covers only information that is collected through this Web site, and does not cover information that may be collected through our mobile applications, social networking applications, or behind the log in on our website.
>
> The program covers only information that is collected through the website and does not cover information that may be collected through downloadable software, SaaS offerings, or mobile applications.

---

[22] *FTC* v. *Javian Karnani and Balls of Kryptonite*, 2009. http://www.ftc.gov/sites/default/files/documents/cases/2009/08/090806karnanitro.pdf

The program covers only information that is collected through these Web Sites, and does not cover information that may be collected behind the log in on our website or client portal websites.

This problem has grown in recent years as cloud services and mobile applications have become popular. Indeed, these additional services are often the core location for EU personal information, but they are excluded from Safe Harbor protection.

The FTC, DOC and European Commission have been aware of this issue for many months, and have been supplied with hundreds of complaints relating to this issue. Safe Harbor compliance will only be achieved when the key authorities acknowledge this issue, warn consumers, and outline how this issue will be addressed.

12.8.3 Trustmarks

Trustmarks play a key role in the Safe Harbor. The Safe Harbor remains a predominantly self-regulatory scheme, and trustmarks provide an outsourced "verification" service for compliance with Principle 7. They also act as independent dispute resolution providers. In 2015, approximately 1,350 Safe Harbor members belonged to a trustmark scheme.

Any drop in the quality and integrity of the trustmark schemes can have a significant impact on Safe Harbor compliance. In practice, the trustmark schemes are performing very poorly in basic areas of Safe Harbor compliance.

Around a quarter of all Safe Harbor false claims come from companies that have also been certified as Safe Harbor compliant by trustmark schemes. It is difficult to see how this is possible, as the trustmark schemes are supposed to be completing annual verification reports for each company in compliance with Safe Harbor Principle 7. The verification reports are supposed to be based on audits and random testing, and need to be signed off each year. However, many false claims involving trustmarks have covered multiple years (the current record is eight years of repeated false claims).

The trustmark schemes used to publish lists of their certified members. This helps consumers verify their certification. However, in recent years, this system has collapsed, and now only one of the Safe Harbor trustmark schemes maintains a public list of certified members.

Bizarrely, one of the schemes now offers a specific Safe Harbor privacy seal that lasts for two years. This is completely inappropriate in a scheme that requires annual certification, and it is no surprise that many organisations are still displaying this particular seal long after their actual Safe Harbor membership has expired.

Finally, two major trustmark schemes have left the Safe Harbor without any warning or notice. In these cases, the relevant Safe Harbor seals tend to "live on" for an extended period, despite the complete lack of protection or coverage that these out-of-date emblems provide.

For most of the history of the Safe Harbor, the FTC only took limited action against trustmark schemes in relation to breaches of the Safe Harbor, despite specific requests to do so.

In the 2009 false claim cases discussed above, six companies were identified as making false claims of Safe Harbor membership. Surprisingly, none of the companies belonged to a trustmark scheme. This statistically unlikely result meant that there was no pressure on trustmark schemes regarding false claims.

In the 2014–2015 false claim cases described above, the FTC identified 29 companies as making false claims of Safe Harbor membership. This time, four of the companies had been certified by a trustmark scheme (TRUSTe[23] in all four cases). This was a better reflection of the proportion of false claimants certified by trustmark schemes, although it does not reflect the large number of false claimants certified by other trustmark schemes such as BBB[24] and eTRUST.[25] Strangely, the 2014–2015 cases included no findings or sanctions against TRUSTe.

Finally, in March 2015, the FTC reached a settlement with TRUSTe regarding public statements made by TRUSTe and TRUSTe-certified companies. According to the final consent order,[26] TRUSTe is required to pay a $200,000 fine for its misleading and deceptive conduct between 2007 and 2013, plus a range of other sanctions, because of its failure to conduct annual re-certifications in key schemes such as the EU-US Safe Harbor and the Children's Online Privacy Protection Act (COPPA) Safe Harbor.[27] FTC Chairwoman Edith Ramirez summed up the FTC's findings as "TRUSTe promised to hold companies accountable for protecting consumer privacy, but it fell short of that pledge."[28]

This case followed a six-year campaign by privacy advocates, and a 24-month formal complaints process, regarding the deceptive practices of TRUSTe. Most of the initial concerns regarding TRUSTe related to the Safe Harbor, although over time, these concerns have spread to other schemes including COPPA and more recently the APEC Cross Border Privacy Rules system (APEC CBPRs). The recent FTC action barely scratches the surface of the conduct complained of to the FTC, but it is still a significant case, and a first step towards improving the conduct of trustmark schemes everywhere.

---

[23] http://www.truste.com/

[24] http://www.bbb.org/council/eusafeharbor/

[25] http://www.etrust.org/

[26] Federal Trade Commission, *In the Matter of True Ultimate Standards Everywhere, Inc., a corporation d/b/a TRUSTe, Inc. – Agreement Containing Consent Order*, 18 March 2015. https://www.ftc.gov/enforcement/cases-proceedings/132-3219/true-ultimate-standards-everywhere-inc-truste-matter

[27] Federal Trade Commission, "TRUSTe Settles FTC Charges it Deceived Consumers Through Its Privacy Seal Program – Company Failed to Conduct Annual Recertifications, Facilitated Misrepresentation as Non-Profit", Media Release, 17 November 2014. http://www.ftc.gov/news-events/press-releases/2014/11/truste-settles-ftc-charges-it-deceived-consumers-through-its

[28] Ibid.

In order to achieve lasting reform in the Safe Harbor, trustmark schemes should be required to take steps to eliminate false claims, to eliminate conflicts of interest, to remove fine print exclusions, to publish accurate lists of certified members and to improve the quality of their annual verification process.

12.8.4 *Complaints of substantive Safe Harbor breaches by data brokers*

In August 2014, the Center for Digital Democracy submitted 30 complaints to the Federal Trade Commission alleging breaches of the Safe Harbor by US data brokers and profilers.[29]

The detailed and comprehensive complaints argue that the 30 selected companies are "compiling, using, and sharing EU consumers' personal information without their awareness and meaningful consent, in violation the Safe Harbor framework".

These "substantive" complaints raise similar issues to those considered in the 2012 and 2013 FTC Safe Harbor cases against Facebook, Google and MySpace discussed above.

At the time of writing, there is no information available on the progress of these cases.

12.8.5 *The use of Safe Harbor as a shield*

One of the most contentious issues surrounding the Safe Harbor is its relationship with national security surveillance. Many EU stakeholders have expressed alarm at the role the Safe Harbor has played in allowing EU data to be transferred to the US, where it has potentially been made available to US security agencies.

However, some US stakeholders have been keen to distance the Safe Harbor from the debate around national security surveillance. Many US stakeholders argue that the Safe Harbor is a commercial arrangement and it should be kept separate from the current debate on national security.

Here are some examples of recent comments defending the Safe Harbor:

> The Safe Harbor framework has been heavily criticized following recent revelations regarding U.S. law enforcement access to EU personal data held by certain Safe Harbor certified entities. This criticism is unwarranted. The critics are inappropriately conflating law enforcement access to personal data once the data are outside of the originating jurisdiction, with the mechanism that was used to transfer the data out of the jurisdiction in the first

---

[29] See:http://www.democraticmedia.org/cdd-files-complaint-useu-safe-harbor-data-privacy-ftc-filing-reveals-failure-us-agreement-protect-eu

place. Unfortunately, this key distinction has been overlooked, as has the fact that other cross-border data transfer mechanisms are similarly vulnerable with respect to access by government agencies once data are in the recipient country.[30]

In addressing national security … Safe Harbor is an easy target but perhaps is not the right target.[31]

Criticisms of the Safe Harbor program are largely unfounded.[32]

The criticism that has been levelled against the [Safe Harbor] program is wholly unfair in my view.[33]

Despite these concerns, the European Commission has asked for the Safe Harbor national security exemption to be tightened and for improvements in disclosure to EU citizens. European and US officials appear close to reaching an agreement on this issue.[34]

The one outstanding (and alarming) feature of the post-Snowden Safe Harbor debate is that the Safe Harbor has specifically been used as a shield to protect US businesses from complaints by EU citizens in relation to national security surveillance.

This has now occurred in Ireland in the Europe v Facebook case[35] and to a lesser extent in Luxembourg (in the Europe v Microsoft and Skype cases[36]). There are reports of similar cases emerging in other jurisdictions.

In the Europe v Facebook case, an EU citizen attempted to bring a complaint regarding the disclosure of personal information to US security agencies via a Safe Harbor member company. The local data protection authority (in this case, the Irish Data Protection Commissioner) refused to consider the case on the basis that the initial disclosure to a Safe Harbor member is allowed, so there is no prospect of a legal challenge to the transfer to the US. It is unclear whether this "defence" was driven by the US companies, or whether it was simply raised by the data protection authorities.

---

[30] Hunton & Williams and the US Chamber of Commerce, *Business Without Borders, The Importance of Cross-Border Data Transfers to Global Prosperity*, Washington 2014, p. 21. https://www.uschamber.com/sites/default/files/documents/files/021384_BusinessWOBorders_final.pdf

[31] Federal Trade Commission, *Privacy Enforcement and Safe Harbor: Comments of FTC Staff to European Commission Review of the U.S.-EU Safe Harbor Framework*, 12 November 2013. http://www.ftc.gov/sites/default/files/documents/public_statements/privacy-enforcement-safe-harbor-comments-ftc-staff-european-commission-review-u.s.eu-safe-harbor-framework/131112europeancommissionsafeharbor.pdf

[32] Future of Privacy Forum (FPF), *The US EU Safe Harbor Framework*, December 2012. http://www.futureofprivacy.org/wp-content/uploads/FPF-Safe-Harbor-Report.pdf

[33] Lisa Sotto, Partner Hunton & Williams, quoted in DataGuidance, 29 May 2014. http://www.dataguidance.com/dataguidance_privacy_this_week.asp?id=2428

[34] European Commission, "EU-U.S. Justice Ministerial in Athens: Vice-President Reding welcomes U.S. announcement on data protection umbrella agreement", Statement 14/208, 25 June 2014. http://ec.europa.eu/commission_2010-2014/reding/multimedia/news/2014/06/20140625_en.htm

[35] See numerous resources at: http://europe-v-facebook.org/EN/en.html

[36] See: http://www.europe-v-facebook.org/PA_18_11_en.pdf

These cases raise two important issues for the Safe Harbor:

The first issue is that the use of the Safe Harbor to shield US companies from complaints regarding national security surveillance completely undermines the argument that the Safe Harbor should somehow be distanced from the Snowden debate. Any argument that the Safe Harbor is not the right target collapses at this point.

The second issue is that the objective of the Safe Harbor was never to extinguish the fundamental rights of EU citizens. Indeed, the Safe Harbor is designed to facilitate the *extension* of those rights in circumstances where companies transfer personal data to the US. Importantly, by signing the Safe Harbor agreement, the US has consented to this extension of European rights. The recent cases, particularly Europe v Facebook, appear to have the impact of extinguishing EU fundamental rights.

Complaints and cases regarding national security should be dealt with on their merits. Using the Safe Harbor as a shield and preventing an EU citizen from even having the matter investigated is a poor outcome for all parties.

The decision of the Irish Data Protection Commissioner in Europe v Facebook has recently been considered by the Irish High Court.[37] It in turn referred the matter to the European Court of Justice. The European Court of Justice concluded its case on 6 October 2015, and declared that the European Commission decision approving the Safe Harbor framework was invalid. Their reasoning was that the Safe Harbor did not include any conditions or restrictions on the surveillance of European citizens, and that European citizens could not access any form of judicial redress in the US in relation to national security surveillance.[38]

At the time of writing, the EU and US authorities are attempting to negotiate a revised Safe Harbor fframework that addresses these two key issues (in addition to the other issues raised in the earlier European Commission report).

12.9 Conclusion

Compliance levels in the Safe Harbor have suffered because of the low level of enforcement activity. There have been long periods (2000–2008, 2010–2011 and 2012–2013) with absolutely no enforcement activity. The rare enforcement activity that has occurred has usually resulted from direct campaigns by privacy and consumer advocates, rather than any general oversight or investigation by the authorities. More than 1,300 Safe Harbor complaints to the FTC have resulted in only 40 successful enforcement cases, and even in those cases, only two companies have faced a monetary sanction.

---

[37] *Schrems v Data Protection Commissioner*, Irish High Court, June 2014, Unofficial transcript at: http://www.europe-v-facebook.org/hcj.pdf

[38] The press release is at http://curia.europa.eu/jcms/upload/docs/application/pdf/2015-10/cp150117en.pdf

This poor enforcement record is the key reason why the Safe Harbor has failed to protect consumers during its 15-year history.

However, after a long history of denying any problems, rejecting any criticism and ignoring any recommendations for reform, it appears that US authorities are finally going to implement some significant reforms and improvements to the Safe Harbor framework, and this may include increased enforcement activity. A principal driver for this change has been the Snowden revelations regarding national security surveillance in May 2013, as all previous efforts to initiate reform had failed.

However, the changes that will now occur reflect many of the issues raised during a long campaign for reform of the Safe Harbor by privacy and consumer advocates. The trigger for the reforms is highly unusual, but the long overdue improvements will be welcome.

There are still some outstanding issues that need to be acknowledged and addressed, and levels of enforcement remain very low, but the mood has changed, and it will be difficult to deny and ignore these issues in the future.

Appendix: Safe Harbor complaints summary

Year	Case	Issue	Sanction	Outcome
2009	Javian Karnani and Balls of Kryptonite http://www.ftc.gov/os/caselist/0923081/	Safe Harbor fraud	Injunction	Never a Safe Harbor member
		Other consumer related claims		
2009	Collectify http://www.ftc.gov/os/caselist/0923142/	False claim of Safe Harbor membership	None	Left the Safe Harbor
2009	Progressive Gaitways http://www.ftc.gov/os/caselist/0923141/	False claim of Safe Harbor membership	None	Left the Safe Harbor
2009	Directors Desk http://www.ftc.gov/os/caselist/0923140/	False claim of Safe Harbor membership	None	Left the Safe Harbor
		Also a complaint of non-compliance with Principle 7 (dismissed)		
2009	Onyx Graphics http://www.ftc.gov/os/caselist/0923139/	False claim of Safe Harbor membership	None	Left the Safe Harbor
2009	ExpatEdge Partners http://www.ftc.gov/os/caselist/0923138/	False claim of Safe Harbor membership	None	Left the Safe Harbor
2009	World Innovators http://www.ftc.gov/os/caselist/0923137/	False claim of Safe Harbor membership	None	Left the Safe Harbor
2011	Facebook http://www.ftc.gov/os/caselist/0923184/	Substantive non-compliance	None	Stayed in the Safe Harbor

(continued)

Year	Case	Issue	Sanction	Outcome
2011	Google (2011) http://www.ftc.gov/os/caselist/1023136/	Substantive non-compliance	None	Stayed in the Safe Harbor
2012	Google (2012) http://www.ftc.gov/enforcement/cases-proceedings/google-inc	Breach of 2011 order	Civil penalty	Stayed in the Safe Harbor
2012	MySpace http://www.ftc.gov/os/caselist/1023058/	Substantive non-compliance	None	Left the Safe Harbor
2014	Apperian, Inc. http://www.ftc.gov/enforcement/cases-and-proceedings/cases/142-3017/apperian-inc-matter	False claim of Safe Harbor membership	None	Re-joined the Safe Harbor
2014	Atlanta Falcons Football Club, LLC http://www.ftc.gov/enforcement/cases-and-proceedings/cases/142-3018/atlanta-falcons-football-club-llc-matter	False claim of Safe Harbor membership	None	Left the Safe Harbor
2014	Baker Tilly Virchow Krause, LLP http://www.ftc.gov/enforcement/cases-and-proceedings/cases/142-3019/baker-tilly-virchow-krause-llp-matter	False claim of Safe Harbor membership	None	Re-joined the Safe Harbor
2014	BitTorrent, Inc. http://www.ftc.gov/enforcement/cases-and-proceedings/cases/142-3020/bittorrent-inc-matter	False claim of Safe Harbor membership	None	Left the Safe Harbor
2014	Charles River Laboratories International, Inc. http://www.ftc.gov/enforcement/cases-and-proceedings/cases/142-3022/charles-river-laboratories-intl-matter	False claim of Safe Harbor membership	None	Re-joined the Safe Harbor
2014	DataMotion, Inc. https://ftcpublic.commentworks.com/ftc/datamotionconsent	False claim of Safe Harbor membership	None	Re-joined the Safe Harbor
2014	DDC Laboratories, Inc. http://www.ftc.gov/enforcement/cases-and-proceedings/cases/142-3023/datamotion-inc-corporation-matter	False claim of Safe Harbor membership	None	Re-joined the Safe Harbor
2014	Level 3 Communications, LLC http://www.ftc.gov/enforcement/cases-and-proceedings/cases/142-3028/level-3-communications-llc-matter	False claim of Safe Harbor membership	None	Left the Safe Harbor

(continued)

Year	Case	Issue	Sanction	Outcome
2014	PDB Sports, Ltd., d/b/a Denver Broncos Football Club http://www.ftc.gov/enforcement/cases-and-proceedings/cases/142-3025/pdb-sports-ltd-dba-denver-broncos-football-club	False claim of Safe Harbor membership	None	Left the Safe Harbor
2014	Reynolds Consumer Products Inc. http://www.ftc.gov/enforcement/cases-and-proceedings/cases/142-3030/reynolds-consumer-products-inc-matter	False claim of Safe Harbor membership	None	Left the Safe Harbor
2014	Receivable Management Services Corporation http://www.ftc.gov/enforcement/cases-and-proceedings/cases/142-3031/receivable-management-services-corporation-matter	False claim of Safe Harbor membership	None	Left the Safe Harbor
2014	Tennessee Football, Inc. http://www.ftc.gov/enforcement/cases-and-proceedings/cases/142-3032/tennessee-football-inc-matter	False claim of Safe Harbor membership	None	Left the Safe Harbor
2014	Fantage.com http://www.ftc.gov/system/files/documents/cases/140107fantageagree.pdf	False claim of Safe Harbor membership	None	Re-joined the Safe Harbor
2014	American Apparel http://www.ftc.gov/enforcement/cases-proceedings/142-3036/american-apparel-inc-matter	False claim of Safe Harbor membership	None	Re-joined the Safe Harbor
2015	TRUSTe https://www.ftc.gov/enforcement/cases-proceedings/132-3219/true-ultimate-standards-everywhere-inc-truste-matter	Numerous instances of misleading and deceptive conduct	$200,000 disgorgement of profit	N/a
2015	TES Franchising https://www.ftc.gov/enforcement/cases-proceedings/152-3015/tes-franchising-llc-matter	False claim of Safe Harbor membership False claim of trustmark certification Threat of expensive dispute resolution	None	Left the Safe Harbor
2015	American International Mail https://www.ftc.gov/enforcement/cases-proceedings/152-3051/american-international-mailing-inc-matter	False claim of Safe Harbor membership	None	Left the Safe Harbor

(continued)

Year	Case	Issue	Sanction	Outcome
2015	Golf Connect, LLC https://www.ftc.gov/system/files/documents/cases/150813golfconnectcmpt.pdf	False claim of Safe Harbor membership	None	Pending
2015	Pinger, Inc. https://www.ftc.gov/system/files/documents/cases/150813pingercmpt.pdf	False claim of Safe Harbor membership	None	Pending
2015	NAICS Association, LLC https://www.ftc.gov/system/files/documents/cases/150813naicscmpt.pdf	False claim of Safe Harbor membership	None	Pending
2015	Jubilant Clinsys, Inc. https://www.ftc.gov/system/files/documents/cases/150813jubilantcmpt.pdf	False claim of Safe Harbor membership	None	Pending
2015	IOActive, Inc. https://www.ftc.gov/system/files/documents/cases/150813ioactivecmpt.pdf	False claim of Safe Harbor membership	None	Pending
2015	Contract Logix, LLC https://www.ftc.gov/system/files/documents/cases/150813ct.pdf	False claim of Safe Harbor membership	None	Pending
2015	Forensics Consulting Solutions, LLC https://www.ftc.gov/system/files/documents/cases/150813forensicscmpt.pdf	False claim of Safe Harbor membership	None	Pending
2015	Dale Jarrett Racing Adventure https://www.ftc.gov/system/files/documents/cases/150813dalejarrettracingcmpt.pdf	Safe Harbor fraud	None	Never a Safe Harbor member
2015	SteriMed Medical Waste Solutions https://www.ftc.gov/system/files/documents/cases/150813sterimedcmpt.pdf	Safe Harbor fraud	None	Never a Safe Harbor member
2015	California Skate-Line https://www.ftc.gov/system/files/documents/cases/150813californiaskatelinecmpt.pdf	Safe Harbor fraud	None	Never a Safe Harbor member
2015	Just Bagels Mfg., Inc. https://www.ftc.gov/system/files/documents/cases/150813justbagelscmpt.pdf	Safe Harbor fraud	None	Never a Safe Harbor member
2015	One Industries Corp. https://www.ftc.gov/system/files/documents/cases/150813oneindustriescmpt.pdf	Safe Harbor fraud	None	Never a Safe Harbor member
2015	Inbox Group, LLC https://www.ftc.gov/system/files/documents/cases/150813inboxgroupcmpt.pdf	Safe Harbor fraud	None	Never a Safe Harbor member

References

Brill, Julie, "At the Crossroads", Keynote Speech at the IAPP Europe Data Protection Congress, Brussels, 11 December 2013. http://www.ftc.gov/sites/default/files/documents/public_statements/crossroads-keynote-address-iapp-europe-data-protection-congress/131211iappkeynote.pdf

Connolly, Chris, *Safe Harbor: Fact or Fiction?*, Galexia, 2008a. http://www.galexia.com/public/research/assets/safe_harbor_fact_or_fiction_2008/print-index.html

Connolly Chris, *Trustmarks Struggle to Protect Privacy*, Galexia, 2008b. http://www.galexia.com/public/research/assets/trustmarks_struggle_20080926/trustmarks_struggle_public-Coverage.html

Connolly, Chris, "Privacy White Lists: Don't Be Fooled", *Privacy Laws and Business International*, Issue 98, 2009. http://www.galexia.com/public/research/articles/research_articles-pa09.html

Department of Commerce, Presentation at *Conference on Cross Border Data Flows, Data Protection and Privacy*, Washington, November 2009, summarised at: http://www.jeitosa.com/wp-content/uploads/2010/12/HARRIS_-_DATA_PRIVACY_12-2009.pdf

Department of Commerce, "Key Points Concerning the Benefits, Oversight, and Enforcement of Safe Harbor", December 2013. http://www.export.gov/static/Safe%20Harbor%20Key%20Points%2012-2013_Latest_eg_main_068867.pdf

Dhont, Jan, María Verónica Pérez Asinari and Prof. Dr. Yves Poullet, *Safe Harbour Decision Implementation Study*, with the assistance of Prof. Dr. Joel R. Reidenberg and Dr. Lee A. Bygrave, for the European Commission, Internal Market DG, 19 April 2004. http://ec.europa.eu/justice/policies/privacy/docs/studies/safe-harbour-2004_en.pdf

European Commission, Commission Decision of 26 July 2000 pursuant to Directive 95/46/EC of the European Parliament and of the Council on the adequacy of the protection provided by the safe harbour privacy principles and related frequently asked questions issued by the US Department of Commerce (2000/520/EC). http://eur-lex.europa.eu/legal-content/EN/TXT/PDF/?uri=CELEX:02000D0520-20000825&from=EN

European Commission, The application of Commission Decision on the adequate protection of personal data provided by the Safe Harbor Privacy Principles, 13 February 2002. http://ec.europa.eu/justice_home/fsj/privacy/docs/adequacy/sec-2002-196/sec-2002-196_en.pdf

European Commission, The implementation of Commission Decision on the adequate protection of personal data provided by the Safe Harbor Privacy Principles, 20 October 2004. http://ec.europa.eu/justice/policies/privacy/docs/studies/safe-harbour-2004_en.pdf

European Commission, Communication from the Commission to the European Parliament and the Council on the Functioning of the Safe Harbour from the Perspective of EU Citizens and Companies Established in the EU, COM (2013) 847 final, Brussels, 27 November 2013. http://ec.europa.eu/justice/data-protection/files/com_2013_847_en.pdf

European Commission, "EU-U.S. Justice Ministerial in Athens: Vice-President Reding welcomes U.S. announcement on data protection umbrella agreement", Statement 14/208, 25 June 2014. http://ec.europa.eu/commission_2010-2014/reding/multimedia/news/2014/06/20140625_en.htm

European Parliament and the Council, Directive 95/46/EC of the European Parliament and of the Council of 24 October 1995 on the protection of individuals with regard to the processing of personal data and on the free movement of such data, O.J.L. 281, 23 November 1995. http://eur-lex.europa.eu/legal-content/EN/TXT/PDF/?uri=CELEX:01995L0046-20031120&from=EN

Federal Trade Commission, Directors Desk LL, 19 January 2010. https://www.ftc.gov/enforcement/cases-proceedings/0923140/directors-desk-ll

Federal Trade Commission, A closer look at the Myspace Order: Part 2, 10 May 2012. https://www.ftc.gov/news-events/blogs/business-blog/2012/05/closer-look-myspace-order-part-2

Federal Trade Commission, Privacy Enforcement and Safe Harbor: Comments of FTC Staff to European Commission Review of the U.S.-EU Safe Harbor Framework, 12 November 2013. http://www.ftc.gov/sites/default/files/documents/public_statements/privacy-enforcement-safe-harbor-comments-ftc-staff-european-commission-review-u.s.eu-safe-harbor-framework/131112europeancommissionsafeharbor.pdf

Federal Trade Commission, "TRUSTe Settles FTC Charges it Deceived Consumers Through Its Privacy Seal Program – Company Failed to Conduct Annual Recertifications, Facilitated Misrepresentation as Non-Profit", Media Release, 17 November 2014. http://www.ftc.gov/news-events/press-releases/2014/11/truste-settles-ftc-charges-it-deceived-consumers-through-its

Federal Trade Commission, *In the Matter of True Ultimate Standards Everywhere, Inc., a corporation d/b/a TRUSTe, Inc. – Agreement Containing Consent Order*, 18 March 2015. https://www.ftc.gov/enforcement/cases-proceedings/132-3219/true-ultimate-standards-everywhere-inc-truste-matter

FTC v. *Javian Karnani and Balls of Kryptonite*, 2009. http://www.ftc.gov/sites/default/files/documents/cases/2009/08/090806karnanitro.pdf

Future of Privacy Forum (FPF), *The US EU Safe Harbor Framework*, December 2012. http://www.futureofprivacy.org/wp-content/uploads/FPF-Safe-Harbor-Report.pdf

Grande, Allison, "EU-US Safe Harbor Members Warned Over Arbitrator's New Fee", Law 360, New York, 5 June 2014 (subscription required). http://www.law360.com/articles/545209/eu-us-safe-harbor-members-warned-over-arbitrator-s-new-fee

Hunton & Williams and the US Chamber of Commerce, *Business Without Borders, The Importance of Cross-Border Data Transfers to Global Prosperity*, Washington 2014. https://www.uschamber.com/sites/default/files/documents/files/021384_BusinessWOBorders_final.pdf

Schrems v Data Protection Commissioner, Irish High Court, June 2014, Unofficial transcript at: http://www.europe-v-facebook.org/hcj.pdf

Working Party on the Protection of Individuals with regard to the Processing of Personal Data, Opinion 7/99 On the Level of Data Protection provided by the "Safe Harbor" Principles as published together with the Frequently Asked Questions (FAQs) and other related documents on 15 and 16 November 1999 by the US Department of Commerce, Adopted on 3 December 1999. http://ec.europa.eu/justice/policies/privacy/docs/wpdocs/1999/wp27en.pdf

Part III
Instruments

Chapter 13
How Effective Are Fines in Enforcing Privacy?

Hazel Grant and Hannah Crowther

13.1 Introduction

This chapter considers how effective monetary penalties are at enforcing privacy, with a particular focus on the monetary penalties issued by the UK Information Commissioner's Office (ICO).

Due to the relative youth of data protection law, and the rapid developments in technology which have led to an explosion in data processing, it is impossible to say with certainty how effective fines are in this area of law. However, the vast fining powers in the new General Data Protection Regulation[1] (GDPR), which will come into force in 2018, suggest that in Europe at least both the legislators and regulators believe that fines can have the desired effect.

Fines, in some form or another, are a feature of most data protection and privacy regimes across the world. Nevertheless, fining does not seem to have been embraced as whole-heartedly in the privacy arena as it has been in the enforcement of many other state-regulated activities. When looked at in the context of the amount of personal data that is processed, issuing sanctions is still a relatively rare occurrence.[2]

[1] European Commission, Proposal for a Regulation of the European Parliament and of the Council on the Protection of Individuals with Regard to the Processing of Personal Data and on the Free Movement of Such Data (General Data Protection Regulation), COM(2012) 11 final, Brussels, 25 January 2012.

[2] By way of an example, between April and December 2013, 1,152 data breach incidents were reported to the ICO whilst only 15 monetary penalty notices were issued during the same period (a

H. Grant (✉)
Privacy and Information Law, Fieldfisher LLP,
Riverbank House, 2 Swan Lane, EC4R 3TT London, UK
e-mail: Hazel.Grant@fieldfisher.com

H. Crowther
Associate Bristows LLP, 100 Victoria Embankment, EC4Y 0DH London, UK
e-mail: hannah.crowther@bristows.com

D. Wright, P. De Hert (eds.), *Enforcing Privacy*, Law, Governance and Technology Series 25, DOI 10.1007/978-3-319-25047-2_13

The UK only amended its data protection law to give the ICO the power to issue fines in 2010.[3] For the 12 years prior to that, the data protection law was enforced only by way of "forward-looking" measures aimed at remedying the practices of the data controller after the breach had occurred.

In comparison to regulators in many of the other EU Member States, the ICO has been one of the more active in terms of the fines it has issued since it was granted these powers. Up to June 2014, it had issued 67 fines against organisations for breach of the data protection laws. However, fines in the UK are still reserved only for the most serious breaches and the ICO continues to rely heavily on the other enforcement mechanisms at its disposal. Furthermore, the ICO's almost complete focus on traditional "security" breaches when issuing fines and the predominance of public sector controllers as the recipients of these penalties lead many to question how effective they are at enforcing privacy on a wider scale.

Formal sanctions (whether monetary or otherwise) imposed by a regulator or a court are certainly not the only means of enforcing privacy. Many controllers prefer (perhaps not surprisingly) more co-operative procedures such as consensual audits, training, public guidance and raising awareness amongst data subjects as more effective means of encouraging good data governance. But these measures are time- and labour-intensive for regulators; and if they do not work, the authorities may need stronger measures. In this chapter, we also consider the importance of the publicity associated with fines and/or the breaches themselves, and whether it is the negative publicity or the fine itself that has the most impact on the controller.

13.2 Legislative background

Legislators around the world have adopted a variety of different "fining models" to enforce privacy obligations. Fines may take the form of an administrative penalty issued by a data protection authority (DPA), a civil penalty ordered by a court or in some cases a criminal penalty (For more on administrative and criminal sanctions, see Chap. 16 this volume). The typical amounts of fines, the sorts of breaches that result in fines, and the typical profile of the recipients of fines also vary significantly between countries.

Across the EU, the statutory basis for issuing fines for breaches of data protection law stems from Article 24 of the Data Protection Directive (95/46/EC), which provides that Member States shall "lay down the sanctions to be imposed in cases of infringement". Of course, "sanctions" does not necessarily mean fines, so there is a distinct measure of discretion here for Member States in their domestic

ratio of approximately 1 in 77 reported breaches resulting in a monetary penalty notice). We can also assume that a large number of breaches go unreported. See ICO Enforcement trends report: http://ico.org.uk/enforcement/trends

[3] Section 55A-E, UK Data Protection Act 1998 and the Data Protection (Monetary Penalties) (Maximum Penalties and Notices) Regulations 2010. The complete text can be found here: http://www.legislation.gov.uk/ukpga/1998/29/contents

legislation. The GDPR is more prescriptive and contains extensive fining powers (discussed in more detail below).

For the purposes of this chapter, we have chosen to focus on the current fining regime in the United Kingdom, as set out in section 55A of the UK Data Protection Act 1998 (the "Act"). When compared with other DPAs in Europe, the ICO is one of the more active (although it has a relatively new penalty regime) and has comparatively high penalties at its disposal.

The ICO has the power to issue a data controller with a Monetary Penalty Notice (MPN) of up to £500,000 in the event of serious contravention of the Act. Since first being given these powers in April 2010, the ICO has issued over 60 MPNs, the largest of which was £325,000.[4]

If a controller fails to pay an MPN when it falls due, it is enforceable as a court order (i.e., failure to pay is considered contempt of court). It is a debatable question whether MPNs in the UK are an administrative sanction or a criminal one. The First Tier Tribunal in *Scottish Borders Council v ICO*[5] commented that there was "an arguable case" for their being criminal proceedings, but decided (perhaps slightly contradictorily) that Parliament intended a civil standard of proof to be applied. The significance of the argument generally centres on the difference from a procedural perspective, for example the impact on the burden of proof and whether the regime is subject to the European Convention on Human Rights. However, it may also have an impact in terms of perception – a criminal sanction is perceived as more serious than an administrative one and therefore may be a greater deterrent, even if the sanction itself is no different. The ICO has now begun referring to monetary penalties as "Civil Monetary Penalties" (CMPs), perhaps in order to discourage any suggestions they may be subject to criminal procedural requirements.

MPNs under s.55A are not the only fines that can be issued under the Act. Unlawfully obtaining or disclosing personal data (or procuring another to do so), failing to register as a data controller with the ICO and failing to comply with an information or enforcement notice are all criminal offences punishable by a fine. So-called "enforced subject access" (i.e., requiring an individual to supply the results of a subject access request made by him or her) was also made a criminal offence in March 2015.[6] Unlike MPNs, these are all specifically expressed in the statute as criminal offences, so the fines can only be imposed by a court after a public prosecution has been brought. Depending on whether these offences are tried in the magistrates' or the crown court, they can potentially result in an unlimited fine.

---

[4] Brighton and Sussex University Hospitals NHS Trust on 28 May 2012.

[5] *Scottish Borders Council v ICO* (EA/2012/0212). The First-Tier Information Tribunal hears appeals from notices issued by the ICO regarding breaches of the law regarding Freedom of Information, Data Protection and the Privacy and Electronic Communications Regulations.

[6] The Data Protection Act 1998 (Commencement No. 4) Order 2015. http://www.legislation.gov.uk/uksi/2015/312/pdfs/uksi_20150312_en.pdf

13.2.1 *How do we want fines to be effective in enforcing privacy?*

Enforcing privacy is a broad concept, and need not be limited to simply stopping controllers from breaching the law. Fines can discourage non-compliance, but they can also act as a positive influence, encouraging good practice and raising awareness of privacy rights. In any discussion of how effective fines are, it is therefore important to consider more precisely the outcome one is hoping to achieve.

As with traditional criminal offences, a fundamental aim behind most fines is to deter re-offending by the controller receiving the fine. Regulators hope that controllers who have been fined will correct their non-compliance, whether by improving their systems and controls, investing in staff training, or even changing the way their business uses personal data in cases where the nature of the breach necessitates this.

We spoke to legal counsel at one organisation that had received a fine who said that the legal team regularly referred to the fine when subsequently advising on the importance of data protection compliance, and that it was particularly helpful in justifying additional expenditure. The spectre of another fine raised data protection from being purely a legal risk to a business one. The budget-holders (who were the key decision-makers) were now far more aware of the risks of non-compliance, and had in fact since become the drivers behind good information management.

Fines are also designed to act as a broader deterrent amongst data controllers more generally, anxious to avoid fines themselves. The primary focus of MPNs in the UK appears to be on deterrence in the wider community (i.e., beyond only the controller concerned), and the ICO takes active steps to obtain media coverage of its enforcement activity. The publicity also provides another potential benefit, by increasing consumer awareness of privacy obligations and their own individual rights. After the MPN regime was first introduced, at least one UK local authority produced a monthly "round-up" for its internal Information Management Committee of the MPNs that had been issued that month – intended as a cautionary tale for its own operations.

In common with the legal counsel at the controller that had received a fine, many data protection officers have commented that the introduction of the MPN regime has increased their profile inside their own organisations and made it easier to convince their employers of the importance of data protection compliance. Being able to point to the risk of incurring a fine is likely to strengthen any business case in favour of investing in privacy controls.

As a specific example, we heard of one organisation that almost immediately began encrypting its hard drives after an MPN of £325,000 was issued against Brighton & Sussex University Hospital for not using encryption technology, amongst other things. For this organisation, the risk of a similar penalty entirely altered the cost/benefit analysis of the extra expenditure on encryption. Although the result may not always be as easily and immediately quantifiable as encryption, similar logic could arguably be applied to other expenditure, such as hiring a consultant or increasing the provision of training.

A fining regime can also be used to influence behaviour. Even in cases where a controller has already committed a serious breach, the threat or issuing of a fine may encourage swift remedial action when the breach is discovered. Regulators can encourage positive behaviour such as voluntary self-reporting, informing affected individuals and committing to future improvements, by taking these into account as mitigating factors when deciding whether or how much to fine a controller.

The ability to fine can also increase the standing of the DPA, and therefore potentially its influence. Certainly, the ICO appears keen to utilise its enforcement activities to strengthen the public's perception of its work. Its policy on communicating enforcement activities "is driven by the reputation the ICO wants to have as the authoritative arbiter of information rights, an educator and an influencer".[7] Fines also provide an indication of the legislator's view of the importance of data privacy. The €20 million fines in the GDPR have been seen by many as a message from the EU to the larger (often US-based) corporations in the wake of the Edward Snowden revelations.

Finally, the *proceeds* of fines can have an effect. The resulting revenue stream could be used to fund other privacy-related projects or used to compensate affected individuals, although this is not the model that has been adopted in the UK. The proceeds of MPNs in the UK are paid into the Consolidated Fund (the government's central account), and thus cannot be ring-fenced for specific data protection purposes or to provide compensation for data protection breaches. One adjustment to this model might be for the ICO to recover its costs in conducting the investigation, but this is not the case currently. Compensation for data subjects is provided for separately under the UK Act by way of a civil claim.

In some instances, the rationale behind a fine (or the particular amount of a fine) is to deprive the controller of any profits generated as a result of the breach. In the UK, there is little evidence of MPNs being used in this manner, although this may be more a reflection of the nature of the breaches being subject to a fine rather than a specific policy of the ICO. The overwhelming majority of MPNs concern security breaches that would not have resulted in a profit for the data controller. Recovery of profits has, however, been cited in MPNs for breaches of the marketing restrictions in the Privacy and Electronic Communications Regulations 2003 (PECR) (which implement the ePrivacy Directive).[8] One could also foresee its potential relevance in cases concerning purpose limitation or data retention (for example, if the controller had used the data unlawfully to generate a profit).

---

[7] Information Commissioner's Office, Communicating enforcement activities, ICO Corporate Affairs policy, Version 5 final, Wilmslow, 11 November 2010. https://stewartroom.co.uk/wp-content/uploads/2014/08/UK-ICO-Communicating-Enf-Activities-Nov-2010.pdf

[8] See, for example, the MPN issued against Gary McNeish on 26 November 2012 (the 'Tetrus Telecoms' case).

13.3 Deciding when to issue a fine, and how much it should be

Ensuring fines are used effectively means the courts and/or DPAs must consider a variety of factors in determining, first, whether to issue a fine in any given instance and, second, how much that fine should be. In this respect, the considerations are not dissimilar to those faced by regulators in any other body of law: fines should be sufficiently high to act as a deterrent without causing undue hardship, should be proportionate to the breach and should reflect the regulator's view of the severity of the misconduct.

The ICO's power to issue an MPN is reserved for only the most serious breaches of the Act. The controller must have committed a "serious contravention" of a kind which was likely to cause "substantial damage or substantial distress" *and* the controller must have known or ought to have known that this would be the likely outcome, and failed to take reasonable steps to prevent the contravention.

Until recently, the same standard applied for MPNs issued for breaches of PECR. However, the ICO began to express significant concern that the requirement for "substantial damage or distress" was too high a threshold, acknowledging that receiving a text message or e-mail is only very rarely going to cause "substantial" damage or distress.[9] It successfully lobbied for a change in the law and, in April 2015, the standard was revised to delete the requirement of substantial damage or distress.[10] Going forward, a person must merely have committed a serious contravention of PECR *and* knew or ought to have known that there was a risk that the contravention would occur and failed to take reasonable steps to prevent the contravention.

In exploring under what circumstances the ICO considers the requirements of the Act to have been met, we can pick out certain key factors. In cases where the ICO decides to issue an MPN, these factors will usually continue to be relevant in determining the amount of the MPN. We have considered the most significant of these factors below.

13.3.1 The nature of the incident

The UK legislator chose to adopt fines only as a means of preventing "serious" contraventions of the law that have a "substantial impact". The ICO has no power to issue a penalty for minor breaches. This decision may have been a recognition of the

[9] In October 2013, Christopher Niebel successfully had his MPN of £300,000, issued for sending unsolicited spam text messages, overturned by the First-Tier Information Tribunal on this basis.

[10] UK Department for Culture, Media and Sport, Privacy and Electronic Communications (EC Directive) (Amendment) Regulations 2015, 24 February 2015. http://www.legislation.gov.uk/uksi/2015/355/pdfs/uksi_20150355_en.pdf

administrative resources that are involved each time the ICO issues a fine — but we would argue this should be the *result* of the high statutory test, rather than an inevitable accompaniment of a fining regime. Under an alternative model, a regulator could have the power to issue a fixed penalty for certain designated "minor" breaches, such as failing to have an online privacy policy or not responding to a subject access request within a 40-day period. With the current high threshold, it is questionable whether the MPN regime has much impact on these more low-level compliance issues.

The counter-argument to this is that the MPN regime increases the profile of data protection more generally, and the risk of a fine for a serious breach encourages organisations to conduct a review of their compliance across the board. Whilst this may be the case in organisations handling large amounts of data and where there is a real risk that a breach could cause substantial damage or distress, it is doubtful whether the same logic applies to a small controller handling non-sensitive data. In these latter cases, it seems more likely that the organisation could regard the risk of receiving an MPN as extremely low – even if its compliance generally was not particularly good.

In accordance with the statutory test, the ICO will consider the nature of the breach to determine whether it is sufficiently serious. This will involve looking at the type of data, the nature of the data subjects (how many, if they were vulnerable individuals, etc.) and, ultimately, the contravention itself: its duration and severity, its impact and whether it was deliberate or foreseeable. (The power applies if the failure is deliberate OR foreseeable and not avoided; it does not need to be both deliberate *and* foreseeable.)

It is interesting to examine the sorts of incidents that have most commonly been the subject of an MPN. More than three-quarters of MPNs have been issued for breach of the requirement to provide appropriate technical and organisational measures to protect the data. In contrast, no MPNs have been issued for breach of the requirement for fair and lawful processing, purpose limitation or processing data in accordance with the rights of data subjects. The MPNs also continue to be for fairly "traditional" security breaches – stolen laptops, the sale of hardware or filing cabinets which still contain data, faxes and e-mails sent to the wrong address – rather than large-scale hacks.

Various explanations for the dominance of security breaches have been suggested. It may be an indication of the ICO's view of the importance of this obligation – so the one that most justifies an MPN – on the basis that a security breach has the greatest potential to adversely affect individuals. If the protection of privacy is the driving force behind the ICO's aims, the negative impact of breaches where the data remains secure within the controller's organisation (even if used for an unlawful purpose, inaccurate or kept for too long) will, as a general rule, be less severe.

From an evidentiary standpoint, security failures are often the easiest to establish and are often reported by the data controllers themselves, something unlikely to occur in the case of failure to provide notice, for example. Indeed, certain public sector organisations in the health and social care sector (which have been the primary target for MPNs) are required to report security incidents by government policy.

Another factor in the prevalence of MPNs for breach of the security obligations might be that it is an area where the ICO considers fines to be most effective at guiding behaviour. Security breaches can often be caused by negligence and a lack of systems and controls within the controller's organisation – something that should be relatively easy to fix if appropriate focus is given to data protection compliance. These steps often require financial outlay on the part of the controller (whether on IT systems, training or consultancy) – and the threat of a fine would support a business case for such investment. Of course, issuing a significant fine at the same time as requiring investment in security systems may not be realistic, especially if the controller has limited resources. Many consider that the aims of privacy would be better served by making the controller spend the amount of the fine on its own internal compliance rather than paying this money to the state.

Legal counsel at an organisation that had received an MPN for a security breach commented that it was difficult to leverage the threat of another fine in the context of other data protection obligations, such as subject access requests. The perception amongst some non-specialists was that fines were only available for breaches of the security obligation and, without any examples to the contrary, it is difficult to counter this contention.

The dominance of MPNs for security breaches has also been criticised because some cases have involved the intervening acts of a third party, usually a thief or hacker. To name three examples, Croydon Council was fined £100,000 in February 2012 after an employee's handbag was stolen; the MPN of £250,000 issued against Sony in January 2013 was a consequence of a sophisticated systems hack; and in June 2013, Glasgow City Council was fined £150,000 after the theft of two unencrypted laptops from the Council offices. Although the controller is being sanctioned for failing to protect the data from the theft or hack, this is not always the perception of non-privacy specialists. As a consequence, there have been suggestions that MPNs should focus more on cases of deliberate bad behaviour. Arguably, a controller that feels it has been fined unfairly is less likely to respond positively by taking steps to improve its compliance.

Looking briefly at the PECR regime, so far MPNs have been reserved for cases of obviously wrongful behaviour. Unsolicited calls or spam text messages or e-mails for direct marketing can be characterised as wilful acts by an organisation, rather than merely a failure to have the correct systems in place.[11] In 2014, the ICO focused a significant amount of attention on so-called "nuisance" calls and text messages. One effect on this has been an increase in fines to the private sector, as these organisations are generally far more likely to conduct significant marketing. Now that the threshold for MPNs for breaches of PECR has been lowered, we expect to see far more fines being issued for these sorts of activities in the future.

[11] We are not suggesting this would always be the case, as there are instances where the PECR could be breached by an omission or a negligent act, for example, by failing to adequately maintain opt-outs.

13.3.2 The antecedent behaviour of the data controller

The ICO will consider whether a breach by a data controller is part of a continuing pattern of behaviour or only a one-off incident. In some cases, of course, the specific incident may be indicative of broader failings within the organisation. If the data controller has previously attracted the attention of the ICO, this would also weigh in favour of an MPN. As yet, however, no organisation has received more than one MPN (evidence perhaps of their efficacy?). In one case where the ICO investigated four incidents within the same data controller, it decided to pursue only the most serious breach and issue an informal warning regarding the others.

Amongst other factors, the ICO will consider whether the organisation has training and appropriate policies in place (and whether they have been recently updated), whether it has a data protection officer in place, and whether senior management considers data protection.

If the incident was the result of a rogue employee acting entirely without the knowledge of the employing controller, it might be more appropriate to pursue that individual rather than the controller. Provided the ICO is satisfied that the controller had adequate systems in place and could not reasonably have been expected to know about the actions of the employee, the ICO might choose to instead bring a criminal prosecution under section 55 of the Act (for unlawfully obtaining and/or disclosing data).

13.3.3 The subsequent behaviour of the data controller

In taking the behaviour of the data controller after the breach into consideration, the ICO cannot of course increase the deterrent effect of the fine. However, it can hope to promote quick remedial action. According to the ICO's guidance on MPNs,[12] the subsequent behaviour of the data controller is more significant in determining the *amount* of an MPN than whether to issue one in the first place; of the 25 MPNs issued in 2012, 21 were self-reported by the data controller. It would appear therefore that a data controller cannot absolve himself entirely from a serious breach by his efforts to fix the problem ex post facto.

Self-reporting, submitting voluntarily to audit by the ICO and offering compensation to data subjects may all serve to reduce the amount of an MPN. In contrast, unnecessary delays or attempting to conceal the breach are likely to increase it. Prior to issuing an MPN, the ICO must issue a Notice of Intent to which the data controller may respond with representations in its defence. At this point, the

[12] For the Information Commissioner's guidance about the issue of monetary penalties prepared and issued under section 55C (1) of the Data Protection Act 1998, issued 2012, see Information Commissioner's Office, Guide to data protection, 2.2.20, Wilmslow, 31 March 2015. http://ico.org.uk/enforcement/~/media/documents/library/Data_Protection/Detailed_specialist_guides/ico_guidance_on_monetary_penalties.pdf

controller has an opportunity to set out all of the steps it has taken to mitigate the breach, with a view to reducing the amount of any MPN that is imposed.

The ICO also has a formal process in place to encourage prompt payments: a data controller who pays within 28 days will receive a 20 per cent discount. This was raised as an issue on appeal[13] by one data controller in the First-Tier Information Tribunal – whether by paying promptly a controller effectively forfeited its right to appeal. The Tribunal commented that the question of whether this constitutes an unfair obstacle to access to the judiciary was one that may have to be answered at some point but, for now at least, the prompt payment scheme remains in place.

13.3.4 The circumstances of the data controller

The ICO has stressed the importance of preserving flexibility in issuing MPNs, on the basis that a set formula for the calculation would not serve the aims of either fairness or efficacy. Regardless of the nature of the breach itself, it is sometimes necessary for the ICO to adjust the fine to take account of the circumstances of the controller.

In this regard, each documented MPN must include the "impact on the data controller" as a potential aggravating or mitigating factor in determining the amount of the penalty. In May 2011, the ICO reduced an MPN of £200,000 to £1,000, because the data controller was an individual of limited means and his ability to pay was taken into account.[14] At the other end of the scale, the MPN of £250,000 issued against Sony Computer Entertainment Europe Limited noted that the data controller had "sufficient financial resources to pay a monetary penalty up to the maximum without causing undue financial hardship".[15] Although the ICO has not expressly stated this, it is safe to assume that a very well-resourced organisation will inevitably attract a larger MPN to ensure it can have sufficient deterrent effect.

In the UK, a brief look at the statistics to date immediately shows that an organisation is far more likely to receive an MPN if it operates in the public sector. Almost half of the MPNs issued to date have been against local authorities, and a large proportion of the others were against other public sector bodies.

The ICO would resist any suggestion that this is the result of a private sector bias, arguing instead that this is an inevitable result of the far larger amounts of sensitive data held by the public sector in the UK (e.g., health records, social care, prison records). Also, the ICO has observed that private sector organisations are often simply better at security – whether because they have more money to invest in it or are more strongly incentivised by the commercial necessity of maintaining customer confidence. It is interesting to note that a very different pattern exists in Spain, where the overwhelming majority of fines are issued to the private sector (see Chap. 6

[13] *Scottish Borders Council v ICO* (EA/2012/0212).

[14] MPN issued against Andrew Crossley trading as ACS Law, 9 May 2011.

[15] MPN issued against Sony Computer Entertainment Europe Limited, 14 January 2013.

for further discussion of this). As mentioned above, it seems likely that the recent changes to the threshold for MPNs under PECR will result in more action being taken against private sector organisations, as they are more likely to be conducting direct marketing.

13.3.5 *Factors external to the data controller*

The decision to issue and the amount of an MPN should reflect the ICO's position as to the seriousness of the breach. This is where precedent and public perception come into play, and there is an element of tactics in the ICO's deployment of fines. If too many are issued, they will cease to be newsworthy. The ICO's policy is to adopt a baseline minimum MPN of £40,000, in order to maintain the perception of MPNs as being a substantial penalty. This will only be reduced if the individual circumstances of the controller merit it (i.e., their ability to pay). However, the ICO wishes to leave itself headroom at the upper end of the scale. To date, the largest MPN issued was for £325,000[16] – so there is a significant scope for higher penalties in future, especially when the new Data Protection Regulation comes into force in early 2018 with potential penalties ranging up to four per cent of a company's turnover.

Other external factors can include a need to maximise the deterrent effect or to send a particularly strong message – for example, if the breach is in an area of high public concern. This was cited as an aggravating factor in the MPNs issued to two individuals in November 2012 for sending spam text messages. The ICO recognised in the formal Notice that "the receipt of unsolicited direct marketing texts has become an issue of significant public importance".[17]

Precedents play a crucial role in determining both the amount of an MPN and whether to issue one in the first place. The ICO has commented that when MPNs were first introduced, the decisions were very difficult, without any past experience on which to rely. The first two MPNs (issued on the same day) were for £60,000 and £100,000, the first for a stolen laptop that contained unencrypted data and the second for faxes sent to the wrong recipient.[18] These appear broadly commensurate with subsequent MPNs for similar incidents (£80,000 for an unencrypted USB stick in October 2013,[19] for example), and so would seem to have set a workable standard.

Before an MPN is issued, the Deputy Commissioner for Data Protection will consider the case as a whole. The purpose of this review, by someone who has not been involved in the case beforehand, is to consider whether the MPN meets the

---

[16] Brighton and Sussex University Hospitals NHS Trust in June 2012.

[17] The "Tetrus Telecoms" case, in November 2012.

[18] MPNs issued against A4e Limited and Hertfordshire County Council, respectively, on 22 Nov 2010.

[19] MPN issued against North East Lincolnshire Council, 15 October 2013.

underlying objective of the ICO's enforcement powers and whether it is consistent with previous MPNs.

13.4 The importance of combining fines with other measures

The most commonly accepted model of data protection enforcement appears to be a regime where fines are used in combination with other forward-looking enforcement measures. Sometimes these can be issued in conjunction with a fine or as an initial step with the threat of a fine if the data controller does not comply. In Chap. 6, Artemi Rallo discusses the introduction in Spain of the first written warning, prior to issuing a monetary sanction.

The best-case scenario is presumably that a fine will provide a sufficient incentive for a controller to act independently to improve its compliance. However, there appears to be an appetite amongst the authorities to play a role in subsequently addressing the root cause of the breach. In some cases, issuing a fine may not, on its own, offer sufficient guarantees that systemic failings will be remedied. There is also concern that well-resourced data controllers should not be able to treat a fine as a "parking ticket", which they can simply pay and walk away from. This can also work the other way; where an organisation is fined but provided with no practical guidance as to how to improve, it can be left unsure how to improve their compliance to a level that will satisfy the fining authority.

In the UK, the ICO has the power under section 40 of the Act to issue an enforcement notice, ordering the controller to take or refrain from taking certain specified steps within a given period. The ICO has utilised enforcement notices to place often quite granular obligations on data controllers in order to achieve compliance. Previous examples include requiring a police constabulary to appoint a Senior Information Risk Owner, conduct annual training, encrypt its laptops[20] and require a city council to create a new register of assets.[21]

In one form, an enforcement notice has the potential to have a far greater influence on a controller than even the heftiest fine: an order to cease processing personal data altogether. Whether the order only relates to certain types of data, or is confined to a limited period (for example, until the controller improves its compliance more generally), it has the potential to shut down a business for the duration of the notice. Consequently, this power is often regarded as the strongest weapon that the ICO has in its arsenal.

Failure to comply with an enforcement notice is punishable by a fine, and constitutes a criminal offence. This means that any subsequent fine is potentially unlimited, but would have to be the subject of formal proceedings before a criminal court (entailing, amongst other things, that the offence be proved beyond reasonable

[20] Enforcement Notice served on Chief Constable of Derbyshire Police, 18 June 2013.

[21] Enforcement Notice served on Glasgow City Council, 4 June 2013.

doubt). At the time of writing, we are not aware of any criminal proceedings having been pursued for breach of an enforcement notice.

The ICO has also leveraged the threat of MPNs to utilise an alternative enforcement mechanism: seeking contractual undertakings from data controllers to take certain remedial steps. Although the practice began before MPNs were initially introduced, undertakings can now be offered to data controllers as a means of avoiding an MPN and the accompanying media coverage that a fine is more likely to provoke (although since undertakings are still published this cannot be guaranteed). Undertakings have significant advantages from the ICO's perspective as well; as a more "co-operative" solution, they are far less open to challenge by the controller, and are significantly quicker and simpler to put in place. The ICO entered into more than 40 undertakings in 2014 (which compares to 11 MPNs and 10 enforcement notices), which suggests that the *threat* of an MPN may be an effective means to drive remedial action, at least *after* a breach has occurred.

In most cases, the ICO has not considered it necessary to issue an MPN as well as an enforcement notice or undertaking. The data controller has usually taken steps after the breach to remedy the situation, so the role of the MPN would appear to be primarily as a public statement that the behaviour was unlawful. However, the *process* of issuing an MPN also encourages remedial steps: part of the ICO's investigation prior to issuing an MPN will involve asking controllers what measures they are taking to address the breach; as discussed above, these may also be taken into account as mitigation in determining the amount of the MPN.

Accordingly, enforcement notices or undertakings will only be necessary when the ICO does not have confidence that the MPN alone will rectify the problem. This can be a particular concern amongst large public sector organisations where remedial action may be confined to the part of the organisation that committed the breach. In these cases, the ICO is able to use undertakings and enforcement notices to compel controllers to adopt a more widespread review of their compliance measures.

13.5 The power of publicity

In the UK, as in much of Europe and the US, the negative publicity surrounding fines is frequently of equal importance in terms of a deterrent as the fines themselves – if not more so. In the case of well-resourced, multinational organisations, the publicity that the regulatory action generates is likely to be more damaging than the fine itself. The media coverage of data breaches and fines also serves to improve awareness of data protection laws more generally, so that non-specialists within data controllers see it as an increasingly important issue.

The ICO and other DPAs clearly recognise the power of publicity, as evidenced by their willingness to co-operate with the media. The ICO does not simply post MPNs on its website for journalists to find, but frequently issues press releases, briefs journalists and uses social media. The ICO's public policy statement on communicating enforcement activities states that "the ICO aims to get media coverage for enforcement activities".[22] The policy contains a list of circumstances where the ICO is likely to seek publicity, including where it is a "new, extreme or first" instance, where publicity is likely to deter others, or where there is an opportunity for education and/or prevention. In France, this element of the penalty is formalised in the French Data Protection Act, under Article 46 of which the Commission nationale de l'informatique et des libertés (CNIL)[23] has a statutory power to seek publication of the penalty in newspapers and other media.

There are two aspects to the negative publicity generated by a fine. First, it publicises the fact of regulatory action being taken against the organisation; it has acted in a way that a regulator considers to be unlawful. Second, the news story will inevitably give details of the breach itself, potentially further damaging public confidence in the organisation. In cases where the breach already attracted significant publicity at the time it occurred, the fine will provide yet another press cycle for the story.

But are fines necessary to generate this press interest? Security breaches are often reported at the time they occur, before the ICO has even opened a formal investigation. A number of major breaches, such as the 'Ring of Steel' of CCTV cameras around Royston,[24] have attracted significant publicity even without an MPN. There were press stories about privacy before the introduction of the MPN regime, and media interest in this area has increased more generally in recent years, for example, as part of the Leveson Inquiry and subsequent trials for phone-hacking at the *News of the World* and *Mirror Group* newspapers. This notwithstanding, it seems indisputable that a fine (or even only the threat of a fine) is more attention-grabbing than a contractual undertaking or an enforcement notice requiring a controller to update its systems.

The ICO includes the reputational impact already suffered by the controller, i.e., in relation to the breach alone, as a mitigating factor when determining the amount of an MPN. An individual to whom we spoke at one local authority that had received an MPN was clear that the negative publicity attracted by the *breach* had a significantly greater impact than having to pay the fine itself. In this particular case, the breach was of a sort that would inevitably attract press interest, with numerous affected individuals, sensitive data and a "story" to tell. Circumstances might be different in a case with fewer media-friendly facts.

Managing publicity can serve as a critical incentive for controllers to take remedial steps after a breach has occurred. Even if some level of fine is inevitable, a lower fine will attract less press attention; a record fine will generate far more headlines than one that is (even if only marginally) below an earlier one. Evidence of remediation can also be deployed in response to negative media reports (for exam-

[22] Information Commissioner's Office, Communicating enforcement activities, ICO Corporate Affairs policy, Version 5 final, Wilmslow, 11 November 2010. https://stewartroom.co.uk/wp-content/uploads/2014/08/UK-ICO-Communicating-Enf-Activities-Nov-2010.pdf

[23] www.cnil.fr/english/

[24] Information Commissioner's Office, "Police use of 'Ring of Steel' is disproportionate and must be reviewed", news release, 24 July 2013. http://ico.org.uk/news/latest_news/2013/Police-use-of-Ring-of-Steel-is-disproportionate-and-must-be-reviewed-24072013

ple, it is clearly helpful if the data controller can issue a statement saying that all affected individuals have now been offered compensation).

13.6 Are the UK's fines too low to be effective?

The question of whether it is the fine or the corresponding publicity that has most impact on the data controller may be answered very differently in jurisdictions where the fines are potentially much higher than in the UK. The US Federal Trade Commission appears to lead the way in terms of the size of privacy-related fines, imposing penalties of $32.5 million and $22.5 million on Apple[25] and Google[26] respectively in 2013 and 2014. In these examples, it would seem unlikely that payment of the fine was a mere secondary consideration in comparison to the adverse publicity that accompanied it.

In Europe, the fines imposed under the existing Directive (at least those issued by the DPAs rather the courts) are markedly lower than those in the US–at least until the new Regulation comes into force. The UK MPN can be up to £500,000; the Spanish DPA has a maximum fining power of €900,000; the French CNIL (one of the most active of the EU DPAs) only €150,000 (or €300,000 for a repeat offence).

There has been some concern that these amounts are simply not enough to act as an effective deterrent to large-scale multinationals. In a speech in January 2014, former European Commissioner Viviane Reding dismissed a €150,000 fine issued by the CNIL against Google as "pocket money".[27] Recently, the Dutch Personal Data Authority, which could previously only issue administrative fines of up to €4,500 for most breaches, obtained an enormous increase in its fining powers. It can now issue penalties of up to €810,000 – closer to the amounts set out in the Regulation.[28]

When compared to the fining power of other regulatory authorities in the EU, the protection given to privacy also starts to look somewhat weak. The EU Competition Commission's penalties frequently amount to tens or even hundreds of millions of euro; the UK Financial Conduct Authority fined organisations more than £470 million in 2013.[29] It is, however, difficult to compare apples with oranges. By their very nature, competition law and financial services regulation concern enormously

---

[25] http://www.ftc.gov/news-events/press-releases/2014/01/apple-inc-will-provide-full-consumer-refunds-least-325-million

[26] http://www.ftc.gov/news-events/press-releases/2012/08/google-will-pay-225-million-settle-ftc-charges-it-misrepresented

[27] Reding, Viviane, "The EU Data protection reform: helping businesses thrive in a digital economy", SPEECH/14/37, European Commission, 19 Jan 2014. http://europa.eu/rapid/press-release_SPEECH-14-37_en.htm

[28] http://www.eerstekamer.nl/behandeling/20150210/gewijzigd_voorstel_van_wet

[29] Financial Conduction Authority, 2014 fines. http://www.fca.org.uk/firms/being-regulated/enforcement/fines/2014

high-revenue companies. It is vital that the fines these regulators mete out deprive companies of the often huge profits they would have made from the unlawful behaviour. Whilst the trend in the enforcement of data protection law (at least in the UK) continues to focus on "traditional" accidental security failures (theft of laptops, data sent to the wrong person), recovery of profits is unlikely to be a driving factor.

As mentioned above, the ICO's baseline for all MPNs is £40,000, on the basis that (in the absence of special circumstances), anything below this would not be sufficient to reflect the seriousness of the breach. Notwithstanding the ICO's desire to retain some headroom at the top, the fact that no MPN has yet reached anywhere near the maximum threshold would perhaps suggest that this amount is sufficient.

However, the new GDPR shows that there is an appetite amongst at least some of the EU DPAs for significantly increased penalties to be imposed. After debating fining powers ranging from a maximum of €1 million to €100 million, the final text of the GDPR permits DPAs to issue penalties of up to €20 million or 4 per cent of global turnover. These fines are available for any breach of specified articles of the GDPR (with no threshold of severity), including a breach of the basic principles for processing, infringement of data subjects' rights, or transfers of personal data. A reduced fining power of €10 million or 2 % of turnover is available for other provisions of the GDPR, including specific security obligations, and the obligations imposed on a certification or monitoring body. The GDPR will also extend the enforcement regime to cover data processors. The extent to which the higher fining thresholds will be used by the DPAs still, of course, remains to be seen. However it seems inevitable that, at least in some Member States, there will be significant increases.

13.7 The limitation on fines (and what are the alternatives?)

It is, of course, worth remembering that the current UK Act was in place for 12 years without the ICO's having the power to issue MPNs. Up until 2010, fines were only available for criminal offences under the Act. The ICO's continued use of other enforcement tools, and the important role played by publicity, clearly indicate that the deterrent effect of a fine, on its own, has limits. So might there be more effective methods of enforcing privacy?

Certainly, fines are not without their disadvantages. One consideration is that fines are more likely to be appealed than consensual measures such as undertakings or audits. Appeals are costly for all concerned (including the regulator) and may delay the implementation of practical remedies whilst the case is still ongoing. Appeals in the UK, however, are still relatively rare (and only two have been successful to date), suggesting there is broad acceptance of the ICO's use of MPNs amongst affected controllers.

One problem with continuing to rely on the publicity generated by a fine (rather than the breach itself) is that it may not be sustainable. MPNs are still relatively new in the UK, and therefore newsworthy. As more fines are issued, this may change. Certainly, the first time the ICO fines a controller the maximum amount (if it ever does) will make headlines – but what about the second, third or 10th time? DPAs may need to keep increasing the level of fines in order to maintain press interest. Even now, there are suggestions that MPNs have lost the "shock-value" they had when the powers were first introduced.

In some cases, the negative financial impact of the fine on the controller may outweigh the deterrent effect. In the case of a local authority, charity or civil society organisation (CSO), the drain on resources might even increase the risk to privacy – if expenditure on staff, training or IT systems was squeezed. In these cases, an audit might be a more appropriate method of improving data governance within an organisation. Several local authorities to whom we spoke voiced a strong preference for audits over fines, and felt they were a far more effective tool. One authority, which accepted a consensual audit instead of an MPN, estimated it had spent a similar amount preparing for the audit as it would have been charged under an MPN – but the money was channelled directly into improving data protection within the authority. Although a "privacy positive" outcome was reached in that case, it does feel somewhat counter-intuitive that the most serious breaches may in fact be the ones where the ICO is the most reluctant to issue a fine – because of the punitive effect such a large fine would have on the controller.

Audits may indeed be a more useful tool in achieving compliance within an organisation. They allow the ICO to take an in-depth look at organisation and practical steps for improvement. However, one cannot disregard the substantial resources required to complete each individual audit. There are more than 370,000 data controllers registered with the ICO, and it would be impossible for the ICO to conduct audits of anything beyond a handful of these. In the UK, therefore, audits tend to be reserved for organisations where the ICO has a particular concern about data protection within that organisation.

One local authority said that its breach resulted in a massive change in the way the organisation viewed data protection; it became a priority, led by the Chief Executive. However, the employee to whom we spoke thought that this change was not driven by the threat of a fine, but by the reputational damage caused by the breach itself. The impact of the breach on the controller's employees was amplified by the fact that the affected data subjects and the controller were based in the same area, so many of the employees knew someone personally who had been affected by the breach.

Arguably, private companies have the best incentive to avoid reduced profit margins or a loss in consumer confidence – both of which could follow from a large fine and the accompanying headlines. Ironically, therefore (in view of the ICO's fining history), fines may be most effective against private sector companies.

This is not to suggest that the public sector and CSOs are not concerned with these issues, but only that other considerations may be of higher priority, and their resources more limited. The ICO's history of fining the public sector has led to some criticism that money is simply being moved around the public purse – diverted from vital public services such as health and social care back into the Consolidated Fund – when what these organisations need is practical advice in achieving compliance. Private companies have the resources to help themselves to meet their obligations, whether by obtaining legal advice, investing in a good IT system or employing consultants. If they choose not to spend their resources in this manner, perhaps the best way of penalising them is indeed to damage their profits. This argument may not be so powerful in the public sector, which (in the UK model at least) has no such profits, and where the allocation of stretched resources between the services they offer is always going to be a challenge.

13.8 Final thoughts

We have chosen not to head this section "conclusion", because it would suggest we had found a definitive answer to the question posed. As with other punitive regimes, the extent to which fines drive behaviour is likely to vary significantly between data controllers. Some people do not commit crimes because they will get punished if caught; others are more influenced by the shame that would ensue or their own moral judgement. This notwithstanding, our analysis does suggest that fines play a valuable role in enhancing the business case for privacy compliance and raising awareness of data protection law, both amongst data subjects and within controller organisations.

Unfortunately, it is impossible to accurately measure whether compliance with the UK Act has improved since the introduction of MPNs in 2010. The pace of technological change and the vast increase in the amount of data collected mean that the challenges for data protection and privacy are increasing exponentially. In 1998 (when the Act was passed in the UK), the majority of data was still collected via paper forms; the dominance of the online world and the emergence of new concepts such as cloud computing and big data mean that the steps required to achieve compliance look very different now to 17 years ago.

Fines would appear to be at their most effective in cases where there has been an element of *choice* on the part of the data controller, which then led to a breach. This could be a choice as to whether to devote attention and resources to data privacy – to write policies or update the IT system – as opposed to overlooking this area and spending the resources elsewhere. In other cases, the choice may be more starkly non-compliant, for example, the decision to send unsolicited marketing messages. The aim is that other data controllers making similar decisions in future would have the risk of incurring a fine in mind, and be encouraged to opt for the more privacy-compliant choice.

It is more questionable how effective fines can be against breaches that result from a lack of awareness or action. This sort of behaviour would be better remedied by more forward-looking enforcement mechanisms – audits, guidance and enforcement notices. The problem, however, is that these alternative measures require far more resources on the part of the authorities: they cannot watch over all data controllers all of time. It is unrealistic therefore to rely on these means alone, without some incentive for controllers to self-discipline.

What seems most apparent is that fines cannot exist in a vacuum. They will only be effective if people know about them. We would suggest that the negative publicity generated by fines is at least as much of a deterrent to data controllers as the fines themselves. The media stories are also vital in increasing awareness of privacy laws in the population as a whole. One can only imagine the headlines that will be generated if and when the first €20 million fine is issued under the new EU Regulation.

References

European Commission, Proposal for a Regulation of the European Parliament and of the Council on the Protection of Individuals with Regard to the Processing of Personal Data and on the Free Movement of Such Data (General Data Protection Regulation), COM(2012) 11 final, Brussels, 25 January 2012. The version of the Regulation agreed by the European Parliament, Council and Commission on 15 December 2015 can be found here: http://www.haerting.de/sites/default/files/pdfs/proposal-eudatap-regulation-final-compromise-151216.pdf

Financial Conduction Authority, 2014 fines. http://www.fca.org.uk/firms/being-regulated/enforcement/fines/2014

Information Commissioner's Office, Data breach trends: http://ico.org.uk/enforcement/trends

Information Commissioner's Office, Communicating enforcement activities, ICO Corporate Affairs policy, Version 5 final, Wilmslow, 11 November 2010. https://stewartroom.co.uk/wp-content/uploads/2014/08/UK-ICO-Communicating-Enf-Activities-Nov-2010.pdf

Information Commissioner's Office, "Police use of 'Ring of Steel' is disproportionate and must be reviewed", news release, Wilmslow, UK, 24 July 2013. http://ico.org.uk/news/latest_news/2013/Police-use-of-Ring-of-Steel-is-disproportionate-and-must-be-reviewed-24072013

Information Commissioner's Office, Guide to data protection, 2.2.20, Wilmslow, 31 March 2015. http://ico.org.uk/enforcement/~/media/documents/library/Data_Protection/Detailed_specialist_guides/ico_guidance_on_monetary_penalties.pdf

Reding, Viviane, "The EU Data protection reform: helping businesses thrive in a digital economy", SPEECH/14/37, European Commission, 19 Jan 2014. http://europa.eu/rapid/press-release_SPEECH-14-37_en.htm

Scottish Borders Council v ICO (EA/2012/0212).

UK Data Protection Act 1998 and the Data Protection (Monetary Penalties) (Maximum Penalties and Notices) Regulations 2010: http://www.legislation.gov.uk/ukpga/1998/29/contents

UK Department for Culture, Media and Sport, Privacy and Electronic Communications (EC Directive) (Amendment) Regulations 2015, 24 February 2015. http://www.legislation.gov.uk/uksi/2015/355/pdfs/uksi_20150355_en.pdf

UK Government, Data Protection Act 1998 (Commencement No. 4) Order 2015. http://www.legislation.gov.uk/uksi/2015/312/pdfs/uksi_20150312_en.pdf

[illegible] by [illegible] of a [illegible] to data controllers as the [illegible] ... the [illegible] in the [illegible] ... the [illegible] under the new EU Regulation.

References

European Commission: Proposal for a Regulation of the European Parliament and of the Council on the Protection of Individuals with Regard to the Processing of Personal Data and on the Free Movement of Such Data (General Data Protection Regulation). COM(2012) 11 final, Brussels, 25 January 2012. [illegible]

[illegible]

[illegible]

[illegible]

[illegible]

[illegible]

[illegible]

Chapter 14
Enforcing Privacy Rights: Class Action Litigation and the Challenge of *cy pres*

Marc Rotenberg and David Jacobs

14.1 Introduction

The enforcement of rights is a critical requirement of privacy law. Absent actual enforcement, there is little meaningful incentive for companies to comply with privacy requirements. Enforcement helps to ensure that the individuals whose privacy is placed at risk are fairly compensated. In matters involving a large number of consumers, allowing enforcement by each user affected by a company's practice is a difficult and often inefficient undertaking. For this reason, courts in the United States provide for "class action" litigation, lawsuits brought on behalf of a large number of individuals in similar circumstances. The theory is that it is more efficient to merge all of the suits that might otherwise be brought individually.

But class action litigation has its own shortcomings. Attorneys who claim to represent injured consumers frequently settle cases and agree to terms that provide benefits to themselves, such as hefty attorney's fees, and the defendant company, such as eliminating the possibility of future lawsuits. As a consequence, the rights of the actual consumers are often sacrificed in these settlements. US courts are sensitive to the problem of collusion between the lawyers in class action settlements and scrutinise these agreements to ensure that the settlements protect the interests of consumers and are consistent with the purposes for which the lawsuit was brought. In the area of consumer privacy, the problem is particularly serious as class action attorneys increasingly trade the rights of Internet users for their own compensation. As a consequence, consumer privacy organisations in the United States are now challenging consumer privacy settlements. One advocacy organisation recently turned down a substantial *cy pres* award, stating that the proposed settlement is

M. Rotenberg • D. Jacobs (✉)
Electronic Privacy Information Center (formerly EPIC Consumer Protection Counsel),
1718 Connecticut Ave, N.W. Suite 200, Washington, DC 20009, USA
e-mail: rotenberg@epic.org; davidjacobs84@gmail.com;
http://www.epic.org

D. Wright, P. De Hert (eds.), *Enforcing Privacy*, Law, Governance and Technology Series 25, DOI 10.1007/978-3-319-25047-2_14

"actually worse than no settlement. It harms vulnerable teenagers and their families under the guise of helping them. Its purported protections are largely illusory and it will actually undermine future efforts to protect minors on Facebook."

14.2 Background

In December 2013, US retailing company Target experienced one of the largest data breaches in US history.[1] Finding that Target's systems were "astonishingly open", computer criminals had covertly installed malware that infected the point-of-sale terminals consumers used to swipe their credit and debit cards.[2] Consumers watched the extent of the breach grow. First, the number of affected consumers was revised upward from 40 million to 110 million – a number as large as one third of the adult American population.[3] Then, the scope of the stolen personal data increased to include not just credit and debit card numbers, expiration dates and three-digit security codes – but also names, mailing and e-mail addresses and phone numbers.[4] Shortly after news of the Target breach, Neiman Marcus, a luxury retailer, reported that it too had experienced a data breach that may have extended back to July 2013.[5]

The day after Target's data breach became public, a class action lawsuit was filed against the company.[6] In early 2014, Target faced nearly 70 class action lawsuits alleging that the company failed to take reasonable steps to secure consumers' personal information.[7] We expect that these various claims, brought by private attorneys on behalf of Target customers, will be consolidated in a single proceeding. It is therefore likely that the claims involving the millions of consumers impacted by the Target data breach will be heard by a single judge.

In the United States, which lacks a public agency specialising in data protection, class action lawsuits could be an important mechanism of privacy enforcement. These lawsuits should stop business practices that harm consumers, compensate individuals for injuries suffered and deter future misconduct. The class action pro-

---

[1] See generally Data Breach FAQ: https://corporate.target.com/about/shopping-experience/payment-card-issue-FAQ

[2] Harris, Elizabeth, et al. "A Sneaky Path into Target Customers' Wallets", *The New York Times*, 18 Jan 2014b

[3] Harris, Elizabeth, and Nicole Perlroth, "For Target, the Breach Numbers Grow", *The New York Times*, 11 Jan 2014a

[4] Ibid.

[5] Reuters, "Neiman Marcus data breach occurred as far back as July", published in *The Chicago Tribune*, 17 Jan 2014 http://articles.chicagotribune.com/2014-01-17/business/chi-neiman-marcus-data-breach-occurred-as-far-back-as-july-20140117_1_cyber-attack-neiman-marcus-ginger-reeder

[6] Roberts, Jeff John, "Target hit with dozens of lawsuits over mass data breach", GigaOm, 27 Dec 2013b http://gigaom.com/2013/12/27/target-hit-with-dozens-of-lawsuits-over-mass-data-breach/

[7] Schectman, Joel, "Target Faces Nearly 70 Lawsuits Over Breach", *The Wall Street Journal*, 15 Jan 2014. http://blogs.wsj.com/riskandcompliance/2014/01/15/target-faces-nearly-70-lawsuits-overbreach/

cedure allows individual legal claims to be aggregated, thereby promoting efficiency, minimising burdens on the courts and enabling actions where the recovery is too small to justify bringing claims individually. Class action lawsuits are important for consumer privacy cases, where the level of harms is often difficult to quantify and statutory damages may be relatively small.

But there are risks and limitations in this type of litigation. The interests of the lawyers representing the class often diverge from the individuals represented. For example, attorneys who bring these cases often seek to settle quickly to obtain their legal fees. As a consequence, the legal interests of the class on whose behalf the case was brought may not be adequately represented. Settlements also offer defendants the possibility of escaping liability – even for future misconduct – with only superficial changes to their business practices. And class action attorneys will some times agree to allow companies to engage in practices that threaten the privacy interests of consumers. Surprisingly, courts have approved settlements where the defendant company is permitted to engage in the practice after settlement that was the reason for the original lawsuit.

Class action lawsuits also present the challenge of *cy pres* allocation – a doctrine used by courts to put unclaimed funds to a use "as near as possible"[8] to direct compensation: payment to charities and other public interest organisations. *Cy pres* arises often in consumer privacy lawsuits because the total settlement amounts tend to be small relative to the size of the class. Where direct payment is impracticable and *cy pres* recipients are aligned with the purposes of the underlying litigation, *cy pres* allocations help advance the interests of the class and fulfill the purpose of the litigation. However, where *cy pres* recipients are poorly chosen, there is no benefit to the class. In some instances, lawyers for defendants have even diverted *cy pres* funds to organisations and research institutions aligned with the interests of the defendant. Lawyers for the class who should object to this practice have largely remained silent so as not to jeopardise the fees that they obtain from the settlement agreement.

The use of *cy pres* in privacy lawsuits has attracted considerable attention in the US from the courts that oversee these cases, advocacy organisations that work to defend the privacy interests of consumers and those concerned about the misuse of the class action procedure. In 2013, the US Supreme Court almost addressed the fairness of consumer privacy class action settlements. In the case *Lane v. Facebook*, the Court was asked to consider whether the defendant in a consumer privacy case could use the funds that would otherwise go to the class members or consumer privacy organisations to instead establish a foundation over which the defendant company would exercise control for distributions. The settlement had been vigorously contested in the lower courts, with judicial panels often divided as to the appropriate outcome. Although the Supreme Court ultimately declined to hear the case, which is not unusual given the number of appeals it receives, Chief Justice Roberts issued an opinion in which he noted the "fundamental concerns" surrounding *cy pres*, including:

[8] *Cy pres* is a corruption of the French *si près* (so near).

> when, if ever, such relief should be considered; how to assess its fairness as a general matter; whether new entities may be established as part of such relief; if not, how existing entities should be selected; what the respective roles of the judge and parties are in shaping a cy pres remedy; how closely the goals of any enlisted organization must correspond to the interests of the class; and so on.[9]

The issues outlined by Chief Justice Roberts in the *Lane* matter speak to the fundamental challenge of ensuring the fairness of class action settlements in consumer privacy cases. The US Supreme Court will likely address this issue in the near future and it may also arise in other countries where legal remedies involving *cy pres* are established.[10]

This Chapter explores the enforcement of privacy rights in the United States by means of class action lawsuits. Section 14.3 provides a brief description of the outline and purpose of the class action device. Section 14.4 reviews the growing judicial concern over the misuse of *cy pres* in privacy lawsuits. Finally, Sect. 14.5 proposes a framework for the appropriate use of the *cy pres* remedy. Chief Justice Roberts was correct to call attention to the "fundamental questions" concerning the use of the *cy pres* remedy. However, with careful judicial oversight and attention to the need for a close nexus between the plaintiff class and the proposed beneficiaries, *cy pres* awards can serve an important role in the private enforcement of privacy law. And the lessons learned from the experiences in the US can help ensure that similar remedies in other countries will be fair to consumers and help ensure the protection of privacy.

14.3 Privacy class action lawsuits generally

14.3.1 The class action device

In a class action lawsuit in the United States, plaintiffs proceed "as representative parties on behalf of all members" of the class.[11] This litigation device serves important policy goals. Class actions allow plaintiffs to take advantage of the efficiencies enabled by aggregate litigation. Class action rules also seek to ensure that these efficiencies are balanced against the due process rights of those who choose not to participate in the case as a member of the class.

---

[9] *Marek v. Lane*, 134 S. Ct. 8, 8–9 (2013).

[10] A recent news report indicates that Germany will soon allow consumer organisations to bring claims for violations of the national data protection law. *Privacy Laws and Business*, "German Consumer Protection Organizations to be Empowered to Sue Businesses for Data Protection Law Violations", 14 Feb 2014. www.bitkom.org/de/presse/8477_78620.aspx (in German, announcing the draft law) www.vzbv.de/12880.htm (in German, the VZBW's 13 February 2014 statement welcoming of the Minister of Justice's announcement of 11 Feb 2013).

[11] Fed. R. Civ. P. 23(a).

The federal rules of civil procedures (FRCP) set out the requirement for class action litigation: (1) the class must be "so numerous that joinder of all members is impracticable"; (2) there must be "questions of law or fact common to the class"; (3) the claims of the representative parties must be "typical of the claims or defenses of the class"; and (4) the representative parties must "fairly and adequately protect the interests of the class".[12] Additionally, each class must be certified by a court before the case may go forward. Three circumstances allow for class action certification: (1) where class members' rights are inextricably linked; (2) where "final injunctive relief or corresponding declaratory relief is appropriate respecting the class as a whole"; and (3) where "questions of law or fact common to class members predominate over any questions affecting only individual members".[13] There are circumstances where attorneys will try to pursue class action claims but are unable to persuade a judge to allow the case to go forward because one of these necessary criteria cannot be established.

The federal rules also contain protections for other parties' interests because judgments in the case are binding on all class members. Absent class members may also be bound by the terms of settlements. For this reason, any such settlement requires notice to class members, an opportunity to object, a finding by the court that the settlement is "fair, reasonable, and adequate" and, for non-mandatory classes, an opportunity for class members to opt out of the settlement.[14] The design of the rule thus evidences various purposes, including "the protection of the defendant from inconsistent obligations, the protection of the interests of absentees, the provision of a convenient and economical means for disposing of similar lawsuits, and the facilitation of the spreading of litigation costs among numerous litigants with similar claims".[15]

14.3.2 *Purposes of the class action*

One principal purpose of the class action procedures is to promote judicial economy and efficient litigation.[16] Where violations cause relatively small harms to individual class members, the disincentive to litigate would allow harmful business practices

---

[12] Fed. R. Civ. P. 23(a)(1)–(4).

[13] Fed. R. Civ. P. 23(b)

[14] Fed. R. Civ. P. 23(e).

[15] *Geraghty*, 445 U.S., pp. 402–03; see also *Re Gen. Motors Corp. Pick-Up Truck Fuel Tank Products Liab. Litig.*, 55 F.3d 768, 785 (3d Cir. 1995) ("The rule thus represents a measured response to the issues of how the due process rights of absentee interests can be protected and how absentees' represented status can be reconciled with a litigation system premised on traditional bipolar litigation.").

[16] See, e.g., *Amchem Products, Inc. v. Windsor*, 521 U.S. 591, 617, 117 S.Ct. 2231, 138 L.Ed.2d 689 (1997) ("The policy at the very core of the class action mechanism is to overcome the problem that small recoveries do not provide the incentive for any individual to bring a solo action prosecuting his or her rights. A class action solves this problem by aggregating the relatively paltry poten-

to continue, even where the individual claims are strong and the aggregate harm is substantial.[17] Furthermore, there are cost advantages when individual claims are aggregated.[18] Class actions thus permit both the vindication of individual rights and the conservation of judicial resources.

These advantages are particularly important in privacy cases because the underlying consumer interest is well established. Modern privacy law is based on the concept of Fair Information Practices, which assigns rights and responsibilities in the collection and use of personal information.[19] The concept of Fair Information Practices was first set out in the influential 1973 report *Records, Computers, and the Rights of Citizens*.[20] The Code of Fair Information Practices describes basic privacy practices, such as:

- There must be no personal-data record-keeping systems whose very existence is secret.
- There must be a way for an individual to find out what information about him is in a record and how it is used.
- There must be a way for an individual to prevent information obtained about him for one purpose from being used or made available for other purposes without his consent.
- There must be a way for an individual to correct or amend a record of identifiable information about him.
- Any organisation creating, maintaining, using or disseminating records of identifiable personal data must assure the reliability of the data for their intended use and must take reasonable precautions to prevent misuse of the data.[21]

---

tial recoveries into something worth someone's (usually an attorney's) labor.") (quoting *Mace v. Van Ru Credit Corp.*, 109 F.3d 338, 344 (7th Cir.1997)); *Abdullah v. U.S. Sec. Associates*, Inc., 731 F.3d 952, 963–64 (9th Cir. 2013); *Allison v. Citgo Petroleum Corp.*, 151 F.3d 402, 410 (5th Cir. 1998) ("It is important to remember that the class action device exists primarily, if not solely, to achieve a measure of judicial economy, which benefits the parties as well as the entire judicial system. It preserves the resources of both the courts and the parties by permitting issues affecting all class members to be litigated in an efficient, expedited, and manageable fashion.").

[17] *Thorogood v. Sears, Roebuck & Co.*, 547 F.3d 742, 744–45 (7th Cir. 2008) ("If every small claim had to be litigated separately, the vindication of small claims would be rare. The fixed costs of litigation make it impossible to litigate a $50 claim (our guess; there is no evidence of what the average claim of a member of the plaintiff's class in this case might be worth) at a cost that would not exceed the value of the claim by many times."); *Murray v. GMAC Mortgage Corp.*, 434 F.3d 948, 953 (7th Cir. 2006) ("Rule 23(b)(3) was designed for situations such as this, in which the potential recovery is too slight to support individual suits, but injury is substantial in the aggregate.").

[18] See *Re Amino Acid Lysine Antitrust Litig.*, 918 F. Supp. 1190, 1196 (N.D. Ill. 1996) (referring to economies of scale available through the class actions device).

[19] Rotenberg, Marc, "Fair Information Practices and the Architecture of Privacy", *Stanford Technology Law Review*, February 2001. http://stlr.stanford.edu/pdf/rotenberg-fair-info-practices.pdf

[20] US Department of Health, Education and Welfare (HEW), *Records, Computers and the Rights of Citizens*, Report of the Secretary's Advisory Committee on Automated Personal Data Systems, Washington, DC, 1973. http://epic.org/privacy/hew1973report/

[21] Ibid., p. 41.

The FIPs have since formed the basis of modern privacy frameworks[22] and US statutes, such as the Privacy Act,[23] the Fair Credit Reporting Act,[24] the Electronic Communications Privacy Act,[25] the Video Privacy Protection Act[26] and the Driver's Privacy Protection Act.[27] Most other national and international privacy laws share a similar conceptual framework. Furthermore, violations of the FIPs codified in these laws often involve harms – such as mental and emotional distress, increased risk of identity theft or physical attack, and loss of reputation or trust – that are difficult to quantify. For these reason, many privacy statutes contain private rights of action and provide for statutory damages.[28] These damage provisions deter privacy violations and ensure that individuals can seek compensation for wrongs. In class action settlements, these statutory damages are not available and the burden falls on the attorneys representing the interests of class members to ensure that they are reasonably compensated. Separately, there are also new challenges to the ability to bring class action lawsuits as companies have devised new ways to avoid legal claims and several of these ways, which appear contrary to law, have been upheld by the US Supreme Court.

14.3.3 US Supreme Court less receptive to class action claims in general

Recent Supreme Court cases have raised some concerns about the future of class action litigation in the United States. The Supreme Court has increasingly deferred to private companies that try to minimise the risk of class action even in circumstances where harm to a large number of consumers may be at issue. In *AT&T Mobility LLC v. Concepcion*, the Supreme Court struck down a state common law rule invalidating unconscionable arbitration clauses on the grounds that it conflicted with the Federal Arbitration Act.[29] *Concepcion* concerned AT&T's form contract

---

[22] See, e.g., The White House, Consumer Data Privacy in a Networked World: A Framework for Protecting Privacy and Promoting Innovation in the Global Digital Economy, 2012; Federal Trade Commission (FTC), *Protecting Consumer Privacy in an Era of Rapid Change:Recommendations for businesses and policymakers*, March 2012. http://online.wsj.com/public/resources/documents/PrivacyReport_FINAL.pdf

[23] 5 U.S.C. § 552.

[24] 15 U.S.C. § 1681.

[25] 18 U.S.C. § 2510.

[26] 18 U.S.C. § 2710.

[27] 18 U.S.C. § 2721.

[28] See, e.g., 18 U.S.C. § 2520(c)(2) ("(A) the sum of the actual damages suffered by the plaintiff and any profits made by the violator as a result of the violation; or (B) statutory damages of whichever is the greater of $100 a day for each day of violation or $10,000."); 15 U.S.C. § 1681n(a)(1)(A) (setting damages as "any actual damages sustained by the consumer as a result of the failure or damages of not less than $100 and not more than $1,000.").

[29] 131 S.Ct. 1740 (2011).

for cellular phones that included both an arbitration clause and a class action waiver agreement.[30] Despite promising a "free" cell phone, AT&T charged them $30.22 in sales tax based on the phone's value, and the Concepcions sued in federal court for, inter alia, false advertising and fraud.[31] After their case was consolidated with similar cases, AT&T sought to enforce the arbitration clause, which the plaintiffs opposed on the ground that it was unconscionable under California's Discover Bank Rule, which invalidates any pre-dispute agreement purporting to waive the right to pursue a class action.[32]

The Supreme Court held that the Federal Arbitration Act pre-empted the California rule because the rule represented "an obstacle to the accomplishment and execution of the full purposes and objectives of Congress".[33] Thus, adhesionary contracts – such as the clickwrap or browsewrap agreements[34] that consumers agree to when using almost any digital product or service – may bind consumers to arbitration agreements that preclude them from availing themselves of the private rights of action that exist in many privacy laws.

More recently, in *American Express Co. v. Italian Colors Restaurant*, the Supreme Court upheld a class action waiver provision contained in an arbitration agreement, despite the fact that the plaintiffs had demonstrated that pursuing the claims individually would be prohibitively expensive.[35] *Italian Colors* involved the business practices of American Express, which requires merchants who wish to accept American Express cards to allow American Express to withhold a "merchant discount fee" from each transaction.[36] American Express required merchants to sign form contracts containing an "Honor All Cards" provision requiring merchants to accept both the discount fee and the company's credit cards.[37] The form contracts also contained arbitration clauses mandating the arbitration of all claims arising out of the contract and prohibiting the use of the class action procedure.[38] Several merchants filed suit against American Express, alleging that the discount fees constituted a violation of section 1 of the Sherman Act.[39] The merchants attempted to resist bilateral arbitration by arguing that it would impose such high costs as to

[30] *Concepcion*, 131 S. Ct, p. 1744.

[31] Ibid.

[32] Ibid., pp. 1745–46.

[33] Ibid.

[34] According to Wikipedia, a clickwrap agreement (also known as a "clickthrough" agreement or clickwrap licence) is a common type of agreement often used in connection with software licences. A browsewrap agreement refers to a contract or licence agreement on access to or use of materials on a website or downloadable product.

[35] 133 S. Ct. 2304 (2013).

[36] *Re Am. Express Merchs. Litig.*, No. 03 CV 9592, 2006 WL 662341, at *1 (S.D.N.Y., 16 Mar 2006).

[37] Ibid.

[38] Ibid. at *2.

[39] Ibid. at *1.

preclude vindication in that forum.[40] To support their argument, the merchants presented an affidavit from an economics expert stating that although it would cost several hundred thousand dollars to generate an expert report, the most any individual plaintiff could recover was $38,549.[41]

The Supreme Court held for American Express.[42] The Court was not persuaded by the claim that the plaintiffs could not effectively vindicate their rights through bilateral arbitration, writing that the effective vindication doctrine was a "judge-made exception to the FAA [Federal Arbitration Act]", and that "the fact that it is not worth the expense involved in proving a statutory remedy does not constitute the elimination of the right to pursue that remedy".[43] The dissent, written by Justice Kagan, criticised the majority for "flaunt[ing]" its answer of "[t]oo darn bad" with "barely" an explanation.[44] *Italian Colors* thus represents the further erosion of the limits on class action waivers in the arbitration context.

Not all of the costs associated with class action lawsuits have come from judicial interpretation. Indeed, many inhere in the structure of the class action device. In a class action, the interests of class counsel often diverge from the interests of the class. Class counsel's primary interest is in maximising their legal fees, while the primary interest of class members is in obtaining relief from harms suffered.[45] Exacerbating the conflict between the lawyers' interest in compensation and the class members' interest in relief is the fact that the stakes for the individual class members are often too low to incentivise adequate supervision of their attorneys. Furthermore, defendants, facing the threat of ruinous judgments, are under pressure to settle cases.[46] Settlements are also attractive to defendants because they preclude subsequent lawsuits by class members asserting the same claim.[47] Many recent settlements also release defendants from liability for violations not yet committed,

[40] Ibid. at *3.

[41] *Re Am. Express Merchs. Litig.*, 554 F.3d 300, 317 (2d Cir. 2009).

[42] 133 S. Ct. 2304 (2013).

[43] Ibid., p. 2311.

[44] Ibid., p. 2313 (Kagan, J., dissenting).

[45] See Koniak, Susan P., and George M. Cohen, "Under Cloak of Settlement", *Virginia Law Review*, Vol. 82, No. 2, 1996, pp. 1051, 1054 (describing "class lawyers in the GM Truck, who negotiated a settlement in which the lawyers would receive $9.5 million in fees, while their clients were to get coupons to buy another GM Truck" and "class lawyers in the Ford Bronco II case, who requested $4 million in fees for negotiating a settlement in which their clients were to receive a warning sticker, a safe driving videotape, a road atlas, an owner's manual, a flashlight and a free vehicle inspection (but not free vehicle repairs) as compensation for having purchased a vehicle that allegedly was prone to roll over"); *Jeff D. v. Evans*, 743 F.2d 648, 651 (9th Cir. 1984) rev'd, 475 U.S. 717 (1986) ("When attorney's fees are negotiated as part of a class action settlement, a conflict frequently exists between the class lawyers' interest in compensation and the class members' interest in relief.").

[46] Hay, Bruce, and David Rosenberg, "'Sweetheart' and 'Blackmail' Settlements in Class Actions: Reality and Remedy", *Notre Dame Law Review*, Vol. 75, Issue 4, 2000, pp. 1377–1408.

[47] See *Pelt v. Utah*, 539 F.3d 1271, 1284 (10th Cir. 2008) (noting that "[i]t is well settled that a class action judgment is binding on all class members" provided that "absent members were 'in fact' adequately represented by parties who are present").

offering them the opportunity to purchase inexpensively the right to "commit trespasses, create nuisances, adopt poison pills, and perhaps even violate the antitrust laws".[48] As a result of the "community of interest between class counsel, who control the plaintiff's side of the case, and the defendants",[49] class action lawsuits may end up producing high-fee, low-damage settlements that benefit everyone involved but the injured class members.

These costs have been evident in many privacy class actions. In *Lane*, the class members challenged a Facebook advertising program, "Beacon", that disclosed information about users' commercial activity on third-party websites such as Overstock.com, eBay and Blockbuster.[50] The settlement agreement ultimately approved provided no monetary relief to the class; barred class members from bringing any claims related to Beacon; paid the class's lawyers $2.3 million; created a $10 million settlement fund to be administered by an organisation with no prior experience in privacy protection, the board of which would consist of three directors agreed upon by Facebook and the class counsel, and left Facebook free to revive the Beacon program under a different name.[51] When the matter came before the appeals court, Judge Kleinfeld dissented and described the outcome of a failed process: "The attorneys for the class have obtained a judgment for millions of dollars in fees. The defendant, Facebook, has obtained a judgment that bars claims by millions of people victimized by its conduct. So have the other companies involved in Beacon. The victims, on the other hand, have obtained nothing. Under the settlement, Facebook even preserved the right to do the same thing to them again."[52] The appeals court almost reconsidered the case, but let the earlier decision stand by a narrow one-vote majority. Six judges argued against the opinion upholding the settlement, stating that "the majority in this case creates a significant loophole in our case law that will confuse litigants and judges, while endorsing *cy pres* settlements that in no way benefit class members".[53]

In *Fraley v. Facebook*,[54] a class action case challenging the exploitation of the images and names of Facebook for commercial endorsement, the lower court rejected a preliminary settlement agreement because it provided no direct benefit to consumers.[55] The proposed settlement provided no monetary relief to class mem-

---

[48] Grimmelmann, James, "Future Conduct and the Limits of Class-Action Settlements", *North Carolina Law Review*, Vol. 91, Issue 2, 2013, pp. 387–474. http://www.nclawreview.org/category/archives/91/issue-2/

[49] *Thorogood v. Sears, Roebuck & Co.*, 547 F.3d 742, 745 (7th Cir. 2008).

[50] https://epic.org/amicus/blockbuster/default.html

[51] *Lane v. Facebook, Inc.*, 696 F.3d 811, 828 (9th Cir. 2012) cert. denied, 134 S. Ct. 8 (U.S. 2013).

[52] *Lane v. Facebook, Inc.*, 696 F.3d 811, 830 (9th Cir. 2012) cert. denied, 134 S. Ct. 8 (U.S. 2013).

[53] *Lane v. Facebook, Inc.*, 709 F.3d 791, 793 (9th Cir. 2013).

[54] No. 11-1726 (N.D. Cal. filed 8 Apr 2011).

[55] Sponsored Stories are commercial messages that republish actions users have taken on Facebook, such as: likes on a page; likes, shares or comments on a page's post; votes on a question; check-ins at a location; joins of an event; installs of an app; uses or plays of an app; likes or shares of a website. See Facebook, "What actions can be turned into Sponsored Stories?". https://www.facebook.com/help/326113794144384/. In addition to merely republishing a user's interaction or content,

bers, gave up to $10 million to class counsel, and allowed Facebook to continue engaging in the challenged conduct known as "Sponsored Stories".[56] In rejecting the preliminary settlement, the court noted that "Merely pointing to the infeasibility of dividing up the agreed-to $10 million recovery, or the relatively small per-use revenue Facebook derived, is insufficient, standing alone, to justify resort to purely *cy pres* payments."[57] The settlement ultimately approved by the court provided $15 to each class member who filed a claim.[58] However, this monetary award was made available to only a small number of individuals whose images would be used by the company for commercial endorsement, and surprisingly the settlement allowed the company to continue the disputed practice. As a result, a new challenge has been brought to the settlement. The *Fraley* case is now on appeal.[59]

The problem of companies continuing to engage in practices that class action litigation is supposed to end is not unusual. The attorneys for the class and for the defendant Google in a proposed settlement concerning Google's disclosure of a user's search queries stated bluntly that "Google will not be required or requested to make any changes to its homepage www.google.com or to the practices or functionality of Google Search, Google Adwords, Google Analytics, or Google Web History."[60] The class would have to settle for the relief provided by Google's modification of its privacy policy.[61] Google Search, the service that provided the basis for the lawsuit, would undergo no substantive changes.

14.4 The challenge of *cy pres*

Of the risks using the class action device, the problem of *cy pres* settlements that fail to benefit the class is particularly relevant to privacy cases. While courts use *cy pres* remedies to provide the "next best" relief to class members in situations where

---

Sponsored Stories can include additional advertiser content that the user may have never encountered, let alone endorsed, under the category of a "Related Post". See Gayle, Damien, "Is Facebook 'impersonating' users to promote stories they've never seen to all their friends?", *Daily Mail*, 24 Jan 2013. http://www.dailymail.co.uk/sciencetech/article-2267575/Is-Facebook-impersonating-users-promote-stories-theyve-seen-friends.html

[56] Motion for Preliminary Approval of Class Action Settlement at 6–8, *Fraley v. Facebook*, No. 11-1726 (N.D. Cal. filed 8 Apr 2011).

[57] Order denying motion for preliminary approval of settlement agreement at 3, *Fraley v. Facebook*, No. 11-01726 (N.D. Cal. filed 8 Apr 2011).

[58] Order Granting Motion for Final Approval of Settlement Agreement, *Fraley v. Facebook*, No. 11-1726 (N.D. Cal. filed 8 Apr 2011).

[59] Goel, Vindu, "Facebook Privacy Deal is Under Attack," *The New York Times*, 13 Feb 2014. http://www.nytimes.com/2014/02/13/technology/facebook-deal-on-privacy-is-under-attack.html. See generally *Fraley v. Facebook*, http://www.fraleyfacebooksettlement.com/

[60] Agreement, at 7, *Re Google Referrer Header Privacy Litigation*, No. 10-4809 (N.D. Cal. filed 25 Oct 2010).

[61] Mot. Prelim. Approval, Dkt. 52, at 5.

direct compensation is infeasible, the use of *cy pres* in privacy cases has provoked considerable judicial controversy.

14.4.1 Cy pres *doctrine*

Cy pres – an abbreviated form of *cy près comme possible*; literally, "as near as possible" – is a legal doctrine that allows courts to approve settlements that benefit the class indirectly by providing payment to third parties and other forms of relief when direct monetary payment to the class would be impractical. Modern *cy pres* originated as a means of distributing unclaimed property in trusts, where it was used to approve a bequest to an alternative charity if the testator's original choice was no longer in existence.[62] The use of *cy pres* for class action purposes began in the 1970s, when courts and academics were searching for distributions of unclaimed funds that did not involve reversion back to the defendant. One early commentator suggested that "[w]hen distribution problems arise in large class actions, courts may seek to apply their own version of cy pres by effectuating as closely as possible the intent of the legislature in providing the legal remedies on which the main cause of action was based".[63] Others advocated class action remainders to charitable organisations.[64] In 1974, a federal district court in New York instituted the first judicial use of class action *cy pres* by directing funds to the trustee of a retirement plan rather than to the shareholders of the company in a case concerning securities fraud.[65]

There are benefits to *cy pres* distributions. In certain cases, the costs of distributing the settlement fund to each individual class member exceeds the amount to which each member is entitled. In cases where fund distribution is burdensome or inefficient, *cy pres* may be the "next best" option: reversion to the defendant removes much of the deterrent effect of the lawsuit; distribution to part of the class through some selection mechanism leaves many absent class members without any benefit; and distribution to the state may involve funding programs with an attenuated connection to the issues involved in the underlying action.[66] But the challenge of

[62] Fisch, Edith L., *The Cy Pres Doctrine in the United States*, Matthew Bender, New York, 1950, § 1.00. *Cy pres* is an ancient device, originating as far back as sixth century Rome; see Gray, Hamish, "The History and Development in England of the Cy-Pres Principle in Charities", *Boston University Law Review*, Vol. 33, 1953, pp. 30–51 [p. 32], and being incorporated into English common law, either as a reflection of a preference for charities over other institutions or a consequence of the close relationship between the church and the courts. See ibid.

[63] Shepherd, Stewart R., "Damage Distribution in Class Actions: The Cy Pres Remedy", *University of Chicago Law Review*, Vol. 39, No. 2, Winter 1972, pp. 448–465 [p. 452]. http://www.jstor.org/stable/1599010

[64] Barnett, Kerry, "Equitable Trusts: An Effective Remedy in Consumer Class Actions", *Yale Law Journal*, Vol. 96, No. 7, June 1987, pp. 1591–1614. http://www.jstor.org/stable/796495; DeJarlais, Natalie A., "The Consumer Trust Fund: A Cy Pres Solution to Undistributed Funds in Consumer Class Actions", *Hastings Law Journal*, Vol. 38, April 1987, pp. 729–767 [p. 732].

[65] *Miller v. Steinbach*, No. 66 Civ. 356, 1974 WL 350, at *2 (S.D.N.Y. 3 Jan 1974).

[66] Shepherd, supra note 63, at pp. 453–57.

cy pres has been ensuring that the settlement funds are truly put to the next best available use. To this end, courts require some nexus between the interests of the class and the *cy pres* beneficiaries.[67] Courts in the United States require, for example, that a *cy pres* award be guided by the "objectives of the underlying statute" and "the interests of the silent class members".[68] Only where "it would be onerous or impossible to locate class members or each class member's recovery would be so small as to make an individual distribution economically impracticable" should *cy pres* be employed.[69]

14.4.2 Growing judicial concern

Despite judicial oversight of the distribution of *cy pres*, many class action settlements have distributed funds to organisations with attenuated connections to the interests of the class. For example, a case involving alleged antitrust violations resulting from the advertised price of compact discs produced a $271,000 *cy pres* award to the National Guild of the Community School of the Arts.[70] A case involving infant formula price fixing resulted in a $700,000 *cy pres* award to the American Red Cross Hurricane Katrina Disaster Relief Fund. In each of these cases, the recipient organisations were perfectly legitimate charities, but they did not represent the best indirect compensation to the victims of the challenged practices.

Indeed, in some cases, *cy pres* distributions may even benefit the defendants. In *Park v. Thomson*, plaintiffs sued BARBRI under the Sherman Act[71] for unlawfully tying its "bar review classes for the state-specific portion of the bar exam to the purchase of a review class for the Multistate Bar Examination".[72] The settlement initially proposed distributed the bulk of the settlement to the "BARBRI Public Interest Law Fund", a fund that, although administered by the American Bar

---

[67] *S.E.C. v. Bear, Stearns & Co. Inc.*, 626 F. Supp. 2d 402, 414 (S.D.N.Y. 2009) ("The purpose of the cy pres distribution is to 'put the unclaimed fund to its next best compensation use, e.g., for the aggregate, indirect, prospective benefit of the class.'") (quoting *Masters v. Wilhelmina Model Agency, Inc.*, 473 F.3d 423, 436 (2d Cir. 2007).

[68] *Nachshin v. AOL*, LLC, 663 F.3d 1034, 1036 (9th Cir. 2011); see also *Dennis v. Kellogg Co.*, 697 F.3d 858, 865 (9th Cir. 2012) (noting that the "choice of charity and its relation to the class members and class claims—or lack thereof—*figure*[*s*] *heavily* in our analysis"); *Klier v. Elf Atochem N. Am., Inc.*, 658 F.3d 468, 474–75 (5th Cir. 2011) (considering *cy pres* relief appropriate only if "the unclaimed funds should be distributed for a purpose as near as possible to the legitimate objectives underlying the lawsuit, the interests of class members, and the interests of those similarly situated").

[69] *Masters v. Wilhelmina Model Agency, Inc.*, 473 F.3d 423, 436 (2d Cir. 2007).

[70] See *Re Compact Disc Minimum Advertised Price Antitrust Litigation*, No. MDL 1361, 2005 WL 1923446 (D.Me. 9 Aug 2005).

[71] The Sherman Act, passed by Congress in 1890, was a landmark in antitrust legislation.

[72] *Park v. The Thomson Corp.*, 05 CIV.2931 (WHP), 2008 WL 4684232 (S.D.N.Y. Oct. 22, 2008).

Association, was clearly connected to the defendant.[73] Even where defendants have no interest in the chosen *cy pres* recipients, they often receive the goodwill of donating to charitable organisations.[74]

The potential abuses associated with *cy pres* have prompted growing judicial concern, and many courts are turning increased scrutiny toward the connection between the class' interests and the activities of the recipients. In 1990, the influential Ninth Circuit court of appeals considered a settlement involving a class of undocumented Mexican workers who had settled Fair Labor Contractor Registration Act claims against a group of fruit farmers for $1,846,500.[75] The settlement directed unclaimed funds to be distributed to the Inter–American Fund for indirect humanitarian assistance in Mexico.[76] The Ninth Circuit rejected the settlement, explaining that the "proposal benefits a group far too remote from the plaintiff class".[77]

The Ninth Circuit followed the *Six Mexican Workers* decision with the opinion in *Nachshin*, where the court rejected a proposed settlement arising from AOL's alleged misuse of data from users' outgoing e-mails.[78] That proposed settlement agreement would have given a class of 66 million AOL subscribers no direct compensation, provided only minor notice changes and the creation of an opt-out on AOL's part (a requirement that represents a significant improvement over the agreement before this Court), and distributed $75,000 in *cy pres* payments. Because class and defence counsel "claimed they could not identify any charitable organisation that would benefit the class or be specifically germane to the issues in the case",[79] the district court selected three organisations as recipients: (1) the Legal Aid Foundation of Los Angeles, (2) the Federal Judicial Center Foundation, and (3) the Boys and Girls Club of America (shared between the chapters in Los Angeles and Santa Monica).

The Ninth Circuit reversed the decision of the lower court, holding that the groups were "geographically isolated and substantively unrelated charities", and focusing on the latter issue.[80] The court noted that some courts "appear to have abandoned the 'next best use' principle implicit in the *cy pres* doctrine. These courts have awarded *cy pres* distributions to myriad charities which, though no doubt pursuing virtuous goals, have little or nothing to do with the purposes of the underlying lawsuit or the class of plaintiffs involved."[81] The court held that because the action

---

[73] Ibid. at *2. The final settlement "provided that Class Members would receive the entirety of the Fund. Only the residue of uncashed claimants' checks or a surplus resulting from lower than anticipated administration costs would devolve to a *cy pres* fund."

[74] *S.E.C. v. Bear, Stearns & Co. Inc.*, 626 F. Supp. 2d 402, 415 (S.D.N.Y. 2009).

[75] *Six (6) Mexican Workers v. Arizona Citrus Growers*, 904 F.2d 1301, 1303–04 (9th Cir. 1990).

[76] Ibid., p. 1304.

[77] Ibid., p. 1308.

[78] 663 F.3d 1034 (9th Cir. 2011).

[79] Ibid., p. 1037.

[80] Ibid., p. 1034.

[81] Ibid., p. 1038, citing *Re Motorsports Merch. Antitrust Litig.*, 160 F.Supp.2d 1392, 1396–99 (N.D. Ga. 2001) (distributing $1.85 million remaining from a price-fixing class action settlement

arose from the alleged online misdeeds of AOL, appropriate *cy pres* relief *must* include organisations that actively work against online misdeeds:

> It is clear that all members of the class share two things in common: (1) they use the internet, and (2) their claims against AOL arise from a purportedly unlawful advertising campaign that exploited users' outgoing e-mail messages. The parties should not have trouble selecting beneficiaries from any number of non-profit organizations that work to protect internet users from fraud, predation, and other forms of online malfeasance.[82]

Given the renewed focus on the interests of the class members in *cy pres* distribution, the outcome in *Lane v. Facebook* presented a startling aberration. *Lane* involved a class action lawsuit over Beacon, a Facebook program "updating a member's personal profile to reflect certain actions the member had taken on websites belonging to companies that had contracted with Facebook to participate in the Beacon program".[83] The lawsuit produced a settlement that included a *cy pres* distribution of $6.5 million to "a new charity organisation called the Digital Trust Foundation ("DTF")".[84] The DTF would "promote the cause of online privacy, safety, and security" and have three directors, "chosen by mutual agreement of the parties".[85] However, the terms of the settlement dictated that at least one of the board members was a current employee of Facebook, and the two other directors chosen had financial ties to Facebook. The foundation would also have a two-member Board of Legal Advisors, who will "offer nonbinding advice on compliance with the provisions of this Agreement, attend all formal meetings and offer nonbinding advice to the officers and directors".[86] The initial Advisors would be the counsel of record for Facebook, and one of two counsels of record for the representative plaintiffs.[87]

Despite the proposed DTF's close connection to Facebook and precedent warning that careless selection of *cy pres* beneficiaries "may answer to the whims and self-interests of the parties, their counsel, or the court".[88] A divided appeals court approved the settlement. The majority of the judges explained that "[w]e do not require as part of that doctrine that settling parties select a cy pres recipient that the

---

relating to merchandise sold at professional stock car races to 10 organisations including the Duke Children's Hospital and Health Center, the Make-a-Wish Foundation, the American Red Cross and the Susan G. Komen Breast Cancer Foundation); *Superior Beverage Co., Inc. v. Owens-Illinois, Inc.*, 827 F. Supp. 477, 480 (N.D. Ill. 1993) (awarding $2 million from an antitrust class action settlement to 15 applicants, including the San Jose Museum of Art, the American Jewish Congress, a public television station, and the Roger Baldwin Foundation of the American Civil Liberties Union of Illinois).

[82] Ibid., p. 1041.

[83] *Lane v. Facebook, Inc.*, 696 F.3d 811, 816 (9th Cir. 2012) cert. denied, 134 S. Ct. 8 (U.S. 2013).

[84] Ibid., p. 817.

[85] Settlement Agreement at 12, *Lane v. Facebook*, No. 08-03845 (N.D. Cal. filed 12 August 2008).

[86] Ibid.

[87] Ibid.

[88] *Nachshin*, 663 F.3d at 1039.

court or class members would find ideal".[89] Instead, the use of *cy pres* funds must only bear a "substantial nexus to the interests of the class members", and the DTF's activities – "promot[ing] the causes of online privacy and security" – satisfied this objective.[90] The court also dismissed arguments that the *cy pres* distribution was fatally flawed because of DTF's lack of service record and because of the presence of a Facebook employee on the foundation's board. Settlements, the court said, "will necessarily reflect the interests of both parties to the settlement",[91] and "a settlement agreement that provides for the formation of a new grant-making organisation is not subject to a more stringent fairness standard".[92]

The opinion prompted a sharp dissent by Judge Kleinfeld, who suspected that the DTF's activities would fail to benefit class members and might even "fund nothing but an 'educational program' amounting to an advertising campaign for Facebook".[93] Other judges voiced similar concerns when the Ninth Circuit denied a petition for en banc review over the dissenting views of six judges.[94] Judge Smith, writing for the dissent, took issue with the DTF's lack of service record, explaining that only by examining factors other than a recipient's mission statement could one evaluate the benefit to the class from a *cy pres* distribution to that recipient.[95] Furthermore, Judge Smith explained that "an appropriate cy pres recipient must be dedicated to protecting consumers from the precise wrongful conduct about which plaintiffs complain".[96] In *Lane*, the class alleged violations of several privacy statutes focused on "preventing the *unauthorized* access or disclosure of private information".[97] DTF's mission, however, was limited to improving consumer education and control. To Judge Smith, this mismatch doomed the settlement because:

> an organization that focuses on protecting privacy solely through "user control" can *never* prevent unauthorized access or disclosure of private information where the alleged wrongdoer *already has unfettered access* to a user's records. The DTF can teach Facebook users how to create strong passwords, tinker with their privacy settings, and generally be more cautious online, but it can't teach users how to protect themselves from Facebook's deliberate misconduct. Unless of course the DTF teaches Facebook users not to use Facebook.[98]

---

[89] *Lane v. Facebook, Inc.*, 696 F.3d 811, 820–21 (9th Cir. 2012) cert. denied, 134 S. Ct. 8 (U.S. 2013).

[90] Ibid., p. 821.

[91] Ibid., p. 821.

[92] Ibid., p. 822.

[93] Ibid., p. 834 (Kleinfeld, J., dissenting).

[94] *Lane v. Facebook, Inc.*, 709 F.3d 791, 793 (9th Cir. 2013) (Smith, Kozinski, O'Scannlain, Bybee, Bea and Ikuta, dissenting). An en banc review is one where a case is heard before all the judges of a court rather than by a panel selected from them.

[95] Ibid., p. 794 ("Rather, a potential donor must look to other factors, such as the MacArthur Foundation's past record of service or its specific list of projects, to determine whether it is reasonably certain that a donation will truly bring about the promised effects.").

[96] Ibid.

[97] Ibid.

[98] Ibid., pp. 794–95.

The split decision was appealed to the US Supreme Court. Although the Supreme Court declined to hear the case, Chief Justice Roberts issued a non-binding opinion regarding the matter.[99] Justice Roberts noted the "unusual" allocation of funds in the settlement and stated that the Court would eventually need to address "fundamental concerns" surrounding *cy pres*, including:

> when, if ever, such relief should be considered; how to assess its fairness as a general matter; whether new entities may be established as part of such relief; if not, how existing entities should be selected; what the respective roles of the judge and parties are in shaping a cy pres remedy; how closely the goals of any enlisted organization must correspond to the interests of the class; and so on.[100]

Justice Roberts expressed particular concern over the Facebook Beacon settlement because, in the end, "the vast majority of Beacon's victims got neither" damages nor injunctive relief prohibiting the unlawful conduct that injured them.[101] This was the case because Facebook only promised to "discontinue the 'Beacon' program itself", and counsel even "conceded at the fairness hearing in the District Court that nothing in the settlement would preclude Facebook from reinstituting the same program with a new name". The parties also agreed to "expand the settlement class barred from future litigation" to include both the "opt-out" class proposed in the original complaint and any potential future "opt-in" class. Justice Roberts went on to explain that "the Court may need to clarify the limits on the use of such remedies".

14.5 Reforming *cy pres* decision-making

Although the Supreme Court did not resolve the concerns raised by the class action settlement in the *Lane* case, the issues identified by Chief Justice Roberts provide a framework for appropriate use of the *cy pres* remedy and a more general understanding of how best to enforce privacy rights though class action litigation. Three primary issues concern (1) when *cy pres* relief is appropriate in the first place; (2) the nexus between the recipient organisation and the interests of the class; and (3) the importance of judicial oversight in the selection process.

14.5.1 When cy pres *should be considered*

The risks inherent in *cy pres* have led some to conclude that such relief should never be used.[102] There are, however, circumstances where locating class members is onerous or impossible, or a direct distribution to class members would be

[99] *Marek v. Lane*, 134 S. Ct. 8 (2013).

[100] Ibid., p. 9.

[101] Ibid.

[102] See Redish, Martin H., et. al., "Cy Pres Relief and the Pathologies of the Modern Class Action: A Normative and Empirical Analysis", *Florida Law Review*, Vol. 62, No. 3, July 2010, pp. 617–666. http://www.floridalawreview.com/wp-content/uploads/2010/01/Redish_BOOK.pdf

inefficient. In these cases, a *cy pres* fund, properly distributed, can provide substantial indirect benefits to the class. This position accords with the prestigious American Law Institute's Principles of Law of Aggregate Litigation, which states that courts should try to identify, and distribute funds directly to, individual class members.[103] Only if individual class members cannot be identified, individual distributions would not be economically viable or "specific reasons exist that would make further distributions impossible or unfair" may a court use a *cy pres* approach.[104] Thus, *cy pres* distributions are appropriate as a last resort, to be used only when further distributions to the class are infeasible.[105]

Because the individual recovery is often small or difficult to ascertain, settlements in privacy class actions are often too quick to resort to indirect relief. Indeed, many recent privacy settlements proposed no direct compensation to individual class members.[106] Here, a greater effort to ensure that direct compensation is infeasible should be made. The approach of the district court in *Fraley v. Facebook* is partly instructive. *Fraley*'s preliminary settlement involved no direct compensation to the class.[107] The court denied preliminary approval on the grounds that, inter alia, class counsel had failed to adequately explain no monetary relief was proposed for the class.[108] The court found the lack of monetary relief particularly problematic in part because the law under which the plaintiffs sued provided statutory damages of $750.[109] Thus, "[m]erely pointing to the infeasibility of dividing up the agreed-to $10 million recovery, or the relatively small per-use revenue Facebook derived, is insufficient, standing alone, to justify resort to purely *cy pres* payments", wrote the Court.[110] The settlement finally approved by the court allowed each claimant to receive $15.[111] About 600,000 class members filed claims, producing a total pay-

[103] See American Law Institute, *Principles of the Law of Aggregate Litigation*, 2010, § 3.07. http://www.ali.org/index.cfm?fuseaction=publications.ppage&node_id=80

[104] Ibid. at § 3.07(c).

[105] See *Perkins v. Am. Nat'l Ins. Co.*, No. 3:05–CV–100 (CDL) (M.D. Ga. 10 July 2012) (considering first whether a "reasonably diligent effort has been made to locate class members who are the direct beneficiaries of the class action settlement" and whether "existing identified class members have been fully compensated" before considering *cy pres*); *Mace v. Van Ru Credit Corp.*, 109 F.3d 338, 345 (7th Cir. 1997)("cy pres recovery should be reserved for unusual circumstances").

[106] See, e.g., *Re Google Referrer Header Privacy Litigation*, No. 10-4809 (N.D. Cal. filed 25 Oct 2010); *Berry* et al. *v. LexisNexis Risk & Analytics Group Inc.*, No. 11-00754 (E.D. Va. 2011); *Re Netflix Privacy Litigation*, No. 11-00379 (N.D. Cal. filed 26 Jan 2011); *Re Google Buzz Privacy Litig.*, C 10-00672 JW, 2011 WL 7460099 (N.D. Cal. 2 June 2011).

[107] See Order Denying Motion for Preliminary Approval of Settlement, *Fraley v. Facebook*, No. 11-01726 (N.D. Cal. filed 8 Apr 2011).

[108] Ibid.

[109] Ibid., p. 3.

[110] Ibid.

[111] Order Granting Motion for Final Approval of Settlement Agreement, *Fraley v. Facebook*, No. 11-1726 (N.D. Cal. filed 8 Apr 2011).

ment to the class of $9.2 million.[112] However, this represented a small number of the total individuals impacted by the firm's practices and left unresolved the question as to whether Facebook could continue to engage in the disputed practices.

14.5.2 The nexus between the recipients and the class

US courts permitting the use of *cy pres* require a close connection between the purposes of the lawsuit and the activities of the *cy pres* recipients. The Ninth Circuit, for example, requires a "driving nexus between the plaintiff class and the cy pres beneficiaries".[113] Specifically, the Ninth Circuit considers the objectives of the underlying statute and the interests of the silent class members.[114] Similarly, the First Circuit recently adopted the "reasonable approximation" test for evaluating the distribution of *cy pres* awards.[115] The test considers a number of factors, including:

> the purposes of the underlying statutes claimed to have been violated, the nature of the injury to the class members, the characteristics and interests of the class members, the geographical scope of the class, the reasons why the settlement funds have gone unclaimed, and the closeness of the fit between the class and the cy pres recipient.[116]

Although these tests are formally strong, their application in consumer privacy cases reveals several common failure points. First, courts tend to assume that educating consumers and challenging misconduct are interchangeable in terms of the benefit they provide to the class. This mistake appears to result from a misconception of privacy as "notice and choice" rather than as "Fair Information Practices".[117] If privacy is conceptualised as notice and choice, then educating consumers and increasing awareness – e.g., more "notice" – are sufficient to minimise privacy violations. But most privacy laws are designed to protect against misconduct by data controllers. More notice, therefore, is of little benefit to the class members in most privacy lawsuits. In fact, notice tends to operate as a waiver or disclaimer, diminishing the privacy expectations that consumers might otherwise reasonably expect. As Judge Smith correctly observed in *Lane*, "[p]laintiffs' claims … have nothing to do

---

112 Ibid.

113 *Nachshin*, 663 F.3d at 1038.

114 See *Lane v. Facebook, Inc.*, 696 F.3d 811, 819–20 (9th Cir. 2012); *Nachshin v. AOL, LLC*, 663 F.3d 1034, 1039 (9th Cir. 2011); *Six (6) Mexican Workers v. Ariz. Citrus Growers*, 904 F.2d 1301, 1307 (9th Cir. 1990).

115 *Re Lupron Mktg. & Sales Practices Litig.*, 677 F.3d 21 (1st Cir. 2012) cert. denied, 133 S. Ct. 338, 184 L. Ed. 2d 239 (US 2012).

116 *Re Lupron Mktg. & Sales Practices Litig.*, 677 F.3d 21, 33 (1st Cir. 2012) cert. denied, 133 S. Ct. 338, 184 L. Ed. 2d 239 (US 2012).

117 Indeed, one recent settlement in a privacy class action lawsuit defended the selection of *cy pres* recipients on precisely this ground. See Supplemental Declaration of Kassra Nassiri. at 4, *Re Google Referrer Header Privacy Litigation*, No. 10-4809 (N.D. Cal. filed 25 Oct 2010) ("Plaintiffs have contended that the [Stored Communications Act] is, like other privacy protections, based on a 'notice and choice' approach.").

with users' lack of 'education' or 'control.' Instead, they relate to *misconduct* by Internet companies that wrongfully exposes private information in ways that even educated users cannot anticipate, prevent, or direct."[118] Privacy statutes focused on prohibiting misconduct require *cy pres* recipients who are willing to challenge misconduct. So long as organisations that actively challenge business misconduct concerning personal data exist, distributions for education or research cannot represent the "next best" use of settlement funds.

A second, and related, mistake occurs when insufficient attention is paid to the track record of the proposed recipient. The most egregious example of this was *Lane*, which saw *cy pres* funds go to a "bespoke creation of this settlement" with "*no* record of service".[119] Many other settlements, however, have directed funds to organisations and law school clinics that are cyber law "generalists" committed to a broad range of issues, such as robotics, intellectual property, free speech and so on. These institutions are no doubt capable of establishing and implementing privacy programs in order to receive *cy pres* funds. But a court looking to best accomplish the purposes underlying the lawsuit should not necessarily prioritise them to organisations specialising in privacy.

Finally, the defendant's interest in, or pre-existing funding for, the *cy pres* recipients seems to carry almost no weight with courts. Settlements frequently include *cy pres* awards to organisations that defendant corporations routinely support anyway for their own benefit.[120] As courts have observed, "[w]hen selection of *cy pres* beneficiaries is not tethered to the nature of the lawsuit and the interests of the silent class members, the selection process may answer to the whims and self interests of the parties, their counsel, or the court."[121] Thus, the influence of defendants on the selection process should be scrutinised to determine the fit between the proposed recipient and the interests of the class.

Mindful of the above considerations, some charities have removed themselves from flawed *cy pres* distributions. In one consumer privacy case, the MacArthur Foundation withdrew from the settlement proposal. The foundation noted that it was not an appropriate *cy pres* recipient and asked that the funds be "redirected to other non-profit organisations engaged in the underlying issues".[122] In the same case, a children's advocacy organisation that was designated to receive a substantial award withdrew from the *cy pres* allocation. In explaining the decision to turn down an award equal to almost the group's annual budget, the Campaign for Commercial-Free Childhood wrote:

---

[118] *Lane v. Facebook, Inc.*, 709 F.3d 791, 794 (9th Cir. 2013).

[119] *Lane v. Facebook, Inc.*, 709 F.3d 791, 793 (9th Cir. 2013).

[120] See, e.g., *Re Google Referrer Header Privacy Litigation*, No. 10-4809 (N.D. Cal. filed 25 Oct 2010); *Fraley v. Facebook*, No. 11-1726, 830 F. Supp. 2d 785 (N.D. Cal. 2011).

[121] *Nashchin*, 663 F.3d at 1039 (citing *Bear Stearns*, 626 F.Supp.2d at p. 415).

[122] Roberts, Jeff John, "Why privacy settlements like Facebook's "Sponsored Stories" lawsuit aren't working", *GigaOm*, 19 Sept 2013a. http://gigaom.com/2013/09/19/why-privacy-settlements-like-facebooks-sponsored-stories-lawsuit-arent-working/

> We knew that all settlements are compromises, but we initially believed this one would help protect teens on Facebook. But after reading objections from other advocacy groups we began to have doubts. …
>
> We now believe that this settlement is actually worse than no settlement. It harms vulnerable teenagers and their families under the guise of helping them. Its purported protections are largely illusory and it will actually undermine future efforts to protect minors on Facebook. In fact, it is in direct violation of our mission to help parents raise healthy families by limiting commercial access to children.[123]

The group wrote a letter to the Ninth Circuit in which it explained its decision and asked the court to overturn the settlement and negotiate an agreement that will "really protect minors".[124] The settlement is still under review.[125]

14.5.3 *Judicial oversight*

Ensuring that a class action settlement will meaningfully enforce privacy requires strict judicial oversight. There should be a clear nexus between the interests of the class and the work of *cy pres* recipients. Courts should satisfy themselves that the recipient organisation's interests align with those pursued by the class before approving a settlement. Here again, the approach of the court in *Fraley* is instructive. The settlement directed a *cy pres* payment of several million dollars to organisations involved in "consumer protection, research, education regarding online privacy".[126] However, the court noted that it was "difficult to say that providing funds to these recipients is precisely aligned with the 'purpose' of the lawsuit" before concluding that the proposed *cy pres* organisations addressed issues "closely related to the matters raised in the complaint".[127] The court's failure to definitively resolve the question of whether the purpose of the lawsuit aligned with the choice of recipients represents an inadequate level of judicial oversight.

A judicially-administered application process with recipients selected pursuant to objective criteria could help courts resolve these questions. Indeed, in some privacy cases, courts have employed similar criteria. In *Re Google Buzz Privacy Litigation*, for example, the parties initially proposed that Google would identify recipients of *cy pres* funds and the final recipients would be selected through a

[123] Campaign for a Commercial Free Childhood, "Why we turned down $290,000", 13 Feb 2014. http://www.commercialfreechildhood.org/blog/why-we-turned-down-money

[124] Letter of *Amicus Curiae* Campaign for a Commercial Free Childhood Supporting the Objector-Appellants Schachter et al., 12 Feb 2014. http://www.commercialfreechildhood.org/sites/default/files/CCFCAmicusLetter.pdf

[125] Fraley v. Facebook, http://www.fraleyfacebooksettlement.com/; EPIC, Fraley v. Facebook. http://epic.org/amicus/facebook/fraley/

[126] Ibid., p. 10.

[127] Ibid.

determination of counsel.[128] The court found that this process "lacked specificity and oversight required to provide a reasonable benefit to the Class".[129] Instead, the court ordered the parties to "nominate the cy pres recipients" based on the following criteria:

(i) The organisation's name and address;
(ii) A description of an established program currently undertaking policy or education efforts directed specifically at Internet privacy;
(iii) The number of years that the program has been established and focused on Internet privacy;
(iv) A short statement as to how the particular program will benefit the Class;
(v) The annual operating budget of the organisation as a whole and the specific Internet privacy or education program; and
(vi) The amount received, if any, in contributions from Google, Inc. in 2010, independent of the Settlement.[130]

More recently, in *Re Netflix Privacy Litigation*, the parties have proposed a settlement agreement that includes an objective nomination process.[131] The application process requests certain detailed information from potential recipients, including:

(i) The organisation's name and address;
(ii) A description of an established program currently undertaking policy or education efforts directed specifically at issues of technology, law and privacy;
(iii) A short statement describing how the program benefits the Class;
(iv) The overall annual operating budget of the organisation and of the specific program;
(v) The total amount of the *cy pres* distribution sought;
(vi) Disclosure of any connections, monetary or otherwise, between the organisations and the parties;
(vii) Disclosure of any connections, monetary or otherwise, between the organisation and Class Counsel and Supporting Counsel; and

---

[128] Notice of Motion and Memorandum in Support of Motion for Order Granting Final Approval of Class Settlement, Certifying Settlement Class, and Appointing Class Representatives and Class Counsel, *Re Google Buzz Privacy Litigation*, 2011 WL 7460099 (No. 10-00672 JW) (N.D. Cal. entered Feb. 16, 2011), p. 6.

[129] Order re. Nomination Process for *Cy Pres* Recipients, *supra* n. 45 at 1.

[130] Ibid., p. 2. The court made explicit its concern that, absent such procedures, worthwhile recipients could be improperly excluded. See ibid. In the 31 May 2011 Order granting final approval of the settlement, the Court acknowledged objections to the proposed *cy pres* distribution of counsel and set out a "few necessary modifications" to ensure that "the nominations list adequately represents the interests of the class…." Order Granting Final Approval of Class Action Settlement; Approval of *Cy Pres* Awards; and Awarding Attorney Fees, *Re Google Buzz Privacy Litigation*, 2011 WL 7460099 (No. 10-00672 JW) (N.D. Cal. entered 31 Mar 2011), p. 2. http://epic.org/privacy/ftc/googlebuzz/EPIC_Google_Buzz_Settlement.pdf

[131] *Re Netflix Privacy Litigation*, 5:11-CV-00379 EJD, 2013 WL 1120801 (N.D. Cal. 18 Mar 2013).

(viii) Disclosure of the amount received, if any, in contributions from the Parties or their counsel in 2011.[132]

The objective checklist in *Netflix* is more detailed than that in *Google Buzz*, although it lacks the latter's degree of judicial involvement. Nevertheless, the use of objective application processes can aid courts in determining whether the proposed distribution would accomplish the purposes of the underlying lawsuit. The authors, with the support of other consumer privacy organisations, have urged federal courts considering *cy pres* allocations to establish similar objective criteria that would require *cy pres* recipients to establish their eligibility to receive *cy pres* funds and to explain how such funds will be used.[133]

14.5.4 *The ethical obligations of* cy pres *recipients*

The withdrawal of a small consumer organisation from a *cy pres* settlement that would have provided substantial benefit to the organisation focuses attention on the legal and ethical obligations of organisations that are designated to receive *cy pres* funds. A simple view of corporate responsibility states that corporations should engage in activities that further the interests of the corporation, particularly the ability to increase net revenue. But non-profit corporations in the United States are granted favourable tax treatment because they are pursuing an important educational or charitable mission. When an organisation is designated to receive *cy pres* funds arising from a matter that is inconsistent with its charitable mission, it is appropriate to decline participation. This explains the recent decision of the MacArthur Foundation, which determined that it did not pursue work in the consumer privacy field that would justify allocation from a *cy pres* settlement fund.

A more difficult problem is posed when the interests of the organisation are aligned with the interests of the class members but the settlement is ultimately a setback for the class and the constituents of the organisation. This is the dilemma that the Campaign for a Commercial-Free Childhood (CCFC) confronted. It could have kept the funds and pursued important work consistent with the purpose of the litigation but it chose instead to reject the funding and opposed the settlement. It is an inspiring example. We recommend that every organisation designated to receive *cy pres* funds engage in a similar considered determination as to whether the settlement terms will further the interests of the class and the mission of the organisation. Organisations should be encouraged to describe in writing the purpose of the

---

132 Class Action Settlement Agreement, *Re Netflix Privacy Litigation* (No. 11-00379 entered 25 May 2012), pp. 13–14.

133 See, e.g., Letter to Judge Lucy H. Kohn concerning *Fraley v. Facebook* Proposed Settlement, No. 11-01726 from EPIC Executive Director Marc Rotenberg, on behalf of the Electronic Privacy Information Center, the Center for Digital Democracy, the Privacy Rights Clearinghouse and the Institute for Public Representation, Georgetown University Law Center, 11 July 2012. http://www.epic.org/privacy/EPIC-et-al-Fraley-Cy-Prs-Ltr-7-12-12.pdf

litigation, the interests of the class members, and how the *cy pres* funds will be used by the organisation. Such statements should be made publicly available for review, particularly by those on whose behalf the case was brought. In those circumstances where courts have established objective criteria for review of *cy pres* applications, as we propose above, the statements to the court will fulfill this purpose and should be made readily available to the public.

A related problem that the CCFC objection raises is whether it is ever appropriate for a *cy pres* recipient to indicate support for a proposed settlement agreement. Too frequently, organisations and research institutions in the United States are asked to present to a judge that, in their opinion, it is a fair settlement and should be approved. We disfavour this practice. The conflict of interest is too great when an organisation that stands to receive a substantial amount of funding is asked to make a judgement to protect the interests of others. We believe that designated *cy pres* recipients should express no opinion as to the adequacy of the settlement and only state how they will use the funds received to advance the interests of class members in a way that is consistent with the underlying litigation. Thus, the decision will remain with the court to assess fairness of the settlement and the responsibility will remain with the *cy pres* designees to provide the "next best" relief for class members.

14.6 Conclusion

Class action lawsuits in the United States present numerous challenges for courts, commentators and class members. Of these challenges, the use of *cy pres* to distribute unclaimed funds has attracted considerable attention. Although *cy pres* distributions raise fundamental questions, they offer an important benefit to class members where direct compensation is unavailable.

US courts should scrutinise these agreements closely for fairness to the class members, ensure that the settlements advance the interests of consumers and are consistent with the purpose of the original legal claim. Regarding the allocation of funds from such settlements, courts should adopt objective criteria to ensure that the monies will be distributed for purposes that serve the interests of the class and are consistent with the reason for the litigation. These factors are the fundamental requirements for just and fair allocations in class action settlements. The US experience will be helpful in other countries where privacy rights are enforced through private litigation and class actions. The experience in the United States suggests that class action litigation can be an effective way to enforce privacy rights, but it is necessary to examine the final settlements to ensure that they are fair to the class members and advance the aims of privacy protection.

With careful judicial oversight and attention to the need for a close nexus between the plaintiff class and the proposed beneficiaries, *cy pres* awards can accomplish their intended purpose as the "next best" available relief.

References

American Law Institute, *Principles of the Law of Aggregate Litigation*, 2010. http://www.ali.org/index.cfm?fuseaction=publications.ppage&node_id=80

Barnett, Kerry, "Equitable Trusts: An Effective Remedy in Consumer Class Actions", *Yale Law Journal*, Vol. 96, No. 7, June 1987, pp. 1591–1614. http://www.jstor.org/stable/796495;

Campaign for a Commercial Free Childhood, Letter of *Amicus Curiae,* Supporting the Objector-Appellants Schachter et al., 12 Feb 2014. http://www.commercialfreechildhood.org/sites/default/files/CCFCAmicusLetter.pdf

Campaign for a Commercial Free Childhood, "Why we turned down $290,000", 13 Feb 2014. http://www.commercialfreechildhood.org/blog/why-we-turned-down-money

DeJarlais, Natalie A., "The Consumer Trust Fund: A Cy Pres Solution to Undistributed Funds in Consumer Class Actions", *Hastings Law Journal*, Vol. 38, April 1987, pp. 729–767.

EPIC, Fraley v. Facebook, http://epic.org/amicus/facebook/fraley/

Federal Rules of Civil Procedure (FRCP).

Federal Trade Commission (FTC), *Protecting Consumer Privacy in an Era of Rapid Change: Recommendations for businesses and policymakers*, March 2012. http://online.wsj.com/public/resources/documents/PrivacyReport_FINAL.pdf

Fisch, Edith L., *The Cy Pres Doctrine in the United States*, Matthew Bender, New York, 1950.

Gayle, Damien, "Is Facebook 'impersonating' users to promote stories they've never seen to all their friends?", *Daily Mail*, 24 Jan 2013. http://www.dailymail.co.uk/sciencetech/article-2267575/Is-Facebook-impersonating-users-promote-stories-theyve-seen-friends.html

Goel, Vindu, "Facebook Privacy Deal is Under Attack," *The New York Times*, 13 Feb 2014. http://www.nytimes.com/2014/02/13/technology/facebook-deal-on-privacy-is-under-attack.html

Gray, Hamish, "The History and Development in England of the Cy-Pres Principle in Charities", *Boston University Law Review*, Vol. 33, 1953, pp. 30–51.

Grimmelmann, James, "Future Conduct and the Limits of Class-Action Settlements", *North Carolina Law Review*, Vol. 91, Issue 2, 2013, pp. 387–474. http://www.nclawreview.org/category/archives/91/issue-2/

Harris, Elizabeth, and Nicole Perlroth, "For Target, the Breach Numbers Grow", *The New York Times*, 11 Jan 2014.

Harris, Elizabeth, et al., "A Sneaky Path into Target Customers' Wallets", *The New York Times*, 18 Jan 2014.

Hay, Bruce, and David Rosenberg, "'Sweetheart' and 'Blackmail' Settlements in Class Actions: Reality and Remedy", *Notre Dame Law Review*, Vol. 75, Issue 4, 2000, pp. 1377–1408.

Koniak, Susan P., and George M. Cohen, "Under Cloak of Settlement", *Virginia Law Review*, Vol. 82, No. 2, 1996.

Privacy Laws and Business, "German Consumer Protection Organizations to be Empowered to Sue Businesses for Data Protection Law Violations", 14 Feb 2014. www.bitkom.org/de/presse/8477_78620.aspx

Redish, Martin H., et. al., "Cy Pres Relief and the Pathologies of the Modern Class Action: A Normative and Empirical Analysis", *Florida Law Review*, Vol. 62, No. 3, July 2010, pp. 617–666. http://www.floridalawreview.com/wp-content/uploads/2010/01/Redish_BOOK.pdf

Reuters, "Neiman Marcus data breach occurred as far back as July", published in *The Chicago Tribune*, 17 Jan 2014. http://articles.chicagotribune.com/2014-01-17/business/chi-neiman-marcus-data-breach-occurred-as-far-back-as-july-20140117_1_cyber-attack-neiman-marcus-ginger-reeder

Roberts, Jeff John, "Why privacy settlements like Facebook's 'Sponsored Stories' lawsuit aren't working", *GigaOm*, 19 Sept 2013. http://gigaom.com/2013/09/19/why-privacy-settlements-like-facebooks-sponsored-stories-lawsuit-arent-working/

Roberts, Jeff John, "Target hit with dozens of lawsuits over mass data breach", *GigaOm*, 27 Dec 2013. http://gigaom.com/2013/12/27/target-hit-with-dozens-of-lawsuits-over-mass-data-breach/

Rotenberg, Marc, "Fair Information Practices and the Architecture of Privacy", *Stanford Technology Law Review*, February 2001. http://stlr.stanford.edu/pdf/rotenberg-fair-info-practices.pdf

Rotenberg, Marc, Letter to Judge Lucy H. Kohn concerning *Fraley v. Facebook* Proposed Settlement, No. 11-01726 from EPIC Executive Director Marc Rotenberg, on behalf of the Electronic Privacy Information Center, the Center for Digital Democracy, the Privacy Rights Clearinghouse and the Institute for Public Representation, Georgetown University Law Center, 11 July 2012. http://www.epic.org/privacy/EPIC-et-al-Fraley-Cy-Prs-Ltr-7-12-12.pdf

Schectman, Joel, "Target Faces Nearly 70 Lawsuits Over Breach", *The Wall Street Journal*, 15 Jan 2014. http://blogs.wsj.com/riskandcompliance/2014/01/15/target-faces-nearly-70-lawsuits-over-breach/

Shepherd, Stewart R., "Damage Distribution in Class Actions: The Cy Pres Remedy", *University of Chicago Law Review*, Vol. 39, No. 2, Winter 1972, pp. 448–465. http://www.jstor.org/stable/1599010

The White House, Consumer Data Privacy in a Networked World: A Framework for Protecting Privacy and Promoting Innovation in the Global Digital Economy, 2012.

US Department of Health, Education and Welfare (HEW), *Records, Computers and the Rights of Citizens*, Report of the Secretary's Advisory Committee on Automated Personal Data Systems, Washington, DC, 1973. http://epic.org/privacy/hew1973report/

Court cases

Abdullah v. U.S. Sec. Associates, Inc., 731 F.3d 952, 963–64 (9th Cir. 2013).

Allison v. Citgo Petroleum Corp., 151 F.3d 402, 410 (5th Cir. 1998).

Amchem Products, Inc. v. Windsor, 521 U.S. 591, 617, 117 S.Ct. 2231, 138 L.Ed.2d 689 (1997).

Berry et al. *v. LexisNexis Risk & Analytics Group Inc.*, No. 11-00754 (E.D. Va. 2011).

Dennis v. Kellogg Co., 697 F.3d 858, 865 (9th Cir. 2012).

Fraley v. Facebook, No. 11-1726 (N.D. Cal. filed 8 Apr 2011).

Geraghty, 445 U.S., pp. 402–03.

Jeff D. v. Evans, 743 F.2d 648, 651 (9th Cir. 1984) rev'd, 475 U.S. 717 (1986).

Klier v. Elf Atochem N. Am., Inc., 658 F.3d 468, 474–75 (5th Cir. 2011).

Lane v. Facebook, Inc., 696 F.3d 811, 828 (9th Cir. 2012) cert. denied, 134 S. Ct. 8 (U.S. 2013).

Mace v. Van Ru Credit Corp., 109 F.3d 338, 344 (7th Cir.1997).

Marek v. Lane, 134 S. Ct. 8, 8–9 (2013).

Masters v. Wilhelmina Model Agency, Inc., 473 F.3d 423, 436 (2d Cir. 2007).

Miller v. Steinbach, No. 66 Civ. 356, 1974 WL 350, at *2 (S.D.N.Y. 3 Jan 1974).

Murray v. GMAC Mortgage Corp., 434 F.3d 948, 953 (7th Cir. 2006).

Nachshin v. AOL, LLC, 663 F.3d 1034, 1036 (9th Cir. 2011).

Park v. The Thomson Corp., 05 CIV.2931 (WHP), 2008 WL 4684232 (S.D.N.Y. Oct. 22, 2008).

Perkins v. Am. Nat'l Ins. Co., No. 3:05–CV–100 (CDL) (M.D. Ga. 10 July 2012).

Pelt v. Utah, 539 F.3d 1271, 1284 (10th Cir. 2008).

Re Am. Express Merchs. Litig., No. 03 CV 9592, 2006 WL 662341, at *1 (S.D.N.Y., 16 Mar 2006).

Re Amino Acid Lysine Antitrust Litig., 918 F. Supp. 1190, 1196 (N.D. Ill. 1996).

Re Gen. Motors Corp. Pick-Up Truck Fuel Tank Products Liab. Litig., 55 F.3d 768, 785 (3d Cir. 1995).

Re Google Referrer Header Privacy Litigation, No. 10-4809 (N.D. Cal. filed 25 Oct 2010).

Re Compact Disc Minimum Advertised Price Antitrust Litigation, No. MDL 1361, 2005 WL 1923446 (D.Me. 9 Aug 2005).

Re Google Buzz Privacy Litig., C 10-00672 JW, 2011 WL 7460099 (N.D. Cal. 2 June 2011).

Re Google Referrer Header Privacy Litigation, No. 10-4809 (N.D. Cal. filed 25 Oct 2010).

Re Lupron Mktg. & Sales Practices Litig., 677 F.3d 21 (1st Cir. 2012) cert. denied, 133 S. Ct. 338, 184 L. Ed. 2d 239 (US 2012).
Re Motorsports Merch. Antitrust Litig., 160 F.Supp.2d 1392, 1396–99 (N.D. Ga. 2001).
Re Netflix Privacy Litigation, No. 11–00379 (N.D. Cal. filed 26 Jan 2011).
S.E.C. v. Bear, Stearns & Co. Inc., 626 F. Supp. 2d 402, 414 (S.D.N.Y. 2009).
Six (6) Mexican Workers v. Arizona Citrus Growers, 904 F.2d 1301, 1303–04 (9th Cir. 1990).
Superior Beverage Co., Inc. v. Owens-Illinois, Inc., 827 F. Supp. 477, 480 (N.D. Ill. 1993).
Thorogood v. Sears, Roebuck & Co., 547 F.3d 742, 744–45 (7th Cir. 2008).

Additional references not mentioned in the chapter, but germane to the subject:

Allen, Anita, and Marc Rotenberg, eds., *Privacy Law and Society*, 3d. ed., West, 2016.
JDSupra, "EPIC Objects to Facebook Settlement, Cites Failure to Benefit Class Members (Letter two)", 16 July 2012.
Marketwatch, "Five Public Interest Groups Underscore Opposition To Settlement In Google Privacy Suit", 16 Oct 2013.
Roberts, Chief Justice John, Statement respecting the denial of certiorari, Mark v. Lane, 571 U.S. ___ (2013).
Rotenberg, Marc, Julia Horwitz and Jeramie Scott (eds.), *Privacy in the Modern Age: The Search for Solutions*, The New Press, 2015.
The Register, "Judge: Google class action 'usual suspects' cash-fling 'smells': Proposed payout gives class members nothing – objectors", 5 Sept 2014.

Chapter 15
Data Protection Certification: Decorative or Effective Instrument? Audit and Seals as a Way to Enforce Privacy

Kirsten Bock

15.1 Introduction

Data protection in the 21st century is confronted with so-called "big data" and globally active organisations, which call for rethinking traditional approaches. Data protection authorities as well as industry struggle to meet the expectations inherent in free democratic societies, i.e., functionally differentiated societies, for the processing and control of personal data and its oversight. It is evident that the fundamental right to data protection can only be achieved in an information society by integration of data protection into technology at its core, a concise data protection management system (DPMS), and consistent and reliable control mechanisms.[1] In addition to the toolbox of negative instruments for data protection oversight, positive incentives are necessary to produce market-supported changes towards more data protection friendly and enhancing technology and behaviour of organisations.

Instruments to produce such incentives are data protection certification and data protection audits. Both have been investigated in the 1990s, especially by Rossnagel and Bäumler, and were put into practice and legislation first in Japan[2] and in Germany by Schleswig-Holstein and Bremen.[3] Soon afterwards, a number of very

---

[1] Dix, Alexander, "Betroffenenrechte im Datenschutz", in Jan-Hinrik Schmidt and Thilo Weichert (eds.), *Datenschutz, Bundeszentrale für politische Bildung*, Bonn, 2012, pp. 290–297 [p. 296].

[2] The Japan Information Processing Development Center (JIPDEC) established, and has been operating, the "PrivacyMark System" since 1 April 1998, cf. http://english.jipdec.or.jp/pmark.html

[3] Rossnagel, Alexander, "Datenschutz-Audit", *Datenschutz und Datensicherheit DuD*, 2007, pp. 505 ff.; Bäumler, Helmut, "Datenschutzgesetze der dritten Generation", in Helmut Bäumler and Albert von Mutius (eds.), *Datenschutzgesetze der dritten Generation*, Luchterhand, Neuwied, Kriftel, 1999, p. 7. Schleswig-Holsteinisches Gesetz zum Schutz personenbezogener Informationen (Landesdatenschutzgesetz) of 9 February 2000, GVBl, 2000, p. 169.

K. Bock (✉)
ULD, Holstenstr. 98, 24103 Kiel, Germany
e-mail: kbock@datenschutzzentrum.de

D. Wright, P. De Hert (eds.), *Enforcing Privacy*, Law, Governance and Technology Series 25, DOI 10.1007/978-3-319-25047-2_15

heterogeneous, mostly private-sector-initiated, trust seals appeared, characterised by either a regional approach, by a lack of focus on data protection or by lack of relevance.[4] To that end, the European Commission proposed a new article on certification in the General Data Protection Regulation[5] and tendered a study on EU privacy seals to investigate the possibilities[6] after the European Parliament in a resolution had called on the European Commission to "develop an EU website labelling system modelled on the European Privacy Seal".[7] Eventually, the UK Information Commissioner's Office (ICO) launched a call for a privacy seal scheme in a given framework and thereby became the second EU country to endorse a dedicated data protection seal system following the French "label".[8]

This chapter proposes an approach that could enable data protection authorities to use data protection certification as a means to enforce privacy and to facilitate their work as oversight bodies. It proposes that certification produces relevant documentation and at the same time enables organisations to effectively manage and control the processing of personal data to gain operative protection. To become such an effective instrument, certification must comprise essential elements, as discussed below. Also discussed are the means by which authorities and organisations can benefit from such an approach.

15.2 Enforcement by certification

Among diverse tools to encourage companies to comply with data protection law, certification and audit can be useful tools if applied wisely. There is already well-grounded experience in process audits and product and service evaluation. Process or performance audits refer to a systematic examination of a precisely defined target. They confirm whether an organisation's monitoring procedures are defined, in place and linked to effective action. This allows a determination if the organisation

[4] Cf. Connolly, Chris, *Trustmark Schemes Struggle to Protect Privacy*, Pyrmont, Australia, 2008, pp. 22 f.

[5] Article 39, European Commission, Proposal for a Regulation of the European Parliament and of the Council on the protection of individuals with regard to the processing of personal data and on the free movement of such data (General Data Protection Regulation), COM(2012) 11 final, Brussels, 25 January 2012.

[6] Cf. Wright et al., *EU Privacy seals study, Inventory and analysis of privacy certification schemes, Final Report*, Study Deliverable 1.4, Luxembourg, 2013.

[7] European Parliament Resolution of 15 December 2010 on the impact of advertising on consumer behaviour, 2010/2052(INI). http://www.europarl.europa.eu/sides/getDoc.do?type=TA&reference=P7-TA-2010-0484&language=EN

[8] Germany introduced the possibility of data protection certification and audits in section 9a of the Federal Data Protection Act of 2003, yet failed to introduce a running system ever since. In 2012, the German parliament set aside a fund to sponsor a seal system by initiating the "Stiftung Datenschutz". From the beginning, it was clear that neither the monetary means nor the funded number of stuff would be in a position to actually produce a running system.

complies with its defined processes and can involve procedural or results-based assessment criteria. Product and service certification verifies the quality of a (sample) product or service. Certificates in the area of data protection vary in value depending on the relevance of certification criteria, the independence and expertise of the evaluator and auditor. The main objective of a certificate is to produce an attestation of quality and thereby to create trust.

The first generation of trust marks led to mixed responses and is frequently called a failure in terms of "real protection".[9] The discussions about trust marks focus on the question whether and to which degree a regulation is necessary to govern message, procedure and issuance. While the private sector seems to favour as much self-regulation as possible, existing schemes have been initiated reluctantly and without much influence.[10] With its proposal for a general data protection regulation, the European Commission sought in its Article 39 to "encourage" the establishment of certification mechanisms,[11] yet postponed regulating the particulars. The compromise proposal made by the European Parliament,[12] taking account of the reluctance of industry to focus on data subjects' fundamental rights,[13] consequently added key aspects such as financial and factual independence as well as proficiency in data protection of the issuing organisation. Article 39 also sets out further requirements for procedure (new para. 2), scope, content (new para. 1b) and presentation of (summary) findings to the public (new para. 1 a)[14] to provide at least a basic framework for certification schemes.[15] In May 2015, the Presidency published the Council's draft proposal[16] shifting from the more data-subject-focussed concretisation of the Parliament to a more detailed determination of the accreditation requirements

[9] McCarthy, Jamie, "TRUSTe decides its own fate today", *Slashdot*, 8 Nov 1999. http://yro.slashdot.org/story/99/11/05/1021214/truste-decides-its-own-fate-today

[10] Connolly, 2008, p. 22.; Feik, Sebastian, and Kai von Lewinski, "Der Markt für Datenschutz-Zertifizierungen", *BvD-News*, Issue 2, 2014, pp. 47–50.

[11] European Commission, Proposal for a Regulation of the European Parliament and the Council on the protection of individuals with regard to the processing of personal data and on the free movement of such data (General Data Protection Regulation), Brussels, COM(2012) 11 final, 25 January 2012, Article 39, Recital 77.

[12] European Parliament, Committee on Civil Liberties, Justice and Home Affairs, Draft Report on the proposal for a regulation of the European Parliament and of the Council on the protection of individuals with regard to the processing of personal data and on the free movement of such data (General Data Protection Regulation),COM(2012)0011 – C7-0025/2012–2012/0011(COD) 2012/0011 (COD), 17 December 2012.

[13] Bock, Kirsten, "Marktwirtschaftlicher Datenschutz", pp. 310–321 [p. 312].

[14] The wording of Article 39 and 39a as proposed by the Council of the European Union as achieved under the Greek presidency constricts the scope to audits, i.e., internal processing operations, without acknowledging certification of products and services which form a substantial number of targets of certification (privacy by design) with much influence on the data processing operations.

[15] Bock, Kirsten, "Marktwirtschaftlicher Datenschutz", pp. 310–321 [310 f].

[16] Council of the European Union, Proposal for a Regulation of the European Parliament and the Council on the protection of individuals with regard to the processing of personal data and on the free movement of such data (General Data Protection Regulation), Brussels, 9398/15, 29 May 2015.

of certification bodies in a new Article 39a. This proposal surprisingly stresses even more strongly the purpose of certification: to demonstrate compliance with the Regulation. It states the key elements of certification as (1) approved certification criteria (Article 39 2a.), (2) granted by an accredited independent certification body with expertise in data protection (Article 39a). The final compromise of December 2015 further specifies the scope of applicants and the duration of accreditation of certification bodies and certification. In a new Art. 39 1a and 1b data subjects' rights and transparency are especially highlighted. By including the National Accreditation Bodies into the accreditation process for certification bodies in Art. 39a 1(b), it opens the accreditation process. It will be the task of the European Data Protection Board to assure transparency and compatibility of criteria, seals and certification processes. The newly introduced Art. 39 2a even opens a possibility for a common European Data Protection Seal.

While data protection authorities in Europe are not too enthusiastic about becoming active players in a new certification scheme, they join the legislator in its opinion that any certification should demonstrate compliance with data protection regulation.

15.2.1 Compliance

Compliance is a term often used when it comes to fulfilment of legal requirements. Of course – at least for the past – the vast majority of companies claimed to achieve legal compliance in their business. However, with technology moving forward at light speed, it is often not clear whether whole business models are still in line with "the law". And it seems that we have left the aspect of offering a product or service in line with the law behind. Not only "code is law", but also "what can be done, will be done" rules the international market, especially if enforcement is slow or absent.

In order to make use of privacy seals, trust marks and labels as a way to enforce data protection,[17] it is crucial to determine the design of the scheme along the lines of data protection law. Compliance is the key buzzword and I am not aware of any scheme that does not at least claim compliance. Seal schemes that do not *demand* actual compliance with the legal obligations of its seal-holders are of no use unless authorities use these schemes to select the seal-holders as next in line for

[17] I follow the distinction of privacy and data protection made in the EU Charter of Fundamental Rights as explicated by Kokott and Sobotta (2013): Privacy "does not necessarily include all information on identified or identifiable persons" [p. 225], it concentrates on the individual to fight back against infringements of private life. Data protection refers to the social context of information processing which addresses the (informational) asymmetry in power to safeguard self-determination and privacy by preventing organisations to (mis-)use their power advantage towards individuals in their respective roles as citizens, patients, employees, etc.

inspections.[18] There is in fact no other option besides compliance for an authority because it cannot seriously support a scheme that promotes companies, products or services that do not achieve the threshold set out by the law. Just imagine the underlying message of such a seal: "This product is not as bad as the rest – it is only trespassing the law a little bit" or "They steal your data, but they don't do the awful things others do to it; they treat your data (sorry, not your rights) nicely". However, this does unfortunately not prevent organisations from offering and using such schemes.

The success of a privacy seal scheme depends on its relevance, quality, manageability, trustworthiness and message. Any scheme that does not require full compliance with data protection regulations will be meaningless in its effort to protect user privacy.[19]

When considering compliance, two general issues matter: First, shall it be necessary for a whole product or service to be within the scope of a certificate or is it sufficient that certain aspects or parts of a service fulfil legal requirements? Second, to what degree are the requirements to be fulfilled? Will it be sufficient to barely pass all of the requirements or shall there be only certain aspects not very important to a product or service that may not be achieved to a higher level? Or should a certified target "demonstrate a positive approach to the adoption of good practice,"[20] rather than just compliance with the letter of the law?

Certification in general and especially consumer-oriented certifications are only meaningful if the scope of the target makes sense to the customer, consumer or user addressed. If a part of a processing or service that cannot be purchased or chosen as such receives a trust mark, it is worthless. If a consumer chooses a service to print digital images and only the storage of the picture is subject to certification but not its customer address management, in fact, the company even shares customer data without notice or consent, a data protection trust mark would be misleading. On the other hand, if a product is composed of two different options of which only one passes the certification criteria, it is misleading to certify the product en bloc.[21]

[18] A suggestion introduced by Connolly 2008, p. 18 ff.

[19] Cf. European Commission, Communication to the European Parliament and the Council on Promoting Data Protection by Privacy-enhancing Technologies (PETs), COM (2007) 228 final, Brussels, 2 May 2007. Connolly, Chris, *Benchmarks for global Privacy Standards – Working Paper*, Pyrmont, November 2009, p. 6; Rossnagel, A., p. 511 f.

[20] Information Commissioner's Office (ICO), Framework criteria for an ICO-endorsed privacy seal scheme, draft for consultation, Vol. 3, 2 Sept 2014. http://ico.org.uk/about_us/consultations/~/media/documents/library/Data_Protection/Research_and_reports/framework-criteria-for-an-ico-endorsed-privacy-seal-scheme.pdf

[21] Cf. ULD Guetesiegel for TGPopen v2.0, Short Public Report, p. 5. https://www.datenschutzzentrum.de/guetesiegel/kurzgutachten/g090805/090805-kurzgutachten-tgpopen_2013.pdf; TeamDrive v3 only applicable to its versions TeamDrive Free, TeamDrive Personal and TeamDrive Professional. https://www.datenschutzzentrum.de/guetesiegel/register.htm; short public report, https://www.datenschutzzentrum.de/guetesiegel/kurzgutachten/g050302/g050302-rezertifizierang-teamdrive-2013.pdf

15.2.2 Measuring compliance

If a processing operation is in conflict with the law, it is unlawful. There is no in-between. It is either in or out. One fault is inherited by the whole system or product. Thus, a product or service of which any aspect is in conflict with a legal obligation cannot receive the result of overall compliance. Another question is whether an authority will fine the controller or processor. It will always have to make a decision whether the processing operation in question is tolerable and thus "in" or whether something *has* to be done about it because it is "out". "Barely tolerable" is not an amiable goal and a certified product or service should consist of a healthy composition of excellent, good and only very few tolerable rankings in fulfilment of criteria and thus compliance.

15.2.3 Demonstrating compliance

To demonstrate compliance – especially towards multi-national requirements in cross-border environments with different oversight bodies – it is essential to focus on key requirements. In order to demonstrate compliance successfully, a certification or audit scheme needs to demonstrate three main elements:

- a systematic method for evaluation,
- a set of pre-defined, binding criteria based on all relevant legal requirements,
- a binding certification or audit procedure governed by an independent certification or audit authority.

Many privacy and data protection certificates are merely decorative. They lack transparency in criteria, evaluation method and significance in results.[22] Neither general criteria and methods nor individual evaluation reports are published or available to oversight bodies.[23] Consequently, such a certification or audit neither demonstrates compliance open to scrutiny nor does it facilitate trust.[24]

In order to be effective in enforcing data protection, a certification and audit scheme must be able to demonstrate its significance in data protection. Sufficiently relevant and systemised documentation of a scheme's components facilitates transparency for the organisation and pro re nata oversight bodies.

---

[22] Wright et al.

[23] Especially ISO security evaluation reports are hard to obtain. Also cf. Privacy Seals Study TASK 4 – Proposals and evaluation of policy options, May 2014, p. 77ff.

[24] To generate trust, certification needs to be directed to the public, which is an aspect of transparency. Cf. Bock, Kirsten, "EuroPriSe Trust Certification", *Datenschutz und Datensicherheit – DuD*, 2008, p. 610 ff.

Certification and audit schemes[25] promise effectiveness in terms of fundamental rights enforcement if they can demonstrate that

- Evaluation methods are consistent, coherent and executed and directed to safeguard the fundamental right to data protection.
- Criteria meet the protection needs vested in the fundamental right to data protection.
- An impartial and independent third party validates the evaluation results.

15.3 Data protection evaluation

This section describes the components of data protection evaluation and its functional interactions as a precondition for certification. The result of data protection evaluation must provide answers to whether and how an evaluation target affects or may affect and protect the fundamental right to data protection, i.e., self-determination of individuals.

An evaluation for certification usually starts at a point where a preliminary examination of essential elements of the target of evaluation and the organisation applying for certification shows that in principle the organisation will pass the evaluation successfully. A crucial precondition of a successful evaluation is a mutual understanding and determination of the target of evaluation, the criteria catalogue applied and the evaluation depth and methods.

15.3.1 Target of Evaluation (ToE)

The first thing to determine in an evaluation is the object of evaluation: an already existing product or system (product certification) or a process or procedure (audit) or a concept for a system or procedure (concept audit),[26] followed by a detailed definition of the target of evaluation (ToE), including its interfaces. In cases of an application for a data protection certificate, the issuing agency should indicate explicitly the difference between it and a security evaluation. To conduct a data protection evaluation means to always consider not only the security properties of a product or service but also the properties of the use case in the evaluation. In a strict sense, it is only possible to conduct an evaluation in the form of an audit (evaluation of a procedure). Either the use case can be recognised in the evaluation because the product and its properties are already used in a particular auditable context or a typical use

[25] The distinction between a data protection certification or audit and an inspection by a data protection authority consists in a mutual understanding between the parties involved that the evaluation is conducted voluntarily and on a co-operative basis. Voluntary evaluation does not imply legal sanctions, which is why evaluations are more likely to identify serious shortcomings.

[26] Bock, Kirsten, "Marktwirtschaftlicher Datenschutz", p. 315f.

case must be defined for products and services. A certification body bound to data protection compliance such as a data protection authority will in an evaluation of a product insist on a relevant use case scenario that is reasonably typical and realistic.

15.3.2 Evaluation

The core activity of an evaluation is to examine. Examination means in general to compare a predefined benchmark with its current status.[27] To this end, the evaluator condenses facts to essentials and comparability in order to facilitate a correlation of the predefined benchmark with the current facts. From the assessment of differences, the evaluator can derive specific requirements that indicate the corrective measures necessary to meet the benchmark.

Criteria

The criteria forming the substantial part of a certification or audit scheme need to be pre-defined, binding and freely available for transparency purposes. To demonstrate compliance, the issuing party[28] commonly generates criteria which are stated in a normative catalogue and which are based on data protection law and regulations derived from sector specific regulations and from regional or European data protection law.[29]

In terms of compliance, the only certifications qualified to claim the term data protection are those that assess the properties of an evaluation target with respect to the risks and protection of the self-determination of data subjects.[30] In the following, we will therefore proceed on the assumption that evaluation criteria reflect data protection law. In order to meet the basic legal data protection requirements, the applicant must be able to answer the following questions concerning the evaluation target:

---

[27] Rodrigues et al., p. 100.

[28] Certification criteria generated by the applicant or by the issuer exclusively for the applicant usually lack overall substance and are therefore not discussed in this paper.

[29] Criteria catalogues based on common standards such as ISO do not facilitate compliance with European data protection law per se due to a lack of comprehensiveness and accumulation of rather unspecific measures.

[30] With respect to current developments, e.g., of big data, not only risks concerning the individual but risks towards society should be considered. However, policy-makers in Europe have been reluctant so far to acknowledge societal threats (e.g., risks for the solidarity principle regarding health insurance by discounts for consent to monitor behaviour, or accumulation of and access to knowledge) to data protection laws and jurisdiction in Europe.

- Does it enable a strict purpose limitation of data processing observing a legal basis?
- Does it enable a data processing that is not excessive and limited to the necessary?
- Can data subjects' rights be implemented including processes to information, access, correction, blocking, erasure and objection of personal data?
- Is the evaluation target auditable, distinguishing the controller or processor, the evaluator (in-house, external, data protection authority) and the data subject?
- Does it assure data security of components used for data processing?

Operationalising these essential protection requirements into technical functions and organisational rules of a ToE can be accomplished by systematically applying the concept of fundamental protection goals to the design of a criteria catalogue.[31] Protection goals are capable of comprehensively translating the normative requirements. They express the value properties necessary to address the risks facing data subjects from organisational procedures. Therefore, six protection goals are integral to a meaningful criteria catalogue for a data protection evaluation. The six protection goals are: availability, integrity, confidentiality, transparency, intervenability and unlinkability.[32] The advantage of protection goals in comparison to risk-based approaches[33] is their normative determination mirroring the legal requirements.[34] In our DPA practice, they have proven to be fully capable of providing a coherent framework to facilitate protective measures which in turn allows the moulding and designing of operative procedures. They have been introduced in a few data protection acts already.[35]

[31] For a first, but not yet systematic attempt to include protection goals into a non-binding criteria catalogue, see http://www.datenschutzzentrum.de/uploads/guetesiegel/guetesiegel-anforderungs-katalog.pdf

[32] Cf. Federrath, Hannes, and Andreas Pfitzmann, "Gliederung und Systematisierung von Schutzzielen in IT-Systemen", *Datenschutz und Datensicherheit – DuD*, Vol. 26, Issue 12, 2000, pp. 704–710. Rost, Martin, and Andreas Pfitzmann, "Datenschutz-Schutzziele revisited", *Datenschutz und Datensicherheit – DuD*, Vol. 33, Issue 6, 2009, pp. 353–358.

[33] For example, see Centre for Information Policy Leadership, Hunton & Williams, "The role of risk management in data protection", November 2014. See http://www.informationpolicycentre.com/files/Uploads/Documents/Centre/Role_of_Risk_Management_in_Data_Protection.pdf, which neglects to mention that in Europe personal data processing is subject to permission.

[34] Bock, Kirsten, and Sebastian Meissner, "Datenschutz-Schutzziele im Recht – Zum normativen Gehalt der Datenschutz-Schutzziele", *Datenschutz und Datensicherheit – DuD*, Vol. 36, Issue 6, p. 425ff.

[35] Cf. section 5, para 1, No. 1–6, Data Protection Act Schleswig-Holstein, Gesetz- und Verordnungsblatt (GVOBl), 2000, p. 169; and concerning transparency, intervenability and unlinkability, see Article 10, para 2, (a)–(c), Data Protection Act Lichtenstein. https://www.gesetze.li/DisplayLGBl.jsp?Jahr=2002&Nr=102

Protection goals

The approach described here systematises on the basis of protection goals in order to help data controllers to plan and implement the necessary measures. Consequently, it facilitates a data protection compliant design and organisation of information technology systems and applications. The approach also provides data protection authorities with a uniform, systematised toolkit to attain a transparent, understandable, reliable overall assessment of a process and its components.

The protection goals are well equipped to form the basic foundation of any data protection criteria catalogue,[36] because they meet the legal data protection requirements on the one hand and on the other they form a superset to the "Global Privacy Standards" used in the framework of privacy by design[37] and the privacy principles listed in ISO 29100.[38] A privacy audit or certificate substantially based on ISO 29100 and 29101, however, is not sufficiently mirroring the legal data protection requirements in Germany and Europe.[39]

The protection goal **availability** refers to the requirement that personal data are available and can be used according to the rules in a designated process respecting the rights of the data subjects. For that to happen, personal data must be accessible for the authorised, and the methods foreseen must be applicable to the processing, which requires that the methods must be able to process the data formats. Availability includes not only findability of data and the ability of the systems used to depict them properly but also the intelligibility of data (semantic ascertainability).

The protection goal **integrity** requires IT processes and systems to continuously satisfy the specifications set out to guarantee performance of their purposive functions and to guarantee that processed data remain accurate, complete and up to date. Controllers must eliminate or take into account and deal with any side effects. This protection goal includes the requirement that there is congruence between the predefined and current status, both in technical detail and in the aggregate of the procedures and purposes.

The protection goal **confidentiality** refers to the requirement that no unauthorised person shall gain knowledge about personal data. Acknowledgment is often already obtained by merely accessing a system because the context in which storing takes place provides enough information to identify a data subject. The unauthorised

[36] They can, of course, also be used for data protection inspections or by the legislator to compose data protection legislative propositions or to check existing data protection legislation in terms of completeness.

[37] Cf. Rost and Bock, "Privacy by Design and the New Protection Goals", in: *Datenschutz und Datensicherheit DuD*, 2011/01.

[38] Cf. Rost and Bock 2012, p. 243f.

[39] Even though the 11 principles in ISO 29100 convey some truth, as a set of principles they lack legal foundation. Their nature as well as the relationship between each other is unclear. ISO does not provide an approach for balancing the principles and its interpretation is non-binding. Different from the protection goals, which always require a whole-set approach, the missing relationships between the principles does not induce an emphasis on any one of them. However, the principles are useful when privacy and data protection are not provided by fundamental rights.

are not only third parties to the data controller, regardless of their criminal or honest intentions, but also employees of technical support providers who do not need access to personal data providing their services, or personnel within organisation units who are unrelated and without connection to the respective procedures or data subjects.

These three aforementioned protection goals are usually describing purposes of IT security and thus relate to measures to facilitate secure operation for procedures and business processes. Organisations must protect their business processes against attacks, regardless of whether internal or external personnel perform these attacks. From a data protection point of view, all parties must understand to which extent the respective measures contribute to secure privacy and whether security measures are in conflict with the interests of data subjects. Operative data protection and IT security do not match easily. The protection goals of data protection require a broader understanding. Data protection implies an additional protective perspective by taking into account risks for data subjects deriving from the activities of an organisation inside and outside of its business processes. Therefore, operational scenarios are indispensable for any data protection evaluation.

The protection goal of **unlinkability**[40] refers to the requirement that data are only processed and used for the purposes for which they have been collected. Data is principally apt to be used for further purposes and be linked to other, even publicly accessible data. The bigger and more relevant the database is, the bigger the likelihood that data are misused or used out of context. In Europe, such further exploitation is eligible only under narrowly defined rules. Data protection law requires that processing is conducted separately according to purposes (functional separation), that data is stored separately according to its purpose (data separation or isolation). As the circumstances require, databases must be duplicated or reduced according to the necessities of the new additional purpose.

The protection goal of **transparency** refers to the requirement according to which data subjects, system operators and the relevant oversight body can identify which data are collected and processed and for which purpose, which systems and processes are used, where the data is going, for which purpose, and who is legally responsible for the data and the systems during the different phases of data processing. Transparency is necessary in order to monitor and navigate data, processes and systems from the cradle to deletion and a prerequisite for data processing to facilitate conformity with the law and if necessary the data subject's consent. Transparency of the whole data processing operation and all entities involved allows stakeholders to identify deficiencies and to initiate modifications.

The protection goal of **intervenability** refers to the obligation of the processing entity to grant to the data subject the right to notification, information, rectification, blocking and erasure effective at any time and to implement the respective measures. This requires the controller to be able to intervene in the data processing operation at any time – from the collection to the erasure of data.

---

[40] CNIL.

The aim of data protection evaluation is to provide answers with respect to the ToE guided by the six essential protection goals. Methodically, controllers can achieve this by balancing and weighing all six goals for inspection and guidance purposes with respect to IT procedures and specific data protection measures in a standardised model enabling comparison and consistent implementation of data protection law.

Standardised data protection model

The standardised data protection model (SDM) deploys the protection goals introduced above to link the normative aspect of data protection law with specific technical and organisational protection or countermeasures perfect for evaluation purposes. An SDM differentiates specific measures for data, IT systems and processes. It distinguishes three levels of protection needs (normal, high, very high). In doing so, the model allows controllers to identify the protection needs from the perspective of the data subject and fundamental rights holder. Hereby, controllers can derive a systematic catalogue of questions and typical protective measures whose essential components will be introduced in the following.[41]

Typical measures to guarantee **availability** are:

- Back-up copies of data, process status, configuration, data structure, history of transactions, etc., in line with a tested concept,
- Protection against external threats (malware, sabotage, force majeure),
- Documentation of syntax and semantics of data,
- Redundancy of hardware and software as well as infrastructure,
- Implementation of strategies for repair and evasive processes,
- Substitution rules for absent personnel.

Typical measures to guarantee **integrity** are:

- Restriction of write and change management rights,
- Use of checksum, electronic seals and signatures in data processing processes according to a crypto concept,
- Documented rights and roles,
- Processes to keep data up to date,
- Pre-determination of processes and regular testing to assess and document functionality, risks as well as security holes and side effects.

Regarding integrity, stakeholders must determine whether an evaluation is actually effective with respect to the data subject. If the examination concerns only the less relevant within a small scope, the result of an evaluation may be highly integer, yet the protection and self-determination of the data subject will gain only little.

[41] Cf. Probst, Thomas, "Generische Schutzmaßnahmen für Datenschutz-Schutzziele", *Datenschutz und Datensicherheit – DuD*, Vol. 36, Issue 6, p. 439 ff.

Typical measures to guarantee confidentiality are:

- Determination of a rights-and-roles concept according to the need-to-know principle on the basis of an identity management by the controller and secure authentication,
- Limitation of authorised personnel who are verifiably responsible (locally, professionally, professionally), qualified, reliable pro re nata (vetted) and formally admitted as well as not subjected to conflicts of interest,
- Determination and control of use of resources especially communication channels,
- Specified and appropriate environment (building, rooms),
- Determination and control of organisational procedures, internal regulations and contractual obligations (e.g., confidentiality),
- Encryption of stored and transferred data as well as processes to administer and protect cryptographic information (crypto concept),
- Protection against external risks (e.g., espionage).

Typical measures to guarantee unlinkability are:

- Limitation of processing, use and transfer rights,
- Blocking and closure of interfaces in procedures and components,
- Regulations to prohibit backdoors as well as quality assuring revision of compliance for software development,
- Separation according to organisation and department,
- Separation by role concepts with differentiated access rights based on identity management by the controller and a secure authentication mechanism,
- Admission of a user-controlled identity management by the processing entity,
- Use of purpose-specific pseudonyms, anonymisation services, anonymised credentials, processing of pseudomised and anonymised data,
- Regulated procedures for change of purpose.

Typical measures to guarantee transparency are:

- Documentation of procedures including business processes, databases, data transfers, IT systems deployed, operational procedures, interaction with other procedures,
- Documentation of test, release and pro re nata prior authorisation of new or changed procedures,
- Documentation of contracts with employees, and contracts with external service providers and third parties from whom data is imported or to whom data is transferred, distribution-of-business plan, and schedule of responsibilities,
- Documentation of consent and objection,
- Protocol for access and change or alteration,
- Proof of data sources (authenticity),
- Versioning,
- Documentation of processing operations by protocol on the basis of a protocol and evaluation concept.

Typical measures to guarantee intervenability are:

- Differentiated consent, withdrawal and objection options,
- Enabling necessary data fields to indicate blocking, notification, consent and/or objection,
- Documented handling of trouble, trouble-shooting and alterations in the procedure as well as in countermeasures of IT security and data protection,
- Possibility to deactivate single functionalities without interruption of the total system,
- Implementation of standardised prompts and dialogue interfaces for data subjects to assert and/or press for claims,
- Monitoring of activities of the controller to guarantee the data subject's rights
- Recognition of the data subject's right to notification in the protocol and evaluation concept,
- Implementation of a single point of contact for data subjects,
- Operational processes to produce, rectify consistently, block and erase all data concerning an individual,
- Possibility of access for the data protection officer of the controller and for the data protection authority.

The existence of these measures can be checked in a systematic process similar to a checklist. Whether the actual measures are sufficient depends on the pre-defined protection needs of the data. In cases of a high protection need, higher and more effective measures to protect IT systems and processes become necessary. This approach also allows an organisation, knowing the measures, to modulate a project and to estimate the financial needs for a project already in its design stage.[42]

15.3.3 Evaluation method

At the beginning of an evaluation, one usually starts to identify the processing operations, their purposes and the data involved. Personal data can either be primary data directly related to the purpose of the processing or secondary, "hidden" data produced incidentally during the operation (e.g., log files, statistical and configuration data, etc.). In order to determine the legal requirements, controllers have to sort data by type followed by a decision on the protection needs (sensitivity) of the data and identification of the entities responsible for data collection, the data, its processing and transfer as well as its erasure (cradle-to-grave procedure).

The protection requirements of the data determine the protection needs of the overall IT system and the processes involved. This bears consequences concerning

[42] Rost, Martin, "Standardisierte Datenschutzmodellierung", *Datenschutz und Datensicherheit DuD*, Vol. 36, Issue 6, June 2012, pp. 433–438. Rost, Martin, "Datenschutz in 3D – Daten, Prozesse und Schutzziele in einem Modell", *Datenschutz und Datensicherheit DuD*, Vol. 35, Issue 5, May 2011, pp. 351–355.

the selection and dimensioning of processes and the respective protective measures. As a next step, controllers need to identify responsibilities from which they can derive rights and obligations and map them to the role-based access control (RBAC) concept.[43]

It also matters whether stakeholders collect the properties of a ToE from the documentation only or whether an evaluator actively and personally collects information on-site. For documentation, it is important to record whether the manufacturer of a product or service produced the information or the organisation using it for the purpose of documentation of a procedure. If there is a data protection management system active, an important audit component will be to conduct an integrity check of the data protection management system (DPMS). Not only from a data protection authority's point of view, it would be desirable in the future for evaluators to concentrate on investigations of standardised DPMS in a data protection evaluation. It would also contribute considerably to an organisation's risk management.

15.3.4 *Evaluation depths*

The evaluator should determine the profoundness of examination at the beginning of an evaluation. Especially for security of IT products, it is difficult to identify system properties without enormous efforts. This will, for example, be the case if not only the external performance of a program but the underlying code is subject to investigation. Methodically, such an examination depth would be one level below the user end of a software program. Another layer below, one could examine the properties of hardware on which a program is running. Apart from tailoring the ToE, the determination of evaluation depth consequently is an important aspect to regulate the complexity of the evaluation target and examination efforts. By reducing the ToE and profoundness of examination deliberately for pragmatic purposes, a data protection evaluation will lose its significance. By tailoring both aspects to a too wide scope, it will quickly surpass the financial opportunities of the applicant and often the capability of evaluators and auditors.

It is not so crucial for a data protection evaluation of IT systems to reach high resolution in the depth of the system if one considers the seven layers of the Open Systems Interconnection (OSI) model for networks. In fact, for data protection, it seems rather relevant to drive profoundness "to the top" and consider the organisation and its regulations for an eighth layer.

An evaluation can stay on the surface and concentrate on verifiability of evaluation and its success factors. This will generally be considered a pre-audit or pre-evaluation which can, of course, be a relevant phase.

---

[43] Mandatory document, cf., e.g., section 6, para 1, State Data Protection Act (LDSG) in connection with section 3, para 2, nr. 5, Data Protection Ordinance (DSVO) Schleswig-Holstein, Germany. An Active Directory or a Lightweight Directory Access Protocol (LDAP) is a tool for such allocations.

In a first step, the evaluator can concentrate on completeness of documentation of the ToE. The result of examination can therefore be to declare documentation as formally incomplete and to mandate its completion. Deficient documentation means that a ToE is not adequately auditable. The essential function of documentation is to produce transparency for the evaluation process.

In a second step, when documentation is complete and the properties of the ToE are fully understood, greater depth can be achieved. In this state, documentation delivers answers to questions concerning the requirements set out by law. An evaluation on the basis of complete documentation already reaches a maturity level that is seldom met.

The final stage to be achieved for certification facilitates an examination depth that allows matching the documentation with the actual status onsite or "as is", enabling the evaluator to evaluate the differences. This is the kind of profoundness data protection authorities wish to see. A DPA will, of course, assess the risks and protective effects in a final validation procedure.

15.4 Intervention

The objective of certification or audit is basically a question concerning the consequences that are drawn from an evaluation.

It is important to distinguish the objective from the motives to enter into a certification or audit process. An internal audit can be motivated by a brutally honest attempt to identify and gain knowledge about shortcomings. The motive of an organisation to go through an external, impartial certification or audit is often to produce evidence about the organisation's compliance claims and trust towards customers. From the point of view of a data protection authority, certification and audit are to eliminate identified shortcomings in the legal, technical and organisational aspects of an organisation.

On the other hand, an evaluation may, even from the point of view of a DPA, be limited to produce transparency about the actual status. The consequences from a result that identifies shortcomings and inefficiencies and the interventions that are to follow may be decided at a later time. Once a DPA has gained knowledge from a voluntary evaluation and the deficiencies identified, it will at least ask for a project plan scheduling the deadlines to correct the defects.

Whenever a certificate is issued, deficiencies must be corrected and the results of evaluation must be validated *before* granting the certificate.[44]

[44] In Germany, an attempt to pass an audit act failed in July 2009 mainly because the certificate was to be issued before an evaluation took place. See http://dip21.bundestag.de/dip21/btd/16/120/1612011.pdf; http://dip21.bundestag.de/dip21/btd/16/136/1613657.pdf. Self-assertion to comply with the Safe Harbor requirements (US-EU Safe Harbor Framework, Guide to self-certification, p. 4) has been qualified as ineffective. http://www.datenschutz-berlin.de/attachments/710/Resolution_DuesseldorfCircle_28_04_2010EN.pdf?1285316129

In a typical data protection evaluation, the pre-defined requirements and the actual status are balanced during the evaluation procedure. From the valuation of identified differences, specific "to dos" can be gained that provide a starting point for consultation. Especially for a DPA, consultation should not be a third mode next to inspection and intervention. Consultation is based on inspection and should therefore be a "soft" form of intervention.[45] To remain impartial, the evaluator should never participate in the implementation of consultation results.

A poor consultation consists of a poor inspection and unspecific advice. Good consultation within an evaluation process of a certification or audit requires a substantial and exhaustive examination based on all relevant criteria and sufficient examination depth. Sustainable consultation proceeds continuously by means of interim requirements, which may constitute another project phase. An evaluation should produce in terms of improvement a strategy or a project plan on how to remedy shortcomings. Additionally, a final examination should be at least outlined. It would assess whether the final pre-defined status has been reached or not.

A good data protection certification scheme therefore consists of several phases of consultation and evaluation of balances and results. Typically, several iterations are necessary to elaborate the implementation of requirements and each time checks are necessary for revision. This procedure essentially resembles the Plan-Do-Check-Act mechanism of a Deming cycle. And because data protection is a continuous process, it may be reasonable and sustainable to use a data protection evaluation to start a data protection management system.

15.5 Validation of evaluation results

Validation is necessary to produce consistent value for a certification scheme.

Criteria catalogues based systematically on the six protection goals will vary only to minor degree. Using the criteria goals, it will even be easy to compare different schemes in terms of completeness. Deploying the standard data protection model promises to produce more consistent evaluation reports and results than conventional schemes. However, in an evaluation, decisions have to be reasoned by the evaluator. In order to ensure consistent and complete application of the criteria within a certification scheme, validation is necessary. Evaluations based on the standard data protection model will produce less effort for the validating body.[46]

The message and quality of a certificate is only as good as the trustworthiness and expertise of the issuing entity. A certification body should therefore be financially independent, impartial and have profound expertise in data protection. It should be able and willing to follow and put into action the decisions of the courts

---

45 Cf. section 38 paragraph 1 sentence 2, Federal Data Protection Act of Germany; Art. 28 para 3, second bullet, 95/46/EU.

46 As there are currently no formally approved standard measures catalogues available, it will be left to the future to assess the effectiveness.

and the data protection authorities. Certification bodies that, on the contrary, adhere to opinions popular among representatives of industry lobby groups or depend on funding from such groups are not likely to produce this kind of effective certification.

15.6 Evaluation report

Evaluation procedure, criteria, methods and results must be documented in order to deliver sufficient substantiation.

In conclusion, the final result of a data protection evaluation must produce the following proofs and – where applicable – reasoning in a report:

- Statement of objective,
- Statement of type (certification or audit),
- Definition of Target of Evaluation (ToE) including use case for product certification and concept audit,
- Criteria catalogue,
- Examination methods,
- Statement on examination depth,
- Statement on application of criteria,
- Detailed evaluation report,
- Publishable summary of findings.

Only if these requirements are met will a DPA be able to use the evaluation results as the pre-defined requirement against which it can conduct an investigation with reduced efforts. For an organisation, the evaluation report will provide all answers necessary to substantiate data protection compliance.

15.7 Certification

Certification concludes a validated evaluation procedure. Whenever a certificate is issued, deficiencies must be corrected and the results of evaluation must be validated *before* the certification body grants the certificate.[47]

A certificate, a seal or a trustmark are usually, and with good reason, issued *after* an evaluation process has concluded with the result that the requirements set out by

[47] In Germany, an attempt to pass an audit act failed in July 2009 mainly because the certificate was to be issued before an evaluation took place. http://dip21.bundestag.de/dip21/btd/16/120/1612011.pdf; http://dip21.bundestag.de/dip21/btd/16/136/1613657.pdf. In the US-EU Safe Harbor, self-assertion to comply with the Safe Harbor requirements (US-EU Safe Harbor Framework, Guide to self-certification, p. 4) is ineffective. http://www.datenschutz-berlin.de/attachments/710/Resolution_DuesseldorfCircle_28_04_2010EN.pdf?1285316129

the scheme are fulfilled to a certain degree of satisfaction. Any shortcomings should not yield to make a processing operation illegitimate. Certification should only be the result if the target of evaluation is fully in compliance. This is especially true for consumer-facing schemes and those schemes that aim for trust. If a certificate is issued *before* an evaluation has taken place,[48] a consumer or customers will question whether the criteria are met at all. This practice would cause considerable risk for users who rely on the validity of the certificate and confusion if certificates were withdrawn following certification.[49]

As changes in IT services and procedures proceed with an unprecedented speed, certification schemes need to respond and offer ongoing or frequent monitoring of evaluation results. Evaluations and consequently certifications are always referring to a specific point or period in time. Thus, a certificate needs to indicate the evaluation period.

A certification scheme needs to foresee a procedure to handle changes in a product or service that invalidate the evaluation results and the certificate. Not each and every change in a service or product will have implications for a current certificate. In fact, some changes will become necessary in order to maintain evaluation results as the state of the art moves on. A reliable procedure to address this consumer- and user-facing issue is indispensable. The SDM as described here offers a consistent, reasonable and effective model for revision.

The trust value of a certificate depends on the credibility of the certification scheme, the criteria and the validation process by an impartial and trustworthy certification authority. A certification body must ensure that criteria are relevant and that independent knowledgeable evaluators apply them in a consistent manner. Evaluators as well as the validating entity must likewise be skilled and vested with expert knowledge in data protection from a technical and legal point of view. Financial independence of the certification body is probably the most critical aspect. If a certification body lowers requirements in order to successfully finalise certifications, then it jeopardises the scheme. Consequently, a certification scheme should not be criticised by the number of certifications. In fact, not only a single certification project but the certification scheme too must fulfil all the requirements of an SDM. If the results of a successful certification are available in a public report that can be matched against its criteria fulfilling the requirements set out by the protection goal model in a comprehensible manner, a certification scheme is more than likely to earn consumer and user trust. A certificate issued by such a scheme will provide management with all relevant information on data protection issues in a reliable and controllable manner enabling management to control, revise and optimise its procedures.

---

[48] The most well known example is the Safe Harbor self-certification process that does not provide a third-party evaluation at all.

[49] Cf. German BT-DRs. 4/09, p. 4f.

15.8 Conclusions

Random evaluation as well as certification without proper documentation, which are both still common practice in many schemes, are very difficult to re-examine and are often fragmented and incomplete. Meaningful certifications enforcing data protection law rely on a sound and consistent procedure to evaluate against data protection regulations. Relevant criteria anchored in data protection law and financially independent third-party evaluations are prerequisites. The new General Data Protection Regulation requires in its Art. 39a paragraphs 4 and 5 an "assessment" and "reasons for granting or withdrawing the requested certification". Yet, it fails to provide the frame for proper documentation of assessments. The above analysis based on practical work in oversight, consultation and certification has shown that the six data protection goals of availability, integrity, confidentiality, unlinkability, transparency and intervenability implemented in a standard data protection model (SDM) addressing data, systems and procedures of personal data processing operations ensures a consistent and coherent approach for enforcing privacy and for delivering reliable and relevant documentation for the management of an organisation. Such a documented evaluation will ease efforts for investigation on the one hand and will provide an organisation with a powerful compliance tool on the other.

The SDM approach in certification allows one to verify the existence of objective evidence showing compliance to required processes, to assess how successfully processes have been implemented and to judge the effectiveness of achieving the defined target levels. It is able to identify and provide evidence concerning reduction and elimination of problem areas and, with its measures, provides a hands-on management tool for achieving compliance in an organisation. It benefits the organisation by identifying non-compliance and proposing corrective actions, highlighting areas of good practice and providing evidence of overall compliance.

As the SDM provides a holistic approach to bridge the gap between objectives from legal norms and operation, it facilitates audits and evaluations as well as privacy by design. The SDM and especially the protection goals can be implemented in diverse certification and audit schemes and in legislation. Legislation in Europe that is based on a fundamental rights approach for privacy and data protection already recognises the fundamental protection goals in essence. Legislators are called to check especially sector specific laws for full recognition of the data subject's rights by deploying the six fundamental data protection goals and to appoint responsible organisations to identify appropriate technical and organisational measures to support the protection goals on three protection levels for data, systems and processes. Not only would legislation on certification become more transparent if it would point out the data protection goals by name as has been already the case in some German state data protection acts. Organisations as well as individuals in their many roles as customers, patients, citizens, etc. would also profit from a reliable and transparent certification ensuring their fundamental right to data protection and privacy.

References

Bäumler, Helmut, "Datenschutzgesetze der dritten Generation", in Helmut Bäumler and Albert von Mutius (eds.), *Datenschutzgesetze der dritten Generation*, Luchterhand, Neuwied, Kriftel 1999, pp. 1–9.

Bock, Kirsten, "Marktwirtschaftlicher Datenschutz", in Jan-Hinrik Schmidt and Thilo Weichert (eds.), *Datenschutz*, Bundeszentrale für politische Bildung, Bonn, 2012, pp. 310–321.

Bock, Kirsten, EuroPriSe Trust Certification, *Datenschutz und Datensicherheit - DuD*, Vol. 32, Issue 9, September 2008, pp. 610–614.

Bock, Kirsten, and Sebastian Meissner, "Datenschutz-Schutzziele im Recht - Zum normativen Gehalt der Datenschutz-Schutzziele", *Datenschutz und Datensicherheit – DuD*, Vol. 36, Issue 6, June 2012, pp. 425–431. http://www.maroki.de/pub/other/2012-06-DuD-SDMRecht.html.

Centre for Information Policy Leadership, Hunton & Williams, *The role of risk management in data protection, Paper 2 of the Project on Privacy Risk Framework and Risk based Approach to Privacy*, Brussels, November 2014. http://www.informationpolicycentre.com/files/Uploads/Documents/Centre/Role_of_Risk_Management_in_Data_Protection.pdf

Connolly, Chris, *Trustmark Schemes Struggle to Protect Privacy*, Pyrmont, Australia, 2008.

Connolly, Chris, *Benchmarks for Global Privacy Standards – Working Paper*, Pyrmont, November 2009.

Council of the European Union, Proposal for a Regulation of the European Parliament and the Council on the protection of individuals with regard to the processing of personal data and on the free movement of such data (General Data Protection Regulation), Brussels, 9398/15, 29 May 2015.

Council of the European Union, Proposal for a Regulation of the European Parliament and the Council on the protection of individuals with regard to the processing of personal data and on the free movement of such data (General Data Protection Regulation), Brussels, 15039/15, 15 December 2015.

Dix, Alexander, "Betroffenenrechte im Datenschutz", in Jan-Hinrik Schmidt and Thilo Weichert (eds.), *Datenschutz*, Bundeszentrale für politische Bildung, Bonn 2012, pp. 290–297.

European Commission, Communication to the European Parliament and the Council on Promoting Data Protection by Privacy-enhancing Technologies (PETs), COM (2007) 228 final, Brussels, 2 May 2007.

European Commission, Joint Research Centre, Institute for the Protection and Security of the Citizen, EU Privacy seals study, Inventory and analysis of privacy certification schemes, Final Report Study Deliverable 1.4, Luxembourg, 2013. http://trilateralresearch.com/tenders/#eu-study-on-privacy-seals

European Commission, Proposal for a Regulation of the European Parliament and of the Council on the protection of individuals with regard to the processing of personal data and on the free movement of such data, COM(2012) 11/final, Brussels, 25 January 2012.

European Parliament and the Council, Directive 95/46/EC of 24.10.1995 on the protection of individuals with regard to the processing of personal data and on the free movement of such data, OJ L 281, Brussels, 23 November 1995.

Feik, Sebastian, and Kai von Lewinski, "Der Markt für Datenschutz-Zertifizierungen", *BvD-News*, Issue 2, 2014, pp. 47–50.

Kokott, Juliane, and Christoph Sobotta, "The distinction between privacy and data protection in the jurisprudence of the CJEU and the ECtHR", *International Data Privacy Law*, Vol. 3, No. 4, 2013, pp. 222–228.

Probst, Thomas, "Generische Schutzmaßnahmen für Datenschutz-Schutzziele", *Datenschutz und Datensicherheit – DuD*, Vol. 36, Issue 6, June 2012, pp. 439–444.

Rodrigues, Rowena, David Wright and Kush Wadhwa, "Developing a privacy seal scheme (that works)", *International Data Privacy Law*, Vol. 3, Issue 2, February 2013, pp. 100–116.

Rossnagel, Alexander, "Datenschutz-Audit", *Datenschutz und Datensicherheit – DuD*, Vol. 21, Issue 9, September 1997, pp. 505–515.

Rost, Martin, "Schutzziele", in Jan-Hinrik Schmidt and Thilo Weichert (eds.), *Datenschutz*, Bundeszentrale für politische Bildung, Bonn, 2012, pp. 353–362.

Rost, Martin, "Standardisierte Datenschutzmodellierung", *Datenschutz und Datensicherheit DuD*, Vol. 36, Issue 6, June 2012, pp. 433–438. http://www.maroki.de/pub/privacy/2012-06-DuD-SDM.html

Rost, Martin, "Datenschutz in 3D – Daten, Prozesse und Schutzziele in einem Modell", *Datenschutz und Datensicherheit DuD*, Vol. 35, Issue 5, May 2011, pp. 351–355. http://www.maroki.de/pub/privacy/DuD2011-05_DP-3D.html

Rost, Martin, and Andreas Pfitzmann, "Datenschutz-Schutzziele – revisited", *Datenschutz und Datensicherheit – DuD*, Vol. 33, Issue 6, July 2009, pp. 353–358.

Rost, Martin, and Kirsten Bock, "Privacy By Design und die Neuen Schutzziele – Grundsätze, Ziele und Anforderungen", *Datenschutz und Datensicherheit – DuD*, Vol. 35, Issue 1, January 2011, pp. 30–35. EN: "Privacy by Design and the New Protection Goals – Principles, Goals, and Requirements". http://www.maroki.de/pub/privacy/BockRost_PbD_DPG_en_v1f.html

Rost, Martin, and Kirsten Bock, "Impact Assessment im Lichte des Standard-Datenschutzmodells", *Datenschutz und Datensicherheit – DuD*, Vol. 36, Issue 10, October 2012, pp. 472–477. http://www.maroki.de/pub/privacy/2012-10_DuD-PIA.html

US Department of Commerce, *US-EU Safe Harbor Framework, Guide to self-certification*, Washington DC, March 2009.

Chapter 16
The Co-existence of Administrative and Criminal Law Approaches to Data Protection Wrongs

Paul De Hert and Gertjan Boulet

[A]ll data protection Acts stipulate a variety of sanctions and remedies for breach of their provisions. Provision is usually made for a combination of penalties (fines and/or imprisonment), compensatory damages and, where applicable, revocation of licences and deregistration. Sometimes, strict objective liability for harm is stipulated. Sometimes too allowance is made for the imposition of ongoing enforcement damages during the time in which a data controller fails to comply with the orders of a data protection authority. In many cases, compensation may be awarded for non-economic immaterial injury (emotional distress) as well as economic loss. In a very few cases, allowance is made for class actions to be brought.[1]

16.1 Introduction

This chapter focuses on public law approaches (administrative and criminal law) to data protection wrongs in EU data protection law and in the data protection Acts of the Member States. The scope is limited to data protection laws in the former first pillar (Community) matters, not in the former third pillar areas corresponding to police and judicial co-operation in criminal matters. We discuss the use of criminal law sanctions and the need to be prudent with these sanctions when alternative systems of enforcement exist. We also look in more depth at the development towards more enforcement of data protection laws through administrative sanctions in the

[1] Bygrave, Lee, *Data Protection Law. Approaching Its Rationale, Logic and Limits*, Kluwer Law International, The Hague, 2002, p. 77.

P. De Hert (✉)
Faculty of Law and Criminology, Vrije Universiteit Brussel, Brussels, Belgium
e-mail: paul.de.hert@vub.ac.be; paul.de.hert@uvt.nl

G. Boulet
Law, Science, Technology and Society, Vrije Universiteit Brussel, Pleinlaan 2, 1050 Brussels, Belgium
e-mail: gertjan.boulet@vub.ac.be

D. Wright, P. De Hert (eds.), *Enforcing Privacy*, Law, Governance and Technology Series 25, DOI 10.1007/978-3-319-25047-2_16

EU. Reference is made to similar developments in other areas of law, such as competition law, market abuse (securities and insider dealing) and environmental law.

The first section discusses the silence on enforcement under the current European data protection legal framework, consisting of the Council of Europe's 1981 Convention 108[2] and the EU 1995 Data Protection Directive.[3] These texts leave the discretion to the Member States. They can either opt for criminal law provisions or administrative or civil law provisions, or a combination. Why and how and when nowhere further explained in the basic texts. The Court of Justice gave some guidance to the Member States, whatever kind of sanctions they apply, in the 1989 *Greek Maize* case: the principles of effectiveness, proportionality and dissuasiveness.

The second section of this chapter discusses the way Member States have organised their enforcement of data protection law. Under the existing framework, there are Member States with only criminal sanctions and Member States with a mixed system of criminal and administrative enforcement.

The third section addresses the reform of the 1995 Directive and of Convention 108.[4] The General Data Protection Regulation[5] distinguishes criminal and administrative sanctions but again leaves the Member States full discretion regarding the use of criminal sanctions.

The fourth section tries to understand the EU's soft approach in harmonising all aspects of enforcement and, in particular, its silence on the use of criminal sanctions in data protection law. The fifth and sixth sections reflect upon the criteria that regulators take or should take into account in enforcing privacy when choosing between an administrative and/or criminal approach to data protection wrongs. Considering the lack of shared criteria between regulators, the seventh section provides a theoretical framework on criminalisation and some guidance for Member States that choose to enact or maintain criminal law provisions in data protection law.

The conclusion (section eight) provides a summary and ideas for further reflection.

---

[2] Council of Europe, Convention for the Protection of Individuals with regard to Automatic Processing of Personal Data, Strasbourg [ETS 108], Strasbourg, 28 January 1981. http://conventions.coe.int/Treaty/en/Treaties/Html/108.htm; Additional Protocol to the Convention for the Protection of Individuals with regard to Automatic Processing of Personal Data regarding supervisory authorities and transborder data flows [ETS 181], Strasbourg, 8 November 2001. http://conventions.coe.int/Treaty/en/Treaties/Html/181.htm

[3] European Parliament and the Council of the European Union, Directive 95/46/EC of the European Parliament and Council of 24 October 1995 on the protection of individuals with regard to the processing of personal data and on the free movement of such data, *OJ* L 281, 23 November 1995, pp. 31–50.

[4] Council of Europe, The Consultative Committee of the Convention for the Protection of Individuals with regard to Automatic Processing of Personal Data [ETS no. 108], Propositions of modernisation, Strasbourg, 18 December 2012.

[5] European Commission, Proposal for a Regulation of the European Parliament and of the Council on the protection of individuals with regard to the processing of personal data and on the free movement of such data (General Data Protection Regulation), COM(2012) 11 final, Brussels, 25 January 2012.

16.2 Criminal law in the 1981 Council of Europe Data Protection Convention and the 1995 EU Data Protection Directive

Both Europe's basic regulatory texts, the EU Data Protection Directive and the Council of Europe's Convention 108, have surprisingly little to say on enforcement in general and on the use of criminal law in particular. Article 10 of Convention 108, on sanctions and remedies, provides that "[e]ach Party undertakes to establish appropriate sanctions and remedies for violations of provisions of domestic law giving effect to the basic principles for data protection set out in this chapter". The Additional Protocol does not add anything to the text of Article 10 of Convention 108.

Article 24 (on sanctions) of the EU 1995 Directive provides that "[t]he member states shall adopt suitable measures to ensure the full implementation of the provisions of this Directive and shall in particular lay down the sanctions to be imposed in case of infringement of the provisions adopted pursuant to this Directive".

These provisions, thus, leave the choice of the enforcement regime to the Member States, including the establishment of appropriate sanctions and remedies via criminal law provisions. "Suitability" seems to be the only requirement.

The lack of focus on criminal law and the broader issue of enforcement in the Council of Europe Convention are in line with its general and early nature. The lack of focus on criminal law in the more recent 1995 Directive is more puzzling. Was there in 1995 still no urge to consider enforcement? Probably, but one other factor equally accounts for the lack of attention to the provisions on enforcement: a lack of clarity in the 1990s about the powers of the EU to regulate in areas connected to criminal law. In fact, until the 2005 environmental law and 2007 ship pollution cases, the EU, in the general perception of most observers, had no possibility to criminalise behaviour in former first pillar (Community) matters.

Things fundamentally evolved in 2005 when the European Commission crossed a line by claiming criminal law competence, even in light of the silence on the use of criminal law by the European institutions in the founding treaties. The Court of Justice agreed with the European Commission, which questioned the use of a framework decision (former third pillar instrument) instead of a directive (a former first pillar instrument). It ruled that the framework decision 2003/80/JHA of 27 January 2003 on the protection of the environment through criminal law[6] created partial harmonisation of the criminal laws of the Member States, in particular, regarding the constituent elements of various criminal offences committed to the detriment of

---

[6] Council of the European Union, Council Framework Decision 2003/80/JHA of 27 January 2003 on the protection of the environment through criminal law, *OJ* L 029, 5 February 2002, pp. 55–58.

the environment. The apparent lack of the Community's competence in the field of criminal law and the rules of criminal procedure, the Court observed,

> does not prevent the Community legislature, when the application of effective, proportionate and dissuasive criminal penalties by the competent national authorities is an essential measure for combating **serious** environmental offences, from taking measures which relate to the criminal law of the member states which it considers necessary in order to ensure that the rules which it lays down on environmental protection are fully effective [emphasis added].[7]

The 2005 judgment is particularly important for the history of European criminal law. For the first time, Court of Justice envisaged a competence in criminal matters for the Community.[8] However, the Court did not say how far the European institutions could go and what was left for the Member States in terms of criminalisation powers. Should criminal law regulation within the first pillar be very limited or, on the other hand, be open for more intensive and deeper regulation, involving, e.g., the type and level of the criminal penalties prescribed? Are the implied criminal competences of the European institutions restricted to the area of environmental protection only or do they extend to (at least) all other Community areas?

In 2007, the Court clarified its position in the *ship pollution* judgment[9] and stated that there are limits to the power of the Community institutions to oblige Member States to prescribe sanctions. A 2005 directive[10] setting out the principles and definitions of maritime pollution infringements caused by ships was supplemented by a 2005 framework decision on ship pollution to strengthen the criminal law framework.[11] Just as in the environmental law case, the European Commission questioned the use of a framework decision instead of a directive. It should be noted, however, that, in contrast to the framework decision in the environmental law case, Articles 4 and 6 of the framework decision on ship pollution also prescribed in more detail the type and maximum level of penalties. The Court accepted this, arguing that the

[7] Court of Justice of the EU, Commission of the European Communities v. Council of the European Union, C-176/03, 13 September 2005, §§ 47–48.

[8] García described the benefits that can be qualified from this judgment as colossal, more particularly "with respect to the new legislative procedure that will apply, the legal effects of the measures adopted and the jurisdiction of the ECJ. The Community method will apply in its entirety: the Commission will have the exclusive right of initiative, the Parliament will participate in the decision-making process as co-legislator; the directives adopted will be able to entail direct effect; and the ECJ will have full jurisdiction to control the member states' implementation of legal instruments and, eventually, to impose penalty payments in cases of non-compliance". See García, José F. Castillo, "The Power of the European Community to Impose Criminal Penalties", *Eipascope*, No. 3, 2005, pp. 1–8 [p. 6].

[9] Court of Justice of the EU, Commission of the European Communities v. Council of the European Union, C-440/05, 23 October 2007.

[10] European Parliament and the Council of the European Union, Directive 2005/35/EC of the European Parliament and of the Council of 7 September 2005 on ship-source pollution and on the introduction of penalties for infringements, *OJ* L 255, 30 September 2005, pp. 1–21.

[11] Council of the European Union, Council Framework Decision 2005/667/JHA of 12 July 2005 to strengthen the criminal-law framework for the enforcement of the law against ship-source pollution, *OJ* L 255, 30 September 2005, pp. 164–167.

Community did not have the competence to enact these kinds of provisions in a first pillar instrument such as a directive. However, just as in the environmental law case, the Court ruled that the Community had the competence to adopt directives with other, more general kinds of provisions of a criminal law nature, but was not competent to enact detailed kinds of provisions with regard to the type and maximum level of penalties in a first pillar instrument such as a directive.[12] "Criminalisation via a directive is allowed, but leave the details to the Member States" is what the Court seemed to think.

This complex situation of forced interplay would simplify with the 2009 Treaty of Lisbon, creating explicit powers for the EU to impose criminal law obligations via directives voted in the European Parliament and the European Council and binding upon all Member States, even when no unanimity was reached at the level of the EU (Article 83.2 of the Treaty on the Functioning of the European Union).[13]

16.3 Criminal and/or administrative law in member states' data protection acts

The foregoing shows that there was no clear mandate for the EU to impose or harmonise the use of criminal law in the 1995 Directive. Discretion was left to the Member States in their choice of criminal law provisions, administrative provisions or other (civil or tort law) provisions or a mix. Considering that the 1995 Directive left the choice of the enforcement regime to the discretion of the Member States, the use of criminal sanctions varies from one country to another. Whereas some States only criminalised some data protection wrongs and mainly used civil law or administrative sanctions, others opted for an extensive set of data protection crimes. Some countries (e.g., Belgium) have exclusively opted for criminal law.[14] In 2013, the European Union Fundamental Rights Agency (FRA) found that "in almost all

[12] More particularly, Article 2 on criminal offences, Article 3 on aiding, abetting and inciting, and Article 5 on liability of legal persons.

[13] Consolidated version of the Treaty on the Functioning of the European Union, *OJ* C 326, 26 October 2012, pp. 47–390.

[14] If a country opts for criminal law sanctions, these are almost always to be found in the respective data protection acts, with the exception of France. A 1992 French law moved the sanctions of the 1978 general data protection law to the criminal code, more particularly to a section on "Des atteintes aux droits de la personne résultant des fichiers ou des traitements informatiques". For instance, article 226–18 of the criminal code provides that "le fait de collecter des données à caractère personnel par un moyen frauduleux, déloyal ou illicite est puni de cinq ans d'emprisonnement et de 300 000 Euros d'amende". See http://www.legifrance.gouv.fr/initRechCodeArticle.do. The change seemed logical at the time, since the French data protection act was mainly based on a criminal law approach with only some provisions dealing with administrative sanctions. Comp. Claire Bernier, "Overview and definition of personal data offences: impact of criminal aspects", International Federation of Computer Law Association, Antwerp, June 2014.

member states criminal sanctions can be imposed, in the form of a fine or imprisonment”.[15]

Looking at the kind of data protection crimes that were created gives the following picture[16]: the majority of EU Member States criminalised the failure to notify data processing. Austria, Finland, Spain and Luxembourg also criminalised the violation of the duty to confidentiality. Belgium, Denmark, Italy, Spain and Sweden criminalised the illegitimate processing of sensitive data. Austria, Denmark, Finland, Italy, Spain and Luxembourg criminalised the failure to fulfil security obligations. Enforced subject access request, i.e., bypassing the legal regime for criminal records disclosures (for instance, by an employer) to access someone’s criminal record, is an offence in Ireland since July 2014,[17] and in the UK since March 2015.[18] Grant and Crowther (see their chapter, this book) refer to the following other criminal offences in the UK: unlawfully obtaining or disclosing personal data (or procuring another to do so), failing to register as a data controller with the data protection authority [the Information Commissioner’s Office (ICO)] and failing to comply with an information or enforcement notice on the basis of section 40 of the Data Protection Act (ordering the controller to take or refrain from taking certain specified steps within a given period).

As observed before, Belgium can serve as an example of a country that has chosen extensive criminalisation. The 1992 Belgian Data Protection Act, amended in 1998, contains a whole range of sanctions for the data controller in case he fails to meet his obligations. Article 39 of the Belgian Privacy Act is unattractive and more common in complex administrative regulations with sanctions: in a general way, it criminalises violations of a long series of provisions,[19] without there being any

[15] European Union Agency for Fundamental Rights, Access to data protection remedies in EU member states, Publications Office of the European Union, Luxembourg, 2013, pp. 1–64 [p. 7]. http://fra.europa.eu/en/publication/2014/access-data-protection-remedies-eu-member-states. The FRA adds that “sanctions that data protection authorities are empowered to impose differ between member states. […] The duration of a sentence and the amount of a fine also vary across member states” (Ibid. p. 7).

[16] Nouwt, Sjaak, “Tijd voor een nieuw punitief sluitstuk in de WBP?”, *Privacy & Informatie*, No. 6, December 2005, pp. 253–257 [p. 254] (hereinafter: “Time for a punitive chapter”); Nouwt, Sjaak, and Ton Schudelaro, “Hij die gegevens misbruikt wordt gestraft … of toch niet? Een onderzoek naar de vraag of misbruik van persoonsgegevens strafbaar moet worden gesteld”, Sdu Uitgeverij Den Haag, The Hague, 2006, p. 120 (hereinafter: “He who abuses data will be punished”).

[17] Data Protection Commissioner, “Enforced Subject Access now an Offence”, 29 July 2014. http://www.dataprotection.ie/docs/29-07-14-Enforced-Subject-Access-now-an-Offence/1453.htm

[18] Information Commissioner’s Office, “Law change outlaws ‘back door’ criminal record check”, 9 March 2015. https://ico.org.uk/about-the-ico/news-and-events/news-and-blogs/2015/03/law-change-outlaws-back-door-criminal-record-check/

[19] Art. 39, Act of 8 December 1992 concerning the protection of privacy in relation to the processing of personal data, *Belgian Official Journal*, 18 March 1993. http://www.privacycommission.be/sites/privacycommission/files/documents/Privacy_Act_1992.pdf. See also De Hert, Paul, and Gertjan Boulet, “Cybercrime report for Belgium”, *International Review of Penal Law* (*RIDP/IRPL*), Issue 84, No. 1–2, 2013, pp. 12–59. http://www.penal.org/en/ridp-irpl-2013-1-2; *Electronic Review of the International Association of Penal* Law, 2013. http://www.penal.org/sites/default/

attempt to call the illegitimate conduct by its name. Remarkable about the Belgian law is its privileging of criminal fines.[20] A similar choice to privilege fines and not imprisonment is also found in the Croatian Act on Personal Data Protection and the Spanish Organic Law 15/1999 of 13 December on the Protection of Personal Data. Other countries such as Sweden and Poland prescribe fines *or* imprisonment up to two (Sweden) or three (Poland) years.

Most data protection acts mix approaches. An example is given in chapter 10 of the Austrian Federal Act concerning the Protection of Personal Data (DSG 2000). The chapter contains a crime of using data with the intention to make a profit or to cause harm in § 51. (1), and a long list of administrative crimes in § 52. (1–3) that can be imposed "insofar as the act does not realize the legal elements of a criminal offence subject to the jurisdiction of the courts of law and is not subject to more severe penalties according to another administrative provision".

The Austrian approach has a certain charm, especially compared to the Belgian Act; the Austrian Act identifies the conduct that is either criminalised or subjected to administrative fines and proposes a rule of co-ordination between the systems ("Insofar as the act does not realize the legal elements of a criminal offence subject to the jurisdiction of the courts of law"). Another element that adds to the charm, and might puzzle the impartial spectator, is that a series of conduct that is criminalised in Belgium is (only) subjected to administrative fines in Austria (e.g., not fulfilling duties to notify), a choice that might indicate a more reflective approach towards criminalisation (see below).

The Austrian Act moreover clarifies that an administrative court imposes an administrative sanction (in this case, the District Administrative Authority) whereas in most other data protection acts, the data protection authority imposes administrative sanctions.[21] For instance, the UK Data Protection Act provides for both monetary penalty notices and criminal sanctions. The use of monetary penalty notices falls under the competence of the data protection authority (ICO). The use of criminal sanctions falls under the exclusive competence of the courts.

This state of things highlights one feature of administrative law: it comprises fewer stakeholders compared to criminal law where one needs to work with victims, data protection authorities (DPAs), police, prosecutors and criminal courts, whereas in administrative law, most roles are played by the data protection authorities

files/files/RV-2.pdf. De Hert, Paul, and Frédéric Van Leeuw, "Cybercrime Legislation in Belgium", in Eric Dirix and Yves-Henri Leleu (eds.), *The Belgian reports at the Congress of Washington of the International Academy of Comparative Law*, Bruylant, Brussels, 2011, pp. 869–956 [p. 884].

[20] This is remarkable in the light of other privacy-related provisions in Belgium law, for instance, in the Belgium criminal code with provisions on illegitimate interception of telecommunications or hacking, punished both with fines *and* imprisonment.

[21] These Acts usually do not clarify to what courts controllers need to turn in case they disagree with the decision to sanction taken by the Data Protection Authority, but this matter is often dealt with in more general laws on administrative procedural law.

(decision to investigate, decision to prosecute and decision to sanction) and the administrative courts (a posteriori controls).[22]

Section 55C of the UK Data Protection Act provides that the Commissioner must issue guidance on how he proposes to exercise his power to impose monetary penalties and, in particular, deal with "the circumstances in which he would consider it appropriate to issue a monetary penalty notice, and how he will determine the amount of the penalty".

This provision is a welcome exception, since most other national acts give no guidance regarding the discretion of the data protection authorities to impose administrative sanctions. Such discretion for data protection authorities might raise questions, especially in the light of a trend towards high administrative fines in the EU Member States. The Fundamental Rights Agency scaled the amount of the administrative fines that a data protection authority can issue. At the lower end is the Romanian data protection authority with fines up to €12,000, and at the upper end, the data protection authorities of France, UK and Spain, with fines up to respectively €300,000, €500,000, €600,000.[23] The Hungarian data protection authority holds the power to impose fines between HUF 100,000 (approximately €320) and HUF 10,000,000 (approximately €32,039).[24]

Some real life examples illustrate the trend towards high fines and more administrative enforcement highlighted above. In April 2014, the Italian data protection authority (Garante) announced that Google agreed to pay a fine of €1 million for privacy breaches related to data collection by the Google Street View cars.[25] The Garante made use of section 164-bis 64§4 of the Italian Personal Data Protection

[22] In general, there are, to our knowledge, few data protection authorities competent to impose criminal sanctions, with the exception of the Estonian and Macedonian data protection authorities competent to impose misdemeanour fines. This is exceptional since as a rule criminal sanctions fall under the competence of prosecutors and criminal courts to whom data protection authorities and citizens have to turn in case of a presumed crime. Compare with article 42(4) of the Estonian Personal Data Protection Act of 2 March 2011, which provides that "the Data Protection Inspectorate is the extra-judicial body which conducts proceedings in matters of misdemeanours provided for in this section". http://www.legaltext.ee/et/andmebaas/tekst.asp?loc=text&dok=XXXX041K1&keel=en&pg=1&ptyyp=RT&tyyp=X&query=isikuandmete+kaitse+seadus; Article 41 of the Macedonian Law on Personal Data Protection (25 January 2005) provides that the Directorate shall have the competence to conduct a misdemeanour procedure. http://www.ceecprivacy.org/pdf/Law%20on%20Personal%20Data%20Protection.pdf

[23] European Union Agency for Fundamental Rights, Access to data protection remedies in EU member states, Publications Office of the European Union, Luxembourg, 2013, pp. 1–64 [p. 21]. http://fra.europa.eu/en/publication/2014/access-data-protection-remedies-eu-member-states

[24] Section 61 of the Act CXII on the Right of Informational Self-determination and Freedom of Information, 2011. http://www.naih.hu/files/Privacy_Act-CXII-of-2011_EN_201310.pdf. In 11 cases, the Hungarian data protection authority would have made use of its power to impose a fine. See Domokos, Márton, "Hungary – Highlights from the new DPA's 'Year One'", International Association of Privacy Professionals, 18 June 2013. https://www.privacyassociation.org/publications/hungary_highlights_from_the_new_dpas_year_one

[25] Italian Data Protection Authority, "Google paga una multa da 1 milione di euro inflitta dal Garante privacy per il servizio", Rome, 3 April 2014. http://www.garanteprivacy.it/web/guest/home/docweb/-/docweb-display/docweb/3033237

Code, on "Less Serious Cases and Aggravating Circumstances", which provides that "[t]he fines referred to in this Chapter may be increased by up to four times if they may prove ineffective on account of the offender's economic status."[26]

The ICO has suggested to increase its use of administrative sanctions by lowering the threshold from "substantial damage or distress" to "irritation and nuisance", in order to impose fines on business that sends unsolicited marketing communications under the Privacy and Electronic Communications Regulations.[27]

And in July 2014, the Brazilian Department of Consumer Protection and Defence issued a fine of €1.2 million on the Brazilian telecoms provider Oi for notification breaches in relation to the tracking of browsing activities and sale to third-party advertisers.[28]

In practice, one sees that the criminal law provisions in countries where they exist are seldom used. In the Netherlands, Nouwt observed in 2006, no criminal prosecutions had been initiated on the basis of the Dutch Personal Data Protection Act.[29] Little has changed today and we are not aware of many criminal cases with regard to data protection in the EU Member States. Turning to criminal law implies that the data protection authorities lose control of a case.[30] We already observed that most countries vest only prosecutors and courts with investigation and adjudication powers, including imposition of criminal sanctions. Yet, this kind of transfers occurs rarely. For instance, not only does the Belgian data protection authority prefer to handle cases itself,[31] it also lacks sufficient support from the criminal law authorities once it opts for a criminal law approach. In the Google Street View case, the Belgian

[26] Personal Data Protection Code, Legislative Decree no. 196 of 30 June 2003. http://www.garanteprivacy.it/documents/10160/2012405/DataProtectionCode-2003.pdf

[27] Out-Law.com, "Government considering making it easier for the ICO to levy privacy fines", 14 November 2013. http://www.out-law.com/en/articles/2013/november/government-considering-making-it-easier-for-the-ico-to-levy-privacy-fines/

[28] DataGuidance, "Brazil: Telecom giant fined €1.2 million", 31 July 2014. http://www.dataguidance.com/dataguidance_privacy_this_week.asp?id=2670

[29] Nouwt and Schudelaro, "He who abuses data will be punished", op. cit., p. 13.

[30] The EU Fundamental Rights Agency stated that "in sufficiently serious cases, some data protection authorities can refer the case to either the courts of the public prosecutor of the relevant EU Member state". See European Union Agency for Fundamental Rights, Access to data protection remedies in EU member states, Publications Office of the European Union, Luxembourg, 2013, p. 21. http://fra.europa.eu/en/publication/2014/access-data-protection-remedies-eu-member-states

[31] In Belgium, following two data breaches, a data leak with the Belgian national railway company NMSB, and the hacking of Belgium's major telecom provider Belgacom, the Belgian data protection authority announced its intent to investigate more privacy infringements. The president of the Belgian data protection authority Willem Debeuckelaere explicitly said that the current prosecution by the public prosecutor is overkill. Compare with Vanhecke, Nikolas, "Commissie maakt werk van privacy-politie", *De Standaard*, 21 October 2013. http://www.standaard.be/cnt/dmf20131020_016. See also Parrilli, Davide Maria, "Belgium: Will the Privacy Commission become a Privacy Police?", *time.lex*, 24 November 2013. http://www.timelex.eu/en/blog/detail/belgium-will-the-privacy-commission-become-a-privacy-police. The Belgian data protection authority would also be able to impose alternative measures, such as the prohibition for infringing companies to continue the processing of certain data, to access a certain database or to revoke the licence to create a database.

data protection authority, convinced that criminal law was needed, referred the case to a local public prosecutor, who imposed a settlement.

Thus, the lack of criminal law enforcement may be explained by the lack of an adequate institutional framework, as there may be institutional resistance from prosecutors and courts against criminal sanctions. Nouwt notes that

> [t]he Public Prosecutor is overburdened and therefore the protection of personal and company data is not one of their priorities. However, there are a number of specialized supervisors which have much more expertise in these areas. In practice, the enforcement of an increasing number of specialist legal areas is therefore relegated to administration bodies like the Netherlands Authority for the Financial Markets (AFM), the Netherlands Competition Authority (NMA), the Independent Post and Telecommunications Authority (OPTA) and the Dutch Data Protection Authority (CBP).[32]

Thus, as the trend towards more enforcement (see above) is of a recent date, there is currently also very little case law in the European Union on the use of administrative sanctions.

Perhaps the future will give us another picture (even on the basis of existing powers) and we will witness a Europe keen on using all sorts of sanctions, including criminal law sanctions. More enforcement will undoubtedly produce more case law. Indeed, there seems to be a growing appetite among data protection authorities for more law enforcement powers.

Of note are the public calls to endow the data protection authorities with more administrative powers and with (some) criminal law powers. In 2014, the UK government started a review of the sanctions in the Data Protection Act. In the reply to a questionnaire, the ICO said it would welcome the legal power to impose custodial sentences on "a person knowingly or recklessly obtaining, procuring or otherwise processing personal data unlawfully" (section 55 of the UK Data Protection Act).[33] Furthermore, during the 2013 International Conference of Data Protection and Privacy Commissioners,[34] Yoram HaCohen, former Director of Israel's data protection authority, stated that "data protection authorities are established in order to protect privacy, and if a breach or privacy is due to a criminal offence, then they should not leave it to others".[35]

---

[32] Nouwt, Sjaak, and Ton Schudelaro, "He who abuses data will be punished", p. 123.

[33] PHAEDRA project. http://www.phaedra-project.eu/. See also Out-Law.com, "UK review of data protection sanctions should include consideration of increasing £500,000 fine threshold, says expert", 5 March 2014. http://www.out-law.com/en/articles/2014/march/uk-review-of-data-protection-sanctions-should-include-consideration-of-increasing-500000-fine-threshold-says-expert/: "Under the Criminal Justice and Immigration Act (CJIA) the justice secretary has the power to introduce new regulations that would allow a custodial sentence penalty to be available for the offences under section 55 of the DPA, but those powers have yet to be used. In 2008 the Act came into force without those powers being immediately available."

[34] 35th International Conference of Data Protection and Privacy Commissioners, "Privacy: A Compass in Turbulent World", Warsaw, 23–26 September 2013. https://privacyconference2013.org/

[35] Dresner, Stewart, "The case for the use of criminal law enforcement powers by DPAs", *Privacy Laws & Business International Report*, No. 126, December 2013, p. 19.

16.4 Reform of the 1995 Directive and Convention 108

Calls for more enforcement powers have reached the policy agenda. In 2010, both Europe's basic regulatory texts, the EU Data Protection Directive and the Council of Europe's Convention 108, were placed under an amendment process, having served individual data protection for many years and witnessed in the meantime technological developments that threatened to make their provisions obsolete.[36] The new draft of Convention 108 is available. A final draft of a new EU regulation replacing the 1995 Directive has also seen the light: the original proposal made public by the Commission in January 2012 (the Commission proposal) has been the object of a report of the Parliamentary LIBE Committee (LIBE report), and votes in the LIBE Committee (LIBE version), the European Parliament (European Parliament version), and the EU Council of Ministers (Council version). A consolidated version (final compromise) was adopted during the trilogue between the European Parliament, the Council and the European Commission on December 2015.[37]

The Council of Europe Convention 108 prefers to keep it very short with regard to enforcement. Article 10 of the Propositions for modernisation of Convention 108 (on "sanctions and remedies") provides that "[e]ach Party undertakes to establish appropriate judicial and non-judicial sanctions and remedies for violations of domestic law giving effect to the provisions of this Convention". Implicitly, this provision seems to make a distinction between criminal and other enforcement mechanisms.

Contrary to the 1995 Directive, the proposed Regulation now explicitly distinguishes criminal and administrative sanctions. Regarding criminal sanctions, Article 78 (on "penalties") of the provides the following:

---

[36] See Gunasekara, Gehan, "Paddling in unison or just paddling? International trends in reforming information privacy law", *International Journal of Law and Information Technology*, Vol. 22, No. 2, 2013, pp. 1–37; De Hert, Paul, and Vagelis Papakonstantinou, "Three Scenarios for International Governance of Data Privacy: Towards an International Data Privacy Organization, Preferably a UN Agency?", *I/S: A Journal of Law and Policy for the Information Society*, Vol. 9, No. 2, 2013, pp. 271–327; Greenleaf, Graham, "'Modernising' Data Protection Convention 108: A Safe Basis for a Global Privacy Treaty?", *Computer Law & Security Review*, Vol. 29, No. 4, 2013, pp. 433–437.

[37] European Commission, Proposal for a Regulation of the European Parliament and of the Council on the protection of individuals with regard to the processing of personal data and on the free movement of such data (General Data Protection Regulation), COM(2012) 11 final, Brussels, 25 January 2012. The analysis below includes the following proposed amendments to the original proposal for a General Data Protection Regulation of the European Commission: (1) the 2012 report of Jan Philipp Albrecht, rapporteur for the General Data Protection Regulation, for the Civil Liberties, Justice and Home Affairs Committee (LIBE) of the European Parliament (hereinafter: LIBE report); (2) the 2013 consolidated version after the LIBE committee vote (hereinafter: LIBE version); (3) the 2014 amended version after vote in the European Parliament (hereinafter: European Parliament version); (4) the 2015 approved version by the EU Council of Ministers (hereinafter: Council version). and the 2015 consolidated version after the trilogue between the European Parliament, the Council and the European Commission (hereinafter: final compromise).

Article 78 ***Penalties***

1. Member States shall lay down the rules on penalties, applicable to infringements of the provisions of this Regulation and shall take all measures necessary to ensure that they are implemented, including where the controller did not comply with the obligation to designate a representative. The penalties provided for must be effective, proportionate and dissuasive.
2. Where the controller has established a representative, any penalties shall be applied to the representative, without prejudice to any penalties which could be initiated against the controller.
3. Each Member State shall notify to the Commission those provisions of its law which it adopts pursuant to paragraph 1, by the date specified in Article 91(2) at the latest and, without delay, any subsequent amendment affecting them.

The LIBE report add a new paragraph 2a to Article 78§1 of the Commission proposal: "in applying the penalties referred to in paragraph 1 Member states shall show full respect for the principle of *ne bis in idem*, meaning that penalties may not be imposed twice regarding the same infringement of this Regulation". The LIBE version and the European Parliament version move the reference to the principle of ne bis in idem from the Regulation's text to the Preamble (recital 119), which also complements the general (Greek Maize) principles (effective, proportionate and dissuasive) provided in recital 119 and Article 78 §1 of the Commission proposal[38] with general human rights protection: "The rules on penalties should be subject to appropriate procedural safeguards in conformity with the general principles of Union law and the Charter of Fundamental Rights, including those concerning the right to an effective judicial remedy, due process and the principle of *ne bis in idem*." The Council version and the final compromise (recital 118b and Article 79 §4) retain the reference to general human rights protection, but this time for *both* penalties *and* administrative fines.

Both the LIBE and European Parliament version repeat the principle of *ne bis in idem* in a new recital 119a, which provides that "in applying penalties, Member States should show full respect for appropriate procedural safeguards, including the right to an effective judicial remedy, due process, and the principle of *ne bis in idem*." Recital 119 of the Council version and of the final compromise demand that "the imposition of criminal sanctions for infringements of such national rules [adopted pursuant to and within the limits of the Regulation] *and of administrative sanctions* should not lead to the breach of the principle of *ne bis in idem*, as interpreted by the Court of Justice." On the other hand, the Council version and the final compromise explicitly allow a cumulation of sanctions and other (non-punitive) measures foreseen in the Regulation (see recitals 118b and 120, and Article 79 §2a).

The text of Article 78 of the Commission proposal has dispersed over various provisions of the Council version and final compromise. Article 79b §1 of the Council version and final compromise add to the original text of Article 78§1 of the

[38] Recital 119 of the Commission proposal reads as follows: "Penalties should be imposed to any person, whether governed by private or public law, who fails to comply with this Regulation. Member States should ensure that the penalties should be effective, proportionate and dissuasive and should take all measures to implement the penalties."

Commission proposal that the obligation of the Member States to lay down the rules on penalties exists "in particular for infringements which are not subject to administrative fines. The Council version also repeats the Greek Maize principles in the new recitals 118b and 120a, and in Article 79 §1. Article 78§2 Commission proposal (application of penalties to the representative of a controller) moved to recital 63 of the Council version and final compromise providing that "[t]he designated representative should be subjected to enforcement actions in case of non-compliance by the controller". Article 79b §3 of the Council version and final compromise is identical to Article 78 §3 of the Commission proposal (notification of the European Commission about the penalties adopted).

The Council version adds that, where the national law (legal system) of a Member State does not provide for administrative fines and, by the date of application of the Regulation (two years after its entry into force),[39] already provides criminal sanctions for the administrative wrongs provided in Article 79a, it may abstain from providing administrative fines for these wrongs "while ensuring that these criminal sanctions are effective, proportionate and dissuasive, taking into account the level of administrative fines provided for in this Regulation" (recital 118b and Article 79 §5). Article 79 §5 of the final compromise, on the other hand, does not justify this general waiver (with the exception of Denmark and Estonia) for providing administrative fines. When the legal system does not provide administrative fines, so the final compromise says, the courts themselves may apply the administrative sanction:

> Where the legal system of the Member State does not provide for administrative fines, Article 79 may be applied in such a manner that the fine is initiated by the competent supervisory authority and imposed by competent national courts, while ensuring that these legal remedies are effective and have an equivalent effect to the administrative fines imposed by supervisory authorities. In any event, the fines imposed shall be effective, proportionate and dissuasive.

New recital 120 of the final compromise exceptionally allows a criminal law only approach for two countries: Denmark and Estonia.

> The legal systems of Denmark and Estonia do not allow for administrative fines as set out in this Regulation. The rules on administrative fines may be applied in such a manner that in Denmark, the fine is imposed by competent national courts as a criminal sanction and in Estonia, the fine is imposed by the supervisory authority in the framework of a misdemeanor procedure, provided that such an application of the rules in those Member States has an equivalent effect to administrative fines imposed by supervisory authorities. Therefore the competent national courts should take into account the recommendation by the supervisory authority initiating the fine. In any event, the fines imposed should be effective, proportionate and dissuasive.

[39] See Article 91 of the Council version: "1. This Regulation shall enter into force on the twentieth day following that of its publication in the *Official Journal of the European Union*. 2. It shall apply from [*two years from the date referred to in paragraph 1*]."

Furthermore, recital 120a of the Council version and final compromise endow the Member States with discretion to choose criminal sanctions where the "Regulation does not harmonize administrative penalties or where necessary in other cases":

> Where this Regulation does not harmonise administrative penalties or where necessary in other cases, for example, in cases of serious infringements of the Regulation, Member States should implement a system that provides for effective, proportionate and dissuasive penalties. The nature of such penalties (criminal or administrative) should be determined by national law.

Regarding administrative sanctions to be imposed by data protection authorities, recital 120 of the Commission proposal (as retained in the LIBE report, LIBE version and European Parliament version) reads as follows:

> In order to strengthen and harmonise administrative sanctions against infringements of this Regulation, each supervisory authority should have the power to sanction administrative offences. This Regulation should indicate these offences and the upper limit for the related administrative fines, which should be fixed in each individual case proportionate to the specific situation, with due regard in particular to the nature, gravity and duration of the breach. The consistency mechanism may also be used to cover divergences in the application of administrative sanctions.

The Council version and final compromise made three amendments to recital 120. First, provide that the administrative sanctions should be fixed "taking into account all relevant circumstances of the specific situation, with due regard in particular to the nature, gravity and duration of the breach, and of its consequences and the measures taken to ensure compliance with the obligations under the Regulation and to prevent or mitigate the consequences of the infringement". Second, for non-commercial undertakings, it provides that "[w]here the fines are imposed on persons that are not a commercial undertaking, the supervisory authority should take account of the general level of income in the Member State in considering the appropriate amount of fine." The final compromise adds that also "the economic situation of the person" should be taken into account when determining the appropriate amount of a fine. Recital 118b of the Council version and final compromise add that "[i]n a case of a minor infringement or if the fine likely to be imposed would constitute an disproportionate burden to a natural person, a reprimand may be issued instead of a fine". Third, regarding public authorities, recital 120 of the Council version and final compromise does not refer to any criteria at all, but leaves it to the Member States to determine whether and to what extent public authorities and bodies should be subject to administrative fines (see recital 120 and Article 79 §3b).

With the Commission proposal, administrative sanctions are made explicitly possible and mandatory in a long provision (Article 79) with several extensive paragraphs that have been the object of many amendments.

Article 79§1 opens with a duty for states to arm their data protection authorities with administrative sanctions. The proposed text partly restricts the discretion of the Member States under the 1995 Directive to choose the nature of sanctions, by setting out guidelines for the administrative sanctions that Member States can introduce. The provision reads like a criminal code with provisions about how administrative sanctions should be determined and a list of "administrative wrongs" grouped in respective paragraphs (paras 3–6) with the amounts of the fines going up in relation to the increasingly evil character of the wrong. A quick count of the provisions that are related to fines gives a list of almost 50 administrative data protection wrongs.

Article 79 of the Commission proposal provides for the following sanctions: warnings, the imposition of a fine up to €1 million or, in case of an enterprise, up to 2 % of its annual worldwide turnover. Article 79§1(2a) of the LIBE version and European Parliament version add regular periodic data protection audits to the list of available sanctions, and raise the amount of fines to €100 million or 5 % of a company's annual worldwide turnover. The Council version, however, resets the maximum amounts and available sanctions to the initial settings in the Commission proposal. The final compromise shows its true nature as a compromise between the previous versions of the regulation when it comes to determining the amount of the administrative fines: up to €20 million or 4 % of a company's annual worldwide turnover. Recital 119 of the Council version also adds that the use of criminal sanctions "may also allow for the deprivation of the profits obtained through infringements of this Regulation".

Article 79§2 of the Commission proposal contains the general (Greek Maize) principles (effective, proportionate and dissuasive) and nine general principles for determining in practice the amount of the fines: the nature, gravity, duration of the breach, intentional or negligent character of the infringement, the degree of responsibility of the natural or legal person and of previous breaches by this person, the technical and organisational measures and procedures implemented and the degree of co-operation with the supervisory authority. Article 79§2 of the LIBE report complements this list of nine criteria, with several additional criteria, which are retained in the LIBE version and European Parliament version. However, the Council version (recital 118b) deletes the following criteria from the list: the repetitive nature of the infringement; the degree of co-operation with the supervisory authority, in order to remedy the infringement and mitigate the possible adverse effects of the infringement; the specific categories of personal data affected by the infringement; the level of harm or damage suffered by the data subject; the financial benefits intended or gained, or losses avoided, from the infringement; and the refusal to cooperate with or obstruction of inspections, audits and controls carried out by the supervisory authority. Article 79§2a of the Council version, also deletes three additional technical and organisational measures and procedures proposed in the LIBE version and European Parliament version: data protection impact assessments, data protection compliance reviews and the designation of the data protection officer. The final compromise retrieves two criteria from the LIBE report: the degree of co-operation with the supervisory authority, in order to remedy the infringement and mitigate the possible adverse effects of the infringement and the categories of personal data affected by the infringement.

Article 79§7 of the Commission proposal empowers the European Commission to adopt delegated acts for the purpose of updating the amounts of administrative fines, with consideration of the criteria in Article 79§2. The LIBE report adds, first, the requirement for the European Commission to request the opinion of the European

Data Protection Board (EDPB); second, that the power to update the amounts only concerns the "absolute" amounts; and third, to take into account the development of standard costs of living. Only the second amendment was retained by the LIBE version and European Parliament version. The Council version, and final compromise, however, delete the reference to delegated acts in relation to sanctions.

The reform of Directive 1995 only slightly touches upon the subject of harmonisation of administrative sanctions. Recital 120 of the Commission proposal, LIBE report, LIBE version, European Parliament version and the Council version provide that "the consistency mechanism may also be used to cover divergences in the application of administrative sanctions". The LIBE version and European Parliament version add to the text of Article 79§1 of the Commission proposal that the supervisory authorities shall co-operate in accordance with the consistency mechanism in order to guarantee a harmonised level of (administrative) sanctions within the Union. The Council version and final compromise move the reference to the consistency mechanism to recital 120 of the Preamble, which provides that "[t]he consistency mechanism may also be used to promote a consistent application of administrative fines".

The foregoing analysis of the Regulation shows a lot of regulatory activity with regard to the administrative sanctioning powers of the data protection authorities, but almost no activity with respect to the criminal law side of the data protection story. Article 78 on the criminal law contains no list or grouping of wrongs and almost nothing on the sanctions (imprisonment or no?) or on the principles to be applied. The provision ends with a short paragraph obliging the Member States to inform the Commission about their use of criminal law. So far for the harmonisation of criminal law in the reform!

16.5 Explaining EU silence about the use of criminal law in data protection

The investment of the European Union in a harmonised system of administrative sanctions and its reluctance to harmonise criminal sanctions is striking and, in our view, not defendable. In theory, a future of sustained differences between Member States goes against the aim of a regulation to establish a uniform data protection framework. The lack of harmonisation also creates legal uncertainty for companies and the data subject. US companies in particular are intimidated by the use of criminal law, independent of its actual enforcement and the sheer existence of these provisions in some EU Member States might influence their decisions. Furthermore, the lack of harmonisation might invite forum shopping, i.e., companies can move their main establishment to a Member State with the most flexible sanction powers.

We are under the impression that the EU legislator simply has overlooked addressing the criminal law aspects of data protection offences, considering the scarce case law on the matter (see above). The European Commission implementation reports that have prepared the reform were also silent on the issue.[40]

The sensitivity of using criminal law in Community areas (discussed above) might have played a part too. Only with the 2005 environmental law and 2007 ship pollution cases did it become clear that the EU had some power to criminalise behaviour in Community (former first pillar) matters. The 2005 and 2007 judgments recognised the power of the EU to provide criminal sanctions in environmental (Community) matters, but many questions remained. Only with the recent Treaty of Lisbon was the power of the European Union to use criminal law in all EU policy areas given formal recognition. Perhaps this was a too-recent development for the drafters of the proposed regulation. In the 2010 Communication entitled "A comprehensive approach on personal data protection in the European Union", the Commission said that it will "assess the need for strengthening the existing provisions on sanctions, for example by explicitly including criminal sanctions in case of serious data protection violations, in order to make them more effective".[41] Yet, in the 2011 Communication entitled "Towards an EU Criminal Policy – ensuring the effective implementation of EU policies through criminal law",[42] the European Commission did not list data protection as a policy area where EU criminal law measures are required, but as a policy area where criminal law enforcement could be explored further.

16.6 Networks of sanctions and the seven characteristics of criminal law

The foregoing indicates that fragmentation will continue to exist with regard to the criminal law aspects of data protection law. What guidance could possibly be given to Member States implementing the Regulation and having to choose between distinct approaches to data protection wrongs? The choice is between a solely

[40] The 2003 and 2007 implementation reports of the Data Protection Directive are available here: http://europa.eu/legislation_summaries/information_society/data_protection/l14012_en.htm; Commission of the European Communities, Report from the Commission, First report on the implementation of the Data Protection Directive (95/46/EC), COM(2003) 265 final, Brussels, 15 May 2003; Commission of the European Communities, Communication from the Commission to the European Parliament and the Council on the follow-up of the Work Programme for better implementation of the Data Protection Directive, COM(2007) 87 final, Brussels, 7 March 2007.

[41] European Commission, Communication from the Commission to the European Parliament, the Council, the Economic and Social Committee and the Committee of the Regions, A comprehensive approach on personal data protection in the European Union, COM (2010) 609, Brussels, 4 November 2010, p. 9. http://ec.europa.eu/justice/news/consulting_public/0006/com_2010_609_en.pdf

[42] European Commission, Communication from the Commission to the European Parliament, the Council, the European Economic and Social Committee and the Committee of the Regions, Towards an EU Criminal Policy: Ensuring the effective implementation of EU policies through criminal law, COM(2011) 573 final, Brussels, 20 September 2011, p. 10.

administrative approach and a mixed approach combining administrative and criminal law. Article 78 read together with Article 79 of the proposed Regulation leaves no other choice. Although the proposed text of Convention 108 would not preclude it, Article 79 of the proposed Regulation bars a purely criminal approach without administrative sanctioning powers for the data protection authorities as exist today in some countries (e.g., Belgium, Denmark, Finland, Liechtenstein).[43]

Let us first recall the basics about the co-existence in today's legal systems of administrative, criminal (and civil) enforcement apparently being very alike in purpose (sanctioning wrongs). In many countries, criminal law is indeed but one of the existing enforcement models or instruments.[44] US federal antitrust laws, for example, are enforced in three main ways, each time driven by different actors: criminal enforcement actions are brought by the Antitrust Division of the Department of Justice and state attorneys, civil enforcement actions are brought by the Federal Trade Commission and civil law suits are brought by private parties asserting damage claims.[45] Not all countries have this American diversity of tools. The Irish Constitution does not allow the use of administrative fines and, thus, privileges the use of the criminal law system.[46] Many countries do not have a system of punitive torts or punitive damages. All countries (except Ireland), however, have in place administrative sanctioning systems in addition to criminal law systems.

---

[43] Note the contrast with the market abuse directive, which imposes mandatory criminal sanctions for serious breaches of market abuse rules, and exempts Member States from providing administrative sanctions if they opt for criminal law alone. See Luchtman, Michiel, and John Vervaele, "Enforcing the market abuse regime: towards an integrated model of criminal and administrative law enforcement in the European Union", *New Journal of European Criminal Law*, Vol. 4, No. 2, 2014, p. 210.

[44] For a study on criminal sanction legislation in the Member States, see European Commission, Study on criminal sanction legislation and practice in representative Member States, Tender JUST/2011/JPEN/PR/0066/A4, final report, November 2013. http://ec.europa.eu/justice/criminal/document/files/sanctions_delivery_en.pdf

[45] Cseres, Katalin, Maarten Schinkel and Floris Vogelaar, "Law and Economics of Criminal Antitrust Enforcement: An Introduction", in Katalin Cseres, Maarten Schinkel and Floris Vogelaar (eds.), *Criminalization of Competition Law Enforcement. Economic and Legal Implications for the EU Member States*, Edward Elgar, Cheltenham, 2006, p. 3.

[46] Massey, Patrick, "Criminalization and Leniency: Will the Combination Favourably affect Cartel Stability?", in Katalin Cseres, Maarten Schinkel and Floris Vogelaar (eds.), *Criminalization of Competition Law Enforcement. Economic and Legal Implications for the EU Member States*, Edward Elgar, Cheltenham, 2006, pp. 176–195 [p. 177]: "Article 34.1 of the Irish Constitution gives the Courts sole and exclusive power (subject to Article 37) to administer justice. Article 37 allows certain bodies other than courts to perform limited types of judicial function. Limited means that the effects of the exercise of such a function should not be unduly serious in their impact. The net effect of these provisions is that fines may only be imposed on individuals and undertakings convicted of a criminal offence by the Courts. As a result Irish competition law provides that breaches of national and EU competition law constitute a criminal offence. In contrast, UK legislation distinguishes between administrative fines which can be imposed on companies for breaches of competition law by the Director General of Fair Trading and which are not defined as criminal and criminal sanctions including imprisonment in the case of individuals found guilty of engaging in cartels."

Ost and van de Kerchove speak about networks of sanctions (réseaux de sanctions) that exist next to each other, each having fuzzy limits and all having uncertain articulations from one to the other.[47] These features are particularly relevant for understanding the relationship between criminal and administrative sanctions. The legal system hesitates between recognising complete independence to both sanction systems (because even with some administrative sanctions having punitive goals, differences remain) and co-ordinating them (because both can have punitive effects). After a detailed analysis, Ost and Van De Kerchove conclude that simple answers are yet not available. There is both autonomy and unity of these systems. Human rights law has created a movement towards unity and co-ordination, but this movement is far from completed.[48] Article 52 of the EU Charter on Fundamental Rights, for example, organises a right to be protected against more than one conviction for the same facts,[49] but this *ne bis in idem* prohibition refers to cumulation of two penalties of the same kind, that is to say, criminal law penalties, and does not protect against cumulation of criminal sanctions with other sanctions.

How to make sense of this fuzzy situation where several systems or networks of sanctions exist (and something without co-ordination or hierarchy)? In literature, a plurality of characteristics is identified to distinguish criminal law from enforcement of a civil or administrative nature.[50] We briefly recall these characteristics.

First, there is the *principle of legality nulla poena nulla crimen sine lege* in criminal law according to which offences and sanctions need to be based on precisely drafted law. The principle of legality is presumed to govern all areas of law, but the required level of precision is higher in criminal law, and is characterised by the hard treatment and intrusiveness of its measures compared to other enforcement systems.[51] Vague sanctions can be introduced in civil and administrative law, but never in criminal law.

---

[47] Ost, François, and Michel van de Kerchove, *De la pyramide au réseau*?, Publications des Facultés universitaires Saint-Louis, Brussels, 2010, p. 243.

[48] Ibid., p. 263.

[49] "No one shall be liable to be tried or punished again in criminal proceedings for an offence for which he or she has already been finally acquitted or convicted within the Union in accordance with the law."

[50] Wils, Wouter P.J., "Is Criminalization of EU Competition Law the Answer?", in Katalin Cseres, Maarten Schinkel and Floris Vogelaar (eds.), *Criminalization of Competition Law Enforcement. Economic and Legal Implications for the EU Member States*, Edward Elgar, Cheltenham, 2006, pp. 60–109 [pp. 61–63]; Asp, Petter, "Blacklisting Sanctions and Principles of Criminal Law", in Iain Cameron (ed.), *EU Sanctions: Law and Policy Issues Concerning Restrictive Measures*, Intersentia, Cambridge, 2013, pp. 131–137.

[51] On the brutishness of criminal law, see Asp, Petter, "Blacklisting Sanctions and Principles of Criminal Law", ibid., p. 132; Gutwirth, Serge, and Paul De Hert, "Een theoretische onderbouw voor een legitiem strafproces. Reflecties over procesculturen, de doelstellingen van de straf, de plaats van het strafrecht en de rol van slachtoffers" [A theoretical framework for a legitimate criminal proces. Reflections about process cultures, the function of punishment, the position of criminal law and the role of victims], *Delikt en Delinkwent*, Vol. 31, No. 10, December 2001, pp. 1048–1087.

Second, under criminal law, a *plurality of actors* are involved (police, prosecutors, courts) which tend to have *stronger investigative powers*. The number of actors involved in administrative enforcement is lower: everything turns around the administration involved.

Third, criminal procedures tend to have *stronger procedural protections*, designed to avoid false convictions. For instance, the commission of a criminal offence usually requires that the prohibited act be committed with a *guilty state of mind* (*criminal intent*), not by mere negligence. Also, criminal law systems mostly accept justification, exculpation or excuse grounds.

Fourth, there is the *expressive function of criminal law* with more stigma for the *targeted individual*. Criminal enforcement has a stronger message-sending role or expressive function than civil or administrative enforcement.

Fifth, the expressive function of criminal law explains the *quite loose relationship in criminal law between the size of the penalty and the size of the harm* caused. Wils explains that "[t]his appears to reflect the idea that criminal law does not seek to price certain behaviour (by making the actor bear the external costs of his behaviour) but rather to prohibit it (unconditionally, that is, irrespective of the actual size of the external costs)."[52]

Sixth, there is reserved use of *imprisonment* for criminal law, a *sanctioning tool with a higher stigmatising effect or symbolic value*. All three enforcement systems rely on fines, but only criminal law puts people in jail. Corporations and other legal persons cannot go to jail and that probably explains why criminal enforcement tends to make relatively more use of penalties imposed on individuals (natural persons), and relatively less of penalties imposed on corporate entities or legal persons.

Seventh, there are more *modalities of sanctioning tools* available in the criminal law apparatus, such as leniency programs where the demand for amnesty would reduce the amount of a high fine, settlements between the parties, extenuating or aggravating circumstances, automatic sanctions, postponement of sanctions, etc.

16.7 Using these characteristics against or in favour of criminal law use in data protection

Based on these characteristics of criminal sanctions and powers, one might raise several objections about turning certain wrongs into criminal wrongs and implying the criminal apparatus. A first argument against the use of criminal law would be the *plurality of actors* in the criminal law apparatus. Administrative procedures would be faster and less costly considering the control by the data protection authority, whereas use of criminal law would imply the involvement of only ministry officials instead of police, prosecutors, investigative and trial judges. A related argument

[52] Wils, Wouter P.J., "Is Criminalization of EU Competition Law the Answer?", op. cit., p. 62.

against the use of criminal law would be that the past shows a certain *institutional resistance against criminal law enforcement* for data protection offences (see above).

A second argument against criminalisation, related to the plurality of actors, are the *higher procedural safeguards* in criminal law. In general, criminal law principles do not apply in the field of administrative law, with the consequent risk of lower legal protection when being confronted with an administrative sanction. This is, of course, a very pragmatic, even cynical argument but in practice, it has a lot of weight in all areas of law. In the area of securities, for instance, Alexander has observed a move to introduce a civil or administrative regime because of the more flexible evidence rules and according greater ease of proof.[53] In the area of competition law, Wils has contrasted the criminal law requirement of a guilty state of mind (criminal intent) with the less strict administrative law requirement of mere negligence,[54] and has also underlined the differences in the context of evidence law: in the English-speaking countries, criminal convictions normally require proof beyond reasonable doubt, whereas civil or administrative findings can normally be made by a preponderance of the evidence or a balance of probabilities.

Third, for Reindl and Spagnolo, imprisonment as a sanctioning tool entails high indirect (innocents in jail…) and direct (resources…) *costs*.[55]

One can, of course, based on the list of differences between the enforcement systems, also advance arguments in favour of using criminal law for a particular problem or legal area.

First, Delmas-Marty noted that the *principle of legality* is practically never required in administrative law,[56] and from a defence rights perspective, one might therefore prefer a criminal law approach with its insistence on legal certainty and detailed legal provisions.

Second, the *plurality of actors* in criminal law, described above as an argument against criminalisation, could also be seen as an argument in favour of criminalisation as it entails a *variety of investigative tools.*

Third, the *higher procedural safeguards* in criminal law (such as the higher standards of proof) may be considered as an argument in favor of criminalisation. In competition law, Wils opines that "criminal procedures tend to have stronger

53 Alexander, R.C.H., *Insider dealing and money laundering in the EU: law and regulation*, Ashgate, Aldershot, 2007, p. 202.

54 Wils, op. cit., pp. 61–63.

55 Spagnolo, Giancarlo, "Criminalization of Cartels and their Internal Organization", in Katalin Cseres, Maarten Schinkel and Floris Vogelaar (eds.), *Criminalization of Competition Law Enforcement. Economic and Legal Implications for the EU Member States*, Edward Elgar, Cheltenham, 2006, pp. 133–149 [pp. 135–136]; Reindl, Andres P., "How Strong is the Case for Criminal Sanctions in Cartel Cases?", in Katalin Cseres, Maarten Schinkel and Floris Vogelaar (eds.), *Criminalization of Competition Law Enforcement. Economic and Legal Implications for the EU Member States*, Edward Elgar, Cheltenham, 2006, pp. 110–132 [pp. 121–124].

56 Delmas-Marty, Mireille, "Introduction: différenciation des systèmes juridiques de sanctions à dominante pénale ou administrative", *International Review of Penal Law*, Vol. 59, semesters 1–2, 1988, pp. 27–64 [p. 36].

procedural protections, designed to avoid false convictions. In particular, in criminal enforcement systems, the adjudicative or decision-making function is always separated from the investigative and prosecutorial function or functions."[57]

Fourth, the *expressive function of criminal law* with more stigma for the *targeting of individuals* is lacking in administrative law, which is essentially targeted at the corporation. Speaking (again) for competition law, Cseres finds that corporate penalties may "not constitute the appropriate sanction, because it is the individuals within the corporation who take the decision and, hence, actually commit the corporate crimes".[58]

Fifth, the *quite loose relationship in criminal law between the size of the penalty and the size of the harm* may allow more flexibility in imposing a criminal sanction. We recall, however, that there are neither any real limits to the level of administrative sanctions, apart from the Greek Maize criteria and the provisions in the reform of the 1995 Directive.

A sixth set of arguments relate to the *sanctioning tools with a higher stigmatising effect or symbolic value* available under the criminal law apparatus, such as prison sanctions and entry in the criminal records. Sometimes, governments need to strike hard and need to use criminal law. In competition law, Massey is averse to the use of fines only: even if fines were high enough, then the risk of bankruptcy would penalise all of the firm's employees and, potentially, its customers too. Imprisonment, on the other hand, would avoid potential reimbursement of the convicted and, if the threat is perceived as real, "may provide individuals with a greater incentive to resist corporate pressure to engage in unlawful activities".[59] Wils, arguing for the use of criminal law in European cartel law, refers to the moral condemnation posed by criminal sanctions, which would have "a stronger message-sending role or expressive function than civil or administrative enforcement".[60]

Michael Sandel has written a breathtaking book on commercialisation of our social life ("commodification of everyday life") and the need to draw lines to stop certain forms of market logic.[61] In his book, Sandel advances an objection based on the corruptive effects of making everything for sale. Markets are not morally neutral and erode our understanding of certain common values essential to the cohesion of democracies. One of the areas that Sandel discusses is criminal law and our understanding of right and wrong. Turning crimes into administrative wrongs is transforming the social into the commercial. By simply paying the administrative fine,

[57] Wils, op. cit., p. 62.

[58] Cseres, Schinkel and Vogelaar, "Law and Economics of Criminal Antitrust Enforcement: An Introduction", op. cit., pp. 7–8.

[59] Massey, op. cit. However, the institutional resistance against criminal enforcement, or even more, the lack of political support for criminal sanctions would prevent effective criminal enforcement, hence, affect the perception of criminal sanctions as a real threat, and thus result in a lower deterrent effect (op. cit., pp. 185, 189, 190).

[60] Wils, op. cit., pp. 61–63.

[61] Sandel, Michael J., *What Money Can't Buy: The Moral Limits of Markets*, Farrar, Straus and Giroux, New York, 2012.

the company can solve its problem with no criminal public record to remind society about the wrong done by a controller that has paid his fine. However, Sandel says the negative impact on our moral compass should not be overlooked.[62]

A seventh set of arguments relates to the larger set of *modalities of sanctioning tools* available in the criminal law apparatus. Most administrative laws, as also seen in our discussion of administrative sanctions, do not contain (yet) an elaborate set of principles that allows us to postpone (using warnings) or fine-tune administrative sanctions or to deal with real life situations where several persons have contributed to the wrongful conduct but not in equal terms.

In light of these arguments and the advantages of the respective systems, it does not come as a surprise that many states in Europe do not want to privilege one approach but combine and use mixed systems, including criminal law even when seldom applied.[63] Very similar to what we have seen in the EU data protection documents analysed above, the 1989 insider dealing directive[64] prohibits insider dealing but makes criminalisation optional, not mandatory. In practice, all Member States (except Spain) have criminalised insider dealing, and work with mixed enforcement systems that, in principle, allow choice between civil or administrative sanctions.[65] The 1989 directive was repealed by the 2003 EU market abuse directive.[66] This 2003 directive was subsequently repealed by the 2014 market abuse regulation[67] and a complementary 2014 directive on criminal sanctions introducing mandatory criminal sanctions for the most serious violations of market abuse rules, including prison sentences of a minimum four years.[68]

---

62 See also on "the fiscalisation" of sanctions and the impact on the perception of the citizen, Ost and van de Kerchove, op. cit., p. 231.

63 Alexander, op. cit., pp. 231–232. This author quotes Professor Barry Rider, former Head of the Commercial Crime Unit of the Commonwealth Secretariat, stating that the criminal sanction should be kept as an option as its higher deterrent could be explained by the threat of imprisonment and the stigma of a criminal conviction: "Very probably, the criminal provisions will over time rarely be used (as indeed they are in practice rarely used at present). But the fact that they can be used, that those who engage in insider dealing know that there is a risk of being prosecuted, does provide a deterrent that mere civil sanctions do not."

64 Council of the European Union, Council Directive 89/592/EEC of 13 November 1989 coordinating regulations on insider dealing, *OJ* L 334, 17 November 1989, pp. 30–32.

65 Alexander, op. cit., p. 114.

66 European Parliament and the Council of the European Union, Directive 2003/6/EC of the European Parliament and of the Council of 28 January 2003 on insider dealing and market manipulation (market abuse), *OJ* L 96, 14 April 2003, pp. 16–25. See also Alexander, R.C.H., *Insider dealing and money laundering in the EU*, p. xvii.

67 European Parliament and the Council of the European Union, Regulation (EU) No 596/2014 of the European Parliament and of the Council of 16 April 2014 on market abuse (market abuse regulation) and repealing Directive 2003/6/EC of the European Parliament and of the Council and Commission Directives 2003/124/EC, 2003/125/EC and 2004/72/EC, *OJ* L 173, 12 June 2014, pp. 1–61.

68 European Parliament and the Council of the European Union, Directive 2014/57/EU of the European Parliament and of the Council of 16 April 2014 on criminal sanctions for market abuse (market abuse directive), *OJ* L 173, 12 June 2014, pp. 179–189.

16.8 Principles of criminalisation as guidance?

The foregoing might surprise some impartial observers from outside the EU. Is it normal that two (or three) more or less similar systems of enforcement co-exist in a given legal system and that there is a choice for one or the other, or a mix free from constraints?

In principle, from the academic criminal lawyer point of view, the answer is "no". The literature on criminal law identifies principles of criminalisation with a view to understanding the correct use of criminal law, next to other available alternative enforcement systems. These principles are based on the last resort argument that argues for limiting the use of criminal law considered as the more brutal means of enforcement available in democracies. Already in 2006, data protection expert Jacques Nouwt turned to these principles to determine whether data protection law was in need of (more) criminal law. Borrowing from the work of legal theorists, such as Haveman, on the issue, Nouwt identifies the following questions that need to be used as a basis for every (de-)criminalisation debate: (1) Is there a problematic situation that needs a public reaction? (2) Should the government play a role in this? (3) Are there adequate non-criminal alternatives? (4) Can criminal law provide an adequate answer?[69]

For Nouwt, the answer to these questions when looking at data protection wrongs depends on several factors: the importance of the protection of the legal interests at stake, the seriousness of a breach of these interests, whether the sense of justice demands punishment; and, on practical considerations that have to do with differences in the way enforcement happens in civil law, administrative law and criminal law.

Overseeing the harsh investigative powers in criminal law, one should consider this system a last resort, also in data protection law, Nouwt holds[70] only criminal sanctions when really needed and always well and precisely defined and distinguished from administrative offences. The UK Data Protection Act can be seen as a model as it distinguishes monetary penalty notices from criminal sanctions.

The last resort argument is a powerful argument in favour of more administrative enforcement,[71] but it cannot, however, be used to turn administrative law into a quasi-criminal law system.[72] So in order to avoid criminal law, pumping up admin-

[69] Nouwt and Schudelaro, "He who abuses data will be punished", op. cit., p. 121.

[70] Ibid., p. 122

[71] Compare with Ost and van de Kerchove, op. cit., p. 244, referring to the work of R. Roth and L. Dupont.

[72] Compare with "Isn't it true that the Rule of Law, the principle of legality and the lex certa principle demand an explicit and clear power to impose punitive sanctions, which makes a discussion about the character of a sanction redundant (apparently not!)?." See Bröring, H.E., "Book review: Oswald Jansen (ed.), Administrative Sanctions in the European Union, (Cambridge: Intersentia 2013)", *Review of European Administrative Law*, Vol. 6, No. 2, 2013, pp. 87–91 [p. 88]. Bröring, after reading the book, concludes that the use of administrative punitive sanctions like (sometimes high) fines are the object of a widespread and fundamental discussion in the countries involved (Ibid., p. 90).

istrative law is no option. Relevant here is a 1990 Resolution of the International Congress of Penal Law, on "The legal and practical problems posed by the difference between criminal law and administrative penal law".[73] The Resolution highlights the expansion of the field of administrative penal law and explains this development by pointing at two phenomena: the expansion of state intervention in more and more areas, and the international trend towards decriminalisation, or removing violations of minor social importance from criminal law to administrative penal law.

The Resolution adds that, although decriminalisation of transgressions is in accordance with the principle of subsidiarity of penal law and thus welcomed, an inflation of administrative penal law is not desirable. Therefore, the legislator and legal science should "devote increased care to defining the proper limits of as well as the guiding principles applicable to administrative penal law".[74] The Resolution further provides that whether certain conduct should properly be punished according to criminal law or to administrative penal law cannot be determined categorically.

> It is therefore in most cases for the legislature to decide what conduct is to be sanctioned criminally or by administrative penal law. In making that decision, legislatures should consider several criteria, especially the importance of the social interest affected by the conduct in question, the gravity of endangerment or harm to that interest, and the kind and degree of fault on the part of the offender.[75]

We would like to underline an additional element to be taken into consideration while going through and applying the criminalisation principles: the open nature of many data protection norms. Not all provisions in data protection law are clear and unambiguous. Notions about proportionality and the appropriate level of security are often the object of interpretation and case-by-case deliberation and this happens quite often in a process or dialogue between processors and supervisory authorities. This dialogue on the application of open norms does not sit comfortably together with a punitive approach.[76] Criminal law may therefore not always be the appropriate

---

[73] XIV International Congress of Penal Law, Resolutions, section I: The legal and practical problems posed by the difference between criminal law and administrative penal law, *International Review of Penal Law*, Vol. 61, semesters 1–2, 1990, pp. 112–114.

[74] Ibid., p. 112, §2.

[75] Ibid., p. 112, §3.

[76] Winston states that "co-regulation is a system under which a state-sponsored institution, such as a government agency or independent regulatory authority, creates a framework within which private actors discuss and if possible agree on regulatory measures. Co-regulation is like self-regulation, except that in co-regulation the government or regulatory authority has some influence over how the rules are developed, and/or how they are enforced. This is supposed to make the rulemaking process more legitimate and effective compared to purely self-regulatory solutions. It is more legitimate because the process is supervised by officials who are accountable to the democratically-elected legislator. It is more effective because the resources of the state can be used to enforce the rules." See Maxwell, Winston J., "Global Privacy Governance: A Comparison of Regulatory Models in the US and Europe, and the Emergence of Accountability as a Global Norm", in Carine Dartiguepeyrou (ed.), *The Futures of Privacy*, Cahier de prospective, Futur Numérique, February 2014, pp. 63–70 [pp. 65–68].

enforcement mechanism in legal areas with open norms such as data protection, but be seen as a last resort.[77] Instead, administrative law may turn out to be more accommodated to the dynamic character of data protection,[78] in some but not all cases.[79]

This important exercise of principle, reflecting on last resort arguments *and* the open or closed nature of norms that one would like to see enforced, should for some authors best be done in a bottom-up way, and not in a blind, good-for-all, sweeping, supranational move.[80]

---

[77] Faure, Goodwin and Weber argue that two trends – towards the increasing use of open or flexible regulation or vaguely worded standards and towards criminal sanctions – "when combined raise serious concerns in relation to the principle of lex certa, or legal certainty". See Faure, Michael, Morag Goodwin and Franziska Weber, "The Regulator's Dilemma: Caught between the Need for Flexibility & the Demands of Foreseeability. Reassessing the Lex Certa Principle", *Albany Journal of Science & Technology*, Vol. 24, No. 2, 2014, pp. 283–364 [pp. 284, 289, 299, 303].

[78] Compare with competition law. Cseres, Schinkel and Vogelaar identify a fundamental criticism of the criminalisation of competition law enforcement, namely that harsh criminal sanctions do not suit the nature of competition law enforcement. "Competition rules have a dynamic interpretation, and over time, as economic insight has progressed, have been enforced with shifting emphases.... In other words, the criminalization of competition law enforcement is likely to require a rethinking of the entire enforcement system as well as the checks and balances that go with it." See Cseres, Schinkel and Vogelaar, "Law and Economics of Criminal Antitrust Enforcement: An Introduction", op. cit., pp. 10–12. The authors add that "it seems important that the European Commission formulates a position on this subject. Such a discussion might possibly follow a bottom-up approach, as has also been the case with the uniformisation of substantive competition laws within the member states.... this bottom-up approach may result in EC harmonization in the future as there would then be a common understanding of "indispensability" amongst the member states.... Effective enforcement of competition laws is best achieved through a mix of public enforcement, leniency programmes, criminal sanctions and private damage suits" (Ibid., pp. 6, 17).

[79] Compare with Nouwt who states that civil enforcement is preferable in horizontal relationships, but thoughtfully adds that this is not always possible because the opposite party is not always known and, furthermore, there is often a difference in the balance of power. "In that case a choice must be made between enforcement by administrative law or by criminal law. This choice depends on: the symbolic value of criminal enforcement; the desirable and realistic enforcement capacity of the parties involved; the intended effectiveness of enforcement (process forms, possibility of reaching an arrangement out of court, 'tit for tat' effects); the societal evaluation of the injustice; and the desired protection mechanisms in investigation and punishment." See Nouwt and Schudelaro, "He who abuses data will be punished", op. cit., p. 122 with reference to Simmelink, J.B.H.M., "Over misdrijven, overtredingen en administratieve gedragingen", in M.S. Groenhuijsen and J.B.H.M. Simmelink (eds.), *Glijdende schalen, Liber Amicorum, J. de Hullu*, Wolf Legal Publishers, Nijmegen, 2003, pp. 511–535 [pp. 528–529].

[80] Reindl, writing in the context of competition law, opposes automatic exportability of criminal sanctions from one country to another, and makes a beautiful plea for a bottom-up development: "What we can assume is that a country's enforcement environment will influence whether criminal sanctions lead to better rates of law compliance. … The US criminal system works within a unique procedural and institutional framework that substantially contributes to the success of US anti-cartel enforcement. In the absence of those conditions in other countries, a criminal enforcement system may deliver far fewer of the perceived benefits. … The most important features include strong investigatory tools including grand jury subpoenas, grand jury investigations and indictments, a competition authority that is also the prosecuting authority and therefore does not have to rely on public prosecutors, and a plea-bargaining system. … In most European jurisdiction, a similar procedural framework does not exist. … Member states would be a good place to focus on the

The different ratios between administrative law and criminal law should always be kept in mind when selecting the appropriate enforcement regime. In our view, according to the criminal law principle of last resort, criminalisation would only be acceptable for serious or grave wrongs.[81] The use of criminal law should be reserved for serious cases, where the right to privacy is at stake, via threats posed by powerful actors. This may also avoid or limit institutional resistance of traditional criminal law actors such as prosecutors. This argument is partially reflected in the contribution of Grant and Crowther, elsewhere in this book, who opine that fines could remedy wilful wrongful behaviour and more alternative sanctions could remedy failure to act.

It is equally important to understand the theoretical nature of the foregoing reflection. Addressing these issues and applying criminalisation principles should always happen in an informed way, taking into consideration the actual context of the debate, and bring in reality.[82] Nouwt rightly notes that theory dictates that the confidentiality of personal and company data, information and secrets must be protected by criminal law, but practice dictates that the confidentiality of personal and company data, information and secrets would be better off in the hands of the expert specialist supervisors than in those of the already overburdened public prosecutor.[83]

A good (more or less) objective or indicator for defining criminal behaviour is given by existing crimes for similar conduct. For instance, in Belgium, hacking is a

discussion of criminal sanctions, experiment with different regimes as well as institutional and procedural set-ups to obtain better cost-benefit outcomes, develop expertise in criminal enforcement, and build public support for a criminal enforcement system." See Reindl, "How Strong is the Case for Criminal Sanctions in Cartel Cases?", pp. 118–127.

81 In competition law, Wils argues that "criminal antitrust enforcement, in its strongest form, relying on imprisonment, can only work or only makes sense if its limited to hard-core cartels, complementing other penalties for companies and for less antitrust violations… one could conclude that prison sentences should only exist for wilful violations of the law, where there is evidence that the individuals knew that they were violating the law or acted with flagrant disregard of for the law … the United Kingdom, with its combination of a criminal cartel offence with a system of administrative fines and director disqualification for all types of antitrust violations, would in my view appear to have struck the balance exactly right." See Wils, W.P.J., "Is Criminalization of EU Competition Law the Answer?", op. cit., pp. 76, 85, 87, 90. Compare also with Massey who adds that "when addressing the issue of criminal sanctions, it is important to distinguish between cartels and other types of anti-competitive practices. Many areas of competition law constitute grey areas. There is often a very thin dividing line between abuse of dominance and aggressive competition.... There is a widespread agreement among economists that cartels are inevitably harmful.... The serious harm caused by cartels arguably provides a justification for subjecting them to more stringent penalties than other types of anticompetitive behaviour." See Massey, P., "Criminalization and Leniency", op. cit., p. 179.

82 Compare Reindl's critique on the plea of Wils to criminalise certain wrongs in competition law: what "Wils characterizes as 'ample evidence' of the deterrent effects of criminal sanctions, however, appears to be based mostly on intuition, hearsay, anecdotes, and personal perceptions." See Reindl, "How Strong is the Case for Criminal Sanctions in Cartel Cases?", op. cit., p. 116.

83 Nouwt and Schudelaro, "He who abuses data will be punished", op. cit., p. 123.

computer crime. Data protection wrongs similar to hacking qualify for a criminal approach.

A second indicator is more complex but also objective. If the legislator has chosen the administrative approach for a certain wrong, there is in principle no need to add criminal law and apply criminalisation. Overseeing the number of wrongs that are dealt with in the administrative approach in Article 79 of the Regulation (see above), one could therefore conclude that there is no need for criminalisation in EU data protection law unless one finds a data protection wrong that is not dealt with in the long list enumerated in Article 79 of the Regulation. This apparently logical reasoning is, however, misleading. Legislators seldom limit themselves to only one approach. Both overlaps between crimes and between criminal wrongs and administrative wrongs are deliberately chosen[84] and, as such, are not always illegitimate, since they allow an approach where the criminal is only used where the administrative fails. In the case of data protection, we would suggest that Member States look closely at the wrongs identified in Article 79 of the Regulation and only selectively, select some (preferably only the more serious ones) for a criminalisation approach. Creating other crimes would, in our view, only be defendable, when a clear case can be made (for instance, the drafters of the Regulation did not see all of the possible data protection wrongs and some of these forgotten wrongs pass the criminalisation test).

16.9 Conclusion

16.9.1 Enforcement left out the harmonisation agenda

Both Europe's basic regulatory texts on data protection, the EU 1995 Directive and the Council of Europe's Convention 108 have surprisingly little to say on enforcement in general and on the use of criminal law in particular. Both instruments leave the choice of the enforcement regime to the Member States, including the establishment of appropriate sanctions and remedies. "Suitability" seems to be the only requirement when Member States have to choose between criminal law, administrative or civil law provisions and sanctions, or for a mix of these systems.

After 1995, most Member States have opted for a mixed system of criminal law and administrative law to enforce data protection rules. Whereas some states have only criminalised some data protection wrongs, others have opted for an extensive list of data protection crimes. Some states have chosen a system with no, some or many administrative sanctions.

In practice, criminal law has proven to be the least evident partner in data protection enforcement. Although the use of criminal sanctions varies from one country to another, in practice, one sees that the criminal law provisions in countries where

[84] On this, see Husak, Douglas, *Overcriminalization: The Limits of the Criminal Law*, Oxford University Press, Oxford, 2008, pp. 11–28.

they exist are seldom used and that administrative procedures controlled by the data protection authorities are preferred.

Most national data protection acts give no guidance on the choice of administrative or criminal sanctions and on the discretion of the data protection authorities to impose administrative sanctions. Such discretion for data protection authorities might raise questions, especially in the light of a trend towards high administrative fines in the EU Member States.

Until the 2005 environmental law and 2007 ship pollution cases, the EU had no possibility to criminalise behaviour in former first pillar (Community) matters. With its 2005 judgment, the Court of Justice explicitly recognised this power, but two years later, in its 2007 judgment, the Court added that the European Union is only competent to define what behaviour should be criminalised by the Member States in (first pillar) legal instruments such as directives or regulations, but not competent to determine the type and level of criminal sanctions. For that kind of detailed criminal law regulation, decisions or framework decisions, instruments controlled by the Member States, had to be adopted to complement the policy options taken in directives or regulations.

With the abolition of the pillar structure by the 2009 Treaty of Lisbon, things have changed and criminal law reform can and is nowadays introduced using directives and regulations. Notwithstanding this new EU competence, one is struck by the observation that the reform of the 1995 Directive through the Regulation, initiated in 2012, (again) is silent on criminal law and (again) leaves full discretion to Member States on the use of criminal sanctions. The focus of the Regulation is clearly elsewhere. The Regulation sets up a powerful administrative system and partly restricts the discretion of the Member States under the 1995 Directive to choose the nature of sanctions, by setting out guidelines for the administrative sanctions that Member States can introduce and general principles for determining in practice the amount of the fines. Articles 78§1 and 79§2 of the Commission proposal recall the general (Greek Maize) principles (effective, proportionate and dissuasive) for penalties respectively administrative sanctions, but apart from these criteria and the principles for determining the amount of the fines, there are hardly any limits to the level of administrative sanctions.

The reform only slightly addresses the issue of harmonisation of administrative sanctions. For criminal sanctions, nothing in the Regulation hints at any harmonisation at all. In theory, a future of sustained differences between Member States goes against the aim of a regulation to establish a uniform data protection framework, and is oblivious the explicit powers for the EU created with the 2009 Treaty of Lisbon to impose criminal law obligations via directives (Article 83.2 of the Treaty on the Functioning of the European Union). The lack of harmonisation also creates legal uncertainty for companies and the data subject. US and other foreign companies in particular are intimidated by the use of criminal law, independent of its actual enforcement and the sheer existence of these provisions in some EU Member States might influence their decisions. Furthermore, it might invite forum shopping, i.e., the fact that companies can move their main establishment to a Member State with the most flexible sanction powers.

Neither do the reform instruments contain any provisions on the use of criteria to be taken into account when choosing between administrative or criminal enforcement.[85]

There is a lack of shared criteria that regulators can take into account when choosing between administrative or criminal enforcement in the field of data protection law. One thing is clear: the use of a criminal approach was not popular in the past. On the one hand, there is evidence of institutional resistance from prosecutors and courts against criminal sanctions. On the other hand, Member States prefer to use administrative law due to some characteristics of criminal law. Administrative law possesses to a certain extent an advantage over criminal law in that there are hardly any limits to the level of administrative sanctions.

16.9.2 Looking critically at criminal sanctions and a fundamental rights agenda for administrative law enforcement

Looking to the future, we recommend Member States define as clearly as possible in their future data protection laws what offences shall be considered criminal or administrative, and enforced by means of criminal and administrative law. Critical and minimal use of criminal law should be amongst the priorities. It is difficult (but not impossible) to argue for the necessity of data protection crimes if neighbouring countries refrain from creating them. The 1990 Resolution of the International Congress of Penal Law provides a first set of elements in the necessary criminalisation exercise, more particularly the importance of the social interest affected by the conduct in question, the gravity of endangerment or harm to that interest, and the kind and degree of fault on the part of the offender. An element that needs to be taken into consideration, and that rallies against the use of criminal law, is the open nature of many data protection norms, often the object of interpretation and case-by-case deliberation and often in a process or dialogue between processors and supervisory authorities. Criminal law may therefore not always offer the appropriate enforcement mechanism, but must instead be seen as a last resort. Administrative law, on the other hand, may turn out to be more accommodated to the dynamic character of data protection, in some but not all cases.

---

[85] There is only certainty about one thing: a purely criminal approach without administrative sanctioning powers for the data protection authorities as exist today in some countries seems no longer possible. Dougan observed that the Greek Maize doctrine applies to every aspect of the enforcement of EU law: not only the nature of the sanction, but also the conditions for its imposition, and even the actual character and level of the penalty imposed. The Court's supervision is not limited to the formal legislative framework established by the Member State, but also extends to scrutinizing whether the actual practices of the national administration fulfil the requirements of equivalence, effectiveness and proportionality." See Dougan, Michael, "From the Velvet Glove to the Iron Fist: Criminal Sanctions for the Enforcement of Union Law", in Marise Cremona (ed.), *Compliance and the Enforcement of EU Law*, Oxford University Press, Oxford, 2013, pp. 74–131 [p. 83].

In our contribution, we have proposed a couple more or less objective indicators for identifying behaviour as (really) criminal. The different ratios of administrative law and criminal law should always be kept in mind when selecting the appropriate enforcement regime: the use of criminal law should be reserved for serious cases, where the right to privacy is at stake, via threats posed by powerful actors. In our view, according to the criminal law principle of last resort, criminalisation would only be acceptable for serious or grave punitive wrongs.[86] Elsewhere, we also said that the EU competence in the area of criminalisation of cybercrime offences should be confined to situations where there is an element of seriousness and a cross-border dimension.[87] Of course, addressing these issues and applying criminalisation principles should always seek to inform itself about the actual context of the debate and bring in reality.

An impact assessment by the European Commission may be welcome in order to determine existing serious data protection wrongs. Although in practice criminal law is not widely used in the Member States, one should continue to take stock of the enforcement practices in the Member States. In case a trend towards more criminalisation becomes apparent, harmonisation of criminal law will have move higher on the EU political ladder.

The future of EU data protection seems indeed to be one of administrative enforcement by data protection authorities, playing several roles at a time (guidance, police, prosecutor, judge...).[88] The turn to administrative law enforcement,

---

[86] The 2005 judgment empowered the EU to use former first pillar instruments for providing criminal sanctions for serious environmental (Community) offences, and although Article 83.2 of the Treaty on the Functioning of the European Union does not explicitly refer to the element of seriousness, in our view, it should be considered when introducing EU criminal sanctions.

[87] De Hert, Paul, Irene Wieczorek and Gertjan Boulet, "Les fondements et objectifs des politiques d'incrimination de l'UE: le cas de la cybercriminalité", in Diane Bernard, Yves Cartuyvels, Christine Guillain, Damien Scalla and Michel van de Kerchove (eds.), *Fondements et objectifs des incriminations et des peines en droit européen et international*, Anthemis, Limal, 2013, pp. 267–282.

[88] In this contribution, we did not look at enforcement of data protection through civil law instruments, but in the light of the growing demand and attention for this system of enforcement; that work needs to be done too. A discretionary choice of the enforcement regime may also have serious implications in this matter. In relation to the Greek Maize case, Dougan noted the difficulties in distinguishing public and private sanctions: "The real question concerns the manner in which these two different perspectives on decentralized enforcement – the public sanction and the private remedy – interact with each other..., questioning the extent to which member states can discharge their own Greek Maize obligation to provide a system of sanctions, by entrusting the enforcement of EU law to private enforcement mechanisms." Dougan, "From the Velvet Glove to the Iron Fist", op. cit., p. 86. In competition law, Cseres et al. state that "in comparison with their American counterparts, European competition authorities have a smaller arsenal or enforcement instruments" and that the number of private damage cases has surpassed public enforcement. In their assessment of the costs and benefits of the criminalisation of competition law (see above), they refer to the potentially greater deterrent effect of non-monetary sanctions such as disqualification orders and naming and shaming. See Cseres, Schinkel and Vogelaar, "Law and Economics of Criminal Antitrust Enforcement: An Introduction", op. cit., p. 3. In a judgment of 14 June 2011, a Belgian criminal court did not specify whether it awarded €1,000 damages on the basis of the Privacy Act or Article 1383 of the civil code (tort) (Correctional Court of Hasselt, 14 June 2011, not published).

advocated in the Regulation, is respectful of the *ultima ratio* argument to minimise criminal law, but should be taken with caution and not to the detriment of legal principles central to due process and the rule of law as they have been developed in criminal law. The combination of roles (police and prosecutor) and the discretion of the data protection authorities to impose administrative sanctions might raise questions, especially in the light of a trend towards high administrative fines in the EU Member States. Most national acts give no guidance to the discretion of the data protection authorities to impose administrative sanctions. The last resort argument for the limited use of criminal law cannot be used to turn administrative law in a quasi-criminal law system with no or fewer guarantees and legal protection than in criminal law.

Let us conclude that the current reform of European data protection regime advances the situation with regard to enforcement. A system of administrative enforcement is made mandatory and a system of criminal enforcement is left optional. The reform pays attention to the kinds of administrative wrongs that Member States need to sanction and creates a framework, including defence principles, that should make administrative enforcement workable.

The lack of harmonisation of the criminal law sanctions strikes us as unsatisfactory. It might very well be that due to the importance of criminal law, some things should be dealt with through the criminal law system. It might also very well be that data protection law is not fit for criminal law logic. Leaving things as they are means fragmentation. The Regulation fails in this respect.

Back in 2002, Bygrave wrote that "[i]n a very few cases, allowance is made for class actions to be brought". Bygrave, Lee A., *Data Protection Law: Approaching Its Rationale, Logic and Limits*, Kluwer Law International, The Hague, 2002, p. 77. Current debates in competition law also include the potential benefits of collective redress. See Juska, Zygimantas, "Obstacles in European competition law enforcement: a potential solution from collective redress", *European Journal of Legal Studies*, Vol. 7, No. 1, 2013, pp. 125–153. http://cadmus.eui.eu/handle/1814/32274. Spagnolo encouraged "some private antitrust law enforcement in the form of class action suits". See Spagnolo, Giancarlo, "Criminalization of Cartels and their Internal Organization", op. cit., p. 140. In 2013, the EU Fundamental Rights Agency argued that in the area of data protection, "more should be done to permit complaints by multiple complainants, as well as to ensure that civil society organisations can bring claims on behalf of victims of discriminatory acts". European Union Agency for Fundamental Rights, *Access to data protection remedies in EU member states*, Publications Office of the European Union, Luxembourg, 2013, p. 7. See also European Union Agency for Fundamental Rights, Opinion of the FRA on the proposed protection reform package, 2/2012, Vienna, 1 October 2012, p. 28. http://fra.europa.eu/en/opinion/2012/fra-opinion-proposed-eu-data-protection-reform-package. Noteworthy in that regard is a class action of 2014, launched against Facebook by Max Schrems, frontman of the Austrian group Europe-v-Facebook. See Essers, Loek, "Austrian court rejects Facebook 'class action' privacy suit, refers it to another court", *PCWorld*, 8 August 2014. http://www.pcworld.com/article/2463120/austrian-court-rejects-facebook-class-action-privacy-suit-refers-it-to-another-*court.html*. The press article clarifies that "under Austrian law, a U.S.-style class action suit in which people can collectively sue a company isn't possible. However, interested parties are allowed to assign their claims to a single person who can then sue on behalf of the third parties and redistribute any damages awarded."

Perhaps things ought to be this way. Criminal law is still a sensitive issue for Member States, and regulations, with their ambition to create detailed uniformity, might be a bridge too far. Directives leave some discretion to Member States when implementing EU law. A future directive, instead of a regulation, may be a more acceptable instrument for harmonisation of criminal data protection wrongs, as is also prescribed by Article 82(2) of the Treaty on the Functioning of the European Union. In fact, this approach was followed in the field of securities, where a directive on criminal sanctions for market abuse complements a recent regulation on market abuse.[89] This approach, to use different instruments for the substantive and enforcement provisions, is also envisaged in the area of environmental law.[90]

References

Act of 8 December 1992 concerning the protection of privacy in relation to the processing of personal data, *Belgian Official Journal*, 18 March 1993. http://www.privacycommission.be/sites/privacycommission/files/documents/Privacy_Act_1992.pdf.

Act CXII on the Right of Informational Self-determination and Freedom of Information (Hungary), 2011. http://www.naih.hu/files/Privacy_Act-CXII-of-2011_EN_201310.pdf

Additional Protocol to the Convention for the Protection of Individuals with regard to Automatic Processing of Personal Data regarding supervisory authorities and transborder data flows [ETS 181], Strasbourg, 8 November 2001. http://conventions.coe.int/Treaty/en/Treaties/Html/181.htm

Alexander, R.C.H., *Insider dealing and money laundering in the EU: law and regulation*, Ashgate, Aldershot, 2007.

Asp, Petter, "Blacklisting Sanctions and Principles of Criminal Law", in Iain Cameron (ed.), *EU Sanctions: Law and Policy Issues Concerning Restrictive Measures*, Intersentia, Cambridge, 2013, pp. 131–137.

---

[89] Not all authors approve of this double regulatory method or *cohabitation forcée*. In 2008, Vervaele regretted the lack of a policy plan for an integrated vision on the relationship between administrative and criminal law enforcement, and said that it would be logical for some policy areas, such as insider dealing and market abuse, to use one Community instrument for both the substantive rules and administrative and criminal law enforcement See Vervaele, J., "The European Community and Harmonization of the Criminal Law Enforcement of Community Policy: Ignoti nulla cupido?", in U. Sieber and K. Tiedemann, *Strafrecht und Wirtschaftsstrafrecht: Dogmatik, Rechtsvergleich, Rechtstatsachen. Festschrift für Klaus Tiedemann zum 70. Geburtstag*, Carl Heymans Verlag, Cologne, 2008, pp. 1353–1384.

[90] "Both the 1961 Single Convention on Narcotic Drugs and 1971 Convention on Psychotropic Substances… contain technical provisions limiting and regulating (amongst other things) the manufacturing, trade and distribution of narcotic drugs and psychotropic substances. The 1988 Convention against Illicit Trafficking in Narcotic Drugs and Psychotropic Substances supplements those prior conventions by regulating the breaches of their provisions and providing a legal framework for the fight against illicit trafficking. To that end the 1988 Convention enumerates a series of offences and sanctions building on the regulations from the previous conventions… To a certain extent, a parallel evolution could now be triggered from the traditional environmental law to a new international environmental criminal law." See Vermeulen, Gert, and Wendy De Bondt, "Exploring the potential of criminal law in protecting the environment", *Revista Eletrônica de Direito Penal*, Vol. 1, No. 1, 2013, [p. 84].

Bernier, Claire, "Overview and definition of personal data offences: impact of criminal aspects", International Federation of Computer Law Association, Antwerp, June 2014.

Bröring, H.E., "Book review: Oswald Jansen (ed.), Administrative Sanctions in the European Union, (Cambridge: Intersentia 2013)", *Review of European Administrative Law*, Vol. 6, No. 2, 2013, pp. 87–91.

Bygrave, Lee, *Data Protection Law. Approaching Its Rationale, Logic and Limits*, Kluwer Law International, The Hague, 2002.

Commission of the European Communities, Report from the Commission, First report on the implementation of the Data Protection Directive (95/46/EC), COM(2003) 265 final, Brussels, 15 May 2003.

Commission of the European Communities, Communication from the Commission to the European Parliament and the Council on the follow-up of the Work Programme for better implementation of the Data Protection Directive, COM(2007) 87 final, Brussels, 7 March 2007.

Consolidated version of the Treaty on the Functioning of the European Union, *OJ* C 326, 26 October 2012, pp. 47–390.

Council of Europe, Convention for the Protection of Individuals with regard to Automatic Processing of Personal Data, Strasbourg [ETS 108], Strasbourg, 28 January 1981. http://conventions.coe.int/Treaty/en/Treaties/Html/108.htm

Council of Europe, The Consultative Committee of the Convention for the Protection of Individuals with regard to Automatic Processing of Personal Data [ETS no. 108], Propositions of modernisation, Strasbourg, 18 December 2012.

Council of the European Union, Council Directive 89/592/EEC of 13 November 1989 coordinating regulations on insider dealing, *OJ* L 334, 17 November 1989, pp. 30–32.

Council of the European Union, Council Framework Decision 2003/80/JHA of 27 January 2003 on the protection of the environment through criminal law, *OJ* L 029, 5 February 2002, pp. 55–58.

Council of the European Union, Council Framework Decision 2005/667/JHA of 12 July 2005 to strengthen the criminal-law framework for the enforcement of the law against ship-source pollution, *OJ* L 255, 30 September 2005, pp. 164–167.

Council of the European Union (Council version), Proposal for a Regulation of the European Parliament and of the Council on the protection of individuals with regard to the processing of personal data and on the free movement of such data (General Data Protection Regulation) – Preparation of a general approach, Brussels, 11 June 2015. http://data.consilium.europa.eu/doc/document/ST-9565-2015-INIT/en/pdf

Court of Justice of the EU, Commission of the European Communities v. Council of the European Union, C-176/03, 13 September 2005.

Court of Justice of the EU, Commission of the European Communities v. Council of the European Union, C-440/05, 23 October 2007.

Cseres, Katalin, Maarten Schinkel and Floris Vogelaar, "Law and Economics of Criminal Antitrust Enforcement: An Introduction", in Katalin Cseres, Maarten Schinkel and Floris Vogelaar (eds.), *Criminalization of Competition Law Enforcement. Economic and Legal Implications for the EU Member States*, Edward Elgar, Cheltenham, 2006, pp. 1–29.

DataGuidance, "Brazil: Telecom giant fined €1.2 million", 31 July 2014. http://www.dataguidance.com/dataguidance_privacy_this_week.asp?id=2670

Data Protection Commissioner, "Enforced Subject Access now an Offence", 29 July 2014. http://www.dataprotection.ie/docs/29-07-14-Enforced-Subject-Access-now-an-Offence/1453.htm

De Hert, Paul, and Frédéric Van Leeuw, "Cybercrime Legislation in Belgium", in Eric Dirix and Yves-Henri Leleu (eds.), *The Belgian reports at the Congress of Washington of the International Academy of Comparative Law*, Bruylant, Brussels, 2011, pp. 869–956.

De Hert, Paul and Gertjan Boulet, "Cybercrime report for Belgium", *International Review of Penal Law (RIDP/IRPL)*, 2013, Issue 84, No. 1–2, pp. 12–59. http://www.penal.org/en/ridp-irpl-2013-1-2; *Electronic Review of the International Association of Penal* Law, 2013. http://www.penal.org/sites/default/files/files/RV-2.pdf

De Hert, Paul, Irene Wieczorek and Gertjan Boulet, “Les fondements et objectifs des politiques d’incrimination de l’UE: le cas de la cybercriminalité”, in Diane Bernard, Yves Cartuyvels, Christine Guillain, Damien Scalla and Michel van de Kerchove (eds.), *Fondements et objectifs des incriminations et des peines en droit européen et international*, Anthemis, Limal, 2013, pp. 267–282.

De Hert, Paul, and Vagelis Papakonstantinou, “Three Scenarios for International Governance of Data Privacy: Towards an International Data Privacy Organization, Preferably a UN Agency?”, *I/S: A Journal of Law and Policy for the Information Society*, Vol. 9, No. 2, 2013, pp. 271–327;

Delmas-Marty, Mireille, “Introduction: différenciation des systèmes juridiques de sanctions à dominante pénale ou administrative”, *International Review of Penal Law*, Vol. 59, semesters 1–2, 1988, pp. 27–64.

Domokos, Márton, “Hungary – Highlights from the new DPA’s ‘Year One’”, International Association of Privacy Professionals, 18 June 2013. https://www.privacyassociation.org/publications/hungary_highlights_from_the_new_dpas_year_one

Dougan, Michael, “From the Velvet Glove to the Iron Fist: Criminal Sanctions for the Enforcement of Union Law”, in Marise Cremona (ed.), *Compliance and the Enforcement of EU Law*, Oxford University Press, Oxford, 2013, pp. 74–131.

Dresner, Stewart, “The case for the use of criminal law enforcement powers by DPAs”, *Privacy Laws & Business International Report*, No. 126, December 2013.

Essers, Loek, “Austrian court rejects Facebook ‘class action’ privacy suit, refers it to another court”, *PCWorld*, 8 August 2014. http://www.pcworld.com/article/2463120/austrian-court-rejects-facebook-class-action-privacy-suit-refers-it-to-another-court.html

Estonian Personal Data Protection Act, 2 March 2011. http://www.legaltext.ee/et/andmebaas/tekst.asp?loc=text&dok=XXXX041K1&keel=en&pg=1&ptyyp=RT&tyyp=X&query=isikuandmete+kaitse+seadus

European Commission, Communication from the Commission to the European Parliament, the Council, the Economic and Social Committee and the Committee of the Regions, A comprehensive approach on personal data protection in the European Union, COM (2010) 609, Brussels, 4 November 2010. http://ec.europa.eu/justice/news/consulting_public/0006/com_2010_609_en.pdf

European Commission, Communication from the Commission to the European Parliament, the Council, the European Economic and Social Committee and the Committee of the Regions, Towards an EU Criminal Policy: Ensuring the effective implementation of EU policies through criminal law, COM(2011) 573 final, Brussels, 20 September 2011.

European Commission, Proposal for a Regulation of the European Parliament and of the Council on the protection of individuals with regard to the processing of personal data and on the free movement of such data (General Data Protection Regulation), COM(2012) 11 final, Brussels, 25 January 2012.

European Commission, Study on criminal sanction legislation and practice in representative Member States, Tender JUST/2011/JPEN/PR/0066/A4, final report, November 2013. http://ec.europa.eu/justice/criminal/document/files/sanctions_delivery_en.pdf

European Parliament (LIBE report), Draft Report on the proposal for a regulation of the European Parliament and of the Council on the protection of individual with regard to the processing of personal data and on the free movement of such data (General Data Protection Regulation), Committee on Civil Liberties, Justice and Home Affairs, rapporteur: Jan Philipp Albrecht, COM(2012)0011 – C7-0025/2012 – 2012/0011(COD).

European Parliament (European Parliament version), legislative resolution of 12 March 2014 on the proposal for a regulation of the European Parliament and of the Council on the protection of individuals with regard to the processing of personal data and on the free movement of such data (General Data Protection Regulation) (COM(2012)0011 – C7-0025/2012 – 2012/0011(COD)), Strasbourg, 12 March 2014. http://www.europarl.europa.eu/sides/getDoc.do?pubRef=-//EP//TEXT+TA+P7-TA-2014-0212+0+DOC+XML+V0//EN

European Parliament and the Council of the European Union, Directive 95/46/EC of the European Parliament and Council of 24 October 1995 on the protection of individuals with regard to the processing of personal data and on the free movement of such data, *OJ* L 281, 23 November 1995, pp. 31–50.

European Parliament and the Council of the European Union, Directive 2003/6/EC of the European Parliament and of the Council of 28 January 2003 on insider dealing and market manipulation (market abuse), *OJ* L 96, 14 April 2003, pp. 16–25.

European Parliament and the Council of the European Union, Directive 2005/35/EC of the European Parliament and of the Council of 7 September 2005 on ship-source pollution and on the introduction of penalties for infringements, *OJ* L 255, 30 September 2005, pp. 1–21.

European Parliament and the Council of the European Union (LIBE version), Inofficial consolidated version after LIBE committee vote provided by the rapporteur 22 October 2013, Regulation of the European Parliament and of the Council on the protection of individuals with regard to the processing of personal data and on the free movement of such data (General Data Protection Regulation). https://www.janalbrecht.eu/fileadmin/material/Dokumente/DPR-Regulation-inofficial-consolidated-LIBE.pdf

European Parliament and the Council of the European Union, Regulation (EU) No 596/2014 of the European Parliament and of the Council of 16 April 2014 on market abuse (market abuse regulation) and repealing Directive 2003/6/EC of the European Parliament and of the Council and Commission Directives 2003/124/EC, 2003/125/EC and 2004/72/EC, *OJ* L 173, 12 June 2014, pp. 1–61.

European Parliament and the Council of the European Union, Directive 2014/57/EU of the European Parliament and of the Council of 16 April 2014 on criminal sanctions for market abuse (market abuse directive), *OJ* L 173, 12 June 2014, pp. 179–189.

European Parliament and the Council of the European Union, Regulation (EU) No XXX/2016 of the European Parliament and of the Council on the protection of individuals with regard to the processing of personal data and on the free movement of such data (General Data Protection Regulation). 15039/15, consolidated text of the General Data Protection Regulation as an outcome of the final trilogue on 15 December 2015. http://www.emeeting.europarl.europa.eu/committees/agenda/201512/LIBE/LIBE%282015%291217_1/sitt-1739884

European Union Agency for Fundamental Rights, Opinion of the FRA on the proposed protection reform package, 2/2012, Vienna, 1 October 2012. http://fra.europa.eu/en/opinion/2012/fra-opinion-proposed-eu-data-protection-reform-package

European Union Agency for Fundamental Rights, Access to data protection remedies in EU member states, Publications Office of the European Union, Luxembourg, 2013, pp. 1–64. http://fra.europa.eu/en/publication/2014/access-data-protection-remedies-eu-member-states

Faure, Michael, Morag Goodwin and Franziska Weber, "The Regulator's Dilemma: Caught between the Need for Flexibility & the Demands of Foreseeability. Reassessing the Lex Certa Principle", *Albany Journal of Science & Technology*, Vol. 24, No. 2, 2014, pp. 283–364.

García, José F. Castillo, "The Power of the European Community to Impose Criminal Penalties", *Eipascope*, No. 3, 2005, pp. 1–8.

Greenleaf, Graham, "'Modernising' Data Protection Convention 108: A Safe Basis for a Global Privacy Treaty?", *Computer Law & Security Review*, Vol. 29, No. 4, 2013, pp. 433–437.

Gunasekara, Gehan, "Paddling in unison or just paddling? International trends in reforming information privacy law", *International Journal of Law and Information Technology*, Vol. 22, No. 2, 2013, pp. 1–37.

Gutwirth, Serge, and Paul De Hert, "Een theoretische onderbouw voor een legitiem strafproces. Reflecties over procesculturen, de doelstellingen van de straf, de plaats van het strafrecht en de rol van slachtoffers" [A theoretical framework for a legitimate criminal proces. Reflections about process cultures, the function of punishment, the position of criminal law and the role of victims], *Delikt en Delinkwent*, Vol. 31, No. 10, December 2001, pp. 1048–1087.

Husak, Douglas, *Overcriminalization: The Limits of the Criminal Law*, Oxford University Press, Oxford, 2008.

Information Commissioner's Office, "Law change outlaws 'back door' criminal record check", 9 March 2015. https://ico.org.uk/about-the-ico/news-and-events/news-and-blogs/2015/03/law-change-outlaws-back-door-criminal-record-check/

Italian Data Protection Authority, "Google paga una multa da 1 milione di euro inflitta dal Garante privacy per il servizio", Rome, 3 April 2014. http://www.garanteprivacy.it/web/guest/home/docweb/-/docweb-display/docweb/3033237

Juska, Zygimantas, "Obstacles in European competition law enforcement: a potential solution from collective redress", *European Journal of Legal Studies*, Vol. 7, No. 1, 2013, pp. 125–153. http://cadmus.eui.eu/handle/1814/32274

Luchtman, Michiel, and John Vervaele, "Enforcing the market abuse regime: towards an integrated model of criminal and administrative law enforcement in the European Union", *New Journal of European Criminal Law*, Vol. 4, No. 2, 2014, pp. 192–220.

Macedonian Law on Personal Data Protection, 25 January 2005. http://www.ceecprivacy.org/pdf/Law%20on%20Personal%20Data%20Protection.pdf

Massey, Patrick, "Criminalization and Leniency: Will the Combination Favourably affect Cartel Stability?", in Katalin Cseres, Maarten Schinkel and Floris Vogelaar (eds.), *Criminalization of Competition Law Enforcement. Economic and Legal Implications for the EU Member States*, Edward Elgar, Cheltenham, 2006, pp. 176–195.

Maxwell, Winston J., "Global Privacy Governance: A Comparison of Regulatory Models in the US and Europe, and the Emergence of Accountability as a Global Norm", in Carine Dartiguepeyrou (ed.), *The Futures of Privacy*, Cahier de prospective, Futur Numérique, February 2014, pp. 63–70.

Nouwt, Sjaak, "Tijd voor een nieuw punitief sluitstuk in de WBP?" (Time for a punitive chapter), *Privacy & Informatie*, No. 6, December 2005, pp. 253–257.

Nouwt, Sjaak, and Ton Schudelaro, "Hij die gegevens misbruikt wordt gestraft … of toch niet? Een onderzoek naar de vraag of misbruik van persoonsgegevens strafbaar moet worden gesteld" (He who abuses data will be punished), Sdu Uitgeverij Den Haag, The Hague, 2006.

Ost, François, and Michel van de Kerchove, *De la pyramide au réseau?*, Publications des Facultés universitaires Saint-Louis, Brussels, 2010.

Out-Law.com, "Government considering making it easier for the ICO to levy privacy fines", 14 November 2013. http://www.out-law.com/en/articles/2013/november/government-considering-making-it-easier-for-the-ico-to-levy-privacy-fines/

Out-Law.com, "UK review of data protection sanctions should include consideration of increasing £500,000 fine threshold, says expert", 5 March 2014. http://www.out-law.com/en/articles/2014/march/uk-review-of-data-protection-sanctions-should-include-consideration-of-increasing-500000-fine-threshold-says-expert/

Parrilli, Davide Maria, "Belgium: Will the Privacy Commission become a Privacy Police?",*time.lex*, 24 November 2013. http://www.timelex.eu/en/blog/detail/belgium-will-the-privacy-commission-become-a-privacy-police

Personal Data Protection Code (Italy), Legislative Decree no. 196 of 30 June 2003. http://www.garanteprivacy.it/documents/10160/2012405/DataProtectionCode-2003.pdf

Reindl, Andres P., "How Strong is the Case for Criminal Sanctions in Cartel Cases?", in Katalin Cseres, Maarten Schinkel and Floris Vogelaar (eds.), *Criminalization of Competition Law Enforcement. Economic and Legal Implications for the EU Member States*, Edward Elgar, Cheltenham, 2006, pp. 110–132.

Sandel, Michael J., *What Money Can't Buy: The Moral Limits of Markets*, Farrar, Straus and Giroux, New York, 2012.

Simmelink, J.B.H.M., "Over misdrijven, overtredingen en administratieve gedragingen", in M.S. Groenhuijsen and J.B.H.M.Simmelink (eds.), *Glijdende schalen, Liber Amicorum, J. de Hullu*, Wolf Legal Publishers, Nijmegen, 2003, pp. 511–535.

Spagnolo, Giancarlo, "Criminalization of Cartels and their Internal Organization", in Katalin Cseres, Maarten Schinkel and Floris Vogelaar (eds.), *Criminalization of Competition Law Enforcement. Economic and Legal Implications for the EU Member States*, Edward Elgar, Cheltenham, 2006, pp. 133–149.

Vanhecke, Nikolas, "Commissie maakt werk van privacy-politie", *De Standaard*, 21 October 2013. http://www.standaard.be/cnt/dmf20131020_016

Vermeulen, Gert, and Wendy De Bondt, "Exploring the potential of criminal law in protecting the environment", *Revista Eletrônica de Direito Penal*, Vol. 1, No. 1, 2013, pp. 81–111.

Vervaele, J., "The European Community and Harmonization of the Criminal Law Enforcement of Community Policy: Ignoti nulla cupido?", in U. Sieber and K. Tiedemann, *Strafrecht und Wirtschaftsstrafrecht: Dogmatik, Rechtsvergleich, Rechtstatsachen. Festschrift für Klaus Tiedemann zum 70. Geburtstag*, Carl Heymans Verlag, Cologne, 2008, pp. 1353–1384.

Wils, Wouter P.J., "Is Criminalization of EU Competition Law the Answer?", in Katalin Cseres, Maarten Schinkel and Floris Vogelaar (eds.), *Criminalization of Competition Law Enforcement. Economic and Legal Implications for the EU Member States*, Edward Elgar, Cheltenham, 2006, pp. 60–109.

XIV International Congress of Penal Law, Resolutions, section I: The legal and practical problems posed by the difference between criminal law and administrative penal law, *International Review of Penal Law,* Vol. 61, semesters 1–2, 1990, pp. 112–114.

Chapter 17
Whom to Trust? Using Technology to Enforce Privacy

Daniel Le Métayer

17.1 Introduction

The fact that the worldwide increase in the adoption of digital services and devices has created many new privacy risks does not mean that all information technologies have a detrimental effect on privacy. Indeed, privacy-enhancing technologies (PETs) have been an active research topic in computer science in the last few decades and a variety of techniques have been proposed to contribute to a better enforcement of privacy rights.[1] Admittedly, the adoption of most of these techniques is still rather limited, even if it is growing, especially in the aftermath of recent privacy breach scandals. However, at a time when privacy risks have never been higher and enforcing privacy rights has never been more challenging, it would probably not be a wise strategy to neglect the potential of available privacy-enhancing technologies.

[1] Goldberg, Ian, David Wagner, Eric A. Brewer, "Privacy-Enhancing Technologies for the Internet", IEEE COMPCON '97, February 1997. Goldberg, Ian, "Privacy-Enhancing Technologies for the Internet III: Ten years later", Chapter 1, in Alessandro Acquisti, Stefanos Gritzalis, Costos Lambrinoudakis, Sabrina di Vimercati (eds.), *Digital Privacy: Theory, Technologies, and Practices*, December 2007. Danezis, George, and Seda Gürses, "A critical review of 10 years of privacy technology" in *Surveillance Cultures: A Global Surveillance Society?*, UK April 2010. Diaz, Claudia, and Seda Gürses, "Understanding the landscape of privacy technologies", Extended abstract of invited talk in proceedings of the Information Security Summit, 2012, pp. 58–63. Gürses, Seda, and Bettina Berendt, "PETs in the surveillance society: a critical review of the potentials and limitations of the privacy as confidentiality paradigm", in Serge Gutwirth, Yves Poullet, Paul De Hert (eds.), CPDP Springer Verlag, 2009. Shen, Yun, and Siani Pearson, "Privacy-enhancing Technologies: A Review", HP Laboratories HPL-2011-113.

D. Le Métayer (✉)
INRIA, Batiment CEI-2 CS 52132, Boulevard Niels Bohr, 56, 69603 Villeurbanne, France
e-mail: daniel.le-metayer@inria.fr

D. Wright, P. De Hert (eds.), *Enforcing Privacy*, Law, Governance and Technology Series 25, DOI 10.1007/978-3-319-25047-2_17

Many factors have an impact on the adoption of privacy-enhancing technologies,[2] including legal requirements, economic incentives, the protection they provide and their usability. Also, privacy is a relatively young and fast developing research area in computer science and much progress and new tools can be expected in the near future. Our objective in this chapter is not to discuss research challenges, but to consider already available technologies and to show how they can effectively contribute to privacy enforcement. We focus on one key aspect of these technologies, namely, the type of trust that they can provide: we discuss in particular the safeguards they offer, the stakeholders involved in their deployment and, among these stakeholders, the parties that have to be trusted. Indeed, one may argue that, at the end of the day, the main benefit of the use of privacy-enhancing technologies is to *reduce the perimeter of trust*. The ideal situation for data subjects should be to have sufficient guarantees about the design of the technologies so that it is not necessary for them to trust any third party.[3] However, it is almost always the case that some level of trust has to be placed in other stakeholders (including data controllers,[4] trusted third parties, peers, not to mention the developers of the technology itself[5]) and the technology can at best help reduce the number of stakeholders to be trusted or provide ways to challenge this trust or to check that it is not misplaced.

This chapter is not intended as an exhaustive or an in-depth technical presentation of the technologies that can be used to enforce privacy[6] but rather as an overview and analysis of privacy-enhancing technologies from a trust and stakeholder perspective. Here, we focus on technologies specifically designed to enhance privacy rather than traditional security technologies.[7] The latter can be used in a

[2] Borking, John J., "Why Adopting Privacy-enhancing Technologies (PETs) Takes so Much Time", in Serge Gutwirth, Yves Poullet, Paul De Hert and Ronald Leenes (eds.), *Computers, Privacy and Data Protection: an Element of Choice*, Springer Verlag, 2011, pp. 309–341.

[3] Diaz Claudia, Omer Tene, Seda F. Guerses, "Hero or Villain: The Data Controller in Privacy Law and Technologies", *Ohio State Law Journal*, Vol. 74, No. 6, 2013.

[4] We use the expression "data controller" in the sense of the entity collecting and processing personal data in this chapter. More precisely, the data controller is defined as "the natural or legal person, public authority, agency or any other body which alone or jointly with others determines the purposes and means of the processing of personal data" by the Directive 95/46/EC of the European Parliament and of the Council of 24 October 1995 on the Protection of Individuals with Regard to the Processing of Personal Data and on the Free Movement of such Data, European Parliament, Brussels, 1995.

[5] A way to enhance trust in the technology is to have all technological components entirely available in source code and open to scrutiny by communities of experts (even though this scrutiny does not bring absolute guarantees either, as illustrated by the famous Heartbleed security bug in the OpenSSL cryptography library: https://en.wikipedia.org/wiki/Heartbleed?oldid=cur

[6] In particular, we do not discuss techniques and protocols dedicated to specific applications such as e-voting, even though they are very challenging and give rise to interesting and potentially wide-ranging research work.

[7] See, for example, Bruce Schneier's cryptography classics library: *Applied cryptography* (Wiley, 1995), *Practical cryptography* (Wiley, 2003) and *Secrets and lies* (Wiley, 2004) or Mao, Wenbo, *Modern cryptography: theory and practice*, HP Professional Series, 2003.

complementary manner, for example, to protect the confidentiality, integrity and authenticity of communications or to secure storage.

We classify the technologies that can be used to enforce privacy into two main categories:

1. Technologies for avoiding or reducing as much as possible the disclosure of personal data, hence enforcing the data minimisation principle (Sect. 17.2);
2. Technologies for enforcing the rights of the subject if personal data is disclosed or processed (Sect. 17.3).

These two categories correspond to two types of privacy rights[8] and to two complementary strategies for individuals: (1) first, reducing as much as possible the disclosure of their personal data (minimisation principle); (2) then enforcing their rights to personal data that is disclosed (if any): consent, rectification, deletion, accountability, etc. This classification is also in line with the distinction made by some authors between *hard privacy* and *soft privacy*,[9] which are associated with different trust assumptions: hard privacy tries to avoid as much as possible placing any trust in a third party (or to reduce this trust), while soft privacy is based on the assumption that the subject will lose control over his data and therefore has no choice but to place a certain amount of trust in the data controller. In the latter situation, technologies for enforcing the rights of the subject can then be seen as compensations for this loss of control (information right, quality, security, etc.) or ways to challenge this trust (accountability). Lastly, even if the notions of privacy and data protection do not coincide,[10] we focus mostly on personal data protection in this chapter and use the word "privacy" in the restricted sense of "information privacy" or "personal data protection". Indeed, it is clear that there are considerable overlaps between the two notions and most "privacy-enhancing technologies" could actually be called "data protection and management technologies".

---

[8] Organisation for Economic Co-operation and Development, *Guidelines on the Protection of Privacy and Transborder Flows of Personal Data*, 1980. See also *Thirty Years After The OECD Privacy Guidelines*, 2011, http://www.oecd.org/sti/ieconomy/49710223.pdf and the latest version of the guidelines: The Recommendation of the OECD Council concerning Guidelines governing the Protection of Privacy and Transborder Flows of Personal Data, July 2013. http://www.oecd.org/sti/ieconomy/2013-oecd-privacy-guidelines.pdf

[9] Deng, Mina, Kim Wuyts, Riccardo Scandariato, Bart Preneel and Wouter Joosen, "A privacy threat analysis framework: supporting the elicitation and fulfillment of privacy requirements", *Requirements Engineering*, Special Issue on Digital Privacy, Vol. 16, Issue 1, March 2011, pp. 3–32.

[10] See, for example, Kokott, Juliane, and Christoph Sobotta, "The distinction between privacy and data protection in the jurisprudence of the CJEU and the ECtHR", *International Data Privacy Law*, Vol. 3, No. 4, 2013.

17.2 Enforcing data minimisation

The recitals of the European General Data Protection Regulation (agreed by the European Parliament, Council and Commission in December 2015) define data minimisation as the requirement that data should be "adequate, relevant and limited to what is necessary in relation to the purposes for which they are processed". In addition, they require that "personal data should only be processed if the purpose of the processing could not be fulfilled by other means".[11] Enforcing data minimisation would be an easy task if the data subject had no need to interact with the outside world. It is a challenge precisely because it is in tension with other requirements, such as the need to access a service, which requires some form of communication and therefore the disclosure of some information. In this section, we start from the original need or requirement (i.e., primary functionality of the system, what it is used for) and structure the presentation of available technologies along four main types of functionalities:

1. *Communication services*: the user of the system just wants to communicate information to another user (or a group of users), for example, sending an e-mail or sharing information with friends in a social network.
2. *Access services*: the user needs to show some kind of credential to get access to a service, for instance, using a transport ticket or showing a badge to get access to a building.
3. *Computation services*: the user needs from a third party a service that requires some kind of computation, for example, paying an electricity fee in a smart metering system or receiving information personalised to his or her location.
4. *Exploitation of databases*: the user wants to receive information from data contained in a database, for instance, information for knowledge-based decision-making or research (e.g., a public transport operator exploiting a passenger travel database to adjust the frequency of the lines).

In the first three types of functionalities, the user of the system is also the data subject (or the person to whom the personal data relate). In the fourth one, data subjects generally contribute to the database; in most cases, the party accessing the records is not a subject whose data needs to be protected but there are also situations in which the entity accessing the records is also a data subject and the request as well as the answer are sensitive information (e.g., users trying to find information about a disease in a medical database).

[11] Regulation of the European Parliament and of the Council on the protection of individuals with regard to the processing of personal data and on the free movement of such data (General Data Protection Regulation), voted by the European Parliament on 12 March 2014.

We could also have considered *storage services*, which is a fast growing field of activity,[12] especially in the context of cloud computing, but the techniques involved[13] are described in the *communication services* subsection. In some sense, storage can be seen as a particular form of communication between a user and herself with no other party (including the server itself, or the cloud service provider) being able to see the content of the data.

The above functionalities are not exclusive. For example, a system may combine the first functionality for communicating with a server: the second one, to get access to server site; and the third one to actually get the desired service. Moreover, certain privacy-enhancing technologies can be used for different types of services. Nevertheless, most technologies can be primarily associated with one type of service; this chapter aims to contribute to achieving a better understanding of the potential of the wide range of available privacy-enhancing technologies.

17.2.1 Communication services

The first situation is when the user of the system needs to communicate information (e.g., e-mail, SMS, micro-blogging message, instant message, social network post, etc.) to a recipient or a group of recipients. The main objectives of the user in terms of privacy are to ensure that[14]:

- The recipient gets the expected information from the sender and nothing more. For example, she does not get the identity of the sender if the latter does not wish to disclose it[15] (*anonymity of the sender*). In other situations, it may be the receiver who does not wish to disclose her identity (*anonymity of the receiver*).
- Third parties (e.g., parties controlling the intermediate nodes in the communication chain or spies listening to the communication channel, etc.) cannot learn anything from this communication, which means that third parties should not be able to observe the content of the information sent or disclosed to the recipient (*confidentiality*) but also that they should not be able to guess that two messages were sent (or received) by the same user (*unlinkability*) or even that a message has been sent (or received) by a given user (*unobservability*).

---

[12] See, for example, Wuala (https://www.wuala.com/en/), Spideroak (https://spideroak.com/) or owncloud (http://owncloud.org/features/).

[13] Local encryption of data before they are transferred to the cloud and no disclosure of the decryption key to the cloud service provider so that users keep full control over their data.

[14] For a survey on data minimisation properties, see: Pfitzmann, Andreas, and Marit Hansen, "A terminology for talking about privacy by data minimization: Anonymity, Unlinkability, Undetectability, Unobservability, Pseudonymity, and Identity Management", Version v0.34, 10 August 2010. https://dud.inf.tu-dresden.de/literatur/Anon_Terminology_v0.34.pdf

[15] More precisely, anonymity is defined as the fact that a subject is not identifiable (i.e., cannot be uniquely characterised) within a set of possible subjects. Indeed, identity is only one of the possible ways of characterising uniquely a subject.

Technically speaking, unobservability is stronger than unlinkability, which is itself stronger than anonymity. Different techniques are available to meet these objectives. First, confidentiality can be enforced using encryption mechanisms: the content of the information is encrypted before being sent in such a way that only the intended receiver(s) can decrypt it. This type of solution requires a collaboration between two parties: the sender and the receiver must have the means to, respectively, encrypt and decrypt messages, which in practice requires them to have similar or compatible tools installed on both sides. This requirement is not too strong though, and a variety of tools are available, such as PGP[16] or GPG[17] to encrypt e-mails or documents,[18] Cryptocat[19] or the OTR[20] technology to protect the content of instant messaging communications.[21] Similarly, the SSL/TLS[22] protocol is widely used to ensure that Internet transactions are encrypted (in both directions) and VPN[23] technologies are deployed by companies and individuals to create private communication channels. Actually, SSL/TLS is a good illustration of the impact of usability on the adoption of privacy-enhancing technologies. Indeed, because all major web browsers and many websites now support SSL/TLS functionalities,[24] they can be used without any effort (and even without users noticing it), which explains why they probably still are the most used privacy-enhancing technologies.[25] PGP, GPG and OTR can also be integrated within e-mail and instant messaging clients to make their use easier, and solutions also exist for other types of communications such as mobile phone conversations, SMS or MMS.

Technologies are also available to protect the content of information in social networks. In this context, communication modes can be more complex, for example, different groups of users being allowed to see different types of information. As an illustration, the Scramble! plug-in[26] allows users to encrypt their contents in such

---

[16] Pretty Good Privacy.

[17] Gnu Privacy Guard.

[18] These tools provide further functionalities, such as signature and authentication but we focus on confidentiality here.

[19] https://crypto.cat/#

[20] Off-the-Record Messaging.

[21] Actually, OTR provides further guarantees including deniability (a user can always deny having sent a message, just as he can deny having said something in a real-life conversation) and perfect forward secrecy (if the computer of a user is compromised or his secrets are stolen, the messages previously sent by other users remain secret).

[22] SSL (Secure Socket Layer) is the ancestor of TLS (Transport Security Layer).

[23] Virtual Private Networks.

[24] Add-ons such as HTTPS Everywhere are also available to force HTTPS versions of websites when they are available.

[25] Goldberg, Ian, "Privacy-Enhancing Technologies for the Internet III: Ten years later", Chapter 1, in Alessandro Acquisti, Stefanos Gritzalis, Costos Lambrinoudakis and Sabrina di Vimercati (eds.), *Digital Privacy: Theory, Technologies, and Practices*, Auerbach Publications, New York, December 2007.

[26] Beato, Filipe, Markulf Kohlweiss and Karel Wouters, "Scramble! Your Social Network Data", in Simone Fischer-Hübner and Nicholas Hopper (eds.), *Privacy-enhancing Technologies*, Proceedings

a way that they are visible only to a limited, pre-selected group of people or receivers. In the same spirit, Hummingbird[27] is a variant of Twitter in which content, interests and hashtags can be selectively encrypted. These solutions provide protection not only against other peers but also against the provider of the service, which does not have to be trusted to comply with the privacy policy of the user.

Concerning anonymity of communications, a wide range of techniques is available. Each of them provides different safeguards and is based on different trust assumptions. However, they all rely on the idea of introducing proxies or intermediate nodes in charge of resending the messages in such a way that it is not possible for the receiver to guess its origin (or for third parties observing the network, or operating nodes to guess the sender-receiver relationship). These techniques vary on the number of intermediate nodes (from 1 in the first generation of remailers – called type-0 – to a chain of nodes in further remailers and onion routers); on the mode of encryption (from no encryption in type-0 remailers to embedded encryptions in onion routers); on the order in which messages are forwarded (e.g., reordering messages and introducing delays to make timing correlation attacks[28] perhaps a footnote to explain briefly what is a timing correlation attack and a size correlation attack? more difficult); on message processing (e.g., dividing messages in fixed-sized packets to make size correlation attacks[29] more difficult); or on the treatment of replies.[30]

Examples of type-0 technology include Anonymizer Universal,[31] which is a proxy offering anonymisation services accessible through an encrypted channel, or search engine proxies such as Ixquick that anonymises search requests before forwarding them to popular search engines, therefore acting as a "metasearch engine".[32] This type of solution requires only one additional stakeholder, the proxy itself, which makes them easy to deploy, but the drawback is that the user must completely trust the proxy as it receives all the information and it takes all the responsibility for

of the 11th International Symposium, PETS 2011, Waterloo, ON, Canada, 27–29 July 2011, Springer, Heidelberg, 2011, pp. 211–225.

[27] De Cristofaro, Emiliano, Claudio Soriente, Gene Tsudik and Andrew Williams, "Hummingbird: Privacy at the Time of Twitter", in IEEE Symposium on Security and Privacy, San Francisco, CA, 21–23 May 2012, pp. 285–299.

[28] A time correlation attack is possible when an attacker watching the network can establish a correlation between different events, for example, the sending of a message and its receipt, based on their times of occurrence.

[29] A size correlation attack is possible when an attacker watching the network can establish a correlation between different events, for example, the sending of a message and its receipt, based on their sizes.

[30] Goldberg, op. cit.

[31] https://www.anonymizer.com/anonymizer_universal.html

[32] Ixquick was awarded the first European Privacy Seal in 2008. It offers an **anonymous proxy browsing** option in which the web pages retrieved after a search also follow the proxy route, which makes the user IP address invisible from the visited page: https://startpage.com and https://www.ixquick.com. Other privacy-preserving search engines are available, such as DuckDuckGo, which does not track users or store (or use except for the search itself) personal data: https://duckduckgo.com/ and is enjoying a growing popularity with more than 5 million queries per day in March 2014 (compared to less than 1 million in January 2012).

not using it for purposes other than forwarding the request, for anonymising the request and for deleting it afterwards.[33] Another limitation is that this type of technology[34] is subject to traffic analysis attacks: a third party observing the network can infer who is communicating with whom, which makes it possible to track the interests and behaviour of the users.

Stronger solutions exist, such as Tor,[35] which are based on the participation of a larger number of stakeholders. The key idea in Tor is to create a random path among the Tor nodes and to encrypt messages and paths in such a way that each relay in the path knows only the relay from which it received the message and the relay to which it has to forward the message. Tor can be used not only to create anonymous communication paths but also to provide anonymous publishing services (e.g., to resist censorship). Its security grows with the number of participants since the number of potential paths then grows exponentially, following the "hiding in the crowd" principle. Tor provides a strong protection allowing users to access services anonymously and without any possibility for the provider to link their sessions (unlinkability). In comparison with type-0 technology, the main advantage of this type of solution is that users do not have to trust a single node;[36] the drawbacks are a more complex infrastructure (requiring the participation of a community of peers to run relay nodes) and a penalty in terms of response time and bandwidth. Although Tor provides a strong protection at the data transport level, identifying information can still be disclosed or inferred at the application level if the user takes no additional measure. For example, the configuration of the computer of the user may be unique and transmitted by his browser,[37] or the user may reveal personal information in his requests. Nevertheless, Tor has succeeded in attracting a large community of users and its number of nodes is constantly growing. Tor is sometimes referred to as a "dark corner of the net" because it can be used for a variety of illegal activities such as selling of controlled substances, money laundering, credit card fraud, identity theft or black market.[38]

The idea of exploiting a peer-to-peer, decentralised architecture to avoid relying on a single third party has also been proposed at the application level. For example,

---

[33] https://ixquick.com/eng/company-background.html

[34] Especially type-0 technology.

[35] The Onion Router: https://www.torproject.org/. See also Syverson, Paul S., David M. Goldschlag, and Michael G. Reed, "Anonymous Connections and Onion Routing", in *Proceedings of the 18th Annual Symposium on Security and Privacy*, IEEE CS Press, May 1997, pp. 44–54. Goldschlag, David, Michael Reed and Paul Syverson, "Onion Routing for Anonymous and Private Internet Connections", *Communications of the ACM*, Vol. 42, No. 2, February 1999, pp. 39–41.

[36] More precisely, this type of system relies on a form of distributed trust: privacy can be breached only in case of collusion between a significant number of malicious nodes. For example, the anonymity of a Tor user can be broken only if all the nodes relaying his communication collude.

[37] Actually, Tor provides an additional functionality to withhold part of this information.

[38] https://en.wikipedia.org/wiki/Tor_%28anonymity_network%29#Licit_and_illicit_uses

the Safebook[39] online social network makes it possible to hide[40] the interactions as well as the friendship relationships between users, and PROPS[41] allows users to generate proofs of their locations through collaboration between neighbours without disclosing their identities.

17.2.2 *Access services*

The second type of service, which we refer to as "access services", corresponds to situations in which a user needs to prove that he is authorised to get access to a resource (e.g., a website, a benefit, information, a metro line or a building). The natural way to proceed in the physical world is to show a document (e.g., transport card, loyalty card, identity card, student card, driver licence, etc.) as a proof of the access right. However, this type of procedure generally leads to the disclosure of the user's identity, in addition to all other personal information contained in the document. In the digital world, this would greatly increase the possibilities of profiling and tracking of the activities of the users in an automated way. Standards have been published for identity management[42] and several solutions have been proposed to allow users to manage different identities and to use them to sign and log into accounts or services.[43] The architectures of these information management systems generally include, in addition to the user and the service provider, one or several identity providers.[44] The identity providers authenticate the user or certify assertions with respect to her identity and the service providers rely on these certificates to grant access to the authorised users. The privacy guarantees for the user in this type of architecture are essentially based on the trustworthiness of the identity manager. For example, collusion between the identity manager and the service provider would lead to a complete disclosure of the activities of the user to the two parties.

Other solutions have been proposed, which rely on a very different trust model. For example, Idemix[45] allows users to get anonymous credentials from an issuing

---

[39] Cutillo, Leucio Antonio, Refik Molva and Thorsten Strufe, "Safebook: a privacy preserving online social network leveraging on real-life trust", *IEEE Communications Magazine*, Vol. 47, No. 12, December 2009. The Diaspora is another example of a decentralised social network hosted by independently owned nodes (called pods); the goals of its creators are to use its distributed design to ensure that "no big corporation will ever control Diaspora" and to ensure that users keep control over their personal data. https://blog.diasporafoundation.org/

[40] With the assumption that an attacker cannot observe the whole network.

[41] http://cappris.inria.fr/wp-content/uploads/2013/04/S%C3%A9bastien-Gambs.pdf

[42] ISO/IEC DIS 24760-2, Information Technology – Security Techniques – A Framework for Identity Management – Part 2: Reference architecture and requirements.

[43] For example, Microsoft Passport, CardSpace and its successor U-Prove, the Liberty Alliance, now integrated within the Kantara Initiative.

[44] Federated Identity Management.

[45] Camenisch, Jan, and Els Van Herreweghen, "Design and Implementation of the Idemix Anonymous Credential System", *Proceedings of the 9th ACM Conference on Computer and Communications Security*, CCS '02, 2002, pp. 21–30.

organisation and to use them to prove their rights to the service provider. The anonymous credential, which contains attributes representing the rights of the user, is issued on a pseudonym under which the user is registered with the issuing organisation. When using the credential to exercise his rights, the user can decide which attributes are revealed to the service provider. In practice, the user does not reveal the credential itself but a probabilistic proof of knowledge[46] of this credential and the associated secret key, thus ensuring the unlinkability of the different uses of the credential. This solution guarantees that the user can remain anonymous towards the service provider, on the proviso that their communication channel supports anonymity (using one of the techniques described in the previous subsection). Idemix makes it also possible to manage the de-anonymisation of credentials to enforce accountability (e.g., to detect misuse of credentials) through the introduction of third parties called "de-anonymisation organisations".[47]

When the design of the system is such that they can be used only once, anonymous credentials can also form the basis of anonymous e-cash solutions. Even though techniques to implement these systems have been available for several decades, they have not been used significantly to our best knowledge,[48] possibly partly due to the fact they have often been associated with illegal activities and online criminal behaviour.[49]

In the same spirit as Idemix, a technique for privacy-preserving national identity cards[50] has been proposed to allow users to prove assertions about themselves (nationality, age, etc.) without disclosing their identity or any other information. This solution also fulfils the unlinkability property, in the sense that it is not possible to link two actions of the user, as well as non-transferability: because the use of the card is controlled by biometrics, only the legitimate user can use it to prove an assertion. However, biometrics itself raises new challenges in terms of privacy, in

[46] The technique used in Idemix is called "zero knowledge proof" because it does not reveal any other information than the veracity of a proof (see Sect. 17.2.3). In addition, a probabilistic algorithm is used to produce the proofs, which is essential to ensure unlinkability (because a new proof is produced for each use).

[47] Actually, true accountability can be guaranteed only if the true identity of the user was authenticated upon registering his pseudonym.

[48] Bitcoin has attracted much attention though, and some initiatives have been taken recently, for example, Expedia's accepting Bitcoin payments for hotel bookings (http://www.bbc.com/news/technology-27810008) or the Monoprix e-commerce branch's announcing its decision to accept Bitcoins before 2015. http://www.latribune.fr/entreprises-finance/services/distribution/20140409trib000824457/pourquoi-monoprix-a-decide-d-accepter-les-bitcoins.html. It should be noted also that the anonymity provided by Bitcoin has been challenged recently: see Meiklejohn, Sarah, Marjori Pomarole, Grant Jordan, Kirill Levchenko, Damon McCoy, Geoffrey M. Voelker and Stefan Savage, "A Fistful of Bitcoins: Characterizing Payments Among Men with No Names",*;login:* The USENIX magazine, Vol. 38, No. 6, December 2013.

[49] https://en.wikipedia.org/wiki/Bitcoin#Criminal_activity

[50] Deswarte, Yves, and Sébastien Gambs, "A proposal for a privacy-preserving national identity card", *Transactions on Data Privacy*, Vol. 3, Issue 3, December 2010, pp. 253–276.

particular, because of the lack of revocability[51] of biometric traits, which may lead to serious risks of identity theft. Techniques have been proposed to address this issue such as "cancellable biometrics"[52] that applies a hard-to-reverse transformation to the original biometric signal so that if one variant of the transformed biometric data is compromised, then a new variant can be created (and the compromised version revoked).

17.2.3 Computation services

The third situation is when the user of the system needs to get a service from a third party and this service requires computations that, by assumption, must involve data possessed by each party. Two main categories of computations can be distinguished depending on the level of accuracy required by the service: the computations may need to be absolutely accurate (for example, the computation of the fee in smart metering or electronic traffic pricing systems), or it may be approximated (for example, the discovery of nearby restaurants in location-based services or network load monitoring for energy suppliers). In the second case, it is often necessary to find a balance between the accuracy of the information disclosed by the user and the value of the service (which is often called the *utility* of the computation).

The main objective of the user in terms of privacy is to ensure that the computation can be done without disclosing any unnecessary information to the service provider. Considering that the computation requires inputs from the service provider and from the user, one option in theory could be to gather all the necessary information on the side of the user so that the computation can be done locally and no personal information is ever disclosed to the service provider (except the result of the computation, for example, the fee in the case of smart metering systems). However, this solution is generally not a real option for a variety of reasons. First, the amount of information that the user would have to collect might be too large (e.g., a database of location information). In addition, the service provider may want to protect the confidentiality of his own information (both the data and the algorithms may represent valuable intellectual property that he wants to hide from his competitors). Even in situations in which it can be considered, this "localisation strategy" is not necessarily easy to implement because the service provider may need strong guarantees that the computation is done correctly. The payment of the fee in a smart metering system is a good illustration of this situation: the algorithm to compute the fee is not secret, so this computation could be done locally, but the electricity provider needs strong guarantees that the user cannot cheat on his fee.

---

[51] Just to take two examples, the fingerprints and the iris are attributes that are, by definition, unique (or almost) to a person and cannot be replaced if they are "stolen" by an impostor.

[52] Ratha, N.K., J.H. Connell and R.M. Bolle, "Enhancing security and privacy in biometrics based authentication systems", *IBM Systems Journal*, Vol. 40, No. 3, 2001, pp. 614–634.

Therefore, in this type of situation, the integrity of the result is a fundamental security requirement that needs to be achieved at the same time as privacy.

General cryptographic techniques have been proposed that make it possible to compute a result without observing the inputs of the computation. For example, *homomorphic encryption* is a type of encryption allowing the receiver of encrypted values (e.g., daily electricity fees) to compute an operation on these encrypted values (e.g., adding the daily fees) without having to decrypt them (hence without observing the daily fees). Even if homomorphic encryption can in theory be applied to any kind of computation,[53] the state-of-the-art schemes[54] are restricted to specific operations (either addition or multiplication).

Commitments are often used in this type of architecture. A commitment can be seen as a locked box containing a value. Commitments provide two key guarantees,[55] (1) a commitment about a value is such that it cannot be opened by the receiver without the help of the sender and (2) it binds the sender (it is not feasible for the sender to later open the commitment to another input value). Commitments can also be homomorphic, allowing the receiver to make calculations on the commitment without having access to the value itself.

Another useful technique in this category is *zero-knowledge proof*[56] (ZKP): in a zero-knowledge-proof-based system, a verifier can check that a property holds (e.g., that the fee has been computed using the correct algorithm and authentic input consumption values) without learning anything else other than this fact (e.g., without learning the input consumption values).

In the same spirit, but in a distributed fashion, *secure multiparty computation*[57] protocols allow several parties to perform a computation on their individual values without having to disclose them to the other parties. For example, two parties can apply a secure multiparty computation protocol to learn which of them earns the highest salary while keeping their own salary secret. Similarly, *private set intersection protocols*[58] allow different parties to find the common items between their individual sets (e.g., sets of preferences or sets of friends) without revealing these sets to the other parties.

[53] Gentry, Craig, "Full Homomorphic Encryption using ideal lattices", in the 41st ACM Symposium on Theory of Computing (STOC), 2009. https://www.cs.cmu.edu/~odonnell/hits09/gentry-homomorphic-encryption.pdf

[54] Paillier, Pascal, "Public-Key Cryptosystems Based on Composite Degree Residuosity Classes", EUROCRYPT, Springer, 1999, pp. 223–238.

[55] Often called the *hiding* and *binding* properties.

[56] Quisquater, Jean-Jacques, Louis C. Guillou and Thomas A. Berson, "How to explain Zero-Knowledge protocols to your children", in *Proceedings on Advances in Cryptology – CRYPTO '89*, Springer-Verlag New York, 1989, pp. 628–631. Goldwasser, Shafi, Silvio Micali and Charles Rackoff, "The knowledge complexity of interactive proof-systems", in Robert Sedgewick (ed.), *Proceedings of 17th Symposium on the Theory of Computation*, Providence, RI, ACM, 1985.

[57] Chi-Chih Yao, Andrew, "Protocols for Secure Computations", Extended Abstract, FOCS 1982, pp. 160–164.

[58] De Cristofaro, Emiliano, and Gene Tsudik, "Practical private set intersection protocols with linear complexity", in *Financial Cryptography*, Springer-Verlag, Berlin, 2010, pp. 143–159.

When the computation of the service does not necessarily require accurate information, techniques modifying the input or output can be used, such as perturbation or obfuscation (deliberately introducing errors to input data or generating fake data), noisy aggregation (aggregating data with error), or approximation (e.g., providing location data at the level of a neighbourhood rather than exact geographical co-ordinates).

In practice, specific privacy-preserving solutions (often integrating several of the above techniques) have been proposed for different types of services. For example, a variety of technologies are available to protect privacy in smart grids.[59] One option for the computation of the fee is to have it done locally (on the user's computer) with a zero-knowledge proof of its correctness. Individual (e.g., daily) fees can be summed up by the operator using a homomorphic scheme. In addition to the fees, the electricity provider receives measurement commitments signed by the smart meter, which are used to check the correctness of the fee without gaining any information on the measurements themselves. In this model, both the user and the operator are assumed to trust the smart meter (which must be a secure component) but they do not need to trust each other. Another solution involves the split of the electricity measurements into shares that are encrypted and distributed (through a data concentrator) to a set of peers (i.e., neighbours).[60] The shares are summed up by the neighbours and by the concentrator using homomorphic encryption. Provided that the neighbourhood is sufficiently large, this protocol makes it possible to detect electricity leakages without disclosing individual measurement values to the concentrator (even if it is malicious). When the result of the computation does not need to be absolutely accurate (e.g., to compute the average load of the system), random noise on the measurement values can be introduced in a careful way, so as to ensure both a high level of protection for the user[61] and an acceptable level of precision for the result of the computation (utility).

As far as privacy is concerned, electronic toll pricing (ETP) and more generally "pay as you drive" systems bear some similarities with payments in smart metering systems and the same kind of technologies can often be applied.[62] One difference is

---

[59] Jawurek, Marek, Florian Kerschbaum and George Danezis, "Privacy Technologies for Smart Grids – A Survey of Options", Microsoft Technical Report, MSR-TR-2012-119, 2012. Rial, Alfredo, and George Danezis, "Privacy-Preserving Smart Metering", *Proceedings of the 2011 ACM Workshop on Privacy in the Electronic Society*, WPES, 2011. Acs, Gergely, and Claude Castelluccia, "I Have a DREAM!: Differentially Private Smart Metering", *Proceedings of the 13th International Conference on Information Hiding*, Springer Verlag, 2011, pp. 118–132.

[60] Garcia, Flavio D., and Bart Jacobs, "Privacy-Friendly Energy-Metering via Homomorphic Encryption", in Jorge Cuellar, Javier Lopez, Gilles Barthe and Alexander Pretschner (eds.), *Security and Trust Management* (STM'2010), Springer, 2011, pp. 226–238.

[61] This level of protection is often measured in terms of differential privacy, a formal privacy metric providing a characterisation of privacy in terms of the knowledge gained by a powerful adversary (possessing all possible auxiliary information).

[62] Josep Balasch, Alfredo Rial, Carmela Troncoso, Christophe Geuens, Bart Preneel and Ingrid Verbauwhede, "PrETP: Privacy-Preserving Electronic Toll Pricing", 19th USENIX Security Symposium, USENIX Association, 2010, pp. 63–78. Troncoso, Carmela, George Danezis, Eleni Kosta and Bart Preneel, "PriPAYD: Privacy Friendly Pay-As You-Drive Insurance", *Proceedings*

that the trust in the input values, which are typically provided by the GPS of the car, is more limited and the on-board equipment is not necessarily considered trusted. As a remedy, these solutions often include *spot checks* that can be conducted by the pricing authority to detect potential misbehaviours of the drivers (e.g., drivers tampering with their GPS device or turning it off). A technique used in several proposals consists in having the on-board equipment (1) sending commitments on the location data to the server of the pricing authority; (2) performing the computation of the fee; and (3) sending this fee to the operator at the end of each period. The authority can initiate a verification protocol after each spot check. If homomorphic encryption is used, the authority can check the consistency between individual fees and their sums. Otherwise, partial sums of the fees have to be disclosed to allow the authority to check that the observed position has been correctly taken into account in the computation of the global fee. In contrast with the previous options, this type of architecture relies on a form of "verified trust" (or "limited trust") in the sense that the trust placed by the pricing authority in the on-board equipment of the vehicle is confirmed by a posteriori verifications.

Other types of solutions have been proposed for other types of services such as the request of an item from a database without the database owner knowing which item is retrieved (private information retrieval or PIR[63]) or online behavioural advertising. Online behavioural advertising is a challenging application because the information flows between the stakeholders are complex and the service is by definition based on very private information, namely, the online behaviour of the user. Nevertheless, several solutions have been proposed, based on the "localisation strategy": the profile of the user is built locally and is never disclosed to the ad broker. Some solutions, like Privad,[64] rely on the existence of a trusted third party in charge of anonymising the ad requests sent by the user (based on his local profile) to the broker. Adnostic[65] is based on a different protocol: the broker serves a set of ads (rather than just one) and the browser uses the local profile to select one of these ads. Adnostic relies on homomorphic encryption and zero knowledge proofs to allow brokers to compute the accounts of the publishers without knowing the individual actions of the users. However, Adnostic does not attempt to protect ad clicks, which remain visible to the broker. In contrast to Privad and Adnostic, the ObliviAd[66]

of the 6th ACM workshop on Privacy in the electronic society (WPES), 2007. de Jonge, Wiebren, and Bart Jacobs, "Privacy-friendly electronic traffic pricing via commits", in P. Degano, J. Guttman and F. Martinelli (eds.), *Formal Aspects in Security and Trust*, Springer, 2009, pp. 143–161.

[63] Chor, Benny, Eyal Kushilevitz, Oded Goldreich and Madhu Sudan, "Private Information Retrieval", *Journal of the ACM*, Vol. 45, No. 6, 1998, pp. 965–981.

[64] Guha, Saikat, Bin Cheng and Paul Francis, "Privad: Practical Privacy in Online Advertising", USENIX Symposium on Networked Systems Design and Implementation, NSDI 2011.

[65] Toubiana, Vincent, Arvind Narayanan, Dan Boneh, Helen Nissenbaum and Solon Barocas, "Adnostic: Privacy Preserving Targeted Advertising", Network and Distributed System Security Symposium 2010.

[66] Backes, Michael, Aniket Kate, Matteo Maffei and Kim Pecina, "*ObliviAd: Provably Secure and Practical Online Behavioral Advertising*", in *Proceedings of 33rd IEEE Symposium on Security and Privacy (S&P 2012)*, 2012, pp. 257–271.

protocol does not make any trust assumption about third parties. ObliviAd is based on the implementation of private information retrieval on a secure hardware-based component. The profile of the user is sent in encrypted form to the secure component on the broker side. The most suitable ad is then selected by the component and returned encrypted to the user without the broker learning any information about the chosen ad. These three solutions provide a good illustration of the range of techniques available to enforce privacy and the importance of the underlying trust assumptions: from an entirely technical solution in ObliviAd (no trust in any third party but trust in the technology, including a secure co-processor) to a trusted third party in Privad and a more limited protection in Adnostic.

An example of application of obfuscation is TrackMeNot,[67] a plug-in that can be added to a search engine to generate fake queries and therefore obfuscate (to some extent) the profile of the user to defeat profiling algorithms. Obfuscation, perturbation, approximation and aggregation are also typically used for location privacy,[68] for example, by degrading the quality of location data or delivering location data at the level of regions. Regions must be defined in such a way that a sufficient number of persons are located in the same region ("spatial cloaking") and it is therefore more difficult to track an individual. The challenge in this context is to find an acceptable trade-off between the privacy guarantees and the utility of the location data with respect to the expected service. This trade-off can be settled by design and measured using privacy metrics[69] or chosen by the user based on their own preferences. Another key issue is the semantics associated with location data. For example, the fact that a given position is close to a hospital or a religious building makes the data more sensitive than a position in the middle of a forest. Some algorithms take these semantics into account to choose the appropriate regions.[70] Other strategies can also be applied to protect location privacy such as anonymity or pseudonymity. A refinement of this idea is to ensure that the pseudonym of a subject is automatically modified when the subject leaves his current region ("mix zone") in order to make it more difficult to trace his successive locations.[71]

Some solutions for location privacy (and other types of services) also rely on a partitioning strategy (sometimes called "separation of trust") consisting in splitting the personal data and disclosing different pieces of information to different actors to ensure that none of them – assuming that they do not collude – will be able to make

---

67 Howe, Daniel C., and Helen Nissenbaum, "TrackMeNot: resisting surveillance in web search", in Ian Kerr, Carole Lucock and Valerie Steeves (eds.), *Lessons from Identity Trail: Privacy, Anonymity and Identity in a Networked Society*, Oxford University Press, Oxford, 2008.

68 Krumm, John, "A survey of computational location privacy", *Personal Ubiquitous Computing*, Vol. 13, 2009, pp. 391–399. Gambs, Sébastien, Marc-Olivier Killijian and Miguel Núñez del Prado Cortez, "GEPETO: A GEoPrivacy-Enhancing TOolkit", AINA Workshops, 2010, pp. 1071–1076.

69 See Sect. 17.2.4.

70 Damiani, Maria Luisa, Elisa Bertino and Claudio Silvestri, "The PROBE framework for the personalized cloaking of private locations", *Transactions on Data Privacy*, Vol. 3, No. 2, 2010, pp. 123–148.

71 Beresford, Alastair R., and F. Stajano, "Location privacy in pervasive computing", *IEEE Pervasive Computing*, Vol. 3, No. 1, 2003, pp. 46–55.

undesired associations.[72] For example, a location-based service provider could see the pseudonym and some transaction information while the mobile operator would know the location data as well as the billing address (but no transaction data). In some cases, third parties (intermediaries or dedicated middleware) are introduced to avoid the communication of personal information to certain actors. Needless to say, the trust model of this type of solution has to be considered carefully since the expected guarantees could be undermined by misplaced trust assumptions (in particular, in the case of collusion between different stakeholders). These solutions can also be associated with the techniques described previously to limit the trust assumptions (e.g., using pseudonyms and obfuscation to prevent information leaks while ensuring the consistency of transactions).

Generally speaking, a sound strategy for the enforcement of data minimisation is to ensure that computations take place as much as possible on the device of the data subject. As mentioned before, it is often the case that this option cannot be pursued in its entirety but the idea of allowing subjects to keep physical control over their personal data using "personal data stores" or "secure personal data servers"[73] has been explored by different research groups in different contexts. It has even been deployed for certain types of services, in particular, in the health sector. Because both the patient and health professionals need to get access to some types of data, a solution consists in combining a central server and secure personal tokens. Personal tokens, which can take the form of USB keys, embed a database system, a local web server and a certificate for their authentication by the central server.[74] Patients can decide on the status of their data and, depending on their level of sensitivity, choose to record them exclusively on their personal token or to have them replicated on the central server. Replication on the central server is useful to enhance sustainability and to allow designated professionals to get access to the data. Health professionals are also equipped with secure tokens and can access the personal data of the patients only with the cryptographic key installed on their tokens.

Other initiatives such as Mydex[75] have been launched to help individuals store and access their personal information on their personal device and enable them to decide "what information they wish to share, with who and for what purpose".[76] The long-term objective of Mydex is to "to offer a radical and practical way of improving

---

[72] See, for example, Kosta, Eleni, Jan Zubuschka, Tobias Scherner and Jos Dumortier, "Legal considerations on privacy-enhancing location based services using PRIME technology", *Computer Law and Security Report*, Vol. 24, Issue 2, 2008, pp. 139–146.

[73] Allard, Tristan, Nicolas Anciaux, Luc Bouganim, Yanli Guo, Lionel Le Folgoc, Benjamin Nguyen, Philippe Pucheral, Indrajit Ray, Indrakshi Ray and Shaoyi Yin, "Secure Personal Data Servers: a Vision Paper", in Elisa Bertino, Paolo Atzeni, Kian Lee Tan, Yi Chen and Y.C. Tay (eds.), *Proceedings of the 36th International Conference on Very Large Data Bases (VLDB)*, Vol. 1, No. 1, 2010, pp. 25–35.

[74] Anciaux, N., M. Benzine, L. Bouganim, K. Jacquemin, P. Pucheral and S. Yin, "Restoring the Patient Control over her Medical History", 21th IEEE International Symposium on Computer-Based Medical Systems (IEEE CBMS), Finland, June 2008.

[75] http://data.gov.uk/library/mydex

[76] The case for personal information empowerment: the rise of the personal data store, Mydex.

relationships with individual customers, cleaning up data and opening up a whole range of new services, based on consumer preference and intent". One may argue that this kind of approach, although well intended, is based on an essentially economic view of privacy and it might lead, considering the imbalance of powers between the parties, to a sell-off of personal data and ultimately to the ruin of privacy. This debate is related to the notion of *privacy as control* discussed in Sect. 17.3.

17.2.4 Exploiting databases

With the advent of "big data" and the development of the "open data" movement in many countries, ever larger amounts of data are available and will be published or made available in the future. Even if not all of these data are personal, various stakeholders already collect huge amounts of personal data, and the exploitation of these data for a variety of purposes (including knowledge-based decision-making, forecasting, identification of trends, medical research, fight against terrorism, intelligence, etc.) becomes a priority for many companies and governments. Even more important, they could also greatly contribute to social well-being and the public good. For example, the exploitation of health data can contribute to expanding knowledge about diseases, identifying appropriate treatments and supporting public health policies.

In contrast with the types of services discussed in the previous sections, in this context, the subject is usually not the user of the service but rather the "provider" of the information collected to populate the databases. Because the exploitation of the database for knowledge mining is generally not the primary purpose of the personal data collection[77] and the users are not necessarily the declared data controllers, the data has to be anonymised. The fast developing research domain called *privacy-preserving data publishing* (PPDP) aims at providing ways to allow *data publishers* to collect personal data from *data subjects* and to release data to *data recipients* (e.g., the public or a specific data miner). Two kinds of trust models can be considered depending on the trustworthiness of the data publisher.[78] If the data publisher is not trusted, then the communication of the initial data from the subject to the data publisher has to be protected and minimised using one of the techniques presented in the previous subsections. In all cases, the data recipient is not trusted and we assume that he may want to extract the maximum amount of information from the data. The challenge is therefore to provide techniques allowing the data publisher to publish data in such a way that he does not breach the privacy of the data subjects yet still retains sufficient utility for the data recipients. As several famous cases have

---

[77] For example, the primary purpose can be the clinical monitoring of patients or payment and the secondary purpose medical research or extraction of buying patterns.

[78] Fung, Benjamin C.M., Ke Wang, Rui Chen and Philip S. Yu, "Privacy-preserving data publishing: A survey of recent developments", *ACM Computing Surveys*, Vol. 42, No. 4, June 2010.

shown,[79] it is not sufficient to remove explicit identifiers such as the names or social security numbers of the subjects because the combination of attributes such as zip code, date of birth and gender can often single out a unique individual.[80] Most works in this area consider four disjointed sets of data record attributes:

1. Explicit identifiers (e.g., name, social security number, IP address, etc.);
2. Quasi-identifiers (e.g., zip code, date of birth, gender) that could potentially single out a subject;
3. Sensitive attributes (e.g., disease, salary, religion, etc.);
4. Non-sensitive attributes that cover all other attributes.

The borderline between these categories is not clear-cut though, and the classification of an attribute is not necessarily an easy task. For example, a quasi-identifier (or a set of quasi-identifiers) can sometimes be used to derive a sensitive attribute (through a "linkability attack") and sensitive or non-sensitive attributes can sometimes be combined to build quasi-identifiers.

The main techniques used to anonymise data records are the following[81]:

- Deletion: the values of specific attributes or entire records are removed from the database.
- Generalisation: some attributes (typically quasi-identifiers) are replaced by a more general value following a pre-defined classification. For example, a date of birth can be generalised into the year of birth, zip codes into region or country codes, etc.
- Noising: a random value (noise) is added to a sensitive attribute to hide the true value (e.g., age or salary). The noise is drawn from a distribution, so that the statistical information that can be computed from the noisy data is not significantly affected.
- Swapping: sensitive attributes of different records are swapped in such a way that statistical information remains as accurate as possible.
- Synthetic data generation: a statistical model of the data is built and used to sample new points that are published in the database instead of the original records.
- Anatomization: the database is released in two parts, a table containing the quasi-identifiers and a table containing sensitive attributes. The two tables are linked by a common attribute, a group identifier, which makes it possible to retain useful information while reducing the possibilities to link a record to a sensitive value (assuming that group identifiers are well chosen).

---

[79] One famous case was the re-identification of the former governor of the state of Massachusetts in a published medical database, through a link with a public voter list.

[80] Eighty-seven per cent of the American population have a unique combination of zip code, date of birth and gender, according to Sweeney, Latanya, "*Re-identification of De-identified Survey Data*", Carnegie Mellon University, School of Computer Science, Data Privacy Laboratory, Technical Report, 2000.

[81] Fung, Benjamin C.M., Ke Wang, Ada Wai-Chee (Fu and Philip S. Yu, *Introduction to Privacy-Preserving Data Publishing: Concepts and Techniques*, Chapman & Hall/CRC, August 2010.

These techniques can be used individually or in combination, depending on the objectives in terms of utility and privacy. For example, deletion, generalisation and anatomisation do not impair the accuracy of the records whereas noising and swapping produce values that do not correspond to any raw record, which can be a drawback in certain situations.[82]

As far as privacy is concerned, a wide range of metrics has been proposed to assess the level of protection ensured by a given algorithm. For example, *k*-anonymity[83] ensures that the record of a user (with regard to his quasi-identifiers) is indistinguishable from the records of at least *k*-1 other user. For example, a medical database meets the 6-anonymity requirement with respect to attributes "zip code" and "gender" if, for any combination of values of these two attributes (for example, "92340" and "male"), there are at least six entries in the database for these attributes. *l*-diversity[84] addresses a weakness of *k*-diversity by requiring that at least *l* values of sensitive attributes appear for every quasi-identifier. Continuing the previous example, if "illness" is considered as a sensitive attribute, then 3-diversity requires that at least three different values of the attribute "illness" occur for records with zip code equal to "92340" and gender equal to "male".[85] The entropy is a measure of the uncertainty of a stakeholder about the value of the data; differential privacy[86] provides strong guarantees: it ensures that the presence of the record of an individual in a database does not affect significantly the output of a query on this database. Therefore, the result of the query does not bring significant additional knowledge about the data subject to a malicious user (disregarding the auxiliary knowledge available to this malicious user).

Whatever the algorithms used, it should be clear that one cannot hope for absolute privacy guarantees. Indeed, given the huge (and always increasing) amount of publicly available data and the power of data mining technologies, linking attacks can never be completely ruled out. In other words, anonymisation techniques can considerably reduce the risks (generally at the price of a loss of utility), and they must be applied before any release of a database built from personal data, but they should not be considered as a silver bullet and should always be integrated within a carefully planned risk assessment and risk management process.

---

[82] Because they may lead to inconsistent databases or break interesting relations between attributes.

[83] Sweeney, Latanya, "k-anonymity: A model for protecting privacy", *International Journal of Uncertainty, Fuzziness and Knowledge-Based Systems*, Vol. 10, No. 5, 2002, pp. 557–570.

[84] Machanavajjhala, Ashwin, Daniel Kifer, Johannes Gehrke and Muthuramakrishnan Venkitasubramaniam, "l-diversity: Privacy beyond k- anonymity", *ACM Transactions on Knowledge Discovery from Data (TKDD)*, Vol. 1, No. 1, March 2007.

[85] If *l*-diversity were not met and, for example, all records with zip code equal to "92340" and gender equal to "male" were such that the associated illness is "cancer", then it would be possible to infer that someone with these quasi-identifiers has cancer, even if *k*-anonymity were met for a given *k*.

[86] Dwork, Cynthia, "Differential privacy", in ICALP (2), 2006, pp. 1–12. Dwork, Cynthia, "A firm foundation for private data analysis", *Communications of the ACM*, Vol. 54, No. 1, 2011, pp. 86–95.

The above techniques can be used by the publisher to anonymise a database before disclosure to the data recipients. Other types of scenarios can be considered, such as the "interactive query model" in which the database is not released directly but the queries are processed interactively so as to meet privacy requirements. Typically, queries can be modified, restricted or even denied depending on the query results already received by the user and the privacy objective (e.g., probability of inferring a sensitive attribute). The problem is complex though and the type of answer (e.g., denial) can in itself leak sensitive information. Another approach, referred to as *privacy preserving data mining* (PPDM),[87] involves techniques which are, to a great extent, similar to those described in this section, but they are targeted at specific data mining algorithms.

17.3 Enforcing the rights of the subject on personal data

In the previous section, we presented techniques that can be used to reduce the disclosure of personal data. However, there are also situations in which data subjects have to disclose some personal data (e.g., to make a purchase) or want to expose personal information (e.g., on a social network site), and they should still be in a position to exercise their rights with regard to these data. In this section, we show how technologies can also contribute to enforcing these rights. We distinguish four types of services provided by these technologies, which cover different aspects of the rights of the subject or obligations of the data controller:

- Decision support: this category includes the techniques and tools that enhance the level of information and understanding of the subject and help her to take really "well informed" decisions about his or her personal data.
- Consent: when she has taken her decision, the subject should be able to express it, which means in particular to provide her informed consent in a precise and specific way. Considering the complexity of the situation (variety of third parties, of potential actions, contexts, etc.), it is of prime importance to have appropriate tools available to help the subject in this task.
- Enforcement: when the subject has expressed her choices, the next stage is to provide ways to ensure that they are respected. Technologies are also available to enforce these rights either locally or on the side of the data controller.
- Accountability: accountability is another obligation of the data controller, which is reinforced in the European General Data Protection Regulation. Accountability is a cross-cutting and complementary measure that can also be supported by appropriate tools.

[87] Verykios, Vassilios S., Elisa Bertino, Igor Nai Fovino, Loredana Parasiliti Provenza, Yucel Saygin and Yannis Theodoridis, "State-of-the-art in Privacy Preserving Data Mining", in *SIGMOD Record*, Vol. 33, No. 1, March 2004, pp. 50–57.

17.3.1 Decision support

The exercise of the rights of the subject generally requires deliberate action by the subject, which means not only that the system should make this action possible but also that it should provide sufficient information to the subject to ensure that she can properly understand the situation and take well-informed decisions. As an illustration, consent is defined in the General Data Protection Regulation as "any freely given, specific, informed and unambiguous indication of his or her wishes by which the data subject, either by a statement or by a clear affirmative action, signifies agreement to personal data relating to them being processed".[88] However, one must admit that obtaining this information as well as understanding all the consequences of a decision is becoming more and more challenging for various reasons. First, a wealth of personal information is disclosed piece by piece to a variety of stakeholders, sometimes directly, sometimes indirectly and under conditions (privacy policies) that are far from clear,[89] sometimes even without the subject's being aware of it.[90] To make things worse, some of these stakeholders are unknown to the subject[91] and they may also share their information with other third parties (of whom the subject is completely unaware). Moreover, the fact that data is collected is not the only useful information for the subject; she should also be aware of the processing logic and the consequences for her (both of the data processing if she provides her consent and of her refusal if she does not provide her consent). Assessing the consequences is particularly challenging with respect to profiling, which can have long-term effects on different aspects of the life of the subject (refusal of a credit, exclusion from a job selection procedure, refusal of a visa, etc.).

As a result, it is difficult to get a clear picture of the situation before taking a decision, and a first type of technology that provides valuable support to the subject are the "transparency-enhancing technologies" (TETs).[92] The simplest type of TET are the "privacy icons", which are visual signs showing the main features of the privacy policy of a website (data collected, purpose, deletion delay, etc.). The next step is to allow users to parameterize their privacy policy in such a way that their browser can automatically check that the policy declared by a site meets their own

---

[88] Regulation of the European Parliament and of the Council on the protection of individuals with regard to the processing of personal data and on the free movement of such data (General Data Protection Regulation), voted by the European Parliament on 12 March 2014.

[89] In addition, they are rarely read by the subject because they often are in the form of long and tedious legal documents that she has neither the time nor the legal background or competence to read.

[90] For example, when she leaves traces of her activities on servers or when third parties use cookies to track her on her own device, or when mobile phone applications plunder her address book or collect her location and forward this information to advertising brokers.

[91] Typically, they can be designated in a generic or deliberately vague way in the privacy policy of the data controller ("our partners", "publishers", "advertisers", "trusted businesses").

[92] Hildebrandt Mireille, and Bert-Jaap Koops, "The Challenges of Ambient Law and Legal Protection in the Profiling Era", *The Modern Law Review*, Vol. 73, Issue 3, May 2010, pp. 428–460.

policy and to inform them (e.g., through specific icons) of the result of the verification.[93]

As far as data collection is concerned, some websites provide a dashboard functionality informing users about the personal data stored[94] and the third parties that can get access to it. However, this kind of site must have carefully designed interfaces to ensure that they do not mislead users.[95] For example, the European PrimeLife project has proposed a Firefox extension called Privacy Dashboard that allows users to know some of the practices of the websites they are using, whether they use cookies, geolocation, third party content or other tracking means. An icon displays a more or less happy face depending on the overall evaluation of the website.[96]

Specific solutions have also been proposed to improve the privacy interfaces of social networks, for example, to reduce unnoticed over-sharing of information, to make it easier to find out to whom a particular attribute is visible[97] or to help users avoid making posts that they may later regret.[98]

As mentioned above, personal data can also be gathered without the subject's being aware of it and by parties of whom she has never heard. This happens typically through cookies created on her computer while she is browsing. Cookies are then used by a variety of companies to track her activities and ultimately to serve her personalised advertisements based on her browsing profile. Users can get a picture of the tracking going on behind their back by using a tool such as Lightbeam[99] (formerly Collusion). Lightbeam is a Firefox add-on recording the events associated with the visited sites and allowing users to display a graph showing the tracking sites and their interactions.

Several tools have also been proposed for smartphones, which represent another major source of leaked personal data. For example, TaintDroid[100] is an extension of the Android operating system tracking the flow of personal information through

[93] Privacy Bird is an example of a browser add-on (for Internet Explorer) that provides this facility.

[94] Google Dashboard includes this feature but it shows only a subset of the collected data, which may actually be misleading for the users.

[95] For example, Scott Lederer et al. identify five pitfalls for designers (obscuring potential information flow, obscuring actual information flow, emphasising configuration over action, lacking coarse-grained control and inhibiting existing practice) and they show how existing systems either fall into these pitfalls or avoid them.

[96] http://primelife.ercim.eu/ (the dashboard does not seem to be maintained any longer).

[97] Paul, Thomas, Daniel Puscher and Thorsten Strufe, "Improving the Usability of Privacy Settings in Facebook", CoRR abs/1109.6046, 2011.

[98] Wang, Yang, Saranga Komanduri, Pedro Leon, Gregory Norcie, Alessandro Acquisti and Lorrie Faith Cranor, "'I regretted the minute I pressed share', A Qualitative Study of Regrets on Facebook", *Proceedings of the Seventh Symposium on Usable Privacy and Security (SOUPS)*, ACM, July 2011.

[99] http://www.mozilla.org/en-US/lightbeam/

[100] Enck, William, Peter Gilbert, Byung-Gon Chun, Landon P. Cox, Jaeyeon Jung, Patrick McDaniel and Anmol N. Sheth, "TaintDroid: An Information-flow Tracking System for Realtime Privacy Monitoring on Smartphones", *Proceedings of the 9th USENIX Conference on Operating Systems Design and Implementation, OSDI'10*, 2010, pp. 1–6.

third-party applications, which can be used to identify misbehaving applications. In the same vein, the Mobilitics[101] project monitors personal data sent to third parties and provides a visualisation tool displaying all personal data stored or sent by the applications, taking also into account potential data aggregations.

Panopticlick[102] provides yet another type of information. Panopticlick tests Internet browsers and shows how unique they are, based on the information shared with the visited sites such as operating system version, browser version, plug-in details, system fonts and language. Panopticlick is an excellent example of a tool enhancing privacy awareness by showing how easily identifiable Internet users may be when they surf the web.[103]

Regardless of the actual level of information that they can obtain, one could argue that individuals are always in a weak position when they have to take decisions about the disclosure of their personal data because they generally do not have the necessary expertise to fully understand all legal and technical aspects of the situation. In addition to a lack of expertise, considering the number of sites they visit every day, they just do not have enough time to devote to this task. As an illustration, a 2012 study has shown that it would take the average Internet user more than 200 h, so more than one working month, to actually read the privacy policies of the websites they visit in a year. One solution to redress this imbalance is to take a more collective approach, for example, by developing a form of collaboration between individuals to help them analyse privacy policies and warn their peers about unacceptable terms. ToS;DR[104] (Terms of Service; Didn't Read), TOSBack[105] and Privacy Critics[106] are examples of efforts in this direction. The goal of ToS;DR is to create a database of analyses of the fairness of privacy policies and to make this information available in the form of explicit icons (general evaluation plus good and bad points), which can be expanded into more detailed explanations. Users can also install a browser add-on to get the ratings directly upon visiting a page. A key aspect of ToS;DR is that users can submit their own analysis for consideration, the goal being that, just like Wikipedia, a group consensus will emerge to provide a reliable assessment of each policy. In the same spirit, TOSBack is a collaboration effort between the Electronic Frontier Foundation (EFF), the Internet Society and ToS;DR, which presents itself as a "terms of service tracker". Contributors check websites' terms and policies to see if any of them has changed and provide a detailed account of the evolution. For its part, Privacy Critics is an architecture to integrate "privacy

[101] Achara, Jagdish Prasad, Franck Baudot, Claude Castelluccia, Geoffrey Delcroix and Vincent Roca, "Mobilitics: analyzing privacy leaks in smart phones", *ERCIM News*, 93, April 2013.

[102] https://panopticlick.eff.org/

[103] Eckersley, Peter, "How Unique Is Your Web Browser?", in Mikhail J. Atallah and Nicholas J. Hopper (eds.), *Privacy-enhancing Technologies*, Springer, 2010, pp. 1–18.

[104] http://tosdr.org/

[105] https://tosback.org/

[106] Ackerman, Mark S., and Lorrie Cranor, "Privacy Critics: UI Components to Safeguard Users' Privacy", CHI '99 Extended Abstracts on Human Factors in Computing Systems, CHI EA' 99, ACM, 1999, pp. 258–259.

critics", which are intelligent agents watching the user's actions and making privacy suggestions. These agents can exploit different types of information coming from different sources such as databases of consumer complaints, advocacy groups or collaborative sites. Ideally, each user should have a range of privacy critics available to take well-informed decisions.

Generally speaking, this last category of tools illustrates a shift in terms of the trust model: trust is placed in a community rather than in a central stakeholder and this trust is not imposed in the sense that each user is free to consult the analysis provided by the group without following its recommendations.

A similar model, albeit at the smaller scale of groups of friends, has been proposed for social networks. For example, "Privacy suites"[107] are abstract specifications of privacy configurations that can be defined by a social network user and imported and customised by her friends, with the hope that the most expert users can have a beneficial influence on their friends and fewer users will just stick with the default privacy configurations. One challenge in this context is to be able to find an appropriate way to express these privacy configurations so that they can be easily understood, shared and instantiated by friends. This issue is addressed in the next subsection.

17.3.2 Consent

When she has reached a decision about her privacy preferences, the next step for the data subject is to express it. Several techniques are available to support her in this task. They differ mostly in terms of scope (general purpose versus specific) and interfaces. On the generic purpose side, various languages have been proposed to express privacy policies.[108] These languages may target citizens, businesses or organisations; they can be used to express individual privacy policies, corporate rules or legal rules. The general principle is that both the subject and the data con-

[107] Bonneau, Joseph, Jonathan Anderson and Luke Church, "Privacy suites: shared privacy for social networks", SOUPS 2009.

[108] See, for example, Barth, Adam, Anupam Datta, John C. Mitchell and Helen Nissenbaum, "Privacy and Contextual Integrity: Framework and Applications", *Proceedings of the 2006 IEEE Symposium on Security and Privacy*, SP '06, IEEE Computer Society, 2006, pp. 184–198. Becker, Moritz Y., Alexander Malkis and Laurent Bussard, "S4P: A Generic Language for Specifying Privacy Preferences and Policies", Technical report MSR-TR-2010-32, Microsoft Research, April 2010. Le Métayer, Daniel, "A formal privacy management framework", in Pierpaolo Degano, Joshua D. Guttman and Fabio Martinelli, *Formal Aspects of Security and Trust*, Proceedings of the FAST'2008 Workshop (IFIP WG 1.7 Workshop on Formal Aspects in Security and Trust), Springer Verlag, Berlin, 2009. Barth, Adam, John C. Mitchell, Adapu. Datta and Sharada Sundaram, "Privacy and utility in business processes", *Proceedings of the 20th IEEE Computer Security Foundations Symposium*, 2007, pp. 279–294. Karjoth, G., M. Schunter and E.V. Herreweghen, "Translating privacy practices into privacy promises, how to promise what you can keep", *Proceedings of the IEEE 4th International Workshop on Policies for Distributed Systems and Networks*, 4–6 June 2003, pp. 135–146.

troller (typically a website) should be able to author privacy policies that are translated into a machine-readable format. The policies can then be processed automatically and matched to ensure that a data controller collects only personal data associated with a privacy policy (defined by the subject) consistent with her own policy. As an illustration, tools such as P3P[109] and Privacy Bird[110] allow websites to declare their privacy policies and visiting users to have these policies analysed and compared with their own preferences. Depending on the result of the matching, different icons can be displayed in order to inform the user and allow her to either accept to visit the site, refuse or look further into the privacy policy (in which case, Privacy Bird can also be used to display the policy in a user-friendly way, starting with a summary). The preferences of the user can be set through a number of panels allowing her to choose different levels of protection for different types of data (health, financial, etc.).

Another illustration of the approach is the Sparcle[111] policy-authoring tool enabling users to express policies in a restricted natural language. This language includes sentence patterns such as "[User Categories] can [Action(s)] [Data Categories] for the purpose(s) of [Purpose(s)] if [(optional) Condition(s)]", which are automatically translated into a valid machine-readable rule. Users can edit rules by selecting elements from pre-defined lists or create them from scratch provided they respect the syntax of the language.

However, this approach raises several challenges. As discussed above, for this kind of consent to be legitimate from a legal point of view, it must be *free*, *specific*, *informed* and *unambiguous*.[112] Freeness is a general condition going beyond the realm of technology, and information has been discussed in the previous subsection, but not all privacy policy languages meet the other two criteria. For example, the categories of data that can be used in P3P or Privacy Bird may be too coarse in many situations and may force users to disclose more data or grant third parties broader rights than they would like. Most languages may also lead to ambiguities or statements that can be interpreted in different ways. Ambiguities may come from the use of vague terms but also from the combination of rules or the existence of default rules.[113] One of the criticisms raised against early privacy frameworks such as P3P was precisely their lack of clarity and the divergent interpretations of privacy

---

109 W3C, Platform for privacy preferences (P3P), W3C recommendation, 2002. http://www.w3.org/TR/P3P/

110 http://www.privacybird.org/

111 Karat, John, Clare-Marie Karat, Caroloyn Brodie and Jinjuan Feng, "Privacy in information technology: designing to enable privacy policy management in organizations", *International Journal of Human-Computer Studies*, Vol. 63, Issues 1–2, July 2005, pp. 153–174.

112 European Parliament and the Council, Directive 95/46/EC of 24 October 1995 on the Protection of Individuals with Regard to the Processing of Personal Data and on the Free Movement of such Data, Brussels, 1995.

113 Brodie, Carolyn A., Clare-Marie Karat and John Karat, "An empirical study of natural language parsing of privacy policy rules using the Sparcle policy workbench", in Symposium On Usable Privacy and Security (SOUPS), 2006.

policies.[114] An option to solve the ambiguity problem is to resort to a sound, mathematical definition of the semantics of the language. This approach has been followed in several proposals. For example, in the SIMPL language,[115] users can express their policies using sentences such as "I consent to disclose my CV to a third party only if this third party has provided the following pieces of information: (1) his identity and this identity belongs to permanent staff of the Company; (2) his privacy policy and this policy includes the following commitments: use only this data for the purpose of human resource management; delete this data within a maximum delay of three months; do not transfer this data to any third party." The benefit of SIMPL is that this kind of sentence is associated with a formal semantics in a mathematical framework, which makes it possible:

- to prove certain properties about the policies (e.g., that a given third party may never receive a given piece of data) and
- to prove that a given implementation is consistent with the semantics[116] – in other words, that the system behaves as expected by the user.

Other frameworks have been proposed to specify and reason about privacy policies such as:

- CI, a temporal logic language inspired by the notion of contextual integrity; CI makes it possible, for example, to express the fact that an agent acts in a given role and context[117];
- S4P, an abstract language based on notions of declaration, permission (e.g., "Company may use e-mail addresses for marketing purpose") and obligation (e.g., "Company will delete any e-mail within 2 weeks").[118]

Even though their scope goes beyond the definition of privacy policies[119] and they may have a strong impact in the future, these academic proposals have not been deployed yet. One reason is the fact that their generality raises new challenges in

---

[114] Reidenberg, Joel, and Lorrie Faith Cranor, "Can User Agents Accurately Represent Privacy Policies?", 30 August 2002. http://ssrn.com/abstract=328860

[115] Le Métayer, Daniel and Shara Monteleone, "Automated consent through privacy agents: Legal requirements and technical architecture", *Computer Law & Security Review*, Vol. 25, Issue 2, 2009 pp. 136–144.

[116] Le Métayer, Daniel, "A formal privacy management framework", in Pierpaolo Degano, Joshua D. Guttman and Fabio Martinelli (eds.), *Formal Aspects in Security and Trust*, Proceedings of the FAST'2008 Workshop, Springer Verlag, 2009, pp. 162–176.

[117] Barth, Adam, Anupam Datta, John C. Mitchell and Helen Nissenbaum, "Privacy and Contextual Integrity: Framework and Applications", Proceedings of the 2006 IEEE Symposium on Security and Privacy, SP' 06, IEEE Computer Society, 2006, pp. 184–198.

[118] Becker, Moritz Y., Alexander Malkis and Laurent Bussard, "S4P: A Generic Language for Specifying Privacy Preferences and Policies", Technical report MSR-TR-2010-32, Microsoft Research, April 2010.

[119] They can be used to specify norms, in a more general sense, for example, CI has been applied to the US HIPPA (Health Insurance Portability and Accountability Act), COPPA (Children's Online Privacy Protection Act) and GLBA (Gramm-Leach-Bliley Act).

terms of user interface. Indeed, to be really usable they should be integrated within tools allowing users to express their choices in a convenient and efficient way. Several options are possible to address this need, such as the integration within specific tools or the existence of pre-defined sets of choices depending on the profile of the user (e.g., his position along a spectrum going from "privacy intransigent" to "unconcerned"). For example, Internet Explorer supports cookie management through P3P cookie policies[120] allowing users to simply choose a sensitivity level or, for example, to decide to accept or deny cookies from specific websites. Other examples of specific tools or services allowing users to manage their privacy protections include ad blockers and the pop-up blocking facilities provided by most browsers. As an illustration, Adblock Plus,[121] a widely used browser extension, blocks certain requests and automatically hides certain texts such as ads on the page displayed to the user. The user can also define filters to decide what information should be hidden. Dedicated browsers have also been proposed with enhanced security and privacy features such as WhiteHat Aviator,[122] Onion Browser[123] and Orweb.[124]

Another option provided by most browsers is the Do Not Track[125] feature that allows users to express the choice not to be tracked in their browsing activities. This opt-out choice is communicated to visited websites through a specific DNT HTTP header sent every time data is requested from the web. Do Not Track makes a difference between "first parties" (sites that are visited directly) and "third parties" (sites that may be visited indirectly, sometimes without the user noticing it, and that also collect personal information). First parties can collect and record personal data but they are not allowed, by default, to transfer this data to the third parties. However, there is no consensus yet on how websites should precisely interpret this DNT signal. As a result, many sites simply ignore them while others limit the amount information that they collect. To address this issue, the W3C[126] has created a working group devoted to DNT in an attempt to create a standard interpretation.[127] The DNT W3C working draft also defines mechanisms for sites to communicate "whether and how they honour a received preference" through use of a specific response header field.[128] In the same spirit, browsers like Mozilla Firefox provide "private browsing" modes allowing users to limit the amount of information stored by the browser itself, such as the list of visited pages (history), search bar entries, passwords, cookies or caches.

[120] http://msdn.microsoft.com/en-us/library/ie/ms537343(v=vs.85).aspx

[121] https://addons.mozilla.org/en-US/firefox/addon/adblock-plus/

[122] https://www.whitehatsec.com/aviator/

[123] https://itunes.apple.com/us/app/onion-browser/id519296448?mt=8

[124] https://guardianproject.info/apps/orweb/

[125] https://www.mozilla.org/en-US/dnt/

[126] World Wide Web Consortium: http://www.w3.org/Consortium/

[127] http://www.w3.org/2011/tracking-protection/

[128] http://www.w3.org/TR/tracking-dnt/

A different strategy is implemented in another browser extension, TrackMeNot, which consists in obfuscating the users' true searches in a stream of automatically generated decoy queries. The generation algorithm is based on popular queries and sets of RSS feeds from popular websites. For the sake of transparency, users can view the generated query list and choose a number of parameters, such as query frequency, to configure the system. An obvious drawback of this kind of solution is that it generates a lot of additional traffic leading to a waste of network bandwidth. According to their authors, however, this "resource usage is relatively low – tiny, in fact, compared with common components of web traffic such as animations, music and video – and consequently it is unlikely to have any appreciable effect on network bandwidth".[129] The effectiveness of TrackMeNot has also been questioned,[130] as it relies entirely on the strength of the randomisation of the generated queries (and their timing) and any weakness in this process could actually make it easy to distinguish the fake queries and recover the profile of the user.

Social networks present another context in which subjects play a key role in the protection of their own privacy. In practice, the definition of privacy settings in a social network is a challenging task in itself, because of the variety of actors involved, the variety of the functionalities of these systems, and their inherent purpose, i.e., allowing users to share information with others. As an illustration, a Facebook user can define, among many others, the following parameters:

- Who can see my profile on web searches?
- Who can see my future posts?
- Who can post on my timeline?
- Who can see what others post on my timeline?
- Who can send me my friend requests?
- Who is in my restricted list of friends (i.e., who does not see all my information)?
- Who is a blocked user (i.e., who cannot be my friend)?
- Who is a blocked app invitation sender?
- Who is a blocked event sender?

To define these parameters, users can use four pre-defined groups[131]: all (public), friends, friends of friends and no one (only me) or define specific (custom) groups of friends (e.g., family, work, music, etc.). The above list is a small sample of the possibilities offered by Facebook. Some options are more complex. For example, the parameters about the applications and their use both by the user herself and by her friends (and what can be disclosed to friends through their use of the applica-

[129] Howe, Daniel C., and Helen Nissenbaum, "TrackMeNot: resisting surveillance in web search", in Ian Kerr, Carole Lucock and Valerie Steeves (eds.), *Lessons from Identity Trail: Privacy, Anonymity and Identity in a Networked Society*, Oxford University Press, Oxford, 2008.

[130] https://www.schneier.com/blog/archives/2006/08/trackmenot_1.html

[131] Users should be careful about the use of these groups though, as they are dynamic by nature: the rights granted to a group such as friends of friends at a given time may no longer be appropriate one year after (because the size of the group may have grown dramatically).

tion). As can be seen from this brief overview, defining an appropriate privacy policy and ensuring that all its consequences are well understood is not an easy task. In addition, many default privacy settings are rather permissive (for example, the list of friends, list of followers and list of followed people are considered public by default), which means that privacy-concerned users should be cautious and should devote sufficient time to define their own settings before they start using the system. In fact, the complexity of the definition of Facebook privacy policies is such that it has given rise to dedicated services to help users understand and fix their privacy settings.[132]

Because the meaning of a privacy parameter is not always obvious and the effect of their combination is difficult to grasp, research work has been carried out to provide formal models of social network privacy policies.[133] This type of model, which generalises the access control paradigm, can be used not only to better understand the effect of a policy but also to investigate alternative options that are not necessarily supported by existing social networks but may prove useful.

Last but not least, it should be stressed that, for centralised social networks such as Facebook, the impact of the choice of privacy settings is limited to the protection of users with regard to other users, and not with respect to the company [Facebook] itself. For example, according to its privacy policy, Facebook retains the right to use the personal data of its users to deliver ads and measure their effectiveness, to provide location-based services, to make suggestions and to provide innovative features and services it develops in the future.[134] In addition, Facebook may change its terms, and the continued use of the service following changes to the terms constitutes acceptance of the amended terms.

To conclude this subsection on consent, it should be noted that the effectiveness of the consent principle itself and its growing importance in privacy theory is a matter for debate.[135] Indeed, this emphasis on consent, which apprehends subjects as responsible for their own "privacy management", and the associated vision of "privacy as control", suffers from limitations, in particular due to the inherent imbalance of power between subjects and data controllers. Before elaborating further on this debate, it is necessary to get some insight on the available mechanisms to ensure that the actual data processing complies with the choices expressed by the user.

---

132 See, for example, http://www.daniel-puscher.de/fpw/ or http://www.privacyfix.com/

133 Fong, Philip W.L., and Mohd Anwar and Zhen Zhao, "A Privacy Preservation Model for Facebook-style Social Network Systems", Proceedings of the 14th European Conference on Research in Computer Security, ESORICS '09, 2009, pp. 303–320.

134 https://www.facebook.com/about/privacy/your-info: "Granting us permission to use your information not only allows us to provide Facebook as it exists today, but it also allows us to provide you with innovative features and services we develop in the future that use the information we receive about you in new ways."

135 Solove, Daniel J., "Privacy Self-Management and the Consent Paradox", *Harvard Law Review*, Vol. 126, No. 7, May 2013, p. 2. http://papers.ssrn.com/sol3/papers.cfm?abstract_id=2171018. Zanfir, Gabriela, "Forgetting About Consent: Why the Focus Should Be on 'Suitable Safeguards' in Data Protection Law", in Serge Gutwirth et al. (eds.), *Reloading Data Protection*, Springer, Dordrecht, 2014.

17.3.3 *Enforcement*

The enforcement of the privacy choices of the data subject depends very much on the localisation of the personal data. Among the different types of consent described in the previous subsection, the only decisions of the data subject that can be enforced locally are the choices concerning cookies, pop-ups or ad blockers. These choices are implemented on the device of the subject as browser (or Flash Player) options or extensions. As long as they know how to do it, subjects can also decide at any time to erase the cookies stored on their computer[136] or their browsing history.

The enforcement of all other types of consent relies on the existence of appropriate technical means on the side of the data controller (and, in some cases, of other stakeholders) and their proper execution. As far as privacy policies are concerned, the first condition for their enforcement is the guarantee that they always remain associated with the content of the data. This principle, which is often called "sticky policies", can be implemented in different ways. For example, the solution proposed by the EnCoRe project[137] relies on a trusted authority storing encrypted personal data with their associated privacy policy. The authority is in charge of disclosing the key to decrypt the data only to organisations authorised by the policy. Policies can specify conditions for the use of the data such as the purpose, type of platform (including security guarantees), deletion delay and authorised third parties. They also include a list of trusted authorities that, in addition to the management of the data, are in charge of keeping track of the requests and promises made by organisations to ensure accountability. It should be clear, however, that this kind of solution does not provide any guarantee that the organisation receiving the data will indeed respect the associated privacy policy. In other words, subjects have to trust data controllers not to misuse their data. Any solution to reduce this over-reliance on the data controller would require strong requirements about the technology used on the controller's side, such as the implementation of DRM-like technology.[138]

The use of DRM technologies has been suggested by several authors to monitor the use of personal data[139] in the same way as digital content such as video or music. It is not clear, however, whether this solution is really viable considering that personal data can easily be copied after it is exported from the DRM system. Experience has also shown that DRM techniques can often be bypassed with moderate effort. As stated by Manuel Hilty, David Basin and Alexander Pretschner, "at the very

---

[136] This may not always be obvious for non-technical users though. For example, they may not be aware of the fact that different types of cookies may be stored on their computer, some of them directly by their browser, others by Adobe Flash Player, which require different actions.

[137] Ensuring Consent and Revocation (EnCoRe) is a research project undertaken by UK industry and academia, to give individuals more control over their personal information: http://www.encore-project.info/

[138] DRM (for Digital Rights Management) technologies are used to protect digital content (for example, music or video) by preventing illegal copies or controlling access.

[139] Mayer-Schönberger, Victor, "Beyond Copyright: Managing Information Rights with DRM", *Denver University Law Review*, Vol. 84, No. 1, 2006, pp. 181–198.

least, DRM can act as a support mechanism … and thereby increase the likelihood that the obligations are fulfilled, or at least prevent unintended violations resulting from carelessness".[140] Another extreme solution would be to require data controllers to use a trusted computing environment to process personal data. Such a trusted platform ensures that the system behaves as expected at the price of having a unique encryption key loaded in the hardware and made inaccessible to the user. This solution has been used in specific cases such as healthcare information processing.[141] It remains to be seen whether it can become a more widely adopted solution considering the controversies about the trusted computing technology itself, which results in a loss of control of the users on their own computers[142] (and an increased control of computer manufacturers and software providers).

Another right of the subject that has received a lot of attention in the last few years is the "right to be forgotten" which amounts, technically speaking, to enforcing data deletion obligations. A conceptually simple (but far-reaching) principle that could be implemented in the operating systems of all devices would be to associate any data with an expiration time and to automatically delete this data when the delay has expired.[143] However, it is not easy to check that remote devices or servers actually enforce this deletion obligation. In the same way as the DRM option mentioned above, this solution would obviously not provide absolute guarantees[144] since ill-intentioned data controllers could still modify such expiration time or copy the data before its deletion. However, as for DRM, it could be a way to ensure that, by default, deletion obligations are fulfilled.

More radical ways to enforce deletion have been proposed, such as the Vanish[145] and EphPub[146] systems, in which data is encrypted and a key escrow mechanism ensures that the key itself is erased after the expiration date defined by the subject. It should be noted, however, that even this type of solution does not prevent the storage of the decryption key or the dissemination of decrypted data by malicious users, in which case data might remain accessible after the expiration time. To conclude on

---

140 Hilty, Manuel, David Basin and Alexander Pretschner, "On obligations", *Proceedings of the 10th European conference on Research in Computer Security* (ESORICS'05), Springer, Dordrecht, 2005, pp. 98–117.

141 http://www.trustedcomputinggroup.org/files/resource_files/3B1360F8-1D09-3519-AD75FFC52338902D/03-000216.1.03_CBIHealth.pdf

142 Which is, admittedly, the intended effect for privacy enforcement when the trusted execution environment is on the side of the data controller, since the objective is to force him to fulfil the sticky privacy policies.

143 Mayer-Schönberger, Victor, *Delete: the virtue of forgetting in the digital age*, Princeton University Press, 2009.

144 Unless they are complemented by the trusted execution environment mentioned above.

145 Geambasu, Roxana, Tadayoshi Kohno, Amit Levy and Henry M. Levy, "Vanish: Increasing Data Privacy with Self-Destructing Data", in Proceedings of the USENIX Security Symposium, 2009.

146 Castelluccia, Claude, Emiliano De Cristofaro, Aurélien Francillon and Mohamed Ali Kâafar, "EphPub: Toward robust Ephemeral Publishing", 19th IEEE Conference on Network Protocols (ICNP 2011), pp. 165–175.

this topic, one must admit that no absolute guarantee about data deletion can be provided by existing technologies[147] but they can still be useful to reduce the risk of accidental or malicious breach of the deletion obligation.

17.3.4 Accountability

As discussed in the previous section, after they have disclosed their personal data to a third party, individuals can generally not get any absolute guarantee that this data is actually used in compliance with the law and the specific conditions possibly agreed with the data controller (as, for example, expressed through a privacy policy). Considering these limitations, the only remaining protection for the data subject is the possibility to have the behaviour of the data controller checked in one way or another.[148] This possibility is in line with the accountability principle introduced three decades ago in the OECD's guidelines,[149] and has been enjoying growing popularity over the last few years as a solution to mitigate this loss of control.[150] The key idea behind the notion of accountability is that data controllers should not merely comply with data protection rules but should also be able to demonstrate compli-

147 See, in particular, Druschel, Peter, Michael Backes and Rodica Tirtea, *The right to be forgotten – between expectations and practice*, ENISA Report, 2011. https://www.enisa.europa.eu/activities/identity-and-trust/library/deliverables/the-right-to-be-forgotten. It should also be stressed that, technically speaking, data erasure is not such a simple task, because of data remanence: a residual representation of the data remains in the computer memory after a simple attempt to erase it, which requires one to resort to more sophisticated techniques or overwriting to make it more difficult to retrieve the data after its "erasure".

148 Computer scientists such as Fred Schneider have also advocated accountability for similar reasons in a more general context: "Accountability, then, could be a plausible alternative to perfection. And while perfection is clearly beyond our capabilities, accountability is not. It's therefore feasible to contemplate an exchange: accountability for perfection." in Schneider, Fred B., "Accountability for perfection", *IEEE Security and Privacy*, March–April, 2009, pp. 3–4.

149 Organisation for Economic Co-operation and Development, *Guidelines on the Protection of Privacy and Transborder Flows of Personal Data*, Paris, 1980. See also *Thirty Years After The OECD Privacy Guidelines*, 2011 (http://www.oecd.org/sti/ieconomy/49710223.pdf) and the latest version of the guidelines: The Recommendation of the OECD Council concerning Guidelines governing the Protection of Privacy and Transborder Flows of Personal Data, July 2013. http://www.oecd.org/sti/ieconomy/2013-oecd-privacy-guidelines.pdf

150 See, for example, Alhadeff, Joseph, Brendan Van Alsenoy and Jos Dumortier, "The accountability principle in data protection regulation: origin, development and future directions", in Daniel Guagnin, Leon Hempel, Carla Ilten, Inga Kroener, Daniel Neyland and Hector Postigo, *Managing privacy through accountability*, Palgrave Macmillan, September 2012. To be fair, however, it should also be noted that accountability has also been questioned as it may sometimes be used by industry as a synonym of self-regulation and a way to avoid more stringent legal obligations. As an illustration of this trend, see Ernst & Young, "Privacy Trends 2012. The case for growing accountability": "To avoid greater regulation, organizations in the retail and consumer products industries and GS1, a supply chain standards organization, are working with privacy commissioners to voluntarily set guidelines that address the privacy implications of using radio frequency identification (RFID) technology in their operations."

ance or "showing how responsibility is exercised and making this verifiable", as stated by the Article 29 Working Party.[151] The General Data Protection Regulation[152] puts the same emphasis on demonstration in its Article 22§1: "The controller shall implement appropriate technical and organisational measures to ensure and be able to demonstrate that the processing of personal data is performed in compliance with this Regulation." It should also be noted that the scope of accountability goes beyond regulation: its goal can also be to improve corporate data governance[153] or to promote ethical practices.

Considering that demonstrability is the core of accountability, the key issues become then:

- What has to be demonstrated?
- Based on what evidence (or "accounts")? and
- How will accountability be demonstrated?

Generally speaking, accountability can take place at several stages leading to different types of evidence. For the sake of clarification, Colin Bennett introduced a useful distinction between three types of accountability, namely, accountability of policy, accountability of procedures and accountability of practice.[154] Roughly speaking, the first type of accountability is purely declarative; the second type adds organisational measures; the third type brings stronger guarantees because it applies to the actual actions carried out on the personal data. Bennett emphasises that excessive focus has been placed on the first and second types of accountability so far, thereby limiting the potential benefits of accountability. Technologies can facilitate accountability of policy through the privacy policy languages and frameworks mentioned in Sect. 17.3.2; they can also support procedures, but the type of accountability to which they can make the greatest contribution is accountability of practice.

Strictly speaking, accountability of practice should put data controllers in a position to demonstrate that their practices, hence their use of personal data, complies with their obligations. The main piece of evidence for accountability of practice should therefore be a file recording all the events that have occurred during the execution of the system (or at least all the events that may have an impact on compliance), which is usually called an *execution log* or *a log*. The key challenges for the implementation of accountability of practice concern the three main stages of

---

151 Article 29 Data Protection Working Party, Opinion 3/2010 on the principle of accountability, 13 July 2010. http://ec.europa.eu/justice/policies/privacy/docs/wpdocs/2010/wp173_en.pdf

152 Regulation of the European Parliament and of the Council on the protection of individuals with regard to the processing of personal data and on the free movement of such data (General Data Protection Regulation), voted by the European Parliament on 12 March 2014.

153 Pearson, Siani, and Andrew Charlesworth, "Accountability as a way forward for privacy protection in the cloud", in M.G. Jaatun, G. Zhao and C. Rong (eds.), *Cloud Computing, Proceedings of CloudCom 2009*, Beijing, Springer, Berlin, 2009, pp. 131–144.

154 Bennett, Colin J., "Implementing Privacy Codes of Practice", (PLUS 8830), Canadian Standards Association, 1995. http://shop.csa.ca/en/canada/privacy/privacy-package/invt/27020152004. See also Bennett, Colin, "International privacy standards: can accountability be adequate?", *Privacy Laws and Business International*, August 2010.

the life cycle of the logs: their construction, their storage and their use to conduct audits. Technologies can support each of these stages.

The main difficulty with respect to the construction of the logs is to determine the proper events to be recorded and to demonstrate that the recorded events are indeed sufficient to establish compliance.[155] The first strategy, which would be to record all possible events of the system (if at all possible), is generally not recommended, both for performance considerations and for privacy protection itself, because recording unnecessary personal data in the logs might introduce additional risks and breach the data minimisation principle. Recent work has shown that it is possible to use formal definitions of privacy policies to derive the minimum amount of data to keep in the logs[156] or even to build "personal data free" logs.[157] Complementary means should be used to demonstrate that the logs indeed contain all the relevant events or, in other words, that they accurately reflect the real actions that have taken place on personal data. More precisely, the logging process itself should be complete and it should not be possible to have it bypassed by malicious data controllers. Formal methods and procedural measures can be used to this aim, but it should be clear that, unless heavy solutions in the style of trusted computing mentioned in the previous subsection are resorted to,[158] accountability cannot bring absolute guarantees. Indeed, its main purpose is to make it more difficult and more risky to breach the rules and so to provide incentives for respectful behaviour.

Assuming that sufficient logs are recorded, the next difficulty is to store them in a secure way. Considering that logs may contain sensitive information both of the data controller (e.g., related to his own algorithms, procedures or business models) and the data subjects, their security is a key requisite. To address this goal, specific techniques have been proposed to enforce forward integrity,[159] which ensures that even if the logging machine is compromised at some stage, it will be impossible for

---

[155] Butin, Denis, Marcos Chicote and Daniel Le Métayer, "Log Design for Accountability", *Proceedings of the 4th International Workshop on Data Usage Management*, IEEE Computer Society, Washington, DC, 2013.

[156] See, for example, for database access policies: Biswas, Debmalya, and Valtteri Niemi, "Transforming Privacy Policies to Auditing Specifications", IEEE 13th International Symposium on High-Assurance Systems Engineering (HASE), 2011, pp. 368–375.

[157] Butin, Denis, and Daniel Le Métayer, "Log Analysis for Data Protection Accountability", in Cliff Jones, Pekka Pihlajasaari and Jun Sun (eds.), *FM 2014: Formal Methods:* 19th International Symposium, Singapore, May 12–16, 2014, Proceedings (Lecture Notes in Computer Science/ Programming and Software Engineering), Springer Verlag, 2014, pp. 163–178.

[158] Mechanisms have also been proposed for "accountable virtual machines" in the context of distributed computing but faults are detected by replaying the execution of the remote processor using a correct copy of its code, which is not really an applicable strategy for privacy accountability because the subject (or even the auditor) does not necessarily know (and should not have to know) the software code running on the controller's side. See Haeberlen, Andreas, Paarijaat Aditya, Rodrigo Rodrigues and Peter Druschel, "Accountable Virtual Machines", Proceedings of the 9th USENIX Conference on Operating Systems Design and Implementation (OSDI 2010), USENIX Association, Berkeley, CA, 2010, pp. 119–134.

[159] Bellare, Mihir, and Bennet S. Yee, "Forward integrity for secure audit logs", Technical report, University of California at San Diego, 1997. Schneier, Bruce, and John Kelsey, "Secure Audit

the attacker to forge log entries appearing before that time.[160] Another important requirement is the possibility to be able to access the logs selectively, depending on the objective of the audit procedure. Standard cryptographic techniques would require the auditor to decrypt all the log data before searching the log, which might be an issue both in terms of efficiency and for security reasons. Techniques relying on identity-based encryption can be used to allow auditors to search audit logs for records associated with specific keywords only.[161]

The last step is the conduct of the audit itself. Considering the typical size of audit logs, one cannot expect auditors to carry out this task without any support tool. Such tools range from simple visualisation of record data in a user-friendly way to the automatic verification that a log meets the compliance criteria, or at least the criteria that can be expressed formally. Recent work has also shown how to combine automatic verification and human verification of additional conditions such as the justification for "break the glass rules"[162] or subjective beliefs.[163]

17.4 Conclusion: in whom do (don't) you trust?

As shown in this chapter, technologies can be instrumental in making privacy rights more effective. Therefore, legal instruments and Data Protection Authorities should create favourable conditions for the development of these technologies and their integration within a global enforcement strategy rather than remaining neutral or even setting up barriers to their adoption.[164]

Logs to Support Computer Forensics", *ACM Transactions on Information and System Security*, Vol. 2, No. 2, 1999, pp. 159–176.

160 Even if, of course, nothing would prevent the attacker from deleting these logs if he has taken control of the machine, but this might not go undetected if the machine has communicated with third parties or if logs have been periodically stored on a backup site.

161 Waters, Brent R., Dirk Balfanz, Glenn Durfee and D.K. Smetters, "Building an encrypted and searchable audit log", presented at the 11th Annual Network and Distributed System Security Symposium, 2004.

162 Exceptional situations or emergencies, for example, when there is a matter of life and death, that can justify a derogation to the general rule.

163 See, for example, Garg, D., L. Jia and A. Datta, "Policy Auditing over Incomplete Logs: Theory, Implementation and Applications", in *Proceedings of 18th ACM Conference on Computer and Communications Security*, October 2011. Butin, Denis, and Daniel Le Métayer, "Log Analysis for Data Protection Accountability", in C. Jones, P. Pihalajasaari and J. Sun (eds.), *Formal Methods 2014*, 19th International Symposium on Formal Methods (FM 2014), Springer Verlag, 2014, pp. 163–178.

164 See, for example, Froomkin, A. Michael, "PETs must be on a leash': how U.S. law (and industry practice) often undermines and even forbids valuable Privacy-enhancing Technology", *Ohio State Law Journal*, Vol. 74, No. 6, 2013, for a critical review of the situation in the US and for a plea in favour of privacy-enhancing technologies, see Diaz, Claudia, Omer Tene and Seda F. Guerses, "Hero or Villain: The Data Controller in Privacy Law and Technologies", *Ohio State Law Journal*, Vol. 74, No. 6, 2013, pp. 923–964. It should be noted that the latter paper defines PETs in a more

As stated in the introduction, the debate in terms of enforcement mostly comes down to the question of where trust should (or should not) be placed to ensure that the rules are complied with. Some take the position that trust assumptions should be as low as possible (and no trust assumption should be made on data controllers or governments)[165]; others place the highest value on the autonomy of the subject and contend that "privacy as control remains the strongest conception of privacy"[166]; others point out the limitations of privacy self-management[167] and believe that too much should not be put on the shoulders of the users because they are not in a strong position to resist or to negotiate[168] (hence the need for some support from governments, typically through DPAs); still others, believe that salvation can neither come from the subject nor from governments but only from communities of peers which constitute the only way to redress this imbalance of powers.[169] Our point in this chapter was neither to take a position in this debate nor to provide arguments in favour of a particular view of what is well placed or misplaced trust, but to show that different kinds of technologies can be used to help implement these different types of approaches. In other words, we do not aim to choose between the techniques presented here: we believe that they are complementary instruments rather than alternatives and they should be selected according to the trust and mistrust assumptions one is ready to make on one hand, and on the utility (in the sense of level of functionality) that they provide on the other hand.

Considering that trust is the core of the problem, one cannot evade the issue of the trust in the technologies themselves. Indeed, recent history has shown that cryptographic tools that were considered as the cornerstone of many secure systems might very well have been either bugged or hacked by secret agencies and might

restricted sense than this chapter, covering essentially a subset of Sect. 17.2. More precisely, it restricts the term "PETs" to "technological solutions that combine three objectives: elimination of the single point of failure inherent with any centralized third party; data minimization; and subjecting protocols and software to community-based public scrutiny".

[165] Diaz, Claudia, Omer Tene and Seda F. Guerses, "Hero or Villain: The Data Controller in Privacy Law and Technologies", *Ohio State Law Journal*, Vol. 74, No. 6, 2013, pp. 923–964.

[166] Birnhack, D. Michael, "A quest for a theory of privacy : context and control", *Jurimetrics: The Journal of Law, Science, and Technology*, Vol. 51, No. 4, 2011.

[167] Solove, J. Daniel, "Privacy self-management and the consent paradox", *Harvard Law Review*, Vol. 126, 2013.

[168] Lazaro, Christophe, and Daniel Le Métayer,"The control over personal data : true remedy or fairy tale ?", *Script-ed*, Vol. 12, Issue 1, pp. 3–34, June 2015, http://script-ed.org/?p=1927. Gabriela Zanfir, "Forgetting about consent. Why the focus should be on "suitable safeguards" in data protection law", 2013. Available at SSRN: http://ssrn.com/abstract=2261973 or http://dx.doi.org/10.2139/ssrn.2261973

[169] ToS;DR (Terms of Service; Didn't Read: http://tosdr.org) is an example of effort in this direction. The goal of ToS;DR is to create a database of analyses of the fairness of privacy policies and to make this information available in the form of explicit icons (general evaluation plus good and bad points) which can be expanded if needed into more detailed explanations. A key aspect of ToS;DR is the fact that users can submit their own analysis for consideration, the goal being that, just like Wikipedia, a group consensus will emerge to provide a reliable assessment of each policy.

thus have been a major source of leak of personal data for years. One cannot expect a simple recipe to ensure that this kind of situation never happens again but there are measures that should contribute to limit such risks. The first one is to make the source code and design documents of the technology available to public scrutiny.[170] It should be clear, however, especially after the revelation of the famous Heartbleed security bug in the OpenSSL cryptography library,[171] that openness is not necessarily a guarantee by itself. The second measure, which complements and strengthens the first one, is to apply formal specification and verification techniques to the most critical components of the systems to ensure that they behave as expected.[172]

Two cautionary notes should be made to conclude this chapter: first, the use of technologies for privacy enforcement cannot be reduced to a simple choice among available off-the-shelf PETs. Privacy considerations should be taken into consideration before the beginning of the design stage, when defining the purpose of a system, through an appropriate privacy impact assessment (PIA), followed by justified design decisions and accountability measures making all design choices traceable. It should be underlined also that privacy impact assessment, privacy by design and privacy-enhancing technologies are very active areas of research and much progress is still to be expected in this area during the next decade. Among the technical, organisational and economic challenges in this respect is to make available reusable design strategies allowing designers to capitalise efforts and ensuring that privacy by design can go from handcraft to industry.[173] Much progress can still be made on the usability of privacy-enhancing technologies, which is a key factor for their large-scale adoption.

Last but not least, great care should always be taken not to over-emphasise the level of protection provided by technology. Protection is never absolute or irrevocable: a technology (e.g., a cryptography software) that may reasonably be perceived as secure at a given time may become unsafe later on because new attacks have been discovered; similarly, a dataset that is supposed to be anonymised using the best available techniques at a given time could possibly be de-anonymised later on, either because new auxiliary data is published or because more powerful data analysis techniques are available. The worst would therefore be to convey a misleading impression of complete protection that would lead individuals to care less about their privacy: technology can play a key role in enforcing privacy but should not be used in isolation or seen as a convenient way to forget about privacy.

---

[170] Ibid.

[171] https://en.wikipedia.org/wiki/Heartbleed?oldid=cur

[172] Daniel Le Métayer, "Privacy by design: a formal framework for the analysis of architectural choices", in ACM Conference on Data and Application Security and Privacy (CODASPY 2013), ACM, 2013, pp. 95–104. Antignac, Thibaud, and Daniel Le Métayer, "Privacy by design: from technologies to architectures", Annual Privacy Forum, Springer Verlag, 2014, pp. 1–17.

[173] Gürses, Seda, Carmela Troncoso and Claudia Diaz, "Engineering Privacy by Design", Presented at the Conference on Computers, Privacy & Data Protection (CPDP), 2011.

Acknowledgement This work was partially funded by the European project PRIPARE / FP7-ICT-2013-1.5 and the Inria Project Lab CAPPRIS (Collaborative Action on the Protection of Privacy Rights in the Information Society). The author also thanks Denis Butin, Mathieu Cunche, Sébastien Gambs and Christophe Lazaro for their comments on an earlier version of this chapter and the editors for their assistance in the preparation of the final version. Their suggestions helped improve and clarify this document.

References

Achara, Jagdish Prasad, Franck Baudot, Claude Castelluccia, Geoffrey Delcroix and Vincent Roca, "Mobilitics: analyzing privacy leaks in smart phones", *ERCIM News*, 93, April 2013.

Acs, Gergely, and Claude Castelluccia, "I Have a DREAM!: Differentially Private Smart Metering", *Proceedings of the 13th International Conference on Information Hiding*, Springer Verlag, 2011, pp. 118–132.

Ackerman, Mark S., and Lorrie Cranor, "Privacy Critics: UI Components to Safeguard Users' Privacy", CHI '99 Extended Abstracts on Human Factors in Computing Systems, CHI EA '99, ACM, 1999, pp. 258–259.

Alhadeff, Joseph, Brendan Van Alsenoy and Jos Dumortier, "The accountability principle in data protection regulation: origin, development and future directions", in Daniel Guagnin, Leon Hempel, Carla Ilten, Inga Kroener, Daniel Neyland and Hector Postigo, *Managing privacy through accountability*, Palgrave Macmillan, September 2012.

Allard, Tristan, Nicolas Anciaux, Luc Bouganim, Yanli Guo, Lionel Le Folgoc, Benjamin Nguyen, Philippe Pucheral, Indrajit Ray, Indrakshi Ray and Shaoyi Yin, "Secure Personal Data Servers: a Vision Paper", in Elisa Bertino, Paolo Atzeni, Kian Lee Tan, Yi Chen and Y.C. Tay (eds.), *Proceedings of the 36th International Conference on Very Large Data Bases (VLDB)*, Vol. 1, No. 1, 2010, pp. 25–35.

Anciaux, Nicolas, Mehdi Benzine, Luc Bouganim, Kevin Jacquemin, Philippe Pucheral and Shaoyi Yin, "Restoring the Patient Control over her Medical History", 21th IEEE International Symposium on Computer-Based Medical Systems (IEEE CBMS), Finland, June 2008, pp. 132–137.

Antignac, Thibaud, and Daniel Le Métayer, "Privacy by design: from technologies to architectures", Annual Privacy Forum, Springer Verlag, 2014, pp. 1–17.

Article 29 Data Protection Working Party, Opinion 3/2010 on the principle of accountability, 13 July 2010. http://ec.europa.eu/justice/policies/privacy/docs/wpdocs/2010/wp173_en.pdf

Backes, Michael, Aniket Kate, Matteo Maffei and Kim Pecina, "ObliviAd: Provably Secure and Practical Online Behavioral Advertising", in *Proceedings of 33rd IEEE Symposium on Security and Privacy (S&P 2012)*, 2012, pp. 257–271.

Balasch, Josep, Alfredo Rial, Carmela Troncoso, Christophe Geuens, Bart Preneel and Ingrid Verbauwhede, "PrETP: Privacy-Preserving Electronic Toll Pricing", 19th USENIX Security Symposium, USENIX Association, 2010, pp. 63–78.

Barth, Adam, Anupam Datta, John C. Mitchell and Helen Nissenbaum, "Privacy and Contextual Integrity: Framework and Applications", *Proceedings of the 2006 IEEE Symposium on Security and Privacy*, SP '06, IEEE Computer Society, 2006, pp. 184–198.

Barth, Adam, John C. Mitchell, Adapu. Datta and Sharada Sundaram, "Privacy and utility in business processes", *Proceedings of the 20th IEEE Computer Security Foundations Symposium*, 2007, pp. 279–294.

Beato, Filipe, Markulf Kohlweiss and Karel Wouters, "Scramble! Your Social Network Data", in Simone Fischer-Hübner and Nicholas Hopper (eds.), *Privacy-enhancing Technologies*, Proceedings of the 11th International Symposium, PETS 2011, Waterloo, ON, Canada, 27–29 July 2011, Springer, Heidelberg, 2011, pp. 211–225.

Becker, Moritz Y., Alexander Malkis and Laurent Bussard, "S4P: A Generic Language for Specifying Privacy Preferences and Policies", Technical report MSR-TR-2010-32, Microsoft Research, April 2010.

Bellare, Mihir, and Bennet S. Yee, "Forward integrity for secure audit logs", Technical report, University of California at San Diego, 1997.

Bennett, Colin J., "Implementing Privacy Codes of Practice", (PLUS 8830), Canadian Standards Association, 1995. http://shop.csa.ca/en/canada/privacy/privacy-package/invt/27020152004

Bennett, Colin, "International privacy standards: can accountability be adequate?", *Privacy Laws and Business International*, August 2010.

Beresford, Alastair R., and F. Stajano, "Location privacy in pervasive computing", *IEEE Pervasive Computing*, Vol. 3, No. 1, 2003, pp. 46–55.

Birnhack, D. Michael, "A quest for a theory of privacy: context and control", *Jurimetrics: The Journal of Law, Science, and Technology*, Vol. 51, No. 4, 2011.

Biswas, Debmalya, and Valtteri Niemi, "Transforming Privacy Policies to Auditing Specifications", IEEE 13th International Symposium on High-Assurance Systems Engineering (HASE), 2011, pp. 368–375.

Bonneau, Joseph, Jonathan Anderson and Luke Church, "Privacy suites: shared privacy for social networks", SOUPS 2009.

Borking, John J., "Why Adopting Privacy-enhancing Technologies (PETs) Takes so Much Time", In *Computers, Privacy and Data Protection: an Element of Choice*, Springer Verlag, 2011, pp. 309–341.

Brodie, Carolyn A., Clare-Marie Karat and John Karat, "An empirical study of natural language parsing of privacy policy rules using the Sparcle policy workbench", in Symposium On Usable Privacy and Security (SOUPS), 2006.

Butin, Denis, Marcos Chicote and Daniel Le Métayer, "Log Design for Accountability", *Proceedings of the 4th International Workshop on Data Usage Management*, IEEE Computer Society, Washington, DC, 2013.

Butin, Denis, and Daniel Le Métayer, "Log Analysis for Data Protection Accountability", in C. Jones, P. Pihalajasaari and J. Sun (eds.), *Formal Methods 2014*, 19th International Symposium on Formal Methods (FM 2014), Springer Verlag, 2014, pp. 163–178.

Butin, Denis, and Daniel Le Métayer, "Log Analysis for Data Protection Accountability", in Cliff Jones, Pekka Pihlajasaari and Jun Sun (eds.), *FM 2014: Formal Methods:* 19th International Symposium, Singapore, May 12–16, 2014, Proceedings (Lecture Notes in Computer Science / Programming and Software Engineering), Springer Verlag, 2014, pp. 163–178.

Camenisch, Jan, and Els Van Herreweghen, "Design and Implementation of the Idemix Anonymous Credential System", *Proceedings of the 9th ACM Conference on Computer and Communications Security*, CCS '02, 2002, pp. 21–30.

Castelluccia, Claude, Emiliano De Cristofaro, Aurélien Francillon and Mohamed Ali Kâafar, "EphPub: Toward robust Ephemeral Publishing", 19th IEEE Conference on Network Protocols (ICNP 2011), pp. 165–175.

Chi-Chih Yao, Andrew, "Protocols for Secure Computations", Extended Abstract, FOCS 1982, pp. 160–164.

Chor, Benny, Eyal Kushilevitz, Oded Goldreich and Madhu Sudan, "Private Information Retrieval", Journal of the ACM, Vol. 45, No. 6, 1998, pp. 965–981.

Cutillo, Leucio Antonio, Refik Molva and Thorsten Strufe, "Safebook: a privacy preserving online social network leveraging on real-life trust", *IEEE Communications Magazine*, Vol. 47, No. 12, December 2009.

Damiani, Maria Luisa, Elisa Bertino and Claudio Silvestri, "The PROBE framework for the personalized cloaking of private locations", *Transactions on Data Privacy*, Vol. 3, No. 2, 2010, pp. 123–148.

Danezis, George, and Seda Gürses, "A critical review of 10 years of privacy technology", in *Surveillance Cultures: A Global Surveillance Society?*, UK, April 2010.

De Cristofaro, Emiliano, and Gene Tsudik, "Practical private set intersection protocols with linear complexity", in *Financial Cryptography*, Springer-Verlag, Berlin, 2010, pp. 143–159.

De Cristofaro, Emiliano, Claudio Soriente, Gene Tsudik and Andrew Williams, "Hummingbird: Privacy at the Time of Twitter", in IEEE Symposium on Security and Privacy, San Francisco, CA, 21–23 May 2012, pp. 285–299.

de Jonge, Wiebren, and Bart Jacobs, "Privacy-friendly electronic traffic pricing via commits", in P. Degano, J. Guttman, and F. Martinelli (eds.), *Formal Aspects in Security and Trust*, Springer, 2009, pp. 143–161.

Deng, Mina, Kim Wuyts, Riccardo Scandariato, Bart Preneel and Wouter Joosen, "A privacy threat analysis framework: supporting the elicitation and fulfillment of privacy requirements", *Requirements Engineering*, Special Issue on Digital Privacy, Vol. 16, Issue 1, March 2011, pp. 3–32.

Deswarte, Yves, and Sébastien Gambs, "A proposal for a privacy-preserving national identity card", *Transactions on Data Privacy*, Vol. 3, Issue 3, December 2010, pp. 253–276.

Diaz, Claudia, and Seda F. Guerses, "Understanding the landscape of privacy technologies", Extended abstract of invited talk in proceedings of the Information Security Summit, 2012, pp. 58–63.

Diaz, Claudia, Omer Tene and Seda F. Guerses, "Hero or Villain: The Data Controller in Privacy Law and Technologies", *Ohio State Law Journal*, Vol. 74, No. 6, 2013.

Druschel, Peter, Michael Backes and Rodica Tirtea, *The right to be forgotten – between expectations and practice*, ENISA Report, 2011. https://www.enisa.europa.eu/activities/identity-and-trust/library/deliverables/the-right-to-be-forgotten

Dwork, Cynthia, "Differential privacy", in ICALP, Vol. 2, 2006, pp. 1–12.

Dwork, Cynthia, "A firm foundation for private data analysis", *Communications of the ACM*, Vol. 54, No. 1, 2011, pp. 86–95.

Eckersley, Peter, "How Unique Is Your Web Browser?", in Mikhail J. Atallah and Nicholas J. Hopper (eds.), *Privacy-enhancing Technologies*, Springer, 2010, pp. 1–18.

Enck, William, Peter Gilbert, Byung-Gon Chun, Landon P. Cox, Jaeyeon Jung, Patrick McDaniel and Anmol N. Sheth, "TaintDroid: An Information-flow Tracking System for Realtime Privacy Monitoring on Smartphones", *Proceedings of the 9th USENIX Conference on Operating Systems Design and Implementation, OSDI'10*, 2010, pp. 1–6.

European Parliament, Regulation of the European Parliament and of the Council on the protection of individuals with regard to the processing of personal data and on the free movement of such data (General Data Protection Regulation), voted by the European Parliament on 12 March 2014.

Fong, Philip W.L., and Mohd Anwar and Zhen Zhao, "A Privacy Preservation Model for Facebook-style Social Network Systems", Proceedings of the 14th European Conference on Research in Computer Security, ESORICS'09, 2009, pp. 303–320.

Froomkin, A. Michael, "'PETs must be on a leash': how U.S. law (and industry practice) often undermines and even forbids valuable Privacy-enhancing Technology", *Ohio State Law Journal*, Vol. 74, No. 6, 2013.

Fung, Benjamin C.M., Ke Wang, Rui Chen and Philip S. Yu, "Privacy-preserving data publishing: A survey of recent developments", *ACM Computing Surveys*, Vol. 42, No. 4, June 2010.

Fung, Benjamin C.M., Ke Wang, Ada Wai-Chee Fu and Philip S. Yu, *Introduction to Privacy-Preserving Data Publishing: Concepts and Techniques*, Chapman & Hall/CRC, August 2010.

Gambs, Sébastien, Marc-Olivier Killijian and Miguel Núñez del Prado Cortez, "GEPETO: A GEoPrivacy-Enhancing TOolkit", AINA Workshops, 2010, pp. 1071–1076.

Garcia, Flavio D., and Bart Jacobs, "Privacy-Friendly Energy-Metering via Homomorphic Encryption", in Jorge Cuellar, Javier Lopez, Gilles Barthe and Alexander Pretschner (eds.), *Security and Trust Management* (STM'2010), Springer, 2011, pp. 226–238.

Garg, D., L. Jia and A. Datta, "Policy Auditing over Incomplete Logs: Theory, Implementation and Applications", in *Proceedings of 18th ACM Conference on Computer and Communications Security*, October 2011.

Geambasu, Roxana, Tadayoshi Kohno, Amit Levy and Henry M. Levy, "Vanish: Increasing Data Privacy with Self-Destructing Data", in Proceedings of the USENIX Security Symposium, 2009.

Gentry, Craig, "Full Homomorphic Encryption using ideal lattices", in the 41st ACM Symposium on Theory of Computing (STOC), 2009. https://www.cs.cmu.edu/~odonnell/hits09/gentry-homomorphic-encryption.pdf

Goldberg, Ian, David Wagner and Eric A. Brewer, "Privacy-Enhancing Technologies for the Internet", IEEE COMPCON '97, February 1997.

Goldberg, Ian, "Privacy-Enhancing Technologies for the Internet III: Ten years later", Chapter 1, in Alessandro Acquisti, Stefanos Gritzalis, Costos Lambrinoudakis, Sabrina di Vimercati (eds.), *Digital Privacy: Theory, Technologies, and Practices*, December 2007.

Goldschlag, David, Michael Reed and Paul Syverson, "Onion Routing for Anonymous and Private Internet Connections", *Communications of the ACM*, Vol. 42, No. 2, February 1999, pp. 39–41.

Goldwasser, Shafi, Silvio Micali and Charles Rackoff, "The knowledge complexity of interactive proof-systems", in Robert Sedgewick (ed.), *Proceedings of 17th Symposium on the Theory of Computation*, Providence, RI, ACM, 1985.

Guha, Saikat, Bin Cheng and Paul Francis, "Privad: Practical Privacy in Online Advertising", USENIX Symposium on Networked Systems Design and Implementation, NSDI 2011.

Gürses, Seda, and Bettina Berendt, "PETs in the surveillance society: a critical review of the potentials and limitations of the privacy as confidentiality paradigm", in Serge Gutwirth, Yves Poullet and Paul De Hert (eds.), *Data Protection in a Profiled World*, Springer Verlag, 2009.

Gürses, Seda, Carmela Troncoso and Claudia Diaz, "Engineering Privacy by Design", Presented at the Conference on Computers, Privacy & Data Protection (CPDP), 2011.

Haeberlen, Andreas, Paarijaat Aditya, Rodrigo Rodrigues and Peter Druschel, "Accountable Virtual Machines", Proceedings of the 9th USENIX Conference on Operating Systems Design and Implementation (OSDI 2010), USENIX Association, Berkeley, CA, 2010, pp. 119–134.

Hildebrandt Mireille, and Bert-Jaap Koops, "The Challenges of Ambient Law and Legal Protection in the Profiling Era", *The Modern Law Review*, Vol. 73, Issue 3, May 2010, pp. 428–460.

Hilty, Manuel, David Basin and Alexander Pretschner, "On obligations", *Proceedings of the 10th European conference on Research in Computer Security* (ESORICS'05), Springer Dordrecht, 2005, pp. 98–117.

Howe, Daniel C., and Helen Nissenbaum, "TrackMeNot: resisting surveillance in web search", in Ian Kerr, Carole Lucock and Valerie Steeves (eds.), *Lessons from the Identity Trail: Privacy, Anonymity and Identity in a Networked Society*, Oxford University Press, Oxford, 2008.

ISO/IEC DIS 24760-2, Information Technology – Security Techniques – A Framework for Identity Management – Part 2: Reference architecture and requirements.

Jawurek, Marek, Florian Kerschbaum and George Danezis, "Privacy Technologies for Smart Grids – A Survey of Options", Microsoft Technical Report, MSR-TR-2012-119, 2012.

Karat, John, Clare-Marie Karat, Caroloyn Brodie and Jinjuan Feng, "Privacy in information technology: designing to enable privacy policy management in organizations", *International Journal of Human-Computer Studies*, Vol. 63, Issues 1–2, July 2005, pp. 153–174.

Karjoth, Günter, Matthias Schunter and Els Van Herreweghen, "Translating privacy practices into privacy promises, how to promise what you can keep", *Proceedings of the IEEE 4th International Workshop on Policies for Distributed Systems and Networks*, 4–6 June 2003, pp. 135–146.

Kokott, Juliane, and Christoph Sobotta, "The distinction between privacy and data protection in the jurisprudence of the CJEU and the ECtHR", *International Data Privacy Law*, Vol. 3, No. 4, 2013.

Kosta, Eleni, Jan Zubuschka, Tobias Scherner and Jos Dumortier, "Legal considerations on privacy-enhancing location based services using PRIME technology", *Computer Law and Security Report*, Vol. 24, Issue 2, 2008, pp. 139–146.

Krumm, John, "A survey of computational location privacy", *Personal Ubiquitous Computing*, Vol. 13, 2009, pp. 391–399.

Lazaro, Christophe, and Daniel Le Métayer, "The control over personal data: true remedy or fairy tale ?", *ScriptEd*, Vol. 12, Issue 1, June 2015, pp. 3–34. http://script-ed.org/?p=1927

Le Métayer, Daniel, and Shara Monteleone, "Automated consent through privacy agents: Legal requirements and technical architecture", *Computer Law & Security Review*, Vol. 25, Issue 2, 2009, pp. 136–144.

Le Métayer, Daniel, "A formal privacy management framework", in Pierpaolo Degano, Joshua D. Guttman and Fabio Martinelli (eds.), *Formal Aspects in Security and Trust*, Proceedings of the FAST'2008 Workshop, Springer Verlag, 2009, pp. 162–176.

Le Métayer, Daniel, "Privacy by design: a formal framework for the analysis of architectural choices", in ACM Conference on Data and Application Security and Privacy (CODASPY 2013), ACM, 2013, pp. 95–104.

Machanavajjhala, Ashwin, Daniel Kifer, Johannes Gehrke and Muthuramakrishnan Venkitasubramaniam, "l-diversity: Privacy beyond k- anonymity", *ACM Transactions on Knowledge Discovery from Data (TKDD)*, Vol. 1, No. 1, March 2007.

Meiklejohn, Sarah, Marjori Pomarole, Grant Jordan, Kirill Levchenko, Damon McCoy, Geoffrey M. Voelker and Stefan Savage, "A Fistful of Bitcoins: Characterizing Payments Among Men with No Names", *;login:* The USENIX magazine, Vol. 38, No. 6, December 2013.

Mao, Wenbo, *Modern cryptography: theory and practice*, HP Professional Series, 2003.

Mayer-Schönberger, Victor, "Beyond Copyright: Managing Information Rights with DRM", *Denver University Law Review*, Vol. 84, No. 1, 2006, pp. 181–198.

Organisation for Economic Co-operation and Development, *Guidelines on the Protection of Privacy and Transborder Flows of Personal Data*, OECD, Paris, 1980.

Organisation for Economic Co-operation and Development, *Thirty Years After The OECD Privacy Guidelines*, OECD, Paris, 2011. http://www.oecd.org/sti/ieconomy/49710223.pdf

Organisation for Economic Co-operation and Development, the recommendation of the OECD Council concerning Guidelines governing the Protection of Privacy and Transborder Flows of Personal Data, OECD, Paris, 2013. http://www.oecd.org/sti/ieconomy/2013-oecd-privacy-guidelines.pdf

Paillier, Pascal, "Public-Key Cryptosystems Based on Composite Degree Residuosity Classes", EUROCRYPT, Springer, 1999, pp. 223–238.

Paul, Thomas, Daniel Puscher and Thorsten Strufe, "Improving the Usability of Privacy Settings in Facebook", CoRR abs/1109.6046, 2011.

Pearson, Siani, and Andrew Charlesworth, "Accountability as a way forward for privacy protection in the cloud", in M.G. Jaatun, G. Zhao and C. Rong (eds.), *Cloud Computing*, Proceedings of CloudCom 2009, Beijing, Springer, Berlin, 2009, pp. 131–144.

Pfitzmann, Andreas, and Marit Hansen, "A terminology for talking about privacy by data minimization: Anonymity, Unlinkability, Undetectability, Unobservability, Pseudonymity, and Identity Management", Version v0.34, 10 August 2010. https://dud.inf.tu-dresden.de/literatur/Anon_Terminology_v0.34.pdf

Quisquater, Jean-Jacques, Louis C. Guillou and Thomas A. Berson, "How to explain Zero-Knowledge protocols to your children", in *Proceedings on Advances in Cryptology – CRYPTO '89*, Springer-Verlag New York, 1989, pp. 628–631.

Ratha, Nalini K., Jonathan H. Connell and Ruud M. Bolle, "Enhancing security and privacy in biometrics based authentication systems", *IBM Systems Journal*, Vol. 40, No. 3, 2001, pp. 614–634.

Reidenberg, Joel, and Lorrie Faith Cranor, "Can User Agents Accurately Represent Privacy Policies?", 30 August 2002. http://ssrn.com/abstract=328860

Rial, Alfredo, and George Danezis, "Privacy-Preserving Smart Metering", *Proceedings of the 2011 ACM Workshop on Privacy in the Electronic Society*, WPES, 2011.

Schneier, Bruce, *Applied cryptography*, Wiley, 1995.

Schneier, Bruce, *Practical cryptography*, Wiley, 2003.

Schneier, Bruce, *Secrets and lies*, Wiley, 2004.

Schneier, Bruce, and John Kelsey, "Secure Audit Logs to Support Computer Forensics", *ACM Transactions on Information and System Security*, Vol. 2, No. 2, 1999, pp. 159–176.

Schneider, Fred B., "Accountability for perfection", *IEEE Security and Privacy*, March-April, 2009, pp. 3–4.

Shen, Yun, and Siani Pearson, "Privacy-enhancing Technologies: A Review", HP Laboratories HPL-2011-113.

Solove, J. Daniel, "Privacy self-management and the consent paradox", *Harvard Law Review*, Vol. 126, 2013.

Sweeney, Latanya, "*Re-identification of De-identified Survey Data*", Carnegie Mellon University, School of Computer Science, Data Privacy Laboratory, Technical Report, 2000.

Sweeney, Latanya, "k-anonymity: A model for protecting privacy", *International Journal of Uncertainty, Fuzziness and Knowledge-Based Systems*, Vol. 10, No. 5, 2002, pp. 557–570.

Syverson, Paul S., David M. Goldschlag and Michael G. Reed, "Anonymous Connections and Onion Routing", in *Proceedings of the 18th Annual Symposium on Security and Privacy*, IEEE CS Press, May 1997, pp. 44–54.

Toubiana, Vincent, Arvind Narayanan, Dan Boneh, Helen Nissenbaum and Solon Barocas, "Adnostic: Privacy Preserving Targeted Advertising", Network and Distributed System Security Symposium 2010.

Troncoso, Carmela, George Danezis, Eleni Kosta and Bart Preneel, "PriPAYD: Privacy Friendly Pay-As You-Drive Insurance", *Proceedings of the 6th ACM workshop on Privacy in the electronic society (WPES)*, 2007.

Verykios, Vassilios S., Elisa Bertino, Igor Nai Fovino, Loredana Parasiliti Provenza, Yucel Saygin and Yannis Theodoridis, "State-of-the-art in Privacy Preserving Data Mining", in *SIGMOD Record*, Vol. 33, No. 1, March 2004, pp. 50–57.

Wang, Yang, Saranga Komanduri, Pedro Leon, Gregory Norcie, Alessandro Acquisti and Lorrie Faith Cranor, "'I regretted the minute I pressed share', A Qualitative Study of Regrets on Facebook", *Proceedings of the Seventh Symposium on Usable Privacy and Security (SOUPS)*, ACM, July 2011.

Waters, Brent R., Dirk Balfanz, Glenn Durfee and D.K. Smetters, "Building an encrypted and searchable audit log", presented at the 11th Annual Network and Distributed System Security Symposium, 2004.

Zanfir, Gabriela, "Forgetting About Consent: Why the Focus Should Be on 'Suitable Safeguards' in Data Protection Law", in Serge Gutwirth et al. (eds.), *Reloading Data Protection*, Springer, Dordrecht, 2014.

Part IV
Challenges for the Future

Chapter 18
The Irish DPA and Its Approach to Data Protection

Billy Hawkes

18.1 Introduction

This chapter explores the methods used and the challenges facing the Irish Data Protection Commissioner (DPC) in enforcing data protection rights. A recent survey of data protection authorities (DPAs) showed that the average number of employees per DPA is about 62. The Irish DPA has 49 directly employed staff with an additional outsourced legal team, while some DPAs have as few as two staff members. In this chapter, the Irish Data Protection Commissioner discusses how the DPC has been able to undertake major investigations of multinational companies such as Facebook and LinkedIn and what instruments the DPC uses to maximise impact, what other steps could be taken to improve the effectiveness of smaller DPAs and how they can leverage their effectiveness, including by means of investigation, raising awareness and audits.

The DPC emphasises the importance of close co-ordination between data protection authorities and anticipates a situation where, under revised EU data protection law, such co-ordination will be the norm where a company is providing services across Europe.

The European Union is made up of Member States with widely different demographic and economic profiles. Ireland is one of the smaller Member States both in terms of population and economic weight. This is reflected in the size of its public service.

Billy Hawkes retired from his role as Irish Data Protection Commissioner in August 2014 and Helen Dixon was subsequently appointed to the role. This chapter was largely prepared by Billy Hawkes with recent inputs from Helen Dixon to bring the information up-to-date.

B. Hawkes (✉)
Office of the Data Protection Commissioner, Canal House, Station Road, Portarlington, Co Laois, Ireland
e-mail: billy.hawkes@icloud.com; info@dataprotection.ie

D. Wright, P. De Hert (eds.), *Enforcing Privacy*, Law, Governance and Technology Series 25, DOI 10.1007/978-3-319-25047-2_18

All Member States are required to fully implement EU law, including the data protection directives. The burden on a data protection authority varies with factors such as the number and complexity of organisations under its jurisdiction and the precise obligations laid down in the national law giving effect to the EU Data Protection Directive (95/46/EC). In the case of the Office of the Data Protection Commissioner, a particular dimension is the number of multinational companies that have based their EU headquarters in Ireland.

This chapter examines the enforcement approach of the DPC, focussing on its use of a combination of "soft" and "hard" enforcement tools. It examines in particular how it has used its audit tool in relation to Ireland-based multinational companies that process personal data in connection with the provision of services across the European Union. It also comments on how the DPC has involved other DPAs in such investigations and how this situation might change under the new EU Regulation on data protection.

18.1.1 Irish data protection law

The Data Protection Act of 1988 gave effect in Irish law to the Council of Europe's 1981 Data Protection Convention (Convention 108). The 1988 Act was amended in 2003 to give effect to the increased obligations imposed on the State by the 1995 EU Data Protection Directive.

Ireland transposed the EU's Electronic Privacy Directive (2002/58/EC, as amended) into law through the Electronic Privacy Regulations (SI 336/2011).

Separate laws designate the DPC as the agency responsible for participating in the data protection oversight arrangements for agencies such as EUROPOL and EUROJUST.

Under the British-Irish Agreement Act of 1999, the DPC shares with the United Kingdom Information Commissioner's Office oversight responsibility for data protection in cross-border bodies established under the Agreement.

18.1.2 Role of the DPC

The legislation assigns four main roles to the DPC:

- An *enforcer* role in relation to the obligations laid down in the law;
- An *ombudsman* role in relation to the resolution of disputes between individuals and organisations about the processing of personal data;
- An *educational* role in disseminating information about data protection rights and responsibilities;

- A *transparency* role in maintaining a public register of major holders of personal data.[1]

While these roles are common to all DPAs, the manner in which they are discharged can vary among them, depending on the content of national law and the legal and administrative traditions of the country. As explained in further detail below, Irish data protection law and practice involve a combination of pro-active engagement with organisations and individuals – particularly through audits and outreach activities – and reactive activity related to complaints and data breach reports. The overall objective is to achieve a high level of protection of personal data across all sectors, public and private – thus "enforcement" in a broad sense.

No sector or organisation is excluded from the DPC's remit which includes the police and armed forces.

Investigation of complaints

Under section 10 of the Data Protection Acts, the DPC must investigate any complaints received from individuals who feel that personal information about them is not being treated in accordance with the Acts, unless the DPC is of the opinion that such complaints are "frivolous or vexatious".[2] The DPC is obliged by law to seek an "amicable resolution" of the complaint in the first instance. Where this cannot be achieved, the Commissioner may make a Decision on whether, in their opinion, there has been a breach of the law. If the complainant disagrees with the DPC's finding, they have the right to appeal the Decision to the Circuit Court.

The duty to seek an "amicable resolution" of complaints can involve extensive interaction with both the complainant and the organisation complained of. The process is usually successful in achieving an "amicable" outcome and can lead to, for example, an apology or an offer of financial compensation. So, while 960 complaints were opened for investigation in 2014, only 27 formal Decisions were issued. If an organisation does not voluntarily co-operate with an investigation, the DPC has extensive powers of compulsion to require such co-operation as described later.

The DPC's main priority, if a complaint is upheld, is that the data controller complies with the law and puts matters right. The DPC does not have the power to award compensation. Section 7 of the Acts provides that "For the purposes of the

---

[1] While the main focus of the annual registration requirement is on transparency, it can also be used as part of the DPC's enforcement strategy as failure to register, or to fully describe personal data being processed, is an offence under the Data Protection Acts. The DPC's power to refuse registration is also relevant as the organisation concerned is prohibited from processing personal data. The DPC has occasionally used or threatened use of these registration-related powers. The registration requirement also generates revenue from fees – however, these go to the general Exchequer rather than to the DPC.

[2] "Frivolous or vexatious" has been interpreted by the High Court as meaning "futile, or misconceived or hopeless in the sense that it was incapable of achieving the desired outcome" in the case *Peter Nowak vs Data Protection Commissioner* [2012] IEHC 449.

law of torts and to the extent that that law does not so provide, a person, being a data controller or a data processor, shall, so far as regards the collection by him of personal data or information intended for inclusion in such data or his dealing with such data, owe a duty of care to the data subject." If a person suffers damage through the mishandling of their personal information, they may therefore be entitled to claim compensation through the courts. The DPC has no function in relation to the taking of such proceedings. Case law suggests that Irish courts are not well disposed towards awarding compensation where the case relies solely on a breach of an organisation's duty towards an individual in relation to processing of personal data.[3]

Data breaches

Under a DPC Code of Practice,[4] any organisation that suffers a data security breach involving personal data above a minimum level is obliged to report the breach to the DPC. The main focus of the Code is on ensuring that affected individuals are informed of the breach and advised of any precautionary measures they should take. The DPC focus is on ensuring that organisations discharge this duty towards affected individuals and take any necessary measures to avoid a recurrence of the breach.

Since 2013, under the revised Electronic Privacy Directive as transposed into Irish law, such reporting is obligatory for telecommunications companies.

Codes of practice

Section 13 of the Data Protection Act provides that the DPC "shall encourage trade associations and other bodies representing categories of data controllers to prepare codes of practice to be complied with by those categories in dealing with personal data." If the DPC agrees that such a code provides adequate data protection for individuals, it will formally approve it and encourage its use in the sector concerned. The DPC may also draw up such a code of practice on its own initiative. The standards laid down in such a code should help organisations to apply the data protection principles to the particular situations that they face in their sector. Examples of such codes include those for the police and for the insurance sector.[5]

---

[3] See *Collins vs FBD Insurance Plc* [2013] IEHC 137.

[4] http://www.dataprotection.ie/docs/Data_Security_Breach_Code_of_Practice/1082.htm

[5] http://www.garda.ie/Controller.aspx?Page=136&Lang=1; http://www.insuranceireland.eu/media/documents/20130626_Code_of_Practice_Final.pdf

Audits

Section 10 (1A) of the Acts provides that "the Commissioner may carry out or cause to be carried out such investigations as he or she considers appropriate in order to ensure compliance with the provisions of this Act and to identify any contravention thereof." These investigations usually take the form of audits of selected organisations. The aim of an audit is to identify any issues of concern about the way the organisation under scrutiny deals with personal data and to recommend solutions. The audit normally includes one or more on-site visits by an audit team from the Office. During these visits, the team will meet with selected staff of the organisation and will usually inspect electronic and manual records. At the end of the audit, the team will prepare a report, which typically includes a set of recommendations. The DPC gives the organisation audited an opportunity to comment on the report before it is finalised. The Office may follow up later on how and whether these recommendations have been implemented. It is only in the event of serious breaches being discovered or failure of the data controller to implement recommendations that coercive enforcement measures would be used.

The DPC carries out the audit in accordance with a standard template[6] which is adapted to the particular circumstances of the entity being audited. In 2014, the DPC carried out 38 audits and inspections, prioritising multinational technology companies and major public-sector organisations.

Educational activity

The DPC devotes significant resources to providing guidance to organisations and individuals on their respective obligations and rights. It operates an active help desk where organisations and individuals can seek guidance by phone or in writing on their respective obligations and rights. A dedicated Compliance Section deals with more in-depth enquiries. The DPC also provides guidance on its website on specific data protection issues; the guidance is updated as necessary to take account of issues arising from complaints or enquiries. It provides speakers for relevant data protection fora and news media. It also publishes an annual report on its activities.

18.1.3 Coercive enforcement powers

Mechanisms such as investigations of complaints and data breaches, audits and codes of practice are "soft" methods of achieving acceptable standards of protection of personal data. These are the main methods used by the DPC. The "soft" mechanisms are complemented by "hard" measures prescribed by law, which are used where organisations fail to voluntarily comply with the law.

[6] http://www.dataprotection.ie/docimages/documents/GuidetoAuditProcessAug2014.pdf

The general approach to enforcement under the Data Protection Acts is corrective rather than punitive. The Acts provide extensive legal powers to the DPC to enforce compliance with the legislation but breaches of the Act are not, in general, offences. In contrast, breaches of the Electronic Privacy Regulations are offences that may be prosecuted summarily by the DPC or on indictment.

Data Protection Act powers

Under section 12 of the Acts, the DPC may require any person to provide it with whatever information it needs to carry out its functions, such as to pursue an investigation. The DPC exercises this power by providing a written notice, called an "information notice", to the person.

Under section 10 of the Acts, the DPC may require a data controller or data processor to take whatever steps the DPC considers appropriate to comply with the terms of the Acts. Such steps could include correcting the data, blocking the data from use for certain purposes, supplementing the data with a statement which the DPC approves, or erasing the data altogether. The DPC exercises this power by providing a written notice, called an "enforcement notice", to the data controller or data processor.

Under section 11 of the Acts, the DPC may prohibit the transfer of personal data from the State to a place outside the European Economic Area. The DPC can exercise this power by providing a written notice, called a "prohibition notice", to the data controller or data processor. In considering whether to exercise this power, the DPC must have regard to the need to facilitate international transfers of information. The DPC must also have regard to decisions of the EU Commission under Article 25 of the Data Protection Directive that a particular country provides an "adequate" level of protection of personal data.[7] A prohibition notice may be absolute, or may prohibit the transfer of personal data until the person concerned takes certain steps to protect the interests of the individuals affected.

Under section 24 of the Acts, the Commissioner may appoint an "authorised officer" to enter and examine the premises of a data controller or data processor to enable the DPC to carry out its functions, such as to pursue an investigation. The authorised officer has the power to:

- enter the premises and inspect any data equipment there;
- require the data controller, data processor or staff to assist in obtaining access to data, and to provide any related information;
- inspect and copy any information;

[7] Following a referral to the Court of Justice of the European Union by the Irish High Court (case c-362/14), the Court ruled that a Commission "adequacy" decision "does not prevent a supervisory authority of a Member State, within the meaning of Article 28 of that directive as amended, from examining the claim of a person concerning the protection of his rights and freedoms in regard to the processing of personal data relating to him which has been transferred from a Member State to that third country when that person contends that the law and practices in force in the third country do not ensure an adequate level of protection."

- require the data controller, data processor or staff to provide information about procedures on complying with the Act, sources of data, purposes for which personal data are kept, persons to whom data are disclosed and data equipment on the premises.

Under section 26 of the Acts, appeals can be made to the Circuit Court against:

- a requirement specified in an information notice;
- a requirement specified in an enforcement notice;
- a prohibition specified in a prohibition notice;
- a refusal by the DPC to accept an application for registration, or for renewal of registration, or for an amendment of registration details;
- a decision of the DPC in relation to a complaint by an individual.

Appeals to the court must normally be made within 21 days from the service of the notice or from the date of receipt of the refusal or decision. The decision of the court is final, although an appeal against the court's decision may be brought to the High Court on a point of law.

Data Protection Acts: offences

Breaches of the data protection rules laid down by the Acts are not, in general, offences. Offences under the Acts relate primarily to failure to comply with statutory notices issued by the DPC. Failure to comply with the registration obligations imposed on certain categories of data controllers and data processors are also offences, as is obstruction of "authorised officers". It is an offence to disclose personal data obtained without authority – in the case of a data processor, without the authority of the data controller. Section 31 provides that offences are punishable by fines – a maximum of €3,000 on summary conviction and €100,000 on conviction on indictment. Section 30 provides that the DPC may bring summary proceedings for an offence under the Acts.

As it is rare for data controllers or processors to fail to co-operate with the DPC, especially when statutory notices have been issued, prosecutions under the Acts are infrequently taken. The DPC does, however, use these powers if necessary and in 2014, the DPC prosecuted nine entities for a total of 162 offences under the Data Protection Acts of 1988 and 2003, and the Privacy in Electronic Communications Regulations of 2011.

Offences under the Electronic Communications Regulations

In contrast to the position under the Data Protection Acts, all breaches of the Electronic Communications Regulations for which the DPC has responsibility[8] are offences. The offences relate primarily to the sending of unsolicited marketing

[8] Enforcement responsibility is shared with the Communications Regulator (ComReg).

communications by electronic means. The offences are punishable by fines – up to €5,000 for each unsolicited message on summary conviction and up to €250,000 on conviction on indictment. The DPC may bring summary proceedings for an offence under the Regulations.

Since 2013, failure by electronic service providers to adopt adequate security measures is also a prosecutable offence.

In recent years, the DPC has made extensive use of the power to bring summary prosecutions in the case of companies that have repeatedly breached the rules on the sending of unsolicited electronic communications. In doing so, it has operated in close co-operation with the Communications Regulator (ComReg). So far, there has been one prosecution for failure by an electronic service provider to adopt adequate security measures.

Enforcement powers: assessment

The DPC approach to enforcement might be described as "enforcement by agreement, where possible". This is evidenced by the focus on "amicable" settlement of complaints, by the use of the audit tool in a generally non-adversarial manner and by the significant resources devoted to guidance activities. However, this approach is backed up by strong enforcement powers of which organisations are fully aware and this undoubtedly influences their efforts to comply. Organisations usually consider it to be in their best interests not to provoke the use of enforcement powers and the negative publicity that usually results – especially where the DPC brings organisations before the courts or names them in its Annual Report. The threat of such enforcement is usually sufficient to elicit a compliant response – especially where an organisation is reminded that its directors or senior officers are also liable to be brought before the courts for non-compliance. The focus of both "soft" and "hard" enforcement measures is to bring about compliance rather than to punish. Even where punitive action is taken through the courts, the objective is always to achieve compliance by the offending organisation and by other organisations in its sector.

Unlike a number of other EU DPAs, the DPC does not have the power to directly impose financial penalties. The granting of such punitive (as opposed to corrective) powers to non-judicial bodies is not common in Ireland.

Enforcement: resource allocation

The DPC is an expanding organisation, with 49 staff and a budget of more than €3.6 million. Its staff-count and budget were increased in 2014, in recognition of the additional responsibilities it has acquired in relation to oversight of information-rich, multinational companies providing services from Ireland across the European Union. This has included the recruitment of specialists in the legal and technological fields. The allocation of extra resources was complemented by a public commitment from the Government that resource needs would be kept under review to ensure that the DPC could meet its EU-wide responsibilities. In addition, Ireland became the first country in Europe in 2014 to appoint a dedicated Minister for Data Protection.

Apart from an obligation on a sub-set of organisations to register annually with the DPC, there are no prior notification requirements under Irish law, hence, the DPC has considerable flexibility in allocating its staffing and other resources. It also benefits from the outsourcing of many functions – IT, finance, human resources – to a shared public services centre and an ability to hire in expertise as required. This ability to hire in expertise has been particularly valuable when dealing with the legal and technological challenges by information-rich Internet companies. Flexibility around resource allocation is an important aspect of the DPC's ability to discharge its oversight responsibilities.

18.1.4 *Enforcement: tools of European and international co-operation*

As business is increasingly done on the Internet and by multinational companies – many processing personal data on a global basis – the need for international co-operation to protect the data protection rights of users has increased considerably. Within the European Union, such co-operation is facilitated by the common requirements laid down in the Data Protection Directive (95/46/EC), including the obligation to co-operate as specified in Article 28.6 of the Directive. In the broader European framework, such co-operation is also facilitated by the Council of Europe Convention 108, with its obligation of mutual assistance between signatories spelled out in its Article 13.

The task of effective international enforcement outside Europe is complicated by the absence of internationally-accepted data protection standards and the potential conflict with the confidentiality obligations laid down in Article 28.7 of the Directive and Article 15 of the Convention. Despite these difficulties, the need for co-operation with non-European regulators is pressing – especially in relation to the United States where many global Internet companies have their main base. The DPC has addressed this issue in various ways. It is an active member of the Global Privacy Enforcement Network (GPEN), which aims to facilitate exchanges of relevant information between organisations charged with enforcement of privacy and data protection. It supports international enforcement efforts being pursued under the aegis both of the International Conference of Data Protection and Privacy Commissioners and of the Organisation for Economic Co-operation and Development (OECD). It has also entered into bilateral Memoranda of Understanding (MOUs) with the US Federal Trade Commission,[9] the Office of the Privacy Commissioner of Canada and the Office of the Australian Information Commissioner.

[9] http://www.dataprotection.ie/documents/MOU/MOU.pdf

For a smaller DPA, being able to work closely with other regulators with similar responsibilities is a significant aid to effectiveness.

18.1.5 *Enforcement: the challenge of multinational companies*

Until 10 years ago, the DPC's responsibilities related almost exclusively to domestic organisations in the private and public sectors. That situation has changed significantly in recent years with the decisions of companies such as Facebook and LinkedIn to establish their European headquarters in Ireland and to designate this entity as the one with which customers enter into agreements.[10] This has resulted in the DPC acquiring significant responsibility for data protection oversight of these companies.[11] Other DPAs increasingly look to the DPC to ensure that these companies comply with the requirements of EU data protection law in their dealings with individuals based in their countries. A significant number of complaints against these companies are also being referred either directly to the DPC or via the local DPA. The data processing activities of many of these companies have been quite controversial, partly due to the fact that their services are offered to users without charge and partly to the fact that personal data processed on the sites is used to target advertising at users.

In response to the challenges presented by such companies, the DPC decided to prioritise them for comprehensive audit. The DPC has informed all such companies of this intention – including at early stages of pre-establishment contact.

Audit of Facebook-Ireland (FB-I): procedure

The first such audit of a major Internet company processing extensive amounts of personal data was of Facebook-Ireland (FB-I), the entity with which users outside the US and Canada enter into agreement. The DPC carried out the audit using its standard methodology for such audits, which involved a combination of desk-based research and on-site investigation.

Given the significance of the audit, the then Deputy Commissioner led the audit team. The team included an external technical consultant, originally provided by

[10] In the case of Facebook, all users outside the US and Canada. In the case of LinkedIn, all users outside the US.

[11] The degree to which, under existing EU law, other European DPAs can assert jurisdiction over entities such as Facebook-Ireland is not entirely clear, linked as it is to interpretations of Article 4 of Directive 95/46/EC, notably the phrase "the processing is carried out in the context of the activities of an establishment of the controller on the territory of the Member State". The DPC, in its audit report, stated that: "it ha(d) jurisdiction over the personal data processing activities of FB-I based on it being established in Ireland" but that this "should not however be interpreted as asserting sole jurisdiction over the activities of Facebook in the EU".

University College Dublin and subsequently engaged on a contract basis. His technical analysis of aspects of Facebook operations was annexed to the audit report.

The audit involved a detailed assessment of the manner in which FB-I complied with the requirements of Irish and EU data protection law. In accordance with DPC standard practice, the report of the audit[12] – which was published in December 2011 with the agreement of FB-I – contained a series of "best practice" recommendations addressed to the company, together with FB-I's initial response to these. Where relevant, the DPC indicated a target implementation date. The audit report stated that the recommendations "do not carry an implication that FB-I's current practices are not in compliance with Irish data protection law" and were not formal DPC decisions on issues raised in complaints that had been taken into account in the audit.

The DPC assessed the degree of implementation of the recommendations in a "re-audit" published in September 2012.[13] This showed that FB-I had complied satisfactorily with most of the recommendations made in the audit. The DPC gave FB-I a short deadline to show progress on the remaining recommendations. It subsequently demonstrated that it had responded satisfactorily to these recommendations.

FB-I's co-operation with the audit process – while vigorously defending its positions on various points – was an example of the use of enforcement powers that did not need to be backed up by more coercive measures. The audit made clear that, as the "best practice" recommendations did not constitute formal decisions under the Data Protection Acts, complainants who did not consider that the result of the audit dealt satisfactorily with the issues they had raised were free to seek formal decisions on their complaints.

Audit of Facebook-Ireland: EU and international co-operation

The audit report stated that it was "built on work carried out by other regulators, notably the Canadian Privacy Commissioner, the US Federal Trade Commission and the Nordic and German Data Protection Authorities". In the course of the audit, the DPC maintained close contact with EU data protection authorities through the Technology sub-group of the Article 29 Working Party. The DPC also contacted the Canadian and US authorities in order to ensure, in so far as possible, that all relevant issues were addressed as part of the audit[14] and that DPC action was complementary to theirs – notably the FTC's requirement for periodic independent audit. These contacts were useful – indeed essential – given the global nature of the service provided by Facebook and the fact that improvements made as a result of the audit were, for the most part, rolled out on a global basis. As a result, all users of Facebook benefited from the protections contained in Irish and EU data protection law.

[12] http://dataprotection.ie/docs/Facbook-Audit/1290.htm

[13] http://dataprotection.ie/docs/Facbook-Audit/1290.htm

[14] As indicated earlier, MoUs have facilitated co-operation with the US and Canadian authorities.

Audit of Facebook-Ireland: assessment

The audit was an example both of "enforcement by agreement" and use of European and international co-operation mechanisms in relation to a company operating on a global basis. This approach was facilitated by the willingness of the company to co-operate with the audit process and to implement the recommendations without the need for coercive enforcement measures. It was clear that the company viewed some of the recommendations as challenging but that, in its own cost-benefit calculus, the merit of being seen to co-operate with its "local" DPA was considered to be of greater importance – as it had been in its dealings with the FTC in the US. This, perhaps ideal, outcome may not necessarily be true of all such global companies; that remains to be seen as the DPC audits other global companies established in Ireland.

The fact that both audit reports were published, with the agreement of the company, was also significant as it allowed others to draw their own conclusions about the basis on which the DPC assessed FB-I's compliance. It may have created an expectation that all such audit reports would be published in full, which may not be possible due to the confidentiality obligations that apply to the DPC and to all EU DPAs.

The ability of the DPC to appoint an external expert to the audit team – using the power provided by law to appoint an "authorised officer" – was important. For the future, it could allow the appointment of such experts for short-term assignments where issues specific to a particular sector arise. Again, flexibility in deployment of a DPA's "tool-box" and an ability and willingness to work closely with other regulators are key enablers for a smaller DPA.

18.1.6 Enforcement: impact of draft revised EU law

In January 2012, the European Commission published its proposals for a significant revision of EU data protection law, reflecting the enhanced status granted to data protection as a fundamental right of EU citizens.[15] One of the most significant revisions is that, instead of a Directive to be transposed into Member State law, there will be a Regulation (directly) applying uniformly across the EU. Failure to comply with its terms would attract severe penalties for intentional or negligent breaches.[16] The proposed Regulation gives each DPA the power to impose such sanctions.

One of the more controversial proposals is for a so-called "one-stop shop" for multinational companies. With a single law applying across the EU, it follows that

[15] Article 8 of the EU Charter of Fundamental Rights.

[16] The compromise text agreed between the Council, Parliament and Commission in December 2015 provides for penalties of up to €20 million or four per cent of an organisation's global turnover.

it should be applied in a uniform manner, without the limited degree of flexibility in application that applies to implementation of the EU Data Protection Directive.[17]

The obligation to co-operate has a provision to include staff from other DPAs in investigations of companies operating across the EU. While this would not be a significant departure for the DPC – which, as described above, co-operated closely with other DPAs in its audit of FB-I and already has the power to appoint persons other than its own staff as "authorised officers" – it could have significant implications for other DPAs. Many major companies in sectors such as transport and financial services that provide services across the EU have their "main establishment" in an EU Member State. The obligation for close co-ordination with other EU DPAs in relation to their supervision could be a significant – even unsettling – development for some DPAs, especially concerning oversight of former State monopolies. Such close co-ordination in order to ensure uniform application of the law would also have significant resource implications both for DPAs and for the European Data Protection Board. Following agreement on the text of the Regulation in December 2015, it is due to enter into force in 2018.

For the DPC, knowledge of the general shape of the future law will encourage a deepening of the EU and international enforcement co-operation model that was applied in the case of Facebook-Ireland. This could include even more active involvement of other DPAs in audits, using the "authorised officer" facility to potentially involve staff of other DPAs – both EU and non-EU – directly in audits of companies providing services to EU users from an Irish base. This might also encourage reciprocal action by other DPAs in relation to the many European multinationals providing services to Irish residents. Such co-operative activity could help to mitigate the resource constraints that apply to a smaller DPA.

The focus in the Regulation on punitive measures such as administrative penalties could involve a significant adjustment in approach for the DPC. Where a company's action impacted on individuals in other countries, it is likely that there would be significant pressure to deploy such measures, rather than the combination of compliance measures – such as guidance and consensual audits – and "hard" measures of legally-binding orders typically used to date by the DPC. A more defensive approach on the part of companies seems likely, especially due to the emphasis on punitive sanctions for a wide variety of breaches of the law. Whether or not the result would be an improved overall level of compliance is hard to predict.

In looking to an uncertain future, one can see that a key focus has to be on further developing effective international enforcement co-operation to match the increase

[17] With regard to the transposition of Directive 95/46/EC into national law, the European Court of Justice has commented that "the harmonisation of those national laws is not limited to minimal harmonisation but amounts to harmonisation which is generally complete". See judgment of 24 November 2011 in relation to Joined Cases C-468/10 and C-469/10 *Asociación Nacional de Establecimientos Financieros de Crédito* (*ASNEF*) (*C-468/10*), *Federación de Comercio Electrónico y Marketing Directo* (*FECEMD*) (*C-469/10*) *vs Administración del Estado* 2012/C 25/30.

in global data flows. Without such co-operation, it will be difficult for individual DPAs to credibly assert that they can meet their obligations to protect the rights of individuals.

18.2 Conclusions

Data protection enforcement is about ensuring that organisations treat the personal data of individuals with respect and, as a minimum, in accordance with the law. There can be significant differences in how DPAs use their enforcement "tool-box" in pursuit of this objective. The DPC has focused more on tools such as guidance, amicable resolution of complaints and consensual audits, backed up by "harder" tools such as legally binding enforcement notices and prosecution through the courts. Planned changes in EU law are likely to lead to a greater emphasis on "hard" enforcement tools such as the direct imposition of administrative penalties – though whether such a punitive approach will actually lead to a higher standard of compliance is open to question. The planned changes are also likely to lead to far closer co-ordination between DPAs in regard to the oversight of companies providing services internationally. The DPC has already experienced closer co-ordination in its oversight of information-rich multinational companies based in Ireland – not only with EU DPAs but also with other enforcement authorities such as the US Federal Trade Commission and other DPAs outside of Europe. For smaller DPAs such as the DPC, closer co-operation through the planned EU "consistency mechanism" – designed to ensure a uniform application of the law – may also offer a way of using the expertise of larger DPAs to address the complex issues raised by the data processing practices of multinational companies.

References

Collins vs FBD Insurance Plc [2013] IEHC 137.

European Parliament, Council and Commission, Charter of Fundamental Rights of the European Union

European Court of Justice, judgment of 24 November 2011 in relation to Joined Cases C-468/10 and C-469/10 *Asociación Nacional de Establecimientos Financieros de Crédito (ASNEF) (C-468/10), Federación de Comercio Electrónico y Marketing Directo (FECEMD) (C-469/10) vs Administración del Estado* 2012/C 25/30.

Peter Nowak vs Data Protection Commissioner [2012] IEHC 449.

Chapter 19
Getting Our Act Together: European Data Protection Authorities Face Up to Silicon Valley

Jacob Kohnstamm

19.1 Introduction

In a world where data are crossing borders like never before, data protection authorities (DPAs) need to work more closely together across borders to be able to ensure that people's privacy and personal data are protected.

In October 2012, the Article 29 Working Party, in which all European Union DPAs are assembled, published its findings on Google's new privacy policy, following an investigation led by the French DPA (CNIL, the Commission Nationale de l'Informatique et des Libertés). The findings included recommendations, several of which were supported by supervisory authorities from other regions of the world, such as North America and the Asia Pacific, urging Google to take effective and public measures to update its privacy policy.

In an ever more globalised world where a few multinationals play a dominant role, can Europe ensure compliance with its high data protection standards? What have the data protection authorities in Europe done so far to ensure compliance by these companies and what are the lessons learned? Given the global nature of the data flows, are global actions successful in ensuring compliance? Will the new EU Data Protection Regulation[1] change things for the better?

This Chapter aims to address such questions, first, by briefly highlighting some joint investigations by European and other DPAs in the past decade or so, and then

---

[1] European Commission, Proposal for a Regulation of the European Parliament and of the Council on the protection of individuals with regard to the processing of personal data and on the free movement of such data (General Data Protection Regulation), COM(2012) 11 final, Brussels, 25 January 2012. http://ec.europa.eu/justice/data-protection/document/review2012/com_2012_11_en.pdf

J. Kohnstamm (✉)
Dutch Data Protection Authority, PO Box 93374,
2500 AJ The Hague, The Netherlands
e-mail: international@cbpweb.nl; j.kohnstamm@cbpweb.nl

D. Wright, P. De Hert (eds.), *Enforcing Privacy*, Law, Governance and Technology Series 25, DOI 10.1007/978-3-319-25047-2_19

by looking to the future to identify what is needed to facilitate better co-operation across borders.

19.2 Joint investigations

19.2.1 Search engines

The struggle to persuade large online enterprises to respect basic privacy rules in a borderless world might be best illustrated by the efforts of data protection authorities over the past 15 years to strengthen the rights of users of search engines. On the international level, the International Conference of Data Protection and Privacy Commissioners (ICDPPC) in 1998 firstly explicitly voiced their joint concern about search engines having the possibility to compile profiles of citizen consumers.[2] This "Common Position on Privacy Protection and Search Engines" was revised and updated in 2006.[3]

Later in that same year, the 28th ICDPPC, held in London on 2 and 3 November 2006, adopted a Resolution on Privacy Protection and Search Engines.[4] The Conference called upon providers of search engines to respect the basic rules of privacy as laid down in national legislation in many countries, as well as in policy documents and treaties, and to change their practices accordingly.

19.2.2 European authorities take a stance

The Article 29 Working Party subsequently adopted an Opinion on issues concerning protection of personal data related to search engines on 4 April 2008,[5] partly based on a questionnaire sent to relevant search engine providers.[6] The Working Party acknowledged the importance of search engines in the current information society, but at the same time noted an increasing number of user complaints regarding possible intrusion of their privacy. Recognising the providers' business interests, the Working Party in its Opinion clarified the circumstances under which organisations must comply with the European legal framework.

The European rules on data protection apply to search engines even if their headquarters are in a country outside the EU. Furthermore, personal data collected by

[2] 23rd International Conference of Data Protection and Privacy Commissioners, "The Common Position on Privacy Protection and Search Engines", Resolution, Hong Kong, 15 April 1998.

[3] 39th Meeting of the International Working Group on Data Protection in Telecommunications, Washington DC, 6–7 April 2006.

[4] www.privacyconference.2006.org

[5] http://ec.europa.eu/justice_home/fsj/privacy/docs/wpdocs/2008/wp148_en.pdf

[6] Annex 2 to Opinion 1/2008 on data protection issues related to search engines

search engines must be deleted as soon as possible, at the latest after six months. Internet users should be clearly informed of their rights. They must also consent to the use of their data for consumer profiling purposes.

Upon publication of the Opinion, the Art. 29 Working Party invited leading search engine providers to offer comments. In February 2009, the Working Party organised a closed hearing, attended by representatives of the major players in the field (Google, Microsoft, Yahoo! and the metasearch engine Ixquick). The hearing focused on three major topics: the retention period of personal data related to searches, including search terms, IP addresses and cookies; the method of deletion or anonymisation of personal data upon expiry of the justified retention period; and the applicability of European data protection law to non-EU based operators.

The operators committed themselves to work with data protection authorities to improve their privacy practices. "However, some operators fear that if search engine providers fail to adopt equivalent practices, they could benefit from an unfair competitive advantage. Therefore, some operators called for a common industry standard that would include, among other features, truly efficient anonymisation and a maximum retention period of six months", according to the Art. 29 WP press release of 12 February 2009.[7] The Working Party welcomed the call for industry standards in online search. Nevertheless, it "has to point out that the European data protection and privacy legislation should be the basis for this initiative". The Working Party regarded the results of its ongoing engagement with the search engine operators from early stages through to the adoption of the Opinion on 11 February 2009 as a "very positive signal that will have an enormous impact on millions of individuals".

The optimism voiced in February turned a bit sour in the following months. In letters of 23 October 2009 to Google, Microsoft and Yahoo,[8] the Working Party welcomed the efforts these operators had made to bring their policy in line with the European data protection legislation, but pointed out some significant shortcomings as well, especially regarding retention periods and the process of anonymisation implemented by the search engines.

19.2.3 FTC involvement

The Working Party has acknowledged the strong international component of this debate. In order to raise the issue to a transatlantic level, it shared its concerns with the US Federal Trade Commission (FTC) and asked it to use its authority to examine the compatibility of the providers' behaviour with section 5 of the Federal Trade Commission Act.[9]

---

[7] http://ec.europa.eu/justice_home/fsj/privacy/workinggroup/index_en.htm

[8] http://ec.eurropa.eu/justice/policies/privacy/news/docs/pr_12_02_09_en.pdf

[9] http://ec.europa.eu/justice/policies/privacy/docs/wpdocs/others/2010_05_26_letter_wp_federal_trade_commission.pdf

Copies of the letters were also sent to the Vice-President of the European Commission in charge of Justice, Fundamental Rights and Citizenship. The Working Party expressed its hope that the exchange would "contribute in a meaningful way to the development and enforcement of adequate, transatlantic data protection principles"[10] and indicated that "key concern for the WP29 is the possibility of enforcement of European data protection principles in a borderless world. Our correspondence with the search engines illustrates the need to pay specific attention to key principles including purpose limitation, independent auditing and retention periods."

19.2.4 Still no full compliance

Did these polite proddings lead to compliance with European data protection law by the search engine operators? According to the Beatles, the long and winding road led to a door. In our case, progress was made, but this did not produce an open door, let alone assure full compliance. Six months later, the Working Party once more sent the operators letters "strongly suggesting" and "urging" them once again to review their retention policies and anonymisation claims.[11] Since then, no further activities have been undertaken vis-à-vis search engine operators.

19.2.5 Google Buzz

In early 2010, Google decided to automatically make all Gmail users members of its new social networking service Google Buzz. This led to a huge public outcry. Users were upset about the publication on their newly created profile of the e-mail addresses of the people whom they had e-mailed, marking them as "followers". Data protection authorities around the world promptly sent a joint letter in which they informed Google that they "were disturbed by your recent rollout of the Google Buzz social networking application, which betrayed a disappointing disregard for fundamental privacy norms and laws. Moreover, this was not the first time you have failed to take adequate account of privacy considerations when launching new services."[12]

The data protection and privacy commissioners did acknowledge that Google had already addressed the most privacy-intrusive aspects of its new service,

[10] http://ec.europa.eu/justice/policies/privacy/docs/wpdocs/others/2010_05_26_letter_wp_vpreding.pdf

[11] http://www.cbpweb.nl/downloads_int/2009_10_23_letter_wp_google.pdf (respectively Microsoft and Yahoo!)

[12] Letter of 19 April 2010, signed by 10 data protection authorities, with seven from Europe, and three from Canada, New Zealand and Israel.

following reactions of outraged Gmail users who were concerned that their personal information was being disclosed. They nevertheless called upon the company to ensure that any new services would comply with fair information principles before they were introduced, to avoid having to repair problems afterwards. This letter was the first action undertaken by data protection authorities from different parts of the world voicing a common concern.

Google responded in a letter on 7 May 2010[13] by reiterating its five privacy principles and gave a short overview of the tools it had developed to enable users to view and control their personal information. Google furthermore stated that "of course we do not get everything 100 % right – that is why we acted so quickly on Google Buzz following the user feedback we received" and that the impact of "user feedback" was appreciated. One could wish that companies would react similarly when confronted by privacy commissioners' admonitions.

In March 2011, the FTC made public that it had reached a settlement with Google following the sudden introduction of social network features within the Google mail system. The FTC's settlement with Google[14] amounted to a comprehensive privacy program imposed on Google. This was a great achievement in jointly addressing an issue of common concern. In October 2011, Google terminated Buzz permanently and launched a different social network called Google Plus.[15] This does not mean, however, that Google had escaped any further regulatory attention.

19.3 A separate investigation: Google Street View

In 2010, almost all European data protection authorities decided to take action regarding the Google Street View service. While Google was driving around all over the world in Street View cars taking pictures for its Street View service, it was also collecting data about and from WiFi access points. The European data protection authorities doubted that the collection of this data was in compliance with the law and therefore concerned authorities undertook immediate action.

Unfortunately, these actions differed substantially. While the data protection authorities from the Netherlands, France, the Czech Republic, Belgium, Italy, Hamburg and Spain ordered Google to hand over the collected data to conduct a thorough investigation, the Irish, Danish and Austrian DPAs ordered Google to destroy all payload data. To complicate the matter even further, in some countries, public prosecutors took the lead in investigations, depending on national criminal law provisions, instead of the data protection authority and in others, the data protection authority, having no sanctioning power itself, had to hand over its preliminary

---

[13] http://www.scribd.com/fullscreen/31056661?access_key=key-np9r7ignhiwjhw2x2i2

[14] http://www.ftc.gov/news-events/press-releases/2011/03/ftc-charges-deceptive-privacy-practices-googles-rollout-its-buzz

[15] Google Official Blog, 14 October 2011. http://googleblog.blogspot.nl/2011/10/fall-sweep.html. Google continued its social networking strategy with Google +.

investigation results to a public prosecutor for follow-up. In still other cases, the data protection authority itself did the investigation and subsequent sanctioning.

For example, in the Netherlands, the Dutch data protection authority found that over a period of two years, Google had systematically and without the data subjects' knowledge, collected the MAC addresses[16] of about 3.6 million different Wi-Fi access points, in combination with their calculated locations, plus snippets of content data (payload), containing personal information. The Dutch DPA ordered Google to inform data subjects within three months about this collection of data and to offer them an online possibility to opt out from the database. Furthermore, after the investigation, the Dutch DPA ordered Google to destroy within four weeks the payload data it had unlawfully collected in the Netherlands. The DPA also issued several administrative orders against Google for incremental penalty payments, stating that if Google did not comply with the administrative orders within three months as from 23 March 2011, the penalty amount would increase to a maximum of one million euros. Google fulfilled the requirements.

Even though efforts were made in the Working Party to co-ordinate the different actions and investigations, there was no co-ordinated single investigation involving all authorities in Europe. This allowed Google to deal individually with the different authorities and with other actors such as public prosecutors, leading to different outcomes of the legal procedures in the concerned Member States.

But this country-specific approach was not all bad, because the European data protection authorities reached consensus with regard to the legal assessment, i.e., that the collection of MAC addresses of WiFi access points, in combination with their calculated location, should be treated as personal data, which can be read in the Opinion on geolocation on smart mobile devices in 2011.[17]

19.4 Common approaches

19.4.1 Facebook

In 2009, the Working Party recognised that social networking had become an important element of online daily life in Europe and adopted an Opinion on social networking outlining, among other things, the importance of free and informed consent and privacy-friendly default settings.[18] In November of the same year, the Working

---

[16] A media access control address (MAC address) is a unique identifier assigned to network interfaces for communications on the physical network segment.

[17] Article 29 Data Protection Working Party, Opinion 13/2011 on Geolocation services on smart mobile devices, WP185, Brussels, Adopted on 16 May 2011, p. 11. http://ec.europa.eu/justice/data-protection/article-29/documentation/opinion-recommendation/files/2011/wp185_en.pdf

[18] Article 29 Data Protection Working Party, Opinion 5/2009 on online social networking, WP 163, Brussels, Adopted on 12 June 2009. http://ec.europa.eu/justice/policies/privacy/docs/wpdocs/2009/wp163_en.pdf

Party organised a hearing with a number of social networking sites, which had signed the “Safer Networking Principles for the EU”[19] a few days before.

In the months after the hearing, Facebook changed the default privacy settings of its users several times, which led to the Working Party reminding Facebook in May 2010 of the key principles outlined in its Opinion on social networking. It told Facebook that it was unacceptable that the company fundamentally changed the default settings on its social networking platform to the detriment of users.[20]

Ireland hosts quite a few European establishments of multinational companies, amongst which is Facebook. This means that, following the understanding at that time, before the judgment of the European Court of Justice in the *Google Spain vs Costeja* case, of the rules on applicable law in the Data Protection Directive, Irish law was deemed the law applicable to the data processing operations of Facebook. Therefore, the Irish data protection authority is in the lead in the EU to supervise the company’s processing of data.

The Irish data protection authority decided to conduct a full audit of Facebook’s privacy practices in 2011 and published the first outcomes on 21 December 2011.[21] To ensure all interested data protection authorities were involved in the process, the Irish data protection authority stayed in close contact with the members of the Article 29 Working Party. In 2013, the Irish authority concluded its audit and made recommendations and issued a set of best practices. At the time of writing, the Irish authority has not yet taken a decision regarding enforcement. Meanwhile, an organisation called “europe-v-facebook.org” started a legal procedure against a decision of the Irish authority.

The Facebook case was yet another step in the right direction. The EU data protection authorities reached a common position and one of the EU data protection authorities undertook an action involving the other interested authorities. At the same time, it also shows that there are still some remaining obstacles that should be overcome if we want to act more effectively against the big and powerful multinationals.

19.4.2 Google privacy policy

In January 2012, Google announced that as of 1 March 2012, it would merge all existing privacy policies of its various services into one comprehensive privacy policy. This would affect a large majority of Internet users in the European Union. In a letter dated 2 February 2012, the Article 29 Working Party announced that it wanted to analyse the new privacy policy and asked Google to delay its introduction, but Google refused. The Art. 29 Working Party then asked CNIL, the French data protection authority, to take the lead and to conduct an extensive investigation.

[19] http://ec.europa.eu/digital-agenda/sites/digital-agenda/files/sn_principles.pdf

[20] http://www.cbpweb.nl/Pages/med_20100513_facebook.aspx

[21] http://dataprotection.ie/viewdoc.asp?DocID=1182

After several months of investigating, CNIL made public the findings, endorsed by all EU DPAs, during a press conference in Paris in October 2012.[22] The EU data protection authorities found that Google should have sought the unambiguous consent of the users for the specific purposes for the combination of data and that Google should have provided clearer information to its users, especially concerning the categories of data the company processes. CNIL also concluded that Google should provide clear and specific retention periods for the categories of personal data it processes.

The letter was signed individually by all – then – 27 European data protection authorities, with support from the Privacy Commissioner of Canada and various members of APPA, the principal forum for privacy authorities in the Asia Pacific Region. This collective action underlined the importance and global nature of the issue.

In February 2013, the Working Party concluded that Google had not implemented all recommendations, or at least not fully. Due to the fact that the EU Data Protection Directive is not directly applicable, but is transposed in national laws, follow-up steps had to be taken on the basis of these national laws. A task force consisting of six DPAs (Spain, the UK, France, Italy, Hamburg and the Netherlands) was set up to co-ordinate the national actions. With the French in the lead, the members of the task force have each started their national procedures, keeping in close contact with each other and with the Working Party as a whole.

Given that enforcement can only be done on the basis of national law and that several authorities have started national procedures, when it comes to enforcement, each member of the task force can impose a fine provided this is possible following national law. Considering Google is a multibillion-dollar company, even the total sum of the fines might not prove to be much of a deterrent, but the fact that various authorities took action together, as well as the reputational damage caused by the investigation and possible enforcement against Google, may prompt the company to reconsider its policy, which would save it a lot of time and energy and may lead to more consumer trust, which is vital for online organisations.

19.4.3 WhatsApp

On Data Protection Day, 28 January 2013, the Canadian and Dutch data protection authorities published their findings following their joint investigation into the processing of personal information by the California-based company WhatsApp Inc.[23] The investigation focused on WhatsApp's popular mobile messaging platform, which allows users to send and receive instant messages over the Internet across various mobile platforms.

[22] http://ec.europa.eu/justice/data-protection/article-29/documentation/otherdocument/files/2012/20121016_letter_to_google_en.pdf

[23] http://www.cbpweb.nl/Pages/pb_20130128-whatsapp.aspx and www.priv.gc.ca

The Canadian and Dutch authorities, who are both bound by their own national laws, signed a Memorandum of Understanding to enable good co-operation between them. The joint investigation, however, still consisted of two different, but parallel investigations, following their respective national laws.

Thc joint investigation revealed that WhatsApp violated several internationally accepted privacy principles, mainly in relation to the retention of personal data, the provision of adequate safeguards and the disclosure of personal data. For instance, most people signing up to the service did not have a choice to use the app without granting it access to their entire address book on their mobile device. The address book contains numbers of users, but also non-users and both should have control over their personal data. In addition, users must be able to freely decide which contact details they wish to share with WhatsApp.

WhatsApp partially responded to these findings by introducing encryption to its mobile messaging service and strengthening its authentication process in September 2012. But not all violations have been remedied yet. The Dutch data protection authority and the Canadian Office of the Privacy Commissioner issued separate reports, respecting each country's data protection law. Following investigation, the Canadian and Dutch authorities will pursue outstanding matters independently.

The Dutch Data Protection Act provides for a second phase in which the Dutch DPA examines whether the breaches of law continue and decides whether it will take further enforcement actions. The Dutch authority cannot directly impose administrative fines, but can force enterprises to comply with Dutch law by imposing incremental penalty payments. The Canadian authority does not have the power to issue orders, but will monitor the company's progress to meet the commitments made in the course of the investigation.

This was the first transatlantic collaboration in investigating breaches of privacy law. Central to the success of this collaboration was a commitment at the highest level to overcome any obstacle they would meet. And by pooling the resources of both investigation teams, the efficiency and effectiveness of the investigation increased.

Of course, not only Canada and the Netherlands had mobile apps on their agenda. The Article 29 Working Party published an Opinion on the matter on 14 March 2013 as well.[24] The Opinion details the specific obligations of app developers and all other parties, for example, app stores, advertising providers, operating system and device manufacturers, involved in the development and distribution of apps under European data protection law. The Opinion stresses the need for co-operation between all these parties to ensure privacy and data protection of the users.

[24] Opinion 02/2013, WP 202, on apps on smart devices. http://www.dutchdpa.nl/Pages/en_pb-20130314-wp29-opinion-on-mobile-apps

19.4.4 Google Glass

If it were up to Silicon Valley, in the future, everyone will be walking around wearing computerised accessories, paid for by one's personal data and used for recording audio and video footage of other people. The prospect of ubiquitous surveillance of individuals by other individuals, whether through such recordings or through other applications which are or will be developed, immediately triggered data protection authorities worldwide to question Google as the developer of Google Glass, the first such device.

In a letter of 18 June 2013, data protection and privacy authorities from across Europe, Australia, New Zealand, Mexico, Israel, Switzerland, Canada, Alberta, Quebec and British Columbia urged Google to engage in a real dialogue about Google Glass with data protection authorities.[25] The authorities reminded Google that they have repeatedly emphasised the need for organisations to build privacy into the development of products and services before they are launched, the so-called principle of privacy by design. Google was requested to answer eight questions relating to privacy issues as well as other broader, ethical issues that arise from wearable computing.

Google responded in a letter on 27 June 2013[26] and provided various data protection authorities with a demonstration of the product. It became clear that Google Glass was not yet ready for consumer release at that time.[27] Google assured the data protection authorities that privacy considerations would be taken into account in its further development. Google wrote: "We have also built some signals into the way Glass is used, with users and non-users in mind. In addition to Glass requiring spoken commands, users touch Glass to scroll through items or press a button on the arm to take a photo or record video – actions that also cause the Glass screen to activate, which is visible to others." At that time, the Commissioners saw no reason for further action.[28]

---

[25] http://ec.europa.eu/justice/data-protection/article-29/documentatio/other-document/files/2013/20130618_letter_to_google_glass_en.pdf

[26] http://www.priv.gc.ca/media/nr-c/2013/let_130627_google_e.asp

[27] A year later, however, the situation has changed. See Prigg, Mark, "Google Glass goes back on sale to the public (although it will still cost $1500)", *Daily Mail* [UK], 14 May 2014. http://www.dailymail.co.uk/sciencetech/article-2627640/Google-Glass-goes-sale-public-cost-1500.html

[28] The recent announcement by Google that it will allow users to simply blink an eye to take a picture contradicts the earlier assurances that such actions would be very visible to people around a person wearing Google Glass. See: Google Blog, 17 December 2013. https://plus.google.com/+GoogleGlass/posts/Eg8PoXk6jXw?cfem=1

19.5 Where do we stand?

All in all, we see that over the past 15 years a lot of energy has been invested in explaining to large global enterprises that respecting the rules and regulations on data protection is not just a legal requirement but necessary to ensure the trust of individuals. The general conclusion is that all these efforts, though necessary and inevitable, have produced limited success. It is a bit like an Echternach Procession.[29] On the plus side, data subjects' awareness has been enhanced, which is perhaps not only the result of the work of data protection authorities, but also of the spin-off from scandals and the misbehaviour of some big companies and public bodies.

What has also improved is the awareness of the legal differences between the European data protection authorities, both with regard to the different national implementations of the same European Directive, and with regard to the investigating and sanctioning powers. These differences make it difficult to reach uniform conclusions quickly and take co-ordinated actions: they do not render an excellent track record.

In my speech given during the APEC Privacy Enforcement Workshop in Auckland in July 2013, I said: "Street View has made us Streetwise". In every country where action was taken, Google told a different story, reflecting the differences between each national legal system. That will have to change. It is clear that the data protection authorities in Europe need to be able to respond quickly to new technological developments that may cause harm to citizens. Given the reality of the global dominance of a few online multinationals, the authorities need to be able to act from a joint legal basis, with sufficient deterrent sanctioning powers.

As the European Union cannot act in splendid isolation, global initiatives are important too. The Global Privacy Enforcement Network (GPEN),[30] for example, which was created in 2010, aims at assisting public authorities with a responsibility for enforcing domestic privacy laws to strengthen their capacities for cross-border co-operation. In May 2013, 15 privacy enforcement authorities joined in a "sweep" to examine companies' duty to provide information on the processing of data. This was another step in joining forces by a relatively large number of authorities in and outside Europe.[31]

Other initiatives for joint investigations, such as the WhatsApp case, also give a boost to facilitating enforcement co-operation across national borders. A binding international agreement on data protection that safeguards human rights by protecting privacy, personal data and the integrity of networks, again called for by the 35th International Conference of Data Protection and Privacy Commissioners in Warsaw

[29] The Echternach Procession is an annual Roman Catholic dancing procession held in Echternach, in eastern Luxembourg. According to Wikipedia, Echternach's is the last traditional dancing procession in Europe.

[30] See www.privacyenforcement.net

[31] http://www.prov.gc.ca/media/nr-c/2013/nr-c_130813_e.asp

in September 2013, is unfortunately not yet in sight in the immediate future.[32] In Europe, however, things have been speeding up, especially since the presentation of a proposed new legal framework for data protection, which should make a difference for the better.

19.5.1 The European Regulation

The European Union's internal market accounts for more than 500 million consumers and to ensure their fundamental right to data protection is respected, a single set of rules directly applicable to both the public and private sectors in all EU states is of utmost importance. I was therefore pleased with the announcement of a revision of the existing law and the presentation in January 2012 by the European Commission of its proposal for a new legal framework for data protection in the EU, consisting of a general data protection Regulation and a Directive for the law enforcement sector.

Especially the fact that the instrument of a Regulation has been proposed to govern data protection in all areas except law enforcement is significant. Where a Directive has to be transposed into national law by the Member States of the EU, leading to similar, though slightly different laws, a Regulation is directly applicable in all Member States. This means that there is one law applicable across the whole of the European Union, one law by which organisations have to abide, leading to more legal security and clarity. Furthermore, the fact that the European Commission proposed a comprehensive framework, covering both the public and the private sectors, was important, as it also contributes to the clarity and legal certainty which are very much needed in today's world.

After the presentation of the proposals in January 2012, the European Parliament and the Council started their respective legislative procedures. In the European Parliament, close to 4,000 amendments were tabled, after which the rapporteurs of the lead Committee, the Civil Liberties, Justice and Home Affairs (LIBE) committee, sought to find compromise amendments. These compromise amendments were put to a vote in the LIBE on 21 October 2013 and were adopted with a great majority. The vote in LIBE on both texts marks a great step forwards in the process of achieving a new comprehensive legal framework on data protection in the EU. The European Parliament endorsed the LIBE version of the Regulation by the vast majority of 621 in favour, 10 against with 22 abstentions on 12 March 2014.

Unfortunately, the Council has made less progress and discussions are still ongoing at the time of writing. One of the biggest stumbling blocks seems to be the reluctance of Member States to hand over powers to each other. This is especially apparent in the discussions regarding the governance, a topic to which I return below. Considering the developments, both with regard to technology and

[32] https://privacyconference2013.org/web/pageFiles/kcfinder/files/5.%20International%20law%20resolution%20EN%281%29.pdf

globalisation, but also looking at the revelations on surveillance activities since the summer of 2013, it is of great importance that the Council also reaches agreement soon, so that the negotiations – or trialogue – can commence to find a consensus between the European Parliament, Council and Commission's versions.

With regard to the new Regulation, I would like to more specifically focus on three subjects that are important in joint enforcement. These are the definitions of personal data and data subject, the consistency mechanism and the competence to impose fines in cases of non-compliance.

19.5.2 *Definition of the data subject*

One of the essential elements of any legal framework, including that on data protection, is the definitions. Providing clear definitions in the new Regulation is important and will help in enhancing co-operation between the data protection authorities.

New technologies make it possible to identify persons by associating them with unique identifiers, for instance, Internet Protocol addresses or unique cookie identifiers. As stated by the Working Party in its Opinion on personal data, a natural person can be considered identifiable when, within a group of persons, he or she can be distinguished from the other members of the group and consequently be treated differently. This view has been supported by Art. 29 Working Party in its Opinion of 23 March 2012,[33] by the FTC in two reports[34] and by the Dutch Parliament.[35] In his comment on the data protection reform package, the European Data Protection Supervisor (EDPS) also insisted on the fact "that as soon as there is a close relation between an identifier and a person this will usually trigger the application of the data protection principles".[36]

The existing Directive already states that data is personal data if an entity other than the controller can identify a natural person. This adds the necessary protection for data subjects, especially in the online world where personal data is ubiquitous.

---

[33] Article 29 Data Protection Working Party, Opinion 01/2012 on the data protection reform proposals, WP 191, p. 9.

[34] Federal Trade Commission, "Protecting Consumer Privacy in an Era of Rapid Change", Preliminary FTC Staff Report, December 2010. See also the likewise titled FTC Report of March 2012.

[35] *Kamerstukken II* 2011/2012, 32 761, nr 37.

[36] Hustinx, Peter, European Data Protection Supervisor, Opinion of the European Data Protection Supervisor on the data protection reform package, Brussels, 7 March 2012, p. 18. http://www.europarl.europa.eu/meetdocs/2009_2014/documents/libe/dv/edpsopinion_/edpsopinion_en.pdf. See also the EDPS recommendations for a good result from the trialogue process. European Data Protection Supervisor, Opinion of 27 July 2015 – Europe's big opportunity, EDPS recommendations on the EU's options for data protection reform. https://secure.edps.europa.eu/EDPSWEB/edps/lang/en/Consultation/Reform_package

Another element of the definition of personal data is the discussion about pseudonymous and anonymous data. I can fully support the use of pseudonymisation as a technique to enhance data protection, but pseudonymising data is disguising identities in a retraceable way, which means that it remains possible to backtrack or (indirectly) identify an individual. Therefore, pseudonymous data is personal data and has to be protected by the provisions in the Regulation. Vice-President Reding put forward a strong point by saying that "pseudonymous data must not become a Trojan horse at the heart of the Regulation, allowing the non-application of its provisions".[37]

Anonymisation, on the other hand, is an irreversible process in which nobody still holds a key or any of the raw original data and I therefore support adhering to the definition that is already provided in the current Directive and in a recital of the proposed Regulation of the European Commission that "The principles of data protection should not apply to data rendered anonymous in such a way that the data subject is no longer identifiable".[38]

19.5.3 Co-operation and the consistency mechanism

As mentioned above, a Directive has to be transposed into national law. In the current situation, under Directive 95/46, an enterprise operating in more than one Member State in the European Union has to deal with several data protection authorities, each of whom may have different sanctioning powers, have slightly different national laws and therefore may take different decisions. A worst case scenario for data protection is that enterprises seek the legal regime that best suits their interests (also known as "forum shopping") to benefit from using this *divide et impera* adagium and choose to have their headquarters in the Member State with the lowest level of protection.

The Google Street View and the Facebook cases were highlighted above to illustrate the negative consequences of the current system for cross border co-operation. The Regulation would bring more harmonisation in the European Union, even though it would probably not be completely void of political stumbling blocks as principles of national sovereignty could stand in the way. But the proposed Regulation is innovative in this regard by ensuring that the data protection authorities can excercise their supervisory activities jointly in data protection issues of common interest.[39]

The proposed Regulation provides for a one-stop shop for companies, which means that, where a controller is established in more than one Member State, it will

---

[37] http://europa.eu/rapid/press-release_SPEECH-13-269_en.htm

[38] http://ec.europa.eu/justice/newsroom/data-protection/news/120125_en.htm

[39] See Kuner, Christopher, "The European Commission's Proposed Data Protection Regulation: A Copernican Revolution in European Data Protection Law", BNA Bloomberg *Privacy and Security Law Report*, 6 Feb 2012, pp. 1–15. http://www.kuner.com/my-publications-and-writing/untitled/kuner-eu-regulation-article.pdf

have to deal with only one data protection authority, the one in the Member State where the company has its main establishment. The one-stop shop, or lead, authority will act as the single contact point for the controller, taking care of the decision-making procedure after having consulted all other concerned data protection authorities in an endeavour to reach consensus, leading to a binding outcome.

To ensure the system is not overburdened and is lean and mean, it is important to stress that local cases should be dealt with locally. It is not necessary to involve the other authorities when it concerns a purely local matter. In cross-border cases, however, there must be a lead supervisory authority that serves as contact point for the company and will be the sole authority to take a legally binding decision. It naturally takes this decision only after having consulted the other concerned authorities in an endeavour to reach consensus. And when a concerned supervisory authority, other than the lead, does not agree with the draft decision proposed by the lead authority, it should have the possibility to appeal to the European Data Protection Board (EDPB), which will be able to adopt an opinion on the matter.

The EDPB, in which all the data protection authorities of the Member States of the EU are assembled and is the successor of the Article 29 Working Party, will have the power to decide whether to adopt an opinion on a specific case. If it decides to do so, this opinion must be taken into account by the lead authority. Naturally, these procedures should not take forever; reasonable deadlines must be inserted.

The system as described above with a lead authority, together with the fact that we will have a Regulation providing one law in the EU, combined with the possibility to impose high fines (the European Parliament proposes 5 % of a company's annual turnover), is the only way to ensure Silicon Valley abides by European rules.

EU data protection authorities should wholeheartedly give the new system a fair try. We must not forget that we should all act together in ensuring a fundamental right, even though it might lead to giving up one's prerogatives and possibly some economic advantage. Anything – well, almost anything – goes to provide incentives to multinational companies to invest from the start in getting data protection right.

19.5.4 *Fines*

Significant fines will help data protection authorities to carry out their task of protecting data more effectively and efficiently. Being able to impose sufficiently high fines can act as a deterrent to data controllers, leading to a higher degree of compliance. Today, not all data protection authorities in the EU have the power to impose (large enough) fines. This means that multinationals can calculate the risk of being confronted with, for instance, incremental penalty payments for non-compliance with national privacy laws and make a decision whether to take that risk. Considering that data protection is a fundamental right, we can see that such consciously-made calculations by companies pose a great risk.

The lack of penalising power is a significant drawback for the efforts of data protection authorities to get enterprises to invest in complying with data protection principles.

In the Netherlands, for instance, notwithstanding a long and incessant battle with the government to change the law, the Dutch DPA still can't impose fines, except for failure to comply with the notification requirement and in future for failure to report data leaks. In 2014, however, the Dutch Parliament called upon the government to introduce a general power for the Dutch data protection authority to impose administrative sanctions,[40] in anticipation of the Regulation, which will likely take several years to come into force. The minister of Justice promised to do so and the bill is currently in progress.

As also mentioned in Opinion 01/2012 of the Working Party,[41] data protection authorities should have a margin of discretion in deciding when to impose a fine. On the other hand, some harmonisation is called for in order to make sure enterprises don't shop around to select those countries that are more likely to impose lesser fines than others in case of violation of data protection principles. So I am in favour of the obligation on supervisory authorities to co-operate to guarantee a harmonised level of sanctions within the Union.

19.6 Future challenges and conclusions

Considering the last two decades have brought many technological possibilities unforeseen 20 years ago, I am sure the future will have many more unexpected technological developments in store for us. Therefore, undoubtedly, the biggest challenge for data protection authorities is getting organisations to acknowledge that privacy by design, transparency and respecting the personal nature of their customers' data are good for business.

Personal data has already become a currency in the online world. It should, however, not be traded without the individual's consent. It will not suffice to adjust the settings or amend the privacy policy following a large number of complaints. The fact that DPAs will be able to impose really impressive fines in case of non-compliance with the new European Regulation will help, of course, but preventing breaches of the law is far better than repairing them. Personal damage is difficult to set right.

World-wide, Europe is still leading the debate on the protection of privacy and personal data. The bottom line of it all is trust. Data subjects must be able to trust organisations to follow the rules. They must *know* that their personal data are safe and not misused for purposes to which they have not consented. They must also be

---

[40] 15 March 2012, TK 2011–2012 32761 no. 22.

[41] Article 29 Data Protection Working Party, Opinion 01/2012 on the data protection reform proposals, Brussels, on 23 March 2012, pp. 18, 24. http://ec.europa.eu/justice/data-protection/article-29/documentation/opinion-recommendation/files/2012/wp191_en.pdf

assured that their data protection authorities, not only the one in their home country, but those across the EU, safeguard the proper use of their data and will enforce the law where necessary. For that purpose, it is just as essential that the European data protection authorities trust one another. If the one-stop-shop system is to become a success, we will have to work together, even in economically difficult times and notwithstanding differences of opinion. Because that is the only way we can achieve our purpose: to effectively protect a fundamental right.

Acknowledgement The author acknowledges with thanks the contributions from Pauline Hoefer-van Dongen and Dominique Hagenauw in the preparation of this chapter.

References

23rd International Conference of Data Protection and Privacy Commissioners, "The Common Position on Privacy Protection and Search Engines", Resolution, Hong Kong, 15 April 1998.

39th Meeting of the International Working Group on Data Protection in Telecommunications, Washington, DC, 6–7 April 2006.

Article 29 Data Protection Working Party, Opinion 5/2009 on online social networking, WP 163, Brussels, Adopted on 12 June 2009. http://ec.europa.eu/justice/policies/privacy/docs/wpdocs/2009/wp163_en.pdf

Article 29 Data Protection Working Party, Opinion 1/2008 on data protection issues related to search engines.

Article 29 Data Protection Working Party, Opinion 13/2011 on Geolocation services on smart mobile devices, WP185, Brussels, Adopted on 16 May 2011, p. 11. http://ec.europa.eu/justice/data-protection/article-29/documentation/opinion-recommendation/files/2011/wp185_en.pdf

Article 29 Data Protection Working Party, Opinion 01/2012 on the data protection reform proposals, Brussels, on 23 March 2012. http://ec.europa.eu/justice/data-protection/article-29/documentation/opinion-recommendation/files/2012/wp191_en.pdf

Dutch Data Protection Authority (College bescherming persoonsgegevens), Opinion 02/2013, WP 202, on apps on smart devices. http://www.dutchdpa.nl/Pages/en_pb-20130314-wp29-opinion-on-mobile-apps

European Commission, Proposal for a Regulation of the European Parliament and of the Council on the protection of individuals with regard to the processing of personal data and on the free movement of such data (General Data Protection Regulation), COM(2012) 11 final, Brussels, 25 January 2012. http://ec.europa.eu/justice/data-protection/document/review2012/com_2012_11_en.pdf

European Data Protection Supervisor, Opinion of 27 July 2015 – Europe's big opportunity, EDPS recommendations on the EU's options for data protection reform. https://secure.edps.europa.eu/EDPSWEB/edps/lang/en/Consultation/Reform_package

Federal Trade Commission, "Protecting Consumer Privacy in an Era of Rapid Change", Preliminary FTC Staff Report, December 2010. See also the likewise titled FTC Report of March 2012.

Google Official Blog, 14 October 2011. http://googleblog.blogspot.nl/2011/10/fall-sweep.html

Google Blog, 17 December 2013. https://plus.google.com/+GoogleGlass/posts/Eg8PoXk6jXw?cfem=1

Hustinx, Peter, European Data Protection Supervisor, Opinion of the European Data Protection Supervisor on the data protection reform package, Brussels, 7 March 2012, p. 18. http://www.europarl.europa.eu/meetdocs/2009_2014/documents/libe/dv/edpsopinion_/edpsopinion_en.pdf

Kamerstukken II 2011/2012, 32 761, nr 37.

Kuner, Christopher, "The European Commission's Proposed Data Protection Regulation: A Copernican Revolution in European Data Protection Law", BNA Bloomberg *Privacy and Security Law Report*, 6 Feb 2012, pp. 1–15. http://www.kuner.com/my-publications-and-writing/untitled/kuner-eu-regulation-article.pdf

Prigg, Mark, "Google Glass goes back on sale to the public (although it will still cost $1500)", *Daily Mail* [UK], 14 May 2014. http://www.dailymail.co.uk/sciencetech/article-2627640/Google-Glass-goes-sale-public-cost-1500.html

Chapter 20
Regaining Control and Sovereignty in the Digital Age

Jan Philipp Albrecht

20.1 Introduction

Because of the rapid pace of technological advances, particularly affecting storage and network capacities, our lives, once almost entirely confined to the analogue world, have – seemingly overnight – been completely digitalised. From browsers to online gaming and smart phones, mostly developed by young IT experts in Silicon Valley, the details behind these new technologies have remained beyond the comprehension of the vast majority of people. It is enough that digitalisation has happened, and that it supposedly makes our lives so much simpler and happier. The focus of our economic and social lives is shifting from actions in the real world to digital communication, but we are failing to prepare a corresponding transformation of the traditional safeguards that operate in a society. The analogue has given way to the digital. Data increasingly determines what happens when and where. In the face of this dramatic revolution taking place in our societies, Silicon Valley tells us that everything will be fine. Nothing can go wrong, because the Googles and Facebooks of this world will take care of us. "We do no harm," they say, as they disempower us not only as customers who consume what they have to offer but also as citizens of democratic societies governed by the rule of law. They dictate their rules to us. This is particularly true of what drives and perpetuates the new economy: our "personal data", which make it possible to deduce our wishes, our capabilities, our way of life and our weaknesses. They gather whatever information about us they can – without consulting us and without even giving us the slightest information about what they are doing. The hard currency of the digital age is, as it were, being filched from our pockets without our even noticing. This process has been going on so surreptitiously and for all practical purposes without regulation

J.P. Albrecht (✉)
ASP 03F 343, European Parliament, Rue Wiertz 60, 1047 Brussels, Belgium
e-mail: jan.albrecht@europarl.europa.eu

D. Wright, P. De Hert (eds.), *Enforcing Privacy*, Law, Governance and Technology Series 25, DOI 10.1007/978-3-319-25047-2_20

that these businesses are now the biggest undertakings in the world. They have greater scope for action and more influence than virtually any business or State in history. If things remain as they are, we shall be completely disenfranchised and easily fleeced in the digitised world. We shall find ourselves living in a totalitarian controlled society, which has come into existence and holds sway because these businesses gather vast amounts of information about us, and are becoming more entrenched in our daily lives.

That political decision-makers have ignored this development for so many years is one of the most serious deficits in recent history. It is true that the history of data protection and the regulation of information technology is marked by legal milestones that have been erected on various occasions, but the real extent of the problem has never been correctly recognised by politicians, judicial authorities, the media, businesses and most of civil society. Despite the surveillance scandals and numerous aberrations in the approach to personal data, data protection has again and again been regarded as a peripheral, technical matter and a low priority politically. Clear rules to govern the digital market are needed, and they have yet to be successfully established. Time and time again, regulatory approaches have been adopted which have missed the mark, for example, with regard to copyright, where better law enforcement has been pursued only by means of more comprehensive protection of copyright works. The only useful instrument to regulate the market was EU competition law, which, thanks to action taken in individual cases by the guardians of competition law, was able to bring about better enforcement of fundamental rules. But in our everyday life, dominated by the digital world, that will not be enough. That is why the Commission set in motion a reform of data protection law with the entry into force of the Lisbon Treaty and the EU Charter of Fundamental Rights. The Commission proposal of 2012 and agreement in the European Parliament in 2014 on its position on an EU Data Protection Regulation represent two major steps towards effective rules for the digital age.

20.2 Power of lobbyists

While big businesses such as Google, Amazon and Facebook extend their market power to new sectors of the economy and even create their own, self-regulated, digital markets, the European Commission and national governments seem to be groping around in the dark. At present, other than data protection reform, there are no serious proposals for regulation of the 'digital internal market'. The long-awaited proposal from the European Commission for a regulation on the telecommunications market,[1] which would unify the rules on Internet services, turned out to be a

[1] European Commission proposal from 11/09/2013: http://eur-lex.europa.eu/legal-content/EN/TXT/PDF/?uri=CELEX:52013PC0627&rid=2, adopted text of the European Parliament: http://www.europarl.europa.eu/sides/getDoc.do?type=TA&language=EN&reference=P7-TA-2014-0281

pure lobbying paper, containing no genuine restrictions with the aim of protecting consumers and smaller market players. The rules that the European Parliament wished to see adopted concerning net neutrality were not included even in rudimentary form. So far, the IT industry lobby, particularly acting on behalf of operators based in the USA, has succeeded in opposing any genuine regulation in Brussels. They are investing millions in lobbying against legislative proposals such as the Data Protection Regulation, because they know very well that their billions' worth of profits are made by breaking the very rules that competitors and consumers would at the very minimum expect in a digital market. Internet giants based in Silicon Valley are in the vanguard of efforts to disseminate a profit-driven ideology that basically aims to defeat any State regulation. Their lobby sees data protection as the last obstacle that it must overcome in order to capitalise areas of life that hitherto have been the most private and intimate and to subject them to its market logic at the cost of our information self-determination and privacy. This means that all of our data are up for sale, and we shall only be able to stop this if we win back sovereignty over our own data.

20.3 The proposed Data Protection Regulation

At the end of January 2012, the European Commission proposed its eagerly anticipated reform of data protection law. After a substantial consultation process, this reform is a major step towards comprehensive legislation on data protection throughout the European Union and, to some extent, even beyond it. The new EU law could bestow great benefits, particularly on users of Facebook and Google or smart phone owners, because hitherto they have in practice hardly enjoyed any protection against their data being stolen and sold to third parties. In an era where personal data are no longer processed in the data subject's own country but are increasingly processed on the Internet, the fragmented legal situation that exists is no longer appropriate. Existing data protection laws are inadequate. Businesses are hardly required to account for their use of personal data, let alone having to fear any consequences. They make self-confident inroads into the market with the new functions built into their products, which process yet more data in new contexts. Those who are using their products or services often have no choice. Who would give up a Gmail account that he or she has been using for years just because they do not agree with a new "feature", such as linkage of search data and e-mail data in order to "optimise" search results? The legal situation which currently applies, governed by the EU Data Protection Directive of 1995, was established at a time when many of these aspects were not yet in any way relevant, as the Internet was then in its infancy. Its basic rules are not wrong on that account: we do not reject them, we want to enforce them better and elucidate their principles for the digitised world of today. This is where the EU should act, and where it has proposed to do so, thereby opening a new chapter in the laying-down of international data protection rules.

The proposals for a fundamental reform of European data protection law are intended to give consumers and citizens a uniform EU standard for the effective protection of their data. Apart from better information and verification options for the individual, in the future there should also be effective penalties for misuse, for example, if data are lost or sold. In view of the self-confidence with which global data gatherers breach existing data protection law, this was a long overdue step. Yet even at the drafting stage of the Commission proposal, some vital demands already fell victim to the interests of big businesses and security authorities.

The influence of the lobby of major IT businesses from Silicon Valley and the powerful advertising industry made itself felt from the outset. As soon as the reform debate began, powerful politicians announced that voluntary commitments by industry were sufficient and that there was essentially no need for stronger European data protection. This is despite the fact that, since the Lisbon Treaty, which entered into force as the EU's new "Constitution" on 1 December 2009, the fundamental right to data protection has been not only an element in the binding EU Charter of Fundamental Rights but also a central principle of EU law. Throughout Europe, data protection is a fundamental right that the State must protect – against both State authorities and private businesses.

20.4 Armies of lawyers looking for loopholes

What the European Commission proposals mean for consumers and citizens is, above all, greater transparency and control over their data. In the case of everyday applications and services, which are storing more and more of our information, deletion and correction should become significantly easier in future. The Commission proposal is, therefore, a good starting point in principle. It aims to secure high standards of data protection which are more harmonised and appropriate to the Internet age, while retaining the fundamentally worthwhile principles of the 1995 Directive: data minimisation, consent of the data subject, a requirement to confine the use of data to the purpose for which they were gathered, and a right to information. From the fundamental rights point of view, the main concern now is to limit the permitted exceptions and flesh out the good ideas. But, for businesses here too, the new rules would represent considerable progress, because at present they have to comply with 28 different sets of data protection rules in the EU's common internal market and thus, despite much bureaucracy, enjoy absolutely no legal certainty. Moreover, they have to compete with Internet giants from Silicon Valley and other data gatherers who employ armies of lawyers to look for loopholes in this obscure jungle of rules, so that they can often evade the regulations. These lawyers were up in arms against the new rules because many of them profit from exploiting the loopholes and inadequacies in existing data protection law. They have also enlisted massive lobbying assistance from the American Chamber of Commerce, which has long regarded European data protection as a thorn in its flesh.

The reform of EU data protection law proposed in January 2012 gives the EU the opportunity to make these provisions into a worldwide standard. Politicians, businesses and non-governmental organisations – across the political spectrum – consider that a reform is needed. Everyone must regain control over his or her own personal data, which are the currency of the digital economy. Like any other currency, it needs confidence in order to be stable. The Snowden revelations regarding the extent of surveillance by the NSA, GCHQ and other intelligence agencies have damaged confidence not only in transatlantic relations but also in the digital economy. It is not only members of the public who are concerned. Gathering, exploiting and transferring personal data also creates an enormous economic potential: in 2011, the data of EU citizens were worth €315 billion, according to research findings.[2] However, people will no longer disclose their data if they do not trust the businesses that are going to process them. Loss of confidence translates into loss of revenue. Data protection reform will help to restore confidence. Union citizens wish to be certain that, in disclosing their personal data, they are not renouncing their rights. Enhancing Europe's high data protection standards means, in addition, creating new business opportunities, as data protection becomes a sales argument and a competitive advantage.

In the meantime, it has become clear to everybody that we can only acquire control over our data by means of an EU-wide guarantee, because in the digital era, information is no longer confined within States. For a long time already, commercial groups and government authorities have been exchanging large quantities of information across borders or locating them in the "cloud". The European Commission proposal was therefore a good basis for linking a stringent data protection standard to a substantial gain in legal certainty for businesses, authorities and consumers, and was sorely needed: the EU's 15-year-old data protection framework cannot confer lasting protection on personal data. In the European internal market, it is unfortunately the country with the weakest data protection laws where the Silicon Valley businesses seek to have their main European establishment. The European Commission was therefore right to seek an EU-wide set of rules that would replace large parts of national data protection laws and require co-operation among data protection authorities. However, this will make it all the more important to set the bar high and make retrospective improvements where the customary level of protection could be reduced in the Member States.

20.5 3999 amendments

After being submitted in January 2012, the Commission proposal was forwarded to the two branches of the EU's legislative authority – the Council of Ministers and the European Parliament – where the appropriate specialist committees have debated it.

[2] See, for example, a study by the Boston Consulting Group: https://www.bcgperspectives.com/content/articles/digital_economy_technology_unlocking_value_personal_data_collection_usage/

Only once both sides have a negotiating mandate can a common position be arrived at under the EU's legislative co-decision procedure. It was originally intended that negotiations between Parliament and the Council should be held in spring 2013, but the adoption of the negotiating positions was delayed on both sides. On 21 October 2013, after more than a year and a half of negotiations, the European Parliament reached agreement on a mandate for the consultations with the Council. Following many rounds of negotiations and after no fewer than 3999 individual amendments had been tabled, a broad majority within the responsible committee, the Committee on Civil Liberties, Justice and Home Affairs (the LIBE committee), agreed on a compromise text which modified virtually every article in the Commission's draft, but which clearly endorsed the proposal's basic aim of establishing a uniform body of EU data protection law. Since then, Members of the European Parliament have been awaiting the beginning of the negotiations with the Council. In adopting its own position, Parliament called on the Council to come to the negotiating table quickly so as to enable a first reading to be held without delay and allow the data protection reform to be adopted before the European elections in May 2014.

However, this did not materialise, as the Ministers of Home Affairs and Justice were unable to agree on large parts of their reform position in October, nor in December 2013 or January 2014. A full two years after the publication of the Commission's proposal, the Council had still not been able to arrive at a common position on the data protection reform. Member States were unable to reach final agreement at the Council meetings in March 2014. This a disappointing and even shocking failure of political responsibility on the part of decision-makers in the EU Member States' governments. How did this happen? Government representatives in the Council took the talks into one extra round after another because some Member States – particularly the UK and Germany – had been delay the negotiations by means of innumerable discussions on matters of principle.

20.6 Enforcement measures vary from one Member State to another

From the outset, the European Parliament was the driving force behind the EU data protection reform. Even in the years before the Commission proposal, MEPs had intensively debated protection of citizens' data in the digital age when discussing the US authorities' access to data from the bank service provider SWIFT and passenger data held by airlines. MEPs had already frequently called for uniform EU data protection laws, as they repeatedly pointed out how incomplete protection was within the EU as well as in relation to third States. In its original resolution on data protection reform, the European Parliament had made better enforcement of EU data protection law in the common internal market one of its main demands, in which connection it particularly had in mind businesses from third countries operating within the EU's internal market. In the course of the ceaseless development of the digital market and the opening of the internal market for businesses from third States – particularly by means of the Safe Harbor declaration for businesses from the USA – it had become increasingly clear that the supervisory authorities of the EU Member States had problems in enforcing data protection laws. In most cases, it is not the data protection authority of our own country that is responsible for protecting our data, but that of a different EU Member State, because it is there that businesses have their main establishment within the EU market. Often, the result is a protracted co-ordination process between supervisory authorities, not uncommonly ending with the finding that the 1995 Directive has simply been enforced differently in the Member States and that in practice enforcement measures still vary enormously between supervisory authorities. In view of the importance attached to data protection as a fundamental right, the vast majority of MEPs have taken the view that this is unacceptable. Their call for the European Commission to propose a uniform data protection law with uniform application and enforcement could not have been expressed more clearly. Moreover, the European Parliament called for such uniformity not only in relation to the EU Member States but also with reference to the various fields of law and application.

The European Parliament was demanding horizontal regulation at EU level allowing departures from it in Member States' legislation only in exceptional cases. The European Parliament decision and the feedback both from the consultation exercise and from the Member States had a big influence over the formulation of the Commission's legislative proposals. In January 2012, when the Commission submitted its proposal for an EU Data Protection Regulation, the feedback from the European Parliament and from European data protection experts was generally positive. This was despite the fact that, even during the internal co-ordination process, some proposals by the Directorate-General for Justice had required modification, such as the requirement of a legal basis in EU law for a transfer of data from within the EU to third-country authorities. These were deleted in response to pressure from other Directorates-General, which had yielded to strong influence from the US Government.[3] This was a foretaste of the altercation with lobbyists representing Silicon Valley, who had by now become powerful, indeed possibly the most powerful lobby group of all, and had already been testing the resilience of regulators on both sides of the Atlantic for years.

The proposed reform does not constitute a substantive revolution and was never intended to. It largely and above all extrapolates from the existing right to data protection with its fundamental definitions and principles.

20.7 Numerous misunderstandings

As a result of the proposal, a lively debate sprang up among experts, although in many cases it was far from a constructive discussion of the Commission proposals and from expressing a desire to improve them. As is often the case when major steps towards integration are being taken, the harmonisation of data protection involved

[3] http://edri.org/US-DPR/ or http://www.spiegel.de/international/business/us-government-and-internet-giants-battle-eu-over-data-privacy-proposal-a-861773.html

the issue of subsidiarity and compatibility with the existing national legal framework. From the beginning, there have been numerous misunderstandings with regard to the relationship between the new Regulation and national laws describing the work of public authorities. But most people realised quickly that there was no alternative to greater harmonisation of data protection and common case law at EU level. Nonetheless, it was months before the prejudices against the proposed EU regulation could be overcome. Unfortunately, Germany's Ministry of the Interior is still trying to fan these prejudices further, in order to delay the adoption of the Data Protection Regulation.[4]

I was appointed as the European Parliament's rapporteur on the EU Data Protection Regulation in March 2012, after which talks began with political groups from the Member States and with the numerous stakeholders on the position to be adopted by Parliament on the Commission's proposal. As the European Parliament's rapporteur, I am one of the Members who have had the most influence on the Regulation. The onslaught of lobbyists that I experienced in the following year was massive. I published on my website a list of the people whom I met during this period leading up to the presentation of my draft report. That report constituted the basis for deciding Parliament's position in January 2013. It aimed to reflect the various points of view on our work. In addition to the many meetings with colleagues within Parliament and representatives of the European Commission and Member States, I met nearly 200 different stakeholders during this period, some 90 per cent of whom were from industry. There could be no plainer indication of the value of our personal data and of data protection rules for all areas of life. It also showed how strong and, in some cases, one-sided, the influence of lobby groups is. A few big companies, particularly from the USA, lobbied massively in Brussels and Strasbourg. They invested large sums in lobbyists and in numerous associations, consultancies and law firms. This enabled them to provide not only me but also more than 750 other MEPs and anyone else involved in the reform with ample information about their positions and arguments, while it was often not clear to members of the public that the future of their fundamental right to data protection was being negotiated here.

Once the draft report was presented, the Members of the committee responsible – the Committee on Civil Liberties, Justice and Home Affairs – had the opportunity to table their own amendments to the Commission proposal. In addition, four other committees, which had been asked to deliver opinions, decided what their positions would be and contributed them to the procedure. By the time of the deadline for tabling amendments in March 2013, the European Parliament had 3999 amendments to consider. As the rules require, all of them were translated into 23 official languages and suddenly appeared in huge stacks outside the committee meeting room. In no other legislative procedure in Strasbourg had so many amendments been tabled. This presented the Rapporteur with the difficult task of finding compromises with the various political groups on the basis of the amendments tabled, the aim being that, when it came to the final vote, a majority of Members would support those compromises.

[4] http://euobserver.com/justice/122853

In principle, Parliament had from the start been fairly unanimous about the Data Protection Regulation. It welcomed the Commission proposal and, together with the Commission, urged that the proposal be adopted quickly with a few clarifications. The original aim was to reach agreement before the end of the parliamentary term, meaning before the European elections in May 2014. However, the reform was repeatedly delayed. Both in the Council of Ministers (discussed in more detail below) and in Parliament, massive lobbying made itself felt from the outset. Big companies such as Google, Microsoft, Amazon, Facebook and IBM invest the most in lobbying, both in Washington, DC, and in Brussels. They spend many millions every year with the aim of bombarding decision-makers with advisers, lawyers and events of all kinds. They try to conceal and camouflage this influence as best they can. Some undertakings simultaneously support several different lobby groups, think tanks and civil society initiatives on data protection and the free movement of data, in order to increase the number of reiterations of invitations, lines of argument and position papers. By means of "AstroTurfing", they seek to use other groups (for example, small and medium-sized enterprises, who are exploited by large companies just as consumers are) to promote their interests or even pretend to be speaking on their behalf. At many meetings with various stakeholders, I heard certain statements and arguments, some of them distorting and tendentious, again and again, put to me in virtually the same words, although the groups had approached me expressing quite different concerns. Things became even more absurd when lobbyists acting on behalf of big businesses did not even mention their own interests but vehemently advocated the alleged interests of consumers and then told me that the latter actually did not want data protection at all. On the contrary, people were happy to give businesses their data and did not want to be consulted as to whether anyone should be allowed to receive them.

Consumer protection organisations, with their totally inadequate resources, described consumers' interests quite differently – and far more accurately – often did not even succeed in reaching Members of the European Parliament with their arguments. Members' agendas were already full of meetings requested by industry lobbyists. The massive pressure that was brought to bear by these lobbyists from the very beginning of this legislative procedure became clear in the summer of 2013, when the website LobbyPlag.eu showed that hundreds of amendments tabled by Members in the European Parliament had been copied word for word from position papers or amendments formulated by large Internet businesses. LobbyPlag.eu had drawn up an overview of all the position papers of big businesses and lobby groups of all kinds and compared them with the thousands of amendments tabled by Members of the European Parliament. After this, some Members vehemently disowned their own amendments, as the public took exception to their having acted so one-sidedly on behalf of large IT businesses, thereby opposing consumers' rights. The former EU Commissioner and current Member of the European Parliament representing the Belgian Liberals, Louis Michel, even dismissed a member of his staff, accusing him of having tabled hundreds of pro-industry amendments in his name without his knowledge or consent.[5]

[5] http://corporateeurope.org/lobbycracy/2013/11/belgian-mep-lobby-amendments-scandal

20.8 A strong compromise

The debates at the European Parliament nonetheless proved highly productive. In the course of more than 50 meetings, it was possible to draw up a strong compromise text with the agreement of all the political group co-ordinators and with the assistance of many members of staff, which was adopted by an overwhelming majority in Parliament. The question that arose again and again was what data protection rules were needed in order for people to gain control over the disclosure and use of their data. Data protection begins even before a service is used. Users need to be unambiguously informed what will happen with their data in order to give their informed consent. But who has ever genuinely read the pages of general terms and conditions that apply to the Internet services they use? Consumers need simple and readily comprehensible conditions of use in the form of standardised symbols, comparable to those that exist for food. The ideas put forward in Parliament ranged from a data protection traffic light system to quite detailed descriptions of all intended uses and methods of use. In the end, Members opted in their negotiating position for a statement of the basic rules of data protection law and marking to indicate if data are to be transferred to third States. In addition, there should also be technical ways in which users can defend themselves against the use of their data for certain purposes by means of a standard setting: if the privacy settings of a browser indicate that the creation of user profiles has not been consented to, service providers should respect this. One way of implementing this would be by means of the do-not-track function, which is already installed in many browsers, but it is not yet widely used. The proposed legislation should change this situation.

On the side of the undertaking too, data protection begins before a service is offered. The reform proposal obliges businesses to design their services in such a way as to minimise the amount of data required, with settings that promote data protection to the maximum. Facebook, for example, currently operates in precisely the opposite way: if someone opens an account, the default privacy settings are the lowest available, and if the user wishes to change the settings, he or she is confronted with information that is often very technical and difficult to comprehend.[6] In encouraging design with built-in data protection, we aim to apply the principle of purpose limitation more thoroughly. In other words, what data are genuinely needed in order to use a service? Is it always necessary to identify the user beyond all shadow of a doubt? These are questions that service providers should put to themselves in advance. Many services also work with anonymous or pseudonymous use. Whether my girlfriend chats with me under her full name or as "spacecommander86" does not in any way affect our communication.

Once personal data are out in the digital world, it is important to retain control over them. Retention periods must therefore be clearly defined, and data must be

[6] Facebook has recently indicated that it is taking privacy more seriously. See Goel, Vindu, "Some Privacy, Please? Facebook, Under Pressure, Gets the Message", *The New York Times*, 22 May 2014. http://www.nytimes.com/2014/05/23/technology/facebook-offers-privacy-checkup-to-all-1-28-billion-users.html?_r=0

deleted again once the purpose for which they were to be processed has been accomplished. It must be easy to exercise and apply the right to deletion and correction that is enhanced by the reform proposal. The debate concerning the "right to be forgotten" which the European Commission has proposed played a central role here, a right which Parliament regards as part of the right of deletion and therefore no longer mentions separately.[7] This is not a matter of technical expiry dates, but a legal right to secure compliance with a request for deletion. A provider may have gathered personal data without user consent, or even passed them on or published them. Providers should comply with user demands for correction or deletion of their personal data. People whose personal information from their youth has unlawfully been communicated over a social network have an interest, quite rightly, in ensuring that, 10 years later, their job opportunities or their chances of obtaining a mortgage no longer depend on it. This, of course, does not apply where a public interest is at stake or where there are issues of freedom of information and opinion. The aim is not to give politicians, for example, a back door method of preventing unwelcome reports from being published. Rather, the purpose is to reduce the impact of the unlawful processing and reprocessing of data.

To this end, the Regulation ought to strengthen rights to information vis-à-vis providers. Individuals should be informed in intelligible language, free of charge and as quickly as possible, who is doing what with their data. Another innovation is the right for individuals to receive their own data in a common electronic form: at the individual's request, service providers should divulge to that individual the data that they hold concerning him or her, in machine-readable format, i.e., digitally and not in the form of hundreds of pages. This would then enable the individual to switch to a competitor whose data protection is more satisfactory.

In order for the Data Protection Regulation not to remain a paper tiger, the proposal for a regulation aims above all to improve enforcement of data protection law. For this purpose, the first step is to give data protection authorities more power. The reform proposal is, therefore, intended to improve co-operation between national data protection authorities, so that my national data protection authority, who speaks my country's language, will always be my contact. What this requires above all is for data protection authorities to be better equipped. The reform proposal also called for financial penalties of up to four per cent. Penalties on this scale can have a real punitive bite.

A cornerstone of the Commission's proposal was the so-called consistency mechanism, which, in conjunction with the "one-stop shop" principle, should create a win-win situation for EU citizens on the one hand, and for data processors on the other hand. Every processor who falls within the scope of the Regulation will have a fixed dialogue partner in the form of the data protection authorities in his or her

---

[7] The "right to be forgotten" has not slipped from our lexicon, however, following the May 2014 judgment of the European Court of Justice. See Travis, Alan, and Charles Arthur, "EU court backs 'right to be forgotten': Google must amend results on request", *The Guardian*, 13 May 2014. http://www.theguardian.com/technology/2014/may/13/right-to-be-forgotten-eu-court-google-search-results

own EU country and will no longer have to argue afresh about the same issues with the authorities in each other country. In addition, the enhanced, binding co-operation at EU level will finally consign to history the inconsistent implementation and application of data protection law, thus, giving citizens a fundamental right to data protection that can be permanently enforced. This was the approach that Parliament had clearly favoured even in advance of the Commission proposal, by focusing on enhanced co-operation in the Article 29 Working Party. In its negotiating position, however, Parliament opted for a slightly different approach to that of the European Commission: unlike in the Commission proposal, Parliament was against giving the last word over a dispute within the newly created European Data Protection Board to the European Commission, and instead favoured empowering the supervisory authorities within the Board to take the decisions that will bind them. This will preserve the autonomy of data protection authorities and at the same time guarantee coherent application of data protection law.

The revelations by Edward Snowden in the summer of 2013 evoked at least one direct political response: in the European Parliament, a broad majority of Members soon backed the reintroduction of the former Article 42 which had figured in an internal preliminary draft of the Commission, which Parliament's rapporteur had reinserted as a new Article 43a. This clause stipulates that the transfer of personal data from the EU to third-country authorities is only permitted on the basis of EU law or of mutual assistance treaties based on EU law. This would mean that the transfer of data, for example, by telecommunications or Internet undertakings, to the security authorities of third States would be explicitly prohibited by the Regulation so long as there was no agreement with the EU on co-operation in this field.

Although a large majority of Members of the European Parliament were in agreement on many points from the outset, the procedure took significantly longer than planned before a negotiating position was agreed for the final negotiations with the Council. The original plan to vote on my report in April 2013 was impossible to adhere to after the deluge of amendments. The postponement of the vote, initially until the summer and then the autumn of the same year, was due to the complex and detailed discussions between the political groups with a view to reaching compromise formulations for each individual article in the Regulation. Only in that way was it possible to ensure that the whole procedure would conclude with a result that would be internally consistent and genuinely supported by a broad majority of the political groups in Parliament.

Ultimately, the interest taken in the work on the Data Protection Regulation by virtually all stakeholders shows that data protection has taken centre stage in the political debate and is now relevant to all areas of life and the economy. Members of the European Parliament know well that many members of the public are monitoring their work on the Regulation. It was, therefore, right to make the debates in the European Parliament as public as possible. Numerous hearings were held in 2012 and 2013, and the co-ordinators from the various political groups and I as rapporteur attended hundreds of events dealing with the various aspects of the data protection reform in parallel with the already packed calendar of meetings of the European Parliament. Unfortunately, however, in the EU's legislative procedure, this is not enough to give people a complete overview of what the main aspects and controversial points are and who is adopting what position, because the Council, with its power of co-decision, whose structures to this day – despite the massive importance of the EU to us all – are built upon diplomatic negotiations behind closed doors, at which the participants themselves feel little burdened by any duty of public accountability for the outcome. It is still the case that the governments of the EU Member States act as if EU decisions were based not on their actions but on the work of an impenetrable bureaucracy in Brussels. In any event, this is the picture they like to present when the decisions taken are assumed to be bad or undesirable. If, on the other hand, decisions manifestly and immediately appear valuable to EU citizens, the way that governments prefer to present them in the Member States is still as if the individual government had dreamed the whole thing up itself and managed to persuade other Member States to support it along the way.

That is why, within the Council, some EU Member States can take the liberty of rejecting certain European Commission proposals not on account of a substantive consideration of the proposed legislation but because they are critical of the EU as a matter of principle or simply because they do not wish to accept proposals that they have not devised themselves. This, regrettably, has also happened with the Data Protection Regulation. From the outset, the discussions within the Justice and Home Affairs Council were marked by fundamental criticisms by the British, Danish, Hungarian and German governments, while Member States such as Spain, Poland, Portugal, Austria and Ireland urged that the Regulation be dealt with and adopted quickly.

20.8.1 Germany's role

The reform was particularly obstructed by the persistence of those who had accommodated themselves to their existing situation. In the negotiations within the Council, it has repeatedly become clear that some government representatives and ministries, while hiding their hands, were playing a double game. One of them, unfortunately, on many occasions, was the German government, whose representatives regarded the EU reform as a general problem and tried to prevent agreement even on interim results. For months, the German government questioned as a matter of principle whether the Regulation – and hence uniform EU data protection – should apply at all in the field of data processing by the authorities, and sought to exclude it from the scope of EU data protection law. This was a particularly absurd attitude, given that, since the 1995 Directive, no distinction between private and public data processing has existed any longer for the purpose of data protection principles. There are good reasons for this, because nowadays private-sector data are also – and particularly – being used for the purposes of the authorities, and authorities now constantly exchange data across borders. It would therefore be illogical and inappropriate to exclude the authorities, of all organisations, from the EU's stringent common data protection standard. Moreover, the EU Data Protection Regulation also provides for a large measure of flexibility in formulating rules on data gathering and data processing by the authorities. The European Parliament had further increased this flexibility at the beginning of the discussions, and the existing rules on whether and under what circumstances the authorities are permitted to gather data at all are still determined by the laws of the Member States.

Why the German government, represented by the Ministry of the Interior, kept repeating this becomes clear if one listens to the other statements that emanated from Berlin on the subject of data protection reform: for example, the suggestion that it would be desirable, in the field of private-sector data processing, to abandon the principle, which has applied under data protection law for more than 30 years, that data may only be processed with consent. Does this mean that, instead of businesses having to ask consumers for permission to process their data or having to demonstrate an overriding legitimate interest in processing the data, Germany's Ministry of the Interior considered that in future they should be allowed simply to gather data like the vastly unregulated Silicon Valley? In return, businesses should (the next demand of the Ministry of the Interior) issue voluntary undertakings and regulate themselves, so that nothing illegal is done with the public's personal data and, in case of doubt, we also receive help if we have a problem. The Ministry's suggestion is that a risk-based approach should be adopted, under which certain rules would only apply where a "risk" existed. However, as yet, the negotiators in the Council have never really been able to say clearly what constitutes such a risk and why. In representing the Federal Republic of Germany and its more than 80 million citizens in the negotiations in Brussels, they are advocating a fundamental rejection of the existing rules of German and European data protection law, which are guaranteed by a fundamental right laid down in the Constitution and the EU Treaties.

Meanwhile, the lobbyists and lawyers employed on behalf of IT companies with international operations celebrate every day that the EU Data Protection Regulation is further delayed. Perish the thought that companies such as Google, Facebook and Amazon, of course, cannot only persuade Members of the European Parliament to table hundreds of amendments that one-sidedly benefit them but can also get to know many people at the ministries of the EU Member States and get them on their side. Indeed, it may even be easier, as the political leadership of ministries is often far more concerned with solving domestic problems than with the technical debates at EU level. And which country in Europe would one choose in order to achieve the abandonment of an inconvenient data protection law? It has made a big impression on the governments of the other EU Member States that Germany – a country that has always been so devoted to data protection – is sniping against the existing data protection rules. And if one bears in mind that it is difficult to get anything adopted in the Council without the consent of the German government, that is enough said.

20.9 Conclusion

Before the European elections in May 2014, the European Parliament overwhelmingly endorsed on 12 March 2014 its version of the Data Protection Regulation, by 621 votes in favour, 10 against and 22 abstentions. With its negotiating position established, the ball for rapid adoption of the EU data protection reform is clearly in the court of the Member States. They must agree on a position as soon as possible and give the new European Parliament a negotiating partner and an opportunity to finally adopt the law. If they cannot even manage this after more than three years and innumerable rounds of negotiations, people in the EU will presumably lose confidence not only in effective protection of their data but also in the ability of their politicians to agree on the common rules that people would like to see at European level. This would also jeopardise the legitimacy of the European Union as a whole and the newly won EU fundamental rights. In view of the many data scandals involving businesses and States, citizens would resignedly turn their backs not only on the digital market but also on democracy that fails to find solutions for today's challenges. At a time when this is an enormous problem, it would be fatal to simply let the window of opportunity slip for agreement on the EU Data Protection Regulation. That the opportunity is already slipping is clear: the new European Parliament includes many new Members whose views on reform at the EU level are not known.

At the moment, many people are taking a far greater interest in data protection than usual. Yet with every day that passes without any enforceable EU data protection, the reality of evasion and undermining of existing rules becomes more manifest. There is a serious danger that one day we shall look around us and notice that the rules that used to apply are no longer being taken seriously by anybody and that the opportunity to place them on an effective footing jointly with other partners (in this case the EU) in time has passed. The longer it takes for us to establish a new legal framework at EU level, the weaker the protection of our self-determination as citizens and consumers in a globalised and digitised world will be. In the period ahead, it will become clear which way the wind is blowing on the reform of European data protection law.

References

European Commission, Proposal for a Regulation of the European Parliament and of the Council laying down measures concerning the European single market for electronic communications and to achieve a Connected Continent, and amending Directives 2002/20/EC, 2002/21/EC and 2002/22/EC and Regulations (EC) No 1211/2009 and (EU) No 531/2012, COM(2013) 627 final, Brussels, 11 Sept 2013. http://eur-lex.europa.eu/legal-content/EN/TXT/PDF/?uri=CELEX:52013PC0627&rid=2

Goel, Vindu, "Some Privacy, Please? Facebook, Under Pressure, Gets the Message", *The New York Times*, 22 May 2014. http://www.nytimes.com/2014/05/23/technology/facebook-offers-privacy-checkup-to-all-1-28-billion-users.html?_r=0

Travis, Alan, and Charles Arthur, "EU court backs 'right to be forgotten': Google must amend results on request", *The Guardian*, 13 May 2014. http://www.theguardian.com/technology/2014/may/13/right-to-be-forgotten-eu-court-google-search-results

World Economic Forum and Boston Consulting Group, Unlocking the Value of Personal Data: From Collection to Usage, February 2013. https://www.bcgperspectives.com/content/articles/digital_economy_technology_unlocking_value_personal_data_collection_usage/

Chapter 21
Privacy Enforcement in Search of Its Base

James B. Rule

21.1 Introduction

The 20 chapters of this book attest eloquently to two things: First, the dedication, resourcefulness and ingenuity of the professionals who enforce privacy codes. In the roughly 40 years since the need for personal data protection agencies first won acceptance, those who staff these organisations have grown into an impressive global community. They have developed shrewd co-operation and shared *savoir faire* on the possibilities for and challenges to privacy protection across many national settings – a knowledge base fully on display in these pages.

Second, these chapters demonstrate the magnitude and complexity of the forces arrayed against their efforts. The tides of social and economic change driving the extension of bureaucratic surveillance are of historic dimensions. Resourceful organisations of the most varied sorts – from retailers to health care providers to tax collection agencies to counter-terrorist organisations – have drawn a single, fateful conclusion. They have understood that fabulous success awaits those who master the most complete, most revealing combinations of personal information on the people with whom they deal. By no coincidence, such organisations operate in a world that constantly generates more and richer personal data on every juncture of everyone's life – from details of people's domestic activities derived from "smart" electrical meters to inferences about political leanings or sexual preferences based on demographic information, social media postings and product choices. Justified or not, these innovative uses of personal data fuel privacy-eroding environments throughout the world's more prosperous societies. Given the breadth and variety of these pressures against privacy, those seeking to defend that endangered value face daunting challenges. In response, many data protection agencies, with small staffs

J.B. Rule (✉)
Center for the Study of Law and Society, School of Law, University of California, Berkeley, 2240 Piedmont Ave., Berkeley, CA 94702, USA
e-mail: jrule@notes.cc.sunysb.edu

D. Wright, P. De Hert (eds.), *Enforcing Privacy*, Law, Governance and Technology Series 25, DOI 10.1007/978-3-319-25047-2_21

and budgets, have won the reputation of "punching above their weight" in their jousts with agencies of corporate and government surveillance. On any reasonable assessment of prospects for ever-expanding surveillance, including the evidence presented in these pages, the agencies had better be prepared to keep punching.

21.1.1 Politics and administration

The preceding chapters focus overwhelmingly on the *palette of administrative techniques and strategies* available for enforcement of privacy codes. But let us agree that administration – from privacy protection to health care administration to war-making – always requires some political context. That is, all governmental bureaucratic action assumes some particular constellation of public consent, funding, legal mechanisms and the like. Those seeking to enforce privacy codes, like all privacy advocates, can be grateful that they have won institutional backing for these enforcement activities in so many countries over just a few decades. But it would be madness to imagine that current claims on state support are immune to shifting political winds. Brutal reversals are possible – as demonstrated in Ivan Szekely's sobering account in Chap. 4 of the undoing of Hungary's privacy protection mechanisms.

Even short of such dramatic defeats, we know that privacy protection efforts are subject to short-circuiting and debilitation, when public support weakens. Once-strong determination to protect people's interests in their information can give way to mechanisms that are little more than legal and administrative fig-leaves. Think of the "self-regulation" structures whose repeated failures Robert Gellman and Pam Dixon document in Chap. 3 – measures never very effective in the first place, then abandoned altogether the moment it appeared that no one was looking. Other debilitating practices include submitting privacy complaints to mediation, where the results of such mediation are not disclosed, thus affording no precedent for future privacy claims. Still others include condoning grossly exaggerated or outlandishly false claims by organisations for their privacy policies – as documented by Chris Connolly and Peter van Dyk in Chap. 12 on EU-US "Safe Harbor" agreements. For specialists in regulation, stories like these have a familiar ring: substantive protections give way to formalities of institutional window-dressing, once the heat is off.

Both in the United States and elsewhere, government regulation – in the form of agencies devoted to interests such as environmental protection, safety in the workplace or consumer protections – are often the precipitate of past social movements. Widespread social agitation and public indignation over newly-decried abuses or failures trigger creation of agencies devoted to upholding and enforcing the endangered values. Privacy policy had such a beginning in America – launched not precisely by any single social movement, but by popular agitation over the fate of personal data in the hands of large institutions. This period culminated in the events of Watergate. That moment of maximum mistrust of government finally led to the dethroning of President Richard Nixon – partly because of real and threatened uses of government-held personal data to attack political enemies. One enduring result of this high-water mark of public indignation was passage of the Privacy Act of 1974, establishing fair information practices over certain forms of personal data held by certain federal agencies. More than 40 years later, it remains America's closest thing to a national privacy law.

In Europe, by contrast, privacy protection seems to have begun more as an elite initiative than in response to grass-roots agitation. But both in Europe and around the globe, occasional "privacy moments" have intruded – episodes of public indignation at or resistance to notably privacy-eroding practices that have fueled subsequent reform efforts. Consider Germany's revolt at plans for the 1983 census, which many found vastly over-detailed and intrusive. Here, too, privacy concerns won the day. As German privacy scholar Wolfgang Kilian commented, "the immediate result was to reduce some 40 million questionnaire forms to a heap of worthless scrap paper".[1] A perhaps even more consequential privacy moment occurred in Australia in 1987, when an unexpected firestorm of public opposition to the Labor government's proposal for a computerised national identity card triggered days of demonstrations in the streets of that country's major cities. Not only did the government hastily withdraw the card proposal, but, as in Watergate, the lingering embarrassments also led to creation of a privacy commission that ultimately became a permanent feature of the government.[2] One can point to similar explosions of privacy consciousness in South Korea, Hungary and elsewhere, often resulting in the establishment or strengthening of privacy institutions.[3]

By far the most dramatic "privacy moment" in recent history is, of course, the one provoked by Edward Snowden's 2013 revelations – a moment we are still experiencing. These closely-documented disclosures of the extraordinary breadth and global penetration of US government surveillance – carried out in concert with surveillance agencies of many allied countries – have triggered repercussions that continue to unfold. Elite political figures at first stumbled over themselves in the attempt either to deny or dissociate themselves from the activities Snowden had revealed. But over the two years since the first revelations, deeper effects of the resulting political clamour have begun to manifest themselves. Public debate on the wisdom and justification of these activities has gained a legitimacy that was impossible during the long period when their very existence could be denied. Public opinion, though hardly united, clearly registers significant anxiety, if not indignation, over the notion that those in power can reach directly into every phone conversation, e-mail exchange, website search or other personal data generated over the Internet. In the United States, after nearly two years of stonewalling and evasion, both the

[1] Kilian, Wolfgang, "Germany", in James B. Rule and Graham Greenleaf (eds.), *Global Privacy Protection; The First Generation*, Edward Elgar, Cheltenham, UK, 2008, p. 80.

[2] Greenleaf, Graham, "Privacy in Australia", in James B. Rule and Graham Greenleaf (eds.), *Global Privacy Protection; The First Generation*. Edward Elgar, Cheltenham, UK, 2008, p. 141.

[3] Park, Whon-Il, "Republic of Korea", and Szekely, Ivan, "Hungary" in James B. Rule and Graham Greenleaf (eds.), *Global Privacy Protection; The First Generation*, Edward Elgar, Cheltenham, UK, 2008.

courts and Congress – but not the Executive Branch – show signs of awakening from the acquiescence that had so long been de facto policy.

So, the episodic, social movement-like demands for privacy protection do produce bursts of political support. And these privacy moments do from time to time yield valuable changes in key legislation, court decisions and institutional realignments. But against these energising moments, countervailing forces focus a different kind of energy. Popular indignation is episodic, dramatic and unpredictable; the forces fostering growth in breadth and penetration of surveillance are quiet, relentless and incremental. Propelled by the steady attractions of profits and bureaucratic aggrandisement, their privacy-eroding advances continue in a ceaseless drip-drip-drip of new sources of personal data, and new ways to exploit it. As the chapters of this book have shown, just anticipating what new demands for personal information are coming next represents a major challenge for privacy enforcement.

Let us be frank: in this historic tension, the forces of privacy face some distinct disadvantages. One is the sheer numbers of surveillance systems, great and small. There was a time when personal data protection authorities could plausibly call for every such system to be registered, and realistically expect at least to take cognisance of each system thus brought to light. That project looks less and less realistic. As in many another regulatory system, the finite attentions of the enforcers cannot track all the activities of interest. Defenders of privacy need to consider measures that will more greatly mobilise the attentions of individual data subjects, so that they can act on their own behalf to combat activities that might escape attention from professional enforcers.

Another disadvantage for institutional privacy protection lies in the terrain on which many day-to-day privacy battles are fought. For many people much of the time, privacy protection manifests itself in the form of irksome advisories and deadening texts – website privacy notices, for example, or terms-of-use contracts on software. It's not just that the language of these communications is tedious and anesthetic to critical thought. Worse, presenting privacy concerns in this way places privacy in the role of a spoiler – a set of issues interposed at the last moment between users of information technology and the services they are seeking. To the delight of the service providers, we impatiently click through these often-impenetrable gatekeeping disclaimers, resolving to worry about privacy another day, if ever. The net result is to convey the message that privacy protection is something designed to stop you from getting on with your life. This is not the association that privacy activists ought to be seeking for their work.

In similar ways, privacy advocates have often allowed their concerns to be portrayed as highly technical specialisms that ordinary mortals cannot expect to penetrate. To a degree, this is unavoidable; enforcing privacy codes does indeed require application of special expertise. But inevitably, even the most privacy-friendly members of the broad public will rarely develop deep interest in ideas like "privacy dashboards" or the weaknesses of protection provided to Europeans' data transferred under the Safe Harbor agreements or the complexities of trans-border data breach requirements. These are indispensable obsessions for professional privacy enforcers, to be sure. But we cannot afford to allow these specialised concepts and activities to remain the main public face of privacy practice. We need to develop hard-hitting, galvanising appeals that will resonate with ordinary people's privacy concerns – and embed themselves in public attention, even in the absence of dramatic events like the Snowden revelations or the Australia card revolt.

21.2 Talking points

Other social movements have capsule slogans that remind everyone of their key demands. Some activists choose names amounting to one-line statements of their goals – Zero Population Growth, for example, or Right to Life, or Marriage Equality. Privacy activists have never come up with such a handle. Indeed, privacy is such a diffuse idea that even its most experienced exponents do not always agree on its central demands. For many, the idea of Fair Information Practices is basic to any privacy reform. But this notion scarcely yields a battle cry likely to stick in the public imagination. Nor is there a consensus interpretation as to what such practices entail.

What we need is a handful of forceful *talking points* – capsule demands that anyone could identify as key privacy affirmations. These should be demands that, if granted, would benefit virtually everyone's privacy interests. Best of all would be a single manifesto of talking points that privacy advocates everywhere could embrace – and that could accordingly be flourished globally as emblematic of privacy activism. We do not yet have such a list, but I believe that doing so is within our grasp. Let me propose three candidates for such talking points, starting with two that are already widely known and enacted, and concluding with one less familiar idea. Consistent with my appeal for simplicity and concision, let me call this mini-manifesto Strong Privacy.

First, *no commerce in personal data without notice and consent.* Where not already restricted by law, private-sector surveillance systems exercise vast influence over the life-chances of ordinary citizens and consumers. In the United States, an entire industry of commercial data-brokerage has grown up, devoted to selling "background" reports of various kinds for use in credit, job screening, marketing, and virtually any other purpose for which someone is willing to pay. Drawing personal data from public records, newspaper and media accounts, product choices registered by vendors and countless other sources, these companies are big business. Added to better-known systems for tracking consumers' desirability as credit customers, insurance applicants and targets of advertising, these systems exert manifest pressures on privacy – much as they also support certain useful services.

Strong Privacy would restrict the sway of these businesses in two ways. First, by making consent by the subject a requirement for inclusion of anyone's personal data in any private-sector data system aiming at commercial sale. And second, by requiring public posting of the existence of any such data system, coupled with easy access for any individual desiring to see his or her record. A website should be established where any member of the public, after proper self-identification, could identify the existence and contents of his or her files. Such access rights should include the right to see the history of sales of information about one's self.

The EU already proscribes many data systems of this kind. In the United States, by contrast, commerce along these lines is rampant, flying under the flag of commercial free speech. This remarkable legal doctrine defines retailing of reports on people's property tax payments, divorce actions, past insurance applications and the like as tantamount in value to the right to advocate for candidates and causes. Strong Privacy would insist on subordinating such *commercialisation* of personal information to a more basic right to remain off the commercial record, for those who wish to do so. Those dissatisfied with their credit records, for example, would have the option of remaining off the radar screen of credit reporting. Those who find the compilation of "investigative reports" about themselves off-putting would have the option of blocking sale of such reports as a default condition, simply by not granting their assent. The result of such rights would be an entirely healthy tension, in which the record-keepers would find it in their interest to make their activities acceptable to as many members of the public as possible.

Second, *no government personal data systems without legislative responsibility and accessibility*. Governments have many legitimate needs for systems of personal information on the governed. But the tracking of citizens by government agencies should never be allowed solely at bureaucratic discretion. Every government personal data system must require specific authorisation by elected officials and must be open to monitoring by those subjected to it. Unwillingness by any government agency to seek approval for its surveillance activities should ipso facto represent a warning that the need for the activities should be reconsidered. Exceptions should be granted – again on legislative authority – only for legitimate investigative activities approved by elected officials. Input from personal data protection officials should be taken very seriously in weighing such exceptions.

As with the parallel right in private-sector record-keeping, application of this principle should make it easy for every citizen and consumer to know what government record systems contain files on himself or herself – and to know when such records have been accessed and what determinations have been made on their basis. A single website should centralise notice of all such systems and provide easy guidance for those seeking to track the existence and use of "their" data. Again, in the EU many of these requirements are already fulfilled – albeit with broad exceptions for national security and other investigative interests. The United States offers some such protections under the Privacy Act of 1974, which applies to a more restricted population of agencies and record systems. In other countries, the idea that government institutions should have to give account of what data on their citizens they are holding, and how they are using it, would constitute a major, privacy-friendly step ahead. Whatever the current state of practice, the notion that all citizens ought to have easy access to the fullest detail of government-held files about themselves is a notion that everyone can understand, and whose benefits everyone can grasp. It is an ideal talking point for Strong Privacy.

Third, *property rights over commercial exploitation of one's own data*. A world reliant on "free" services provided through unauthorised use of personal information represents a disaster-in-the-making for privacy. Strong Privacy requires a new kind of universal property right over commercialisation of one's own data. The default condition would be ridiculously simple: without consent from the subject, no *commercialisation* of personal information should be possible. This means no sale or exchange for value of personal information for purposes like credit reporting, advertising, targeted marketing, employment reporting or the like. If people indeed value commercial services produced through these aggressive uses of their data, they will certainly be willing to grant their consent. Absent such consent, the ultimate opt-in principle should prevail: no commercialisation of any kind.

A right of this kind would require very careful crafting. It should never be interpreted to interfere, for example, with uses (including sale) of personal information in connection with public discourse – in debate over the issues of the day, political campaigns, critical biographies or even cash-for-trash journalism and ordinary gossip. But in strictly commercial contexts, consent from the individual must be indispensable. Moreover, those willing to permit use of "their" data should be able to demand compensation for their consent. Organisations should not be able to predicate access to their services – websites, dating services, restaurant reservation booking systems – on waiver of one's commercial data property rights. To prevent such short-circuiting of the logic of the right, compensation for release of one's data should only be possible in cash.

Again, the EU already provides significant protection in this direction. Since the Data Protection Directive of 1995, Europe has proscribed "secondary use" of personal data – that is, release of data provided to one user for one purpose must not be shared for other uses without express permission from the data subject. What Strong Privacy would add to existing EU protections is a guarantee of the right to demand and accept compensation for use of one's "own" data – which would then really be one's own. In practice, such a right would most likely lead to creation of a new industry devoted to managing, on behalf of individuals, permission for commercialising their data.

Perhaps the greatest virtue of a right like this is that it would transform privacy concerns from a tiresome speed bump in navigating the Internet to a source of power and benefit to everyone. Those categorically dedicated to privacy would see their wishes served simply by doing nothing; without consent, the default condition would always be *no disclosure*. For those willing to extend limited permissions to share – which should always be closely specified as to purpose and readily revocable – this right would offer the possibility in sharing in the wealth generated by exploitation of personal data. This sort of empowerment, based on principles accessible to anyone, is exactly what Strong Privacy needs to promote.

In the United States and other countries, the mere contemplation of a right like this will trigger howls of alarm from Silicon Valley and the rest of the information industry. The counterattack would begin with the charge that any obstacle to the "free flow" of personal data would block "innovation". To this, privacy supporters will have their speech prepared in advance: not all forms of "innovation" are worth having. If ordinary people find the costs of sophisticated commercialisation of their data intolerable in terms of privacy, they must have a right to withdraw from both the benefits and the costs of these processes.

This, I hold, is exactly the kind of speech that privacy supporters should be making more often.

*

None of the ideas behind these three talking points is new. The idea of property in commercialisation of personal data, for example, was broached as early as Alan Westin's landmark *Privacy and Freedom*;[4] the notion has been refined and extended by a number of authors since then.[5] Key elements of the first two talking points – on access to and accountability for personal data held in corporate and government systems – have long been basic in privacy advocacy, and are already incorporated to varying degrees in various national privacy codes.

What I am proposing here, then, is not so much new principles as a new and more aggressive outreach strategy for projecting privacy concerns. Too often, both official enforcers of privacy codes and private activists have found themselves playing a reactive role – protesting new privacy-eroding practices and pleading for their limitation. Such defensive measures are often necessary, but we ought to locate them within a program of positive change that would aim at rolling back existing practices, making everyday life more privacy-friendly for everyone. Strong Privacy talking points like those I've suggested can build bridges to natural allies who will never immerse themselves in the details of privacy enforcement, but who are nevertheless eager for a more private world.

To be sure, all three of these proposed points require much further specification before serving as a basis for policy. For example: should a property right over commercialisation of one's personal data prevent the holder of a bad debt from selling that debt to a collector? (Here my own answer would be no.) Or, how selectively should people be able to opt out of private-sector databases – e.g., only from those reporting results of civil court actions? Many such questions of implementation demand serious consideration. But there's no reason to let the complex nature of such considerations stand in the way of advocating Strong Privacy.

21.3 The future

Imagine that global privacy forces succeed in rallying behind a simple agenda of hard-hitting talking points like those I've proposed. Even in that near-utopian case, administrative *savoir faire* like that documented in this book will always be

[4] Westin, Alan, *Privacy and Freedom*, Atheneum, New York, 1967, pp. 224–25.

[5] E.g., Hunter, Larry, "Public Image: Privacy in the Information Age", *Whole Earth Review*, Vol. 32, January 1985; Laudon, Kenneth, "Markets and Privacy", *Communications of the ACM*, Vol. 92, 1996; Rule, James B., "Toward Strong Privacy; Values, Markets, Mechanisms and Institutions", *University of Toronto Law Journal*, Vol. 54, 2004.

indispensable. Policing the interstices of privacy will always be a complicated and multifarious business, and the work of highly-trained specialists will always be needed. And even where the analytical issues are transparent, professional advocacy will always be needed. Some members of the public will always need help to formulate their needs; some data-holding organisations will yield only to official pressures to open their activities for review. But the talking points above may succeed in widening the range of matters in which ordinary citizens can act on their own initiative.

Like other social movements that rose to prominence in the 1960s and 1970s – environmental protection, for example, or women's rights or prison reform – privacy protection has won some precarious victories. Laws have been enacted; supportive court decisions handed down; new institutions (including regulatory agencies) have been formed. But in none of these cases could anyone imagine that the opposing forces have simply slipped away – on the contrary. Public opinion polls attest to privacy as an enduring and widespread concern. But this shared state of mind does not automatically translate into sustaining support for the day-to-day work of those charged with enforcing privacy codes. Given the potency of the opposition, privacy advocates would do well to develop sources of support capable of sustaining their efforts over a very long haul. A forceful manifesto for Strong Privacy could help solidify an alliance between concerned members of the public and professional privacy advocates that so far has remained a missed opportunity.

References

Greenleaf, Graham, "Privacy in Australia", in James B. Rule and Graham Greenleaf (eds.), *Global Privacy Protection; The First Generation.* Edward Elgar, Cheltenham, UK, 2008.

Hunter, Larry, "Public Image: Privacy in the Information Age", *Whole Earth Review*, Vol. 32, January 1985.

Laudon, Kenneth, "Markets and Privacy", *Communications of the ACM*, Vol. 92, 1996.

Rule, James B., "Toward Strong Privacy; Values, Markets, Mechanisms and Institutions", *University of Toronto Law Journal*, Vol. 54, 2004.

Kilian, Wolfgang, "Germany", in James B. Rule and Graham Greenleaf (eds.), *Global Privacy Protection; The First Generation*, Edward Elgar, Cheltenham, UK, 2008.

Park, Whon-Il, "Republic of Korea", in James B. Rule and Graham Greenleaf (eds.), *Global Privacy Protection; The First Generation*, Edward Elgar, Cheltenham, UK, 2008.

Szekely, Ivan, "Hungary" in James B. Rule and Graham Greenleaf (eds.), *Global Privacy Protection; The First Generation*, Edward Elgar, Cheltenham, UK, 2008.

Westin, Alan, *Privacy and Freedom*, Atheneum, New York, 1967.

Index

D. Wright, P. De Hert (eds.), *Enforcing Privacy*, Law, Governance and Technology Series 25, DOI 10.1007/978-3-319-25047-2

The manufacturer's authorised representative in the EU is Springer Nature Customer Service Centre GmbH, Europaplatz 3, 69115 Heidelberg, Germany. If you have any concerns regarding our products, please contact ProductSafety@springernature.com

Printed and bound by CPI Group (UK) Ltd, Croydon, CR0 4YY
30/09/2026
02225650-0018